GUIDE TO THE
RESEARCH COLLECTIONS
OF THE NEW YORK
PUBLIC LIBRARY

GUIDE TO THE RESEARCH COLLECTIONS OF THE NEW YORK PUBLIC LIBRARY

Compiled by

SAM P. WILLIAMS

under the direction of

WILLIAM VERNON JACKSON

and

JAMES W. HENDERSON

with the editorial assistance of

HARVEY SIMMONDS, ROWE PORTIS

and

WILLIAM L. COAKLEY

AMERICAN LIBRARY ASSOCIATION

Chicago 1975

Library of Congress Cataloging in Publication Data

Williams, Sam P
    Guide to the research collections of the New York
Public Library.

    Replaces A guide to the reference collections of
the New York Public Library, compiled by Karl Brown.
    Includes index.
    1. New York (City). Public Library.
    2. Library resources—New York (City) I. New York
(City). Public Library. A guide to the reference
collections of the New York Public Library. II. Title.
Z733.N6W54   027.4'747'1   75-15878
ISBN 0-8389-0125-5

Printed in the United States of America

DEDICATED TO THE MEMORY OF

KARL BROWN

*and to all those
who have contributed to the greatness
of the research collections of
The New York Public Library*

CONTENTS

(Some chapter subdivisions have been omitted from this
condensed table of contents; the Index should
be consulted for specific subjects.)

CONTENTS

SECTION
II
THE HUMANITIES
PART ONE

PART TWO

CONTENTS

SECTION
III
THE SOCIAL SCIENCES
PART ONE

PART TWO

CONTENTS

SECTION

IV

THE PURE AND APPLIED SCIENCES

PREFACE

The New York Public Library is, in actuality, a universe of libraries containing virtually every kind of library collection and service yet described.

It is not, officially, a national library; but its research collections rank in size, scope, and quality with those of the Library of Congress, the British Museum, and the Bibliothèque Nationale, and constitute a resource of national and international importance.

It devotes itself to no specific faculty or student body; yet its Research Libraries are similar to those of the great university libraries of the United States and Europe, and function as a definitive source in answering the advanced research needs of students and faculty in New York City and other parts of New York State, as well as scholars throughout the nation. The new central facility of the Branch Libraries, the Mid-Manhattan Library, has been designed specifically with service to undergraduate students in mind. And to the academically unaffiliated, the New York Public Library is in itself a university: It is everyman's university.

Although it cannot provide the type of custom service often available from the "special" libraries of business, industrial, and professional organizations, the New York Public Library is, in fact, a conglomerate of special libraries covering almost every subject field (with the exception of law, medicine, theology, and pedagogy). Representatives of the business and professional communities account for at least one quarter of the use of its Research Libraries.

The library is not a school library. Yet both elementary and secondary school students in New York City have found the Branch Libraries to be indispensable, and the need to provide special services to children and young adults for both school-related and extracurricular reading was recognized by the library long ago.

Nor, surprisingly, is the New York Public Library a public library in the traditional meaning of that term.[1] It is a public library because it is for the use of the public, and its Branch Libraries constitute the largest public library

---

1. For a full understanding of the library's functions and complex organizational history, see Harry Miller Lydenberg's *History of The New York Public Library* (The New York Public Library, 1923) and Phyllis Dain's *The New York Public Library; A History of Its*

system in the United States. But that component of the library known as the Research Libraries, which for the most part are privately supported, has no counterpart in size or scope in any other municipal library system in the United States.

It is the research collections in the New York Public Library system that this *Guide* is intended to describe. It will be helpful, therefore, to say a word about the nature of a research library collection.

A research library has two primary functions. First, it is one of the institutions invented by society through which the records and the glories of civilization are preserved. In one respect, therefore, the research library is a museum of books and other documents. Its second function is to make available for the advancement of knowledge the sources of information, the spurs to the imagination, contained within the works it preserves. These two functions often overlap. In acquiring the original manuscript of T. S. Eliot's *The Waste Land*, for example, the New York Public Library was obviously adding a museum piece to its collection. Because the manuscript is so different from the final version published in 1922, and because it contains revisions and remarks by Ezra Pound, it is also a rich resource for scholarly research.

Except for the four subject fields already mentioned—law, medicine, theology, and pedagogy—the Research Libraries of the New York Public Library have developed collections of excellence in most subject fields, and in several areas the collections are of special significance and distinction. In the fields of the humanities and fine arts, the performing arts, the social sciences, and science and technology, the Research Libraries over the past century and a quarter have gradually increased their collections in a fashion impossible to duplicate today. And, except for motion pictures and videotapes, which have been collected only in the fields of black culture, dance, and theatre, no form of document has been excluded. Printed books and pamphlets, serial and periodical publications, broadsides and other printed ephemera, manuscripts and archives, maps, prints, drawings, sheet music, and phonorecords have all been collected. Material that may appear to be relatively insignificant has found a home in the Research Libraries alongside some of the most distinguished collections of rare books and manuscripts in existence. The choice of materials has not been affected by what librarians or the contemporary public regard as good or important. Recognizing that standards of taste and value change with time, curators have made an attempt to record life as it passes, with attention paid to what may seem trivial, vulgar, or evil, as well as to works representing the more obviously significant and agreeable aspects of human experience.

To be usable, library collections must be organized and made accessible. The usual method is to provide, through some scheme of classification, locations for items found in the collections, and descriptions of these items in the form of entries in the library catalog. The catalog is used primarily to determine whether

---

Founding and Early Years (The New York Public Library, 1972). The latter completes the story up to 1913, and will be followed by a second volume (now in preparation) covering subsequent decades.

or not a library has a specific item. Through it, a library's holdings of the works of a given author, or the materials available for a narrow subject, may also be ascertained. Beyond these possibilities, however, the alphabetical or dictionary catalog cannot provide a clear, general picture of a library's holdings or an idea of its strengths and weaknesses.

This *Guide* provides a quite different approach to the collections. Its purpose is to describe them discursively, subject by subject, and evaluate them at the same time. As William V. Jackson points out in his Introduction, few attempts of this kind have been made. One of the most successful was Karl Brown's *Guide to the Reference Collections of The New York Public Library*, published by the library in 1941. Brown's work was panoramic: It was as if he had photographed aerial views of the collections, class by class, zooming in on the most important items as he proceeded. In compiling this *Guide*, Sam P. Williams has been unable to follow Brown's method, because the collections have doubled since the publication of Brown's *Guide*, and also because, beginning in 1956, materials have been shelved by size rather than class in many subject areas. Williams has thus presented his descriptions by broad subject coverage, rather than by following a detailed classification system or a scheme based primarily on the administrative organization of the collections.

The *Guide* will provide the prospective user of the Research Libraries with an idea of what he may expect to find in the collections and where it may be found. It will give the researcher and the scholar an awareness of the inter-relationships of materials in the collections and of important resources that might otherwise be overlooked. It will be useful to new library staff members as they seek to familiarize themselves with the collections, especially in subject fields outside their areas of assignment.

It will serve reference librarians outside the library, and many others in the book world as well, as an aid in referring scholars to particular materials. It will provide a basis for planning, with other libraries, programs of cooperative collection development and cooperative service.

Work on this *Guide* started in 1965 with funds made available from a grant by the Old Dominion Foundation, now superseded by the Andrew W. Mellon Foundation, and was completed with funds bequeathed to the library by Emily E. F. Skeel. Publication was assisted by a grant from the Mellon Foundation. Williams was aided in his compilation by many members of the staff of the library, especially by the chiefs of divisions of the Research Libraries and curators of collections. Lewis M. Stark and the late Gerald D. McDonald helped review many of the chapters, and David V. Erdman, editor of library publications, contributed valuable suggestions. Walter J. Zervas was tireless and resourceful in putting the manuscript into its final draft form. The library is greatly indebted to all who have contributed to the making of this *Guide* to its resources.

JAMES W. HENDERSON
Andrew W. Mellon Director of the
Research Libraries

xix

INTRODUCTION

WILLIAM VERNON JACKSON

In 1941 the New York Public Library published a *Guide to the Reference Collections of the New York Public Library* by Karl Brown. In reviewing the publication, Keyes D. Metcalf, former chief of the Reference Department (as the Research Libraries were named at that time) and then director of the Harvard University Library, called the work "a landmark."[1] This 416-page "guide, index, or handbook" (as Brown put it) has served the library's users and staff, not to mention scholars and librarians outside New York City, as a valuable tool for understanding the wealth of resources assembled over nearly a century. In this volume, under a slightly different title, we present a new guide to a collection greatly enriched over an additional thirty years.

Let us look for a moment at the library world of 1941, when Brown's *Guide* was released as a book (after having appeared *seriatim* in the pages of the library's *Bulletin* from May 1935 to February 1941). At that time there were relatively few similar publications. In 1934 Harvard had issued the fourth edition of A. C. Potter's *The Library of Harvard University: Descriptive and Historical Notes* (of which no later editions have appeared) and other libraries—such as the Newberry Library, the American Antiquarian Society, and the Hoover Institution—had prepared guides or handbooks; but the resources of the Library of Congress and those of such universities as Yale, Columbia, Illinois, and California (Berkeley) were (and remain) undescribed. To be sure, on a different level, in 1938 the American Library Association had published Robert B. Downs's *Resources of Southern Libraries*, the first attempt "to study all classes of library research materials distributed over a large region,"[2] and Downs soon thereafter embarked upon the preparation of *Resources of New York City Libraries*, for which he received permission to draw upon the Brown volume. Attempts to describe and evaluate scholarly collections in the United States predate this period (examples survive from the nineteenth century), but the number of guides to the resources of the nation's large research

1. See "A Guide to the Reference Collections of The New York Public Library, compiled by Karl Brown," *PBSA* 36(1942): 74–77.
2. Robert B. Downs, *Resources of Southern Libraries* (Chicago: American Library Association, 1938), p. xi.

libraries was limited in 1941, and has remained so. Indeed, even now it appears quite unlikely that the near future will see realization of Metcalf's hope for similar works for all members of the Association of Research Libraries.

THE GUIDE TO RESOURCES

Although a precise definition of a "guide to resources" is difficult, such a work is essentially the description—*not* the listing—of special collections and subject strengths in one or more libraries. Using a narrative style, a guide to resources describes holdings in such terms as their nature and extent, language and geographic spread, degree of comprehensiveness, unique materials (e.g., first editions and manuscripts), nonbook items present, special emphases or areas of note within the total field being reviewed, and supporting and related materials in other parts of the collection.

It might be well to discriminate at this point between a guide to resources (as defined above) and works that provide information about resources in other ways. The latter group includes handbooks, checklists, bibliographies, calendars, library surveys, union lists, union catalogs, and printed book catalogs (presently enjoying a renaissance as a result of the application of the techniques of photographic reproduction and the computer to library files). All of these provide information on resources, but focus on specific titles rather than the description of subject collections or other groups of materials.

Each guide to resources varies in the degree to which it resembles the theoretical definition and in the arrangement of its information. Karl Brown, for reasons stated in the Introduction to his *Guide*, found it advantageous to present his material following the classes in the classification schedule devised by John Shaw Billings for the New York Public Library. Although basically a subject arrangement which moves from biography (A), through history (B–I), to geography (K–L), and then to art (M), literature (N), science (O–Q), philology (R), social sciences (S–T), technology (V), medicine (W), law (X), philosophy (Y), and finally religion (Z), this scheme was of course a unique one, reflecting both Billings' ideas and the special characteristics of the library's collections, especially in terms of the "star classes" established to provide for certain subjects (bibliography, *G and libraries, *H), or forms of material (newspapers, *A; periodicals, *D; phonograph records, *L; and microfilms, *Z), or collections chiefly of material in languages not known to the average student (Orientalia, *O; Slavonic, *Q; and Jewish, *P), or groups requiring special administration (rare books, *K), or publications coming from special sources (public documents, *S and museums, *F). Even these two general categories did not include all of the library's material, as they did not make provision for the Manuscripts and Archives Division, the Spencer Collection, and certain other collections.

Brown calls the reader's attention to the fact that the *Guide*, "with the scheme of classification as a basis, is developed by consideration of the following points for each class or sub-class, as division occurs:

1. Statement of extent and character
2. Mention of strength or weakness
3. Related subjects and class marks
4. Special collections
5. Special catalogues, indexes, files of clippings and pamphlets, etc.
6. Reference lists in the *Bulletin*."[3]

The Brown volume remained a standard bibliographic tool, although it lost some currency with the passing of time. In the years which followed, the library made few basic changes in its collecting policies, but gave new emphasis to certain fields such as the performing arts, and continued to increase its resources (from about 2,500,000 to more than 4,000,000 volumes). It received several new special collections, including the Arents Collection of Books Relating to Tobacco, the Arents Collection of Books in Parts, and the Berg Collection of English and American Literature. The library naturally continued to disseminate information about its resources through publications such as the *Bulletin*, its annual report, individual monographs and pamphlets, and later the series of divisional catalogs issued by G. K. Hall.[4] But none of these significantly updated the Brown volume, and circumstances prevented the compilation of the 1940–45 supplement promised in the *Guide*. The preparation of the revised *Guide* was delayed until the fall of 1965, when "The Guide to the Research Collections Project" began operations. At that point some basic decisions on the nature of the project were considered: Would it serve as a supplement to Brown covering the last twenty-five years, or would it be a completely new edition? Would it follow Brown's approach and manner of presentation? What was the most appropriate and efficient methodology for the job at hand? The final decision called for a new edition, rather than a supplement to the *Guide*, thus making it unnecessary for a user to refer to Brown except for special features. A complete rechecking of all Brown's information did not seem feasible, however, so as much of it as possible was utilized in the new *Guide*, with revision when necessary for size, scope, and notable additions, and with an effort to make the statements even more useful to the reader seeking information.

Another major decision was to arrange the new volume according to general subjects, rather than follow the Billings Classification Schedule. Several considerations led to this decision, one of the most important being that since July of 1956, about one-half of the library's accessions have been shelved in fixed order location, rather than according to the Billings Classification Schedule.[5] Also, some holdings are separated from others merely by accident of

3. *A Guide to the Reference Collections of The New York Public Library* (The New York Public Library, 1941), p. x.
4. For a list of published catalogs, see the first Appendix.
5. Rutherford D. Rogers, "Shelving Books by Size," *ALA Bulletin* 51(1958): 435–37.

provenance—e.g., although they may deal with English literature, they may have been acquired for the Berg Collection, or they may have a nonbook form. Thus the person interested in English literature will find the Research Libraries' rich resources described in one section of the *Guide*, even though the sources may be shelved in the general stacks, the Berg Collection, the Rare Book Division, the Spencer Collection, the Manuscripts and Archives Division, or even in the Performing Arts Research Center at Lincoln Center.

METHODOLOGY

With these decisions made, the methodology of preparing this compilation was devised. As was explained previously, the Brown volume furnished the point of departure, and the first task was to obtain information to supplement or modify, where necessary, Brown's statements. Rather than doing this independently for each subject, it seemed wiser and more efficient to perform several preliminary operations to secure overall data which could be used throughout the new *Guide*. How, for example, had the collections of the Research Libraries developed from 1940 through the mid-1960s? To answer that question efficiently involved the utilization, whenever possible, of already published material, and so a literature search for references to the library's resources published during this period was undertaken. First, complete sets of the *Bulletin*, the library's annual report, and those of the library's own publications dealing with holdings were assembled. Second, a careful check was made of Robert B. Downs's *American Library Resources: A Bibliographical Guide* and its supplement,[6] based not only on the index entries under "New York Public Library," but also upon annotations (e.g., "Locates copies in 11 libraries") that suggested the possibility of the library's inclusion in publications covering several research collections. The publications cited were checked to verify the nature and extent of the description, or to see whether an item on various libraries did actually cover the New York Public Library. Although this research incidentally yielded some works which had escaped the assiduous labors of Downs and his helpers, there were few cards indeed to be marked "not in Downs." The file resulting from these efforts was duplicated, one set arranged by author and the other by subject. As another check on publications, all entries from the Public Catalog under "New York Public Library" were also copied. The establishment of this bibliography made possible the development of a Resources File, used to bring together material about the research collections. Items cut from duplicate copies of the *Bulletin* and the annual report, reproductions of pages from monographic studies, as well as copies of memoranda and other documents prepared for internal use (generally taken or copied from the Research Libraries' administrative files), went into folders which were arranged broadly by Dewey Decimal Classification.

These two files, bringing together for the first time material about the collections, constituted the first steps taken to prepare this *Guide*. (Since the

6. The second supplement had not, of course, appeared at the start of the project.

library has continued to incorporate new items into both files, they have become small, specialized additions to its bibliographic instruments.) At this stage occasional conversations with division chiefs and others also provided valuable clues to additional material or subject strengths to be explored later.

A third important preliminary step was to determine the extent of the Research Libraries' holdings in various subjects. Statistics resulting from censuses taken in 1921 and 1930, and the figures published in Brown (basically adjustments of the latter year), were available. Apparently the library had made little or no attempt to maintain such statistics subsequent to 1941. Since holdings of individual subjects in research collections grow at rates which do not entirely correspond with the overall rate of increase, simply projecting growth of each subject at a uniform rate was deemed unsatisfactory. There was also the question of new areas for which statistics were wanted. In order to provide for continuity and some basis of comparison, it seemed useful to utilize figures (corresponding to most of the Billings classmarks) used in 1921, 1930, and 1941—especially for those representing subjects. But a greater breakdown of holdings in science and technology and the social sciences seemed desirable. The final decision was a compromise: figures were thus compiled for many specific subjects, but certain very broad areas (e.g., the Documents, Jewish, Orientalia, and Slavonic collections) were not broken down, because there was no solution that would not be excessively time-consuming. A sampling technique yielded figures both for volumes shelved in fixed-order location and those in the general collection and elsewhere in the library; these were later modified as direct examination of shelves, discussion with division chiefs and other staff members, or other good reasons dictated. The figures presented at the beginning of sections remain, however, careful estimates of the extent of holdings in each subject.

One final preliminary operation was undertaken. Since the reader of this *Guide* might well be unfamiliar with the organization of the Research Libraries in relation to the subjects of interest to him, it appeared desirable to prepare a brief general statement on each division or unit, indicating its collecting responsibilities, the special indexes and files which supplement its resources, major gifts which may have influenced the development of collections, and other pertinent matters. For divisions with responsibility for a single, specific subject it was possible to prepare this at the same time as the description of resources, but for those representing area collections (e.g., Orientalia) or responsible for several subjects (e.g., General Research and Humanities Division), such statements were prepared as a part of the preliminary operations.

PREPARATION OF SUBJECT DESCRIPTIONS

Completion of this essential, if time-consuming, work provided a solid foundation for preparing the descriptions of resources, subject by subject. Although the technique varied somewhat for each discipline, the following steps were common to nearly all:

1. Study and critical review of the description by Brown
2. Examination of standard bibliographies and guides to the literature of the field
3. Review of bibliographic citations and material in the Resources File for clues on general strengths and special features, especially for new or changed emphases and for significant acquisitions in the years since the Brown study; comparison of these data with *Bulletin* articles and checklists cited by Brown
4. Examination of the collection on the shelves
5. Tabulation and study of selected important subject entries in the Public Catalog
6. Consultation with the staff of the division bearing primary responsibility for the development of resources in that area, and use of the division's special indexes and files
7. Investigation of holdings of other divisions (e.g., Spencer, Slavonic, Rare Book, Manuscripts and Archives) to see the extent to which their resources strengthen or supplement the main body of material
8. Review of new statistics of estimated holdings, in comparison with those for 1921, 1930, and 1941
9. Review of the acquisition policy statement for the Research Libraries' current collecting policy.

With these steps taken, writing began. Allowing for differences from section to section, a typical arrangement runs as follows: (1) the extent of holdings, usually giving figures for 1921, 1930, 1941, and 1966 (occasionally for a few earlier years too) as an indication of the quantitative development of the collection; (2) the current acquisition policy, with mention where possible of those areas receiving comprehensive, representative, or selective coverage;[7] (3) bibliographical and reference tools; (4) serials, with both an indication of number and types currently received and of typical back files and the extent of their completeness; and (5) subdivisions or special topics, as appropriate to the subject. Examples of such special categories include subdivisions on local history (within history sections), on major authors (literatures), on higher education (education), on magic (theatre), on Napoleon (French history), and on librarianship abroad (library science). Unique materials such as first editions and manuscripts are mentioned where appropriate. For subjects with materials dispersed in several units, the descriptions often indicate location of those not shelved with the primary group (e.g., "The Berg Collection contains . . . "). Although the guide to resources, as pointed out earlier, is not a listing of authors and titles, the present compilation attempts to avoid vagueness by giving specific information such as the titles representative of serials and the

7. For a definition of these terms, see pages xxx–xxxi.

names of authors and institutions whose publications are present in quantity. But this information should be considered primarily as examples of the type of material available. The reader should not infer that authors, institutions, and topics not discussed are necessarily less well represented: what is significant in the smaller library (e.g., American scholarly journals, standard reference and bibliographical tools—even those of multivolume proportions—and complete works and critical editions of major figures in all Western literatures) can safely be assumed to be in this collection of over 4,000,000 volumes.

Nevertheless it would be a mistake to presuppose that the present *Guide* reveals all things to all men about the collections. More importantly it does not generally compare resources of the Research Libraries with those of other institutions; the use of words such as "strong" and "significant" refers to holdings within the Research Libraries and not in comparison to other libraries. In short, we have attempted to describe accurately the collections as they are. Many of these bibliographical statements are, to some extent, subjective; that is, they are seldom the result of checking bibliographies or lists. Nor does this *Guide* attempt to provide reference to all publications—even those of the library itself—which mention, in one way or another, these resources; that is done in part by entries in the Public Catalog, in part by the Downs compilations, and in part by the bibliographic files assembled during the course of preparing this work.

This *Guide* does not attempt to chronicle the history of the Research Libraries' collections. Numerous historical facts are given because they contribute to a better understanding of present holdings, not as a systematic approach to the evolution of resources; consequently there are no chronological listings of acquisitions as in Brown. Nor does this *Guide* present the financial story of the building of the Research Libraries' holdings by presenting total and specific expenditures over the years, or by discussing endowed book funds and similar topics. The present volume does adhere to Brown's principle of a detailed index, in the hope that the guiding principle of arrangement by subject will cause the user fewer searches for material about each specific topic of interest.

It is the library's expectation that the *Guide*, which covers resources acquired through December 1969, will be kept up-to-date through regular supplements. Indeed, one supplement, for the last six months of the July 1969–June 1970 fiscal and statistical year, has already appeared.[8] It is hoped that this new *Guide* and its supplements will prove as useful as its predecessor to the library's readers and staff, and to scholars and librarians everywhere.

---

8. "Additions to the Resources of The Research Libraries," *BNYPL* 75(1971): 122–42.

GUIDE TO
THE USE OF THIS VOLUME

Following its consolidation as the New York Public Library, Astor, Lenox and Tilden Foundations in 1895, the library was organized into two major components, now called the Branch Libraries and the Research Libraries. The Branch Libraries have responsibility for providing materials for general reference and home use, while the Research Libraries are concerned with collecting, preserving, and providing access to materials of value for advanced reference work and research. Although mention of materials in the Branch Libraries will be made from time to time in this *Guide*, the focus of the discussion is on the collections of the Research Libraries. Unless noted otherwise, the phrase "the library" used in descriptions of holdings in this volume applies to the Research Libraries.

The methods used in preparing and arranging this guide to resources are explained in Jackson's Introduction (especially pp. xxiv–xxvi). Current figures and references to specific subjects and titles indicate the range and relative strengths of the library's collections in the late 1960s. For complete and up-to-date information on the holdings, consult the Public Catalog in Room 315 of the library's Central Building and the published *Dictionary Catalog of The Research Libraries* for new acquisitions since 1971 (see the first Appendix for a detailed listing of the Research Libraries' published catalogs).

In this *Guide* subjects are covered for which the library has notable collections; the catalogs will of course locate materials in many subjects not mentioned here. Unless there is a specific division reference given, titles cited are from the general collections, and can be located through the Public Catalog or *Dictionary Catalog* and requested in Room 315.

Locations of administrative units of the library are given in the Location Chart on page 304, not in the text. The first letters of the titles of administrative divisions are capitalized (Music Division; Berg Collection). For collections forming part of the holdings of a division, lower case is used (for example, the Drexel collection, Music Division). For these, the administrative division is mentioned in the text.

TERMS AND ABBREVIATIONS

For the convenience of the reader, certain terms and abbreviations used by the library and referred to in this volume are defined in the following list. Some terms used to indicate the relative strengths of particular collections are self-evident; however, "comprehensive," "exhaustive," "representative," and "selective" are used precisely to denote the library's acquisition policy: the definitions of these terms are included herein.

analytics, analyze—A cataloging term which indicates full cataloging under author and subject for monographs in series. See "indexing" below.

BNYPL—*Bulletin of The New York Public Library.*

Billings Classification Schedule(s)—The arrangement of works in the Research Libraries devised by John Shaw Billings, the first director of the library. It is basically a subject arrangement, with special "star" classes for special divisions and types of materials. See *Classification Schedules for Printed, Microcopy and Phonorecord Materials in the Reference Department* [now called the Research Libraries] (The New York Public Library, 1955) and "Locations of Classes of Books" charts and pamphlets in each division. See "fixed order" below.

class—One of the main categories of classification or the works therein.

class mark—The series of letters, etc., denoting the classification of a work. It corresponds to "Call Number," etc. in other libraries.

Collection—An administrative unit of the Research Libraries (equivalent to Division) or the Branch Libraries (see Location Chart on p. 304).

collection—A group of materials identified by the name of a donor, collector, or subject, which is not an administrative unit of the library. These collections are listed in the Index; the name of the division or Collection administering them is noted in the text if they are not part of the general collections (see below).

comprehensive—At least 75 percent of what is obtainable.

Division—An administrative unit of the Research Libraries (see Location Chart on p. 304).

exhaustive—Everything obtainable.

Farmington Plan—A voluntary agreement under which major American research libraries have accepted responsibility for collecting in special fields.

fixed order—A system of shelving books by size rather than subject. Fixed order was instituted in 1956 for some materials entering the library's general collections and extended to other collections in later years.

general collections—The book collections housed in the stacks, titles from which may be requested in Room 315 of Central Building. Comprising more than one-half of the total number of books in the Research Libraries, these general collections cover such fields as bibliography, biography, European history, geography, literature, linguistics, the natural sciences, philology, philosophy, psychology, and religion. Also used to describe materials not in the Special Collections of rare books, manuscripts, and prints.

indexing—A cataloging term which indicates that an article in a periodical has been entered in the catalog under subject or author (or both). See "analytics" above.

Lydenberg, *History*—Harry Miller Lydenberg, *History of The New York Public Library* (The New York Public Library, 1923).

n.c.—Not cataloged. Part of a class mark formerly given to volumes of pamphlets, brochures, etc. which were considered worth preserving but not given separate cataloging.

PBSA—*Papers of the Bibliographical Society of America.*

PL 480—Public Law 480, the Agricultural Trade and Development and Assistance Act of 1954, as amended; a program which has provided funds used to purchase foreign currencies to finance acquisition and distribution of books and booklike materials for participating libraries, one of which is the New York Public Library.

p.v.—Pamphlet volume. Part of a class mark used for volumes of pamphlets. Each pamphlet is fully cataloged.

oversize (+, ++)—The symbols are part of the class mark for oversize books, which are usually shelved apart from smaller volumes in the class, but are requested in the normal manner.

representative—From 50 to 75 percent of what is obtainable.

Research Center—A major administrative subdivision of the Research Libraries (see Location Chart on p. 304).

selective—Any amount up to 50 percent of what is obtainable.

Special Collections—A major administrative subdivision (equivalent to Research Center) of the Research Libraries (see Location Chart on p. 304).

stacks—The main shelves of books in the Central Building, primarily the general collections.

star (*)—The symbol is part of the class mark for the "star" classes of the Billings Classification Schedules, which are composed of special forms of materials (e.g., *L for phonograph records) or collections of materials requiring special care (e.g., *K for rare books) or other collections of special materials.

GENERAL MATERIALS

PART ONE

1

GENERAL RESEARCH AND HUMANITIES DIVISION

This division is responsible for the selection of general reference works, for the major part of the book collections housed in the stacks, more than one-half the total book holdings of the Research Libraries, and for periodicals of a general nature and in the Roman and Greek alphabets (see chapter 4). It selects material in these alphabets for such fields as bibliography, biography, European history, geography, literature, linguistics, philosophy, psychology, philology, and religion. It is also responsible for the collections of sports and games, and shorthand.

The division provides general reference service to readers personally and by telephone and letter, maintaining a small collection of books in Room 315 of the Central Building for ready reference which includes almanacs, directories in various fields, indexes and catalogs of books and periodicals, current book-trade lists, and various compilations in fields such as literature, education, and business. The division also administers the Main Reading Room reference collection of 32,500 volumes.

PUBLIC CATALOG, BOOK CATALOGS, INDEXES

In addition to general reference work, a major function of the General Research and Humanities Division is to interpret the massive Public Catalog. Included here are cards for all book and booklike materials in the Roman alphabet and in Greek with the following exceptions: there are no cards for manuscripts, phonorecords, prints and drawings, music scores, sheet music, maps, and moving picture stills; there are no cards here for materials in the Berg Collection or the Arents Collections, and only a partial record of Spencer Collection holdings (these materials must be located through the appropriate subject or special collections of the Research Libraries, with the exception of nonmusical phonorecords, which are listed in a supplementary catalog located in the General Research and Humanities Division). Although the most complete record of newspaper holdings is to be found in the card catalog of the Newspaper Collection, a separate catalog for newspapers is kept at the Information Desk in Room 315; retrospective and current newspaper series are now being added to the Public Catalog. The Research Libraries holdings in the Cyrillic script and in the Oriental languages and Hebrew or Yiddish are recorded in the division catalogs of

the Slavonic Division, the Oriental Division, and the Jewish Division, respectively.

The Public Catalog is a dictionary catalog containing author, title, and subject entries for materials acquired up to 1971. From the library's earliest years, entries have also been prepared which index articles in periodicals and learned journals; ordinarily only subject cards for such articles are made. Since these index entries are largely for material not covered by published indexes, they form an immensely valuable feature of the catalog.

The General Research and Humanities Division keeps at hand the book catalogs of the Manuscripts and Archives, Map, Slavonic, and Oriental Divisions, and those of the Schomburg Center and the Berg and Arents Tobacco Collections, the book catalogs of the drama and World War I collections, as well as the *Dictionary Catalog of The Research Libraries* for post-1970 acquisitions.[1] All printed book catalogs of the collections of the Research Libraries are intended to be located in this division for use in conjunction with the Public Catalog. Near the Public Catalog, too, are kept recent indexes of the *New York Times* and many of the H. W. Wilson periodical indexes, as well as sets of *Cumulative Book Index*, the book catalogs of the Library of Congress, including *The National Union Catalog Pre-1956 Imprints*, the British Museum *General Catalogue of Printed Books*, and other standard bibliographic tools.

THE MAIN READING ROOM

Located on the shelves of the North and South Halls of the Main Reading Room is the library's principal reference collection; the 32,500 volumes shelved here may be consulted without filing call slips. The collection, which supplements and extends the general collections housed in the stacks, is intended to supply a balanced group of the important sources for general topics found by experience to be most used by readers. Limited holdings of standard or general works in each of the fields for which there is also a subject collection are also present for the convenience of readers who use the Research Libraries when the subject divisions are not open.

---

1. The published book catalogs of library holdings are listed, with full bibliographical information, in the first Appendix.

The Main Reading Room contains reference works—dictionaries of the major languages of the world, encyclopedias representing the important countries of the world, and compendiums covering subjects most in demand. Also included are standard histories, biographies, and works on subjects generally in demand but not covered by any of the special reference divisions of the library. As far as possible, books in these collections are in English, although there is a good representation of foreign encyclopedias and dictionaries, and of works in foreign languages offering better presentations of their subjects than those available in English.

Since the Main Reading Room collection attempts fuller coverage of those subjects not strongly represented in the reference collections of other divisions of the Research Libraries, the following subjects receive minimal coverage: art and architecture; economics and finance; Jewish literature; local history and genealogy (there is no representation for these subjects); music; Orientalia; science and technology; Slavonic literature.

The following notes describe reference collection holdings in certain important areas.

Bibliography

The collection is strong in this field. It contains many standard bibliographical works, most of the national bibliographies, and subject lists. Book catalogs of important collections in other libraries are also available. Associated bibliographical collections include reference materials located in the Preparation Services and bibliographies in the Rare Book Division; both are represented by cards in the Public Catalog, and may be requested by call slip.

Biography

This rich collection includes both collective and individual biographies. Other units in the Research Libraries have biographical materials related to their fields.

Book Arts

A working collection of histories of publishing, printing, typography, etc., this represents one of the library's major strengths. Important supplementary materials are found in the Rare Book, Prints, and Manuscripts and Archives Divisions.

Directories

An important and frequently used part of the reference collection, directories fall into four main groups:

1. In the north hall of the Main Reading Room is a collection of approximately 95 percent of all current U.S. telephone directories. The majority of current foreign telephone directories is kept in the stacks.
2. A retrospective file of greater New York City area telephone directories on microform is available in the Microform Reading Room. It extends from 1878, the date of the first telephone directory. The main directory set includes the various communities in the Metropolitan area (Westchester and Rockland Counties, Long Island, New Jersey, Connecticut, etc.).
3. A small collection of current United States city directories is kept in the Main Reading Room.

4. A representative group of foreign and international trade and commercial directories is also available.

History

Standard historical sets and the works of outstanding historians are available in addition to the basic reference works in the field. Most areas of world history are well covered with the exception of United States, Canadian, and South American history, which are represented in the American History Division, and United States and British local history, which are administered by the Local History and Genealogy Division.

Law

Materials in this area are limited to United States and New York State statutes and court reports.

Literature

A comprehensive collection of definitive editions of the standard authors (with the exception of Oriental, Jewish, and Slavonic writers) is available, as well as the more important systematic critical and historical works.

Natural Sciences

A good collection of the standard reference works is maintained for natural history, biology, botany, and zoology, although these are fields in which the Research Libraries do not specialize.

Philology

Containing most of the standard and classic monolingual dictionaries in the Western European languages, the collection includes many bilingual dictionaries and works on etymology.

Philosophy

A working collection of general introductory material, philosophical dictionaries, histories, and other critical works is maintained.

Religion

A basic working collection of materials covering most Christian sects and the Bible, including encyclopedias, dictionaries, handbooks, histories, and commentaries is available. A representative collection of books on liturgy and ritual reflects the latest forms or changes.

Sociology

This portion of the collection is restricted to general treatises and reference works.

Sports

The materials available in this area include sports records, encyclopedias, and histories.

Technology

Cookery, gardening, navigation and naval art, and military art and science constitute the major strengths of this group of materials. Little attempt to cover the broad field of science and technology has been made.

SPECIAL INDEXES AND FILES

American Periodicals 1800–1930

General American periodicals are listed alphabetically by decades during which they were current (2,300 cards). The file does not include specialized periodicals such as historical journals and scientific publications. This classification by ten-year periods facilitates the study of trends of opinion about important historical events, social problems, etc.

British Periodicals 1700–1930

General British periodicals are listed alphabetically by decades during which they were current (1,400 cards).

Bookseller File

A file consisting of the names and addresses of booksellers in the New York City area arranged by subject specialty (1,000 cards).

Bulletin of The New York Public Library Index

The General Research and Humanities Division indexes the *Bulletin* as it is issued; cards are discarded when a cumulative index is published.

Current Periodicals List

A "wheeldex" file listing some of the most commonly used Roman-alphabet magazines, chiefly those indexed in the Wilson indexes (2,000 cards). The library classmark for each title is noted, as well as the division or subject collection in which current issues are held.

Directory Catalog

This file locates and gives bibliographical information for directories throughout the collections of the Research Libraries: subject, commercial, professional, occupational, and many other kinds of directories are included (12,000 cards). The theatrical, musical, and dance directories housed in the library's Performing Arts Research Center at Lincoln Center are also noted.

Literary Form Headings

This file consists of author entries under literary form headings with national subdivisions (e.g., "Fiction, French"; "Drama, Brazilian"; "Poetry, Scottish-Gaelic") (450,000 cards). A full record of the editions of an author's works does not appear here; the reader must consult author entries in the Public Catalog to determine the complete holdings.

Before 1940 literary form headings were maintained in all languages. Since that time they have been partially discontinued with the exception of drama, which has been maintained in all languages. The state of particular files can be approximately determined by spot checking the dates of publication on cards entered under nationality subdivisions of the form in question.

Material on Careers File

An index to occupational monographs arranged by occupation (500 cards).

Newspaper File

An alphabetical record of newspaper holdings arranged by county, state, and city in the United States; and by country and city abroad (4,000 cards, domestic; 2,000 cards, foreign). For holdings of United States newspapers published before 1800 the reader is referred to the Rare Book Division.

Quotation File

A selection of quotations not readily found in standard books of quotations, the file consists in large part of entries from the question and answer column of the *New York Times Book Review* (12,000 cards). Quotations or their source are given, with many cross-references.

"Scrap Box" File

This file, arranged by subject, notes information and sources for quick reference in areas not readily covered by standard tools (3,000 cards). The file is in part an aid for locating items in sections of the Public Catalog with unusually complicated subject headings.

Special Collections File

A card file arranged alphabetically by main entry under the name of selected special collections, detailing the materials in those collections (40 card drawers). A listing of special collections for which there are cards, with an indication of the subject matter of each, follows.

American Alpine Club (mountaineering)
American Jewish Committee (Judaica)
American Scenic and Historic Preservation Society (preservation of natural and historic sites)
Argentine (books published in Argentina)
Bernays, Edward L. (public relations)
Billings, J. S., memorial (miscellaneous)
Black, James (temperance, prohibition)
Blacque, Mrs. Valentine Alexander (fine bindings, for the most part nineteenth-century French)
Blumenthal, George (works by and about Anatole France)
Dueling
Falls, DeWitt Clinton (military uniforms)
Goulston baseball collection
Gregg collection (shorthand, only material not classed in *IDT, *IDTA)
Gress, Edmund G. (typography)
Grossman, Moses H. (general literature)
Hadley, Henry, memorial (U.S. orchestral works)
Hanford, Franklin (naval history, etc.)
Haynes, William DeForest (salmon)
Hooker, Samuel Cox (legerdemain, magic)
Huneker, James G. (music, belles-lettres, etc.)
Johnson, Merle (bibliography, belles-lettres)
Laurie (wit and humor)
Marshall, Frank J. (chess)
Morris, Mrs. Dave H. (Esperanto, universal languages)
Mott memorial collection (religion)
National Temperance Society (temperance)
Pearson, Edmund Lester (fiction, detective stories, crime)
Poetry Society of America (poetry, including that of members of the Society)

Remington, Frederic (works by or illustrated by Remington, or containing Remington autographs)
Russian Historical Archive (Russian manuscript materials)
Schatzki (juvenile literature)
Schwimmer-Lloyd (woman suffrage, labor, etc.)
Sprague, Frank Julian (railways)
Starr, Reginald H. E. (anthropology, language)
Weaver, John V. A. (drama)
White, David McKelvy (Spanish Civil War, 1936–39, Veterans of Abraham Lincoln Brigade)
Williamson (black Freemasonry)
Wolkan (drama)
U.S. Works Progress Administration, New York City (W.P.A. publications)

Theatre Scrapbook File

An arrangement by title of plays performed in New York City itemizing and locating reviews, mainly from newspapers, of each play (10,000 cards). The author, date of performance, and theatre are noted on each card. This file serves as an effective index to the collection of news-paper clippings of dramatic criticism kept in the Theatre Collection at Lincoln Center.

Vertical File

This file is a ready reference collection, arranged by subject, built up as a result of questions from the public (12 file trays). It provides information not readily available in standard books of reference.

Who's Who File

Arranged by general subject and by occupation, this file lists the source and location within the Research Libraries of current biographical sketches.

Inactive Files

A 2,000-card index to the *Dictionary of American Naval Fighting Ships* for the World War II period and a 2,000-card index to articles in books and periodicals on the history of food discontinued after August 1937 have been preserved.

2

GENERAL COLLECTIONS

A Guide to the Reference Collections of The New York Public Library (1941) included a section entitled "General Collections," in which were noted certain large groups of material, divided into two categories: "Segregated Collections" and "Collections Not Segregated." In this revision of the *Guide* the segregated collections (the Berg Collection, the Spencer Collection, and the Stuart Collection now under the administration of the Rare Book Division) receive separate treatment. The collections not segregated, that is, the large general collections which have not been kept together as units, but have instead been absorbed into the various divisions of the Research Libraries, are described below.

ASTOIN COLLECTION

In 1872, Felix Astoin presented his important collection to the Lenox Library; it was received by the library after his death in 1884. In the donor's words, the collection was built up "during a long residence in this city, embracing about 5,000 volumes, all bound and in an excellent state of preservation, of French books, including the best encyclopedias, works of art, and on history, classics, etc., and probably the most complete collection that can be found in this country."[1] Later encyclopedias, bibliographies, etc., have in many instances supplanted those of Astoin's day, but the library is still enriched by having many significant titles pertaining to the historical aspects of learning.

Astoin had little interest in rare books as such. For the 1840–70 period the collection has extensive examples of French imaginative literature; it also added to the library's collection of classical literature in French translations, and few examples, apparently, were overlooked. This is particularly important as translations, except standard translations into English, are not usually purchased by the library.

A checklist of the Astoin collection appeared as number 7 of the Lenox Library's *Short-title Lists* (1887).

BANCROFT COLLECTION

The library of George Bancroft, the American historian, consisting of 11,606 books, 4,648 pamphlets, and 486 volumes of manuscript, was purchased by the Lenox Library in 1894, primarily for its materials on American history, although general literary works were included. The rare items in the collection are found in the historical group; the remainder were characterized as the "works one would expect to find in the library of a man of such a wide experience in affairs as Bancroft."[2] This portion includes 2,000 volumes relating to history and literature, 1,500 volumes of German literature and philosophy, 1,000 volumes of French and Italian literature, 500 volumes of Greek and Roman literature, and a large number of miscellaneous works.

DUYCKINCK COLLECTION

In 1878 the Lenox Library announced the gift of the Evert Augustus Duyckinck collection of 15,164 books and 1,596 pamphlets, together with the Duyckinck papers: it was the accumulation of a Dutch father and two sons—all bookmen,

---

1. See Lydenberg, *History*, p. 100.

2. See Lydenberg, *History*, pp. 125–26.

all New Yorkers—and is of real significance in showing the tastes and interests of the city in the late eighteenth and early nineteenth centuries. The collection contains relatively few titles now considered real rarities, although most of the classical authors are represented, some in early imprints; the 76 editions of Horace, for example, include 1 from the fifteenth century, 4 from the sixteenth, 7 from the seventeenth, and 27 from the eighteenth. In the main, however, the collection remains highly interesting for the number and variety of contemporary English and American editions and for its fine books, illustrated by such artists as Bewick, Cruikshank, and others of the period; there is also an excellent representation of eighteenth-century French works.

"Literature," as far as English and American titles are concerned, must be construed in its broadest sense, including not only imaginative literature, but also biography, travel, and similar materials. Among imaginative works are representations of Shakespeare and older authors in good editions. Most of the eighteenth- and nineteenth-century authors are present in first or early editions. An interesting feature is American imprints of English authors. American writers generally appear in first editions. There are excellent files of American literary periodicals through the first half of the nineteenth century.

Most of the Duyckinck papers are those of Evert A. Duyckinck, accumulated in connection with his editorship of *Arcturus*, the *Literary World*, and the *Cyclopedia of American Literature* (1804–55), but also included are letters to his brother, George Long Duyckinck, from nearly every American man of letters during the period. In addition to other series, there is a mass of private and personal letters, bills, business papers, and account books. Selections from the papers have been printed occasionally in the *Bulletin*; these may be found through the published *Index*.

Check lists of the printed materials in the Duyckinck Collection appear as numbers 8 and 12 of the Lenox Library's *Short-title Lists*, printed in 1887 and 1890.

FORD COLLECTION

In 1899, Worthington Chauncey Ford and Paul Leicester Ford offered the library their collection of printed books as a memorial to their father, Gordon Lester Ford. The gift, estimated at more than 30,000 books, 70,000 pamphlets, and a large number of maps and prints, came partly as a result of the purchase by J. Pierpont Morgan of the Ford collection of manuscripts, from which he made his selection, turning the remainder over to the library.

The principal feature of the Ford collection is American political, constitutional, and economic history in the broadest sense, but with additional notable materials in the fields of finance, taxation, and economics of England and the continent. Gordon Lester Ford collected everything. His selection of books was remarkable; he ranked with Tefft, Cist, and Sprague as an early collector of autographs and historical manuscripts; and his association with Whitelaw Reid taught him "that frequently the trivial, ephemeral pamphlet of today is the important historical document of tomorrow."[3] His sons' enthusiasm continued and they expanded the collection, following their own interests as bibliographers and editors, as well as historians.

While American history and economics are undoubtedly the major features of the collection, hardly a field or topic is not represented. Throughout the library's holdings—in biography, travel, philosophy, philology, literature, religion, even law and medicine—titles from the Ford collection are to be found.

Paul and Worthington Ford and their sister, Mrs. Emily Ellsworth Ford Skeel, added hundreds of volumes to supplement the original gift.

TILDEN COLLECTION

In addition to the funds which constitute the third of the original foundations of the library, Samuel Jones Tilden bequeathed this institution some 15,000 volumes (not including his law library, which went elsewhere). The books have been described as a "collection made for his own use and enjoyment . . . the usual classics one expects to find in a 'gentleman's library' . . . shelving little rubbish."[4]

Included among general materials are bound files of New York City newspapers covering the period from the 1840s through 1886, and runs of economic periodicals for about the same period.

Most of the social sciences are represented, the more important material being in the fields of history and economics. Among rarities in this group is a collection of 225 scarce tracts relating to banking and currency in England, printed from 1683 to 1850. History is for the most part American, ranging from Hakluyt's *Voyages* (1599–1660) and the accounts of other discoverers, to Catlin's *North American Indian Portfolio*. A strong feature is political history; present are the chief publications relating to the various administrations and political parties of the United States; to Congress and congressional affairs; and to political and constitutional conventions, especially those of New York State.

Literature comprises the richest portion of the collection. Included are the first 3 editions of Milton's *Paradise Lost* (1667–78) and the first 3 Shakespeare folios. The portion relating to art, archaeology, and natural history includes the finely illustrated editions popular from the latter part of the eighteenth century through the first half of the nineteenth. Also included are a number of the now famous "Galleries," relating to art and archaeology (as well as the magnificent publications of individual authors), and the folio Audubon *Birds*, which is typical of the natural history publications.

A number of extra-illustrated works are present, including Sir Walter Scott's *Waverley Novels* and such histories and biographies as lent themselves well to this treatment. In addition, unusual collections of portraits, including the works of Birch, Lodge, Caulfield, and others, are represented. The extraordinary collection found in this group is that of Gillray's caricatures dated from 1777 to 1811, representing the entire period of that artist's productivity.

Finally, Tilden's papers were included with the original gift.

---

3. See Lydenberg, *History*, pp. 378–80; see also *BNYPL* 3 (1899): 51–53, 387–89.

4. See Lydenberg, *History*, pp. 129–50; see also *BNYPL* 3 (1899): 4–8.

3

BIBLIOGRAPHY AND ENCYCLOPEDIAS

BIBLIOGRAPHY

Bibliography—writings and compilations which deal with the description of books, and subject lists—is one of the strongest features of the library's collections. The collecting policy is comprehensive for general and national bibliographies, and representative or selective for booksellers' catalogs, auction catalogs, and catalogs of university and college libraries. Most of the general bibliographical works in the Research Libraries are housed in the general collections, but important holdings can be found in the Rare Book, Economic and Public Affairs, and General Research and Humanities Divisions, and in the Preparation Services. A great number of special subjects bibliographies, a particular strength of the library, are classed with subject materials. Most published bibliographies are secured, even those for subjects in which the library makes little or no attempt to specialize. Medicine and law, for example, are both adequately represented bibliographically, although the library has a relatively small representation of the works and journals cited. The only field that may be said to be seriously incomplete is the biological sciences. Although the researcher may find in the bibliographies citations to materials he cannot secure in the Research Libraries, he is able to do much of the initial research in the library; materials lacking are usually to be found in other large or specialized libraries of the city.

Before the widespread publication of periodical indexes, entries for bibliographies appearing in periodical and society publications were prepared for the Public Catalog. Since 1930 only items not likely to be indexed elsewhere have been entered.

The library has been keenly interested in bibliography from the beginning. In addition to building a bibliographical collection in the Astor Library, Dr. Cogswell, a collector and bibliographer as well as librarian, personally acquired many of the works needed in this field. Upon his resignation in 1861 he turned over to the Astor Library his collection of more than 4,000 volumes in the fields of bibliography and literary history, in return for an annuity of $300.00. In 1884 the Lenox Library received the Astoin collection (strong in French bibliography), and in 1890 the Stuart collection containing more than 200 volumes of bibliography and literary history. In addition, there was Lenox's collection of booksellers' catalogs and publishers' lists which he had checked and annotated, particularly important for information on Americana and the Bible. In 1938–39 a collection of French book auction sale catalogs for the period 1730 to 1930 enriched the library's resources. In 1939–40 Wilberforce Eames's personal library of books, manuscripts, and bibliographies came to the library; the Americana section of Eames's collection was particularly good.

The general collections devoted to bibliography have grown over the years as follows:

1921	9,010 volumes
1930	12,196
1941	17,000
1966	45,400

The general collection is wide in scope and varied in content, containing a substantially complete representation of the works of the great bibliographers. Many of the standard bibliographies and current materials are kept in special divisions for greater public convenience. The general collection does not include bibliographies of special subjects, which are classified with subject materials. Some of the larger collections of bibliographies in the special divisions of the Research Libraries are described below.

RARE BOOK DIVISION

This collection numbers some 4,000 volumes. It consists of general and special bibliographies of authors, special presses, and individual printers; and bibliographies of printing in specific cities or geographical areas such as *Rare Kentucky Books, Manuel du bibliographe normand, Oklahoma Imprints 1835–1907.* Materials in the collection have been chosen largely for their value in bibliographical and cataloging research in the field of rare books. Many of the items are duplicated in the general collections.

A subclass of unusual interest was originally intended to provide for the elaborately annotated catalogs and working lists of James Lenox, many of which are a valuable contribution to bibliography, particularly those having to do with Americana and the Bible. The scope of this subclass was later extended to include annotated lists of other bookmen and collectors whose collections have come to the library, or whose work has had some connection with its holdings. The more important of these lists and notes are those of Bancroft, Bryant, Dixon, Myers, and Westwood; those having to do with the South Sea Bubble; and the Tilden shelf inventory of 1887.

PREPARATION SERVICES

The books located in the Preparation Services bear the classmark "Ref. Cat." (Reference Catalog); they are entered in the Public Catalog and may be secured for use in the Main Reading Room by submitting call slips in the usual manner. The section dealing with bibliography numbers about 1,000 volumes. It is composed principally of national bibliographies and the catalogs of important libraries such as the Bibliothèque Nationale, the British Museum, and the Library of Congress. Another collection, kept in the Acquisition Division, is most important for lists and directories of periodicals and serials. They are held for staff use in cataloging the books for the collections.

ECONOMIC AND PUBLIC AFFAIRS DIVISION

The publications in bibliography to be found in the Economic and Public Affairs Division fall into three groups: (1) A group composed of one copy of all Library of Congress bibliographical publications; duplicate copies are located elsewhere in the collections for general use; (2) the official records of books, periodicals, etc., published by governmental agencies throughout the world, and (3) the catalogs of the book, periodical, and other accessions of governmental agencies throughout the world.

GENERAL RESEARCH AND HUMANITIES DIVISION

More than 5,000 bibliographical volumes are kept at the Information Desk near the Public Catalog and in the Main Reading Room. At the Information Desk are the current American and English national bibliographies, large library catalogs, indexes to periodicals, and the various "best books" lists. In the Main Reading Room are subject and national bibliographies, less frequently used periodical indexes, the *U.S. Catalog of Copyright Entries*, and similar materials.

SPECIFIC ASPECTS OF THE BIBLIOGRAPHY COLLECTION

National and Trade Bibliographies

This is a comprehensive collection with complete files of series such as the *Publishers' Trade List Annual, Bibliographie de la France*, and *Reference Catalogue of Current Literature*. Historically the collections have excellent coverage for the United States, England, most European countries, and the USSR. There are substantial holdings of Latin American bibliographies, but only a fair representation for Oriental countries. Currently the library receives 130 national bibliographies, but the holdings from those countries where bibliographical facilities are not well established have many gaps. There is a concentrated effort, however, to keep the files of all national bibliographies as current and complete as possible.

Booksellers', Art and Print Dealers' Catalogs

Although the collecting policy for booksellers' catalogs does not aim for completeness, the library's holdings of this material are unusual. A great number of the dealers' larger compilations are classed by subject in the collections and are not shelved with the general bibliography holdings. The general collection includes important nineteenth-century catalogs of European and American booksellers. One bound series of 31 volumes covers the period from 1801 to 1828; perhaps even more rare are smaller and more general early catalogs. A large number of formerly uncataloged materials of this nature, which as early as 1902 numbered 7,000 items, have now been assimilated into the collections. These items have been cumulated into bindable volumes and a form card has been established in the Public Catalog under the name of the dealer, a card which indicates that numbered or unnumbered catalogs are available, but without further detail. A list of 28 United States, 13 English, and 18 European bookdealers has been established as those whose catalogs are to be retained in the future; other catalogs are discarded after they have been used by the staff for ordering. The list of dealers whose catalogs are retained is subject to constant review and revision. An attempt is made to secure missing catalogs from 1956 onward for dealers on the retention list. The greater part of the collection of booksellers' catalogs is held with other infrequently used materials at the library's Annex. Holdings are noted in the Central Serial Record.

Art dealers' catalogs form one of the stronger holdings in the Art and Architecture Division.

The Prints Division retains all print dealers' catalogs that are received. Current items are retained and certain selected items are bound and added to the collections; mimeographed or other ephemeral materials are filed in envelopes. Form cards are prepared for the division's catalog.

Auction Catalogs

The collection of auction catalogs is representative for United States and English houses, but selective for French and most other European firms. Both priced and unpriced catalogs are retained, the priced being preferred. There is a bound file of the priced catalogs of the American Art Association Galleries from 1880; a fairly complete file for the Anderson Galleries from 1900; for the American Art Association from 1880; for the Parke-Bernet Galleries from 1938; and for Sotheby and Company from 1829, with some earlier scattered numbers. Auction catalogs of other American and European firms are present in large numbers. The larger, more important publications, located in the bibliography collection or classed by subject, are fully cataloged.[1] An attempt is made to secure missing catalogs from 1956 onward of the active galleries and dealers whose catalogs the library currently receives and retains. In addition there are complete files of such auction records as *American Book-Prices Current, Bookman's Price Index*, and *Book-Auction Records*. Both the Art and Architecture and Prints Divisions maintain sales records and retain individual auction catalogs as received.[2]

Manuscripts

In the Manuscripts and Archives Division are materials of bibliographic interest such as the Merle Johnson papers, the George Henry Sargent collection, and the Rodd family papers (1826–59). There is also the thirteen-volume manuscript compilation by H. O. Teisberg entitled "Records of Manuscript and Book Auctions in the United States, 1717–1889," which includes references to newspapers and catalogs.

ENCYCLOPEDIAS

The collecting policy for encyclopedias is comprehensive for all except the Oriental languages. The retrospective collection of encyclopedias is principally of historical interest. There is a good representation of editions of nineteenth- and twentieth-century American titles. Children's encyclopedias of the twentieth century are also present, although this is not a field in which the library has actively collected. Late eighteenth- and early nineteenth-century German children's encyclopedias are found in the Schatzki collection. The British collection includes many of the nineteenth-century "universal" compendiums as well as various editions (English and American) of such

---

1. See George McKay, "American Book Auction Catalogues, 1713–1934," *BNYPL* 39 (1935): 141–66 et seq. Published separately by the library, with revisions, 1937. See also supplements, *BNYPL* 50 (1946): 177–84; 52 (1945): 401–12. Reprinted by Gale Research Co., Detroit, 1967.
2. See Harold Lancour, "American Art Auction Catalogues, 1785–1942: A Union List," *BNYPL* 47 (1943): 3–43 et seq. Published separately by the library, with revisions, 1944.

standard works as the *Encyclopaedia Britannica.* There are generally full representations of works in foreign languages, such as the German "Brockhaus" and "Meyers," and the French "Larousse." The general collections also include the concise compendium or "fact book"; the nineteenth-century representations of this type of reference work are particularly interesting. Of works such as Chambers' *The Book of Days* there are many editions.

The open shelves of the Main Reading Room house most of the recently published or current titles. In keeping with the cosmopolitan character of New York City, the many foreign-language encyclopedias are in constant use. Each year the Main Reading Room replaces a single English-

language title with the current edition to insure that up-to-date information is always available. Among older standard works are complete sets of the Diderot *Encyclopédie* and Johann Heinrich Zedler's *Grosses vollständiges Universal-Lexicon.*

The Oriental Division has English and German editions of the *Encyclopaedia of Islam.* One of the Chinese manuscripts in the Manuscripts and Archives Division is an eighteenth-century copy of sections 15,951 to 15,958 of the Yung Lo Ta Tien of the Ming Dynasty.

Encyclopedias of subject interest, such as those covering the fields of technology or art, are classified with the subject and are generally located in the reference collections of the subject reading rooms.

4

PERIODICALS SECTION AND GENERAL

PERIODICAL RESOURCES

PERIODICALS SECTION

The Periodicals Section of the General Research and Humanities Division collects and houses an extensive number of current periodical titles, most of these in the Roman alphabet. At present there are approximately 10,000 titles. The section also maintains a collection of press directories and current issues of the standard periodical indexes.

The section services only current issues of the periodicals. After binding or filming, the majority of periodicals are located in the general collections. Not all current periodical issues are held in the Periodicals Section; those of special subject interest or in certain foreign languages are held in the subject divisions of the library as follows: In the Central Building are found periodicals of the American History Division, the Economic and Public Affairs Division, the Jewish Division, the Local History and Genealogy Division, the Oriental Division, the Science and Technology Research Center, and the Slavonic Division. In the Performing Arts Research Center are periodicals of the Dance Collection, the Music Division, and the Theatre Collection (including motion pictures, the circus, and allied arts). In the Schomburg Center are periodicals relating to black culture; those in the Patents Collection are in the Annex.

The collecting policy of the Periodicals Section is universal and parallels the strong subject areas of the library's monographic holdings. There is comprehensive coverage in such fields as art, architecture, geography, history, philosophy, poetry, psychology, and belles-lettres, with an attempt to provide research material ranging from learned society and museum publications to illustrated magazines. The life, habits, and thinking of the various national and ethnic groups are thoroughly documented. There are strong holdings of pacifist, photography, travel, and trade union publications, as well as titles in such diverse disciplines as economics, agriculture, the graphic arts, and forestry. The collecting policy is selective in such fields as political opinion and fashion.

The library has always maintained strong holdings in publications from Africa, Great Britain and the Commonwealth Nations, France, Germany, India, Italy, the Netherlands, and the Scandinavian countries. This is true to a lesser degree for other countries, including those of Eastern Europe. Holdings of United States periodicals are more inclusive, ranging from the organs of various pressure groups and underground publications to prison publications. The collection of house organs is good. Trade and professional publications are strongly represented in such fields as advertising, insurance, fire prevention, the garment and food industries, tobacco, and the book trade.

Catalogs

The dictionary catalog of the Periodicals Section is an arrangement by title and subject of the holdings of all current periodicals in the collections of the Research Libraries, not just those available through the Periodicals Section. If a periodical ceases publication, or if it is no longer currently received by the library, the cards for it are removed from this catalog.

A second file in the section is the Geographic Catalog. The periodicals currently received in the Research Libraries are arranged alphabetically by title under the name of the country of origin. There are no subject entries.

The library's Central Serial Record, administered by the Preparation Services, is discussed on page 11.

GENERAL PERIODICAL RESOURCES

Periodicals form one of the notable resources of the library's collections, and have traditionally been collected in all fields of the library's specialization. The general periodical collection in the Roman alphabet, including publications of a general literary nature, is estimated at 83,000 bound volumes. It is with this collection that the following remarks are primarily concerned. Learned society and institutional publications of a general nature are discussed in chapter 6 of this *Guide*.

The library has always had an excellent collection of periodicals. The Astor Library gathered a large general collection, and the Lenox Library received in the Duyckinck collection extensive files of English literary and illustrated periodicals. Many large collections of serial publications have been received as gifts. The collection is noteworthy not only for its long and generally complete files of the important journals, but also for the representation of periodicals of secondary importance.

In September of 1966 the library established a Central Serial Record to provide a current and retrospective record of all serial holdings in the Research Libraries (including annuals, newspapers, and gazettes). This record is not directly accessible to the public; readers in public divisions requiring information not available in the various catalogs should consult a member of the staff to ascertain the exact status of the file, latest issue in the library, issues at the bindery, and similar information.

In the language divisions, particularly the Slavonic and Jewish Divisions, the collections are rich. The Oriental Division has a good collection of periodicals in Asiatic and African languages, and the Schomburg Center for Research in Black Culture has many American and African periodicals in its subject areas. Additional comments are found in the appropriate literature sections of this *Guide*.

INDEXING OF PERIODICALS

The library's policy has long been to make articles in serial publications as readily accessible as books, especially in those subject areas which are of particular interest to its collections. As long ago as 1897/98, Dr. Billings, the first director of the library, was instrumental in starting the cooperative indexing of periodicals by libraries; this task was later assumed by the American Library Association. Billings then selected some 260 periodicals not on the cooperative list for indexing by this library. The present policy is to index articles which represent a major and, presumably, permanent contribution to a subject, or those by outstanding authorities, or those on subjects which are of interest to the Research Libraries, but for which there is little available material. Biographical and autobiographical articles, bibliographies, and important fugitive articles in unexpected sources are also indexed. The library does not index articles in periodicals covered by standard indexing and abstracting services.

At one time the library bound separately the advertising pages of some magazines. This collection covers the period from 1911–21 and includes advertising pages from such periodicals as *American Magazine, Century, Harper's Literary Digest, Review of Reviews, Scribner's,* and *Woman's Home Companion*. The collection is held in the Economic and Public Affairs Division. Present practice is to bind advertising pages with the text.

SPECIAL INDEXES AND FILES

In addition to the Dictionary and Geographical Catalogs noted in the discussion of the Periodicals Section, several important supplementary guides

to periodical resources exist in the library. In Room 315 of the Central Building are located the other General Research and Humanities Division files, including American Periodicals 1800–1931, British Periodicals 1700–1930, and the Current Periodical List, all described in chapter 1 on page 5.

Rare Book Division Files

The Almanac File is a card file (active, 5 card drawers) in two parts, featuring American almanacs published before 1821 and other almanac rarities: (1) An alphabetical file arranged by title of almanac or compiler's name (2 card drawers); and (2) A chronological file arranged by the year for which the almanac was issued. This file is in effect a shelf list of the almanacs in the division (3 card drawers).

Slavonic Division Files

The Current Periodicals and Newspapers file (active, 2 card drawers) is arranged by country, and lists in alphabetical order the newspapers and magazines published in Balto-Slavic languages available in the library. Information given includes the name of the journal or newspaper, its dates, and place of publication.

GENERAL RESOURCES

Bibliographical Aids

Bibliographies, union lists, and indexes of periodicals for the United States, Great Britain, the European countries, South America, Australia, and other countries form an extensive collection, covered by some 1,400 entries in the Public Catalog. These include index entries for listings and other publications which originally appeared in periodicals. A large number of the H. W. Wilson indexes are kept near the Public Catalog in Room 315, and are supplemented by other indexes in the reference collection of the Main Reading Room, including such tools as the *Internationale Bibliographie der Zeitschriftenliteratur aus allen Gebieten des Wissens.*

United States and English Periodicals

Little detail is necessary in a description of a class which is so generally strong as this. Files of titles indexed by the H. W. Wilson indexes are virtually complete. The Rare Book Division's holdings of American periodicals published no later than 1800 has been described as one of the three finest in existence. The representation of political weeklies in the general collections is also noteworthy. The resources are rich in journals of secondary importance or of short duration.

Pulp Magazines

The library has collections of the American popular monthlies now generally known as "pulp magazines." Included are files of titles such as *Cowboy Stories* (1925–33), *Railroad Stories* (1907–), *Argosy* (1926–), and the *National Police Gazette* (1845–), and broken files of others. The library currently collects this type of material only on a selective basis. From 1925 to 1941 a selected group of all types was gathered from news stands and bound each year with the title "Popular Periodicals for the Year. . . ."

Little Magazines and Avant-Garde Literature

The little magazines collection is particularly strong. Little magazines are generally defined as "those periodicals which have been noncommercial though not amateur, inclined to be rebellious and more open to experimental and 'advanced' contributions than their more staid, and more stable, contemporaries."[1] Building on strength, the library in 1968 purchased a collection of 3,000 items including not only little magazines but also monographs by American authors published in the United States primarily in the late 1950s and 1960s. Many of these titles are printed in limited editions, often privately issued by the authors, and in many cases they are not included in standard bibliographies.

Almanacs

Some 2,500 items in the Rare Book Division are principally American printings through 1820, including many rare publications. There are also a number of English almanacs of the seventeenth century in the Division.

Later almanacs in the general collections include materials from all countries, among them such titles as the *Brooklyn Daily Eagle Almanac* and the *Tribune Almanac*. The *World Almanac* is available from 1868. There is a collection of royal almanacs, and a substantial group of nautical almanacs and ephemerides. The latter range from incunabula (Regiomontanus and Zacuto), through sixteenth-century editions of Petrus Apianus and Johann Stöffler, to complete sets of the *Nautical Almanac* (1767–   ) and the *American Ephemeris and Nautical Almanac* (1855–   ). There are many modern nautical almanacs from France, New Zealand, India, and other countries.

Comic almanacs and periodicals form a good collection, with long files of such titles as *Puck*,

Punch, etc., their German counterparts the *Fliegende Blätter* and *Jugend*, and those of other countries. There are, in addition, interesting representations of humorous weeklies such as the brilliant St. Louis *Punch*.

Manuscript Holdings

A number of substantial archives in the Manuscripts and Archives Division relate to American periodicals, and most especially to those published in New York City. Among these are the papers of Richard Rogers Bowker (1848–1933), editor and publisher of book trade periodicals (21 volumes, 170 boxes, and 3 cartons);[2] William Conant Church (1836–1917), editor of the *Galaxy* and of the *United States Army and Navy Journal* (6 boxes); Richard Watson Gilder (1844–1909), editor of *Scribner's Monthly* and the *Century Magazine* (32 boxes and 39 volumes); Albert Shaw (1857–1947), editor of the American *Review of Reviews* (75 linear feet and 32 file drawers); and Charles Hanson Towne (1877–1949), editor of *Harper's Bazaar* (13 boxes and 14 volumes). Two significant German-language periodicals of New York City are also touched upon in the papers of Udo Brachvogel, editor of the *Belletristisches Journal* (6 boxes and 1 volume);[3] and Wilhelm Weitling, editor of *Die Republik der Arbeiter*.[4] In its Century collection the division holds the correspondence of the *Century Magazine* and that of its predecessors *Scribner's Monthly* and *St. Nicholas* (207 boxes).[5] In the late 1930s the library received the editorial correspondence of the Crowell Publishing Company, the publishers of *Woman's Home Companion*, *American Magazine*, *Collier's National Weekly*, and *Country Home*.

---

1. See Carolyn F. Ulrich and Eugenia Patterson, "Little Magazines," *BNYPL* 51 (1947): 3–25. The article is a detailed description of the library's holdings in English from 1890 to 1946.

2. See *BNYPL* 41 (1937): 165–66.
3. See Mabel Clare Weaks, "Gift of Udo Brachvogel Papers," *BNYPL* 31 (1927): 373–76.
4. See *BNYPL* 57 (1953): 358–60.
5. See Mabel Clare Weaks, "The Century Collection," *BNYPL* 38 (1934): 15–16.

5

NEWSPAPER RESOURCES AND JOURNALISM

The General Research and Humanities Division maintains a Newspaper File with 4,000 cards for domestic newspapers and 2,000 cards for foreign newspapers, which duplicates the catalog of the library's Newspaper Collection. It is an alphabetical record of newspaper holdings in the library's collections arranged by county, state, and city for the United States; and by country and city abroad. Holdings of United States newspapers published before 1800 are itemized in the Newspapers Check List in the Rare Book Division.

The Research Libraries have long maintained a policy of not issuing current newspapers to the public; files are usually made available only after they have been processed, either in bound volumes or on microfilm. There are certain exceptions to this rule, most notably the *New York Times*, current issues of which are available in the General Research and Humanities Division in the Central Building; the *Wall Street Journal*, available in the Economic and Public Affairs Division; and current newspapers in the Balto-Slavic and Oriental languages, available in the Slavonic and Oriental Divisions.

It may be well to define the terms "current" and "newspaper" as employed by the library. A newspaper is considered current if the latest issues are made available to the public in their original form as soon as they are received. Newspapers have been defined as "publication[s] appearing daily, weekly, or at other intervals, in sheet form, following conventional newspaper format (masthead, columnar arrangement, headlines), the chief function of which is to report, illustrate, and comment upon current events of either general or special interest."[1] (Trade or professional papers such as *Women's Wear Daily* are discussed in chapter 56 of this *Guide*; government gazettes, treated as public documents, are discussed in chapter 34.)

PRESERVATION POLICY

For preservation, most of the newspaper files in the library are filmed or will be filmed in the future. After filming of the original, files may or may not be retained. In the case of older files on rag paper, for example, files are retained if space permits; but modern titles on newsprint, which deteriorates rapidly, are rarely retained. Newspaper and periodical titles which the library has microfilmed and makes available in positive copies are listed in *Publications in Print and Titles Available on Microfilm* issued annually by the library. A particularly important group of Judaica and Hebraica is included.

COLLECTING POLICY

The Research Libraries acquire or, through cooperative library enterprises, provide access to United States newspapers in all languages from the standard metropolitan areas (as defined by the United States Census Bureau) on a representative basis, and on a selective basis other newspapers which may be important for cultural, economic, political, or sociological reasons. Since this policy, instituted in 1969, represents a change from previous coverage, emphasis is placed on participation in cooperative library newspaper programs (where files are represented in microform) and on purchase of microform newspaper files for titles of particular importance. The existing files of newspapers are being gradually augmented. Long-range plans call for the completion of existing broken files and the microforming of original files as a means of preserving the collection.

The library acquires or provides access to newspapers from other countries on a selective basis; when possible this includes at least one newspaper from every country in the world. Microfilms of lacking titles are borrowed from the Center for Research Libraries in Chicago or elsewhere.

The library maintains for its own collections comprehensive files of New York City newspapers in all languages. If films of these titles are not available through commercial or other sources, the library acquires original issues and undertakes preservation of these titles by microform. The library has always had a comprehensive collection of New York City newspapers, but while recognizing its responsibility to acquire the local and neighborhood newspapers of the city, it had not been able to do so with any great degree of success until 1969. In that year, after the formulation of the new acquisition policy, various library divisions began to make a particular effort to obtain this material, particularly those titles considered to be of cultural, economic, political, or sociological value. These local and neighborhood newspapers are generally the collecting responsi-

bility of the Local History and Genealogy Division, and include complete files on film of two outstanding titles, the *Villager* and the *Village Voice*. Other titles will be added in accordance with the new policy. The Branch Libraries have in various of their units current files of local and neighborhood newspapers which are usually discarded after a short period. The Schomburg Center of the Research Libraries retains a complete file of the *Amsterdam News* (1922–23, 1925–). Under the new acquisition policy, underground newspapers are also to be acquired selectively by the Periodicals Section of the Research Libraries. The Newspaper Collection will, in addition, acquire commercially produced collections of underground newspapers on microfilm.

COLLECTIONS OF NEWSPAPERS
NEWSPAPER COLLECTION

The Newspaper Collection of the Research Libraries, located in the library's Annex at 521 West 43rd Street, contains files of more than 4,000 newspapers published in most areas of the world since 1800. Papers published before 1800 are usually to be found in the Rare Book Division, although some eighteenth-century British files are in the Newspaper Collection. Newspapers in the Balto-Slavic and Oriental languages, and in Hebrew and Yiddish, are generally found in the Slavonic, Oriental, and Jewish Divisions. Most files of foreign newspapers begin in 1900 or later, although there are some earlier files. The holdings of the Newspaper Collection include more than 42,000 reels of microfilm and approximately 22,000 bound volumes. Most of these bound volumes contain older files of newspapers. More than 150 current titles are received from all over the world. A small collection of reference books is maintained, including the standard indexes to the *New York Times*, London *Times*, *Christian Science Monitor*, and the *Wall Street Journal*, along with other materials on journalism and newspaper history.

There are virtually complete files of most general newspapers (as distinguished from those of strictly local or neighborhood distribution) published in New York City from 1801 to the present, in English and other languages. Notable files include the *New York Post* (1801–), *New York Journal of Commerce and Commercial* (1828–), *New York Herald* (1835–1924), *Brooklyn Eagle* (1841–1955), *New York Times* (1851–), *World* (1860–1931), and the *New York Sun* (1833–43, 1861–1950). Foreign language papers published in New York City include the *Atlantis* and *National Herald* (Greek), *El diario-La prensa* (Spanish), *Nordisk Tidende* (Norwegian), and others in Chinese, Japanese, Finnish, Swedish, Italian, and German.

Some of the significant titles received from other cities of the United States are the *Atlanta Constitution* (1945–), *Boston Herald* and *Boston Herald Traveller* (1952–), *Chicago Tribune* (1947–), Honolulu *Star-Bulletin* (1959–), New Orleans *Times-Picayune* (1958–), and *Philadelphia Inquirer* (1860–65, incomplete; 1942–). The collection of California newspapers covers the period from 1850 to the present.

British newspapers include a good file of the *London Chronicle* (1757–98), the London *Times* (1785–), the Manchester *Guardian* (1929–), and others. A special collection of interest includes issues which appeared during the general strike of 1926.

---

1. See Aaron L. Fessler and Saro J. Riccardi, *Current Newspapers, United States and Foreign: A Union List of Newspapers Available in the Libraries of the New York Metropolitan Area* (The New York Public Library, 1957), p. 3.

Continental European newspapers are less numerous, and the files less complete. There are generally representative files beginning about 1900 from most nations. Many others were added at the beginning of World War I, such as the *Frankfurter Zeitung und Handelsblatt* (1900–43). The incomplete file of the Paris *Journal des débats* covers the periods 1814–26, 1841–68, 1879–87, and 1892–1942. Files of other important titles are substantial although frequently incomplete. There is an interesting group of newspapers from all belligerent countries during the period of World War I. Among titles now received are *Figaro* (1880– , incomplete) from Paris, and the Swiss *Neue Zürcher Zeitung* (1900–09; 1914–). The famous *La Prensa* of Argentina is available in a complete run beginning in 1869, and there are copies of Mexico's *El Universal* (1933–), and the *Diario de Centro America* (1949–) from Guatemala.

Catalog and Special Indexes and Files

The catalog of the Newspaper Collection follows a regional arrangement in three main sections: the United States by state; New York City; and foreign countries. There are few subject entries in the catalog, which is primarily an alphabetical listing by title. Cards for materials in various divisions of the Research Libraries are also filed, however, including those from the Rare Book, Economic and Public Affairs, and Slavonic Divisions; and for items in the Center for Research Libraries in Chicago.

Among the special indexes and files in the Newspaper Collection are the following:

Columnists File. An index arranged alphabetically by name of columnists, giving such information as the type or title of newspaper column written, names of newspapers in which it appeared, etc. (inactive, 1 card drawer).

Facts Index. A card index arranged by subject and containing information accumulated in answering reference questions (semi-active, 22 card drawers). For example, under the heading "Hiss-Chambers Case" index cards provide dates and locations for news stories.

Other-than-Newspapers File. An alphabetical index of subject cards pertaining to literature in the newspaper field (active, 1 card drawer). The titles may be found in either the Newspaper Collection or the general collections.

Vertical Files. File folders contain miscellaneous information that may be needed either by the staff or the public (active, 3 file trays). There are folders under such headings as "Strikes—N. Y. City," "Newspapers on microfilm," "Library of Congress current list," and "Steiger Collection of German-American newspapers."

RARE BOOK DIVISION

American newspapers published before 1800, and other newspaper rarities, are kept in the Rare Book Division. The division maintains an active Newspapers Check List in two loose-leaf notebooks arranged by city and town.

Early British newspapers in the division include files of the *St. James's Chronicle* (1768–78), *Lloyd's Evening Post and British Chronicle* (1758–81, incomplete), and the *London Packet* (1772–78), of added interest because they were published during the colonial and Revolutionary periods of American history. Many important examples of early seventeenth-century English newspapers or "newsbooks" came to the division in the Lonsdale collection, purchased in 1947.[2]

Other holdings include a group of facsimiles or later souvenir issues of rare newspapers such as the *Ulster County Gazette*, of which the division has over thirty editions, although lacking the rare original issue of January 4, 1800.[3] There are also the productions of amateur and toy presses, Lilliputian newspapers, and other materials.

This is one of the most important collections in the library. Early files and rare issues are numerous, among them Bradford's *New-York Gazette*, Zenger's *Weekly Journal* (the best file known), Parker's *Post-Boy*, and excellent files of Holt's *Journal*, Gaine's *Mercury*, and Farley's *American Chronicle*. Going beyond New York, the representation of Philadelphia newspapers includes extensive files of Franklin's *Gazette* and Bradford's *Journal*. The library's holdings of newspapers published before 1821 are recorded in Brigham's *History and Bibliography of American Newspapers, 1690–1820* (1947), although some files and issues have been added since its appearance. The division's holdings have been extended by photostat or microfilm files to include North Carolina newspapers before 1800, the *Virginia Gazette*, and the *Kentucky Gazette*.

Later American materials held in the division because of their value include the famous issue of the *Vicksburg Daily Citizen* of July 2, 1864, set by the staff of the newspaper but printed by Union soldiers after the fall of the city. Files of American Indian newspapers include a notable group of Cherokee newspapers for the period from 1828 to 1853.

MICROFORM READING ROOM

In the Microform Reading Room of the Central Building are kept microfilm copies of the *New York Times* (1851–), the *New York Post* (1967–), the *New York Herald Tribune* (1924–66), and the *World Journal Tribune* (1966–67). The *New York Times Index* from 1851 until recent years is also kept here; indexes for the last few years are held in Room 315.

---

2. See Lewis M. Stark, "Lonsdale Collection of English Newspapers," *BNYPL* 52 (1948): 35–36.

3. See R. W. G. Vail, "The Ulster County Gazette and Its Illegitimate Offspring," *BNYPL* 34 (1930): 207–40, with a listing of this and other facsimile newspapers owned by the library; see also "The Ulster County Gazette Found at Last," *BNYPL* 35 (1931): 207–11. Published together separately by the library.

ECONOMIC AND PUBLIC AFFAIRS DIVISION

Issues covering the latest six months or a year of a small number of newspapers on banking and investment are kept in the Economic and Public Affairs Division for consultation in conjunction with periodicals and other publications on these subjects. Older issues are microfilmed or bound and permanently located in the Microform Reading Room or the Newspaper Collection. Included in this group are such titles as the *Wall Street Journal*, *Financial Post* (Toronto), *Financial Times* (London), and *Financial Express* (Bombay).

LOCAL HISTORY AND GENEALOGY DIVISION

A perhaps unique collection of anniversary and special issues of local United States and Canadian newspapers is available. The division is expanding its coverage of local and neighborhood New York City newspapers. Complete files of the *Villager* and the *Village Voice* are on microfilm in the Microform Reading Room (current issues are available through the Periodicals Section).

SCHOMBURG CENTER FOR RESEARCH IN BLACK CULTURE

The Schomburg Center has a good collection of African newspapers on microfilm. The Afro-American newspaper collection includes long, complete runs of newspapers dating from 1827 through World War I, such as the *California Eagle, Cleveland Gazette*, and *Savannah Tribune*. Current issues of black newspapers giving national coverage are microfilmed at the end of each year.

SLAVONIC DIVISION

This division houses some 120 newspaper titles, mostly in Balto-Slavic languages. Approximately 40 of these come from the USSR, including *Pravda* (1917–) and *Izvestiya* (1917–); 4 are from Poland, including *Trybuna Ludu* (1948–); and 1 is from Czechoslovakia, *Rudé Právo* (1948– , incomplete). There are papers from thirteen other countries, with the largest single unit being 52 titles from the United States and Canada. Current issues are available to the public as received; back files are available on microfilm.

ORIENTAL DIVISION

The division has many newspapers on microfilm from the United Arab Republic, Iran, India, Japan, and Korea. A number of titles are received from the People's Republic of China, Georgia, Armenia, and the countries of Soviet Central Asia. Current issues are held in the division for use by the public.

JEWISH DIVISION

This division contains one of the largest collections of Jewish newspapers and periodicals in the United States. The newspapers, which originate in many nations, are collected both in their original form and on microfilm. Many of the filmed titles are available for sale and are listed in the Library's *Publications in Print and Titles Available on Microfilm*, which is published annually. A detailed description of periodical and newspaper holdings in Hebrew, Yiddish, and Ladino is given in chapter 10 of this *Guide*.

MANUSCRIPTS AND ARCHIVES DIVISION

Among the resources of the Manuscripts and Archives Division are collections relating to New York City newspapers, particularly the files of editors and publishers. Among these are the papers of James Gordon Bennett, editor and publisher of the *New York Herald* (2 boxes); John Bigelow, coowner and editor of the *New York Evening Post* (39-volume diary, 24 other volumes, and 38 boxes); Robert Bonner, publisher of the *New York Ledger* (3,500 pieces); Parke Godwin, editor of the *New York Evening Post* (17 boxes); Horace Greeley, editor of the *New York Tribune* (5 boxes); George E. Jones, one of the founders of the *New York Times* (250 pieces); St. Clair McKelway, editor of the *Brooklyn Daily Eagle* (4 file drawers); and Henry J. Raymond, a founder and editor of the *New York Times* (125 pieces).[4]

PRINTS DIVISION

The Prints Division contains a great deal of material pertaining to newspaper cartoons, including original drawings by Thomas Nast and the proofs of the political cartoons of Rollin Kirby and Daniel F. Fitzpatrick. The James Wright Brown cartoon collection contains original editorial cartoons by American artists.

ADDITIONAL RESOURCES

Materials in the general collections include a number of trench and camp newspapers of World War I. Also important is a complete file of *Yank* for both World Wars, and an almost complete file of *Stars and Stripes* in the single edition of World War I and the 30 editions of World War II.[5] The library's extensive holdings of the publications of free and resistance movements and clandestine publications for the World War II period include many newspapers. Papers published in countries formerly occupied by Germany and those published by the Allied occupying forces number approximately 600 separate titles dating between 1945 and 1949; these are augmented by 172 reels of filmed post-World War II German papers administered by the Newspaper Collection. Spanish newspapers of the period immediately preceding the Spanish Civil War are also noteworthy. There is a collection of Hungarian newspapers published during the uprising of 1956.

JOURNALISM

The library's holdings in the field of journalism contain not only texts and treatises on the subject, but also periodicals, directories, and other related material, including a strong collection of bibliographies, union lists, indexes, and directories of newspapers. An important feature is the history of the press (general, international, national,

---

4. See Robert W. Hill, "Gifts: The Henry J. Raymond Papers," *BNYPL* 55 (1951): 512–14.

5. See C. E. Dornbusch, "Stars and Stripes: Check List of the Several Editions," *BNYPL* 52 (1948): 331–40 and supplement, 53 (1949): 335–38; "Yank, The Army Weekly; A Check List," *BNYPL* 54 (1950): 272–79. Each published separately by the library.

and regional), and the history of individual newspapers. The library also has an extensive group of materials published by or relating to schools of journalism. The special files noted above in the discussion of the Newspaper Collection, although of restricted access, supplement the regular hold-ings. Manuscripts and Archives Division holdings related to newspapers are described above; materials in the division relating to Charles Hanson Towne, editor of *Harper's Bazaar*, are more closely related to periodicals and are described in chapter 4 of this *Guide*.

6

LEARNED SOCIETY AND MUSEUM PUBLICATIONS, AND INTERNATIONAL EXHIBITIONS

LEARNED SOCIETY PUBLICATIONS

The general publications of learned societies and institutions, comprehensively collected and one of the strong features of the library's holdings, are represented by approximately 55,370 volumes. Not included are publications of a society or academy devoted wholly to one subject, which are classed and considered with that subject.

Although the common origin of most learned societies seems to have been an interest in natural history in some form, the development of that interest has led to greatly increased scope in many cases, so that the publications of the organizations may now cover everything from belles-lettres to the exact sciences. A trend especially noticeable since World War II is the development by larger organizations of separate publications for the exact sciences. The library seldom separates these series; they are held in integrated sequences under the administration of the General Research and Humanities Division.

Natural history was a subject of considerable interest in the Astor Library, which commenced very early to gather these publications as well as finely illustrated books in the field, and to secure the earlier sets. In 1851, Dr. Cogswell reported that the Astor Library was already rich in the transactions of learned societies, and in 1854 he wrote that it had the "publications of the principal societies in Great Britain, France, Belgium, Holland, Germany, Denmark, Sweden, Norway, Russia, Italy, Spain, and Portugal, and also of the United States. . . ."[1] Interest is not presently centered in material relating to natural history or the biological sciences, but instead is based on the widened interests of the societies which now make their contributions of great value to the library's collection as a whole.

Perhaps the most important subjects featured in the library's general collection of learned society publications are biography, local history and genealogy, anthropology, art and archaeology, and the divisions of the sciences in which the library specializes, such as chemistry and physics.

GENERAL COLLECTION (BILLINGS *E)

Approximately 48,000 volumes represent virtually complete holdings of the publication series of such organizations as the Carnegie Institution of Washington, the Royal Society of London, the Preussische Akademie der Wissenschaften of Berlin, the Institut de France, the Accademia Nazionale dei Lincei, and other national bodies. No distinction in geographical origin is made in the library's collecting; the European representation is as strong as the American and English. Other parts of the world well represented are Africa, Australia, and South America. In addition to national societies and academies, the library actively collects the publications of state and local societies. Since many of the latter are no longer in existence, some of the sets in the library's collection are particularly valuable for research. Chronologically, the general collection of society publications ranges from the later seventeenth century to the present.

In addition to general materials are strong collections of learned society publications in the Jewish Division (either in the Hebrew alphabet or on Judaica as a subject); in the Oriental Division (publications of societies specializing in Oriental studies, as distinguished from scientific contributions such as the *Proceedings* of the Japan Society, which are held in the general collections), and in the Slavonic Division (materials published in Imperial Russia or in the USSR, and other publications in the Cyrillic alphabet).

INDEXING OF LEARNED SOCIETY PUBLICATIONS

To make the contents of learned society publications more readily accessible to readers, the library attempts to index or analyze certain materials in them for the Public Catalog or the appropriate division catalogs.[2] This indexing is selective rather than systematic, and principally covers subjects in which the library is strong. It is more extensive for older, rather than the more recent materials, since there has been a great increase in the number of commercially produced indexes that are readily available in the reading rooms of the Research Libraries.

---

1. Lydenberg, *History*, pp. 20, 27.

2. A distinction is made between the terms "index" and "analyze." Indexing is, in general, subject cataloging only and is used principally for articles in periodicals. Analyzing, which entails cataloging under author and subject, is used principally for monographs in series.

JEWISH DIVISION

The holdings of some 1,100 volumes represent a good cross section of materials in many languages, published in many countries. Examples are found in the Juedisch-theologisches Seminar (Breslau) *Jahresbericht* (1856–1937), Lehranstalt für die Wissenschaft des Judentums (Berlin) *Bericht* (1876–1932), Ferencz József Országos Rabbikepzö Intézet (Budapest) *Jahresbericht* (1878–1946), Mekize Nirdamim *Kovets 'al yad* (1885–), Israelitisch-theologische Lehranstalt (Vienna) *Jahresberichte* (1894–1923), and the American Academy for Jewish Research *Proceedings* (1928–30).

ORIENTAL DIVISION

The holdings of Oriental journals are outstanding; the major part of this collection consists of learned society publications numbering approximately 5,000 bound volumes. The range and diversity of the resources may be determined from the following partial enumeration of titles: American Oriental Society *Journal* (1843–); Deutsche morgenländische Gesellschaft *Zeitschrift* (1847–); Royal Asiatic Society *Journal* (1834–), all branches; Société Asiatique *Journal asiatique* (1822–); and the Asiatic Society of Japan *Transactions* (1872/73–). There are also files of the Società Asiatica Italiana *Giornale*, the *Bijdragen tot de taal-, land-, en volkenkunde van Nederlandsche-Indië*, and various publications of the Koninklijk Bataviaasch Genootschap van Kunsten en Wetenschappen. The holdings are substantially complete in most cases.

SLAVONIC DIVISION

More than 2,000 bound volumes in the Slavonic Division are learned society publications of a general nature. The largest single group is made up of the various publications of the Akademiya Nauk of Leningrad and Moscow, of which the division has a complete set passing through many changes of title and subdivisions, including *Mémoires* (1726–1890), *Bulletin* (1779–), and *Doklady* (1849–). There are, in addition, the publications of the various academies of science of the soviet republics such as those of Armenia, Azerbaijan, Belorussia, Georgia, Kirghiz, Kazak, Tajik, and the Ukraine, among others. The division also has a complete file of the Naukove Tovarystvo Imeny Shevchenka *Zapysky* (1892–).

MUSEUM PUBLICATIONS

Approximately 1,500 card entries in the Public Catalog refer to the subject "Museums" and its subdivisions, locating some 7,300 volumes in the collections; many of the entries are for multi-volume periodical sets. This heading covers only the publications by or about general museums and does not include art galleries or other specialized museums. Institutions such as the Metro-politan Museum of Art are placed under the heading "Art—Collections," the American Museum of Natural History under "Natural History —Museums and Collections," and the Deutsches Museum von Meisterwerken der Naturwissenschaft und Technik in Munich under "Science—Museums." The collecting policy is comprehensive for all subject areas, including those not otherwise acquired in depth, such as zoology.

Museum publications collected by the library include administrative reports, general handbooks, and the publication series of the museums themselves. Holdings are strong but do not always include handbooks or guidebooks in the latest issue. The Art and Architecture Division, however, maintains an up-to-date collection of handbooks for the major art collections of the world. The varied collection of general museum publications includes, for example, those of the Bergens Museum (Norway), the Charleston Museum (South Carolina), the Federated Malay States Museum, the Manchester Museum (England), the New York State Museum, the Transvaal Museum, and many others. Files of serial publications or handbooks are by no means complete, but the representation is substantial.

INTERNATIONAL EXHIBITIONS

A strong collection emphasizes the great international exhibitions held in the period 1851 to 1904, especially those of Philadelphia (1876) and Paris (1900). The collecting policy is comprehensive for book materials from all countries and periods; some 3,500 entries in the Public Catalog identify resources administered by the General Research and Humanities Division. Periodicals are a feature of the holdings, not only those issued by the fairs during their period of operation but also such trade publications as *La Revue de l'exposant* (1964–). A large proportion of the book material is in pamphlet form.

In the Duyckinck collection in the Manuscripts and Archives Division is a scrapbook of 150 trade cards from the Crystal Palace Exhibition held in New York City in 1853; the division also holds two letters by P. T. Barnum relating to the Crystal Palace.[3] The records of the New York World's Fair (1939/40) Corporation cover the period 1936 to 1941, and include the central files for all major departments of the corporation. Additional material includes registers of visitors to the Community Building; miscellaneous papers and ephemera of Ashley T. Cole, a member of the New York State Commission to the Fair; and files of correspondence for the Temple of Religion. The division also has the records of the New York World's Fair (1964/65) Corporation with additional related material in the personal papers of Robert Moses.

---

3. See Earle E. Coleman, "The Exhibition in the Palace; A Bibliographical Essay," *BNYPL* 64 (1960): 459–77.

7

GENERAL PAMPHLETS AND SCRAPBOOKS

PAMPHLETS

As a category of materials often ephemeral in nature pamphlets have always been one of the library's special collecting interests. Three classes of pamphlets are generally recognized according to cataloging treatment: pamphlets given full cataloging; pamphlets placed in "n.c." (not cataloged) volumes; and pamphlets cataloged collectively.

Fully cataloged pamphlets are generally bound together in pamphlet volumes, and from the cataloging point of view are indistinguishable from other monographs, except that their classmarks include the abbreviation "p.v." There are exceptional cases when size, rarity, demand, special interest, or other factors dictate that a piece be separately bound and treated as a book. While the pamplet volume is a convenience from the standpoint of organizing and shelving materials by subject, the practice is currently under review because of the deleterious effect a publication on poor paper may have on those bound with it.

Pamphlets classified as "n.c." are materials which have been retained in the collections but not separately cataloged. Such material has been bound together by subject as closely as possible, and is represented in the public catalogs only by subject cards. Readers making a comprehensive study of a subject are advised to examine these volumes. (This type of cataloging was abandoned after 1945.)

Some pamphlets having a close subject connection have been bound together and cataloged collectively under such titles as "Collection of Pamphlets on Woman Suffrage." These are represented by subject and composite entry cards in the public catalogs of the library. Contents of the collection are in some cases given on the main entry cards.

In this *Guide*, pamphlet holdings are described with subject resources. Although it is impossible to estimate the total size of the pamphlet holdings of the Research Libraries, mention can be made of certain large and important collections. Among these are French revolutionary pamphlets; Dutch historical pamphlets of the sixteenth to eighteenth centuries; English Civil War pamphlets; British historical pamphlets; pamphlets dealing with the American Revolution published in England and colonial America; several hundred nineteenth-century Irish pamphlets, many relating to the land question; and pamphlets concerning the Spanis Civil War of 1936–39. The pamphlets and brochures relating to early automobiles in the United States, England, and Europe are of unusual interest; and there is an extraordinary collection of pamphlets on economics and commerce, transportation, and labor.

In addition to the pamphlets dispersed throughout the library by subject, there is a special classmark assigned in the Billings Classification Schedule (*C) as a general location for miscellaneous pamphlets and miscellaneous monographic series. There are some 22,000 volumes in this classmark, which is no longer in active use.

SCRAPBOOKS

The library has long been interested in certain kinds of scrapbook material. In some cases scrapbooks are valuable in themselves because they contain primary source material; in others they are extremely useful in supplementing books and periodical resources for research. Of the former, the scrapbooks of correspondence and clippings of the American Civil Liberties Union may be cited;[1] of the latter type are scrapbooks relating to William Sulzer, Woodrow Wilson, and Charles Evans Hughes; those in the Spalding baseball collection; and a large number relating to the early stages of World War II. Much of this material, mounted and bound, has come as gifts; some of the volumes have been assembled by the library. The Art and Architecture Division and the Science and Technology Research Center have many volumes and series of this kind, although neither division is now adding to its scrapbook collections.

Scrapbooks are of great importance to the divisions and collections of the Performing Arts Research Center at Lincoln Center, and represent a rapidly growing form of materials there. The staff of the Music Division maintains a "New York Scrapbook" consisting of newspaper clippings on musical events in the City. Scrapbooks received as gifts are generally filmed and cataloged; the originals are then discarded. Scrapbooks are an important part of the extensive holdings of the nonbook materials in the Theatre Collection. The collection has the distinctive practice of referring to cataloged pamphlets bound together as scrapbooks. Scrapbooks relating to the dance are prime sources of information in the Dance Collection, particularly when they have been prepared by the artists or artists' managers, as were those of Agnes de Mille and Sol Hurok, among many others. All scrapbooks in the collection are filmed and the original scrapbooks are retained.

The library's general cataloging procedure treats scrapbooks as monographs, classifying the volumes with related subject materials.

---

1. The originals of these were transferred to Princeton University in 1950 after microfilming by the New York Public Library.

8

GRAPHOLOGY AND BOOK ARTS AND PRODUCTION

The library's general works on book arts number some 30,000 volumes, excluding the numerous examples of fine illustrated books and notable bindings in the collections, and technical works on paper and ink which are the collecting responsibility of the Science and Technology Research Center. The collections in this field are generally strong; the collecting policy is comprehensive for most of the subsections described below. The principal resources in the various fields of the book arts are located in the general collections with the following major exceptions: materials on book illustration (as opposed to illumination) are in the Prints Division; editions noted for their fine illustrations or bindings are collected particularly by the Spencer Collection; and the publications of special presses are a strong feature of the Rare Book Division.

HANDWRITING

Some 1,700 entries in the Public Catalog refer to handwriting. Eighteenth- and nineteenth-century works form the larger part of the collection, but there is an extensive representation of sixteenth- and seventeenth-century titles as well. There are notable groups of general works, textbooks on special systems, and a rich collection of hand-writing specimens. The Spencer Collection holds a number of early writing books including Sigismondo Fanti's *Theorica et Pratica de Modo Scribendi* (Venice, 1514) and Juan de Icíar's *Arte Subtilissima* (1550). The Rare Book Division has a collection of early American writing books.[1]

But handwriting as a subject has many aspects besides copy-book styles, most of which are well represented. The most impressive in number, perhaps, is an interesting group of both historical and current works on character in handwriting. Important gifts in this subject area have related principally to penmanship. In 1911 George H. Shattuck gave 428 works—school copy-books, handbooks, and specimen books—published from 1659 to 1911, and covering very fully the period after 1850. This date approximately marks the change from manuscript copy-books prepared by the individual teacher to engraved books issued by the publisher.

Other resources of interest in this area include a substantially complete group of facsimiles of existing Aztec and Mayan codices in the American History Division. Epigraphy is significantly represented; a strong collection on Egyptology in the Oriental Division contains much of interest relating to Egyptian hieroglyphics.[2] The Manu-

scripts and Archives Division has 624 Sumerian and Babylonian clay and stone tablets.[3] Materials on Chinese characters and other Oriental writings are held by the Oriental Division, with actual examples in the Manuscripts and Archives Division and the Spencer Collection. Works on procedures requiring special techniques, such as illumination, show-card writing, library hand, and many others are classed with the appropriate subject materials.

SHORTHAND

The shorthand collection is one of the outstanding collections of the Research Libraries, with strong historical coverage from the earliest period to 1940.[4] Approximately 8,600 entries covering the subject are listed in the Public Catalog. The collecting policy is comprehensive for historical works but representative for current items, the intention being to provide examples of the latest publications on the established systems, and to include coverage of new systems and developments in the field.

Although a considerable amount of shorthand material was included in the Ford collection (received in 1899), the subject first became of real importance in the library when the National Shorthand Reporters' Association deposited the Charles Currier Beale collection, together with its own library, in 1912. Beale's interest lay principally in the history of English systems. As a result, his collection emphasized works in the English language, and was particularly strong in the textbooks of John Byrom and Benn Pitman. Beale also acquired many curious little books written in shorthand, and he made notable collections of shorthand journals and reports of trials and debates. His interest in manuscripts centered on Phinehas Bailey. The National Shorthand Reporters' Association collection is particularly strong in periodicals and shorthand society publications. It contains some early English and American titles, and makes a larger contribution in textbooks relating to the principal European systems.

New York, 1925," *BNYPL* 45 (1941): 791–820 et seq. Published separately by the library, 1942. See also her "Modern Egypt: A List of References to Material in The New York Public Library," *BNYPL* 32 (1928): 589–634 et seq. Published separately by the library, 1929. Reprinted in 2 vols. as *Ancient Egypt* and *Modern Egypt* by Kraus Reprint Co. (New York, 1969).

3. See Leo Oppenheim, *Catalogue of the Cuneiform Tablets of the Wilberforce Eames Babylonian Collection* (New Haven: American Oriental Society, 1948).

4. See Karl Brown and Daniel C. Haskell, "Shorthand Books in The New York Public Library," *BNYPL* 36 (1932): 243–49 et seq. Published separately by the library, with corrections and additions; reprinted by the library and Arno Press, 1971.

---

1. See Ray Nash, *American Writing Masters and Copybooks* (Boston: The Colonial Society of Massachusetts, 1959), in which the extent of the library's holdings is indicated.

2. See Ida A. Pratt, "Ancient Egypt: A List of References to Material in The New York Public Library," *BNYPL* 27 (1923): 723–66 et seq. Published separately by the library, with additions and index, 1925. See also her "Ancient Egypt: 1925–1941; Supplement to: Ancient Egypt . . .

In 1913 a bronze tablet in honor of Sir Isaac Pitman was placed in the Public Catalog Room of the Central Building by the Isaac Pitman Shorthand Writers' Association of New York, "to commemorate the one hundredth anniversary of the birth of Sir Isaac Pitman and in recognition of the important collection of shorthand literature in the New York Public Library." At that time the association and Clarence A. Pitman presented collections of Pitmanic works to the library.

In the early 1920s John R. Gregg, personally and through the Gregg Writer and the Gregg Publishing Company, initiated the presentation of important gifts of material, including publications on the Gregg system, various American and foreign periodicals, and works on other systems of shorthand. Dr. Gregg checked the holdings of the library and generously supplied from his own library important works not present. Gifts from the Gregg Company and Gregg's widow continued through the 1940s.

With the cooperation of the National Shorthand Reporters' Association, five other notable American collections were acquired by gift and purchase. The David O'Keefe collection of general works, valuable for the addition of many representative works on American systems, came to the library in 1923. The Jerome B. Howard collection, acquired in 1924, was believed by its owner to be the largest collection of English shorthand works in the world. Its rarities are predominantly of the seventeenth and eighteenth centuries. The collection also includes most of the important histories and literary works about shorthand. The Norman P. Heffley collection, acquired in 1925, included European, and particularly German, systems and literature. As Heffley was one of the first American collectors in the field, he was able to secure representative works of considerable diversity. The Julius E. Rockwell collection, acquired in 1927, was notable for its rarities. Rockwell collected particular distinctive, curious, or rare titles, rather than systematic series of editions; these include textbooks, Bibles, Testaments, and prayer books in the various systems of shorthand. William D. Bridge's collection, which was acquired in 1928, contained many of the representative works of earlier English systems but was richest in Pitmanic titles. A large portion of the works published by Isaac Pitman from 1837 onward is included, together with strong holdings of the works of Andrews and Boyle and other early exponents of the system in the United States.

In 1937, John J. Healy gave the collection of manuscripts described below.

RESOURCES

Books and Periodicals

The collection is strongest from the earliest period to 1940. Both general periodicals and those dealing with particular systems, together with the publications of shorthand, stenographic, and reporting organizations, are held in strength. The present collecting policy calls for a representative selection of current materials: eight periodical titles on shorthand are received at present from the United States, England, France, Czechoslovakia, and Poland.

Among the systems, the English and American are more fully represented than the European. The early English representation is very rich, lacking few works, with sets of editions of most of the systems virtually complete. This is equally true for American systems; as these are for the most part reprints and adaptations of English systems, they are less important from the point of view of shorthand history. The catalog adopts the conventional date of 1837, which marks the adoption of Pitman's "Phonography," for the beginning of "modern" shorthand. The representation of both Pitman styles (the English Isaac, and the American Benn) is very full, as is that of the numerous reprints and adaptations. Holdings related to the Gregg system are rich in both historical and contemporary works. An interesting feature of the collection is the manuals of systems, both old and modern, which had little or only local vogue.

Works in shorthand, particularly Bibles, constitute a strong collection. More curious than useful to the student of shorthand are such works as those in Chinook Jargon, an adaptation of the Duployan to this American Indian dialect.

As shorthand is not a subject in which most college and university libraries are interested, the Research Libraries have assumed a continuing collecting interest in the field. There is a heavy reliance upon gifts to maintain the collections of contemporary textbooks and other material.

Manuscripts

In 1937 the library received from John J. Healy, of Buffalo, New York, the correspondence and documents of the Standardization Committee of the National Shorthand Reporters' Association —an accrual of opinion and knowledge, based on experience, which was published in the committee's *The Reporters' Phrasebook of Standardized Shorthand* [Pitmanic] (1934). In addition to the large file of committee correspondence, the collection contains several copies of the dummy used in the final shaping of the shorthand symbols, a large number of clipped magazine articles by members and others prominent in the reporting profession, and other materials relative to this important work. The correspondence has been arranged by Arthur R. Bailey to present in logical form the progress of the movement. A continued attempt is made to collect both original and printed materials covering the standardization from its inception in 1909.

Other manuscripts are, for the most part, related to the English and American systems: many came with the Beale collection described above. A gift from the Gregg Publishing Company of New York City in 1938 included 40 packages of company papers from about 1910 to 1938. Associated with this gift is a purchase of 25 letters written by John Robert Gregg during the period 1924 to 1946. Representative of the other noted system of shorthand, the Manuscripts and Archives Division has the diary in Pitman shorthand of Frederick Pitman, covering roughly the period from 1845 to 1884. Additional materials consist of manuscript shorthand transcriptions of the New Testament, the Book of Common Prayer, etc., in various systems dating from the sixteenth through the early nineteenth centuries. A series of sermons in shorthand transcriptions include some by the Rev. Phinehas Bailey which date from the early nineteenth century. There are also transcripts of court proceedings,[5] autographs of noted shorthand

---

5. See Karl Brown, "The Court Reporter's Job," *BNYPL* 55 (1951): 531–34, describing several dozen pages of records of trials held during the first decade of this century.

writers, manuscripts of books written on short-hand, and many other items. A separate card file, which is not reproduced in the published catalog of the division, records manuscript holdings in this field.

TYPEWRITING

Collecting policy calls for representative acquisition in this subject area. There are approximately 500 references to typewriting in the Public Catalog. Historical materials are particularly interesting, including a number of old manuals of the various systems dating from the nineteenth and early twentieth centuries. A rich source of additional material is found in the collection of shorthand periodicals; these have not, however, been indexed for articles dealing with typewriting.

AUTHORSHIP

Periodicals relating to the marketing of manuscripts are a feature of this relatively small collection, covered by some 700 references in the Public Catalog. The scope is international. Related materials are found classed with such subjects as journalism and philology.

PUBLISHERS AND PUBLISHING

Materials on publishing, both in this country and abroad, constitute strong holdings in a subject area covered by comprehensive collecting. The resources are entered under a number of different headings in the Public Catalog: "Authors and Publishers," "Best Sellers, Literary," "Clandestine Publications," "Censorship, Literary," "Music—Publishing," etc. The collection of more than 100 editions of the *Index librorum prohibitorum* in the Rare Book Division, the earliest dated 1550 with coverage extending to the nineteenth century, is a significant part of the material dealing with censorship. Periodicals are a feature of the general collections on publishing, as are the formal histories of the industry and of individual firms; New York City is especially well covered. A collection of 22 scrapbooks containing examples of book jackets produced in the United States, England, Germany, and other countries illustrates the development of that form. Also included is a small but interesting collection on literary hoaxes entered in the Public Catalog under the heading "Literature—Forgeries, frauds, etc.;" many index entries to periodical articles are included.

Manuscript Resources

Since New York City is the center of publishing activity in the United States, the Manuscripts and Archives Division has made an effort to acquire archives of publishing houses and editors; these supplement the excellent resources in American and English literature. The manuscript "Work Book No. 2" of Benjamin Franklin and David Hall, Philadelphia printers, came to the library in 1929 as the gift of Edward S. Harkness. It is a business record of the firm for the period August 2, 1759 to January 30, 1766.[6] The papers of Richard Rogers Bowker, editor and publisher of book-trade periodicals from 1870 to the 1930s,

consist of 21 volumes, 170 boxes, and 3 cartons of materials.[7] Other extensive records of printing and publishing firms include those of the Century Company from 1880 to 1914 (207 boxes);[8] Alfred A. Knopf, 1930–50 (3 boxes and 10 cartons); the Pynson Press, publishers of the *Colophon*, 1928–33 (14 packages); and the Chiswick Press (England), 1831 to 1933 (3 boxes). The acquisition of the Macmillan Company archives in 1965 gave the library a magnificent collection of editorial correspondence in 119 copy-books for the period from 1889 to 1907, and some 16,000 letters from Macmillan authors during the first half of the twentieth century.[9] The papers are more fully described in the discussion of significant gifts in chapter 20 of this *Guide*. Related manuscript materials on specific aspects of publishing are discussed in the chapters on periodical and newspaper resources.

More than 400 items record the history of the first press of South America, from its establishment in Lima in 1584 by Antonio Ricardo until the death of the second printer, Francisco del Canto, in 1618. The materials, contained in a single large portfolio, include letters, contracts, inventories of the contents of the printing shop, and other documents, with the major portion referring to del Canto. This archive was the gift of Edward S. Harkness.

COPYRIGHT

The library maintains a good collection of historical and contemporary works on this subject. The collection of Major George H. Putnam, given by Mrs. Putnam in 1931, contained a publisher's working library on copyright.

Many items in the Manuscripts and Archives Division relate to the subject. The larger part of the Robert Underwood Johnson papers consist of correspondence during the period 1877 to 1935 between Johnson, as an officer of the American Copyright League, and other organizations working in behalf of copyright legislation. Nine boxes of materials in the Richard Rogers Bowker papers represent Bowker's activities in this field, and supplement his personal papers relating to international copyright, now held by the Library of Congress.[10]

PRINTING

This is a strong collection, which has always been of interest to the library. The collecting policy is comprehensive. There are approximately 7,000 references to the subject in the Public Catalog, including numerous cross-references to related subjects. The periodical collections are substantially complete, both historically and on a current basis, with long runs of such titles as *El arte tipográfico* (1908–), *Inland Printer* (1883–1958), and the *British Printer* (1888–). About 75 international periodical titles are currently received, including publications from Asian and South American countries. The book collections contain excellent holdings on the history of printing and of individual printers. Bibliographies in the field are particularly well represented, both

---

6. See George S. Eddy, "A Work Book of the Printing House of Benjamin Franklin and David Hall, 1759–1766," *BNYPL* 34 (1930): 575–89.

7. See *BNYPL* 41 (1937): 165–66.
8. See Mabel Clare Weaks, "The Century Collection," *BNYPL* 38 (1934): 15–16.
9. See *BNYPL* 71 (1967): 3.
10. See *BNYPL* 41 (1937): 165–66.

in the general collections and in the Rare Book Division; the holdings of the latter are more complete and reflect the division's excellent Americana resources.

TYPOGRAPHICAL SPECIMENS

Several hundred fonts of old-fashioned type faces were presented to the library in 1957 by the Carl and Lily Pforzheimer Foundation, Inc., forming a rich and welcome addition to the small number of existing collections of this kind in the United States. The collection had been acquired by Mr. Pforzheimer from his friend Elrie Robinson, "The Horse and Buggy Printer" of St. Francisville, Louisiana. Nearly all of the fonts are previously unavailable Old Faces of the later nineteenth-century style; there are also 1,440 cuts, borders, and ornaments. A card catalog of the type faces is on file in the Printing Office in the Central Building, with a set of proofs of the cuts, borders, and ornaments. The collection itself, housed in the Central Building, is not available for public inspection except by special arrangement. Proofs may be obtained from the library's Printing Office; there is a small fee for the production of proofs.[11]

The Rare Book Division maintains a collection of fifteenth-century type facsimiles, consisting of 21 file boxes of specimen pages of printing, including material from the Type Facsimile Society, the Burger Monumenta, and similar institutions arranged in folders by city of origin. The division also holds a small but select collection of books on typography and fine printing given by Philip Hofer in 1938.

BOOK ILLUSTRATION

PRINTS DIVISION

The Prints Division is the starting point for an investigation into the excellent resources in this area. Approximately 1,700 entries in the division catalog relate to book illustration; these provide a geographical breakdown, and many index entries for articles in periodicals and learned society publications. The division maintains files of those periodicals exclusively devoted to book illustration. Also much information on individual artists is maintained, with oeuvre catalogs and supporting reference works. Materials dealing with the illumination of books and manuscripts, including an extensive representation of specimens and reproductions, are under the jurisdiction of the General Research and Humanities Division, and are housed with the general collections.

Some 1,200 illustrated books in the Prints Division serve as examples of the illustrator's art in the Western world from the late seventeenth century to the present. Among them is a particularly fine representation of the work of George Cruikshank, the larger part given by Mrs. Henry Draper in 1911, with original wood-block and steel engravings. Thomas Rowlandson is also well represented. The division holds eleven scrapbook volumes of mounted proofs of the wood engravings of Alexander Anderson, the nineteenth-century American illustrator. Among more recent materials are many Denslow drawings for Frank Baum's *Oz* books, and most of the original drawings made by Reginald Marsh for book illustrations. There is a good collection of original woodcut proofs of Fritz Eichenberg's illustrations, as well as published books illustrated by this artist. The Book Illustrators Index in the division locates examples of the work of specific illustrators in the library's collections. The Illustrated Books Index lists notable illustrated books shelved outside the division.

ARENTS COLLECTION OF BOOKS IN PARTS

The collection holds many drawings by nineteenth-century English artists, the originals of illustrations prepared for books acquired by the collection. Among those represented are Rowlandson (nine original drawings for the *English Dance of Death* and other items), George Cruikshank, Hablôt K. Browne ("Phiz"), Millais, and Kate Greenaway. Many books in parts are themselves fine examples of the illustrated book.

BERG COLLECTION

The Berg Collection of English and American Literature contains many illustrated books among its first and early editions, most of them from the nineteenth and twentieth centuries. A number of original drawings for illustrations include two by William Hogarth for the second edition of Sterne's *Tristram Shandy*.[12] The illustrators of Dickens are particularly well represented. Drawings made by authors such as Thackeray and Kipling, often to illustrate their own books, are of interest.[13] There are substantial holdings of the work of Kate Greenaway.

SPENCER COLLECTION

This collection of notable illustrated books and fine bindings from every period and geographical locale is described in chapter 16 of this *Guide*.

ADDITIONAL REMARKS

The examples of illustrated books and original drawings for book illustrations cited here offer no more than a general suggestion of the type of rare and unusual materials available in the Research Libraries. Illustrated books are found in every division or special collection. Descriptions of resources in illustrated books are included in a number of the sections of this *Guide* which discuss various national literatures and subject collections; the chapter on juvenile literature indicates holdings in the Central Children's Room at the Donnell Library Center, among them many drawings and some paintings by such famous illustrators as Randolph Caldecott, Howard Pyle, and N. C. Wyeth.

---

11. See *Old Fashioned Type Specimens in the Robinson-Pforzheimer Collection*, 5th ed. (The New York Public Library, 1969) and *Cuts, Borders, and Ornaments Selected from the Robinson-Pforzheimer Typographical Collection in The New York Public Library* (The New York Public Library, 1962).

12. See William Holtz, "The Journey and the Picture: The Art of Sterne and Hogarth," *BNYPL* 71 (1967): 25–38.

13. See Lola L. Szladits and Harvey Simmonds, *Pen & Brush: The Author as Artist* (The New York Public Library, 1969).

BOOKBINDING

The library has a strong collection dealing with bookbinding in all its aspects, and remarkable holdings of fine bindings. The collecting policy for technical books on the subject is comprehensive. There are approximately 1,800 references to bookbinding in the Public Catalog, including such aspects of the field as armorial binding and bookbinding materials. A number of index entries for periodical articles direct the reader to bookbinding information in periodicals on other subjects. Periodicals devoted wholly or partially to the subject range from the late nineteenth century to the present; the library currently receives nine titles including *La Reliure* (1891–) and the *Schweizerische Fachschrift für Buchbindereien* (1950–). Catalogs of collections or exhibitions of bookbinding are a substantial part of the holdings.

TRADE BINDINGS IN THE GENERAL COLLECTIONS

The General Research and Humanities Division has acquired a selective group of trade bindings which illustrate the development of the industry. These bindings are from many countries, with the United States and England most strongly represented. They cover a period from the early nineteenth century to the present, although few examples were added during the 1940s and 1950s. Acquisitions are made on a very selective basis and include unusual examples such as Marc Saporta's innovative *Composition Nº 1* (1962), the pages of which the reader is invited to shuffle like a deck of cards.

FINE BINDINGS IN THE SPENCER COLLECTION

The collection acquires finely illustrated books in handsome bindings representing the work of the most noted bookbinders of all countries. Examples range from the fifteenth century to the present. The earliest examples include leather-covered missal boxes with woodcuts decorating the inner lids, as well as incunabula in contemporaneous bindings. A girdle book breviary, dated 1454 and bound in a leather pouch to be hung from the belt or girdle is a great rarity.[14] Among the sixteenth-century items is a Grolier binding which came from the collection of Lucius Wilmerding. Seventeenth-century bindings include fine examples of the work of the Englishmen Roger Bartlett and Samuel Mearne. The holdings of eighteenth-century bindings are strongest in French work, with specimens of the bindings of Padeloup, Derôme le Jeune, and others. Many of the books in W. A. Spencer's original collection were bound by the great nineteenth- and twentieth-century French binders; there are also modern bindings from England, Germany, Spain, the United States, and other countries.[15] Unusual bindings in the collection include embroidered, ivory, and jewelled bindings, and those made of leaves from old manuscripts. Oriental books in the collection add lacquered bindings from India, palm leaf bindings, and bindings of painted and tooled leather.

FINE BINDINGS IN THE RARE BOOK DIVISION

The division does not actively collect bindings, but many fine examples have been acquired through gift, and by purchase of books important for their text. There are approximately thirty bindings of the fifteenth century, some with clasps. Of the unsigned bindings, the greatest number are from the sixteenth century; signed bindings date for the most part from the nineteenth century. Curious bindings in the division form an interesting group extending from those made of wallpaper to the cover of a baseball, and from fiber glass to cigar boxes.[16] A treatise on Shakespeare is bound in oak board from Holy Trinity Church, where Shakespeare was baptized and buried. The first Hawaiian hymnal, compiled by William Ellis and Hiram Bingham and printed in Oahu in 1828, is bound in tortoise shell with a leather back.

Two special files maintained in the Rare Book Division relate to bindings:

Bindings File

A card file of books in the division arranged alphabetically by names of binders and owners (as indicated by coats of arms, signatures, etc. on the bindings) (active, 4 card drawers). The alphabetical list is followed by a classed arrangement: by century for unsigned bindings, and by special categories (such as embroidered, silver, curious bindings, fore-edge paintings, etc.). There is also a section containing original and facsimile binders' labels.

Reproductions of Bindings

A vertical file of pictures, most of them clipped from dealers' catalogs, mounted and sourced (active, 11 file boxes). The file is in three parts: pictures of bindings arranged by name of binder (5 boxes); those arranged by special forms, such as chained bindings, embroidered bindings, etc. (3 boxes); and representations of armorial association bindings (3 boxes).

FINE BINDINGS IN THE ARENTS TOBACCO COLLECTION

Among the many notable examples in this collection are English armorial bindings made for Elizabeth I, and for James I and his queen, Anne of Denmark.

BOOKPLATES

This strong collection of bookplate examples from the earliest periods to the present is administered by the Prints Division. The holdings are notable for the work of contemporary American and European artists (mainly from the collection given by Herman T. Radin), but also include such early examples as the Buxheim bookplate (in color) and the earliest Swiss bookplate, that of Balthasar Brennwald (1502). The collection is arranged alphabetically by name of owner. Additions to the collection are made on a selective basis; gifts of such material are screened carefully.

---

14. See Karl Kup, "A Fifteenth-Century Girdle Book," *BNYPL* 43 (1939): 471–84.

15. The dictionary catalog and shelf list of the Spencer Collection has been published in book form in two volumes by G. K. Hall & Co. (Boston, 1970).

---

16. See Lawrence S. Thompson, "Bibliopegia Fantastica," *BNYPL* 51 (1947): 71–90. Published separately by the library.

The Prints Division also maintains a collection of books, bibliographies, and other materials on the subject of bookplates. The collecting policy, while comprehensive for bibliographies and for works on individual artists, is only selective or representative for periodical and society publications, catalogs, and general and miscellaneous works.

9

LIBRARY SCIENCE

Although resources in librarianship have always constituted a small part of the library's total holdings, they have received more attention, for professional reasons, than numerical reports indicate. Over a 45-year period this collection has grown very significantly, as indicated below:

1921	3,212 volumes
1930	5,677
1940	7,500
1966	17,500

Statistics only partially measure the library's resources in this field. For example, since they indicate volumes rather than pieces, they do not reflect the fact that many volumes contain annual reports for a period of years. Moreover, many publications which other institutions classify as library science are classified differently in the Research Libraries (for example, published catalogs and certain bulletins of libraries).

The library's current acquisition policy embraces varying levels of coverage for different areas of librarianship. For bibliography, periodicals, and public services, the policy is comprehensive to the extent that such material is available through normal purchase or exchange channels. Education for librarianship and general works on American, British, French, and German librarianship receive coverage on a representative level. Publications by and about individual libraries in these countries, as well as all publications from other nations, are collected on a selective basis. However, material received under the PL-480 Program provides comprehensive current coverage for titles issued in the countries covered, and the Jewish Division maintains the same level for all library science publications in Hebrew. A policy of generally comprehensive coverage, apparently followed in the library's early years, did not prevail in a later period, probably under the assumption that the comprehensive collecting given to many areas in the field by the School of Library Service at Columbia University made the same degree of coverage unnecessary at the New York Public Library. In general, the Research Libraries have formed a collection which is good to strong in the general monographs and periodicals of the field (although better developed in English than in other languages), but which lacks comprehensive holdings in such special forms as library surveys, annual reports, dissertations, and ephemeral publications. For these types of materials the library makes individual, rather than blanket, selection decisions—it does not, for example, acquire microfilms of doctoral dissertations in the field, but selects individual titles for purchase.

RESOURCES

The bibliographical tools of the field are well covered, although holdings are not comprehensive.

In addition to *Library Literature* and *Library Science Abstracts* are indexing and abstracting services published in France, Hungary, Poland, Sweden, and the USSR. Another indication of this strength is the fact that the collection contains a very good representation of the guides, descriptions, surveys, check lists, etc., cited in *American Library Resources: A Bibliographical Guide* (1951) and its supplement (1962) by Robert B. Downs. The *Dictionary Catalog* of the library of the Columbia University School of Library Service is present, and the holdings of other printed library catalogs are good. For examples of the general catalogs issued by many American libraries in the late nineteenth and early twentieth centuries, those from such academic and special libraries as the American Antiquarian Society, Boston Athenaeum, Columbia, Cornell and Harvard Universities, the John Crerar Library, Massachusetts Historical Society, the University of Michigan, and Wisconsin Historical Society might be cited. Catalogs, book bulletins, and published accession lists of public libraries have come from Boston, Brooklyn, Chicago, Cleveland, Enoch Pratt (Baltimore), Carnegie Library of Pittsburgh, St. Louis, and some smaller cities. From abroad are similar publications from such university libraries as Coimbra, Leiden, Oslo, and Oxford, and from such public and national institutions as those in Bordeaux, Geneva, Rio de Janeiro, and Stockholm. A nearly complete collection of the sets of printed volumes issued in recent years which reproduce the card catalogs of major foreign and domestic collections is also available. Useful for reference purposes is a sizable group of some 200 directories which provide listings of libraries and librarians; about half are foreign publications, covering either individual countries or regions.

The collection of the most important American library periodicals—those indexed in *Library Literature*—is strong. The library currently subscribes, with two or three exceptions, to the entire group (some 100 titles); in the large majority of cases it possesses a full file, while sets are complete for the remaining titles from the point at which the subscription began in the 1940s or 1950s. More selective coverage applies to foreign periodicals, but current subscriptions exceed 50 titles from about 25 countries. There are complete sets of such important journals as *Accademie e biblioteche d'Italia, Archives et bibliothèques de Belgique, Bücherei und Bildung, Bulletin des bibliothèques de France, Indian Librarian, Libri, New Zealand Libraries,* and *Zentralblatt für Bibliothekswesen,* but files of other titles may begin with recent years. The coverage of bulletins of library associations is good, especially those in the British Commonwealth.

Annual reports of American libraries constitute an important feature of the collection. However, in recent years many libraries have ceased publishing reports, or the Research Libraries have found it increasingly difficult to claim items which fail to arrive regularly. For instance, there are files for only about one-third of the institutions composing the Association of Research Libraries (those of some additional universities appear as part of the president's report); with some exceptions (e.g., Harvard, Stanford, Yale, the Huntington E. Hartford Library, and the Boston Public Library) these sets begin only in the 1950s. For large public libraries, such as those in Chicago, Los Angeles, the Carnegie Library of Pittsburgh, and St. Louis, files are complete since their founding. Deserving special mention are long runs of the reports of smaller municipal institutions in southern New England; this group includes Brookline, Fitchburg, Lancaster, Lawrence, Lowell, Lynn, Malden, Northampton, Quincy, Salem, Springfield, Watertown, and Worcester, Massachusetts; Providence, Rhode Island; Hartford and Waterbury, Connecticut. Examples from smaller cities in other parts of the country are also present, but relatively few files extend to the present without gaps. Some 500 cities are represented in this group, with holdings ranging from a single report to a complete file. There are good files of the reports, journals, and other publications of most state library agencies.

Holdings of library surveys are good, but not comprehensive. The Public Catalog contains about 225 entries under the heading "Library Surveys." With the exception of general works on survey methodology, most titles are reports of surveys of individual American public, college, and university libraries, generally undertaken since 1930. Among the authors represented are Robert B. Downs, Nelson Associates, Maurice F. Tauber, Joseph L. Wheeler, and Frederick Wezeman. There are a few studies not dealing with American institutions, nearly all of which refer to the British Commonwealth. These often cover library services in an entire country or portions of it, rather than those of an individual library.

More than 1,000 entries in the Public Catalog are listed for publications of the American Library Association. These include serial titles such as *ALA Membership Directory*, publications resulting from such special programs as the Library Technology Project; and the various reading lists and guides issued over the years. Few of the items which receive limited distribution, such as the minutes of the executive boards and processed publications of the divisions, are retained by the library.

SPECIAL TOPICS

Of the specialized areas within librarianship, holdings are most extensive for that of classification. They embrace not only theoretical and practical works, but also include a good collection of general classification schemes, both those abandoned and those still in use. More than 400 schemes for individual subjects (e.g., agriculture, business, Japanese literature, motion pictures, nursing) are also available. The collection of materials on reference books and reference work is also strong, although less extensive than that on classification. Nearly all guides to and bibliographies of reference materials are present.

For two subareas the library's collecting policy approaches exhaustively. A small group of monographic and serial literature, which includes publications in a wide range of languages, covers the preservation of library materials. Information storage and retrieval systems are covered by the standard journal and monographic works, a sizable number of conference proceedings, and reports emanating from research centers and consulting firms in the information science field.

The area of librarianship education is not strong. While all important monographic studies (e.g., those by Danton, Munn, Reece, Vann, and Williamson) and the serial publications of the Association of American Library Schools are present, holdings of the course announcements, reports, and alumni bulletins of the individual accredited library schools are weak; there has been no attempt to maintain files of such items. An exception is the library's own Library School, which operated from 1911 to 1926. The book collection contains the announcements, reports of the principal, programs of commencement exercises, registers of students, and miscellaneous items; archival materials have been transferred to Columbia University. There is a basic information collection on education for librarianship in other countries.

Resources on the New York Public Library and those institutions which it absorbed are, or course, unique. Published material includes not only the 46 reports (1849–94) of the Astor Library and the 25 (1870–94) of the Lenox, but also those of the Aguilar, Harlem, New York Free Circulating and Washington Heights Free Libraries from their founding until their consolidation with the New York Public Library. A set of the library's own general and financial reports, the *Bulletin*, and other publications, is maintained as a unit in the classified collection (other parts of the collection frequently contain additional copies of individual items). The Manuscripts and Archives Division administers archival collections which bear directly upon the library's history: letters to Joseph Green Cogswell, superintendent of the Astor Library; some 200 letters (1859–73) from James Lenox to Edward G. Allen relating to the purchase of books for Lenox's library, and 33 from various persons to Lenox; the papers of C. A. Nelson, long associated with the Astor Library; and the papers of two New York Public Library directors, John Shaw Billings and Harry Miller Lydenberg; an extensive collection of bibliographical notes and other papers of Wilberforce Eames; the entire collection of manuscripts relating to Andrew Carnegie's gifts for public library development in New York City (including his famous letter of March 12, 1901, about his contribution of $5,200,000 toward the branch library building program).

Coverage of material about other libraries in the city and state is good, although there are noticeable gaps in the files of annual reports. There is a collection of the reports, check lists, and public library statistics of the New York State Library. The Manuscripts and Archives Division also has a group of documents relating to the early years of the Library Company of Philadelphia, the keystone being a "Memorandum of Agreement" with its first librarian, Louis Timothee, dated November 14, 1732, and signed and sealed by Benjamin Franklin and other directors of the company. Several collections—such as those on the Berkshire Republican Library, Stockbridge, Massachusetts; the Union Library, Western, New York; and the Lisbon Library, Newent, Connecticut—pertain to the early history of the American library movement. The division holds the papers of R. R. Bowker, founder and editor of *Library Journal*; and the records of the New York Library Club for the period from 1901 to 1959.

LIBRARIANSHIP ABROAD

Entries in the Public Catalog under the subject heading "Libraries" with geographical subdivisions provide the best single indication of the library's resources on libraries and librarianship abroad; over 3,500 titles appear here, excluding, of course, those under the subdivision for the United States. This figure does not reflect publications in Slavonic and Oriental languages and in Hebrew, whose cards do not appear in the Public Catalog. Publications include long runs of annual reports of important libraries (especially those in the British Commonwealth), surveys, brochures issued for the dedications of new buildings, general histories and the histories of individual libraries, treatises on administration, technical processes, etc. There are relatively few items of less than book length (e.g., surveys of individual libraries and reports by American librarians on their overseas assignments). Although this file contains entries for nearly all foreign countries, the most substantial numbers of entries appear under Australia, Canada, China, Denmark, France, Germany, Great Britain, India, Italy, Japan, New Zealand, Poland, the Soviet Union, Spain, Sweden, and Switzerland; of this group Canada, France, and Great Britain are most extensively covered.

Material on librarianship in Canada includes publications of the Canadian Library Association and the Canadian Library Council, journals of regional associations, and the reports and other publications of the National Library and a number of major university and public libraries. Resources on Great Britain consist of comparable types of material; the reports from the public libraries of such cities as Birmingham, Liverpool, and Manchester extend back more than a century. In addition, there is a large block of publications issued by the British Museum—particularly guides to and catalogs of manuscript holdings and the printed catalogs of the Department of Printed Books.

In addition to general material on libraries in France (some 250 titles), there is an excellent collection of the publications of the Bibliothèque Nationale. Approximately 1,200 titles, some in bound volumes of pamphlets, are held. More than one-third pertain to manuscripts held by the Bibliothèque Nationale; another sizable portion are publications issued by the individual departments (e.g., Maps, Periodicals, Prints) and the published catalogs of the Département des Imprimés; finally, there is an extensive group of exhibition catalogs. Material assembled on such French research libraries as the Arsenal and the National and University Library at Strasbourg are considerably less extensive; these institutions have been relatively inactive in publishing. The same is true of the major libraries of the University of Paris (the Sorbonne, Bibliothèque Sainte-Geneviève, and others), although entries used in the Public Catalog do not bring references to the university's libraries together under a single heading.

The Slavonic Division's holdings consist of general monographic publications, directories and censuses, and yearbooks of major individual libraries. Much of the material is of historical, rather than current, value. For publications from China before 1949 there is a good collection in English and some items in Chinese; few publications from the People's Republic of China are found. For most Asian and African countries the Research Libraries have little nonwestern-language material. Resources in the Jewish Division embrace libraries and librarianship in Israel, and Jewish libraries in other parts of the world.

For comparative librarianship the publications of international organizations active in the field supplement materials dealing with specific countries. In addition to UNESCO publications, the collection contains complete sets of those issued by the International Federation of Library Associations (IFLA) and the International Federation for Documentation (FID). Also available are the various publications of the Pan American Union's Columbus Memorial Library.

PART TWO

10

JEWISH DIVISION AND GENERAL RESOURCES IN JUDAICA AND HEBRAICA

In 115,100 volumes, 550 manuscripts, and 200 letters the Jewish Division presents a comprehensive record in many languages of the Jewish people, and collects books in Hebrew and Yiddish on all subjects. Many thousands of works throughout the library complement the division's resources.[1]

---

1. Abraham Berger, "The Jewish Division of The New York Public Library," *Jewish Book Annual* 23 (1965): 42–47. The historical and general account given here is largely drawn from the article by Berger, former chief of the Jewish Division.

The division holdings include specialized bibliographies and reference works; Jewish Americana; Jewish folklore, history, and social studies; Biblical archaeology; Kabbalistic and Hasidic writings; works by Christian Hebraists; rabbinic responsa; classic and modern Hebrew and Yiddish literature; and one of the largest collections in the world of Jewish newspapers and periodicals, both in their original form and on microfilm. Also worthy of mention are the resources dealing with Samaritans, Karaites, Jewish apologetics, and anti-Semitic writings. In addition to the holdings in Hebrew, Yiddish, and other languages, there is notable material in Ladino (Judeo-Spanish), Aramaic, Judeo-Arabic, and Judeo-Persian. Of the division's 115,000 volumes, about 45,000 are in Hebrew, 15,000 in Yiddish, and the rest in English, German, Russian, French, and other languages.

The policy of collecting material with Hebrew or Yiddish text in all subject categories extends to such items as illustrated art books, music scores, and government documents, ordinarily held in the appropriate subject divisions of the library. Material in the exact sciences in Hebrew received from Israel is also presently kept in the Jewish Division.

HISTORICAL SURVEY

The growth of the Jewish Division during the first seventy years of its existence is shown in the following:

1897	2,000 volumes*
1911	20,000
1921	22,164
1930	33,068
1941	44,000
1966	115,100

(* Figures for 1897, 1911 and 1941 are estimated; figures for 1921, 1930, and 1966 are official census records.)

The Jewish Division was established two years after the formation of the New York Public Library, and Jacob H. Schiff offered $10,000 for the purchase of Semitic literature; his gifts to the library in this field were to total some $100,000—a bequest of $25,000 still yields income used to acquire rare and classic works. Abraham Solomon Freidus, the first chief of the division, brought together from all parts of the Astor Library the Hebrew books and books in other languages on Jewish subjects published after 1600. To these 2,000 volumes, 300 of which were in Hebrew, were added Hebrew treasures from the Lenox Library, including a fine Pentateuch printed on vellum in Bologna in 1482. The working library of Leon Mandelstamm was acquired through A. M. Bank in 1897. Mandelstamm, a scholar and educator, served as secretary to the Russian governmental commission established to draw up an education system for the Jews. He assembled some 2,000 volumes in Hebrew, German, and Russian, giving particular attention to history, literature, and classic Hebrew texts. In 1899 several hundred volumes were added from the library of Meijer Lehren of Amsterdam. These included about 100 volumes of rabbinical responsa, written opinions and decisions by eminent Hebrew authorities, which are a basic resource for the study of Jewish social history; works on Jewish sectarian movements were also notably represented. The Aguilar Free Library, which became part of the Circulation Department (now the Branch Libraries) of the New York Public Library in 1903, had a sizable collection of Yiddish materials. These were transferred to the Jewish Division and formed the nucleus of holdings which have grown to great importance.

The growth of the collection through the past seventy years has been steady and cumulative, rather than by acquisition of large collections. The periods of most rapid growth were 1897 to 1911, and post-1933. In 1964 Israel was incorporated in the PL-480 Project, with the New York Public Library as one of the participating libraries. Under this project the Library of Congress administers appropriations granted under the provisions of Public Law 480 (the Agricultural Trade and Development and Assistance Act of 1954, as amended); these funds are used to purchase foreign currencies to finance an acquisition and distribution program for books and booklike materials for participating United States libraries. By 1966 the Jewish Division was receiving approximately 2,000 titles from Israel annually under the project; Israel was not involved in the project after 1973. "Titles" is not synonymous with "items"; the Library of Congress PL-480 Newsletter no. 9 (March, 1965) indicated an average yearly receipt from Israel of 13,442 pieces per library.

SPECIAL INDEXES AND FILES

Microform Catalog

A listing by title of Hebrew-alphabet materials that have been filmed by the library (active, 5 card drawers).

Picture Index

A subject index to pictures in books shelved in the division (inactive, 14 card drawers). The subjects include archaeology of the Holy Land, biography, history, etc.

Responsa Catalog

A subject index on cards of rabbinical responsa, opinions and decisions rendered by eminent Central European rabbis of the sixteenth and seventeenth centuries on questions submitted to them (inactive, 8 card drawers). The responsa cover a wide range of topics.

The card catalog of the Jewish Division has been published in book form in fourteen volumes by G. K. Hall & Company (Boston, 1960).

RESOURCES

Printed Collections

Perhaps the oldest of the division's printed collections is Ugolino's Thesaurus antiquitatum sacrarum (Venice, 1744–69). Representing, as it does, translations into Latin of classic Hebrew texts, it is still outstanding for its encyclopedic range, and is an important source for the study of Biblical, Talmudic, and early Christian archaeology. There is a full collection of Festschriften in Hebrew and Western European languages. The division's files of publications of learned societies and institutions concerned with the promotion of archaeological study in Biblical lands are virtually complete. Almost all of the great editions of the standard codes of Jewish law and their commentaries are available. Rabbinical decisions and responsa form an outstanding body of material numbering some 2,000 volumes and spanning eighteen centuries.

Periodicals and Newspapers

Periodicals and newspapers make up a large proportion of the deteriorating materials which the library is attempting to preserve by microreproduction. By 1966 approximately 50 newspaper and 250 periodical files from the holdings of the Jewish Division had been filmed, as had some 6,000 pamphlets and books, including hundreds of popular Yiddish novels published in Vilna, Warsaw, and New York at the turn of the century; among the latter are the novels of N. M. Shaikewitz, Auser Blaustein, and Goetzel Selikovitsch, with the translations of Abner Tannenbaum.

The division currently receives some 380 periodical and newspaper titles in Hebrew, Yiddish, and other languages from eighteen countries. By far the greatest number of items come from Israel itself (221 titles). Periodicals and newspapers from other countries include 105 titles from the United States, 11 from Argentina, 8 from France, 5 each from Canada, Great Britain, and South Africa, and 2 from Brazil. All newspapers are filmed on arrival and the originals discarded. In addition, the division acquires microfilm files of newspapers which are not received on a current basis.

Hebrew Periodicals and Newspapers

The mention of a few of the many significant titles contained in the division can offer an indication of the depth of resources in this area. The first successful modern Hebrew periodical, *Hameasef* [The gatherer] (Königsberg, Berlin, Breslau, etc., 1784–1811), is called the voice of the Enlightenment. It is included in the collection, as are the nineteenth-century *Bikkure Ha-'Itim* and *Hashahar*, and the first American Hebrew periodical, *Hatsofe b-Erez Hachadosho* (1871–73). An interesting attempt to romanize the Hebrew alphabet is found in *Deror*, a weekly published in Tel-Aviv in 1933/34. *Haolam*, the official organ of the Zionist movement, is also in the files. Russian newspapers in Hebrew constitute another important resource and include such items as *Hamelitz* (Odessa, 1861–1904) and *Hazeman* (St. Petersburg, 1903–14).

The bulk of current newspapers and periodicals are received from Israel; among the 6 newspaper titles are *Haarets, Hatsofeh*, and *Hayom*, and among 215 periodical titles are *Sinai, Tarbiz, Zion, Molad*, and *Goldene Keit*. Mention should also be made of complete runs of the American Hebrew periodicals *Hadoar* (1921–) and *Bitzaron* (1939–).

Yiddish Periodicals and Newspapers

Yiddish newspapers and periodicals also constitute a strong feature of the division's resources. *Kol mevasser* (Odessa, 1862–70) was the Yiddish supplement to the Hebrew *Hamelitz*; the American Yiddish newspaper *Der Arbeiter* (New York, 1904–11) was the organ of the Socialist Labor Party. The *Jewish Daily Forward* (1897–) was the first newspaper to be filmed in the division's microfilming program. Yiddish newspapers and periodicals are received currently from Australia, Canada, Israel, South Africa, and South America, as well as from various European countries and the United States.

Ladino Periodicals and Newspapers

The division holds a file of *El avenir* (Salonica 1897–1900), *El tiempo* (Constantinople, 1899–1902), and a full run of the American Ladino newspapers *La vara* (1923–48) and *La America* (1910–25). At present it receives *El tiempo* from Israel.

Rare Books

In 1923, when Joshua Bloch became the second chief of the Jewish Division, 2 Hebrew incunabula, and approximately 200 sixteenth-century books

were contained in the division. By 1966 the division had 41 incunabula and more than 1,000 sixteenth-century books. The library owns books published in 253 of the 939 localities of Jewish printing.[2]

The incunabula in the Jewish Division form an impressive group, important not only for their specialized interest but often as examples of the earliest printing in the localities where they were produced. *Arba turim* by Jacob ben Asher, printed in 1475 on vellum in the Italian city Piove de Sacco, may be the earliest dated printed Hebrew book. The division has four of the eight to twelve incunabula printed at Rome, among them the Moses Nahmanides commentary on the Pentateuch, published before 1480; it has been suggested that this may be the first printed Hebrew book. There are examples of incunabula from Naples, another center of Hebrew printing.[3] A commentary on the Pentateuch by Nahmanides dated Lisbon, 1489, is the first book known to have been printed in the capital of Portugal.

Among the books of the sixteenth century in the division are the publications of Daniel Bomberg, a Christian printer of Hebrew books from 1517 to 1549; and virtually all the books in Hebrew printed in Venice during the sixteenth century. A remarkable addition to the Ladino collection in the Jewish Division is Moses Almosnino's *Regimiento de la vida* (Salonica, 1564), the first printed original work in that language. *Sefer middot*, a work on ethics published in Isny, Würtemberg in 1542, represents one of the earliest printed works in Yiddish.

Another noteworthy possession is Martin del Castillo's *Arte hebraispano* (Lyons, 1676). This first American publication dealing with Hebrew grammar was written by the Franciscan monk in Mexico, but printed in France because there was no Hebrew type in America. A possibly unique set of *First Fruits of the West* is dated Kingston, Jamaica, 1844.

Other divisions of the library possess rare Judaica. The Rare Book Division contains fifteenth- and sixteenth-century editions of the Greek and Latin texts of Josephus and Philo Judaeus, Abraham Zacuto's astronomical works, and studies of the Hebrew language and the Kabbala by Johannes Reuchlin. A copy of the first sermon of the Jewish faith preached in America is also in the Rare Book Division. It was delivered in Spanish by Rabbi Haim Isaac Carigal at Newport, Rhode Island on May 28, 1773; the printed version is an English translation.

Manuscripts

Hebrew Manuscripts

Most of the 90 Hebrew manuscripts in the library are Biblical and liturgical texts. Among

---

2. See Aron Freimann, "A Gazetteer of Hebrew Printing," *BNYPL* 49 (1945): 355–74 et seq, which mentions 247 places. Harry M. Rabinowicz, in *The Jewish Literary Treasures of England and America* (New York: Yoseloff, 1962), p. 100, increases the number to 253.

3. See Joshua Bloch, "The Library's Roman Hebrew Incunabula," *BNYPL* 55 (1951): 211–12; see also "Hebrew Printing in Naples," *BNYPL* 46 (1942): 489–514, published separately by the library.

the rarest items is a Samaritan Pentateuch in the Manuscripts and Archives Division consisting of 549 leaves, written in 1231–32. It was acquired by James Lenox in 1895 to cap his very great collection of Bibles in Hebrew and in translation. The Manuscripts and Archives Division holds 12 other Hebrew manuscripts, primarily Pentateuchs or Books of Esther on parchment scrolls of the eighteenth or nineteenth centuries, and texts by Yemenite scribes. In the Spencer Collection the Xanten Bible, an illustrated manuscript in 2 volumes, carries the colophon "I, Joseph of Xanten, son of Kalonymus from Neuss have written and illustrated these twenty-four books for my friend Moses, son of Jacob. . . ."[4] It contains Masora and pen-and-ink drawings. The Spencer Collection has three Hebrew illuminated scrolls of the Book of Esther, dating from the seventeenth and nineteenth centuries.

There are some 70 manuscripts in the Jewish Division in Hebrew, including mahzors, Kabbalistic works of the seventeenth century copied in the eighteenth and nineteenth centuries; Yemenite liturgical texts written in the eighteenth century; manuscripts on folk medicine, magic, and astrology; and manuscripts of modern Hebrew literature, as well as several hundred letters written, for the most part, by twentieth-century Hebrew authors.

The Jewish Division acquired two manuscript mahzors on vellum as a gift from Louis M. Rabinowitz in 1952. Each of the manuscripts represents a compilation of Jewish liturgical and related texts employed in synagogue worship. One is a fourteenth-century work; the more lavishly illuminated of the two, it was used by the Hebrew scholar Samuel David Luzzatto, who supplied a handwritten table of contents in which he indicated those poems not to be found in printed books. The second was written in the fifteenth century and is a striking example of Hebrew calligraphy in red and black.[5]

Among other outstanding manuscripts is a *Beth Israel* by Israel Michelstaedt written in his own hand. This commentary on the Agada (legends and sayings of the Talmud) was started in Cracow and finished in Berlin in 1772; it has never been published. A 1640 manuscript of the *Tsahut bedihuta de-kidushin* [Comedy of betrothal] by Leone Sommo de Portaleone is the third oldest of five known manuscripts of this first Hebrew play, published for the first time in Israel in 1946. In 1961 the library acquired the diary of Abraham Jona, the last rabbi of the Venetian ghetto. The diary records special synagogue services, as well as the critical events which necessitated them during the disorders of 1797–1814, following the abdication of the Venetian government and the formation of a democratic republic by the French.[6]

Yiddish Manuscripts

There are approximately 460 manuscript items in Yiddish; some 300 are from the Boris Thomashefsky collection of works by Thomashefsky, Leon Kobrin, Joseph Lateiner, Osip Dymov, and others, including manuscript versions of about 150 plays, parts of plays, and scenarios performed for the most part in the New York Yiddish theatre. Mr. Thomashefsky was a leading actor and producer of Yiddish plays in New York City. The manuscripts form part of a large collection documenting his stage career and including typescripts of operas and operettas; manuscript orchestral arrangements and sheet music; scrapbooks, photographs, and clippings of Thomashefsky, his family, contemporary actors, and others; and much additional material. Given by Harry Thomashefsky in 1940, the collection has been dispersed through various divisions of the library.

---

4. See Rabinowicz, *Jewish Literary Treasures*, p. 100.
5. See Joshua Bloch, "Two Illuminated Manuscripts of the Mahzor Given by Louis M. Rabinowitz," *BNYPL* 56 (1952): 423–25.

6. See Abraham Berger, "The Diary of Abraham Jona," *BNYPL* 66 (1962): 623–29.

11

ORIENTAL DIVISION AND GENERAL ORIENTAL RESOURCES

Oriental Division holdings number 62,000 volumes. 270 manuscripts in the division are supplemented by more than 1,600 scrolls, manuscripts, tablets, and inscriptions in Oriental languages in the Manuscripts and Archives Division and the Spencer Collection, and a number of manuscripts, journals, and commercial papers in English and Western European languages in the Manuscripts and Archives Division.

The division collects grammars, dictionaries, and the literature of the Orient, in both original texts and translation, in more than 100 languages. It also collects works on Oriental archaeology and

religions. The Orient is defined as the countries of Asia (except Siberia), Ceylon, the islands of Japan, the Malay Archipelago, the Near East, and other areas in which Oriental alphabets, characters, and syllabaries are used. History and description of the Orient are collected when in Oriental languages; otherwise these subjects are the responsibility of the General Research and Humanities Division. Law, with the single exception of Moslem law, is not generally acquired. The division has, in addition, traditionally acquired works in the languages of North Africa, Ethiopia, and those African languages which now use or once used the Arabic script, such as Fulah, Haussa, Somali, Swahili, etc. Some of the non-Indo-European languages of the Soviet Union (with the exception of Finno-Ugrian) are the collecting responsibility of the Oriental Division: Turko-Tataric, Tungus-Manju, and the Mongolic languages, collectively known as the Altaic languages; a quantity of Turkic material collected before World War II is in the Slavonic Division. The Armenian holdings are very strong, and there is a unique collection in the Georgian language.

Material on Oriental archaeology, including works on Egypt, Assyria, the Hittites, and other areas of remote antiquity, is collected by the division; but classical and Byzantine archaeology are the collecting responsibility of the Art and Architecture Division and the General Research and Humanities Division.

The scope of the Oriental Division presents conflicts between the subject and language approach to collecting. Although the Oriental Division is, generally speaking, a humanities division, certain areas in the humanities lie beyond its interest: Oriental government documents are held by the Economic and Public Affairs Division; Oriental patents are found in the Patents Collection; Oriental art is the collecting responsibility of the Art and Architecture Division. In such cases, partial guidance can be found in the Oriental Division catalog. The division of responsibility between the Oriental Division and the Slavonic Division is not always clear in regard to some of the Central Asian languages; nor between it and the Jewish Division in regard to Semitic languages: the Oriental Division collects all the Semitic languages except Hebrew. The Aramaic texts are also divided between these two divisions, with Biblical and Palestinian Aramaic in the Jewish Division, and the others in the Oriental Division. Although these distinctions determine the location of volumes, the reader will find duplicate sets of cards, or at least cross-references, in all divisional catalogs where confusion in subject or language areas might occur.

HISTORICAL SURVEY

When the Oriental Division was formed in 1897, it was one of the smaller, less developed collections in the library; it is now one of the leading resources for Eastern studies. Although the tremendous growth of published materials in the older civilized nations of Asia and the scope of the division preclude comprehensiveness in any single area, the holdings include many unique materials. The following table of the Oriental collections shows that holdings have approximately doubled in size with each quarter century.

1867	Astor Library	3,321 volumes
1911	New York Public Library	15,000
1921		22,000
1930		31,000
1966		63,000

Early interest in Orientalia is evident from Joseph Cogswell's 1854 report on the Astor Library: "[The] greater part of those [families and branches of languages] of Asia and Africa, are represented in the collection. It contains the best works on the Egyptian hieroglyphics, the cuneiform inscriptions, and the other curious records of the ancient nations of the East, which recent discoveries have brought to light." Cogswell mentions two works in the collection never printed for sale, "Seven Seas: a Dictionary and Grammar of the Persian

Language" in seven volumes and "Sabda Kalpa Druma of the Rajah Radhakant Deb," a Sanskrit dictionary.[1] A gift of $10,000 from John Jacob Astor in 1878 was used in part to add important titles in this field.[2]

The Lenox Library did not collect Oriental works extensively, but its librarian, Wilberforce Eames, made a large collection of Chinese literature for his private library. In 1909 he sold to the library about half of his collection, "consisting mostly of the Chinese classics, original texts, and commentaries thereupon, largely examplars from the library of the noted Professor James Legge."[3]

The first chief of the Oriental Division, Dr. Richard Gottheil, a professor of Semitic languages at Columbia University and an editor of Syriac texts, was interested in Arabica. Through the generosity of Jacob M. Schiff during the years from 1900 to 1915, the acquisition of classic Arabic literature and Islamic materials made the division one of the outstanding centers in the country at that time. The income from a $25,000 fund established by Schiff permitted the purchase of 250 Arabic manuscripts in 1934.

From the beginning, Egyptology has been a strong subject area, but it is not now collected in the great depth which marked earlier acquisition policies. The Arabic and Near Eastern collections were also very strong until the 1930s, but since 1950 the collecting emphasis to some extent has swung to the Far East; in 1966 materials relating to Japan formed the fastest growing area. Armenian and Georgian resources are small but represent strong and rapidly developing fields.

The PL-480 Project was established in 1962 for India, Pakistan, and the United Arab Republic; in 1964 Indonesia and Israel were added for several years and in 1966 Nepal. The Library of Congress administers appropriations granted under the provisions of Public Law 480 (The Agricultural Trade and Development and Assistance Act of 1954, as amended); these funds are used to purchase foreign currencies to finance an acquisition and distribution program for books and booklike materials for participating United States libraries. The New York Public Library receives comprehensive sets of government publications at the national and state levels, every commercially published monograph of research value, and a wide selection of commercially published serials from India, Pakistan, and the United Arab Republic; newspapers were received in the early stages of the program from India alone but were not retained. Institutional publications are received from India; this type of material from other

---

1. Quoted in Lydenberg, *History*, p. 29. See *Catalogue of Books in the Astor Library Relating to the Languages and Literature of Asia, Africa and the Oceanic Islands* (New York: Astor Library, 1854).
2. See Lydenberg, *History*, p. 66.
3. Victor Hugo Paltsits in *Bibliographical Essays; a Tribute to Wilberforce Eames* (Cambridge, Mass.: Harvard University Press, 1924; reprinted New York: B. Franklin, 1968), p. 22. Professor Legge died in 1897, and at least portions of his library had been acquired by James Tregaskis, the London bookseller, from whom Eames purchased choice works over a period of time. The other half of the Eames general Chinese collection, of some 1,553 lots, including Korean materials, was purchased by the Case Memorial Library, Hartford, Connecticut.

countries is acquired by the library on international exchange outside the program. By far the largest volume of material has been received from India—approximately 45 percent of the yearly total received (36,000 pieces out of a total of 80,000 at the end of 1964). Not all of the material has been cataloged; in 1966 approximately 20,000 pieces were in a deferred category. However, accession lists and catalog cards prepared by the Library of Congress for the material bear code numbers by means of which materials may be located.

The distribution of materials in the Oriental Division by area shows that the collection of Arabica is numerically the strongest, with the Indian, Ancient Near Eastern, Japanese, and Chinese collections following in that order. The subject groupings are based on those given in the introduction to the division's published *Dictionary Catalog*; figure totals are based on a later census and certain categories (Africana, Ethiopica, and Korea) have been added.

General Oriental studies	6,500 volumes
Ancient Near East	
(Egypt, Mesopotamia, etc.)	7,900
Arabica	14,200
Africana (in languages using	
Arabic script)	200
Ethiopica	400
Indica	9,900
Language, literature and	
civilization of:	
Iran	2,100
Armenia	1,650
Georgia	350
Turkey	1,300
Central Asia	250
Southeast Asia	1,300
China	7,200
Japan	7,700
Korea	850
Total	61,700

SPECIAL INDEXES AND FILES

Arabic Catalog

A card catalog arranged alphabetically by title, in Arabic characters, of the Arabic books in the division (active, 4,200 cards). The books represented by these cards are also entered in the regular catalog of the division, but under author and subject rather than title.

Bibliographie Papyrologique Index

Issued by the Fondation Égyptologique Reine Elisabeth, Brussels, this is a card index to published materials in the field of papyrology (active, 5,500 cards). It begins with the year 1938, and is an alphabetical listing by main entry, useful not only for Oriental materials but also as a catalog of studies in Greek and Latin papyrology.

Chinese Author Information Cards

Published by the Oriental Society of Hanover, Massachusetts, these cards give a condensed biography and list of works of Chinese authors of all periods (1 card drawer). The text is in Chinese, although authors' names are given in Wade-Giles transliteration. The cards are filed by name of author.

Chinese Catalog

A card catalog of the Chinese books in the division arranged by number of strokes in the first Chinese character of the main entry (active, 2,400 cards). The cards are filed, within the total stroke number, alphabetically according to the romanized form of the main entry (Wade-Giles system). The titles are indicated in Chinese characters and in transliteration; at one time an English translation of the title was also given, but this has been discontinued.

Illustration Catalog

A card catalog, arranged alphabetically by subject, of the illustrations of interest to the division located in books and pamphlets shelved in the division and in other parts of the library (inactive, 6,000 cards).

Persia Bibliography

An unfinished bibliography on cards, arranged alphabetically by author, of material in the Oriental Division and elsewhere in the library relating to Persia (inactive, 3,000 cards).

Persian Art Index

An unfinished bibliography on cards, arranged alphabetically by author, of material on Persian art found in the library's collections (inactive, 500 cards).

Portrait Index

An index on cards, arranged alphabetically by subject, to portraits of interest in the Oriental Division in books and pamplets shelved in the division and elsewhere (inactive, 1,100 cards).

PL-480 Materials Catalog

A card index by main entry of the material received from Oriental countries under the PL-480 program (active, 30,000 cards). Each card bears a code number which is marked on the materials as a finding aid.

The card catalog of the Oriental Division has been published in book form in 16 volumes by G. K. Hall & Company (Boston, 1960).

RESOURCES

PERIODICALS

The representation of Oriental journals and society publications is outstanding. For the most part, the files are complete, and include those of the American Oriental Society, the International Congress of Orientalists, the Koninklijk Bataviaasch Genootschap van Kunsten en Wetenschappen, the Royal Asiatic Society, the Deutsche Morgenländische Gesellschaft, etc. Other important titles are *Asiatic Review, Journal asiatique,* and, among recently published materials, *Monumenta Serica* and *Monumenta Nipponica.* Periodical and society publications in special fields are equally notable, such as those of the Egypt Exploration Society, the Service des Antiquités de l'Egypte, *Revue d'Assyriologie et d'archéologie orientale, Zeitschrift für Assyriologie, Calcutta Review,* the publications of the Royal Asiatic Society of Bengal, the present Bihar and Orissa Research Society, and the Asiatic Society of Japan. Of more recent date are *Journal of Cuneiform Studies, Harvard Journal of Asiatic Studies, Journal of Egyptian Archaeology,* and *Journal of Near Eastern Studies,* available in the Oriental Division in substantially complete runs.

Currently the Oriental Division receives well over 1,000 periodical titles from Oriental countries—among them 110 titles from mainland China (both scientific and popular); 144 Chinese language periodicals from outside mainland China; 300 Japanese titles; 250 Arabic titles (mostly PL-480 material); and 150 Korean titles. A substantial representation of Indian, Pakistani, and Indonesian commercially published serials and institutional publications are received (mostly in the PL-480 program). Large newspaper holdings are administered by the division, rather than the Newspaper Collection. Current issues of the more general periodicals on Asian subjects, as for example *Journal of Asian Studies*, are held in the Periodicals Section.

As in other fields, journal articles of special interest are indexed in the catalogs. References to contributions in Oriental studies appear in both the Public Catalog and the Oriental Division catalog. In addition, the Oriental Division adds reference cards for periodical matter of particular interest to its collections or work.

PRINTED COLLECTIONS

Printed collections of materials are principally of two sorts—printings or reprintings of Oriental classics, and monographs (frequently magnificently illustrated quartos or folios) by scholars on various subjects. Of the former are the Yale Oriental Series, the E. J. W. Gibb Memorial Series, the Royal Asiatic Society of Bengal's *Bibliotheca Indica*, the publications of the Musée Guimet and the École des Langues Orientales Vivantes, the Bibliothèque Elzévirienne, *Sacred Books of the East, Kashmir Series of Texts and Studies*, the publications of the Oriental Translation Fund, *Corpus Inscriptionum Semiticarum* of the Académie des Inscriptions et Belles-Lettres, and others. Collections of scholarly monographs include the publications of the Staatliche Museen zu Berlin, the Egypt Exploration Society, the British School of Archeology in Egypt, etc. These series are fully analyzed in the division's catalog.

SUBJECT RESOURCES

Materials on Egypt, both ancient and modern, include such pioneer works as the studies conducted during Napoleon's expedition and published by the Commission des Monuments d'Egypte, the researches of Lepsius, and the mass of publications that have appeared during the nineteenth and twentieth centuries. There is a fine set of Egyptian archaeological maps in the Map Division. PL-480 additions have strengthened the area since 1962.[4]

Another strong group relates to the Arabs, their history, customs, and language. There are extensive periodical resources and an unusual representation of grammars and dictionaries. There is a very full collection of editions of the *Arabian Nights*. Historical resources of unusual richness include archaeological works and other works published in Arabic. Islamic (Muhammadan) law is well represented.

The materials on India in the Oriental Division are also rich. All aspects of Indian life are well covered, particularly Indian law. Modern government publications, including materials reprinted from Indian archives, are located in the Economic and Public Affairs Division. PL-480 additions since 1962 have enriched the Indic holdings in all areas.

Linguistics is an outstanding feature of the Oriental Division's resources. The representation of standard dictionaries and treatises of the principal Oriental tongues is noteworthy, and the library has long made special efforts to collect both critical writings and such printed examples of minor languages as can be found. In the latter field it unquestionably excels.

History, always a major strength of the library's collections, is fully represented for the Oriental countries. Historical materials in Oriental languages are retained in the Oriental Division, while those in Western languages are administered by the General Research and Humanities Division. The Oriental Division holds such special items as Chinese dynastic histories in Chinese and pamphlets issued by the Taiping rebels, discussed more fully in the chapter on Asian history.

All Oriental religions are well covered—Buddhism, Hinduism, etc. The collection of Korans in native languages and in translation is extensive.

MANUSCRIPTS

Oriental Division

Although the Oriental Division does not have special facilities for the storage of manuscripts, 268 bound manuscripts are found on the general book shelves. The great majority of these are Arabic, with several Persian and Turkish items. Included are treatises on religion, medicine, law, and the sciences, ranging from the twelfth to the nineteenth centuries. With the exception of occasional diagrams, they are not illuminated. The earliest and perhaps the most precious manuscript is the "Al-mujmal fi al-lughat," by Ibn Faris, the first part of an Arabic dictionary copied in Medina in 1172.[5]

Chinese items housed in the Oriental Division include 12 manuscript concordances or indexes of Chinese characters and phrases used by James Legge in his translation of *The Chinese Classics* (Hong Kong and London, 1861–72). There are also certain texts prepared by the Chinese scholar Wang T'ao for Legge's use in the same work.[6]

Manuscripts and Archives Division

The Manuscripts and Archives Division holds more than 1,000 manuscripts, tablets, and stone

4. See Ida A. Pratt, "Ancient Egypt; A List of References to Material in The New York Public Library," *BNYPL* 27 (1923): 723–66 et seq. Published separately by the library, with additions and index, 1925. See also her "Ancient Egypt: 1925–1941; Supplement to: Ancient Egypt . . . New York, 1925," *BNYPL* 45 (1941): 791–820 et seq. Published separately by the library, 1942. See also her "Modern Egypt: A List of References to Material in The New York Public Library," *BNYPL* 32 (1928): 589–634 et seq. Published separately by the library, 1929. Reprinted in 2 vols. as *Ancient Egypt and Modern Egypt* by Kraus Reprint Co. (New York, 1969).

5. See "Some Oriental Manuscripts," *BNYPL* 55 (1951): 565–66.

6. See Arthur W. Hummel, *Eminent Chinese of the Ch'ing Period*, 2 vols. (Washington, D.C.: U.S. Library of Congress, Asiatic Division, 1943–44), p. 837.

inscriptions in Oriental languages. Among items of note are an Egyptian stone inscription and papyrus fragments, and 624 Sumerian and Babylonian clay and stone tablets from the collection of Wilberforce Eames.[7] The 26 Arabic manuscripts include copies of the Koran in old Cufic characters dating from the eighth, ninth, and tenth centuries, and an illustrated treatise on the human body dated 1278. Among other manuscripts are 37 texts in Pali of the Tripitakas in Burmese script on palm leaves, 3 Batak soothsayer books on bark or bamboo, and 15 Persian manuscripts, most of them dating from the fifteenth and sixteenth centuries. Eight Ethiopic manuscripts on vellum, some illustrated, represent amulets and psalters, for the most part of the eighteenth century. Among the 4 Chinese manuscripts is an eighteenth-century copy of sections 15,951 to 15,958 of the Yung Lo Ta Tien of the Ming dynasty, the last full copy of which was destroyed in the burning of the Summer Palace near Peking in 1860 at the order of Lord Elgin. A small group of 3 Manchu manuscripts are of some interest, especially a scroll dated 1661 in Manchu and Chinese containing an imperial decree bestowing honors on the mother of a Manchu officer of the second heredity rank.[8]

Relevant manuscripts in English consist of sea journals and logs, correspondence, and commercial papers of firms or persons engaged in trade or travel between the United States and the Far East. The manuscripts range in date from the eighteenth to the early twentieth centuries. Additional materials furnish sources for the study of diplomatic relations of the United States and Eastern powers. Some of the collections of this nature are discussed below; others are scattered in groups of documents and papers in the division.[9]

Among the papers presented to the library by Mrs. Thomas F. Burgess in 1939 are two series of letters written from Persia and the Near East during the years 1827 to 1855 by the brothers Charles and Edward Burgess. These letters provide a history of the adventures and fortunes of Westerners in the Orient.[10]

The letters of the Hon. Townsend Harris, presented by Mrs. Thomas A. Janvier in 1921, were written to her and her mother Mrs. Sandwith Brinker during Harris's sojourn in Japan as the first United States Consul-General, later the first United States Minister during the period 1856 to 1862. The letters do not refer to diplomatic affairs, but to the country, the customs of the people, and incidents of his daily life.[11]

The John Redman Coxe Lewis journal and logbook of the corvette USS *Macedonian* gives a day-by-day account of the expedition of Commodore Matthew Perry to Japan in 1854, with descriptions of Japan and its people.[12] The diary of C. Blue, kept during the author's tour of duty on the U.S. sloop of war *Vandalia* (1853–56), describes Commodore Perry's reception in Japan and incidents in Shanghai during the Taiping Rebellion. A scroll of watercolor sketches by a Japanese artist of the scene on the first day after Perry's arrival at Uraga is in the Spencer Collection. It was the gift of Dr. Frank P. O'Brien.[13]

The Constable-Pierrepont papers (1774–1890) and the papers of Fogg Brothers of Boston (1840–1926) contain documents related to trade with the Orient.

The George C. Foulk papers, consisting of about 1,000 pieces, relate to Korea during the period from 1884 to 1887.[14] The collection was supplemented in 1924 by a gift of 44 volumes and more than 300 separate pieces from Dr. Horace Newton Allen, former minister to Korea, including his personal and official diaries for the period 1884 to 1905, and correspondence, commissions, account books, files of Korean newspapers, and translations.[15] In the gift is a collection of Korean poems dated from 1665 to 1745, illustrated with drawings by a native artist.[16]

In 1965, Mrs. A. Hawkins of Daytona Beach gave 3 boxes of material relating to the Chinese, Japanese, and Korean business of the mercantile firm of Frazar & Company, and to Everett Frazar's activity as Consul-General to the Kingdom of Korea in the United States and member of the American Asiatic Society. The period covered is 1883 to 1948.

Manuscripts pertaining to the Philippines are found in the Obadiah Rich collection. They consist of transcripts, dated about 1800, of sixteenth- and seventeenth-century accounts of voyages to the Philippines, together with historical and descriptive material. Other collections of the division contain an eighteenth-century Spanish naval log book, and papers relating to the attack on the Philippines by the United States and the War of Independence of 1898 and 1899. Also noteworthy are transcripts of the Acts of the Junta de Censura de Imprenta dating from 1866 to 1875.

Spencer Collection

The Spencer Collection's Oriental manuscripts, which number about 600, were collected principally for their illustrative and calligraphic value. These manuscripts are treated in greater detail in the discussion of the Spencer Collection and pertinent subject areas. Outstanding among them are

7. See A. Leo Oppenheim, *Catalogue of the Cuneiform Tablets of the Wilberforce Eames Babylonian Collection* (New Haven: American Oriental Society, 1948). This publication catalogs 393 tablets from the Third Dynasty of Ur.

8. See John L. Mish, "A Manchu-Chinese Scroll," *BNYPL* 52 (1948): 143–44. See also his "Grand Secretary Ortai," *BNYPL* 66 (1962): 535–38, for a transliteration and translation.

9. James W. Snyder in his "A Bibliography for the Early American China Trade, 1784–1815," *Americana* 34 (1940): 297–345, makes mention of some library holdings.

10. See Mabel C. Weaks, "Gift of Anglo-Persian Papers," *BNYPL* 43 (1939): 484. See also Benjamin Schwartz, "The Burgess Persian Letters," *BNYPL* 45 (1941): 351–62 et seq.

11. See *BNYPL* 24 (1920): 213.

12. See Henry F. Graff, ed., "Bluejackets with Perry in Japan," *BNYPL* 54 (1950): 367–83 et seq. Published separately by the library.

13. See Harold A. Mattice, "Perry and Japan," *BNYPL* 46 (1942): 167–84.

14. See *BNYPL* 5 (1901): 332.

15. See *BNYPL* 29 (1925): 208–9. See also Robin L. Winkler, *The Horace Allen Manuscript Collection at The New York Public Library* (Ypsilanti, Mich.: Korean Research Associates, 1950).

16. See J. Le Roy Davidson, "An Unpublished Korean Album," *BNYPL* 39 (1935): 595–604. Translations of the poems are given with descriptions of the pictures.

the Persian manuscripts, including the sumptuously illustrated Shahnāmeh of Firdausi made for Shah Abbas I in 1614;[17] the "Aja-ib al-Makhluquat" [The wonders of the world] by Kazwīnī, completed some time after 1370. Turkish manuscripts include a Shahnāmeh translated into Turkish, perhaps the only complete copy of the Turkish translation in existence.[18] Japanese manuscripts

and scrolls number 235, with such items as the "Iwaya No Soshi" [The princess in the cave, or the stepmother] consisting of 70 full-page miniatures dating from about 1540. *The Catalogue of Japanese Illustrated Books and Manuscripts in the Spencer Collection of The New York Public Library*, compiled by Shigeo Sorimachi, was published in Tokyo in 1968. It is in Japanese, with titles translated into English.

17. See Richard Gottheil, "The Shahnāmeh in in Persian," *BNYPL* 36 (1932): 543–54.
18. See Richard Gottheil, "The Shahnāmeh in Turkish," *BNYPL* 36 (1932), 9–10.

12

SLAVONIC DIVISION AND GENERAL SLAVONIC RESOURCES

Slavonic Division holdings number 166,700 volumes. The division collects in fourteen Indo-European languages, two of which, Latvian and Lithuanian, are not Slavic but Baltic. The other languages include Russian, Belorussian, Ukrainian, Bulgarian, Old Church Slavonic (which survives only in liturgical use), Macedonian, Serbo-Croatian, Slovenian, Polish, Czech, Slovak, and Lusatian (the language of the remaining Slavs in Germany). In addition the collections hold materials in some non-Indo-European languages of the Soviet Union, such as Uzbek, Yakut, Chuvash, and Finno-Ugric. Geographically the division covers a vast area, including Balkan and Eastern European territory, as well as most of the USSR; practically every aspect of life in the nations within this area, including their literature, is represented in the division's resources. The term Balto-Slavic more exactly describes this division of the Research Libraries, but Slavonic has been traditionally applied and is used here.

Specifically the Slavonic Division collections include: (1) Works in any Balto-Slavic language on all subjects (except works on Jews, Music, and American Indians); and public documents in Cyrillic characters that is, Russian, Ukrainian, Belorussian, Bulgarian, Serbian, and Macedonian (other Balto-Slavic public documents are housed in the Economic and Public Affairs Division or in the appropriate subject divisions of the library); (2) All translations from Balto-Slavic belles-lettres; and (3) All works in any non-Balto-Slavic language on Balto-Slavic linguistics or belles-lettres. All other works on Balto-Slavic subjects, such as history, economics, or the arts in non-Balto-Slavic languages, are placed in the appropriate subject division.

This deceptively simple tabulation of the type of material to be found in the Slavonic Division bears close analysis. It can be seen, as an example, that the library's rich collection of materials on Russian history in western languages will not be shelved in the Slavonic Division, although cards for the material will be found in the division's card catalog. Materials on Russian history in the Cyrillic alphabet are housed in the Slavonic Division and represented in the division's catalog, but not in the Public Catalog or in other subject division catalogs. In the same manner, a sizable

group of items on stagecraft in the Cyrillic alphabet will be found in the Slavonic Division and not in the Theatre Collection. It should be noted that the Slavonic Division catalog is generally richer than the Public Catalog in references to periodical articles on Balto-Slavic subjects both in Balto-Slavic and in non-Balto-Slavic languages.

This survey reflects the present organization of the Slavonic Division. Changes are contemplated that would make the division an equivalent of the General Research and Humanities Division, containing material only in the humanities.

HISTORICAL SURVEY

The collections of the Slavonic Division have primarily been developed since the foundation of the New York Public Library. The Astor Library had a small group of Slavic dictionaries and other material, but did not expand in this field as it did in Orientalia and Judaica. The few important accessions of the nineteenth century came principally in the A. M. Bank collection, acquired in 1897. This was the working library of the scholar and educator Leon Mandelstamm, formed in Russia but principally of Jewish interest; the notable additions to Russian holdings were imprints from early and little-known Russian presses.

The Slavonic Division was established in 1899 as the Department of Slavonic Literature. In the early years the collection was overwhelmingly Russian, but in recent decades there has been a concerted attempt to build up other holdings, especially in Polish, Ukrainian, Czech, and the less common languages. The following indicates the growth of the division over the years:

1854 Astor Library	41 volumes (Hungarian and Slavic literatures collectively)	
1899 New York Public Library	1,300	
1917	24,495	
1921	26,711	
1930	44,278	
1941	60,000	
1945	84,963	
1966	166,710	

Table 1 illustrates the relative strengths and growth of the language components of the division, clarifying its basic structure and revealing how the proportion of Russian-language holdings has changed from 1935 to 1966.

TABLE 1. STRENGTHS AND DEVELOPMENT OF SLAVONIC DIVISION

Language	1917	1935*	1945*	1966
Russian	21,395	43,811	61,142	105,484
Polish	2,080	5,773	6,159	19,628
Minor languages†	—	7,598	5,026	—
Czech and Slovak	280	2,844	3,539	12,124
Latvian	80	2,058	2,553	5,062
Ukrainian	100	1,443	2,187	6,606
Serbo-Croation	300	1,932	2,049	8,114
Bulgarian	160	1,005	1,078	4,603
Lithuanian	100	688	644	1,237
Belorussian	—	270	344	1,116
Slovenian	—	235	203	990
Sorbian (Lusatian)	—	31	39	137
Macedonian	—	—	—	100
Non-Indo-European languages	—	—	—	315
Slavistics	—	—	—	1,194‡
Total	24,495	62,688	84,963	166,710

*The figures for 1935 and 1945 are taken from Jadwiga Pulaska, "The Slavonic Division of The New York Public Library" (M.L.S. thesis, School of Library Service, Columbia University, 1953). They reflect a more detailed inventory than those in the preceding list of figures, in which the figure for 1941 is an estimate based on the official census of 1930.

†It is difficult to know what Miss Pulaska meant by "Minor languages."

‡There must have been books in Slavistics (general studies in the Cyrillic languages) in the library in 1935 and 1945. Although the categories in the various inventories do not match exactly, the table presents an accurate picture of the relative growth of the collections.

SPECIAL INDEXES AND FILES

Current Periodicals and Newspapers

Arranged by country, this card file lists in alphabetical order the newspapers and magazines published in Balto-Slavic languages available in the library (2 card drawers). Information includes the name of the journal or newspaper, its dates, and place of publication.

Exhibitions Vertical File

All information relative to the exhibitions prepared by the Slavonic Division is retained (1 file tray). The material consists of labels, notes, and other items. The file was established in 1955. Among the periodic exhibitions, often in commemoration of an anniversary of an important author, have been those devoted to Dostoyevski and Mickiewicz in 1956, Turgenev in 1958, Chekhov in 1960, and Shevchenko in 1961.

Master Negative File

An alphabetical listing, by name of author or issuing institution, of all Slavonic Division materials which have been filmed and for which there is a master negative available. The file was established in 1964 (4 card drawers).

The Slavonic Division Catalog has been published in book form in 44 volumes by G. K. Hall & Company (Boston, 1974).

RESOURCES

GENERAL HOLDINGS

Imaginative literature in all forms is a strong feature of the Slavonic collection, especially outstanding in the Russian holdings. The important editions of the great classic writers such as Turgenev, Dostoyevski, Tolstoi, and Pushkin are present. Children's books of the eighteenth and nineteenth centuries are well represented.

Extensive collections of public documents are included. Among them those of Imperial Russia are particularly notable, containing full sets of the proceedings of the state Imperial Duma, a complete collection of the laws of the Russian Empire, strong files of the annual reports of the ministries, and a complete file of the government gazette. The Soviet regime is represented as far as possible by printed legislative and administrative documents of the central government and the various member states of the federation.

The social sciences, in the broadest sense, are well covered. The library attempts to obtain any original contribution in the exact sciences, especially in mathematics, chemistry, and physics. The applied sciences, on the other hand, are less well covered; little material is collected relating to medicine, a field in which the library does not specialize. The library subscribes to a large and steadily increasing number of scientific and technical periodicals. Until 1964 periodicals in the Balto-Slavic languages were held in the Slavonic Division; some of the more significant titles have been transferred to the Science and Technology Research Center. A contemplated policy change will probably place all science titles in that subject division of the library, regardless of the language in which they are written.

The resources for the history of Russia, Poland, and other Slavic countries are substantial, both in native tongues and in Western languages. The holdings include histories, books of travel, and descriptions of social life with particular emphasis on Russia. Biographies of Russian royalty include important material on Peter the Great and Catherine II. There are also significant items documenting the dynastic, administrative, and political history of the Russian Empire during the last three centuries of its existence. The purchase of some 450 books from the libraries of Czar Nicholas II and other members of the Imperial family began about 1926. In 1931 the library of Grand Duke Vladimir Alexandrovich was acquired. The 2,200 volumes contain valuable documentation on various phases of the history of the Empire and include an outstanding group of regimental histories.[1]

---

1. Avrahm Yarmolinsky, "The Library of Grand Duke Vladimir Alexandrovich (1847–1909)," *BNYPL* 35 (1931): 779–82.

Another large group of material relates to revolutionary movements in Russia and to the Revolution of 1917. Particularly notable are the George Kennan collection and the donations of Miss Isabel Hapgood, which are more fully described below in the description of manuscript resources. The John Reed Russian collection, presented in 1935, consists of material published chiefly in 1917 and 1918.

The division collects the most important publications of Russian émigrés. Books have been acquired from New York, London, and other places, but the chief center of production is Paris. They range from scholarly works to memoirs of former notables, and from imaginative works to political pamphlets.

More than 750 periodical titles and 120 newspapers in all fields are received by the Slavonic Division. Of this total, 294 periodicals and 43 newspapers come from the USSR; 158 periodicals and 4 newspapers from Poland; and 92 periodicals and 1 newspaper from Czechoslovakia. In addition, the division acquires journals and newspapers from 13 other countries, the largest single unit being 94 periodicals and 52 newspapers from the United States and Canada, including materials both in Cyrillic and non-Cyrillic alphabets. Newspapers are housed in the division rather than in the Newspaper Collection. Publications of the national academies and other learned societies, as well as general reviews, are included in the collections, the strongest representation being for the period since 1850.

RARE BOOKS

The Slavonic Division is primarily a working collection of reference and documentary materials, rather than rare books. The Slavonic Reserve Section, however, contains approximately 1,500 items, the large majority of them Russian, including some Petrine editions (the first books printed in the new Russian script introduced by Peter the Great). Other rare and valuable Slavonic publications are housed in the Rare Book Division.

The *Triod tzvetnaya* [The Floral Triodion or Pentecostarion], a liturgical book of the Eastern Orthodox Church, is believed to have been printed in Krakow by Schweitpolt Fiol (Viol) in 1491, the initial date in the history of printing from Cyrillic type. Only four other copies are known. The "Prague Bible," so called because it was printed in that city in 1488, is the earliest complete Bible in Czech; a translation of the Acts of the Apostles, printed in Moscow in 1564, is the first Russian dated book. A fine copy of the *Kormchaya kniga* [Nomocanon], printed in 1653, is a variant of the first edition of the digest of canon law by which the Russian Orthodox Church was guided until well into the nineteenth century. In 1968 a unique collection of nearly 300 pamphlets printed in Poland between 1590 and 1802 was acquired. The majority date from the seventeenth century. For the most part written in Latin, they consist in the main of panegyrics on such state events as royal weddings, declarations of war, and investitures of cardinals, and include much elusive historical and genealogical material. Many of the pamphlets were printed at the Jesuit press in Wilno.

The library's holdings of eighteenth-century "original" Russian publications in the *grazhdanskii* or civil script are strong; 166 titles are found in the Slavonic Division; the Map Division, the Music Division and the general collections.[2] "Original" publications are those written in Russian rather than translations into Russian from another language.

MANUSCRIPTS

The Manuscripts and Archives Division of the Research Libraries houses some Slavonic manuscripts. Perhaps the most remarkable item is an Eastern Orthodox lectionary written in Cyrillic characters on parchment in the fourteenth century by a copyist apparently from northern Muscovy. Another important item is Georg de Hennin's description of the Siberian Metal Works written in 1735.[3] During the second decade of this century, Isabel F. Hapgood presented numerous books and about 100 letters from eminent Russians with whom she had corresponded, including Tolstoi and members of his family, Maxim Gorki, and Alla Nazimova.

During 1919 and 1920 the library received two important gifts from George Kennan, totalling about 650 books and pamphlets, over 700 manuscript pieces, about 500 photographs and pictures, and numbers of magazines and newspapers. Kennan, an American journalist, was noted as an investigator of the Siberian penal system. The letters in the collection were written for the most part in the 1880s and 1890s by political convicts and other people connected with the emancipatory movement; there are many related documents. Also included are copies of 40 letters from Catherine Breshkovsky, known as the "Grandmother" (Babushka) of the Russian Revolution, some of them to Alice Stone Blackwell. Additional sections of the gift include materials for the biographies of convicts and official documents relating to the life of the exiles. The pictorial matter, which complements the manuscripts, contains a group of some 200 photographs of early Russian political exiles and convicts. A further 200 to 300 pictures relate to Siberia, with the exception of a number of pogrom photographs taken in Kishinev in 1903.[4]

The Russian Historical Archives were established in 1940 by Avrahm Yarmolinsky, former chief of the Slavonic Division, and others, but have not grown significantly. Most of the materials relate to Aleksandr V. Adiassewich, a petroleum engineer and writer on historical subjects. There are about 800 pages of Adiassewich's manuscript on Armenia, Turkestan, and the Ukraine in their economic aspects, and an unfinished draft of a book on Turkey. Also in the archives are correspondence, short stories, and articles by Yevenii N. Chirikov, Vasilii Nemirovich Danchenko, and Piotr P. Popov.

There are 174 letters (1923–34) from Catherine Breshkovsky to Mrs. Irene Dietrich discussing their mutual interest in Russian refugees, particularly children. The papers and correspondence of the Russian-American social reformer and Posi-

2. See Edward Kasinec, "Eighteenth-Century Russian Publications in The New York Public Library: A Preliminary Catalogue," *BNYPL* 73 (1969): 599–614, and 75 (1971): 474–94.

3. See Avrahm Yarmolinsky, "A Russian Manuscript Treatise on Metallurgy," *BNYPL* 40 (1936): 1007–11.

4. See Avrahm Yarmolinsky, "The Kennan Collection," *BNYPL* 25 (1921): 71–80.

tivist thinker, William Frey, include letters to and from Russian liberals and revolutionaries, American Communists, and others. The collection of about 375 items centers on Frey's work in founding a community in Cedar Vale, Kansas, during the period from 1860 to 1888. The Emma Goldman collection (1917–28) and the Norman Thomas papers (1916–68) contain material of Russian interest; and several travel diaries of the mid-nineteenth century describe parts of Russia.

13

SCHOMBURG CENTER FOR RESEARCH IN BLACK CULTURE

The Schomburg Center for Research in Black Culture (formerly The Schomburg Collection of Negro Literature and History), located at 103 West 135th Street, is one of the world's largest, most comprehensive, and most heavily used repositories of records documenting the experience of the peoples of African origin and descent.[1] Its collections, international in scope and interest, include more than 58,000 volumes, along with phonodiscs, tape recordings, prints, posters, paintings, sculptures, clippings, periodicals, pamphlets, sheet music, and newspapers, as well as large holdings of manuscript and archival records.[2]

HISTORICAL SURVEY

The present center assumed international prominence as long ago as 1926 with the addition of the personal library of Arthur A. Schomburg. It is therefore fitting to preface a guide to specific holdings with some discussion of how Mr. Schomburg's bibliographical interests provided the impetus for the development of this center for research in black culture. During the early 1920s, a period later referred to as the "Harlem Renaissance,"[3] the 135th Street Branch of the New York Public Library accommodated a growing public interest in what was then described as "Negro writing, art, and music." Due to the efforts of a Citizens' Committee, the branch's extensive reference collection received gifts and loans from the private libraries of figures in the black community as notable as John E. Bruce, Louise Latimer, Hubert H. Harrison, George Young, Dr. Charles D. Martin, and Arthur A. Schomburg. On May 3, 1925, the cooperative work of Miss Ernestine Rose, head of the 135th

Street Branch, and the Citizens' Committee, resulted in the official opening of the Division of Negro Literature, History, and Prints. In outlining the division's plans to the press, Miss Rose pointed out that there were similar collections in the Library of Congress, and at institutions such as the Tuskegee Institute and Howard University, in certain large city reference libraries, and in a few private libraries. The 135th Street Branch Library, however, had the potential and public interest to become the largest and most valuable such collection in the world.

In 1926 the new division assumed international prominence with the addition of the personal library of Arthur A. Schomburg. Consisting of more than 5,000 books, 3,000 manuscripts, 2,000 etchings, and several thousand pamphlets, this collection was purchased from Mr. Schomburg by the Carnegie Corporation, at the suggestion of the Urban League. It was presented to the New York Public Library with the understanding that it would be housed in the 135th Street Branch as a reference collection.

Arthur A. Schomburg was a Puerto Rican of African descent. Born in San Juan in 1874, he was educated in Puerto Rico and the Virgin Islands; he came to New York City in 1891, where he was employed for many years by the Bankers' Trust Company. Schomburg was an expert and zealous collector of works dealing with African and Afro-American history. Through the years he searched book markets in Europe, North Africa, Latin America, and the United States seeking out the books, documents, pamphlets, and art objects which would offer the concrete evidence that the black man indeed has a long and glorious heritage in which his descendants could justifiably take pride.

Among the treasures he unearthed were Ad Catholicum, Juan Latino's Latin verse (Granada, 1573), and his book on the Escorial (1576). Schomburg also acquired copies of the works of Jupiter Hammon, America's first black poet (An Address to the Negroes in the State of New York, 1787); manuscript poems and early editions of the works of Phillis Wheatley of Boston, an American slave; copies of the Almanacs (1792 and 1793) compiled by Benjamin Banneker, an African-American whose unusual abilities had been employed by Thomas Jefferson and others; the scrapbook of Ira Aldridge, the Shakespearean actor who won fame in Europe during the nineteenth century; various editions of William Wells Brown's Clotel; or, The President's Daughter; A Narrative of Slave Life in the United States, the first novel by a black American; George Washing-

---

1. The present chapter relies heavily upon Stanton F. Biddle, "The Schomburg Center for Research in Black Culture: Documenting the Black Experience," *BNYPL* 76 (1972): 21–35.

2. Other divisions of the Research Libraries collect (and often duplicate) subject materials held by the Schomburg Center; such holdings are described in appropriate sections throughout this *Guide*. For example, a significant Duke Ellington manuscript in the Music Division is discussed in chapter 31.

3. See *The Negro in New York: An Informal Social History*, ed. Roi Ottley and William J. Weatherby, with preface by James Baldwin and foreword by Jean Blackwell Hutson (New York: The New York Public Library and Oceana Publications, 1967), 245–64.

ton Williams's *History of the Negro in America from 1619 to 1880* (New York, 1883), said to be the first such history produced in America by an African-American to receive serious attention by white scholars. The list goes on to include rare biographies and autobiographies, texts of sermons, scrapbooks, memoirs, and other items documenting the black man's history and continuing contribution to modern civilization.

In 1932 a grant from the Carnegie Corporation enabled the New York Public Library to hire Arthur A. Schomburg as the first curator of his cherished collection. After his death in 1938, the Negro Division was officially designated the Schomburg Collection. Under Schomburg's successors, the scope and activities of the collection have greatly expanded, with the inclusion of lecture series, exhibits, scheduled programs on special occasions, and the annual Honor Roll in Race Relations Awards. Since its inception, the Schomburg Collection had been a part of the New York Public Library's Branch Library system. In the spring of 1972 the collection became part of the Research Libraries. This action changed the Schomburg's organizational and administrative relationship to the rest of the library from that of a neighborhood branch with a special subject-area concentration to that of a full-fledged reference and research center. In December 1972 the collection was officially designated the Schomburg Center for Research in Black Culture.

RESOURCES

The curators of the prized Schomburg Collection built upon the spirit and tradition of Arthur A. Schomburg and the others who had participated in the movement for a Black Collection in the early 1920s. Today the Schomburg Center stands as a living monument to their efforts and concerns. It has expanded from the original nucleus of reference volumes to a present book stock of over 58,000.[4] In addition it includes a wealth of non-book and even non-textual resources which are of immeasurable value to the scholar.

Of special interest are the histories of ancient African kingdoms—Ghana, Mele, Songhai, Benin—names which have become familiar since independent states have emerged as the "new" Africa. Recent changes in the Caribbean area have brought into prominence Schomburg's extensive holdings in West Indian history, social conditions, poetry, fiction, and folklore. The collection of Haitian literature and history is unique in its comprehensiveness. Other items which suggest the Schomburg Center's holdings include the 81 manuscript volumes of the field notes and memoranda used by Gunnar Myrdal in writing *An American Dilemma*; Claude McKay's manuscripts; the Harry A. Williamson library on the Negro in Masonry; *The Sound of Africa*, a set of 210 long-playing records of African folk music, indexed by tribe, type of song, and instruments; and a file of some 800 newspapers on microfilm offering a reflection of historical and contemporary Negro thought and life, over more than a century. Significant

---

4. The *Dictionary Catalog of the Schomburg Collection of Negro Literature and History* was published in book form in nine volumes in 1962 by G. K. Hall & Co. of Boston; there have been a *First Supplement* in two volumes (1967) and a *Second Supplement* in four volumes (1972).

books and manuscripts from the center's holdings in American literature are described in chapter 23.

The following list is presented in an attempt to illustrate the size and diversity of Schomburg Center materials:

Clipping File

The center maintains a file on some 9,000 subject headings. Included are clippings from newspapers and magazines, playbills, leaflets, pamphlets, book reviews, correspondence, typescripts, and programmes.

Linguistic Materials

Students of African languages will find especially valuable resources in the Schomburg Center. There are notable holdings in some 60 indigenous languages as diverse as Adangme, Nyanja, Sotho, Swahili, and Zulu; the language held in the most strength (59 works) is Xhosa. More than 140 African languages and dialects are documented by dictionaries, grammars, and general studies in English and the European languages (the largest number of these in French). Among extensive phonodisc holdings in the center, the important *The Sound of Africa* series contains 3,000 items in 128 languages which are of linguistic as well as musical significance.

Periodicals and Newspapers

The center subscribes to more than 200 newspapers and magazines. Black and interracial publications are kept in their entirety either in bound volumes or microfilm copies; general publications are clipped, and relevant articles incorporated into the clipping file. Among the periodicals received regularly are *Parade* from Rhodesia, *Nigeria Magazine*, *Ethiopia Observer*, and *Jeune Afrique*, valuable for their sketches of contemporary African personalities and life styles; *Africa*, a scholarly publication of the International African Institute; *Africa Report* and *A Current Bibliography on African Affairs*, both dealing with current affairs in Africa and the United States' relations with African nations. The file of black newspapers on microfilm offers a reflection of contemporary and historical black thought and life. African newspapers, such as the *West African Pilot*, *East African Standard*, *Evening News* (Ghana), and *Central Africa Post*, are now available on microfilm. The Afro-American newspaper collection includes long, complete runs of newspapers dating from 1827 through the First World War, such as the *California Eagle*, *Cleveland Gazette*, and *Savannah Tribune*. Current issues of black newspapers giving national coverage are microfilmed at the end of each year.

Microfilm

The microfilming program at the Schomburg Center has made available copies of some of the center's material to schools and libraries all over the world. It has also provided copies of rare and fragile materials, thus helping to preserve original documents by limiting their direct use. The program has further added to the holdings of the center by acquiring complete runs of black newspapers as well as microfilm copies of the official legislative gazettes of a number of African countries.

Motion Picture Film

A grant from the Urban Center at Columbia University provided the center with the series of more than 100 filmed lectures "Black Heritage: A History of Afro-Americans" which was produced in cooperation with CBS-TV. The grant also marked the beginning of the projected Archives of Black Films, an attempt to document the contributions to and involvement of black people in the motion picture industry.

Phonograph and Tape Recordings

Over the years a sizable collection of phonograph recordings of early blues and jazz, as well as African and West Indian folk music, has developed. Recent grants have enabled the staff to expand the holdings to include contemporary "Soul Music" recordings, prose and poetry readings, and documentary productions as well. Hundreds of reels of tape recordings have been collected. These include poetry readings, lecture series, speeches, musical programs, interviews, and the like.

Photographs

The center maintains a photograph collection of some 15,000 indexed items plus many thousands more unassorted. These include material from the "Harlem on My Mind" Exhibition, picture files from the National Urban League, Farm Security Administration, National Youth Administration, and New York *Amsterdam News*, as well as general donations from interested individuals.

MANUSCRIPTS AND ARCHIVES

Arthur A. Schomburg did not limit his collecting to books and published works. At the time his private library became a part of the New York Public Library it included some 3,000 historical manuscripts. These consisted of addresses, sermons, letters, and poems by such personalities as Alexander Crummell, Paul Laurence Dunbar, Lemuel Haynes, Phillis Wheatley, Frederick Douglass, Booker T. Washington, Edward W. Blyden, and many others. There were also the signed army orders of Toussaint L'Ouverture, the Haitian military genius who drove Napoleon's armies into the sea; slave certificates of registration; bills of sale for the purchase of slaves; a parchment-bound Spanish manuscript by Soley Balsas (1757) recounting in poetry the life of an African girl who became St. Theresa of Salamanca; and many other treasures.

In 1936 the New York City Historical Records Survey, a WPA project, undertook a program to compile the first complete calendar of the manuscript holdings of the Schomburg Collection, the initial stage of which was completed in 1938. *The Calendar of the Manuscripts in the Schomburg Collection of Negro Literature* contained complete entries for some 2,271 record items. These were arranged in eight collections (West Indian, 1716–1817; Slavery, 1700–1890; Abolition, 1787–1876; Alexander Crummell Letters, 1837–98; Alexander Crummell Sermons, 1840–97; Paul Laurence Dunbar Collection, 1892–1902; John E. Bruce Collection, 1872–1927; and Miscellaneous Letters and Papers, 1757–1918). For each item the calendar gave date, author, place, a brief summary of contents, a description of the item

itself (number of pages, autograph document, typed letter signed, autograph letter, etc.), and finally each item was assigned a collection number and a calendar number. In addition to the item descriptions themselves, the Historical Records Survey compiled biographical sketches and a comprehensive index to the entire collection. The calendar itself was never published because of the advent of World War II shortly before its completion in 1942, yet it has served as an invaluable tool in locating and describing manuscript material housed in the Schomburg Center.

Between the completion of the calendar in 1942 and 1967 very little was done in the way of processing or handling manuscripts or archival records on an organized basis, with two exceptions: the Harry A. Williamson collection of Negro Masonry, and the Writers' Program study "Negroes of New York." Harry A. Williamson was a collector somewhat in the tradition of Arthur A. Schomburg. However, his driving interest was in the Black Freemasons movement. He sought to document the legitimacy of the black Prince Hall Lodges which were not recognized by the white Masons, as well as chronicle the many and varied activities of these Masons. By 1936 he had accumulated a considerable amount of material which he donated to the New York Public Library to be housed in what was still the Negro Division of the 135th Street Branch. His collection represented over thirty years of research and included such kinds of records as the proceedings of fifty-nine Grand Lodges of Prince Hall dating from 1860; proceedings of Masonic Congresses; Constitutions of thirty-one Prince Hall Grand Lodges; Masonic periodicals; and scrapbooks of newspaper clippings on Masonic activities. In total it represented the most comprehensive body of material on the black Masonic movement in the country. Between the original donation and his death in 1965, Mr. Williamson added to this collection, keeping it current and continually increasing its importance and significance.

Although the Williamson collection might be viewed as an archival record group, reflecting as it does the interests and activities of black Masonic organizations, it was decided that it should be cataloged as a special book collection and handled accordingly. In 1943 representatives of the library's central Cataloging Office, with the assistance of the Schomburg curator, drew up a classification system which employed the Dewey Decimal numbers 366.10–366.19. The same basic approach was employed in dealing with the manuscripts of the Writers' Program study of Negroes of New York. It was compiled by the workers of the Writers' Program (WPA) in New York City between 1936 and 1941, and deposited in the Schomburg Collection. The surveys analyzed such areas as housing for black people, churches, education, medicine and health, migration, sports, theatre, press, motion pictures, in addition to historical questions relating to economic developments and the development of black communities in each of the city's five boroughs. The entire study was cataloged (974.7 W) with subject entries for each of the individual surveys and cross references for many of the individual personalities treated.[5]

---

5. The "pre-final" manuscript draft of this study was published as *The Negro in New York: An Informal Social History* (see footnote 3, above).

These two instances represent the only major activities relating to the processing of manuscript and archival records in the period between 1942 and 1967. Individual documents which came into the library's possession during that period were routinely added to the still unpublished *Calendar of Manuscripts*. Additions to the Williamson collection were either assigned Dewey numbers under the special classification set up for them or merely placed in storage for future disposition.

Fortunately the acquisition program during the period 1942–67 was active; the collection came into possession of a number of very important bodies of records. Although there was no apparatus available for handling archival records or large manuscript collections, it was felt that it was important nevertheless that the Schomburg Collection accept these materials as they became available rather than allow them to be lost. The first major body of material to be acquired under this philosophy was the records of the National Negro Congress. This group contained not only the records of the executive secretaries of that organization, but also records relating to a number of its affiliates, namely the Joint Committee on National Recovery, Negro Industrial League, and the Negro Labor Victory Committee. The records had been deposited in the Schomburg Collection in the very late 40s and had remained virtually untouched, in their original state, for nearly two decades.

The largest single body of records accepted under this same primary concern for preservation came with the demise of the Civil Rights Congress in 1956. In the resolution officially dissolving the organization, the Civil Rights Congress empowered its past national executive director, William L. Patterson, to dispose of the records "as would best suit the interests of the American People." The material consisted not only of the congress's own records but also included sections of records inherited from several organizations which had merged to form the Civil Rights Congress. The most noteworthy of these was the International Labor Defense, an organization which is primarily remembered for its involvement in the famous Scottsboro Case.

In addition to the organizational records listed above, the Schomburg Collection found itself custodian to a number of other record groups as well. Arthur A. Schomburg himself had left a sizable collection of his own records—primarily correspondence but including unpublished manuscripts, research notes, editorials, and articles. The editors of the short-lived *Negro World Digest* deposited several boxes of their records; the family of William Pickens, one of the founders and officials of the NAACP, gave his personal files, some 21,000 record items; and in 1965 Dr. Hugh Smythe and his wife, both noted scholars and educators, presented many of their personal and professional papers to the Schomburg Collection just before Smythe assumed his post as United States Ambassador to Syria.

By 1967 the Schomburg Collection had in its possession several hundred thousand archival record items and manuscripts. Many of these were still in their original state—packed away in cardboard boxes or rusted metal file cabinets, or simply tied in bundles. Some were partially accessible but most were totally inaccessible. None had been thoroughly analyzed, so there was no way of knowing their full content or significance. With the heightened interest in black studies resulting from the change in emphasis away from integra-

tion as a goal in itself to one stressing instead self-identity and ethnic pride, the potential contribution of such a large body of rare and unique primary sources began to be felt. Therefore, in 1967 two concerned scholars secured a grant for the Schomburg Collection from the Ford Foundation to begin an archival program which would not only make its record resources available for study, but also would help preserve them for future generations. By the summer of 1968 the archival program had been initiated with the work on the National Negro Congress records. Since that time over 1,000,000 record items have been processed. The records themselves include such classes of material as personal and business correspondence, minutes of meetings and conferences, manuscripts of articles and books, galley proofs of books, legal papers, certificates and diplomas, newspaper clippings, organizational publications, financial statements and ledgers, leaflets, pamphlets, petitions, texts of speeches, transcripts of court proceedings, etc. The archives are not restricted to paper documents but also include such other record forms as photographs, phonodiscs, tape recordings, engraved printing plates, X rays, card files, and motion picture film. As of September 1972, 25 major record groups had been fully processed, along with several smaller collections of materials. A number of other bodies of records have been transferred to the archives from other parts of the center; however, it was decided that full processing was not always necessary, but rather in some cases the old systems employed in the *Calendar of Manuscripts* or the library's cataloging could remain in force. The following is a list of some of the material now housed in the archives of the Schomburg Center:

John Edward Bruce collection
Civil Rights Congress record group
Earl Conrad/Harriet Tubman collection
Alexander Crummell collection
Records of the Chief, Schomburg Center
International Labor Defense record group
Oakley Johnson papers
Claude McKay Exhibit material
National Negro Congress record group
Negro Labor Committee record group
Negro World Digest record group
William Pickens papers
Hugh Smythe papers
Universal Negro Improvement Association, Central Division (New York)
Richard Wright collection
Writers' Program, Negroes of New York (typescripts)

With the exception of the records of the chief of the Schomburg Center, all of the above records have been microfilmed by the Schomburg's photographic laboratory. Master negatives are kept in the New York Public Library's photo-vault. Positive microfilm prints are kept at the Schomburg Center itself. Copies of some records not covered by specific restrictions can be obtained from the New York Public Library's Photographic Service.

Currently the archival staff is in the process of transferring other manuscript and archival records from the general collection into the archives. It is also actively pursuing a program of acquiring new bodies of records which are becoming available as knowledge about the program spreads. One such collection is the personal papers of Dr. Robert C. Weaver, former secretary of the Department of Housing and Urban Development, the first African-American to attain a cabinet level position in the federal government. Another is the personal papers of Lawrence Brown, a pianist and composer who was for many years the accompanist of Paul Robeson and Roland Hayes, as well as a widely acknowledged musician in his own right.

The Schomburg Center recently purchased a considerable portion of the private library of Kurt Fisher, an Austrian who fled to Haiti during Hitler's rise to power in Europe. Fisher developed an intense interest in Haitian history and culture, and he assembled an excellent personal library. In addition to the books, many of which are rare editions or autographed copies, the collection contains several thousand very important manuscripts relating to various aspects of Haitian history, life, and culture. They include proclamations and correspondence of a number of Haitian presidents dating back to the Haitian and even French Revolutions, memoranda and orders from high military and government officials, church records, legal documents, charters, property inventories, and other kinds of Haitian historical records which are almost impossible to find elsewhere today. The records of the organizing committee of the 1963 March on Washington for Jobs and Freedom is another recent accession which will prove to be a very valuable primary source once it has been properly arranged and inventoried.

The Schomburg Center has become the repository of the records of a number of special studies and research projects. The two most important are the Carnegie-Myrdal study of the Negro in America and the Writers' Program (WPA) study of "Negroes of New York." Many writers, both black and white, who have produced some of the most widely acclaimed books on the black experience have deposited their research notes and relevant manuscripts in the Schomburg Center.

ART RESOURCES

The Schomburg Center houses a priceless array of art works by black painters and sculptors, as well as an historically important collection of African and African-American artifacts.

Works by a number of black artists have been donated to the center or left on indefinite loan. This has resulted in large part from the efforts of the now defunct Harmon Foundation (which formerly supported the work of African-American artists) as well as individual artists. The works include paintings, sculptures, prints, etchings, and even posters. Some of the American art objects are remnants of the Harlem Art Center (WPA) supplemented by gifts from the Harmon Foundation and by important loans from Richmond Barthé and the estate of Judge Irving Mollison.

Outstanding sculptures and paintings are displayed in every available space, and students come from everywhere to view the works of the important black artists represented, such as Richmond Barthé, William E. Braxton, E. Simms Campbell, Aaron Douglas, Archibald J. Motley, Jr., Augusta Savage, Charles Sebree, Henry O. Tanner, and Charles White.

Artifacts

In addition to art works, collections of artifacts have been donated and lent to the Schomburg Center over the years. The African collection of several hundred pieces of sculpture and other artifacts is based on the Blondiau-Theatre Arts Expedition to Africa in 1927. Professor Alain Locke was instrumental in placing half the result of this expedition in the Schomburg Center and half at Howard University. Also noteworthy are Mrs. Florence Bruce's collection of Nigerian artifacts, and Eric de Kolb's unique collection of African arms and weapons, which was added in the early 1940s.

14

MANUSCRIPTS AND ARCHIVES DIVISION

The collections of the Manuscripts and Archives Division (called until 1972 the Manuscript Division) are estimated to contain more than nine million pieces. The dictionary catalog of the division, which has been published in book form in two volumes by G. K. Hall & Company (Boston, 1967) reproduces about 25,000 cards and represents a guide to the holdings, rather than a detailed listing. In accordance with general practice in manuscript cataloging, the division generally records materials by collection rather than by individual piece. Calendars or inventories of a number of the more important collections are available to the reader.

The Manuscripts and Archives Division is open to the public upon presentation of an admission card obtained from the Research Libraries Administrative Office. The coverage ranges from Sumerian and Babylonian clay and stone tablets to twentieth-century publishers' archives. Among early materials are more than 150 Greek and Latin manuscripts. A concentration of notable individual items and collections falls within the period of the American Revolution, with such holdings as the Olive Branch Petition, unique source materials on Samuel Adams and the local Committees of Correspondence, the Thomas Addis Emmet collection, in which there are three complete sets of autographs of the signers of the Declaration of Independence, and the Theodorus Bailey Myers collection, with one complete set of signers of the Declaration. Reflecting the library's strong interest in the discovery and settlement of the Americas, the Obadiah Rich and other collections provide extensive holdings for Latin American areas prior to their wars of independence.

Personal narratives and diaries are a particular strength of the division. Mercantile papers portray the economic history of New York and its contacts with foreign lands. Ships' logs and journals include the records of both commercial and naval vessels. Literary manuscripts appear as individual items, in autograph collections, and in the large bodies of publishers' correspondence (Century Company records, Crowell-Collier Publishing Company records, Macmillan Company records, etc.), as well as in such holdings as the noteworthy Lewis M. Isaacs collection of Edwin Arlington Robinson materials. Institutional papers include those of the United States Sanitary Commission (the combined Red Cross-USO of the American Civil War), and the major parts of the records of the New York World's Fairs of 1939/40 and 1964/65, the latter not yet open to the public.

The division is not the only repository of manuscripts in the Research Libraries, although it is the largest. Collections in other divisions are merely noted in the following remarks; more complete descriptions appear with the accounts of the particular division or subject resource. Manuscripts in the Berg Collection, for example, relate principally to nineteenth- and twentieth-century American and English authors, and form the greatest concentration of literary manuscripts in the Research Libraries. The manuscripts in the Spencer Collection, collected for their fine illustrations, include superb examples of illuminated manuscripts on vellum and paper, and scrolls and books from Japan and other countries of the Orient. The Arents Tobacco Collection has a wide variety of manuscripts relating to tobacco, including literary material, drawings, etc. The Rare Book Division administers the Oscar Lion collection of Walt Whitman manuscripts and books. The Oriental Division has on its shelves several hundred Arabic manuscripts and a number of Persian and Turkish items. The Jewish Division holds some seventy manuscript mahzors, Kabbalistic works, liturgical texts, and other materials. Each of the divisions of the Research Libraries at Lincoln Center (the Theatre and Dance Collections and the Music Division) contains important groups of manuscripts connected with its field. The Schomburg Center for Research in Black Culture has important manuscript and archival materials, both literary and historical.

COLLECTING POLICY

Since the establishment of the Manuscript and Archival Division in 1914, when the manuscript accumulations of the Astor and Lenox Libraries and the Tilden collection were assembled in a separate area of the new Central Building at Fifth Avenue and 42nd Street, the determinant for the inclusion of materials has been that they be handwritten rather than printed. The typewriter, when used by the author or writer, has been accepted as the modern substitute for the pen and pencil. In general the Manuscripts and Archives Division, as it is now designated, follows the overall acquisition and collecting policies of the Research Libraries which specify that an effort should be made to add materials having relevance to areas where the resources are already strong. In fields where other institutions or agencies pursue an active collecting policy, the Research Libraries gather only complementary collections.

The collections of the Manuscripts and Archives Division may be divided into three major groupings: personal papers and records; records of organizations; and manuscripts, autograph collections, and small collections of unpublished papers.

Each of these involves a different approach to collecting.

Personal papers and records of an individual in public life, or family records, are selectively acquired. The relevance of such papers to the study of the New York metropolitan area, and their interest from personal, sociological, and historical points of view are considered, as well as any connection that may exist with materials already in the collections. The papers of private figures of importance offered for sale rather than as gifts are considered not only with regard to their intrinsic quality and suitability for the collections, but also in relation to the availability of funds.

Records of organizations, including business enterprises, societies, and other agencies, are now acquired on a limited basis for organizations in the New York area. Those which are added to the holdings constitute a sample, covering activities and interests already represented. In the area of publishing, for example, the recent acquisition of the archives of the Macmillan Company supports the library's extensive literary holdings, and the acquisition of the minutes of the New York Typographical Union No. 6 strengthens the library's resources in materials relating to printing technology, the printing industry, and trade unionism and economics. Records of business enterprises are accepted only if they illustrate various types of commercial activity in the region, especially from a retrospective viewpoint. In the fields of the performing and fine arts, the library attempts to secure representative records of creators, performers, commercial enterprises, trade unions, and associations which have been important in the development of the artistic life of the community. Government records in their original form are not collected by the Research Libraries, as it is felt that national, state, and municipal archives are the proper stewards of such papers.

The principles governing the acquisition of personal papers and records and the records of organizations are generally applicable to single manuscripts and small collections of unpublished papers. For these categories, however, the Research Libraries attempts to secure significant material regardless of geographical area, especially material related to subject collections of special strength.

CATALOGS, CALENDARS, AND OTHER GUIDES

As noted in the introductory paragraph of this chapter, the dictionary catalog of the Manuscripts and Archives Division is a guide, rather than an itemized list. Most of the bulky collections are represented by concise descriptions, added subject entries, and numerous cross-references. Inventories or brief listings are generally available for unprocessed material. The division catalog contains no entries for manuscripts in other divisions of the library.

The division follows in practice the subject headings used in the library's Public Catalog; many of these have undergone revision due to the varied nature of manuscript materials. Additional changes arise from cooperation with the *National Union Catalog of Manuscript Collections* and an attempt to conform to that system of entry.

One very important group of materials for which no entries appear in the catalog is the collection of miscellanies. These series include single items or small collections not part of a larger unit and not sufficiently significant to warrant special cataloging. Miscellanies are arranged in alphabetical order by name, subject, and geographical area. This valuable source of original autographs is the nucleus from which individual collections are built by later accessions.

The division maintains a semi-active Letters Catalog (18 card drawers), which provides an alphabetical listing by name of the writers of letters in a few of the collections. Heavily weighted with material from the Emmet collection, the file is far from complete; it is not duplicated in the dictionary catalog.

Additional autograph material is indexed in the Autograph and Provenance File of the Rare Book Division, which locates signatures and manuscript inscriptions in books shelved in the Rare Book Division and in the Spencer Collection.

Typescript calendars or inventories provide detailed information about the contents of some 150 of the more important collections in the Manuscripts and Archives Division. Inventories for many smaller collections are found in the manuscript containers with the material. The catalogs of the important Gansevoort-Lansing papers and the Garrison-McKim-Maloney collection (containing Irish historical material, the Roger Casement papers, etc.) form appendices to the published dictionary catalog of the division.[1]

Among the important separate calendars are the following:

Alfred W. Anthony autograph collection—letters and autographs of literary figures and other prominent persons of the late nineteenth and early twentieth centuries.

Bancroft collection—original papers and transcripts of material dealing with the American Revolution.

Joseph Barondess papers—relating to socioeconomic developments in New York, especially among Jewish workingmen, in the late nineteenth and early twentieth centuries.

Sol Bloom papers—papers of the New York political figure and United States congressman; Edwin Markham material is included.

Bronson papers—papers of a family prominent in the nineteenth-century business community.

Bryant-Godwin collection—letters to William Cullen Bryant, his son-in-law Parke Godwin, and members of their families.

Budke collection—deeds, wills, maps, etc. of Rockland and Orange Counties, New York, and Bergen County, New Jersey.

Victor Francis Calverton papers—correspondence and literary papers of the American radical writer and editor.

Carnegie autograph collection—American literary, historical, and other figures, 1899–1905.

Century Company records—correspondence of contributors to the *Century Magazine* and its predecessors, *Scribner's Monthly* and *St. Nicholas.*

Duyckinck collection—papers of Evert A. and George A. Duyckinck, nineteenth-century editors and publishers of the *Cyclopedia of American Literature* and other works.

Richard Watson Gilder collection—letters received, letter books, diaries, articles for "Topics of the Time," and other papers of the editor of *Scribner's Monthly* and the *Century Magazine.*

Harkness collection—miscellaneous literary and historical manuscripts—American, English, and European; includes Shirley Brooks's albums of manuscripts, drawings, etc. relating to *Punch.*

Washington Irving lists—locate Irvingiana in the library.

Stanley M. Isaacs papers—general correspondence, Borough Presidency papers, City Council papers, scrapbooks, etc.

Lee Kohns memorial collection—autographs of royalty, literary figures, artists, political figures, etc.

Fiorello H. La Guardia papers—Congressional correspondence 1918–33, letters, pamphlets, scrapbooks, etc.

Macmillan Company records—editorial correspondence copy-books 1889–1907, letters from Macmillan authors, etc.

Vito Marcantonio papers—general correspondence, Congressional papers.

Montague collection—literary autographs; American historical autographs; British historical autographs; Robert Fulton materials, etc.

National Civic Federation papers—general correspondence; departmental correspondence (i.e., Immigration, Industrial, etc.); conferences and commissions; annual meetings, etc.

Edward D. Ordway collection—letters dealing with problems in the Philippine Islands at the beginning of this century.

Oriental manuscripts in the Manuscripts and Archives Division (lists manuscripts in Arabic, Armenian, Batak, Chinese, Egyptian, Ethiopic, Hebrew, Pali, Persian, Sanskrit, Siamese, Sinhalese, Tamil, Turkish, etc.).

Personal Miscellaneous—a listing of various smaller collections of personal papers in the division.

John Quinn memorial collection—letters to John Quinn from artists, authors, political figures, etc., with copies of his replies, 1900–24. See footnote 15 below.

Edwin Arlington Robinson collection [Lewis M. Isaacs collection]—a copy of the library's published check list, "Edwin Arlington Robinson: A Descriptive List of the Lewis M. Isaacs Collection of Robinsoniana," *BNYPL* 52 (1948): 211–33, with additions noted.

Albert Shaw papers—correspondence and other papers, including editorial correspondence of the *Review of Reviews,* the manuscript of Shaw's Ph.D. thesis *Icaria* with letters and pamphlets concerning it, etc.

David McNeely Stauffer collection—personal correspondence; literary collection; autographs—officers of the American Revolution, political lawyers, actors and artists, etc.

Joel E. Spingarn collection—papers related to American literary criticism, military history, issue of academic freedom, and the Troutbeck Press.

Norman Thomas papers—a restricted collection which includes general correspondence, speeches, writings, miscellaneous papers; Thomas family papers; manuscripts of books; papers of committees and conferences, etc.

Samuel J. Tilden papers—correspondence; political papers; legal papers; business and real estate; Tilden Estate and Trust materials.

---

1. See also Alice P. Kenney, " 'Evidences of Regard': Three Generations of American Love Letters," *BNYPL* 76 (1972): 92–119, which is a discussion of one aspect of the Gansevoort-Lansing collection.

Carl Van Vechten collection—general correspondence; scrapbooks; drafts of books and correspondence regarding them; broadsides, photographs, etc.

Frank P. Walsh papers—general correspondence; speeches and writings; legal papers including material on the Mooney Case and Irish affairs.

The card catalog of the division has been published in book form in two volumes by G. K. Hall & Company (Boston, 1967). Listed below are a number of additional printed sources of information about the holdings of the Manuscripts and Archives Division which, while not complete in themselves, are serviceable when used in conjunction with the specialized reference assistance provided by the staff of the division.

Calendar of the Emmet Collection of Manuscripts, etc. Relating to American History (The New York Public Library 1900; reprinted by the library, with additions, 1959).

Victor Hugo Paltsits, "Manuscript Collections in The New York Public Library," *BNYPL* 5 (1901): 306–36.

―――― "The Manuscript Division in The New York Public Library," *BNYPL* 19 (1915): 135–65.

Evarts Boutell Greene and Richard B. Morris, *A Guide to the Principal Sources for Early American History (1600–1800) in the City of New York*, 2nd ed. rev. (New York: Columbia University Press, 1953).

Seymour de Ricci and W. J. Wilson, *Census of Medieval and Renaissance Manuscripts in the United States and Canada*, 3 vols. (New York: H. W. Wilson, 1935–40; reprinted by Kraus Reprint Company).

―――― ―――― *Supplement*, originated by C. U. Faye, continued and edited by W. H. Bond (New York: Bibliographical Society of America, 1962; reprinted by Kraus Reprint Company).

Harry James Carman and Arthur W. Thompson, *A Guide to the Principal Sources for American Civilization, 1800–1900, in the City of New York: Manuscripts* (New York: Columbia University Press, 1960).

United States National Historical Publications Commission, *A Guide to Archives and Manuscripts in the United States*, Philip M. Hamer, ed. (New Haven: Yale University Press, 1961).

Modern Language Association of America, *American Literary Manuscripts* (Austin: University of Texas Press, 1961). This is a slightly misleading source. The library reported holdings for over half of the figures listed (1,112 of the 1,960 names), but is often shown as having substantial resources when there are in fact only one or two items for a particular author.

During the period 1915 to 1948 there appeared annually in the *Bulletin* of the library a record of the year's manuscript acquisitions. Numerous articles on important additions have appeared in the *Bulletin* and can be located through the published *Index*. The library began to list new accessions in the *National Union Catalog of Manuscript Collections* in 1963.

RESOURCES

For the purposes of this description, manuscripts may be divided into those which are of paleographic or decorative interest, and those which are essentially valuable for their subject matter. Early holdings in the first category—the illuminated manuscripts—were described in the library's *Bulletin* of February 1915 (pp. 140–42); the prefatory statement that the library "is believed to contain more valuable European illuminated manuscripts than any other public institution in America" is no longer accurate. This is the case not because of any diminution in the quality of the collection (interesting and valuable pieces have since been added and are supplemented by the highly important holdings of the Spencer Collection), but because the status of other institutions has changed. Libraries once private—such as the Pierpont Morgan and the Henry E. Huntington—are now public, in the sense that those collections are available to the public without the restrictions which private ownership implies. Individual treasures in the Manuscripts and Archives Division provide magnificent examples of European and Oriental paleographic art, to which the resources of the Stuart collection and Spencer Collection add notable support. Various individual manuscripts are the subject of articles in the library's *Bulletin*, many of which are cited in this *Guide* in the discussions of the manuscripts as resources in particular subject areas. They are also listed in such standard bibliographical tools as the de Ricci *Census* and its supplement.

In the second category, manuscripts primarily valuable as source material, collecting emphasis has been placed on American history and literature, although there are also notable individual collections in other fields. The following descriptions follow broad subject divisions.

HISTORICAL RECORDS

With the exception of illuminated manuscripts and some literary collections, the greater portion of the manuscript materials which came to the library before the turn of the century were historical. These provide rich representations of original documents and transcripts, pertaining largely to early American history. Descriptions of these and later collections appear in the appropriate subject sections of this *Guide* and are merely noted here. Particularly important collections include the Rich collection (early Spanish America); the Chalmers collection (American colonies, mainly for the period leading to the Revolutionary War); the Hardwicke collection (British archives of the sixteenth to eighteenth centuries relating to America, etc.); the Smyth of Nibley papers (Virginia papers, 1613–79);[2] the Bancroft collection (British colonies and the American Revolution); the Emmet collection (one or more autographs of nearly every distinguished American of the colonial and revolutionary periods and early nineteenth century);[3] the American Loyalists papers (claims for losses and services in the Revolution);[4] the Myers col-

―――――――

2. See "The Smyth of Nibley Papers, 1613–1674," *BNYPL* 1 (1897): 186–90, a calendar of the collection. See also published selections, *BNYPL* 1 (1897): 68–72; 3 (1899): 160–71 et seq.

3. See *Calendar of the Emmet Collection of Manuscripts, etc. Relating to American History* (The New York Public Library, 1900; reprinted by the library, with additions, 1959).

4. See *BNYPL* 3 (1899): 416.

lection (letters and documents of distinguished Americans of the colonial and revolutionary periods and of the nineteenth century, and of distinguished Englishmen, Frenchmen, and Hessian officers);[5] the Ford collection (autographs of the colonial and American revolutionary periods and the nineteenth century); the William Livingston papers (correspondence of the revolutionary period); the Gansevoort-Lansing collection (military and other papers of the eighteenth and nineteenth centuries);[6] and the Schuyler papers (American Revolution, New York State, Indians, etc.). Among notable single manuscripts in the division are the Olive Branch Petition,[7] Thomas Jefferson's draft of the Declaration of Independence, one of seven known copies of the original Bill of Rights, and George Washington's Farewell Address,[8] as well as important holdings of diaries and personal narratives.

During the period from 1900 to 1914, the major increase in the manuscript holdings was in the field of New York City records. By 1915 it could be said that the library had become the depository of a vast aggregation of official records of the city of New York, most of these mayors' papers documenting more than fifty years of the nineteenth century. These official records of the city have been transferred to the Municipal Archives and Records Center, an agency under the Municipal Service Administration of the city of New York.

Among the collections bearing on American relations with other countries are the James Leander Cathcart correspondence (1785–1806) on Tripoli and the Barbary States; the George C. Foulk papers and the Horace N. Allen papers, both of which relate to Korean matters at the close of the last century;[9] the John Bigelow letters (1856–68) relating to France; the Francis Vinton Greene papers relating to Turkey, the Philippines, and other countries at the close of the last century; the papers (1839–88) of William Frey, concerning Russian-American associations; and the Garrison-McKim-Maloney collection which deals, in part, with the role played by individuals in the United States during the struggle which culminated in the Irish Free State.[10] The latter is supplemented by the John Quinn memorial collection, which includes Quinn's correspondence (1900–24)

with members of the Irish Home Rule movement as well as international writers and artists.[11]

Pertinent to national affairs are the Gansevoort-Lansing collection, rich in sources for the study of early American history (national as well as state) for a period of 250 years;[12] the Gideon Welles correspondence (1825–85) concerning his tenure as secretary of the Navy in Lincoln's and Johnson's cabinets; the Samuel J. Tilden papers (1830–86) of interest to New York and national history and to legal affairs; the Brigadier-General John Wolcott Phelps papers and scrapbooks (1838–72) relating to various American wars and troubles; the Horace Greeley papers (1842–70) dealing with politics and legislation in Indiana, New York, and the United States; the Levi P. Morton correspondence (1878–98) containing letters from various important officials and political figures; Charles James Folger's unofficial correspondence as a federal officer (1881–84); the James Schoolcraft Sherman correspondence (1896–1912) dealing in part with national and state matters; and the Sol Bloom papers (1920–49) covering his term as congressman from New York.

Of interest to the history of New York State are the Tilden and the Gansevoort-Lansing collections mentioned above; the William Smith papers (1763–83) of great value for the study of the administrative and political history of the province of New York;[13] and the Timothy S. Williams papers, in part relating to Williams's activities as private secretary to Governors Hill and Flower (1889–94).

Among the library's rich collections of manuscript materials relating to local history are the George H. Budke papers, which are early records of the history of Rockland and old Orange Counties of New York State and of the adjoining Bergen County, New Jersey. The James Riker collection of original seventeenth- and eighteenth-century Dutch and English manuscript records (with translations) documents the villages of Harlem, Newton, New York, Brooklyn, and others; it was collected by this local historian for use in his work. The Hon. Percy G. Childs papers (1817–22) originate in the Cazenovia, New York region. The Stanley M. Isaacs (1889–1962) papers include materials concerning his activities as a New York City politician and leader, and the papers of Lillian D. Wald illustrate the social history of New York from 1894 to 1940. The Robert Moses papers (at present restricted) also bear on New York City history.

The Schomburg Center includes important manuscript and archival resources, such as the papers of Frederick Douglass and Booker T. Washington, the WPA Writers' Program study "Negroes of New York," a comprehensive collection of Haitian records from the library of Kurt Fisher, and the records of the Civil Rights Congress.

5. See *BNYPL* 4 (1900): 112–14.

6. See *Dictionary Catalog of the Manuscript Division*, 2 vols. (Boston: G. K. Hall, 1967), 2:517–75; see also footnote 1 above.

7. See Cornelius W. Wickersham, "The Olive Branch," *BNYPL* 56 (1952): 539–43. See also *The Olive Branch Petition of the American Congress to George III, 1775, and Letters of the American Envoys, August-September 1775. [With Essays by] Cornelius W. Wickersham [and] Gilbert H. Montague* (The New York Public Library 1954).

8. See Victor Hugo Paltsits, ed., *Washington's Farewell Address* (The New York Public Library, 1935; reprinted by the library and Arno Press, 1971).

9. See *BNYPL* 29 (1925): 208–9. See also Robin L. Winkler, *The Horace Allen Manuscript Collection at The New York Public Library* (Ypsilanti, Mich.: Korean Research Associates, 1950).

10. See *Dictionary Catalog of the Manuscript Division*, 2:577–99.

11. See Harvey Simmonds, "John Quinn: An Exhibition to Mark the Gift of the John Quinn Memorial Collection," *BNYPL* 72 (1968): 569–86. Published separately by the library. See also footnote 15 below.

12. See *Dictionary Catalog of the Manuscript Division*, 2:517–75; see also footnote 1 above.

13. See *BNYPL* 24 (1920): 125–26. See also William H. W. Sabine, ed., *[William Smith's] Historical Memoirs*, 2 vols. (New York: Colburn and Tegg, 1956–58).

OTHER FIELDS

Art, Music, Theatre, Sport

With the exception of actual examples in the form of illuminated manuscripts, the collections of the Manuscripts and Archives Division are not particularly strong in material related to the graphic arts. There are, however, autographs of artists and architects, as well as a number of collections of personal papers which are described in chapter 28 of this *Guide*.

Although little theatrical material was received during the earlier years, large gift collections were acquired after the Theatre Collection was established in 1931 and then raised to the status of a full division in 1945. When the Music Division and the Theatre and Dance Collections moved to the Library and Museum of the Performing Arts at Lincoln Center in 1965, the Manuscripts and Archives Division transferred to them all music manuscripts (there were highly important resources in this field) and many theatrical manuscripts, which are described in the chapters on those divisions. There remain in the Manuscripts and Archives Division several important theatrical archives: the Robert H. Burnside papers (1894–1949) document Burnside's career in theatrical production including his long association with the Hippodrome Theatre in New York City; the Charles B. Dillingham correspondence and accounts (1905–27) were accumulated while Dillingham was owner and manager of the Globe Theatre and associated with the Knickerbocker and Hippodrome Theatres in New York City; the Annie Russell papers (1874–1936) consist chiefly of letters from prominent theatrical and literary figures; the Sothern and Marlowe papers (1859–1950) are the archives of the famous Shakespearean acting team of Edward H. Sothern and Julia Marlowe Sothern; the Paul Kester papers (1880–1933) contain 17,000 pieces, largely correspondence with theatrical figures.

Manuscript holdings related to sports are limited. Two collections contain extensive materials on baseball: the Spalding collection and the Swales collection.

Literature and Book Arts

Early gifts included manuscripts by Thackeray, Hawthorne, Irving, and other major authors writing in English; in addition to other extensive Irving holdings, the division administers the important Seligman and Hellman collections of the manuscripts and books of Washington Irving.[14] The remarkable Duyckinck collection of business papers, letters, etc., relates to American literature during the first half of the nineteenth century; the Bryant-Godwin papers consist of letters to William Cullen Bryant, his son-in-law Parke Godwin, and members of their families, from persons in the United States and abroad who were distinguished in literature, the arts, science, and other fields. The John Quinn memorial collection preserves Quinn's correspondence with leading English, Irish, and American literary figures of the first quarter of the twentieth century.[15] The personal and professional correspondence of H. L. Mencken became available to the public in 1971; the papers of Genevieve Taggard, important for the study of Emily Dickinson, are partially restricted until 1985. Carl Van Vechten also presented his rich personal collections, which included much correspondence and many manuscripts, to the library.[16]

In the 1930s and 1940s the Manuscripts and Archives Division sought and accepted from writers and publishing firms many authors' drafts of published works. This resulted in a collection of several hundred literary typescripts, some donated to the Emma Mills collection established in memory of the literary agent; a good representation of literary autographs is also found in the collection.

Publishers' archives found in the division constitute a vast corpus of literary source material beginning with the Century Company papers (1804–1913),[17] and including those of the Crowell-Collier Publishing Company, the Macmillan Company,[18] Alfred A. Knopf, and others. Additional significant holdings include the papers of Paul A. Bennett, the typographic promotion manager of the Mergenthaler Linotype Company and secretary of the Typophiles.

The literary manuscripts in the division are supplemented by the rich resources of the Berg and Arents Tobacco Collections, the Schomburg Center for Research in Black Culture, and the Oscar Lion Walt Whitman collection administered by the Rare Book Division. Detailed descriptions of literary manuscripts are to be found in the chapters on general literature, American literature, and English literature.

Business and Economic History

The collection of business records of New York City firms is especially strong. The library ordinarily accepts only those records which illustrate the various types of commercial activity in this region, especially from a retrospective viewpoint. Collections of business records received by the library before 1915 were for the most part eighteenth- and nineteenth-century American and British materials. Later additions include the Constable-Pierrepont papers (1774–1890)[19] covering the mercantile trade between New York and Philadelphia, and New York and the Orient, realty in southern and northern New York, and other matters; the papers of Brown Brothers of

14. See "Catalogue of the Seligman Collection of Irvingiana," *BNYPL* 30 (1926): 83–109; published separately by the library as *The Seligman Collection of Irvingiana*. See also "The Hellman Collection of Irvingiana," *BNYPL* 33 (1929): 207–19; published separately by the library. A later publication is H. L. Kleinfield, "A Census of Washington Irving Manuscripts," *BNYPL* 68 (1964): 13–32; unpublished lists of Irving holdings in the Manuscripts and Archives Division provide further information.

15. See Simmonds, *John Quinn*. See also B. L. Reid, *The Man from New York: John Quinn and His Friends* (New York: Oxford Univ. Press, 1968). See also Francis O. Mattson, "The John Quinn Memorial Collection: An Inventory and Index," *BNYPL* 78 (1975): 145–230.

16. See John D. Gordan, "Carl Van Vechten: Notes for an Exhibition in Honor of His Seventy-fifth Birthday," *BNYPL* 59 (1955): 331–66.

17. See Mabel Clare Weaks, "The Century Collection," *BNYPL* 38 (1934): 15–16.

18. See *BNYPL* 71 (1967): 3.

19. See *BNYPL* 47 (1943): 93; 48 (1944): 402.

New York and London, bankers (1825–80);[20] the papers and account books of Moses Taylor and Company of New York, merchants and bankers (1832–88);[21] the papers of Brewster and Company, manufacturers of carriages and automobile bodies in New York and New Haven (1837–1924); and the papers of Fogg Brothers of Boston (1840–1926) concerning the China trade and especially cotton cloth. An outstanding collection relating to Henry George, including letters, diaries, and other materials, covers the second half of the nineteenth century.[22] The library holds the voluminous records of the New York World's Fairs of 1939/40 and 1964/65, the latter not yet open to the public. Additional resources are noted in the commerce section of the chapter on economics and business administration.

Law, Politics, and Sociology

Many of the collections received before 1915 and described with historical records and business materials contain resources of importance to legal, political, and sociological studies. These subjects developed as a separate collecting field somewhat later.

Among notable holdings are documents relating to estate administration in New York (1771–1866);[23] the George Croghan papers (1812–48); the correspondence and letter books (1892–1917) of William Bourke Cockran relating to his law practice, political activities, etc.; the Emma Goldman papers (1812–48); the Norman Thomas papers (1905–67) including family papers, letters, speeches, articles, etc.; and the papers of congressmen Sol Bloom (1920s–49) and Vito Marcantonio (1935–56). The minute books and manuscript materials from various chapters of Delta Upsilon Fraternity cover the period from the 1850s to the 1890s. The division holds the papers (1896–1939) of Frank P. Walsh, labor representative, protagonist of public utility ownership, advocate of Irish independence, and public official. The George Kennan collection, which was received in 1920, is one of the most important assemblages of Russian material ever presented to the library. It contains letters, papers, pictures, and books of interest for the period from the 1880s through the early 1890s and from 1910 to 1912.[24] The papers of Pierre Toussaint, Haitian ex-slave and humanitarian, reflect a unique phase of social life in New York City in the first half of the nineteenth century. The selected papers of Carrie Chapman Catt and of the National American Woman Suffrage Association relate to the strong collection on women in the library.

The Schomburg Center holds the papers of several civil rights organizations, including the Civil Rights Congress and the organizing committee of the 1963 March on Washington for Peace and Freedom.

Church records in the division, so often of value as genealogical and historical sources, include the Methodist Historical Society's collections of records of discontinued churches in New York City and environs, the Dutch Lutheran Church records,[25] and Shaker manuscript records (1780–1929), in addition to collections of the letters of leading American clergymen and the papers of American educational and religious leaders.

Science and Applied Arts

An important group of more than seventy manuscripts and drawings by Robert Fulton in the Parsons[26] and Montague collections documents the development of the steamboat and the use of steam vessels as instruments of war. The papers of the United States Sanitary Commission consist of more than 1,000 boxes of material covering the period 1862 to 1867. Among the largest groups of material are the papers of the Army and Navy Claim Agency, the Army and Navy pay claim archives, the Washington Hospital Directory archives, and condensed historical matter consisting of reports, plans, maps, newspapers, clippings, etc. The Frank Julian Sprague papers on the development of the electric trolley and the electrification of railroads are an important resource. The William John Wilgus collection contains material on the AEF Transportation Corps, the New York Central Railroad, the Holland and Narrows tunnels, etc.[27] Other materials are described in subject discussions, particularly in the chapter on technology.

---

20. See Victor Hugo Paltsits, "Business Records of Brown Brothers & Co., New York—1825–1880," *BNYPL* 40 (1936): 495–98.

21. See Wilmer R. Leech, "The Moses Taylor Papers," *BNYPL* 35 (1931): 259–61.

22. See Rollin Alger Sawyer, "Henry George and the Single Tax: A List of References to Material in The New York Public Library," *BNYPL* 30 (1926): 481–503 et seq. Published separately by the library. See also "Henry George Exhibition," *BNYPL* 31 (1927): 899–903.

23. See Robert W. Hill, "The Robert Troup Papers," *BNYPL* 37 (1933): 574–76.

24. See Avrahm Yarmolinsky, "The Kennan Collection," *BNYPL* 25 (1921): 71–80.

25. See Arnold J. H. vanLaer, "The Lutheran Church in New York, 1649–1772: Records in the Lutheran Church Archives at Amsterdam, Holland," *BNYPL* 48 (1944): 31–60 et seq.

26. See "Catalogue of the William Barclay Parsons Collection," *BNYPL* 45 (1941): 95–108, 585–658. Published separately by the library.

27. See *BNYPL* 42 (1938): 40.

15

RARE BOOK DIVISION

The Rare Book Division contains approximately 91,000 volumes (including books, pamphlets, and bound volumes of newspapers), 20,000 broadsides (including broadside ballads, proclamations, and newscarriers' addresses), and miscellaneous items (such as globes, medals, badges, campaign buttons, etc.). It is open to the public upon presentation of an admission card obtained from the Research Libraries Administrative Office.

The Rare Book Division has developed from the collection of Americana, early Bibles, and voyages and travels formed by James Lenox. With the exceptions noted in the following paragraph, the division houses all books in the library published before 1601 in Europe, before 1641 in England, and before 1801 in the Americas, in addition to many other rare or valuable items of all periods including the present (such as modern examples of fine printing and private press books).

This division might be called the "general" rare book division, as other rare books in the Research Libraries are housed according to language, special subject interest, or format. Books in Hebrew, for example, are housed in the Jewish Division, books in the Cyrillic alphabet in the Slavonic Division, books in Oriental languages in the Oriental Division, and books on black culture are kept in the Schomburg Center. In the area of special subject interests, books on music are found in the Music Division, books on the dance in the Dance Collection, American and English literary first and significant editions and manuscripts are kept in the Berg Collection, and books relating to tobacco are found in the Arents Tobacco Collection. Books in fine bindings or notable for their illustrations are housed in the Spencer Collection, while books in parts are found in the Arents Collection of Books in Parts. The Rare Book Division does, however, include materials in certain of these categories, such as American literary first editions and books in parts.

The chief strength of the Rare Book Division is Americana, especially materials published before 1801. The holdings are particularly rich in the earliest period, 1493 to 1550; in English Americana before 1641; and in publications dealing with the American Revolution. Among outstanding rarities in these categories are the only known copy of the Columbus letter to Luis de Santangel (Barcelona, 1493) announcing the discovery of a new world; the Bay Psalm Book (1640), the first book printed in what is now the United States; and the first printing of the Declaration of Independence (Philadelphia, 1776), as well as one of two known copies of the first New York edition, printed by John Holt.

Other specialties of the division are:

1. Voyages and travels, including probably the most extensive collection of De Bry, and one of the finest sets of the Canadian "Jesuit Relations."
2. Early Bibles, including the first Gutenberg Bible brought to this country.
3. Eighteenth-century American newspapers and periodicals such as William Bradford's *New-York Gazette* and Hugh Gaine's *New-York Mercury*.
4. American and English literary first and significant editions, with notable collections of Shakespeare, Milton, Izaak Walton's *Compleat Angler*, Bunyan's *Pilgrim's Progress*, and the Oscar Lion collection of Walt Whitman.
5. Modern fine printing, including a complete collection of the Kelmscott Press books and nearly complete runs of such other important private and special presses as the Ashendene, Doves, Golden Cockerel, Grabhorn, Nonesuch, and Vale; and what is probably the most extensive institutional collection of books designed by Bruce Rogers.

This listing indicates particular strengths of the division, but is far from exhaustive. Mention may also be made of some 700 incunabula from the total of about 850 in the library. There are also block books, a strong collection of early editions of Sacro Bosco's *Sphaera Mundi*, the Whitney collection of early English cookbooks, the Beadle and Adams dime novel collection, children's books, chapbooks, and many other materials.

Most of the world's famous books are to be found in the library, either in original editions, later editions, reprints, or some kind of facsimile. In cases where the original edition is in the collections, an effort is made to provide the work in some less valuable form for general use. The method of this *Guide* is to consider rare and valuable materials, together with general holdings, as resources for research, and to discuss them in connection with relevant subject areas. The following remarks on the Rare Book Division attempt no more than a summary description of the collection.

HISTORICAL SURVEY

The nucleus of the Rare Book Division is the library of James Lenox. The other predecessor collections, the Astor Library and the Tilden collection, made important but secondary contributions. Scarce and valuable works have been collected through the years as they could be secured; many have come as gifts, the most notable large groups being the Duyckinck, Myers, and Ford collections.

Features of James Lenox's collection were the famous Bibles, early editions of English literature, first printed accounts of early voyages, and most especially rare Americana. In the twelfth annual report of the trustees (1881), the Lenox Library was said to contain "some of the most rare and precious monuments and memorials of typographic art and the historic past as have escaped the wreck and been preserved to this day"—a characterization that needs no modification. In 1890 the Lenox Library received from Margaret Wolfe Duyckinck (widow of Evert A. Duyckinck) a legacy of the valuable printed books, manuscripts, and engravings which her husband had gathered.[1] The Stuart collection, described in detail in the section on Rare Book Division resources, came to the Lenox Library in 1892; it is particularly rich in materials on natural history, general history, theology and ecclesiastical history, and the fine arts. In 1897 Alexander Maitland gave more than 220 volumes of rare Americana, approximately half of which were published before 1550; these included some of the rarest treasures of the noted collector Martin Kalbfleisch, purchased from his son through J. O. Wright.[2] Maitland also established a purchase fund for Americana and cartography.

The Tilden collection, which together with funds of the Tilden Trust formed a part of the original foundation, contained individual rarities. Although Samuel Jones Tilden's library was not given entirely to the New York Public Library, among works received were three issues of the first edition of Milton's *Paradise Lost* (1667–68), and the first three folio editions of Shakespeare (1623, 1632, and 1664).[3]

The Astor Library, though it acquired rare works, was not a collector's but a reference library, with resources not usually found elsewhere in the city. Dr. Cogswell, the superintendent responsible for the development of the Astor Library, was guided in his purchases by the concept of securing the *finest* edition of any works collected; during the last half of the nineteenth century, this usually indicated a first edition. Therefore, while he did secure a first folio Shakespeare and an *editio princeps* of Homer, as he reported in 1849, most books were chosen primarily for their value to scholarship, rather than as treasures. This point of view continued to guide the policy of the Astor Library. J. J. Astor, for example, gave the Hepworth Dixon collection of about 500 English Civil War pamphlets (1640–50) which, together with other notable accessions of the preceding year, prompted Robbins Little, then superintendent, to describe the Astor Library in his annual report of 1880 as one "to encourage high studies and assist in the reform of popular instruction."[4] Treasures were not, however, entirely neglected. In 1884, Mr. Astor gave early printed books mainly of the fifteenth and sixteenth centuries, some of which were primarily interesting as rarities.

In 1922, Dr. Frank P. O'Brien gave the library his Beadle Dime Novel collection numbering about 1,400 pieces, and in 1963 C. V. Clare gave approximately 900 examples of *Diamond Dick Weekly* and other successors to Beadle.[5] More than 100 rare books and manuscripts came as a gift of Mrs. Felix M. Warburg in 1941.[6] The Whitney collection of cookbooks also came to the library in 1941, under the terms of the will of Mrs. Helen Hay Whitney. This important gift included seventeen manuscripts and more than 200 printed books, largely English, ranging in date from the fifteenth to the twentieth centuries.[7] In 1947, Gabriel Wells, the New York rare book dealer, gave the library, through the terms of his will, the privilege of selecting rare books and manuscripts to the value of $10,000.[8]

The bequests of Edward S. Harkness in 1950, and of his widow, Mary Stillman Harkness, in 1951, brought many rare volumes to the division, including a fine copy of the first edition of T. E. Lawrence's *Seven Pillars of Wisdom* and a set of the four folio editions of Shakespeare.[9] Mrs. Francis Minot Weld presented in 1950, in memory of her husband, rarities in general literature, reference books, and first editions, together with a purchase fund.[10]

The Oscar Lion Whitman collection, of great importance for the study of Walt Whitman, was placed on deposit by Lion in 1953; by 1960 the full collection had been transferred to the library.[11] The purchase in 1958 of the Sir William Stirling-Maxwell collection of 59 contemporary books and pamphlets celebrating the battle of Lepanto formed the core of a growing group of materials relating to this key victory of Don Juan of Austria.

In addition to these and other notable rare book gifts, several special funds have been established for the purchase of materials for the division. The De Vinne Memorial Fund was the bequest of Alfred E. Ommen in 1950 for the purchase of books related to the art of printing and finely printed books of all ages. The Eames Fund, created by the will of Dr. Wilberforce Eames, provides funds for the purchase of Americana published before 1801. The Ford Fund (No. 1) was established by Emily Ellsworth Ford Skeel in memory of her parents Gordon Lester Ford and Emily Ellsworth Fowler Ford for the purchase of books, manuscripts, and papers to be added to the Ford collection. Under the will of Mrs. Lathrop C. Harper, four funds were established: Harper Fund No. 1 is used for the purchase of incunabula, and Harper Fund No. 2 for the purchase of books over 100 years old, other than incunabula, primarily Americana; Harper

---

1. See *BNYPL* 1 (1897): 6. The Lenox Library's *Short-Title Lists* nos. 8 and 12 (1887, 1890) are devoted to the collection.

2. See Lydenberg, *History*, p. 186. See also "Early Books, Mostly Relating to America, Presented . . . by Alexander Maitland," *BNYPL* 3 (1899): 9–22.

3. See *BNYPL* 3 (1899): 5–6.

4. Quoted in Lydenberg, *History*, pp. 71–72. For contents of the Hepworth Dixon collection see *Dixon Collection; A Collection of Pamphlets . . .* (New York: Astor Library, 1880?)

5. See "The Beadle Collection," *BNYPL* 26 (1922): 555–628. Published separately by the library.

6. See Lewis M. Stark, "The Warburg Collection," *BNYPL* 45 (1941): 941–43.

7. See Lewis M. Stark, "The Whitney Cookery Collection," *BNYPL* 50 (1946): 103–26. Published separately by the library with corrections, 1946; 2d ed. rev. 1959.

8. See Lewis M. Stark, "Gabriel Wells Bequest," *BNYPL* 51 (1947): 320–24.

9. See Robert W. Hill and Lewis M. Stark, "The Edward S. Harkness Collection," *BNYPL* 54 (1950): 585–94; and "The Bequest of Mary Stillman Harkness," *BNYPL* 55 (1951): 213–24.

10. See Lewis M. Stark, "The Weld Memorial Collection," *BNYPL* 54 (1950): 350–52.

11. See "Walt Whitman: The Oscar Lion Collection," *BNYPL* 58 (1954): 213–29. Published separately by the library. The famous "Blue Book" (the 1860–61 *Leaves of Grass* with Whitman's manuscript additions and revisions) from this collection was published in facsimile by the library in 1968, with a volume of textual analysis by Arthur Golden.

Funds Nos. 3 and 4, for the purchase of books on jewelry and precious stones and on the graphic arts, are administered by the Art and Architecture Division. A bequest under the will of Alexander Maitland in 1911 makes funds available for the purchase of early Americana and cartography.

SPECIAL INDEXES AND FILES

The dictionary catalog of the Rare Book Division has been published in book form in 21 volumes by G. K. Hall & Company (Boston, 1971); it is supplemented and analyzed by many useful special indexes and files.

Almanac File

A card file (active, 5 card drawers) in two parts of American almanacs published before 1821 and other almanac rarities: (1) An alphabetical file arranged by title of almanac or compiler's name (2 card drawers), and (2) A chronological file arranged by the year for which the almanac was issued. This file is in effect a shelf list of the almanacs in the division (3 card drawers).

Autograph and Provenance File

A card file arranged alphabetically by names which appear as signatures or as manuscript inscriptions in books shelved in the Rare Book Division and the Spencer Collection (active, 15 card drawers). The names may be those of author, illustrator, etc., or of previous owners (personal or institutional).

Bibliographical References File

This is a typed-slip file which contains short form references to bibliographies cited on catalog cards for Rare Book Division and Spencer Collection books (active, 1 card drawer). It provides the library's classmark for the cited bibliography, allowing the reader to obtain more detailed bibliographical information than can be included in cataloging.

Bindings File

A card file of books in the division arranged alphabetically by names of binders and owners (as indicated by coats of arms, signatures, etc. on the bindings) (active, 4 card drawers). The alphabetical list is followed by a classed arrangement by century for unsigned bindings, and by special categories (such as embroidered, silver, curious bindings, fore-edge paintings, etc.). There is also a section containing original and facsimile binders' labels.

Books Printed on Colored Paper

An alphabetical list by author of books in the Rare Book Division, the Spencer Collection, and elsewhere in the library that are printed on colored paper (active, 250 cards). The color of the paper is indicated in each case. Some newspapers, broadsides, and other types of material are also listed.

Books Printed on Vellum

A card index for *printed* books on vellum in the Rare Book Division, Spencer Collection, Music Division, and elsewhere in the library, arranged alphabetically by author (active, 200 cards).

Broadsides File

A card file arranged chronologically by year, month, and day of broadsides in the Rare Book Division and certain other locations in the library (active, 11 card drawers). Since the broadside collection is not yet fully cataloged, the cards in this file serve as an official record of a portion of the library's holdings; it is included in the printed catalog of the Rare Book Division.

Carriers' Address File

This small file is of much curiosity and interest (active, 1 card drawer). It was formerly the custom of newspapers, particularly in the United States, to prepare a poem at the beginning of each year for carriers to present to customers in the expectation of a monetary reward for the past year's services. Such addresses were printed as broadsides or, much less frequently, as pamphlets. The Rare Book Division's holdings extend from the mid-eighteenth century to the time when the custom fell into general disuse around 1900. The card index file is divided into three parts: (1) A chronological arrangement subdivided by name of newspaper; (2) an arrangement by place of printing; and (3) an arrangement by title of newspaper.

Chapbooks File

A card file of the chapbooks in the Rare Book Division arranged under main entry (author or title) (active, 3 card drawers). It includes some material shelved elsewhere in the library, particularly in the Central Children's Room of the Branch Libraries.

Check List of the Documents of the First Fourteen Congresses

The library's holdings, which with few exceptions are in the Rare Book Division, are checked in an interleaved copy of A. W. Greely's *Public Documents of the First Fourteen Congresses, 1789–1817* (1900). These checked volumes form the library's official record. There is also an incomplete alphabetical index to subjects and names of persons and corporate bodies in six card drawers (active).

Check List of State Documents

The Rare Book Division's holdings of U.S. territorial and state documents printed before 1801, or during territorial status, are checked in Grace E. MacDonald's *Check-List of Session Laws, Preliminary Check-List Statutes,* and *Preliminary Check-list of Legislative Journals* (1936–37). These checked volumes form the official record of the library's holdings (active).

Christmas Books File

A card file of books and pamplets sent out by individuals or firms as Christmas greetings, arranged alphabetically by name of sender (active, 1 card drawer). Material shelved in the Rare Book Division and elsewhere in the library is noted.

Date File

A chronological catalog of books printed through 1800 shelved in the Rare Book Division, the Spencer Collection, and in certain other locations such as the Special Collections Reading Room of the Music Division (active, 49 card drawers).

Ephemera Collection

Miscellaneous material not individually cataloged is placed in envelopes arranged alphabetically under subjects such as "Authors," "Churches," or "Tickets." A typed list of subject headings is maintained (active, approximately 300 envelopes).

Imprint Catalog

This is the largest and most important special index in the Rare Book Division (active, 261 card drawers). It is arranged alphabetically by place of printing and by date of imprint under each place. It includes cards for books and broadsides in the division and in the Spencer Collection, as well as for early or unusual imprints in other parts of the library, such as American imprints from 1801 to 1820. Newspapers and federal and state statutes and journals, which are not cataloged on cards, do not appear in this catalog; the Rare Book Division notes its holdings in standard printed bibliographies or check lists, and maintains a separate Newspapers Check List (noted below).

A number of cards for books not in the library are also filed in the Imprint Catalog to establish the record of printing in a city or because the book is important and a record is wanted. The latter volumes of Sabin's *Dictionary of Books Relating to America* were prepared at the library, and many entries from the proof sheets of that portion of the work covering Smith to the end of the alphabet have been cut, pasted on cards, and filed in the Imprint Catalog.

This catalog was commenced by Wilberforce Eames, as librarian of the Lenox Library, and developed by L. Nelson Nichols and others. It was established in its present form in December, 1912, when various date, place, and historical printing cards were brought together into one file. In the winter of 1914 the Imprint Catalog contained twelve trays of cards. Entirely separate from the official dictionary catalog of the Rare Book Division, it was first planned to serve as a check list of rarities in the library, but now includes a record of all important or unusual imprints that come to the staff's attention. It covers the history of printing of more than 10,000 places. No attempt has been made to include a complete card record of printing under any one place with the exception of English cities through 1640, by means of the cards for University Microfilms' reproductions of English imprints through that year. The earliest imprints of a given place have naturally been emphasized, as have printing in the United States and Latin America. A typed and manuscript index to this catalog is arranged alphabetically by country and state, listing each city and town with a note of the earliest recorded date of printing and the earliest imprint date represented in the library.

Landauer Collection of Title Pages, Colophons, etc.

In 1926, Mrs. Bella C. Landauer gave the library 24 scrapbooks of actual title pages, type ornaments, and colophons (inactive, 24 scrap-

books). This collection richly covers French and Italian typography from the sixteenth to the eighteenth centuries. There is a typed contents list which gives such information as the number of items by century, the chronology of the imprints, imprints by place, etc. The complete title pages are represented by cards in the Imprint Catalog.

Newspapers Check List

A check list of newspapers in the Rare Book Division arranged by cities and towns (active, 2 loose-leaf notebooks). This is the official record of newspapers held by the division.

Presidential Campaign Buttons File

A card index, arranged chronologically by campaign year, of holdings of coins, ribbons, buttons, name tags, etc. for U.S. presidential elections (100 cards). Material for both presidents and unsuccessful candidates for office is included.

Printers before 1521 Index

A card file listing books in the library printed before 1521, arranged alphabetically by the names of the printers and chronologically under each printer (active, 6 card drawers).

Reproductions of Bindings

A vertical file of pictures, most of them clipped from dealers' catalogs, mounted and sourced (active, 11 file boxes). The file is in three parts: pictures of bindings arranged by name of binder (5 boxes); those arranged by special forms, such as chained bindings, embroidered bindings, etc. (3 boxes); and representations of armorial association bindings (3 boxes).

Special Press Catalog

A card file of books and pamphlets printed by special and private presses, a strong collecting interest of the Rare Book Division (active, 18 card drawers). Most of the cards represent material shelved in the division but include some items shelved elsewhere in the library. References to other entries in the division's dictionary catalog pertaining to special presses are included. A printed list of the presses, book clubs, and book designers represented in the special press collection of the division is issued periodically in revised form for internal use by the library as a Preparation Services Technical Order; the most recent is Technical Order 72-9 of March 24, 1972.

RESOURCES

This discussion of specific resources follows the subdivisions of the Billings Classification Schedule, classmark *K. The classes and subclasses, which indicate the shelving sequence of the books, often follow a form or chronological order rather than a subject arrangement. The dictionary catalog of the division and the Public Catalog provide the necessary subject approach.

BIBLIOGRAPHY COLLECTION (BILLINGS *KA)

This important group of some 4,000 volumes consists of general and special bibliographies; catalogs of libraries and of private collections of rare books; bibliographies of authors, special presses, and individual printers; and bibliographies of printing in specific cities or geographical areas. Materials in the collection have been chosen largely for their value in bibliographical and cataloging research in the field of rare books; many are duplicated in the general collections.

A subclass of unusual interest is *KAY, originally intended to provide for the elaborately annotated catalogs and working lists of James Lenox. Many of Lenox's notes are valuable contributions to bibliography, particularly those having to do with Americana and the Bible. The scope of this subclass was later extended to include annotated lists of other bookmen and collectors whose collections have come to this library, or whose work has some connection with its holdings. The more important of these lists and notes are those of Bancroft, Bryant, Dixon, Myers, Westwood; those having to do with the South Sea Bubble; and the Tilden shelf inventory of 1887.

BOOKS PRINTED IN EUROPE, GREAT BRITAIN, AND ASIA THROUGH 1750 (BILLINGS *KB-*KC)

The library has some 850 incunabula, of which 700 are in the Rare Book Division. There are 8 fifteenth-century block books in the division,[12] the first Gutenberg Bible to come to this country, and 11 Caxtons (which with 2 in the Berg Collection make a total of 13 in the library). There are about 150 Aldines in the collections. The library's holdings are noted in Frederick R. Goff's *Third Census of Incunabula in American Libraries* (1964).

The division holds some 7,800 sixteenth-century printed works, of which about 6,700 are from European presses and 1,100 are English publications. Seventeenth-century imprints number approximately 10,700: 4,200 European and 6,500 English.[13] The Rare Book Division retains only those imprints published after 1600 in Europe and after 1640 in England that are scarce, costly, or can be considered Americana. A total of 3,180 eighteenth-century imprints up to 1750 include 1,330 European and 1,850 English titles.

Geography and history are strong subjects. A notable collection of voyages made during the age of discovery was built up by James Lenox. These include not only collected editions but original printings of the works embraced in them. There are notable representations of De Bry, Hulsius, and Thévenot.[14]

Lenox's enthusiasm for Americana led him to make a remarkable collection with such features

as a nearly complete set of the Canadian "Jesuit Relations," discussed with Canadian resources in chapter 52 of this *Guide*. Lenox considered a work to be Americana if it contained even a slight reference to the Americas; his collection is documented in the Lenox Library *Short-Title List* No. 3 (1887), *Americana*. The library has continued intensive collecting in this field.

The foremost item of Americana in the division is the unique Spanish folio edition of the Columbus letter, dated February 15/March 14, 1493, announcing to Luis de Santangel, treasurer of Aragon, the discovery of a new world; the letter was printed in Barcelona. There are also in the division 5 of the 8 separate Latin editions published in 1493 (including the only known complete copy of the Basel illustrated edition) and the German translation of 1497.[15]

Other rare Americana include most of the works recorded in Henry Harrisse's *Bibliotheca Americana Vetustissima* (works published before 1551 containing references to America), a field in which the library excels. Publications which it has not been possible to obtain in original editions are often present in facsimile.

Additional subjects represented in classmarks *KB-*KC include scientific works. An outstanding group of more than 100 editions of Joannes de Sacro Bosco's *Sphaera Mundi* includes the first printed in Venice in 1472. There is a fourteenth-century manuscript of the work in the Manuscripts and Archives Division entitled "Opera Astronomica et Mathematica."

Religion is represented by an extensive and remarkable collection of Bibles, built on the library of James Lenox. Included are copies of nearly every famous Bible that has been printed, and original editions of versions in various languages. They are discussed more fully in chapter 19 of this *Guide*. The library has about 125 editions of the *Index Librorum Prohibitorum*, a sizable number of which were printed before 1750.

The rich holdings of materials on angling, which include books from the collection made by Thomas Westwood, contain the first five editions of Walton's *Compleat Angler*, issued during the author's lifetime. These and other accessions are described in the seventh and eighth of the *Contributions to a Catalogue of the Lenox Library*, and are more fully discussed in chapter 41 of this *Guide*.

BOOKS PRINTED IN NORTH AMERICA AND THE WEST INDIES THROUGH 1800 (BILLINGS *KD)

Early American printing is well represented.[16] Books in English before 1801 number over 9,100 titles. These include such rarities as the Bay Psalm Book. Good collections of German-Americana printed before 1801 include the Saur Bible of 1743 and Braght's *Der blutige Schau-Platz* (1748). Early printing in New York is of great interest to the library, and many fine examples

---

12. There is a small but interesting collection of Chinese block books, the earliest dating from the Sung or Yuan Dynasty, and others printed by the Jesuits in China in the seventeenth and first years of the eighteenth centuries.

13. For an early listing, see "Check-List of Early English Printing, 1475–1640, in The New York Public Library," *BNYPL* 29 (1925): 484–512, et seq. Published separately by the library.

14. The first and third of the *Contributions to a Catalogue of the Lenox Library* were collations of the different editions of the voyages of Hulsius and Thévenot respectively. In 1934 the Rare Book Division prepared a typewritten check list of Thévenot Relations. A catalog of the De Bry voyages appeared in the library's *Bulletin* for May, 1904.

15. See Wilberforce Eames, "Columbus' Letter on the Discovery of America (1493–1497)," *BNYPL* 28 (1924): 595–99. Several facsimiles have been published, the most recent in 1956.

16. See Lewis M. Stark, "Printing from Coast to Coast; An Exhibition of Early American Imprints," *BNYPL* 62 (1958): 388–406. Published separately by the library in a slightly expanded version.

are in the collection,[17] including an important representation of seventeenth- and eighteenth-century sermons, 1660 to 1800. In American literature, the library has a fine collection of literary works written in America before 1800, such as those of Anne Bradstreet (first three editions), Edward Wigglesworth, Timothy Dwight, and others. Checked copies of Oscar Wegelin's *Early American Plays* (1905) and *Early American Poetry* (1930) in the division indicate its holdings. The Theodorus Bailey Myers collection of books and manuscripts, received in 1900, included some rare and valuable Americana of the eighteenth century.[18]

BOOKS PRINTED IN LATIN AMERICA THROUGH 1800 (BILLINGS *KE)

The library has well over 1,000 works in this group, including many fine examples. The collection began with James Lenox's interest in Americana.

The collection of Mexican imprints is outstanding, the earliest dated 1543, and followed by others of which there are few known copies. The holdings include more than a hundred rare printings in the Mexican Indian languages. This rich collection was considerably augmented in 1914 by the purchase of selections from the library of Paul Wilkinson, consisting for the most part of seventeenth- and eighteenth-century imprints.[19] The other most important single sources have been the major bequest of Thomas A. Janvier and the gifts of Mrs. Catherine Janvier (1915–18), containing many scarce and valuable titles. An exceptional group of Latin American imprints, with a large number of Peruvian books, was given by Edward S. Harkness.

BOOKS (EXCEPT LITERATURE) PRINTED AFTER THE FINAL DATES OF *KB-*KE (BILLINGS *KF)

This class, while large, is too miscellaneous to permit detailed description. Among the rare and valuable Americana of dates later than provided for in the classifications *KB-*KE is a group of more than 520 pieces issued by southern presses during the Confederacy; approximately 360 items are official publications (described below with *KR materials) and 160 are unofficial publications, including textbooks, almanacs, newspapers, and periodicals, but excluding sheet music, the publications of fraternal organizations, and religious publications. These holdings are checked in a copy of Marjorie Lyle Crandall's *Confederate Imprints* (1955).

ASSOCIATION COLLECTIONS (BILLINGS *KG)

This class contains over 4,300 items. Notable subclasses include the following.

*KGA, Beadle Collection

The Beadle Dime Novel collection was given to the library in 1922 by Dr. Frank P. O'Brien.[20]

It includes nearly 70 of the famous original yellow-back novels which began to appear in 1850. Seventeen of the first 25 titles of this series are in the collection, including a first edition of Edward Ellis's celebrated *Seth Jones*, a story of the New York wilderness in 1785. The 1,400 items in the original collection were supplemented in 1963 by C. V. Clare's gift of some 900 examples of the *Diamond Dick Weekly* and the *Wild West Weekly*, later series inspired by the Beadle Dime novels.

*KGB, Bancroft Collection

The greater part of this collection, purchased by the Lenox Library in 1894, was added to the general collections. The Rare Book Division houses in *KGB rare and valuable books with pencilled annotations by Bancroft that are not duplicated in the general collections; books from the collection with few or unimportant notations are mainly in *KF. Bancroft's sets of his *History of the United States*, annotated and revised for later editions, are housed in the Manuscripts and Archives Division.

*KGC, Bunyan Collection

The Bunyan collection, which is discussed in chapter 24 of this *Guide*, is particularly notable for its remarkable sequence of editions of *Pilgrim's Progress*, beginning with the first. The more valuable of these are shelved in this subclass.[21]

*KGF, False Association: Forgeries, Frauds, etc.

The library's collections as a whole in this area are described in the section of chapter 20 of this *Guide* dealing with literary forgeries. The important feature of this collection is false inscriptions attributed to authors or historical personages. There are also a number of fraudulent imprints, including a Columbus letter to Santangel (1497/1882) and several of the Thomas J. Wise nineteenth-century pamphlets.

Of related interest, although not located in this classmark, are genuine association copies. Among a great many notable examples in the Rare Book Division are Ben Jonson's copy of Thomas Scott's *An Experimentall Discoverie of Spanish Practises* (1623–24); Milton's copy of Benedetto Varchi's *Sonetti* (1555); George Washington's copy of Voltaire's *Letters* (1770); Martha Washington's collection of 35 pamphlets eulogizing her husband; Wordsworth's copy of Milton's *Paradise Lost* (1678); and the discoverer Sir Ferdinando Gorges's copy of Hakluyt's *Principal Navigations* (1598–1600).

The Autograph and Provenance File of the Rare Book Division provides an alphabetical listing of names which appear as signatures or in inscriptions in the holdings of the division and the Spencer Collection. Many early accessions which predate the file are not included; important signatures are usually indicated in the division's dictionary catalog.

*KGS, Spingarn Collection

This subclass consists of 40 of the more valuable works selected from the Spingarn gift of

17. See Wilberforce Eames, "The First Year of Printing in New York: May, 1693–April 1694," *BNYPL* 32 (1928): 3–24.

18. See *BNYPL* 4 (1900): 112–14.

19. See *BNYPL* 18 (1914): 201–02.

20. See "The Beadle Collection," *BNYPL* 26 (1922): 555–628.

21. James Lenox's collection of *Pilgrim's Progress* is described in the fourth of the *Contributions to a Catalogue of the Lenox Library* (1879).

materials relating to literary criticism, principally sixteenth-century Italian publications. The greater part of the gift was added to the general collections and is described in the chapter on general literature.

*KGW, Washington Collection

The principal features of this collection, which numbers about 700 items, are many early editions of Washington's Farewell Address and some 285 eulogies and funeral orations.[22] There are several books from Washington's personal library. Related to biographical material in the general collections is the large and unusual representation in the Rare Book Division of Mason L. Weems's curious biography of Washington, most of them collected by Paul Leicester Ford.[23] This collection includes one of the 3 located copies of the fifth edition, published in Augusta, Georgia in 1806, the first to contain the famous story of the hatchet and the cherry tree.[24] The most important single item relating to Washington is the original manuscript of his Farewell Address in the Manuscripts and Archives Division.[25]

LITERATURE: ALL LITERATURE AFTER FINAL DATES OF *KB-*KE (BILLINGS *KL)

Rare editions of literary works do not form one of the more remarkable features of the division's collections. This classmark covers about 5,700 volumes, exclusive of material in the Oscar Lion Whitman collection of over 500 pieces, which is the most important representation of a single author in the division. There are also outstanding groups of Cooper's and Melville's works; earlier literary materials are found in *KC and *KD. The most extensive holdings of rare English and American literary printed and manuscript materials in the Research Libraries are to be found in the Berg Collection of English and American Literature, discussed in chapter 20 of this *Guide*. Resources in this area are supplemented by the large general collections and by the holdings of the Manuscripts and Archives Division, which include the notable Hellman and Seligman collections of Washington Irving materials.

NUMISMATICS (BILLINGS *KM)

This classmark represents actual coins and medals. The library has occasionally received coins, medals, tokens, and paper money. Books on the subject of numismatics are not in the Rare Book Division unless qualified to be there through rarity or imprint date, but are classified

in the general collections. The division's holdings of paper money are notable, particularly for colonial and Confederate currency, and include some 270 pieces received with the Myers collection, mounted in eight folio volumes and titled "A Complete Series of the Paper Money Issued by the Continental Congress during the Revolution, with Specimens of Colonial and State Issues." A Chinese mulberry-bark banknote of the Ming dynasty is an isolated rarity.[26]

About 1,100 coins in the holdings include examples of European, British, colonial American, and Latin American coins, as well as U.S. copper, silver, and gold coinage. There are about 800 medals classified into such categories as Americana, U.S. historical and presidential, New York history, medallion portraits of the kings of France, etc. There is a collection of C. C. Wright's early American work and some 365 copper and brass tokens of the U.S. Civil War period.

The paper money collection, numbering an estimated 10,500 pieces, is enumerated below:

United States (estimated 3,350 pieces)

American colonies	1,250
Revolutionary	260
Confederate	1,750
U.S. state banks (counterfeits)	50
U.S. college banks (specie currency, mostly from New York State in the 1860s)	20
U.S. scrip (mostly of the 1930s)	20

Foreign (estimated 7,150 pieces)

Belgium (World War I, local currency issued during the German occupation)	80
Austria ("Notgeld," emergency paper currency issued in the 1920s)	2,800
Germany ("Notgeld," issued 1914–20s)	3,350
(scrip, issued early 1930s)	620
Miscellaneous (currency from 15 countries)	300

GLOBES (BILLINGS *KN)

Three globes are located in this classmark; the oldest of them, the Hunt-Lenox globe, is one of the library's greatest treasures. It is probably the earliest surviving globe from the period immediately following the discovery of the new world.[27] The other globes date from the eighteenth century: one is by Nathaniel Hill (1754); the second, from Germany, shows the path of Captain Cook's second and third voyages. A fine group of sixteenth-century globe gores in the division forms a supplementary resource.

PRESSES AND BOOK CLUBS (BILLINGS *KP)

This collection contains the work of private and special presses, ranging in date from Horace Walpole's eighteenth-century Strawberry Hill Press and famous nineteenth-century presses such as William Morris's Kelmscott Press and the Doves Press of T. J. Cobden-Sanderson, to modern presses such as Allen, Grabhorn and Officina

22. See Margaret Bingham Stillwell, "Checklist of Eulogies and Funeral Orations on the Death of George Washington," *BNYPL* 20 (1916): 403–50. Published separately by the library, with alterations, as *Washington Eulogies; A Checklist*.
23. See Alice Hollister Lerch, "A Brief for Parson Weems," *BNYPL* 33 (1929): 139–45.
24. See Lewis M. Stark, "The 'Cherry Tree' Edition of Weems' *Life of Washington*," *BNYPL* 75 (1971): 7–8.
25. See Victor Hugo Paltsits, ed., *Washington's Farewell Address* (The New York Public Library, 1935); reprinted by the library and Arno Press, 1971.

26. See Benjamin Schwartz, "A Chinese Paper Bank Note," *BNYPL* 42 (1938): 750–51.
27. See Robert W. Hill, "The Lenox Globe," *BNYPL* 41 (1937): 523–25; Frederick J. Pohl, "The Fourth Continent on the Lenox Globe," *BNYPL* 67 (1963): 465–69.

Bodoni. Some 1,000 special presses, book clubs, and book designers are represented, in a collection numbering about 12,500 volumes. The collecting policy is comprehensive in the range of presses included, but only representative in the individual publications of most of the presses. There are particularly good collections of the work of Bruce Rogers and Frederic W. Goudy; a gift made by Ivan Somerville in 1954 added much valuable Goudy material. Additions to the special press collection are often purchased with income from a fund established under the bequest of Alfred E. Ommen as a memorial to Theodore Low De Vinne. The division maintains a Special Press Catalog and a printed list of the names of the special presses, book clubs, and book designers represented in the collection is issued in revised form at irregular intervals.

A special collection in this class is *KPC, Christmas books, issued as gifts of individuals, publishers, and presses. It includes mainly privately printed material. There are about 500 books and pamphlets in addition to boxes of greeting cards. The division maintains as a card index the Christmas Books File, arranged by the name of the sender. Christmas cards are collected as examples of graphic art by the Art and Architecture and the Prints Divisions.

AMERICAN GOVERNMENT DOCUMENTS (BILLINGS *KR)

This group, numbering over 5,000 pieces represents one of the richest collections in the library. The principal materials are session laws, collected statutes, and legislative journals. Not only individual documents, but early volumes in series ordinarily located in the general collections, are to be found in the Rare Book Division if they are scarce or valuable.

No terminal date is set for inclusion in the Rare Book Division's collection of documents. Generally speaking all colonial, provincial, state and federal documents before 1801 are located here. Also included are documents published by the federal government through the first fourteen congresses; a checked copy of A. W. Greely's *Public Documents of the First Fourteen Congresses, 1789–1817* (1900), which serves as the division's official record, shows a strong collection in this field. The executive and legislative documents of the various states are also noteworthy. If the library does not have and cannot secure original printings it attempts to provide photographic reproductions of this early material. Grace E. MacDonald's three check lists, *Check-list of Session Laws*, *Preliminary Check-list of Statutes*, and *Preliminary Check-list of Legislative Journals* (1936–37), marked to show the division's holdings, serve as the official record. Approximately 300 documents bound in 5 volumes once belonged to Thomas Jefferson.

Documents in the division issued by the Confederate States of America number about 360 pieces and consist of a rather scattered grouping of presidential messages, senate bills, acts, and statutes; and reports. There is also material from a number of the separate states of the Confederacy.

Further comments on the Research Libraries' entire rich collection of these materials appears in chapter 36 of this *Guide* and in connection with such various subject areas as American history, law, etc.

SERIALS (BILLINGS *KS)

Except for individual rarities, the terminal date of 1800 is used in the Rare Book Division's collection of serials. Numbering about 10,350 pieces, the collection includes some 1,800 volumes of bound newspapers and 4,000 issues of unbound newspapers; 2,000 periodicals; 2,500 almanacs; and some 50 directories.

The extensive holdings of almanacs include the only known copy of the 1649 edition of Danforth's *Almanack*, printed at Cambridge, Massachusetts. There is a special catalog for American almanacs published before 1821 and other rare almanacs in the division.

The directories in the Rare Book Division include those printed in America before 1801 and a few later nineteenth-century rarities. The major collection of U.S. city directories through 1869 is in the Local History and Genealogy Division. There are numerous other types of directories in other divisions of the library.

Newspapers in the division constitute one of the library's important collections. Early files and rare issues are numerous, among them Bradford's *New-York Gazette*, Zenger's *Weekly Journal* (the best file known), Parker's *Post-Boy*, and excellent files of Holt's *Journal*, Gaine's *Mercury*, and Farley's *American Chronicle*. Going beyond New York, the representation of Philadelphia newspapers includes extensive files of Franklin's *Gazette* and Bradford's *Journal*. The library's holdings of newspapers before 1821 are recorded in Brigham's *History and Bibliography of American Newspapers, 1690–1820* (1947), although some files and issues have been added since its appearance. The division's holdings have been extended by photostat or microfilm files, including North Carolina newspapers before 1800, *Virginia Gazette*, and *Kentucky Gazette*.

Later American materials held in the division because of their value include the famous issue of the *Vicksburg Daily Citizen* of July 2, 1864, set by the staff of the newspaper but printed by Union soldiers after the fall of the city. Files of American Indian newspapers include a notable group of Cherokee newspapers for the period from 1828 to 1853.

Early British newspapers in the division include files of *St. James's Chronicle* (1768–78), *Lloyd's Evening Post and British Chronicle* (1758–81, incomplete), and *London Packet* (1772–80), of added interest because they were published during the colonial and revolutionary periods of American history. Many important examples of early seventeenth-century English newspapers or "newsbooks" came to the division in the Lonsdale collection.[28] The division's complete file of *The London Gazette* (1665–1800) is continued to date on film in the general collections.

Other holdings include a group of facsimiles or later souvenir issues of rare newspapers such as the *Ulster County Gazette*, of which the division has over 30 editions, although lacking the rare original issue of January 4, 1800.[29] There are also

---

28. See Lewis M. Stark, "Lonsdale Collection of English Newspapers," *BNYPL* 52 (1948): 35–36.

29. See R. W. G. Vail, "The Ulster County Gazette and Its Illegitimate Offspring," *BNYPL* 34 (1930): 207–40, with a listing of this and other facsimile newspapers owned by the library. See also his "The Ulster County Gazette Found

the productions of amateur presses, toy presses, Lilliputian newspapers, etc. The full resources of the library in this field are discussed in chapter 5 of this *Guide*.

The library's collection of rare American periodicals is excellent, with particular strength in eighteenth-century sets. Holdings are recorded in W. Beer's *Checklist of American Periodicals, 1741–1800* (1923), although other titles and volumes have since been added. Only very rare or irreplaceable material is held in this small subclass. Descriptions of the periodical holdings in the library appear in a separate chapter and in the discussion of subject fields in which there are noteworthy collections.

AMERICAN CODICES (FACSIMILE) (BILLINGS *KTA)

This is a small collection of Central American codices in facsimile. The major collection in the library is in the American History Division.

BOXED MATERIAL (BILLINGS *KVA-*KVZ)

These classmarks serve to cover a heterogeneous group of material including broadsides, cards, chapbooks, cries, New England primers, hornbooks, miniature books, peculiar printing, etc., much of it of considerable rarity and interest. Children's book rarities are well represented in the library and are discussed at length in chapter 21 of this *Guide*. Chapbooks are treated in chapter 40: some 2,650 items are in the Research Libraries and the Central Children's Room of the Branch Libraries. About 1,000 are in the Rare Book Division (classed under *KVD); the division's card index Chapbooks File is the official record. Schoolbooks are also an important feature. There is an outstanding collection of New England primers; the 139 examples include the *New-England Primer Enlarged* (Boston, 1727), the only known copy of the earliest surviving edition of this famed children's book. Textbooks issued in the Southern States during the reconstruction period are also of considerable interest.

The 20,000 broadsides are a strong feature of the division's holdings. The principal representation is American, in original and photostat form, including broadside ballads, proclamations, and carriers' addresses, the latter described in some detail in the section above on Rare Book Division special indexes and files. Included are 94 broadsides of the Continental Congress given by Worthington C. and Paul Leicester Ford in 1902 and 1907, and an acquisition of 86 pieces on the American Revolution from the Bancker collection.[30]

Broadside ballads form an attractive and cosmopolitan group. Collections of English and Irish street ballads of the nineteenth century and Confederate ballads of the Civil War in the Rare Book Division are supplemented by scrapbooks of broadside sea songs and sea ballads and about 500 mid-nineteenth-century American broadsides in the Drexel collection of the Music Division, and 6 albums of bound song sheets of nineteenth-century Florentine *romanze d'amore* and other forms in the Prints Division.

Miniature books (defined by the Rare Book Division as books under four inches in height) constitute an unusual collection of some 900 pieces. These include a gift from S. P. Avery in 1896 which contained John Taylor's "Thumb Bible" (169–), the *Bible in Miniature* (1780), and a number of other minute volumes and specimens of microscopic printing. Also included is an unusual collection of miniature Bibles in shorthand. J. D. Henderson's *Lilliputian Newspapers* (Worcester, Mass., 1936) shows the library to have an important representation in this field, with some unique copies. A number of the library's rarities are described in notes on an exhibition held in conjunction with the microbibliophilic group "The LXIVMOS."[31]

The library some years ago established a collection of "typographical small wares"—ephemeral bits of printing such as ballots, blotters, bookmarks, calling cards, dance programmes, lottery tickets, rewards of merit, trade cards and similar materials which reflect printing styles during various periods.

BOOKS OF PLATES (BILLINGS *KW)

This collection of several hundred volumes is segregated largely because of difficulty in shelving. It consists of scrapbooks, portfolios, and other materials without text. Finely illustrated books, of which the library has an unusual collection, are ordinarily classed by subject.

EXTRA-ILLUSTRATED BOOKS (BILLINGS *KX-*KZ)

The library has a notable collection of extra-illustrated books largely derived from the Lenox Library. These are published works to which owners have added supplementary illustrative material. Of some 450 volumes, about 100 are in the Rare Book Division (classed under *KX) and the remainder (classed under *KZ) are shelved in the stacks and administered by the General Research and Humanities Division. *KZ is the only subclass of *K that is not administered by the Rare Book Division. Extra-illustrated books were also acquired in the Duyckinck, Stuart, Tilden, Myers, and Ford collections, and the gift of Miss E. D. Brainerd in 1936.

The most important single group of extra-illustrated books in the library, the Emmet collection presented by John S. Kennedy in 1896, is administered by the Manuscripts and Archives Division. It consists of a large group of illustrated works relating to the early history of the United States, the volumes being extended by the insertion of thousands of illustrations, autographs, facsimiles, and other material relating to Americans of note before 1800. The *Catalogue of the Library Belonging to Thomas Addis Emmet* (1868), of which the library has several copies, analyzes this collection.

STUART COLLECTION

The Stuart collection of books and manuscripts, paintings, and natural history specimens—the bequest of Robert Leighton Stuart—was received

---

at Last," *BNYPL* 35 (1931): 207–11. Published together separately by the library.

30. See "American Broadsides, Etc., 1774–1864 purchased in December 1898," *BNYPL* 3 (1899): 43–44.

31. R. W. G. Vail, "A Lilliputian Library," *BNYPL* 33 (1929): 3–7.

by the Lenox Library in 1892.[32] It is retained as a separate unit outside the Billings Classification Schedule; although it has been under the administration of the Rare Book Division since the late 1960s, it is serviced for reasons of convenience by the Art and Architecture Division. The original collection consisted of 11,888 books, 1,963 pamphlets, 240 paintings, a large collection of minerals, shells, and other objects of natural history, and many art curiosities. Nonbook materials which were part of the gift are now on indefinite loan to other institutions. In order to avoid inconvenience to readers, while meeting the stipulation of the bequest that materials from the collection not be made available for use on Sunday, the larger proportion of the books has been duplicated in the regular collections of the library. Cards for book materials in the Stuart collection appear in the Public Catalog.

The most notable part of the collection relates to natural history. Included are the elephant folio of Audubon, magnificent sets of John Gould's *Birds*, and the splendid productions of the American naturalist Daniel G. Elliot. There are many other finely illustrated works on natural history and botany.

The representation of histories and works in related fields is admirable. For the European countries, there are a number of standard treatises of the nineteenth century. Biography is represented by Edmund Lodge's *Portraits* and similar works; description and travel by John Britton's famous illustrated works on England and Wales, Adolf Closs's *Switzerland*, and many others.

Some 2,000 volumes relate to American history. For the most part, they are the scholarly productions of the nineteenth century, though there is also an interesting selection of titles published in both England and America during the eighteenth century, and such rarities as De Bry's "America," parts 1–9 (Frankfort, 1590), Louis Hennepin's *New Discovery* (London, 1698), and Samuel Purchas's *Pilgrimage* (London, 1613). Indians are well represented, both descriptively and historically, by such works as George Catlin's writings, William Hubbard's *The Present State of New England*, and similar titles. Most of the contemporaneously published general and state histories are present, and there are such pre-Revolutionary titles as *The History of the British Dominions in North America* (London, 1773), Captain John Smith's *The Generall Historie of Virginia* (Lon-

don, 1632), William Smith's *History of the Province of New York* (London, 1757). The same characterization may be made of works of description and travel, ranging from Thomas Peake's *America* (London, 1655), and John Ogilby's *America* (London, 1671), to Mary (Grey) Duncan's *America as I Found It* (New York, 1852), and later works. Individual biographies of illustrious Americans are generally present—not only those published during the second and third quarters of the nineteenth century, but also such rarities as Cotton Mather's *Pietas in Patriam* (London, 1697), the life of Sir William Phips.

Theology and ecclesiastical history number about 2,000 volumes. There are 400 editions of the Bible, including some of the historically famous, such as the "Breeches Bible" (six editions between 1607–15) and the "Bishops' Bible." Most of the more than 50 manuscripts in the collection consist of horae, missals, and other liturgical texts, many of them fine examples, principally of the fifteenth and sixteenth centuries. Sermons are another feature, rich in first editions, as of the Mathers. Church and denominational history in various countries is also worthy of note.

The fine arts, architecture, and archaeology constitute a third major group. Art is richly represented by the publications of such galleries as Munich, Versailles, Dresden, the Vatican, Düsseldorf, Pitti Palace, the Musée Français, and the Musée Royal. Architecture is represented by the folios of Luigi Rossini and other magnificently illustrated works. Archaeological materials cover many phases of the subject, as shown by the presence of John S. Stanhope's *Olympia*, Lord Kingsborough's 9 folio volumes of *Antiquities of Mexico*, and Ephraim Squier's *Antiquities of the State of New York*.

Finally, there is a rich collection of what may be called "general literature." In this group are a number of volumes interesting for the presses they represent—Aldus, Elzevir, Bodoni, Baskerville, and others—and an impressive selection of imaginative literature in first and early editions. The English classics are present from the early seventeenth century to Dickens and Thackeray. Drama, especially Elizabethan, includes such early imprints as the 1640 folio of Ben Jonson and the 1679 edition of Beaumont and Fletcher. English poets from Chaucer to Tennyson are represented by early and textually important editions. American authors are usually to be found in first editions. Bibliographical essays, such as those of Thomas F. Dibdin and Edward Edwards, and the bibliographical compilations of Henry Harrisse, Obadiah Rich, and others number some 200 volumes.

---

32. See *Catalogue of the Library of Robert L. Stuart* (New York: J. J. Little & Co., 1884); and Lydenberg, *History*, pp. 121–23.

16

SPENCER COLLECTION

The Spencer Collection was created in 1913 by the bequest of William Augustus Spencer, a collector of finely illustrated books who had lost his life in the *Titanic* disaster of April 1912. The bequest included Spencer's own collection of books and an endowment fund. The will instructs

that the income from the endowment be used to purchase "the finest illustrated books that can be procured, of any country and in any language, and that these books be bound in handsome bindings representing the work of the most noted book-binders of all countries, thus constituting a collection representative of the arts of illustration and bookbinding." Spencer also directed that books containing the original designs, drawings, or paintings made by the illustrators be acquired as opportunity offered. The collection now numbers some 8,000 volumes and more than 750 manuscripts, with a number of drawings. (It is available to the public upon presentation of an admission card obtained from the Research Libraries Administrative Office.)

In carrying out the terms of the Spencer bequest, the library has attempted to strengthen its overall resources in many special fields by adding materials which meet the standards set for the Spencer Collection but which could not normally be acquired from general funds or other special funds. This supplementary function is an important part of the Spencer Collection's program. Duplication of material in other divisions is avoided. Quality is the principal factor determining purchase; the collection makes a particular point of obtaining not simply a copy of a finely illustrated book, but the best available copy, as for example the best state of the edition, or a special association copy.

Spencer's personal collection, which formed the nucleus of the Spencer Collection, contained 232 illustrated French books for the most part of the period 1880 to 1910. Many of these were bound by the great French binders of the time, and some of the bindings were made from Spencer's own designs; a manuscript catalog of the original gift is held in the collection. The income from the bequest became available in 1917; by 1921 the collection had grown to 364 titles. The earliest additions were Medieval and Renaissance illuminated manuscripts and illustrated incunabula. Examples of Western book illustration from the sixteenth century to the twentieth century were also acquired. By 1930 the collection had reached 600 volumes. During the war period from 1942 to 1945 it was removed from the library for safekeeping; nevertheless it continued to grow, reaching 1,800 volumes by 1947. After World War II fine examples of Oriental book illustration were acquired, with an emphasis on China, Japan, India, Persia, and other Asian civilizations. With the books came many splendid illustrated manuscript scrolls enriching the collection in yet another area.

Fifty-one exhibitions of treasures from the collection were held in the period from 1934 to 1966. Notable recent exhibitions include those on the book of India and the book of Japan in 1960, Venice in 1961, and Picasso and his contemporaries as book illustrators in 1962. The collection maintains no special indexes or files beyond its regular card catalog and separate shelf lists for manuscripts and books. The *Dictionary Catalog and Shelf List of the Spencer Collection of Illustrated Books and Manuscripts and Fine Bindings* was issued in book form in two volumes by G. K. Hall & Company (Boston, 1970); other published lists and descriptions appear in the final section of this chapter.

RESOURCES

The subject matter of books in the Spencer Collection includes fields as diverse as literature, science, art, religion, history, and the performing arts. Among important individual groups of materials are the portrait collections, festival books, emblem books, books on architecture, views, heraldry, and certain in-depth collections such as Aesop and the Dance of Death. Acquisitions have been selected to present an international sampling of the book arts in all their forms—illustration, typography, binding, etc.

WESTERN MANUSCRIPTS

Although in the early stages of the development of the collection a number of outstanding manuscripts on vellum were purchased, for the most part religious in nature, subsequent development has emphasized the secular illustrated manuscript on paper; there are now some 180 Western manuscripts in the collection. Illuminated manuscripts on vellum include an "Apocalypse" (Ms. 57), a "Bible historiée" from thirteenth-century northern France (Ms. 22), and the fourteenth-century "Les heures de Blanche de France" (Ms. 56). The famous Tickhill Psalter is a beautifully illuminated English manuscript of about 1310 (Ms. 26). The "Bologna Missal" was commissioned by Galeacci Marescotti about 1490 (Ms. 64); the finest of the group of Aesops in the collection is a manuscript of the same period in Greek (Ms. 50). Of principal importance among Western manuscripts is a book of Minor Prophets with saints' lives, written and illuminated in the Abbey of Weingarten between 1215 and 1232 (Ms. 1).

Illustrated manuscripts on paper include such fine fifteenth-century examples as Rudolf von Ems "Weltchronik" (Ms. 38), Noë Bianchi's "Journey to the Holy Land" (Ms. 62), and the "Tacuinum Sanitatis" (Ms. 65) with drawings of plants, simples, occupations, etc. The Spencer Collection copy of Ulrich von Richenthal's "Chronicle of the Council of Constance" (Ms. 32) is the second-oldest version of the chronicle known, and was copied from a manuscript now lost.

WESTERN DRAWINGS

The collection has acquired a number of drawings which served as models for the engravings of Western book illustration from the seventeenth century onward. Among these are examples of the work of Charles Nicolas Cochin for Tasso's *La Gerusalemme liberata* (Paris, 1784–88). There are twenty-two drawings by Arthur Rackham which reflect his work on 17 different books. Examples of drawings by a number of contemporary American artists for children's books include the work of James Daugherty, Fritz Eichenberg, and Fritz Kredel. Thomas Rowlandson's drawings for *The English Dance of Death* (1815–16), 33 in number, are also noteworthy.

WESTERN ILLUSTRATED BOOKS

Fifteenth Century

There are about 130 illustrated incunabula from five countries, most of them religious. Fine examples of the Cologne, Lubeck, and Malermi (1493) Bibles are present, as well as classics of the Italian printed book, including a magnificent copy on vellum of the *Hypnerotomachia poliphili* (1499). There is a copy of the first book on military science published in French, *L'Art de chevalerie selon Vegece* (1488), the notable Lyon edition of *Mer des histoires* (1491), and Antoine Vérard's edition of *Therence en frãcois* (1500?). The illustrated book in the Netherlands is exemplified by the Culenborg, 1483, edition of *Speculum humanae salvationis* with illustrations made up from earlier block books, and the Gouda, 1480, book of fables, *Dialogus creaturarum*. From Germany come splendid copies of Bishop Sánchez de Arévalo's *Spiegel des menschlichen Lebens* (Augsburg, 1497), and a Ptolemy *Cosmographia* on vellum (Ulm, 1482), beautifully colored by hand, and formerly in the collection of Prince Eugene of Savoy and Sir George Lindsay Holford.

Sixteenth Century

The group of nearly 700 books from eight countries is strongest in the literature of France, Germany, and Italy. Many of the earliest festival books produced are included, particularly those of the triumphal entries of French kings and queens. Other books are on military architecture, such as Androuet de Cerceau's *Bastiments de France* (1576–1607); travel; typography, such as Geoffroy Tory's *Champfleury* (1529); and the cartography of France, exemplified by Bouguereau's *Le Theatre francois* (1594). Albrecht Dürer's three "great books" of 1511 (*Apocalipsis cū figuris; Epitome in divae parthenices Mariae historiam; Passio Christi*), long recognized as landmarks of book illustration, are present in a contemporaneous binding as issued. The Spencer copy of the *Theuerdank* (1517) came from the library of Robert Hoe. One of the many Aesops in the collection is that printed in Freiburg in 1535. From Italy there is the Figino edition of Dante's *Divina commedia* (Venice, 1512); and from Spain Lucio Marineo's *De primis Aragonie regibus* (Saragossa, 1509). Fine bindings include one produced for Jean Grolier on a copy of Girolamo Cardano's *De subtilitate libri XXI* (Nuremberg, 1550).

Seventeenth Century

The baroque books of Spain, Italy, the Netherlands, and Germany are well represented. A preponderance of the very strong collection of festival books date from this period. There are also some splendid works on cartography. Jacob Schrenck von Nozing's *Augustissimorum imperatorum . . . imagines* (1601) illustrates the armor of the period, and a similar work from Italy, *Il torneo de Bonaventura Pistofilo* (1627), contains etchings of men in armor going through tournament movements. An excellent group of English bindings includes the work of Samuel Mearne, and bindings in his style, including a copy of Jeremy Taylor's *Antiquitates Christianae* (1675) bound by the "Queen's Binder B." A Bible of 1680 is bound by Roger Bartlett.

Eighteenth Century

The holdings for this period mirror the French literature of the age and include many volumes of illustrated poetry. Two editions of La Fontaine are among the most sumptuous works of the century: *Fables choisies* (1755–59) in four folio volumes, illustrated with 276 engravings after J. B. Oudry, with a second copy of volume I in a Padeloup binding made for King Augustus III of Poland; and the *Contes et nouvelles* (1762), the celebrated edition printed at the expense of the Fermiers Généraux. The Spencer copy of Bernardin de Saint Pierre's *Paul et Virginie* (1789) is one of four or five copies printed on vellum and contains, bound in, the original watercolor drawings, four by Moreau le Jeune and one supposedly by Vernet, after which the plates for this edition were made. Other fine works are the *Geistreiche*

Gesänge und Lieder (1725–26) and Tasso's *La Gerusalemme liberata* (1745).

Nineteenth Century

Illustrated books in the Spencer Collection cover the basic literature of the various nationalities of the Western world. They also reflect the change in book production during the century. A splendid copy of the 1806 edition of Bernardin de Saint Pierre's *Paul et Virginie*, the last to appear during the author's lifetime, contains complete sets of the plates in three states, with sets of proofs of the engravings of the 1789 edition redone in octavo size. Bound in with the copy is a charcoal drawing by Prud'hon for the plate "Naufrage de Virginie" and another sepia drawing by Vernet. In folio size, the work is bound by Thouvenin in plum-colored morocco elaborately ornamented. Editions of Krylov's *Fables* (Moscow, 1834) and Manzoni's *I promessi sposi* (Milan, 1840) are other fine examples of the nineteenth-century book. Kugler's *Geschichte Friedrichs des Grossen* (1840–42) contains the 379 wood engravings made after the designs of Adolph Menzel. Also included are copies of the Kelmscott Chaucer of 1896, and Renard's *Histoires naturelles* (1899) with lithographs by Toulouse-Lautrec.

Twentieth Century

The renewed effort by individual artists during the first half of the century to illustrate texts with original graphics is reflected in the collection. The production of French book artists is exceptionally well represented and includes such works as Verlaine's *Parallèlement* (1900) with Bonnard's illustrations; and Matisse's illustrations for the *Poèmes* of Charles, Duke of Orléans (1950), as well as *Jazz* (1947), in which Matisse appears as artist and author. The substantially complete holdings of books illustrated by Picasso include Balzac's *Le Chef-d'oeuvre inconnu* (1931), *Eaux-fortes originales pour des textes de Buffon* (1942), José Delgado's *La Tauromaquia* (1959), and *Le frere mendiant* by Ilya Zdanevitch (1959).

ORIENTAL MANUSCRIPTS

There are some 600 Oriental manuscripts in the collection. Early Oriental manuscript scrolls and printed matter are mostly religious in nature. Examples in the Spencer Collection are mainly illustrated Buddhist, Taoist, and Shinto writings. It was only in later centuries that illustrated secular works were produced.

The collection of nearly 300 Japanese items includes a number of Heian scrolls; manuscripts of the "Tale of Genji" and the Japanese anthology of the "Thirty-six Great Poets" range from the thirteenth to the eighteenth centuries. The holdings of Persian manuscripts are notable for their miniatures and calligraphy; illuminated Firdausi and Nizami texts include Firdausi's *Shahnāmeh* dated 1614, illustrated with forty-four paintings in the style of the 1430 Bayshungur *Shahnāmeh* in the collection of the Gulestan Palace Library in Teheran.

Among Persian manuscripts in Arabic is an important fourteenth-century cosmography (Kazwīnī) with colored pen-and-ink drawings of animals, trees, plants, and mythological beings. Turkish manuscripts include a *Shahnāmeh* of about 1550 and a late sixteenth-century *Siyar-e Nabi* (Life of the Prophet Mohammed). A collection of 86 Indian manuscripts ranges from a tenth-century palm leaf manuscript of northern India to the productions of mid-nineteenth-century Rajasthan. Other materials include several palm leaf manuscripts from Orissa, and paintings from Malwa, Merwar, Kangra, and other centers. Sixteen items relate to the Moghul Indian period. Many of the manuscripts mentioned in this paragraph are in fine bindings of lacquered wood or of leather with tooled or painted decoration. The Spencer Collection also owns four Hebrew manuscripts, among which the "Xanten Bible" (1294) is an early and very rare example of an illuminated manuscript in that language.

ORIENTAL PRINTED BOOKS

Japanese examples are by far the most numerous among the Oriental printed books in the collection. The earliest printed work in the library is a Buddhist charm made for the Empress Shotoku about 770 A.D. Later items mirror the history of Japanese literature from the *Ise Monogatari* (1608) through the works of Sai Kaku and Bakin. Artists of the book represented include Moronobu; Masanobu; and painters of the *ukiyo-ye* school— Utamaro (with examples of his famous shell and insect books), Hokusai, and Hiroshige; and the contemporary artist Kichiemon Okamura. China is represented by early printings of the drawing books of the *Mustard Seed Garden* and the *Ten Bamboo Hall*, and other Ming dynasty illustrated books.

BIBLIOGRAPHY

A catalog of the collection was issued in the library's *Bulletin* in 1914, and reprinted in the same year; a revised edition appeared in 1928. The Japanese holdings are described in Japanese, with titles translated into English, in Shigeo Sorimachi's *Catalogue of Japanese Illustrated Books and Manuscripts in the Spencer Collection of The New York Public Library* (Tokyo, 1968). G. K. Hall & Company of Boston published the Spencer Collection card catalog and shelf list in book form in two volumes in 1970.

Important descriptions of individual books and manuscripts in the collection published in the *Bulletin* are listed below; additional articles may be located through the *Index* to the *Bulletin*.

"Aesop in Russia," 58 (1954): 3–5.

"The Affiliations of the Spencer Collection's Corvinus *Livy*," 42 (1938): 324–26. Published separately by the library.

"Archibald Robertson's Diaries and Drawings in America," 37 (1933): 7–37 et seq. (This work

was preprinted in 1930 with a slightly variant title. An extensive index is available in the separate publication, which was reprinted as *Archibald Robertson: His Diaries and Sketches in America, 1762–1780* (New York Public Library and Arno Press, 1971).

"Caricature Heads after Leonardo da Vinci in the Spencer Collection," 62 (1958): 279–99.

"The Christmas Story in Medieval and Renaissance Manuscripts from the Spencer Collection," 73 (1969): 625–746. Published separately by the library.

"A Fifteenth-Century Girdle Book," 43 (1939): 471–84.

"A First Edition of Struwelpeter," 37 (1933): 3–6.

"The Four Corvinus Manuscripts in the United States," 42 (1938): 315–23. Published separately by the library.

"An Italian Edition of the *Ars Moriendi*," 39 (1935): 927–30.

"The Malermi Bible and the Spencer Collection" 33 (1929): 779–88.

"The Petworth Manuscript of *Grace Dieu*; or, *The Pilgrimage of the Soul*. An English Illuminated Manuscript of the Fifteenth Century," 32 (1928): 715–20. Published separately by the library.

"A Renaissance Illuminated Manuscript of Valerius Maximus from the Library of the Aragonese Kings of Naples," 33 (1929): 847–53.

"The Shahnāmeh in Persian: An Illuminated Manuscript in the Spencer Collection," 36 (1932): 543–54.

"The Shahnāmeh in Turkish: An Illuminated Manuscript in the Spencer Collection," 36 (1932): 9–10.

"A Thirteenth Century Illuminated Manuscript *Minor Prophets and Lives of the Saints*, Identified as a Relative of the Berthold Missal," 32 (1928): 647–54. Published separately by the library.

"The Three Great Woodcut Books of Albrecht Dürer," 35 (1931): 459–64.

"The Tickhill Psalter: An English Illuminated Manuscript of the Early Fourteenth Century," 36 (1932): 663–78. (An extensive study, *The Tickhill Psalter and Related Manuscripts* by Donald Drew Egbert, was published under the joint auspices of the New York Public Library and the Department of Art and Archaeology of Princeton University, 1940.)

"Ulrich von Richental's *Chronicle of the Council of Constance*," 40 (1936): 303–19. Published separately by the library.

"Variant Copies of the 1499 Poliphilus," 36 (1932): 475–86.

17

RESEARCH FACILITIES OF THE BRANCH LIBRARIES

Public library facilities in New York City consist of three separate systems. The Brooklyn Public Library and Queens Borough Public Library serve their respective boroughs, and the New York Public Library serves Manhattan, the

Bronx, and Staten Island (Borough of Richmond).

In considering the New York Public Library, however, the organic connection between the Research Libraries and the Branch Libraries must be understood. The New York Public Library, a corporation operating under state charter, has two major contracts with the city of New York. The first covers the arrangement by which the Research Libraries, supported in the main by private funds, occupy the building at Fifth Avenue and 42nd Street rent-free; the second details the stipulations under which the library operates the Branch Libraries for the city, primarily with city funds. (Other contracts relate to the library's operation of the Library and Museum of the Performing Arts at Lincoln Center, which encompasses units of both the Research Libraries and the Branch Libraries.) The two systems, the Research Libraries and the Branch Libraries, are separate collections designed to serve two widely different but equally important functions; common ideals of public service are assured by a single Board of Trustees and single administration. This relationship, frequently confusing to the public, is further outlined in the following paragraphs in an attempt to clarify the respective responsibilities of the two departments.

The Research Libraries, maintained largely by endowment and annual gifts, operate in addition to general, special, and subject collections in the Central Building, an Annex on West 43rd Street, the Performing Arts Research Center in the New York Public Library at Lincoln Center, and the Schomburg Center for Research in Black Culture in Harlem.

The Branch Libraries operate more than 80 circulating branches and 5 bookmobiles in Manhattan, the Bronx, and Staten Island. They include such specialized collections as the circulating and information collections at the General Library & Museum of the Performing Arts at Lincoln Center; the Picture Collection in the Central Building; the foreign-language collections, the Central Children's Room, and the Nathan Straus Young Adult Library at the Donnell Library Center; the Library for the Blind and Physically Handicapped; and the Mid-Manhattan Library. There is a total of more than 3,000,000 books in the Branch Libraries,[1] with almost 2,000,000 pictures, over 90,000 phonorecords, and large numbers of talking books, tapes, films, etc.

A major confusion arises from the assumption that the Research Libraries are the "main branch" of the system, from which books may be borrowed as they are from neighborhood branches of the Branch Libraries. (Since 1970 the large publicly supported Mid-Manhattan Library has served such a function.) A common supposition is that as taxpayers, all should have the privilege of borrowing books from the Research Libraries. The Research Libraries' policy was most fully explained in the statement of the Executive Committee of the Board of Trustees, approved December 10, 1913:

The Reference Department [now the Research Libraries] . . . is frequently asked to lend books for outside use. These requests it must refuse, because the Reference Department is supported in the main from funds given with the understanding that books bought therefrom be used within the building. . . .

As early as 1857 the Trustees of the Astor Library adopted a resolution declaring it to be "the settled and unchangeable basis of administering the library that its contents should remain in the library rooms, for use by readers there, and should not be lent out or allowed to be taken from the rooms." The same policy, though never formally declared, was pursued by the Lenox Library; and it has also been the policy of The New York Public Library. One result of this has been that scholars from all parts of the United States have felt confidence that they would be sure of finding in this building, at all times, whatever books of reference the library might possess. . . .

Thus, no one has the privilege of withdrawing books from the collections of the Research Libraries, and no staff member is authorized to grant such privilege. Exceptions to this policy are made in the case of loans to other institutions for exhibition purposes, and in the case of the United Nations and federal, state, and municipal officials in New York City. Photocopies may be provided, however, under certain circumstances and with the approval of the officer of the Research Libraries having curatorial responsibility for the material to be copied.

The collections of the Branch Libraries, on the other hand, are largely for circulating purposes, and anyone who lives, works, or goes to school in New York State is entitled to a free borrower's card. Visitors from other states may borrow from the circulating collections by showing a local library card or by paying a fee for a nonresident borrower's card. Through the system of interbranch loans, books in most branches are available for issue from any other branch. A card is valid in any branch of the system.

For the Branch Libraries, a Union Catalog for materials catalogued before November 1972 (except those in the Mid-Manhattan Library and new branches) and published book catalogs for newly catalogued and Mid-Manhattan Library materials list the works in the branches (the Bronx, Manhattan, and Staten Island) and indicate their locations.[2] Books in the non-Roman alphabets are cataloged and added only to the Union Catalog. The largest libraries in each borough provide extensive reference, advisory, and lending services. Ready reference service is available in every branch. Supplementing the advanced research collections in the Research Libraries, the Mid-Manhattan Library and some of the larger and more strategically located branch libraries, known as Library Centers and Regional Branches, have larger book collections and information files than the average neighborhood branch library. Most branch libraries have collections of

---

1. These are for the most part works in English. The Donnell Foreign Language Library has about 43,000 volumes in foreign languages; a number of the branches maintain foreign-language collections; and rotating collections of books in French, German, Italian, Spanish, and Yiddish are available to any branch on request.

---

2. For the New York Public Library's Branch Libraries, a multivolume, computer-produced book catalog of adult materials and a *Children's Catalog* have been issued; they are divided into three parts according to type of entry (name, title, subject). Supplements and cumulations of the basic volumes are published regularly. For periodicals an annually issued *Periodicals in The Branch Libraries* (except Mid-Manhattan Library) and a revised catalog, *Periodicals in the Mid-Manhattan Library* (The New York Public Library, The Branch Libraries, 1973; supplement, 1975), have been published.

current periodicals, but Library Centers and Regional Branches maintain files of back issues of many of the most widely indexed periodicals. A list of periodical holdings is available for consultation in every branch library.

The Branch Libraries offer a wide range of library services in addition to collections of books, such as readers' advisory services; adult education activities; extension work with schools; and loan facilities for phonorecords, orchestral scores, and sixteen-millimeter films, etc.

Although this *Guide* is primarily a description of the resources of the Research Libraries, a number of the specialized collections of the Branch Libraries of particular importance for research are described in conjunction with subject materials of the Research Libraries: the Picture Collection (in chapter 29); the Central Children's Room (in chapter 21); and the collections of the General Library of the Performing Arts at Lincoln Center (in the chapters on the Music Division and the Dance and Theatre Collections).

The largest and newest unit of the Branch Libraries is the Mid-Manhattan Library primarily at 8 East 40th Street, which houses more than 300,000 volumes including 2,500 periodical titles with 40,000 bound volumes of back issues and 15,000 microfilm reels. All books are on open shelves. The library consists of four departments: (1) a General Reference Service with a basic reference collection of books, indexes, and bibliographical tools in all subject fields; (2) a Science Department comprising materials in the fields of the life and physical sciences both pure and applied; periodicals include English translations of some major foreign publications; (3) a History and Social Science Department (the largest department) covering sociology, education, economics, business and industrial relations, psychology, philosophy and religion, history and government, and geography and travel; and (4) a Literature and Language Department (located in the Central Building) containing extensive collections of American and English literature and foreign literature in translation, including important works of fiction and current novels, nonfiction, and belles-lettres. Most books in the library are in English. In addition to standard reference books, one copy of most nonfiction titles is held in the library at all times for use by readers. There is, as noted above, a computer-produced book catalog of the collections.

SECTION

II

THE HUMANITIES

PART ONE

18

PHILOSOPHY, PSYCHOLOGY, AND
RELATED MATERIALS

COLLECTING POLICY

The varied holdings in philosophy, psychology, and related disciplines include fields such as ethics, moral philosophy, the occult sciences, New Thought, mental healing, and mysticism. Although the general collecting policy is comprehensive, specific exceptions should be noted. Chinese philosophy is collected on a representative basis, and Russian philosophy in the Balto-Slavic languages is acquired selectively. Systems and manuals in the field of psychology and material on psychological laboratories are collected on a representative basis; in the field of ethics, systems, manuals, and material on temperance are collected selectively. Dissertations and theses from American universities are acquired on a representative basis, while those from foreign universities are acquired selectively.

HISTORICAL SURVEY

The growth of the collections in the broad field of philosophy, psychology, and related subjects is indicated by the following:

1854	Astor Library	1,500 volumes[1]
1921	New York Public Library	19,158
1930		25,888
1941		33,000
1966		57,200

In 1852–53, the Astor Library acquired a philosophical and miscellaneous collection of between 4,000 and 5,000 pieces. The Bancroft collection, purchased by the Lenox Library in 1894, was strong in the field of German philosophy. Among gifts bearing directly on this field is the James Black temperance collection presented in 1917 by the National Temperance Society. In 1948–49 the library received the Clarence Evans James collection of about 1,000 books and pamphlets chiefly on astrology, but also including nineteenth-century works on occultism, theosophy, and similar subjects. Other important gifts and acquisitions bearing indirectly on these areas are discussed below.

GENERAL DESCRIPTION

Resources devoted to philosophy are excellent. Existentialism is particularly well represented, and

---

1. Ethical and metaphysical sciences only. See Lydenberg, *History*, pp. 27–28.

full collections of both primary and secondary materials for the study of the German philosophers are present. Among the most notable working collections are those devoted to Spinoza and Kant.

Psychology is represented by a good collection in its nonclinical aspects. Included are many interesting works in the fields of phrenology and physiognomy. In the field of ethics, particularly in materials dealing with war and peace, dueling, and temperance, the collection is representative.

The Research Libraries have long collected materials in the broad area of philosophy and psychology not generally acquired by other learned institutions. Such subjects as parapsychology, spiritualism, clairvoyance, poltergeists, occultism, and witchcraft are represented. There is a substantial collection of material on New Thought. The Jewish Division holds important collections on the Kabbala and Hasidism. The periodical holdings are substantially complete with many lesser-known journals held in files very rarely found in this country. Philosophy textbooks are not generally collected.

TRANSLATIONS

Translations into English of the works of foreign philosophers, and critical material about them, are acquired regularly, in addition to texts in the original languages. Translations into other languages of material written originally in English are, however, seldom acquired. For example, few of the numerous translations of Bertrand Russell's writings have been acquired, although there is an extensive collection of his works in English, and critical material in all languages. An exception is made in the case of the Slavonic Division, which regularly acquires translations into Russian of material in the lesser-known Balto-Slavic languages.

PHILOSOPHY

RESOURCES

Periodical holdings are substantial for most countries; the large majority of the world's important philosophical journals are available. The resources include complete runs of *Archiv für Philosophie* (1947–), *Aristotelian Society Proceedings* (1887–), *Journal of Philosophy* (1904–), *Revue philosophique* (1876–), and many others. The Research Libraries currently receive approximately 110 periodical titles in this area.

The collections for western philosophy are strong. The Public Catalog contains entries for individual philosophers and for schools of philosophy; for instance there are approximately 80 entries in the card catalog under the heading "Stoicism," but a number of references lead to individual Stoic philosophers such as Cleanthes, Musonius, Seneca, and Marcus Aurelius; further, there are 78 entries for Marcus Aurelius and 66 entries for works about him. Similarly, Scholasticism receives some 170 entries, with the major figures, Saint Thomas Aquinas and Saint Bonaventure, having 650 and 90 entries. Philosophy holdings in the Jewish Division center on some 500 volumes of the works of Moses Maimonides and Judah ha-Levi in Hebrew texts and exegeses. Modern western philosophy is well represented, with about 400 entries treating Existentialism as a subject, excluding the works of individual philosophers. Holdings of the works of such figures as Martin Heidegger, Jean-Paul Sartre, and Gabriel Marcel are almost complete both in the original languages and in translation.

ORIENTAL PHILOSOPHY

Philosophical materials in the Oriental Division make up a good working collection, although one that is not as detailed or complete as the resources in other language areas. Arabic, Chinese, and Indian philosophy are the strongest collections. A preponderance of some 380 texts and critical works in Arabic philosophy are in Arabic, with parallel translations in certain cases. Chinese philosophical texts and critical works number about 240 items, including texts in Chinese. Classics in this field are held in a great number of editions and translations. There are some 360 Indian philosophical titles. The majority of the texts in Sanskrit are in the various printed collections and series that are an outstanding feature of the Oriental Division, among them the *Poona Oriental Series* and the *Bibliotheca Indica*. Yoga and Vedanta are the best represented of the six schools of Indian philosophy.

SPINOZA AND KANT

The holdings of works by and about Spinoza make up a particularly good working collection, numbering about 100 original works and some 450 critical books and journal articles. The Rare Book Division has two states of the first edition of *Tractatus theologico-politicus* (1670); there is also a French translation entitled *Reflections curieuses . . .* (1678) in the general collections. There are late seventeenth- and early eighteenth-century refutations of Spinoza's theories, and translations of his works. Among collected editions are the Latin edition of Paulus (1802–03), the "Supplementum" in Latin and Dutch of 1862, the German edition of Schaarschmidt and Baensch (1888–1905), the editions of Van Vloten and Land (1882–83), Carl Gebhardt (1924), and others. Periodicals related to Spinoza include the *Spinozistisch Bulletin* (1938–40), and *Biosophical Review* (1931–54).

The collection of materials by and about Immanuel Kant includes some 200 works by the philosopher and an additional 475 about him. First and early editions are included in the collection; for example, the first (1781) third, fifth, and sixth editions of *Critik der reinen Vernuft*,

and a first edition of *Die Religion Innerhalb der Grenzen der blossen Vernuft* (1793), are included. The standard collected edition of the Berlin Academy in 21 volumes (1900–38) is present, as is a run of *Kantstudien* (1897–1919, 1920–43, 1953–).

THEOSOPHY

The collection of theosophical materials numbers 600 titles, including 70 periodical files, of which 9 were current in 1966. Among the older periodicals is a run of *Theosophical Review* (London, 1887–1909), and among current publications are *Theosophist* (Madras, 1879–), and *Theosophy* (Los Angeles, 1912–). The book materials include collected and other editions of the works of Helene Petrovna Blavatsky, Jakob Böhme and others. A significant amount of material is regularly added to the collection.

RARITIES AND MANUSCRIPTS

In addition to the first and early Spinoza and Kant editions mentioned in the preceding paragraphs, possibly the most noteworthy rarity is a first edition of René Descartes' *Discours de la méthode*. In the Rare Book Division are two copies of a *Biblia pauperum* (Strasbourg, 1490) said to have been compiled by Saint Bonaventure, who is also the purported author of the *Speculum beatae Mariae Virginis* (Augsburg, 1476) and the established author of *De triplici via* (Cologne, 1475). Among other incunabula in the division relating to philosophy are Saint Thomas Aquinas' *Summa contra Gentiles* (Venice, 1480) and his *Quaestiones de duodecim quodlibet* (Venice, 1476), Ibn Sina's *Metaphysica Avicenne* (1495), William Ockham's *Quodlibeta* (Paris, 1487), Boethius' *De consolatione Philosophiae* (Toulouse, 1481), and Plato's *Opera* (Venice, 1491).

This is not a field in which the Manuscripts and Archives Division has sought out or collected manuscripts, but many modern figures of significance are represented by one or more letters in autograph collections and collections of personal correspondence in the division. Included, for example, are 138 letters of John Dewey, 74 of Josiah Royce, and 18 of William James. Medieval manuscripts include Boethius's "De consolatione Philosophiae" written in Lombardy and dated December 29, 1381, and 2 fifteenth-century versions of Aristotle's "De virtutibus et vitiis."

PSYCHOLOGY

RESOURCES: BOOKS

Psychology in its nonclinical aspects is one of the library's strong subjects, with approximately 14,100 volumes. Psychiatry as a branch of medicine is collected only selectively; specific medical areas of the subject, such as nervous diseases or epilepsy, are not collected at all. Periodical holdings are substantial on an international level, with such titles in the subject area of psychology as *Archives de psychologie* (1901–), *Imago* (1912–34), and *Journal of General Psychology* (1928–); in psychiatry, titles such as *Mental Hygiene* (1917–) and *American Journal of Psychiatry* (1921–). The library receives some 115 journals in psychology, applied psychology, social psychology, and related fields, and fewer than 10 titles in psychiatry. The book collections contain full holdings for major figures, as well as many secondary works. There are the standard editions of the leading theorists, Sigmund Freud, Carl Gustav Jung, Alfred Adler, and others, with many individual original and critical works. Also included are a number of early psychological and psychiatric books, including a French translation of Robert Whytt's work on nervous, hypochondriac, and hysteric diseases entitled *Les Vapeurs* (Paris, 1767).

Dreams, clairvoyance, somnambulism, and hypnotism form another important subject area; among relevant materials is *Revue de l'hypnotisme* (1887–1913). The collection of early American dream books has been described by Harry Weiss.[2] The General Research and Humanities Division continues to collect dream books in hard covers, but does not acquire the many ephemeral paperback publications on the subject. Hypnotism as a stage subject is of considerable interest to the Theatre Collection. In the collection of the Society of American Magicians there are the press books of the American magician Howard Thurston; the Theatre Collection also holds 25 volumes of manuscripts, letters, articles, and clippings for the period 1855–1909 relating to magic, hypnotism, spiritualism, legerdemain, and ventriloquism gathered by Dr. Saram R. Ellison. The collection maintains clipping files of reviews, photographs, and similar material filed under the name of individual hynotists. There is also a card catalog subject entry under the heading "Drama—Subjects—Hypnotism" which provides references to reviews and pictures of theatrical performances dealing with hypnotism.

The New York Public Library collection of materials on phrenology is significant. It numbers about 375 books and pamphlets and includes a run of *Phrenological Journal and Magazine of Moral Science* (Edinburgh, 1823–47).

RESOURCES: MANUSCRIPTS

An extensive group of the papers of Max Wertheimer, founder of Gestalt psychology, are in the Manuscripts and Archives Division. Typescripts of articles and correspondence of James Oppenheim in the division relate to psychoanalysis, as do similar materials by Robert West and Otto Juliusburger. A 127-page typescript of Sigmund Freud's *Der Mann Moses und der Monotheismus* is accompanied by page proofs and the printed text of sections translated into English and published in 1939.

The papers of the Willow Springs Phrenological Society of Willow Springs, Illinois, consist of the records of proceedings from 1847 to 1851. These give much incidental information on the activities of the Society.

ETHICS

Three collections totalling 10,700 volumes are prominent in this resource area of the Research Libraries: temperance, dueling, and war and peace.

TEMPERANCE

The temperance holdings number some 4,000 volumes. Most aspects of this subject are collected on a selective basis; only bibliography, history,

and items relating to the Prohibition Party are collected comprehensively.

Entries in the Public Catalog provide such categories as lectures, addresses, and sermons; biblical arguments for temperance; fiction, drama, poetry; and songs and music related to the subject. The periodical holdings are of importance, numbering some 450 titles, mostly from the nineteenth century. The Research Libraries currently receive some 15 titles from six countries, including *American Issue* (1926, 1928–), *Canadian Forward* (1927–), and the Finnish *Alkoholikysmys* (1954–). The files of the *Minutes of the Annual Meeting of the Woman's Christian Temperance Union* and the *Anti-Saloon League Yearbook*, are substantially complete. Timothy Shay Arthur's classic *Ten Nights in a Bar-room* (1854) is in the Rare Book Division; a copy of Walt Whitman's *Franklin Evans; or the Inebriate* (1842) in original wrappers is in the Berg Collection.

The James Black temperance collection presented by the National Temperance Society in 1917 has an unusual range of historical materials, including a number of scarce pamphlets. The society added to the gift in 1941 with a further large collection consisting of 357 volumes, 538 pamphlets, about 3,000 separate periodicals, 51 post cards, and 15 framed portraits of former presidents of the society.

Several collections in the Manuscripts and Archives Division relate to temperance. Most prominent are 8 boxes of correspondence of Mary Hannah Hunt, educator and temperance reformer of Massachusetts, covering the years of her service with the International Woman's Christian Temperance Union, 1890 to 1906. The archive also includes the correspondence and papers of the Scientific Temperance Federation of Boston during the years 1906 to 1918. Other material on temperance is in the Malone theatre collection, in the Smith family papers of Peterboro, New York (especially in the papers of Gerrit Smith), and in the Cyrus Williams papers.

DUELING

A collection of over 500 volumes ranges from titles of the sixteenth century, including the works of Andrea Alciati and Girolamo Muzio, to the present. The library continues to collect comprehensively in this area. Of note are seventeenth- to nineteenth-century volumes of ordinances, court decisions, laws, and proclamations against dueling in England, Europe, Mexico, and Argentina. There are no related manuscripts.

WAR AND PEACE

The holdings include a large collection of books, as well as extensive files of periodicals and serial publications of organizations promoting peace, both American and foreign. Among the periodical holdings are such items as Noah Worcester's *Friend of Peace* (1815–27), *World Affairs* [*Advocate of Peace*, etc.] (1854– , incomplete), and the year books and annual reports of the Carnegie Endowment for International Peace (1911–). More than 50 international periodical titles are currently received, including *Survival* (London, 1959–), *Journal of Peace Research* (Oslo, 1964–), and *Baris Dünyasi* (Istanbul, 1962–). A substantial proportion of the book material bears on the first and second International Peace Conferences at The Hague in 1899 and 1907, and on the Paris Peace Confer-

---

2. See Harry B. Weiss, "Oneirocritica Americana," *BNYPL* 48 (1944): 519–40 et seq.

ence of 1919. Material on conscientious objectors and other subjects related to war and peace is also collected in depth by the Research Libraries. Handbills and other fugitive materials are acquired when available, and housed in the ephemera collection of the Rare Book Division.

In the Manuscripts and Archives Division the Women's Peace Union papers in 9 boxes contain correspondence, publicity material, petitions to Congress, and minutes for the period 1920 to 1941. In addition, the selected papers of Carrie Chapman Catt, lecturer and American woman suffrage leader, are concerned with peace, particularly for the period 1913 to 1941. Items from the Norman Thomas papers cover peace activities from 1905 onward. The feminist, peace, and world government movements of modern times are substantially documented in manuscripts and in printed matter in the Schwimmer-Lloyd Collection of 1,777 boxes and 420 linear feet of material. Included are the correspondence and papers of Rosika Schwimmer (1877–1948), Hungarian feminist and pacifist, and Lola Maverick Lloyd (1875–1944), American suffragist and pacifist. Files include those of the Ford Peace Expedition and Neutral Conference, the International Committee for Immediate Mediation, and the Campaign for World Government. The collection is multilingual with correspondence and printed matter in English, German, Hungarian, and other languages; access was restricted until January 1, 1974.[3]

Cruelty to Animals

The catalog entry "Animals—Treatment" locates materials which include many periodical and society publications from the early nineteenth century to the present. Seven current periodical runs include the *National Humane Review* (1913–).

OCCULT SCIENCES

Occultism is particularly well represented in materials on magic and witchcraft. Magic is discussed with the holdings of the Theatre Collection. Witchcraft is one of the richer collections of historical materials, particularly in records of early trials, both American and European.[4] Certain books on Oriental customs in the Oriental Division deal with witchcraft.

Periodical holdings in the occult field are extensive and varied, with such titles as *Revue spirite* (1858–), *Rosicrucian Fellowship Magazine* (1913–), and *Journal of Parapsychology* (1937–).

The Manuscripts and Archives Division has 8 examinations, charges, and indictments for witchcraft of late seventeenth-century Massachusetts,

among them the "Examination of Tittuba the Indian Woman. March 1 and 2, 1691/2."

The Spencer Collection has associated materials, among them 2 illustrated paper manuscripts from nineteenth-century Thailand, one a fortune teller's notebook (probably made for his own use) and the other a sorcerer's handbook, folded in accordion style, with illustrations of fortune telling, witchcraft, and sorcery.

NEW THOUGHT

Approximately 700 titles (1,400 volumes) bear on this popular philosophical movement. Examples of the works of O. S. Marden, Ralph Waldo Trine, and others are present. Some 62 separate periodical files are a major feature of the holdings in this field; only 2, *The Aquarian Age* (1918–) and *Science of Mind Magazine* (1927–), are current.

MYSTICISM

This is a good working collection of 2,200 volumes with strong holdings on the Kabbala and Hasidism in the Jewish Division. The Slavonic Division collects works on Russian mystics primarily as examples of literature and only secondarily for their philosophical or religious aspects. A rare title edited by Johann Amos Comenius entitled *Lux in tenebris* (1657) was acquired in 1952. Described at the time of its acquisition as probably the only copy in this country, the book deals with prophecies made by three seventeenth-century seers.[5]

The Kabbala and Hasidism

Approximately 550 entries in the card catalog cover works on the Kabbala and editions of kabbalistic works from incunabula to the present day. Moses Nahmanides' commentary on the Pentateuch is in the kabbalistic manner; three of the Jewish Division's incunabula are editions of the work, published in Rome (ca. 1480), Lisbon (1489), and Naples (1490). A similar commentary by Bahya ben Asher, printed in Naples in 1492, is also in the division. Another significant group of material consists of texts of the Zohar (called the Kabbalistic Bible) from its first editions in Mantua and Cremona (1558–60) to the most recent printings. Further items are devoted to the renaissance of the Kabbala in sixteenth-century Palestine, primarily in the works of Moses Cordovero. The division has a first edition of his *Pardes Rimonim* [Garden of Pomegranates] (Krakow, 1591), and works from the school of Isaac Luria. The Isaac Meyer collection in the Manuscripts and Archives Division also deals with the Kabbala.

The Research Libraries have a full collection, numbering over 500 book and journal article titles, of legends and works issued since the founding of the Hasidic movement in the eighteenth century. Among them is the first printed work of Hasidism, that of Jacob Joseph, ha-Kohen, of Polonnoye issued in Koretz in 1780; also copies of the first collection of legends about the founder, Israel Baal Shem Tob, issued simultaneously in Berditchev and in Kopys in 1815. The modern literature of the movement is well represented. There are some 250 critical studies and exegeses.

---

3. See Robert W. Hill, "The Schwimmer-Lloyd Collection," *BNYPL* 47 (1943): 307–09.

4. See Charles F. McCombs, "The Massachusetts Bay Exhibition," *BNYPL* 35 (1931): 465–71. George F. Black, "List of Works in The New York Public Library Relating to Witchcraft in the United States," *BNYPL* 12 (1908): 658–75; "List of Works in The New York Public Library Relating to Witchcraft in Europe," *BNYPL* 15 (1911): 727–55; "A Calendar of Cases of Witchcraft in Scotland, 1510–1727," *BNYPL* 41 (1937); 811–47 et seq.; 42 (1938): 34–74, published separately by the library, reprinted by the library and Arno Press, 1971.

5. See Avrahm Yarmolinsky, "A Rare Comenius Title," *BNYPL* 57 (1953): 149–51.

19

RELIGION

COLLECTING POLICY AND HISTORICAL SURVEY

The collections of the Research Libraries in the area of religion emphasize the impact of religion on society rather than individual religious experience. Intensive coverage of the subject is considered to be the province of the theological libraries of the community. Nevertheless, the total resources of the library number almost 100,000 volumes, and there is an attempt to be comprehensive in the fields of history of religion, biography of religious figures, bibliographies, and clerical lists. Certain religious sects such as the Shakers, the Mormons, the Society of Friends (Quakers), the Seventh Day Adventists, and the Christian Scientists are given particular attention, since some are indigenous religions and all have played a part in the development of the United States. In most other aspects of the subject, the collecting policy is selective, with variations noted in the more detailed discussions that follow.

A brief listing indicates the development of the holdings in this area:

1854	Astor Library	3,752 volumes
1921	New York Public Library	58,592
1930		73,282
1941		92,000
1966		99,300

In 1855 the Astor Library's collection on theology was described as

including the best editions of the Hebrew and Greek Scriptures, the Walton Polyglott, various editions of the Vulgate, and numerous versions of the whole Bible, and parts of it, in the principal languages of Europe and the East. The collection of the Fathers is full, but not absolutely complete, and contains most of the Benedictine editions, the Bibliotheca Maxima of Despont, the Patres Apostolici of Cotelerius, and many other works of this class of less note. It is equally well provided with works on the Councils, including Colet's edition of Labbé, in 29 volumes; the Concilia Maxima, in 37 volumes folio; Beveridge's Synodicon, Lorenzana, Concilianos provinciales, etc. It is also respectable in scholastic, dogmatic, parenetic and polemic theology, including the early and more recent English Divines in the best editions.[1]

By 1877 theology as a collecting field had been deemphasized by the Astor Library since other libraries of the city covered this field. In 1883, however, a gift from John Jacob Astor made possible needed additions. The Lenox Library had an unusually extensive file of the "Jesuit Relations" relating to both America and the Far East; a list of books on this subject appeared as No. II of the *Contributions to a Catalogue of the Lenox Library*. The Stuart Collection, which came to the Lenox Library in 1892, contained some 2,000 volumes relating to theology and ecclesiastical

history; many of these titles are now duplicated in the library's general collections. In 1894 purchases at the George H. Moore library and Livermore sales added important catechisms.

In 1897 the library secured the Reverend W. H. Treadway's collection of sermons, about 20,000 pieces. In 1899, Helen Miller Gould (Mrs. Finly Shepard) presented the Berrian collection on Mormonism with materials on the Reorganized Church, and on James J. Strang.

In 1914, Miss Isabel Hapgood was instrumental in the library's receiving over 500 theological works, presented by the Holy Synod of the Russian Church through the courtesy of the Most Reverend Platon. In 1923, Frank A. Peterson gave a large collection relating to the Seventh Day Adventists, including the publications of that group, a collection to which he subsequently added. In the same year the library purchased a collection of 5,000 publications issued by the American Board of Commissioners for Foreign Missions, consisting of catechisms, tracts, portions of the Gospels, the Bible, and other religious books in native dialects of India, Africa, and other parts of the world.

RELIGIONS

RESOURCES IN RELIGIONS

Materials which deal in a general way with the religions of the world number some 5,000 volumes. Dictionaries, encyclopedias, and the bibliography and history of religion are collected comprehensively; periodical and society publications are acquired selectively. Periodical holdings include such titles as *Archiv für Religionswissenschaft* (1898–1934), *Hibbert Journal* (1902–) and *Recherches de science réligieuse* (1910–34). Files are usually complete for issues through 1934, when a number of subscriptions were discontinued. Noteworthy features are the philosophy of religion, manuals, and comparative studies, with representative nineteenth- and twentieth-century works. There are rich pamphlet collections of eighteenth- to twentieth-century essays and miscellanies.

Among non-Christian religions the holdings are particularly extensive for the classical religions and are complemented by associated materials in archaeology and anthropology. Teutonic religions are also well represented, not only by a good collection of formal treatises but also by substantial holdings of sagas and an unusual group of periodicals, both literary and historical. Oriental religions and Judaism are treated separately in the following section.

Oriental Religions

Only general works on Oriental religions and Islamic theology are collected comprehensively by the Oriental Division; other religions are given representative or selective treatment. A number of spiritual disciplines or philosophical systems that have religious elements are treated in the discussion of Oriental philosophy in chapter 18 of this *Guide*.

---

1. Lydenberg, *History*, p. 26.

Approximately 1,000 volumes on the Islamic religion are available, including about 160 editions of the Koran in Arabic and fifteen other languages. The earliest examples are fragments in the Manuscripts and Archives Division dating probably from the eighth to tenth centuries, in Kufic characters. Other rarities include English, Latin, and German translations from the sixteenth and seventeenth centuries. Also found are some 400 works on the Koran, 200 on the lives of the prophets, and 200 on Islamic tradition. The 150 volumes on pilgrimages include a first edition of Sir Richard Burton's celebrated *Personal Narrative* (1855), describing his journey to Mecca. The works of Theodore Gaster and Henri Frankfort are representative of more recent material on Oriental religions.

Beginning with ancient Egypt (with an emphasis on religion's archaeological aspect), the resources of the Oriental Division follow the course of religious thought through Zoroastrianism, Manichaeism, Hinduism, Brahminism, Sikhism, Buddhism (a strong collection covering all of Asia), Lamaism and the Bon religion of Tibet, Taoism and Confucianism in China, and Shintoism in Japan. A comprehensive collection of the Persian liturgical texts in Avestan and Pahlevi is available. There is also a good deal of material on Christianity in the Orient, including Nestorianism and the Ethiopian, Maronite, and Melchite Churches. Printed collections produced by various learned societies such as the Pali Text Society reinforce the holdings of monographs.

Pictorial and textual information on the rituals and liturgies of the Oriental religions may be found in the Spencer Collection.

Judaism

The Judaic religion is well covered in the Jewish Division, although no attempt is made to achieve the comprehensive coverage provided by theological seminary libraries. There are about 12,500 volumes in the holdings. The collecting policy is generally representative or selective.

The Talmud and Talmudic literature comprise about 2,900 volumes, including editions published in Pesaro and Venice in the sixteenth century. There is also a first edition of the Jerusalem Talmud (Venice, 1523) and commentaries by Solomon ben Adret (Venice, 1522).

About 2,200 volumes represent the halacha and responsa. Among them are Jacob ben Asher's *Arbaah Turim* (Piove di Sacco, 1475), the second dated book printed in Hebrew. Another code of religious law written by Moses Maimonides dates from 1490, and a similar work by Moses ben Jacob of Coucy is dated Soncino, 1488. These works are all available in later editions as well. Notable among the collections of responsa, for which there is a card index, are those of Solomon ben Adret, chief rabbi of Barcelona (Rome, 1480), and of Asher ben Jehiel (Constantinople, 1517).

Two manuscript mahzors of the thirteenth and fourteenth centuries according to the Ashkenazic (German) rite are among the treasures of the Research Libraries. They form part of some 1,800 volumes on liturgy and ritual in the Jewish Division. A mahzor according to the Roman rite was printed in Soncino in 1485. With the Hebrew manuscripts in the Manuscripts and Archives Division are a number of Yemeni liturgical texts written in the eighteenth century.

Homiletic literature and sermons number about 2,000 volumes, mostly in Hebrew, but including materials in Yiddish and English. Midrashim are a feature of the holdings. Isaac ben Moses Arama's sermons, published in Salonica in 1522, are noteworthy. Individual sermons are classed by author and by subject (i.e., "Sermons, American"; "Sermons, Hebrew") in the Jewish Division Catalog. This is no longer a feature of the Public Catalog.

The various Jewish sects, ancient and modern, are well represented. The writings pertaining to the Pharisees, the Sadducees, the Essenes, and so on are of wide interest. The oldest Jewish sect is that of the Samaritans; the collections contain virtually everything obtainable in printed form written by and about them. Next in point of age is the sect known as the Karaites, whose early history lies in obscurity. There is an almost complete collection of the known printed texts produced by writers of this sect, with equally complete resources about it.

Hasidism and the Kabbalah, both of which are strongly represented in the collections of the Jewish Division, are discussed in chapters 10 and 18 of this *Guide*.

Christianity

The collections attempt comprehensive coverage of the history of Christianity with the exception of essays, miscellanies, and periodical and society publications, which are acquired selectively. Holdings are particularly strong in biographical material, bibliographies, directories, and church histories. There has been no attempt to build resources in the field of Christian theology, and apart from such standard works as the *Acta Sanctorum* and other writings of the early Fathers, little theological material is to be found.

Material of specific interest includes a growing collection of books about Saint Rose of Lima, the first American to be canonized, and the Berg Collection copy of the first English edition of John Foxe's *Actes and Monuments of These Latter and Perillous Dayes* (1563), better known as Foxe's *Book of Martyrs*.

Materials associated with the celebration of Christmas include original works of graphic art issued as Christmas cards, collected by the Prints Division, and privately printed Christmas greetings produced in limited editions, collected by the Rare Book Division. There are some 1,400 of the latter, documented in a special card file. The Spencer Collection has strong holdings in the iconography of the Nativity.

Jesus Christ: A strong collection, extensively subdivided and documented by 5,000 card entries in the Public Catalog, relates to Jesus Christ. Although only biographical materials are now acquired comprehensively, the library has always collected extensively in the iconography of Christian art. "Christus in Arte," an unusual collection in the Art and Architecture Division, consists of 25 bound volumes of pictorial documents dealing with the life of the Savior. The first group of 15 bound volumes was given in 1920 by John Powell Lenox of Oak Park, Illinois.[2] In 1951 Madame Lucie Lenox-Darcy and her husband Emery Darcy added 800 pictures, several unframed originals, and a bound volume of letters, press clippings,

---

2. See Frank Weitenkampf, "Christ in Art," *BNYPL* 24 (1920): 207–12.

and illustrations.[3] Resources in this area are arranged by form rather than by subject: prints are to be found in the Prints Division and art books in the Art and Architecture Division. Notable in this very extensive archive are original works by Dürer, Cranach, and Urs Graf.

In accordance with the attempt of the Research Libraries to document all sides of a question, materials hostile to Christianity are collected comprehensively and number some 2,000 books and pamphlets, including a good selection of items on and by Thomas Paine, Robert Ingersoll, Charles Bradlaugh, and Annie Besant. Among notable items are Anthony Collins's *Discourse of Freethinking* (1713) with Jonathan Swift's version in "plain English" of the same year, and a copy of Ethan Allen's *Reason the Only Oracle of Man* (1784). The Irving Levy collection of pamphlets and other literature on free thought was given in 1923.

Sermons: The holding of sermons is extensive. Current collecting policy assures selective acquisition of published sermons delivered in New York City or by internationally known preachers such as William Ashley (Billy) Sunday or William Franklin (Billy) Graham. The most important group of sermons is from the United States. The Reverend W. H. Treadway's collection of sermons, about 20,000 pieces, was secured in 1897. The great mass of these sermons are bound in pamphlet volumes: there are also scrapbooks of sermons clipped from newspapers, pictures, portraits, and other material. Only collections appear under the subject heading "Sermons" in the Public Catalog; individual sermons must be located through the name of the author. Entries for sermons as a literary form subdivided by country are found in file drawers located on the balcony of Room 315. The entries cover material acquired before 1940 when the use of literary form headings in the major languages was discontinued. The Jewish Division continues to catalog sermons of Jewish interest under the form heading "Sermons."

The collections of sermons in the Rare Book Division include at least one incunabulum: Bernard of Clairvaux's sermons, dated 1494. A strong group of election sermons, preached each year at the opening session of the legislature, are most extensive for Massachusetts and Connecticut and range in date from 1663 to 1884.[4] A number of Mexican sermons are interesting examples of early imprints. Sermons by individual preachers include a copy of Robert Cushman's *A Sermon Preached at Plimmoth* (London, 1622), probably the first printed sermon delivered by a North American preacher, and sermons by George Whitfield. A particularly extensive collection of Jonathan Edwards' works includes first printings of *Sinners in the Hands of an Angry God* and *God Glorified in the Work of Redemption*. The Manuscripts and Archives Division holds additional North American sermons.

Missions: About 7,000 volumes on Christian missions include periodicals, the publications and reports of societies and organizations, and a notable representation of publications of the missions themselves. Material on the American Indian is of particular note, as is the collection of some

5,000 titles issued by the American Board of Commissioners for Foreign Missions, consisting of catechisms, tracts, portions of the Gospels, the Bible, and other religious books in native dialects. Supplementary sources include an excellent collection of colonial governmental reports issued by supervisory bureaus for missions.

The collection of Jesuit letters from North American missions ("Jesuit Relations") is one of the finest in existence, being founded on the acquisitions of James Lenox. Among the most prized items are the 1632 Le Jeune edition (McCoy 1); the Le Mercier edition of 1656 (McCoy 96); and the Lallemant edition of 1660 (McCoy 104).[5] There are also strong holdings of Jesuit letters from missions in the East. Dating from the late sixteenth through the eighteenth centuries, the reports cover such countries as Mexico, Peru, Chile, Ethiopia, China, India, and Japan. The Rare Book Division fills gaps in these holdings when possible. The division's total resources listed under Jesuits and Jesuitism numbers about 900 separate title entries. A list of the original Lenox holdings appeared as No. II of the Lenox Library's *Contributions to a Catalogue of the Lenox Library*.

RESOURCES IN CHRISTIAN DENOMINATIONS

Holdings in Christian denominations are strongest in the area of history, and less comprehensive in matters of doctrine and other aspects of the subject. There is a conscious effort, however, to acquire all material documenting changes in church polity, such as the publications of the Vatican Councils.

General church history is well covered, with such standard sets as the *Gallia Christiana* and *España Sagrada*. Materials for the English churches include parish and diocesan registers, the publications of the Canterbury, York, and Cantilupe Societies, and the volumes issued by local record societies. The national convention reports of the United States denominations and the reports of regional New York conventions are collected.

Extensive materials relating to individual American and foreign churches are located in the Local History and Genealogy Division, while works on ecclesiastical art and architecture are held by the Art and Architecture Division. The publications of learned societies, which are often indexed in the library's catalogs, frequently provide information in these areas.

Eastern Orthodox Churches

The Slavonic Division catalog holds some 1,200 entries for the Eastern Orthodox Church. The extensive collections of works of Old Church Slavonic are notable for their linguistic value, but the resources also contain numerous liturgical works. The Spencer Collection holds other illustrated examples of liturgical manuscripts, as well as manuscript texts used in the Armenian Church.

Roman Catholic Church

In the Research Libraries are found some 15,400 volumes on the Roman Catholic Church. Comprehensive collections are maintained in the field

---

3. See Muriel Baldwin, "Christus in Arte," *BNYPL* 55 (1951): 515.

4. See R. W. G. Vail, "A Check List of New England Election Sermons," *American Antiquarian Society Proceedings*, n.s. 45 (1935): 233–66.

5. See James C. McCoy, *Jesuit Relations of Canada 1632–1673* (Paris: A. Rau, 1937).

of Church history and in the history of individual orders, particularly the Jesuits and specifically Saints Ignatius Loyola and Francis Xavier: an unusual set of the "Jesuit Relations" documents the early work of the order in world missions. Clerical lists and directories are also collected comprehensively; materials in other categories are collected on a representative or selective basis. The publications of the Church and of religious orders are collected. Among historic Catholic parties, the Jansenists are especially well represented, with supportive literary and educational material. A noteworthy collection relating to Church policy and canon law includes some 125 editions of *Index Librorum Prohibitorum*, the earliest dated 1550. A remarkable example of pictorial materials documenting the affairs of the Church exists in the Spencer Collection's manuscript copy of Ulrich von Richental's "Chronicle of the Council of Constance," written in the South-German dialect and illustrated by a contemporary artist about 1450–60.[6]

Materials on the Inquisition are comprehensively collected. Among strong holdings for Mexico and the South American countries are a number of broadsides of the early nineteenth century (in the Rare Book Division) and a group of manuscript documents in Spanish which relate to the edicts and proceedings of the Inquisition in Mexico between 1622 and 1680 (in the Manuscripts and Archives Division).

Histories of local parishes and individual churches, printed church records, and ecclesiastical heraldry are collected by the Local History and Genealogy Division.

Protestantism

The history and bibliography of the Protestant Churches are collected comprehensively. A collection relating to the Anglican Churches is of considerable historical interest; there is a good representation of the reports of diocesan conventions of the Protestant Episcopal Church, and excellent pamphlet materials dealing with the history of the Church of Scotland. The published histories and the writings of founders and principal leaders of the Protestant denominations are usually present, and there are special materials for some denominations: historical works relating to the Baptists were purchased from the library of the Reverend W. R. Williams in 1896; holdings for the New Jerusalem Church include an excellent collection of Swedenborg's works. Of particular note, and given separate attention below, are the resources for the Shakers, the Mormons, the Seventh Day Adventists, the Society of Friends (Quakers), and the Christian Scientists.

The Local History and Genealogy Division collects comprehensively and retrospectively printed parish registers from the United States, Canada, and the British Isles, including Northern Ireland. It acquires few similar records for Europe or South America, although any materials received are cataloged. British parish registers are best represented; more material of this type has been published in Great Britain than elsewhere, the larger part of it from the late nineteenth century to the present. In recent years many church records have been published in historical and genealogical periodicals. Indexing of this material in the library's card catalogs is confined to records of New York City. Much of the material over a wider geographical area can be found in commercial indexes.

The Research Libraries' holdings of early titles printed in the United States and England as listed in H. M. Dexter's *The Congregationalism of the Last Three Hundred Years as Seen in Its Literature* (1880) are creditable.

Manuscripts: The Methodist Historical Society has placed on deposit with the New York Public Library the records of the Methodist Episcopal Church in New York City, as well as records of many congregations in Long Island, Westchester County, New York State, and New Jersey. Covering the period 1784 to 1937, the archive consists of nearly 500 volumes and boxes of material. Further papers were donated by Mrs. Gino Speranza in 1949, including 6 roll books of St. Paul's Methodist Episcopal Church in New York City, and various papers and records of St. Luke's Methodist Episcopal Church in the city, also miscellaneous papers of the Church Extension Society of Philadelphia, Pennsylvania. The period covered is from 1861 to 1904. Further church records include a volume of Kingston, New York, church records for the period 1681 to 1683, and the New Harlem Deacon's Book in 9 volumes for the period 1672 to 1674; both are written in Dutch. They were donated by the Title Guarantee and Trust Company of New York in 1917, as part of the James Riker papers.

The library holds photostats and typewritten transcripts of original letters and documents exchanged between the Consistory of the Lutheran Church in Amsterdam and the congregation in Manhattan for the period 1649 to 1772. Translations, photostats of which are on file, were published in the library's *Bulletin*.[7]

Papers of religious leaders in the Manuscripts and Archives Division include those of Horace N. Allen (Presbyterian missionary to China and Korea; Minister to Korea); Joseph Anderson, Henry Ward Beecher, John Davenport,[8] and Jedidiah Morse (Congregational clergymen); Alfred Williams Anthony and John Betts Calvert (Baptist clergymen); Richard Heber Newton and Henry Dana Ward (Episcopal clergymen); Caroline Augusta (Mrs. Henry) Soulé (Universalist clergywoman); William Adams Brown (Presbyterian clergyman and professor of theology); Isaac Langworthy (Congregational clergyman); James Chrystal (Episcopal clergyman); and Theodoric and John Brodhead Romeyn (Dutch Reformed clergymen). Other papers relating to religious activities include a collection of letters of leading American clergymen. Manuscript material on the Mormons, the Society of Friends (Quakers), the Shakers, and the Seventh Day Adventists is discussed under separate headings.

Mormons: The history and belles lettres of Mormonism are now collected comprehensively; other materials relating to the sect are acquired selectively. The holdings number some 2,200 entries in the Public Catalog and are built around

---

6. See Karl Kup, "Ulrich von Richental's Chronicle of the Council of Constance," *BNYPL* 40 (1936): 303–20. Published separately by the library.

7. Arnold J. H. van Laer, "The Lutheran Church in New York, 1649–1772; Records in the Lutheran Church Archives at Amsterdam, Holland," *BNYPL* 48 (1944): 31–60 et seq.

8. See "Winthrop-Davenport Papers," *BNYPL* 3 (1899): 393–408.

the Berrian collection presented in 1899 by Helen Miller Gould (Mrs. Finley Shepard). It was at that time considered to be one of three or four ranking collections in this country. The collection represents many years of work by William C. Berrian of Brooklyn; it is composed of 800 books and pamphlets, including many early rarities, a large number of bound and unbound newspapers, and scrapbooks of clippings, portraits, photographs, and similar material, relating to Mormonism from its beginnings to 1880. The collection also contains materials on the Reorganized Church and on James J. Strang.[9] The holdings have been steadily increased by gift and purchase. Associated materials include an excellent collection of public documents bearing on Utah and Mormonism.

Among the rarities in the library are most of the early American and European editions of *The Book of Mormon*, including the first (Palmyra, New York, 1830); one of the library's 2 copies has the scarce four-page index. The Rare Book Division copy of *The Book of Commandments* (Zion [Independence, Mo.], 1833) is 1 of the 4 known examples. Forty-three newspaper files include such titles as the *Evening and Morning Star* (1832–34, 1900–), scattered issues of the *Wasp* (1842–), and the *Nauvoo Neighbor* (1843–45). Of some 60 periodical and society publications relating to Mormonism, 4 are current, including the *Saints' Herald* (1860–) in an incomplete run, and the *Relief Society Magazine* (1914–).

Material in the Manuscripts and Archives Division includes the diaries of Albert Tracy, 1858–62, and of Brigham Young, Jr., 1900–02. There is also material relating to the Mormon mission to Japan during the period 1901–05.

Fictional treatment of Mormons is found in first and early editions and typescripts of Joaquin Miller's *First Fam'lies of the Sierras* (1876) and and an 1882 edition retitled *The Danites in the Sierras.*

Seventh Day Adventists: The holdings of materials on the Seventh Day Adventists are based on the collection given by Frank A. Peterson in 1923. The original gift, to which Peterson made subsequent additions, consists of 745 books, 2707 pamphlets, 782 periodicals, 320 sheets, and 6 boxes of manuscripts.[10] It is especially strong in periodicals, with some 150 titles covering denominational, missionary, and conference papers. Of note are sets of *The Midnight Cry* (1842–45) and *Quarterly Journal of Prophecy* (1847–73). Most of the periodical runs were discontinued in the early 1940s; currently only 1 journal is received in the Periodicals Section, *Message Magazine* (1935–), a leading missionary magazine. Books and pamphlets include notable collections of the writings of Mrs. Ellen G. White, virtual head of the Church from its beginning in 1845 to her death in 1915, and of such writers as James White and Uriah Smith. Most of the material is housed at the library's Annex at Forty-third Street.

Shakers: Because of the strength of its manuscript materials, the library is a leading center of source material on the Shakers. Book materials in the bibliography and history of the sect are collected comprehensively, and other materials are acquired selectively. Many of the earlier items in the library have interest or value as imprints of a typical American sect.

The Manuscripts and Archives and the Rare Book Divisions hold copies of Joseph Meacham's *A Concise Statement of the Principles of the Only True Church* (Bennington, Vt., 1790), the first Shaker pamphlet printed in this country. In the Manuscripts and Archives Divisions are extensive collections of manuscript materials, the largest being 118 volumes of records of the Shaker Church in the United States from 1780 to 1934. The volumes include a record of the daily events in Shaker communities, diaries, recollections, accounts of seances, spirit messages, songs, poems, and church laws. In 1961 the library acquired 39 reminiscent or autobiographical letters by Angell Matthewson telling of his conversion and early years of membership in the Shaker community at New Lebanon, New York, during the period 1780 to 1813.

Dancing, a characteristic of Shaker worship, is documented in the Dance Collection through contemporary lithographs; modern representations of Shaker dancing by Doris Humphrey are preserved in still photographs and motion picture films. The Music Division holds a number of Shaker hymnals.[11]

Society of Friends (Quakers): Some 3,200 entries in the Public Catalog cover the library's fair representation of the great body of writings by and about this sect. History, biography, and general works about the Society of Friends are collected comprehensively; other materials are collected only selectively. Holdings of seventeenth-, eighteenth-, and nineteenth-century pamphlets are notable, including works by George Fox and William Penn, among them a first printing of Penn's *To the Children of Light* (London, 1776) and the later American printing (Philadelphia, 1776). The Bowne collection in the Manuscripts and Archives Division contains the account book of John Bowne dated 1649 to 1703 with financial records of the Society of Friends at Flushing, New York.

Christian Science: A good collection of Christian Science materials includes a first edition of Mrs. Eddy's *Science and Health* (1875) and numerous later editions. There is a complete set of the *Christian Science Monitor* (1908–) and extensive files of periodicals, including most of the foreign-language versions of *The Herald of Christian Science*. There are many numbers of the *Christian Science Series* (1889–91). The collecting policy is selective in this area; in earlier years, however, the policy was comprehensive, reflecting an emphasis on this native American religion.

Other Religious Sects: Material on the Mennonites includes interesting early imprints and unusual historical items. There is a complete file of the *Watchtower* of the Jehovah's Witnesses from 1879 to the present.

LITURGY AND RITUAL

JEWISH LITURGY AND RITUAL

The collection of materials on liturgy and ritual in the Jewish Division is representative rather than comprehensive. There are examples of the

---

9. See "List of Works in The New York Public Library Relating to the Mormons," *BNYPL* 13 (1909): 183–239.

10. See *BNYPL* 27 (1923): 459–60.

---

11. See "List of Works in The New York Public Library Relating to Shakers," *BNYPL* 8 (1904): 550–59.

prayer and festival books for the Sephardic and Ashkenasic rites, and for Orthodox, Conservative, and Reformed Judaism, with the variations within these rites and groups. A description of particularly noteworthy manuscripts and books is found in chapter 10 of this *Guide*.

CHRISTIAN LITURGY AND RITUAL

The General Research and Humanities Division maintains a collection of current books of devotion in the Main Reading Room for the Christian religion as practiced in the United States. The division is careful to acquire new materials that reflect changes in ritual. Among materials collected comprehensively by the division are the breviary, the *Book of Common Prayer* of the Church of England and the Protestant Episcopal Church, and the *Prayer Book* of the Reformed Episcopal Church.

The general collections include standard works and publications devoted to liturgy, such as those of the Henry Bradshaw Society. Denominational hymns and the poetical works of individual hymn writers are numerous; the collection of hymn books in the Music Division holds much associated material. Sunday observance is well covered and is particularly interesting for its historical materials. There is a noteworthy collection of devotional and meditative works. Reports and other publications of theological schools in the United States are interesting mainly for the older material. Homiletics is extensively covered.

Books of Hours

Approximately 40 manuscript books of hours are found in the Manuscripts and Archives Division, the larger number French fifteenth-century illuminated works on vellum. The Spencer Collection manuscript *horae* include distinguished examples of English, French, Flemish, Dutch, and Italian work.[12] Outstanding among the 15 examples in the collection is the Wingfield Hours (Spencer Ms. 3), 2 distinct manuscripts bound together, the first consisting of a calendar and Latin prayers, the second being a Latin psalter. This is a mid-fifteenth-century illuminated English manuscript on vellum, the second part of which was written for Lady Anne Neville, wife of the first Duke of Buckingham; its name derives from a later owner, Sir Richard Wingfield. Another fine book of hours is that written and illuminated on vellum for Blanche de France, Duchess of Orleans (Spencer Ms. 56). This is northern French work, probably Parisian, from the end of the fourteenth century. Of 23 printed books of hours in the Spencer Collection, one of the most celebrated is the *Hore in Laudem Beatissime Virginis Marie* printed in Paris by Simon du Bois in 1527 with woodcut illustrations and borders. There are other books of hours in the Arents Collection.

Psalters and Psalm Books

The earliest manuscript psalter in the Spencer Collection is in Latin, written and illuminated

on vellum in South-Western Germany, perhaps Augsburg or Bamberg, about 1235 (Spencer Ms. 11). The La Twyere Psalter (Spencer Ms. 2) is a fine example of English work on vellum, with thirteen pages of miniatures, dated around 1320 and possibly from Yorkshire. Perhaps the greatest treasure of the collection is the Tickhill Psalter (Spencer Ms. 26), so called because it was written and gilded by John Tickhill, Prior of the Abbey of Worksop (now Radnor) near Coventry in the early fourteenth century.[13] With its wealth of illuminations, some in various states of completion, it is one of the most important surviving examples of English Gothic illumination. It was purchased in 1932 from the libraries of the Marquess of Lothian through the Spencer Fund and with the generous aid of an anonymous trustee. Another outstanding psalter (Spencer Ms. 130) was written and illuminated on vellum by Matteo Felice of Naples about 1475. In the Manuscripts and Archives Division there are 4 psalters of the thirteenth through the fifteenth centuries.

There are notable examples of printed psalters and their descendants, psalm books, in both the Spencer Collection and the Rare Book Division. The famous "Bay Psalm Book," *The Whole Book of Psalmes Faithfully Translated into English Metre* (Cambridge, Mass., 1640), was the first book printed in what is now the United States, and forms a cornerstone of the Americana collection of the Research Libraries. The Rare Book Division's example is 1 of 11 known copies.[14] A later version also in the division, entitled *The Psalms Hymns and Spiritual Songs of the Old and New Testaments* (Cambridge, Mass., 1651), is the only copy known to exist of 2,000 originally printed.[15] The first psalm book of John Wesley, *A Collection of Psalms and Hymns* (Charleston, 1737), is 1 of 2 copies known to have survived.[16]

Missals

The Manuscripts and Archives Division owns a folio missal on vellum of the fourteenth century. It is written in large Gothic letters in black and red and illuminated with a single large illustration, historiated initials, and leaf-scroll decorations. Three other missals on vellum date from the fifteenth century. In the Spencer Collection a magnificent and richly ornamented missal from Bologna (Spencer Ms. 64), dating from the latter half of the fifteenth century, has miniatures and initial letters by Bartolommeo Bossi and others. The Spencer Collection printed missals range from incunabula (such as *Missale Brixinense*) to illustrated examples of the eighteenth century.

---

12. Illustrations from these and other illuminated manuscripts are reproduced in Karl Kup, "The Christmas Story in Medieval and Renaissance Manuscripts from the Spencer Collection," *BNYPL* 73 (1969): 625–746. Published separately by the library.

13. See Donald Drew Egbert, "The Tickhill Psalter," *BNYPL* 36 (1932): 663–78, and *The Tickhill Psalter and Related Manuscripts*, (The New York Public Library and the Department of Art and Archaeology of Princeton University, 1940).

14. See Stevens, *Lenox*, pp. 44–9. See also Bradford F. Swan, "Some Thoughts on the Bay Psalm Book," *Yale University Library Gazette* 22 (1948): 51–76.

15. See Stevens, *Lenox*, p. 137.

16. See Martha Winburn England, "The First Wesley Hymn Book," *BNYPL* 68 (1964): 225–38.

Other Devotionals, *ars moriendi*, etc.

The Spencer Collection houses numerous fine examples of illustrated devotional books, both manuscript and printed, including such interesting items as a "girdle book" breviary written by Brother Sebaldus of the monastery of Kastl, near Eichstätt, Germany, dated 1454 (Spencer Ms. 39). Psalms, hymns, prayers, and canticles are found in an Armenian manuscript dated before 1489. A Melchite *horologion* printed in Fano, September 12, 1514, is the first book printed in Arabic characters. The Spencer Collection's copy is printed in red and black with woodcut borders. An *ordinarium* printed in Mexico in 1556 in the Rare Book Division contains the first music printed in the New World, and is one of two known copies. There are also manuscripts from Ethiopia, and a book of prayers of the seventeenth century.

Among 7 fifteenth-century *ars moriendi* printed in Germany and France are a block book printed in Latin in Germany in 1470 (Rare Book Division) and a Leipzig printed version of 1495 (Spencer Collection). Other examples span the sixteenth century.

Book of Common Prayer

The collections of the Church of England *Book of Common Prayer* begin with the edition of 1604. The Protestant Episcopal Church of America editions include those of 1790 and 1793 and many later editions. Three eighteenth-century translations made by the Society for the Propagation of the Gospel in Foreign Parts into the Mohawk (Mahaque Indian) language are of note, the earliest dated 1715 and printed by William Bradford. Decorated copies of the seventeenth century are to be found in the Spencer Collection.

BIBLES

COLLECTING POLICY AND HISTORICAL SURVEY

Works about the Bible, the history of the Bible, bibliographies, dictionaries, and encyclopedias of the Bible are collected comprehensively; other aspects of the subject are representatively or selectively covered. Although the Research Libraries do not attempt specialization in this field, the representation of Bibles in the special collections is unusually rich and extensive, and there is a wide range of translations in the general collections. Most of the Bible rarities were acquired by James Lenox.[17]

A tabulation of the census figures for Bibles and biblical literature in the Research Libraries will give some indication of the growth of the collections in this area:

1921	11,695 volumes
1930	12,787
1941	10,000[18]
1966	17,100

In the 1853 report of the Astor Library, Joseph Cogswell notes the presence of "the best editions of the Hebrew and Greek Scriptures, the Walton Polyglott, various editions of the Vulgate, and numerous versions of the whole Bible, and of parts of it, in the principal languages of Europe

and the East."[19] The consolidation of the Astor and Lenox Libraries in 1895 brought the Lenox Bible rarities together with the Astor standard works and other rarities that had been added, principally in the 1880s. An interesting collection deposited by the American Bible Society in 1897 was withdrawn in 1937 when the society was able to provide adequate space for the collection in a new building.

The Spencer Collection, which came to the Research Libraries in 1913, added a further group of illustrated Bibles, many in fine bindings. In 1929 Edward S. Harkness gave a ninth-century Gospels in Latin, the Landevennec Gospels, described on page 76. The collection of examples of African, Oceanic, and Indic dialects was materially increased and strengthened in 1932 by the purchase of Bibles used in missionary work from the American Board of Commissioners for Foreign Missions.

RESOURCES

Although the Research Libraries do not attempt specialization in this field, as do the Union Theological Seminary and the General Theological Seminary, an idea of the great extent of the collection can be gained by noting that some 44 card catalog trays are required for references on the Bible—an estimated total of 33,700 cards. The range of holdings is demonstrated by estimates of the number of editions of the English Bible available: 80 editions of the sixteenth century, 260 of the seventeenth century, 200 of the eighteenth century, and over 970 of the nineteenth century. This generous representation is due to a policy of retaining every imprint before 1900, even if only slight variations are apparent. All important twentieth-century editions are also present, and texts in foreign languages are well represented. Expository and biographical works meet the research needs of the layman and are frequently useful to the scholar.

Curiosities are not lacking. There is an outstanding collection of Bibles in shorthand in various English systems, beginning with William Addy's in the sixteenth century and continuing to the current systems of the twentieth, as well as in the systems of continental Europe.[20] Also included is an interesting representation of miniature Bibles.[21]

The Jewish Division holds approximately 4,000 volumes of Biblical editions and critical commentaries. Works are found in Hebrew, Yiddish, Ladino, and other languages, as well as in the Western European tongues. The collecting policies are similar to the general policy of the Research Libraries.

Two additional features of the Bible collection are noteworthy: the Local History and Genealogy Division records all Bibles in which family history and vital records have been entered; some 1,140 references to notable illustrated editions appear in the Public Catalog.

Translations

One of the particular strengths of the Bible collections is the wide range of languages into

---

17. Stevens, *Lenox*, pp. 33, 36.

18. The figure for 1941 reflects the withdrawal by the American Bible Society of its deposit collection in 1937.

19. Lydenberg, *History*, p. 26.

20. See *BNYPL* 38 (1934): 746–95, 866–96.

21. See Victor Hugo Paltsits, "An Exhibition of Bibles of Ancient and Modern Times in Various Languages," *BNYPL* 27 (1923): 3–18.

which the Biblical texts have been translated. Some idea of the variety of languages can be gained from an enumeration of languages and dialects entered in the catalog for the first four letters of the alphabet, A–D: the Old Testament appears in five tongues, the New Testament in thirty-five, and the complete Bible in nineteen. Among minor languages and dialects, those of the American Indian and of African and Indic languages are best represented.

The Slavonic Division has very rare Gospel translations into Mordvinian and Mari made by the Russian Bible Society in 1821 before these languages became literary, New Testaments translated into Livornian in the early nineteenth century, and a first edition of the Bible in Lettish (Riga, 1685–89). The Berg Collection holds the only translation of the Gospels into the Gypsy language in the collections: a translation of the Gospel of St. Luke made by George Borrow (1837). A copy of the second edition (1871) in proof sheets has alterations and corrections in Borrow's hand.

Rarities

Printed Bibles: Most of the early Bibles or Testaments in the Research Libraries were acquired by James Lenox. The most important is the so-called Gutenberg, or 42-line Bible, the first book executed in Europe from movable metal type. The Lenox copy, now in the Rare Book Division, was purchased in 1847 for £500; it was the first Gutenberg Bible to come to the United States. On paper, rubricated but without illumination, it is bound in two volumes. Until 1923 it lacked the first four leaves. In that year Gabriel Wells presented the library with the originals of leaves two, three, and four in the book's first setting of 40-lines; the first leaf is still lacking.[22]

Block books are considered among the rarest of fifteenth-century publications; six of them in the Rare Book Division are Biblical texts: three *Biblia Pauperum*, "Bibles of the Poor," the earliest dated 1465 and printed in the Netherlands; and three copies of the *Apocalypsis Sancti Johannis*, the earliest dated 1465 and printed in Germany.

Other Bibles in the Rare Book Division include the first printings in Arabic, Dutch, French, Hebrew, Bohemian, English, Swedish, Danish, and Armenian; Luther's translation of the New Testament, the first of all the many subsequent Protestant Testaments and Bibles; and the first Catholic Bibles in English. Indicative of the richness of the resources of the Research Libraries not only in Bibles but in American Indian languages are the copies of the first Bible printed in America, the translation into the language of the Massachuset Indians made by the Reverend John Eliot, often called Eliot's Indian Bible—the Rare Book Division holds copies of the New Testament (1661) and the complete Bible (1663); there is a copy of the New Testament in the Berg Collection.

The Pitcairn Bible (Edinburgh, 1764), a Bible of unusual interest as an association copy, was presented to the library in 1924 by Eliza H. Lord, Daniel M. Lord, Herbert G. Lord, and Harriet Lord Bradford. Carried aboard H.M.S. *Bounty* in 1787, it stayed on the ship until taken off at Pitcairn Island, where it remained for almost fifty years until it was brought to the United States and came into the possession of the Lord family.[23]

Curious examples of the Bible in the collections are the so-called Vinegar Bible, the Murderer's Bible, the Ear Bible, Cromwell's Souldiers Pocket Bible, and the Wicked Bible. In the latter, published in London, 1631, there are many gross and scandalous typographical errors, among them the omission of the important word "not" in the Seventh Commandment. The Lenox copy is one of six known.[24] Equally rare is a German Wicked Bible (Halle, 1731).

The Spencer Collection's holdings of illustrated Bibles include the famous Malermi Bible (Venice, 1493), which takes its name from Niccolò Malermi who translated it into Italian,[25] the Cologne Bible of 1478, copies of two notable Augsburg imprints, the Sorg Bible of 1480 and the Schönsperger Bible of 1487, the Lübeck Bible of 1494, and other later editions collected for their illustrations or fine bindings.

Manuscript Bibles: Many of the manuscript Bibles and Testaments in the Research Libraries are among their greatest treasures. The earliest medieval manuscript in the Manuscripts and Archives Division, and one of the finest in the United States, is an "Evangelistarium, sive Lectiones ex Evangeliis" (De Ricci, NYPL 1), written for a monastery dedicated to St. Michael, doubtless in Germany. It is on vellum with many pages written in gold on purple.[26] The ninth-century Landevennec Gospels (De Ricci, NYPL 115), presented by Edward S. Harkness in 1929, was written in Brittany and illustrated with rough colored drawings.[27] A thirteenth-century Pentateuch is one of the oldest manuscripts of the Samaritans of Nablus. There are 12 Latin Bibles of the thirteenth and fourteenth centuries in the Manuscripts and Archives Division, of English, French, and Italian workmanship. There is also the oldest extant complete manuscript (fourteenth century) of Wycliffe's New Testament (De Ricci, NYPL 67). Fifteenth-century manuscripts on vellum include 4 copies of Purvey's revision of Wycliffe's New Testament, and an Apocalypse of the early part of the century (De Ricci, NYPL 15). The "Lectionarium Evangeliorum" written in Italy about 1540 contains 6 large and several small miniatures of great beauty by Giulio Clovio. It was executed for Cardinal Alessandro Farnese, who presented

---

22. See Stevens, *Lenox*, pp. 20–23. See also Lewis M. Stark, "The Lenox Gutenberg Bible; 1847–1947," *BNYPL* 51 (1947): 583–5; Victor Hugo Paltsits, "The First Printed Bible," *BNYPL* 56 (1952): 487–92. Other descriptions of rare Bibles include Victor Hugo Paltsits, "An Exhibition of Bibles of Ancient and Modern Times in Various Languages," *BNYPL* 27 (1923): 3–18; Lewis M. Stark, "Twenty-five Rare Bibles 1455–1782; An Exhibition from the Reserve Division," *BNYPL* 61 (1957): 605–10; Lewis M. Stark and Maud D. Cole, "Bibles in Many Languages 1455–1966," *BNYPL* 70 (1966): 495–504.

23. See "The Pitcairn Bible," *BNYPL* 28 (1924): 443–52.

24. See Stevens, *Lenox*, pp. 27–32.

25. See Frank Weitenkampf, "The Malermi Bible and the Spencer Collection," *BNYPL* 33 (1929): 779–88. The Spencer copy is the very rare rival edition of 1493, not the first illustrated edition of 1490.

26. See Victor Hugo Paltsits, "The Manuscript Division in The New York Public Library," *BNYPL* 19 (1915): 141.

27. See C. R. Morey, "The Landevennec Gospels," *BNYPL* 33 (1929): 643–53.

it to Pope Paul III. The Lenox Library acquired this masterwork in 1888; it is sometimes called the Towneley Lectionary, the name taken from a former owner.

Several of the manuscript Bibles in the Spencer Collection are also of great interest. An early thirteenth-century illuminated manuscript of the Minor Prophets and Lives of the Saints (De Ricci, Spencer 1) has been identified as coming from the Benedictine Monastery of Weingarten in Swabia.[28] A "Bible historiée et vies des saints" (De Ricci, Spencer 22) in French on vellum was produced in northern France about 1300 and contains over 800 miniatures.

_____

28. See Hanns Swarzenski, "A 13th Century Illuminated Manuscript Minor Prophets and Lives of Saints," *BNYPL* 32 (1928): 647–52.

PART TWO

20

GENERAL LITERATURE

(Including the Berg Collection and the Arents
Collection of Books in Parts)

GENERAL ACQUISITION POLICY

Literature is one of the special strengths of the Research Libraries. Perhaps 25 percent of the volumes in the collections are concentrated here, with notable accumulations of rare and unique materials. The size and scope of the collections make necessary the arrangement of the following chapters in four sections:
1. A general survey of collecting policy by languages and by literary forms.[1]
2. A discussion of this policy in terms of specific administrative units.
3. A description of the general resources in literature, including juvenile literature.
4. Separate descriptions of resources for specific national literatures.

The library collects materials of literary merit (belles-lettres) on a comprehensive basis.[2] The policy of comprehensive collection applies to American, European, and Latin American literature. For the British Commonwealth countries (Canada, Australia, New Zealand, and South Africa), as well as for Scottish literature in both Gaelic and English, and Welsh literature in Celtic, the library attempts representative coverage.

The selection of monographs and serials is systematic for those countries where there are developed bibliographical tools or reliable dealers, but somewhat less systematic for countries where such aids are not available and it is necessary to rely on domestic book selection tools.

Literary texts are normally available in preferred editions. As a rule, the library attempts to

_____

1. The general collecting policies for literatures in non-Roman alphabets (Slavic, Hebrew, Yiddish, and the Oriental languages) are considered in the chapters which deal with the library's resources in those areas.

2. For the purposes of the library the term *belles-lettres* is defined as literature, more especially that body of writing comprising drama, poetry, fiction, criticism, and essays, which lives because of inherent imaginative and artistic rather than scientific or philosophic qualities.

secure the first edition of every book wanted and every subsequent edition which adds something to the first through revision, editing, or the addition of exegeses. There are a great number of collected editions of major authors, in addition to the separately published editions of their individual works. The library also acquires the minor works of major literary figures. The Berg Collection collects first appearances in print of the works of English and American authors; since these are often in journals, the collection contains incomplete runs of a number of serial publications.

Literary criticism and biographies of authors form other strong aspects of the literature collection. For major authors, the library collects criticism in all languages, although the literary work itself may be available only in the original language and in English translation (if a translation has been made). The "appreciative" work, designed to introduce an author or literary work to students, is rarely purchased. Textbooks are not usually acquired since the library's research collections are designed for the use of the serious researcher at a mature level.

In contrast to the general policy outlined above, the library deliberately acquires all American literature.

TRANSLATIONS

The library attempts to acquire in its original language every work collected. For major literary figures and writers of nonfiction used in literary studies it acquires the principal English translations, not only because modes of translation change, but also because each translator, consciously or unconsciously, brings to the translation a style of his own. A variant-language edition of a work already in the library is usually added if the variant is (1) in the original language of the work, or (2) in English, or (3) in a language more appropriate for reference use than the edition already in the collection, such as a translation from Finnish into German, or (4) when the translation has significant literary, historical, ideological, or critical interest. The single exception in literature is that made for dramatic texts: the library's holdings in this field are of such strength and depth that these are collected exhaustively.

SELECTION POLICY FOR SPECIFIC GENRES

FICTION

By the definition already given, the library's resources include for the most part fiction of literary distinction; nevertheless all works by recognized authors, whatever their merit, are acquired. American fiction of lesser quality is acquired because it presents local color or reflects social and cultural values; this is also the policy with English fiction, to a somewhat lesser degree. The Berg Collection purchases first and important editions and manuscripts of English and American authors. The Arents Collection of Books in Parts is, as its name indicates, primarily concerned with the acquisition of books issued in parts, regardless of their subject matter; as a great deal of fiction has been issued in this form, particularly in the nineteenth century, the collection helps to enrich resources in this area. The Arents Collection also has a steadily growing group of "shilling shockers" and "penny dreadfuls." A large group of Beadle dime novels is found in the Rare Book Division; these are discussed in full in chapter 23 of this *Guide*. English language science fiction of the late nineteenth and early twentieth centuries is also a feature of the fiction holdings. The Slavonic Division acquires a sampling of current science fiction published in the USSR.

DRAMA

Drama in the Western European languages is a subject which the library attempts to collect exhaustively. In this instance the collecting policy does not take into account the literary merit of the piece. As explained above, dramatic texts in translation are added to the collections when possible regardless of language. Plays of fewer than twenty-five pages have not been acquired in the past. Although the Theatre Collection moved to Lincoln Center in 1965, the collection of printed plays and books about the theatre remains under the jurisdiction of the General Research and Humanities Division. For information about holdings of dramatic texts, the Theatre Collection must rely upon a printed catalog[3] and its extensive holdings of typescripts and prompt-books (described in chapter 33), many of which represent unpublished plays. The Theatre Collection's holdings of the shooting scripts of motion pictures and radio and television scripts are also extensive.

In 1950 the Library was assigned the Farmington Plan[4] responsibility for drama in general, i.e., collections and works on the drama as a literary genre. Drama for individual countries remains the responsibility of other libraries assigned to national literatures, but this has not affected the efforts of the Research Libraries in this field.

---

3. The New York Public Library, the Research Libraries, *Catalog of the Theatre and Drama Collections; Part I, Drama Collection: Listing by Cultural Origin, Author Listing; Part II, Theatre Collection: Books on the Theatre* (Boston: G. K. Hall & Co., 1967).

4. The Farmington Plan is a voluntary agreement under which major American research libraries have accepted responsibilities for collecting in specific fields as a means of increasing the nation's total resources for research.

POETRY

Following the rule established for literature, the library collects the work of established poets or poets of literary quality. English, American, and Russian poetry are collected comprehensively, French and German representatively, and poetry in other languages selectively. Anthologies, except those designed for school use, are usually secured as they appear. Most older editions of a poet's work are available in the library's holdings, but new editions are purchased only if the critical approach presents a new point of view or includes new materials. As in the case of all literary publications, special press editions are often secured. This is particularly true in the field of poetry, and the Rare Book Division has a significant collection of these publications.

ESSAYS, LETTERS, ETC.

Volumes of essays (except those designed as school textbooks and reprints) are generally secured. Most collections of letters are purchased, since they represent source materials for the critical study of literature and are closely allied to biography, a subject well covered in the collections.

Literature in all languages forms a vast subject area and is the responsibility of many divisions and special collections within the library. The General Research and Humanities Division has the major responsibility for the library's resources in this field: this includes the literature of America and England, the literature of Europe (except that written in the Cyrillic alphabet), and classical literature. The Slavonic Division collects and houses the Balto-Slavic literature (in the Cyrillic alphabet and in translation), and the Oriental Division is responsible for literature written in the Near and Far Eastern languages. The Jewish Division collects and houses Hebrew and Yiddish literature in the original languages and in translation, as well as material in any language relating to Jews and Judaism.

The Spencer Collection acquires fine illustrated books. The Arents Collection of Books in Parts purchases book material of any kind issued in parts. Originally the collection acquired material in the English language, but over the years its policy has widened to include books in parts in other languages. The Arents Tobacco Collection includes almost every important historical work dealing directly with tobacco, but also contains many literary works in which references to tobacco are only incidental; examples are Edmund Spenser's *The Faerie Queene* (1590), with the first known reference in English poetry to tobacco ("diuine Tobacco" and "Soueraine weede"); Charles Lamb's "A Farewell to Tobacco" in manuscript, dated about 1805; Sir Walter Scott's "The Minstrel's Pipe" (ca. 1806), also in holograph; and among more contemporary materials William Faulkner's manuscript "Father Abraham," a first draft of his novel *The Hamlet*, in which chewing tobacco figures prominently.

The Berg Collection collects first and important editions and manuscripts in English and American literature. The collection is strong in nineteenth-century authors. The Rare Book Division has restricted its purchases of first editions in English and American literature in order not to duplicate the holdings of the Berg Collection, but it continues to acquire first editions and literary rarities in other languages. The division maintains a strong collection of literary bibliographies. The Manuscripts and Archives Division is actively seeking to build up its already extensive resources in English and American authors of the nineteenth and twentieth centuries and modern Irish authors. It solicits the editorial files of publishing houses which furnish a wealth of primary source material in the correspondence of authors and editors. Since New York City is a center of authorship and publishing, the Manuscripts and Archives Division assumes the responsibility for gathering examples of the literature of the different periods in the city's history.

Many divisions of the library, described fully in other sections of this *Guide*, are involved in the acquiring of literature as a specific part of their full collecting responsibilities. In the following section only those special collections which are most strongly connected with literature in the Roman alphabet will be considered: the Berg Collection and the Arents Collection of Books in Parts.

THE BERG COLLECTION OF ENGLISH AND AMERICAN LITERATURE

The Berg Collection contains first and important editions, original manuscripts, and autograph letters in the field of English and American literature (some 70,000 pieces). Its particular strength is in the nineteenth and twentieth centuries. The collection is open to the public upon presentation of an admission card obtained from the Research Libraries Administrative Office.

A history of the Berg Collection reveals the development of its present structure. Shortly before the death of Dr. Henry W. Berg in 1938, a younger brother, Dr. Albert A. Berg, approached the New York Public Library to discuss the donation of their collection of rare books.[5] After the death of Henry W. Berg, his brother presented in his memory the 3,500 items which they had accumulated over the course of three decades. This initial gift in February 1940 was the beginning of the memorial Henry W. and Albert A. Berg Collection. One of the conditions of the gift was that the library should allocate special rooms for the collection, the upkeep of which would be provided from a fund established by Berg. The gift consisted of a good collection of first editions of Dickens and Thackeray, early favorites of the brothers, as well as first editions of other nineteenth-century authors. There were also a number of manuscripts.

Berg's desire to build the collection increased. In September 1940 he purchased and presented to the library the collection of William Thomas Hildrup Howe, late president of the American Book Company. The Howe collection consisted of 16,000 pieces, including first and early editions, presentation copies, manuscripts, and important autograph letters, particularly of the nineteenth and early twentieth centuries. Individual items of outstanding importance are the famous Roseberry

copy of Keats's *Endymion* (1818) presented to Leigh Hunt by the author; Cooper's own copy of *The Spy* (1827) interleaved with manuscript corrections and additions; a first edition of Edgar Allan Poe's *Tamerlane* (1827); many Thackerary letters, literary manuscripts, sketchbooks, and drawings; and Dickens's own public reading copies of *The Chimes, A Christmas Carol, David Copperfield, Nicholas Nickleby at the Yorkshire School*, and other works.[6]

Shortly thereafter Dr. Berg learned that Owen D. Young, formerly chairman of the board of the General Electric Company, wished to sell his collection. Berg arranged to purchase an undivided half-interest in the Young collection for the library, and Young presented the remainder. Described as of "almost fabulous proportions," the Young collection numbered between 10,000 and 15,000 books, manuscripts, and other English and American literary treasures. Beginning with the fifteenth century, it included the Pynson printing (1490) of *Canterbury Tales*; 4 Shakespeare folios (including the Dean Sage copy of the first folio); a 1640 edition of Shakespeare's poems; Bacon's own copy, with his crest, of *Instauratio magna* (1620); Alexander Pope's copy of Milton's *Poems* (1645), and a first edition of "Comus" (1637); William Blake's hand-colored *Songs of Innocence* (1789) and *The Book of Thel* (1789)[7]; the Kilmarnock edition of Robert Burns's *Poems* (1786); 1 of the finest of 12 known copies of Poe's *Tamerlane* (1827); "Alice's copy" of the withdrawn first edition of *Alice's Adventures in Wonderland* (1866); and the dedication copy of Thackeray's *Vanity Fair* (1848). Among the original manuscripts are the extensive literary archive (some 2,500 items) of Fanny Burney (Frances Burney d'Arblay), Keats's final letter to Fanny Brawne, and Samuel Clemens's manuscripts of *A Connecticut Yankee in King Arthur's Court* and *Following the Equator*.

By 1941 the Berg Collection had become a rare book and manuscript collection of first

---

5. Dr. Henry W. Berg (1858–1938) was a specialist in the treatment of smallpox and diphtheria, and a teacher at Columbia University and Mount Sinai Hospital. Dr. Albert A. Berg (1872–1950) was an authority on the treatment of cancer and ulcer of the stomach, and a consulting surgeon at Mount Sinai and Montefiori Hospitals.

6. See *A Christmas Carol: The Public Reading Version*, a facsimile, with introduction and notes by Philip Collins (The New York Public Library, 1971); and *Mrs. Gamp; A Facsimile of the Author's Prompt Copy*, with introduction and notes by John D. Gordan (The New York Public Library, 1956). See also Philip Collins, "The Texts of Dickens' Readings," *BNYPL* 74 (1970): 360–80, and *BNYPL* 75 (1971): 63.

7. See *The Book of Thel; A Facsimile and a Critical Text*, ed. by Nancy Bogen (The New York Public Library and Brown Univ. Press, 1971). Other Young treasures are described in a memorial catalog published by the library in 1974.

8. See John D. Gordan, "A Doctor's Benefaction," *PBSA* 38 (1954): 303–14. For bibliographical descriptions of the collection's holdings, see Gordan's exhibition catalogues, which are listed in *BNYPL* 72 (1968): 285–87; and those by Lola L. Szladits published since 1968: "New in the Berg Collection: 1962–1964," *BNYPL* 73 (1969): 227–52; *Pen & Brush: The Author as Artist*, with Harvey Simmonds (The New York Public Library, 1969); *Charles Dickens 1812–1870; An Anthology . . . from Materials in the Berg Collection* (The New York Public Library and Arno Press, 1970); "New in the Berg Collection: 1965–1969," *BNYPL* 75 (1971): 9–29, published separately by the library, with additions; *1922: A*

quality.[8] In another twenty years of growth notable author collections were built up (Arnold Bennett, Joseph Conrad, George Gissing, Thomas Hardy, John Masefield, Bernard Shaw); among important literary archives which have come into the collection are those of Lady Gregory, Sir Edward Marsh, Sean O'Casey, and Virginia Woolf.

SPECIAL INDEXES AND FILES

The Berg's Collection's holdings have not been incorporated into the Public Catalog of the Research Libraries. The collection maintains its own catalog (which was published in book form in five volumes by G. K. Hall & Company of Boston in 1969); but in the future new book acquisitions will be included in the *Dictionary Catalog of the Research Libraries*. Catalog cards detail bibliographical points; the letters "H," "Y," and "B" identify material from the Howe collection, the Young collection, and the original Berg collection.

There are three special files in the collection. The Correspondent File provides a record of letters under the name of the recipient. The Provenance File lists a selection of association copies and manuscripts under the name of the recipient, or under the name of the donor and recipient if the donor is other than the author of the work. The Portrait File locates portraits in the collection.

THE ARENTS COLLECTION OF BOOKS IN PARTS

The Arents Tobacco Collection was deposited in the library in 1944. In 1923 George Arents had started a companion collection of books in parts which he gave to the library in 1957, adding to it each year until his death in 1961. Since that time this collection has doubled in size to 1,273 pieces, including books and associated items; it is housed in the room adjacent to the tobacco collection and is open to the public upon presentation of an admission card obtained from the Research Libraries Administrative Office. In the description and checklist of the collection published by the library in 1957, the first curator, Sarah A. Dickson, pointed out that "So far as has been ascertained this is the only library assembled on the principle that the books therein appeared serially in separate numbers and are still in their original state. Books in parts may be defined as works by an author or authors which are published piecemeal over a period of time, each unit having its separate cover." From the beginning it was the policy to collect also associated material such as manuscripts, original drawings, and illustrations.

Only items in the English language were acquired at first, but in time the policy was relaxed (with Arents's permission) to include items in other languages. Dr. Dickson remarked that "the most striking feature of the literature which was issued in parts is its great diversity. Almost every type of book and author is represented in the Arents collection."

The earliest item in the collection is *Musica Transalpina, Madrigales Translated of Foure, Five and Sixe Parts* by Yonge (1588). The excessive rarity of seventeenth- and eighteenth-century books in parts has interested the collection in endeavoring to build up its resources in this area. The Victorian authors Dickens, Charles Lever, Thackeray, and Anthony Trollope are heavily represented, as is Sir Walter Scott. Twentieth century works issued in parts are also included. The checklist of the collection appeared in 1957,[9] supplemented in 1964.[10]

SIGNIFICANT GIFTS

Certain important gifts are listed alphabetically below. All of these are literary in nature, some exclusively and others predominantly.

DeCoursey Fales Collection of Literary Manuscripts

Consisting of 9 boxes and 9 volumes of holograph letters, manuscripts, and other materials of English and American literary personages of the eighteenth to twentieth centuries, the collection was donated during the period 1951 to 1963. Among the authors represented are Thomas Burke, Robert W. Chambers, Bret Harte, Emile Zola, Julia Ward Howe, Charlotte Yonge, Edward Bulwer-Lytton, Douglas Jerrold, and Wilkie Collins.

Harkness Collection

The 700-volume bequest in 1950 from the library of the late Edward S. Harkness, a trustee of the library from 1919 to 1929, was a valuable addition to the library's literature collections.[11] The group comprises miscellaneous literature, art reference books, extra-illustrated sets, important first editions, association books, and original drawings, in addition to manuscripts. Among them is a famous modern rarity—a fine copy of T. E. Lawrence's *Seven Pillars of Wisdom* privately printed for the author in 1926. One of the choicest volumes is a copy of the first edition of Shakespeare's *Poems* (1640). There are some 95 original pencil or watercolor drawings, including some by Hablôt K. Browne ("Phiz"). The 21 volumes from George Washington's library are perhaps the most significant in the group; all but 2 have Washington's bold signature.

There are 6 literary manuscripts, holographs of Thackeray, Whittier, Thoreau, and Mark Twain. Among the Revolutionary manuscripts are 2 letters from George Washington. Harkness gave other manuscript items over the course of the years, among the most important of which are the fifteenth-century "Livre du Petit Artus" and

---

Vintage Year (The New York Public Library, 1972); and *Documents: Famous & Infamous* (The New York Public Library, 1972). See also *BNYPL* for other descriptions of important acquisitions, for example, "O'Casey Papers Acquired," 73 (1969): 357–58; Ronald Ayling, "A Note on Sean O'Casey's Manuscripts and His Working Methods," 73 (1969): 359–67; and "The Writer's Diary" [Virginia Woolf], 75 (1971): 7.

9. Sarah Augusta Dickson, *The Arents Collection of Books in Parts and Associated Literature; A Complete Checklist* (The New York Public Library, 1957).

10. Perry O'Neil, *The Arents Collection of Books in Parts and Associated Literature; A Supplement to the Checklist 1957–1963* (The New York Public Library, 1964).

11. See Robert W. Hill and Lewis M. Stark, "The Edward S. Harkness Collection," *BNYPL* 54 (1950): 585–94.

a valuable collection relating to sixteenth- and early seventeenth-century printers, mainly Peruvian.

MARY STILLMAN HARKNESS COLLECTION

In 1951, Mary Stillman Harkness, widow of Edward Harkness, bequeathed her collection to the library.[12] Like her husband's gift, it contains general literature, first editions, manuscripts, and original drawings. The outstanding feature is a set of the 4 folio editions of Shakespeare's *Comedies, Histories and Tragedies,* published in 1623, 1632, 1664, and 1685. Several nineteenth- and twentieth-century English authors are represented, particularly Dickens, Thackeray, and Conrad: the 40 Conrad first editions supplement 15 in Harkness's bequest. Mrs. Harkness's collection contains a large number of important nineteenth- and twentieth-century illustrated books. Among these books are 36 volumes illustrated by Arthur Rackham and 23 original watercolor drawings by Rackham, now housed in the Spencer Collection. The manuscripts include a superb group of 13 letters and documents, either in the hand of Benjamin Franklin or bearing his signature. The literary manuscripts in the Americana portion are dominated by a series of holograph essays by Edgar Allan Poe. There are manuscripts by Ruskin, Dickens, and Walter Crane.

LITERARY TYPESCRIPTS

The Manuscripts and Archives Division houses a large collection of typescripts, amounting to approximately 450 items and representing a great number of subjects ranging from belles-lettres to sociology. Dating for the most part from the late 1930s and 1940s, they represent the effort made at that time to accumulate typescripts, principally those of contemporary American authors. The Emma Mills memorial collection represents contributions of typescripts in memory of the late literary agent, starting from 1956. More recently acquired items include works by Marchette Chute, Beatrice J. Chute, and William Inge.

MACMILLAN ARCHIVES

In 1965 the Macmillan Company turned over its archives to the New York Public Library. These archives, housed in the Manuscripts and Archives Division, consist of 119 copy-books for editorial correspondence over the period from 1889 to 1907. In addition are approximately 16,000 letters from Macmillan authors during the first half of the twentieth century. Notable among the 710 included are: Gertrude Atherton (405 letters), Liberty Hyde Bailey (992 letters), the American author Winston Churchill (459 letters), Jack London (279 letters), John Masefield (443 letters), Edgar Lee Masters (159 letters), Marianne Moore (51 letters), H. G. Wells (235 letters), and Owen Wister (412 letters). Two bestselling novels are documented by extensive files, Margaret Mitchell's *Gone with the Wind* and Kathleen Winsor's *Forever Amber.*[13]

JOHN QUINN MEMORIAL COLLECTION

The John Quinn memorial collection in the Manuscripts and Archives Division, consisting of some 10,000 letters and 30 correspondence copybooks, was given to the library by Quinn's niece and goddaughter, Mrs. Thomas F. Conroy, beginning in 1962.[14] The collection comprises the correspondence to and from Quinn dating from about 1900 to his death in 1924. It reflects his years of friendship with members of the Irish Literary Renaissance and the Irish Home Rule Movement, with English and American literary figures, and with art dealers and artists of France, England, and the United States. It also gives insight into the social and professional life of a successful lawyer of that period. In 1936 the estate of John Quinn presented to the library a typewritten transcript, in 13 volumes, of an edited selection of the correspondence. The originals of these letters, included in the memorial collection, represent only a small part of the whole.

Of central importance in the correspondence are letters from such Irish notables as William Butler Yeats (127 items, with several hundred letters from other members of the Yeats family), Maud Gonne MacBride (56 items), Lady Gregory (148 items), George W. Russell (103 items), James Stephens (23 items), Douglas Hyde (131 items), Sir Roger Casement (21 items), James Joyce (32 items). English and American literary figures include Arthur Symons (122 items), Joseph Conrad (72 items), Frank Harris (30 items), Wyndham Lewis (17 items), James G. Huneker (200 items), Ezra Pound (253 items), and T. S. Eliot (27 items).

A large body of the correspondence relates to Quinn's assembling of what was certainly one of the most important private collections of paintings of contemporary artists, a collection which was dispersed within three years of his death. Correspondence with art dealers, with Henri-Pierre Roché who served as Quinn's adviser in France, and with Walter Pach who acted in a similar capacity in the United States, as well as with the artists themselves, is described in chapter 28 of this *Guide.*

THE J. E. SPINGARN COLLECTION OF CRITICISM AND LITERARY THEORY

The library's collection of literary criticism was strengthened in 1926 by Dr. Joel Spingarn's gift of approximately 1,000 books and pamphlets relating to literary criticism, literature, and aesthetics, including some important early works.[15] In 1955, Mrs. Spingarn presented her late husband's papers and documents bearing on American literary criticism, military history, and issues of academic freedom.[16] Correspondence relating to Spingarn's Troutbeck Press is also included.

WARBURG COLLECTION

The library acquired in 1941, as the gift of Mrs. Felix M. Warburg, a collection of over 100 rare books and manuscripts, ranging from fif-

---

12. See Lewis M. Stark and Robert W. Hill, "The Bequest of Mary Stillman Harkness," *BNYPL* 55 (1951): 213–24.

13. See *BNYPL* 71 (1967): 3.

14. See Harvey Simmonds, "John Quinn . . . ," *BNYPL* 72 (1968): 569–86. Published separately by the library. An inventory and index were published in *BNYPL* 78 (1975): 145–230.

15. See *BNYPL* 30 (1926): 225.

16. See *BNYPL* 59 (1955): 99.

teenth-century illuminated Books of Hours to a set of Thackeray's *The Newcomes* in the original parts. The collection is general in character and not confined to a single field of collecting. It contains manuscripts, examples of early printing, Americana, first editions, and fine bindings.[17]

WELD MEMORIAL COLLECTION

In memory of her husband, Mrs. Francis Minot Weld presented to the library in 1950 more than 1,600 volumes from his collection of general literature, reference books, and first editions, together with a fund for the purchase of books in the fields in which Weld was interested, especially French and German literature.[18] The earliest book in the group is Joachim Du Bellay's *Les Oevvres Françoises* (1569). There are first editions of Molière and Victor Hugo. Weld's collection of German authors contained numerous first editions of Goethe, Schiller, Heine, Grillparzer, and Lessing. There are also important English and American first editions.

WELLS BEQUEST

In 1947, Gabriel Wells, a prominent New York book dealer, stipulated in his will that the library might select from his shelves rare books and manuscripts to the value of $10,000.[19] Among other items chosen were the first and second editions of Richard de Bury's *Philobiblon* (1473, 1483), the first translations of Seneca into English by Jasper Heywood, and the *Quadripartitum* of Claudius Ptolemaeus (1484). Manuscript items include material relating to the early history of New York, as well as holograph items of Washington Irving and Robert Louis Stevenson.

GENERAL HOLDINGS

LITERARY BIBLIOGRAPHIES

It is the library's aim to be comprehensive in this all-important field. A full discussion of bibliographies will be found in chapter 3 of this *Guide*; considered here are only bibliographies in the field of literature. The general collections of national and trade bibliographies of Germany, France, Spain, and other countries are shelved in the Main Reading Room. Also in this location are bibliographies of a number of literary forms and special subjects, such as the *Bibliographie des recueils collectifs de poésies*, the *Catalogue of Manuscripts Containing Anglo-Saxon*, etc. An extensive collection of bibliographies of individual authors is found in the Rare Book Division (*KA-). In addition to author bibliographies, this collection covers incunabula, places (arranged by city, state, and country), individual presses and printers, and other nonliterary subject areas. There is a limited duplication of the author bibliographies in the general collections.

PERIODICAL AND SOCIETY PUBLICATIONS

This is a strong group, numbering about 500 titles with generally complete files of such journals as the Dutch *De Boekzaal* (1692–1863); the *Allgemeine deutsche Bibliothek*; the *Allgemeine Literatur-Zeitung*, the *Analytical Review*, the *Critical Review*, the *Monthly Review*, and others beginning in the eighteenth century; the *Jahrbücher der Literatur*, the *Revue critique d'histoire et de littérature*, and others commencing in the nineteenth century. The library also has rich collections of American university literary studies and philological journals. Supplementing the periodical and society publications are the various newspaper book reviews—the New York *Herald Tribune's Books*, the London *Times Literary Supplement*, the *New York Times Book Review*, and others. In cases of incomplete files full runs can be consulted in the Newspaper Collection either in their original form or on microfilm. Related sources for reviews are an extensive collection of general periodicals commencing in the eighteenth century.

More than 50 general literary periodicals are currently received. Most of them are from the United States, England, or Western Europe, although titles from other countries include the *East-West Review* (Kyoto, 1964–   ), the *Literary Criterion* (Mysore, 1961–   ), *Inostrannaya literatura* (Moscow, 1956–   ), and a partial film record of *El libro* (Buenos Aires, 1953–   ). A far greater number of literary periodicals are discussed in the sections on the various national literatures.

Literary annuals and gift books are well represented in the library's holdings. Of some 700 titles, most of which appeared during the period 1823–65 when annuals and gift books were most popular, 350 are American publications.[20] They include *The Atlantic Souvenir* (1826–32), *The Token* (1828–42), and *The Talisman* (1828–30). In addition the chief of the American antislavery gift books, *The Liberty Bell* (1839–58), is available. British annuals are not quite so well represented, although, among other items, there is a representative set of the first English title of this genre: the *Forget-me-not* (1826–46). German titles include the early *Musen Almanach* (1775–1804). Also included are a number of Mexican gift annuals of the mid-nineteenth century. The collection is being expanded in order to fill in gaps, most particularly in the files of American publications.

FICTION

This section includes general fiction, criticism, works on technique, and numerous collections of "best" stories. There are also older collections, such as the *Bibliothèque universelle des Romans . . .* (1775–89). Serials containing fiction appear as well, for example *Short Stories; a Magazine of Select Fiction* (1890–1918). Supplementing serials are the extensive collection of general periodicals, and college and university publications. Associated with fiction in many ways are the library's extensive resources in folklore.

Gifts of fiction have always been an important source for completing the library's holdings in this area. In 1938 and again in 1949–50 the New York Society Library deposited over 13,000 examples of nineteenth-century American fiction. Charles Scribner's Sons in 1952 donated some

17. See Lewis M. Stark, "The Warburg Collection," *BNYPL* 45 (1941): 941–43.

18. See Lewis M. Stark, "The Weld Memorial Collection," *BNYPL* 54 (1950): 350–52.

19. See Lewis M. Stark, "Gabriel Wells Bequest," *BNYPL* 51 (1947): 320–24.

20. The greater part of this collection of annuals was brought together by John Robinson of Salem, Massachusetts, from whom they were secured by Mrs. Henry Draper and presented to the library. See "Catalogue of Literary Annuals and Gift Books in The New York Public Library," *BNYPL* 6 (1902): 270–75.

4,000 volumes representing nearly a complete set of Scribner publications from about 1849 to 1924. Although many of the items were already in the library, the gift filled gaps and replaced worn copies.

POETRY

Certain key acquisitions add distinction to the library's holdings in this literary form. In 1948 the Poetry Society of America deposited with the library, as the first part of a continuing gift which terminated in 1961, a collection of books (many privately printed and difficult to obtain), monthly bulletins, and important papers of the society. A gift received in 1951 consisted of over 100 poems, holographs and typescripts, many of which are believed to be the favorite compositions of their authors. The works of leading American poets are included.

In 1948 the library's extensive holdings of American and English poetry were further enriched by the addition of nearly 300 volumes from the library of Richard Watson Gilder, presented as a gift by his daughters, Miss Rosamond Gilder and Mrs. W. W. Palmer, and his son Rodman Gilder. The gift contains the works of most of the poets of the second half of the nineteenth century in their original bindings; more than half are inscribed by the authors. In 1952, 1957, 1960, and 1962, the gift was increased by a total of about 85 volumes. The collection is kept in the Rare Book Division.[21]

Another donation consists of some 400 volumes of poetry used in preparing Edith Granger's *An Index to Poetry and Recitation* (1904).

DRAMA

General works on drama are contained in this section; drama of each national literature is covered in the appropriate chapters. The section includes certain serial publications, such as the Drama League of America's *Course, Theatergeschichtliche Forschungen*, etc. (General periodicals and journals on the theatre are under the jurisdiction of the Theatre Collection and are discussed under that heading in this *Guide*.) Important materials relating to criticism and playwriting and the religious drama, as well as numerous collections of plays, are included. In addition to contemporary "best plays" (including the one-act), selected by various editors, there are such compilations as the *Spectatoriaale Schouwburg*, the *Teaterbibliotek* of the Svenska Teaterföreningen in Finland, *Det Kongelige Theaters Repertoire*, and others, both early and recent.

These compilations form part of the library's collection of dramas written in the western languages, estimated in 1967 at over 120,000 titles. In that year G. K. Hall & Company published the *Catalog of the Theatre and Drama Collections*.[22] A reasonable estimate of drama holdings in the various national literatures at that time is as follows: American, 20,000; Dutch, 2,800; English, 21,000; French, 22,000; German, 14,000; Italian, 7,100; Portuguese, 3,000; Norwegian and Swedish, 4,400; Spanish, 16,000. Danish and Walloon each have over 1,000 catalog entries, and among those of less than 1,000 but with appreciable numbers are Bohemian, Catalan, Flemish, Polish, and Russian in translation; Scottish, Spanish-American, and others. Many translations of Hebrew and Oriental plays are included.

Jewish, Oriental, and Slavonic drama are discussed with the literatures of these subject areas. In addition to the library's holdings of published dramas, the Theatre Collection possesses a strong and continually growing archive of typescripts and promptbooks of American plays, many of which have never been published; these include the Becks collection of promptbooks, the Dramatists' Guild collections, and individual copies of promptbooks and typescripts, including motion picture scenarios and screen plays. The Theatre Collection also maintains vertical files comprising materials relevant to the drama.

COMPARATIVE LITERATURE

An examination of the entries classed under "Literature, Comparative" in the Public Catalog does not disclose the richness of the library's holdings in this field. Many related titles are classed under such subject headings as "English Literature—Foreign Influence on, French," or "English Literature—Foreign Influence of." The holdings are strong for research in the interrelationships of all national literatures.

Periodicals and society publications in the field are well represented for all countries and include the proceedings of international congresses. They are reinforced by the excellent journal resources in such related areas as folklore, philology, and the various literatures of the world. Reference to periodical articles in comparative literature must be located through the general and specific periodical indexes; there are few index entry cards in the Public Catalog.

LITERARY FORGERIES

The library has a small collection of materials on forgery acquired by gift, but it does not actively seek to expand its holdings. In the Rare Book Division are approximately 80 examples of literary forgeries and false association copies. Most of the material consists of forged signatures in books rather than forged books, with the exception of such items as a Columbus letter to Santangel (1497/1882) and several of the well-known Thomas J. Wise nineteenth-century pamphlets. The Manuscripts and Archives Division has a collection of 3 boxes of forged letters and manuscripts of poems. A great number are forged sixteenth-, seventeenth-, and eighteenth-century Scottish pseudo-historical documents, and spurious manuscripts of Robert Burns's poems made by Alexander Howland "Antique" Smith. Some specimens of the work of Robert Spring in forged Washington and Franklin holographs are included in this group. Representing the work of the modern forger are some false letters of Lincoln and Edgar Allan Poe made by Joseph Cosey, and other curiosities.[23]

---

21. See Lewis M. Stark, "Gilder Poetry Collection," *BNYPL* 52 (1948): 341–54; 56 (1952): 321–23; 61 (1957): 604; 64 (1960): 87; 66 (1962): 383–85.

22. The New York Public Library, the Research Libraries, *Catalog of the Theatre and Drama Collections; Part I, Drama Collection: Listing by Cultural Origin, Author Listing; Part II, Theatre Collection: Books on the Theatre* (Boston: G. K. Hall & Co., 1967).

23. See Gerald D. McDonald, "Association Books from the Library of William Harris Arnold," *BNYPL* 35 (1931): 847–51; "The Shelf of Forgeries," *BNYPL* 37 (1933): 200–04; "Forgeries in the Library," *BNYPL* 41 (1937): 623–28.

21

JUVENILE LITERATURE

GENERAL REMARKS AND COLLECTING POLICY

In the field of juvenile literature, the book selection policies of the Research Libraries bear directly upon the policy of the Central Children's Room in the Donnell Library Center of the Branch Libraries. The original policy of the Research Libraries was to acquire selectively only foreign children's literature, leaving the selection of English and American children's books entirely to the Central Children's Room, along with the general acquisition of books in other languages. This policy has changed considerably. By 1965 the General Research and Humanities Division of the Research Libraries (responsible for book selection in the field of the humanities in Western European languages and in English) was acquiring selectively English and American children's books representative of book production and illustration. Only in German was any systematic selection of children's books as literature being made. Old or rare children's books were not acquired. These Research Libraries collecting guidelines were qualified as follows:

1. Children's books in the native language by an established author of books for adults are purchased.
2. The library will purchase or accept as a gift a new significant edition of a children's book that has become a classic.
3. The library will comprehensively purchase works in English and Western European languages about juvenile literature and juvenile authors.
4. The library will acquire the works of children as authors. (These materials supplement a good collection of books written and illustrated by children in the Central Children's Room.)
5. The library will acquire one current juvenile biography of a United States president for the biography collection.

Other divisions also acquire children's material of specialized subject interest. The American History Division is particularly interested in children's books about American Indians, while the Local History and Genealogy Division is concerned with those about New York City and, to a lesser extent, children's books about heraldry. Works in series which have a reputation of being well illustrated, such as the Junior American Heritage series in the American History Division, are obtained. Art books for children are not acquired. Very few purchases are made of old or rare children's books, although many have been accumulated over the years by the Rare Book Division. Purchases made by that division are in the field of English and American books. The Berg and Arents Collections have no interest in children's books unless the books fall within their collecting fields. The Oriental and Slavonic Divisions do not purchase current children's books unless they are by an established author of adult works, illustrated by a well-known illustrator, or represent a significant edition of a classic. Occasionally a textbook is acquired if it illustrates a historical change in the language. The Jewish Division buys selectively in Hebrew and Yiddish children's literature.

The Economic and Public Affairs Division is highly selective in its acquisition of children's books; for example, it will buy a book on communism written for children or one on the New York Stock Exchange written for teen-agers. The Science and Technology Research Center does not buy or accept current children's books. The Map Division contains a representative selection of books on the elementary techniques of map making and map reading written for children.

Plays written for children are not acquired unless they have been professionally produced, but material about the amateur and professional productions of children's plays and material about any kind of professional entertainment—magic, puppet shows, children's films—is acquired by the Theatre Collection. The Music Division only occasionally acquires children's books. The Dance Collection is highly selective in acquiring children's materials which can be used by the teacher; these include books on singing games and dances at an elementary level, and ballet plots, synopses, and biographies at a junior high school and high school level. These materials are supplemented by a good collection of children's play, music, and folk songs in the Central Children's Room.

CHILDREN'S PERIODICALS

The Research Libraries own a possibly unique file of the very early *Youth's News Paper* (1797), as well as other early American children's periodicals. In addition C. F. Weisse's *Der Kinderfreund* (1775–81) and a partial set of the *Deutsche Jugendzeitung* (Dresden, 1832–48) typify holdings in early European children's periodicals. Some early Russian children's periodicals are available in the Slavonic Division, such as *Detskoĭ* (St. Petersburg, 1815). Both the Central Children's Room of the Branch Libraries and the Research Libraries own substantial runs of one of the best-known of children's magazines in the United States, *St. Nicholas*. Other periodicals available are broken runs of the *Juvenile Miscellany* and the *Youth's Companion*. A most significant acquisition in 1957 was the *Giornale per i bambini* (Rome, 1881–83) which contains the first appearance of Carlo Lovenzini's *La storia di un burratino* ("Pinocchio"). A substantial collection of amateur periodicals is presently housed in the library's Annex, with a supplementary, noncurrent collection located in the Periodicals Section. Extending in date from the last quarter of the nineteenth century through the 1950s, the material consists chiefly of collections formed by Bertram Adler, Charles R. Heins, and Charles W. Smith. These holdings are of interest as they contain examples of children's and young people's writing. Listed in the Public Catalog under the heading "Periodicals, Amateur," the collection has a typed index.

The magazines *Seventeen* (1958–) and *Horn Book* (1933–) are currently available in the Research Libraries; for other juvenile titles the public is referred to the Central Children's Room of the Branch Libraries. Several current periodicals are available in the Jewish, Oriental, and

Slavonic Divisions, although these divisions place no stress on this type of material.

EARLY CHILDREN'S LITERATURE

EDUCATIONAL

Two interesting early horn books are in the library's collections. One in the Rare Book Division, possibly of the eighteenth century, is of wood covered with brick-red paper, with the lesson sheet on the front covered with horn and the back stamped in black with the device of a double-headed eagle. The other, for which there is no indication of date or place of origin, is in the Berg Collection; it is of ivory, paddle-shaped, with alphabet and vowels engraved on the front. There are designs and pictures (including the head of a dog with a pipe in its mouth) on the handle, sides, and back.

In the Spencer Collection is found an early book designed strictly for children, *Catechismus Pro Pueris et Iuventute* (1539), designed to teach the Lutheran catechism to the young. Of similar intent, although intended for Puritan children, is the Rare Book Division copy of John Cotton's *Spiritual Milk for Boston Babes in Either England. Drawn out of the Breasts of both Testaments for their Souls Nourishment* (Cambridg [sic], 1656). This is the only known copy of the earliest American edition. Other religious catechisms are mainly American, ranging from the seventeenth to the nineteenth centuries. Another well-known item in the Rare Book Division is the earliest extant edition of the *New-England Primer Enlarged* (1727). It is the first in an important collection of New England primers of the eighteenth and nineteenth centuries. Also found in the division are primers for American Indian children. Noah Webster's *A Grammatical Institute of the English Language* (1783), better known as Webster's "Spelling Book" or "Blue-backed Speller," forms part of an extensive collection of schoolbooks by this great educator, many of them his personal copies. The collection of Confederate school books in the Rare Book Division is also of interest, both in content and as examples of printing.

The Schatzki collection of children's books was purchased in 1932. Consisting of approximately 700 pieces, the collection was given the special class mark 8-NASZ. Some 15 items in the stacks were transferred to the Rare Book Division, and the outstanding book, an original edition of *Struwwelpeter*, is in the Spencer Collection. Most of the material is in German, published in the seventeenth to nineteenth centuries. Some 100 titles in French and English are from the eighteenth and nineteenth centuries. Also included are a number of German encyclopedic picture books of the second half of the eighteenth and early nineteenth centuries, finely illustrated with hand-colored engravings of the period, among them *Bilder-Akademie für die Jugend* (Nürnberg, 1782). There are also a number of German children's alphabet books and almanacs of the eighteenth century.

The C. C. Darton collection of 427 children's books, most of which bear the Darton publishing imprint, was acquired in 1940. Dating from the late eighteenth to the mid-nineteenth centuries, the majority of the books are of an instructional or moral nature.[1]

CHAPBOOKS, FAIRY TALES, AND OTHER MATERIAL

The collection of English, Scottish, American, and foreign chapbooks numbers about 2,500 pieces, ranging primarily from 1750 to about 1850.[2] A chapbook may be defined as any printed material, from a broadside to a good-sized book, that was carried for sale by a chapman, or peddler. Many chapbooks were designed for children. An alphabetical card catalog of all the chapbooks in the Research Libraries is located in the Rare Book Division, where most of the collection is housed.

Also in the Rare Book Division is a first edition of *Histoires ou contes du temps passé* (1697) of Charles Perrault, perhaps better known as "Mère Loye" (Mother Goose). The Spencer Collection has a second edition of this famous work dated 1700 and a copy of the 1786 edition, which was the first with woodcuts, the earlier editions having been illustrated with engravings.

The Life of Washington the Great (Augusta, Georgia, 1806), by Mason Locke (Parson) Weems, is a much sought-after item. The first four editions of this work were factual biography, but with the fifth the author rewrote the book, inventing the hatchet story and other "very curious anecdotes" which made him and his book famous. William Roscoe's *The Butterfly's Ball* (1807), which broke with the current tradition of the moral tale, is in the Spencer Collection, with a set of original drawings in pen and wash by the artist, William Mulready. Another nursery classic in the Spencer Collection is a first edition of Heinrich Hoffmann-Donner's *Lustige Geschichten und drollige Bilder* (1845), more familiar as *Struwwelpeter* or *Slovenly Peter*. The rarer first edition of the book in English, entitled *The English Struwwelpeter or Pretty Stories and Funny Pictures for Little Children* (Leipsic [sic], 1848), is also in the Spencer Collection.

The Slavonic Division houses a number of early Russian children's books dating from 1740 to the mid-nineteenth century. Among them are bibliographical rarities and specimens of fine printing and illustration.

The Beadle Dime Novel collection was given to the library in 1922 by Dr. Frank P. O'Brien. It includes, among the varied series in which these novels were issued, 68 of the famous "original yellow back novels" which began to appear in 1850. Seventeen of the first 25 titles of this series are in the collection, including a first edition of Edward Ellis's celebrated *Seth Jones*, a story of the New York wilderness in 1785. There were 1,400 items in the collection, now housed in the Rare Book Division, which has not been greatly augmented in succeeding years.[3] In 1963, C. V. Clare gave approximately 900 issues of the *Diamond Dick Weekly* and the *Wild West Weekly*, which serve to supplement the holdings of publications inspired by the Beadle imprints.

---

lished: C. C. Darton, *A Check List of the C. C. Darton Collection of Children's Books* (London: G. Michelmore & Co., 193–?).

2. See Harry B. Weiss, "A Catalogue of the American, English, and Foreign Chapbooks in The New York Public Library," *BNYPL* 39 (1935): 3–34 et seq. Since 1935 the chapbook collection has been augmented, mainly by gift. There is also a collection of chapbooks in the Central Children's Room of the Branch Libraries.

3. "The Beadle Collection," *BNYPL* 26 (1922): 555–628.

---

1. The collection has been assigned the separate class mark 9-NASY. A check list has been pub-

RECENT CHILDREN'S LITERATURE

The holdings of later nineteenth- and early twentieth-century children's fiction are extensive. The William T. Adams stories, written under the pseudonym of Oliver Optic, are complete, and there are substantial runs of the Horatio Alger series, G. A. Henty, Martha Finley, L. Frank Baum, and many others. The Arents Collection of Books in Parts holds a first edition of *The Wonderful Wizard of Oz*, dedicated by the author to his mother, and a series of proofs for illustrations of the work.

The Berg Collection supports the general holdings of the Research Libraries with a number of first editions of classical children's literature, many in multiple copies. For example, the Berg Collection copy of Lewis Carroll's *Alice's Adventures in Wonderland* (1865) is one of a small number of located copies of the first edition withdrawn because of the dissatisfaction of the artist and author with the printing of the pictures. The collection also has seven copies of the second edition, dated London, 1866, and three copies of the earliest American edition of the same year. Two copies of the London, 1866 edition are presentation copies; one to Alice Pleasance Liddell, the original Alice, bound for her in blue morocco with her initials; the second inscribed to her sister, Lorina Charlotte Liddell.

The holdings of twentieth-century children's literature in the Research Libraries are selective. More complete collections of children's fiction in English are to be found in the Central Children's Room of the Branch Libraries. Nonfiction holdings roughly parallel fictional holdings in scope and extent.

PICTURE BOOKS

Kate Greenaway is perhaps the best-represented great children's book illustrator of the late nineteenth century. The Prints Division has a complete set of her *Almanacks* (London, 1883–97, except 1896, not published), and 10 of the 13 issues of the French *Almanach de Kate Greenaway* (Paris, 1885–86, 1888–95). The Arents Collection of Books in Parts, in addition to a complete set of the *Almanacks*, owns several other Kate Greenaway picture books. The Arents Collections also have all the Randolph Caldecott *Picture Books* published from 1878 to 1885. In the Spencer Collection are many books illustrated by Arthur Rackham, Walter Crane Edmund Dulac, and others. Russian picture books in the Slavonic Division number some 350 items and range from the late 1920s to the present. The Research Libraries do not attempt, however, to collect children's picture books except on a very limited basis, and then primarily for their artistic or typographic interest. The most complete holdings of picture books are located in the Central Children's Room of the Branch Libraries.

DRAWINGS BY CHILDREN'S BOOK ARTISTS; LETTERS; MANUSCRIPTS

Although the Mulready drawings for William Roscoe's *The Butterfly's Ball* in the Spencer Collection, and a number of original drawings by George Cruikshank (some of which were intended for children's books) in the Berg Collection are notable, the library's strongest holdings of original drawings center on the English book artists of the late nineteenth century—Randolph Caldecott, Walter Crane, Kate Greenaway, and

Beatrix Potter. The Central Children's Room of the Branch Libraries holds six original drawings in pen-and-ink by Randolph Caldecott for his picture book *The Diverting History of John Gilpin* (1878). In the Arents Collection of Books in Parts are original drawings for nine of the uncolored plates for another of Caldecott's picture books, *Ride a Cock Horse to Banbury Cross* (1894). The Spencer Collection has ten of Walter Crane's holograph pencil sketches for the Grimm *Household Stories* (1882) bound in with a copy of the book; also included is a group of watercolors made by Crane for his daughter Beatrice during a stay in Rome in 1882 and 1883, entitled *Beatrice's Birthplace*; these drawings have probably never been published. In the Manuscripts and Archives Division and in the Berg Collection are an illustrated manuscript diary, maps, and other related material on Walter Crane's trip to India from 1906 to 1907.

About one hundred Kate Greenaway drawings, watercolors, and designs for illustrations and Christmas cards are in the Berg Collection, while the Arents Collection of Books in Parts holds the complete set of original watercolors and drawings by the artist for her *Mother Goose*, with the original manuscript of the poems and rhymes. In addition to these are many other drawings, including a number done for the almanacs.

Although Beatrix Potter is represented by a single drawing in the library's collections—a watercolor entitled "Winter" in the Central Children's Room—the Manuscripts and Archives Division has two boxes of correspondence, Christmas cards, and photographs exchanged by Miss Potter and Anne Carroll Moore. This correspondence was part of a gift made to the library in 1961 by S. B. Lunt, Miss Moore's nephew. Also included were the layout for *The Art of Beatrix Potter* for which Miss Moore wrote the introduction, and correspondence with the children's book artist L. Leslie Brooke and many other authors with whom Miss Moore was associated.

Striking items in the Berg Collection include two original watercolor drawings for Thackeray's *The Rose and the Ring* (1885) and an original Tenniel drawing for Lewis Carroll's *Through the Looking Glass*. The Spencer Collection holds four gouache drawings by Edmund Dulac for his illustrations to Hawthorne's *Tanglewood Tales* (1919), twenty-two original Arthur Rackham drawings bound in a volume, and a manuscript of *A Midsummer Night's Dream* with original illustrations and decorations by Rackham. The Spencer Collection has purchased two sets of original drawings and sketches to accompany copies of Thomas Handforth's *Mei Li* (1938) and James Daugherty's *Andy and the Lion* (1938).

Among outstanding manuscripts is the pen-and-pencil holograph of Frances Hodgson Burnett's *The Secret Garden* (1911) in the Manuscripts and Archives Division, where it is joined by the original manuscript of "The Proud Little Grain of Wheat," a story published in *St. Nicholas* for January 1880. A group of twenty-two autograph letters by Lewis Carroll range in date from 1873 to 1891; the majority of the letters are addressed to Mrs. Blakemore.

THE BRANCH LIBRARIES

CENTRAL CHILDREN'S ROOM

Certain units of the Branch Libraries must be mentioned in any *Guide* to the library's research resources. Since its opening on May 24, 1911, the Central Children's Room (now in the Donnell Library Center) has been an international center of information about children's books and reading, and has been used by adults as well as children. There are now 1,000 bound periodicals and 79,000 books, including an old book collection of more than 2,100 items. Material is selected in accordance with the recommendations of the Office of Children's Services of the Branch Libraries. Careful consideration is given each new title, and every edition of a recommended title is treated as a new book. Factors of good design, illustration, and format, as well as literary quality, are taken into consideration.

In the total book collection are 47,000 volumes of noncirculating reference books and 8,000 foreign-language books in fifty different languages. Audiovisual materials in the collection include more than 2,000 phonograph records both musical and spoken, a small collection of cassettes, and film strips. Particular strengths are the collections of picture books (both English and American) of the late nineteenth and twentieth centuries, material on children's book illustration, and folklore.

Outstanding among the room's noncirculating holdings is a group of French deluxe picture books of the late nineteenth century, including Louis Maurice Boutet de Monvel's charming *Nos enfants* (1886), *Jeanne d'Arc* (1897), and *Filles et garçons* (1915). Of equal interest is a series of nine titles published by the imperial Russian government in the early years of the twentieth century and illustrated by Ivan Bilibin. A series of Soviet picture books of the immediate post-Revolutionary period are of some rarity. In 1961 the Children's Room received a gift of modern Soviet children's books. Both fiction and non-fiction are included, and there are many translations of the great children's classics into Russian. Among the many specimens of modern European children's books, a group of the books of Bruno Munari are examples of inventive modern work. Also included is a first edition of Jean de Brunhoff's classic, *Histoire de Babar le petit éléphant* (1931).

The Central Children's Room is also rich in nonbook material. Of importance in the history of American book illustration is a complete set of the original line drawings by Howard Pyle for his *The Merry Adventures of Robin Hood* (1883) given by the publishers, Charles Scribner's Sons. There is also a complete set of the N. C. Wyeth oil paintings which served as illustrations for his edition of *Robin Hood* (1917), five illustrations for *Kidnapped* (1913), and two for *Treasure Island* (1911). The great English children's illustrators of the late nineteenth and early twentieth centuries are represented in drawings by Kate Greenaway, Beatrix Potter, Walter Crane, and Randolph Caldecott. A growing collection of paintings by children includes work from Spain, Sweden, Belgium, Japan, the United States, China, and other countries. There is also children's sculpture done as part of a WPA project, as well as a collection of valentines, mostly of the nineteenth century.

Representing a much-collected field are holdings of the toy theatre sheets of England, sometimes referred to as "penny plain, twopence coloured." The Children's Room has, for the most part, the "twopence coloured" sheets published by Benjamin Pollock. There are uncut sheets of figures and scenery, with sheets of theatre prosce-

niums and transformations for a number of dramas, among them *Timour the Tartar*, *The Miller and His Men*, *Aladdin*, and *The Battle of Waterloo*; included are the little books of the plays. There is also a nineteenth-century toy theatre constructed in England. Other three-dimensional items include collections of toys and games, many from Japan, and small figures of characters from famous children's books in bronze, porcelain, and other materials.

The Central Children's Room holds frequent exhibits, one of which is an exhibition of children's books suggested as holiday gifts shown during November and December. An annual catalog is published for free distribution through the branch libraries and for sale as a library publication by mail.

Some Notable Gifts

Mary Gould Davis, for many years supervisor of storytelling, built up a collection of folk tales, source books on folklore, and picture books including many autographs and presentation copies with original drawings. The collection, amounting to over 750 items, was presented after her death by her sister, Mrs. Perley Bryant Davis.

Approximately one thousand items from the library of Anne Carroll Moore, superintendent of Work with Children from 1906 to 1941, were given by her nephew, S. B. Lunt, in 1961 after Miss Moore's death. The material consisted of books, manuscripts, letters, original drawings, and presentation copies of children's books.

Susan D. Bliss has given, over a period of years, many fine and first editions of the classics and of children's books, games toys, drawings, and other material. Of particular interest are two original découpages made by Hans Christian Andersen.

Elizabeth Ball has donated battledores and other material to the Central Children's Room. The old valentine collection has developed almost entirely through gifts, many of them having been presented by the widow of Arthur B. Hopkins. Frederic Melcher gave the Children's Room toys, games, and children's books, and after his death his son, Daniel Melcher, presented his father's collection of Japanese children's books. In October 1972 the books displayed in the exhibition of *Japanese Children's Books, Past and Present* were given to the Central Children's Room by the Japanese Book Publishers' Association. Another outstanding gift is a collection of children's picture books from the nineteenth century presented by Lincoln Kirstein.

COUNTEE CULLEN REGIONAL BRANCH

The James Weldon Johnson collection of books for children about the black experience is kept on permanent reserve at the Countee Cullen Regional Branch at 104 West 136th Street for use in the Children's Room there.[4] Most of the titles are also available for circulation in children's rooms throughout the city.

GENERAL LIBRARY OF THE PERFORMING ARTS

The Children's Library of the General Library of the Performing Arts at Lincoln Center contains

---

4. See Barbara Rollock, *The Black Experience in Children's Books* (The New York Public Library, 1974).

a reading room collection of books, phonodiscs and cassettes, and sheet music relating to children's theatre, music, dance, and storytelling. Musical and nonmusical recordings include dramatizations of Newbery Medal books. Also of interest is the collection of manuscripts and memorabilia of the Broadway child-star Elsie Leslie.

22

GREEK AND LATIN LITERATURE

In 1854 the Greek and Latin literature department of the Astor Library was described as "neither a very strong nor a weak department of the Library: it is just about as it ought to be. The whole number of volumes, in both languages, with the *apparatus criticus* pertaining to them, is three thousand one hundred."[1] The growth of the collections in this area is shown in the following tabulation:

1854 Astor Library	3,100 volumes
1921 New York Public Library	7,677
1930	7,923
1941	10,000
1966	15,900

In 1868, W. B. Astor gave the Astor Library $5,000 for additions to the Classical Department. In 1884, Felix Astoin's gift of his library added important works. The Lenox purchase of the George Bancroft collection in 1894 increased the holdings of Greek and Latin literature by some 500 volumes. In 1924 the library received a gift of $1,000 from Mrs. Charles H. Russell and Mrs. Conrad Chapman to establish the Charles Howland Russell Fund, the income to be used for the purchase of books relating to classical literature, history, and Mediterranean antiquities. Among the treasures unearthed by Arthur A. Schomburg, the renowned collector and first curator of the Schomburg Collection, were volumes of Juan Latino's Latin verse (Granada, 1573) and his book on the Escorial (1576). Wilberforce Eames's bequest of manuscripts in 1940 included copies of the classics. The collections have continued to grow under a policy of comprehensive acquisition.

The holdings, now approximately 15,900 volumes, include histories, critical works, and various standard editions of authors both in the original languages and in translation; the selection, however, of contemporary editions is limited to those making notable contributions to scholarship, and textbooks are seldom acquired. Classical journals, both literary and philological, are an important feature. The library receives approximately 45 journals in the field of classical studies, including the related fields of classical archaeology, epigraphy, etc. Among them are *Hermes* (1866–), *Maia* (1948–), and the *Classical Journal* (1905–). Standard sets of the classics are also available. The *Loeb Classical Library* is located on the shelves of the North Main Reading Room. Although the *Bibliotheca Teubneriana* is not complete, gaps are being filled as the set is reprinted or republished under its new title, *Bibliotheca Scriptorum Graecorum et Romanorum Teubneriana*.

The strength of the classical literature collection cannot be estimated without reference to other sections of this *Guide*. Works by classical historians are discussed in chapter 49; the rich classical folklore holdings, excepting Aesop, are described in chapter 40; classical archaeology in chapter 45; and the works of the Greek philosophers in chapter 18.

TRANSLATIONS

A notable feature of the collections is the number of standard translations of the classics into the major European languages, as well as translations into other languages such as Esperanto and Icelandic. Translations into the English form the largest group. First editions of many of these translations can be found in the Berg Collection and in the Rare Book Division.

Called by Moses Coit Tyler "the first utterance of the conscious literary spirit articulated in America,"[2] George Sandys's translation of Ovid's *Metamorphoses* is represented in the library by copies of each of the first eight editions of the entire fifteen books (1626–90). Two-thirds of the translation was made on Sandys's voyage to Virginia and in Virginia itself, where he acted as treasurer of the colony.

ALDINE EDITIONS

From the Astor Library comes an *editio princeps* Homer (Florence, 1488) and *Anthologia Graeca* (Florence, 1494). Many of the 150 Aldine editions in the library are classical works; 65 date from the period 1494 to 1515 when the press in Venice was under the management of Aldus Pius Manutius. The Greek titles include an Aristophanes (1498), a Sophocles (1502), a Homer (1514), and an Aeschylus (1518). Among Latin authors are Virgil, Horace, and Martial, all of 1501, an Ovid (1502), and a Cicero (1512).

MANUSCRIPTS

The Manuscripts and Archives Division owns copies on paper of Aesop, Hesiod, and Lucan's *Pharsalia* dating from the fifteenth century. In 1940 a bequest by Wilberforce Eames brought twenty-three manuscripts to the library, including in the classical texts Cicero, Terence, Sallust and Eutropius. A vellum Horace *Opera* in the Spencer Collection is ascribed to the calligrapher Bartolomeo San Vito of Padua and dated in the late

---

1. See Lydenberg, *History*, pp. 29–30.

2. See Moses C. Tyler, *A History of American Literature During the Colonial Time* vol. 1 (New York: Putnam, 1897), p. 54.

fifteenth century. It combines elegant penmanship with beautifully illuminated letters, borders, ornaments, and incidental decorations. A manuscript Aesop in the Spencer Collection is described in the following section.

AESOP'S *FABLES*

Of particular significance are the many translations of Aesop's *Fables*. There are translations into a great many languages, and even transcriptions into shorthand. A fifteenth-century manuscript on paper, the gift of John Jacob Astor, is in the Manuscripts and Archives Division. Aesopic incunabula in the Rare Book Division include a Naples *editio princeps* in Latin and Italian of 1485 (the Tuppo Aesop) with fine woodcut borders. Also in the division is the Aldine edition of 1505 in Greek with a Latin translation.

The Spencer Collection, with its emphasis on fine illustrated books, has added the greatest number of rare Aesopic editions to the collections, including a splendid manuscript of about 1500, written in Greek with innumerable miniatures in the style of Florentine book illumination of the Renaissance. Among the many illustrated Aesops are the Italian (Milan, 1498) and German (Basel, 1500?) editions; also fine copies of the polyglot editions (French, English, and Latin) illustrated by Francis Barlow and published in 1666 and 1687 are to be found. John Ogilby's editions of Aesop with copper plate engravings are also notable; the 1651 edition in quarto is the rarest, although the 1665 folio edition is the most elaborately illustrated.[3] A copy of *Zhitie ostroumanova Esopa* (The Life of Sharp-Witted Aesop) is illustrated with *lubki*, the Russian equivalent of French *imagerie populaire*; it is an eighteenth-century abridgement of the fictionalized life of Aesop (ca. 1300) by Maximum Planudes.[4] Among the Japanese holdings is the *Isoho Monogatari*, the earliest printed Oriental Aesop, dated 1659 and including both the life and the fables.

NEO-LATIN; MEDIEVAL AND MODERN GREEK

The neo-Latin collection has received greater attention in recent years as a result of the revival of interest in this field of studies after about 1945. New editions and critical studies are added to the resources as they are issued.

Medieval and modern Greek literature are adequately represented in the holdings. Collecting interest in this field was slight during the 1920s to the late 1950s, when greater emphasis began to be placed on the acquisition of modern Greek literary material. Although no attempt has been made to fill gaps, new editions of older works are purchased as they appear. Literary history and philology are more fully represented than belles-lettres.

---

3. See Marian Eames, "John Ogilby and His Aesop" *BNYPL* 65 (1961): 73–88.

4. See Avrahm Yarmolinsky, "Aesop in Russia," *BNYPL* 58 (1954): 3–5.

23

AMERICAN LITERATURE

American literature is collected comprehensively in all genres.[1] The rate of growth of the collections administered by the General Research and Humanities Division is indicated by the following tabulation:[2]

1921	20,721 volumes
1930	31,969
1941	42,000
1966	60,000

In addition to the holdings of single and collected works of major and minor writers, critical and historical studies, biographical materials, and literary periodicals to be consulted in the Main Reading Room, are the extensive collections including multiple copies and variants of first and important editions in the Berg Collection and the Rare Book Division. Extensive holdings of literary manuscripts are found in the Berg Collection and Manuscripts and Archives Division, including authors' correspondence.

The library does not attempt to acquire translations of all American literary works, but translations and critical editions of major authors in foreign languages are added.

NOTABLE GIFTS

In 1878 the Lenox Library announced the gift of the Evert A. Duyckinck collection of 15,164 books, 1,596 pamphlets, and the Duyckinck pa-

---

1. For reference to the collections of the New York Public Library mentioned in this chapter, see the following publications of G. K. Hall & Co., Boston: *Catalog of the Theatre and Drama Collections* (1967), 21 vols., to be supplemented; *Dictionary Catalog of the Henry W. and Albert A. Berg Collection of English and American Literature* (1969), 5 vols.; *Dictionary Catalog of the Manuscript Division* (1967) 2 vols.; *Dictionary Catalog of the Rare Book Division* (1971), 21 vols.; *Dictionary Catalog of the Schomburg Collection of Negro Literature and History* (1962), 9 vols., with *First Supplement* (1967), 2 vols. and *Second Supplement* (1972), 4 vols; and *Dictionary Catalog and Shelf List of the Spencer Collection of Illustrated Books and Manuscripts in Fine Bindings* (1970), 2 vols.

2. Astor Library figures, given in the case of other literatures, have not been given here. Joseph Cogswell indicated only one figure of 3,400 volumes for English literature, by which it is assumed he meant literature in the English language. See Lydenberg, *History*, p. 30.

pers. The collection is most important for its nineteenth-century English and American authors and fine illustrated books. Files of American literary periodicals are excellent for the first half of the nineteenth century. The larger part of the Duyckinck papers consists of the correspondence of Evert A. Duyckinck, accumulated in connection with his editorship of *Arcturus, Literary World* (New York), and the *Cyclopaedia of American Literature* (1855–66). In the papers are letters to Evert A. Duyckinck and his brother George Long Duyckinck from almost every American writer of the period; as well as correspondence between the brothers, and a mass of personal and family papers. Of more than 100 boxes of manuscript material in the collection, 23 form the group termed the Literary Correspondence, which contains large holdings of William Gilmore Simms and Herman Melville items, in addition to letters from Lowell, Longfellow, Poe, Hawthorne, Holmes, Margaret Fuller, and others. Checklists of the printed materials in the Duyckinck collection appear as numbers 8 and 12 of the Lenox Library *Short-title Lists*, printed in 1887 and 1890.

In 1945, William C. Church donated six boxes of material pertaining to *Galaxy* (1866–78). Among the correspondents represented are John Burroughs, Helen Hunt Jackson, Walt Whitman, and Emma Lazarus. The Crowell-Collier Publishing Company (Crowell Publishing Company) has presented the library with typescripts of stories and articles used in *Collier's Magazine*, together with all make-up, layout, and editorial correspondence for the period 1936–52. The Manuscripts and Archives Division retains correspondence and authors' manuscripts for *Century Magazine* and some of its predecessors, among them *Scribner's Magazine* and *St. Nicholas*. Additional material pertains to the *Century War Series*. This collection covers the period from the 1870s until World War I, and consists of literary and editorial, rather than financial or business, correspondence. Prominent personalities represented, most of them editors of Century publications, include Josiah Gilbert Holland, Robert Underwood Johnson, and Clarence Clough Buel.

An important era in American book publishing is represented in the Manuscripts and Archives Division by the correspondence of Mr. and Mrs. Alfred A. Knopf for 1919 through 1951, presented to the library between 1953 and 1958, and by Knopf publishing house records, presented in 1966. The Macmillan archives, donated in 1965, consist of correspondence, copy-books covering the period 1889–1907, and letters from Macmillan authors during the first half of the twentieth century. Included are such notable figures as Gertrude Atherton, Liberty Hyde Bailey, Winston Churchill, Jack London, John Masefield, Edgar Lee Masters, Marianne Moore, H. G. Wells, Owen Wister, Margaret Mitchell, and Kathleen Winsor.

A notable holding in the Manuscripts and Archives Division is the large collection of papers and correspondence of the American poet and editor Richard Watson Gilder (1844–1909), given to the library between 1950 and 1968 by Miss Rosamond Gilder and Mrs. Walter W. Palmer. Also administered by that division is a memorial collection of the papers (1902–24) of John Quinn, the prominent Irish-American lawyer and man of letters who was instrumental in organizing the famous Armory Show of 1913; the collection was donated by Mrs. Thomas F. Conroy, beginning in 1962.

The Arents Tobacco Collection has acquired first editions, typescripts, holograph manuscripts, and correspondence containing references to tobacco or smoking made by noted American authors. A surprising number of authors are represented. Some indication of the material available to researchers is indicated under the studies of individual authors given below.

RESOURCES

BIBLIOGRAPHIES

The library's holdings in this section consist of standard bibliographical works, certain exhibition and sales catalogs, auction catalogs, and check lists printed in limited editions. A number of the bibliographies are on the open shelves in the Main Reading Room. More specialized bibliographical material on individual authors and geographical areas is found in the Rare Book Division's bibliography collection of some 200 volumes, with occasional duplication in the general collections.

COLLECTED WORKS

The collected works of major American authors, collections of letters, and general anthologies are found in both the general collections and the Main Reading Room. Also available for ready access in this reading area are the significant critical and biographical studies, as well as the historical studies of literary periods and movements.

PERIODICALS

The library's extensive holdings of American literary periodicals include all those of importance mentioned in Spiller's *Literary History of the United States*, for the most part in complete runs. One of the earliest magazines which included the work of native writers on patriotic grounds, *American Museum* (1787–92), is in the library, as are *Pennsylvania Magazine* (1775–76), *Columbian Magazine* (1786–92), and *Port Folio* (1801–27). There are complete runs of all the important literary magazines of the nineteenth and twentieth centuries, among them *Century Magazine, Dial, New-England Magazine, Southern Review, Harper's Magazine, Atlantic Monthly*, and *American Mercury*. The Berg Collection may acquire individual issues or volumes of periodicals containing authors' first publications, but does not attempt to obtain complete runs.

A helpful feature of the library's Public Catalog is the presence of index entries for articles in learned journals. These entries, as a rule, supplement rather than duplicate information found in the larger commercially published indexes.

Little Magazines

The library's collection of little magazines is one of the largest accumulations of such material in the United States. Little magazines are generally defined as "those periodicals which have been noncommercial though not amateur, inclined to be rebellious and more open to experimental and 'advanced' contributions than their more staid, and more stable, contemporaries."[3] The most re-

---

3. See Carolyn F. Ulrich and Eugenia Patterson, "Little Magazines," *BNYPL* 51 (1947): 3–25.

cent count of little magazines revealed 550 titles, the larger part United States publications but including representative English, Irish, and Canadian titles. A 1968 acquisition of some 3,000 items has substantially strengthened these holdings. New titles are acquired in all Western European languages.

SIGNIFICANT HOLDINGS

Certain significant holdings for specific areas in American literature and for American authors are detailed in the following pages. The descriptions give an indication of the library's holdings for a number of major authors and unusually extensive holdings for minor ones. Although unique and rare items are specifically described, it should be understood that holdings of standard editions and critical material in the general collections are comprehensive.

American Indian Literature

The American History Division collects as a matter of policy all literature written by American Indians regardless of language; the library holds substantial collections of American Indian literature arranged by language. The majority of the volumes are philological studies or translations of religious works into the Indian tongues; there are, however, many original works in languages such as Quechua, Maya, and Nahuatl, in addition to critical studies in Western European languages. Under the catalog entry "Manuscripts, Indian— American" are found facsimiles, translations, and studies of the existing Mayan, Mexican, and North American manuscripts. This section, consisting of approximately 350 titles, is in large part Aztec and Mayan, and features the accordion-folded reproductions of the important codices now in Europe.

In the Arents Tobacco Collection are 12 pen-and-ink and watercolor drawings made by Ariel Baynes in 1938 and 1939 after Mexican manuscripts reproduced in Lord Kingsborough's *Antiquities of Mexico* (1831–48). The Spencer Collection has the Mexican *Codex of St. Maria Zolotepec* in the Nahuatl language on paper made from the maguey plant. Dating probably from 1535 and written in the Roman alphabet, it describes the division of land among the Indian tribes ordered by Cortés and contains gold illustrations in brush and wash and some color. In the Manuscripts and Archives Division is a damaged leaf of maguey paper which bears writing in an Indian dialect from the province of Guadalupe in Mexico, along with similar transcripts of an unknown date.[4]

Literature of the American Negro

American Negro literature is documented in the general and special collections of the Research Libraries, most notably in the Schomburg Center, a center for research which includes works of history, literature, music and dance, drama, religion, linguistics, science, psychology, and the fine arts, anthropological and sociological studies, and materials for the study of African and other black cultures, slavery in the Americas, and missionary and colonizing efforts. Since the Schomburg Center was part of the Branch Libraries until 1972, and the Research Libraries attempted to acquire one copy of every book judged to be of permanent reference value, much of the less recently published printed material in the Schomburg Center has been duplicated in the general collections of the Research Libraries.[5] The holdings of novels, poems, plays, and essays are extensive; the Schomburg Center has emphasized the acquisition of rarities, older first editions, literary manuscripts, and autograph letters.

Entries in the Schomburg Center catalog approximately double those in the general collections for most major figures. Many of the Schomburg Center entries represent analytical references to book and periodical articles, phonodiscs of readings, and similar matter; others refer to multiple editions of particular works, typescripts of unpublished theses, and other specialized material not in the general collections. The general collections of the Research Libraries have acquired most of the individual works of the major authors. Definitive research in this field requires the use of both catalogs.

The Schomburg Center: The center's holdings are international in scope, covering all parts of the world where blacks have lived in significant numbers. It is built around Arthur A. Schomburg's distinguished private library of rarities and treasures, which the library purchased with funds made available by the Carnegie Corporation of New York in 1926. It was originally placed in the 135th Street Branch of the Branch Libraries and is now located at 103 West 135th Street. Schomburg was curator of the center until his death on June 10, 1938. Approximately half of the more than 50,000 bound volumes in the center relate to peoples on the continent of Africa. The largest number are in English, with a considerable volume of works in French, German, and Spanish. There are also extensive holdings of manuscripts, prints, and pamphlets. Periodical files are extensive, and there is an archive of some 200 Negro newspapers on microfilm, including American newspapers dating from 1827. Additional materials consist of photographs, newspaper clippings, playbills, programmes, and broadsides, as well as sheet music and recordings of music composed or performed by blacks.

Among notable rarities in the Schomburg Center are textbooks from the Republic of Liberia, grammars of the various African languages, the 81 manuscript volumes of the field notes and memoranda used by Gunnar Myrdal in writing *An American Dilemma*, the Eric de Kolb collection of African arms and war weapons, the extensive Harry A. Williamson collection on black Masonry, and records compiled between 1936 and 1941 by the Federal Writers Program (WPA) to document the Negro experience in New York City.[6]

The article is a detailed description of the library's holdings in English from 1890 to 1946.

4. In *Monumentos Guadalupanos*, vol. 1, p. 213. This set contains holograph manuscripts of the sixteenth through nineteenth centuries relating to the worship of the Virgin of Guadalupe.

5. See Peter Duignan, *Handbook of American Resources for African Studies* (Stanford: The Hoover Institution on War, Revolution, and Peace, 1967), pp. 99–104.

6. Manuscripts originally prepared by the Federal Writers Project of the WPA were published in 1967 by the Library and Oceana Publications, Inc., under the title *The Negro in New York: An*

Schomburg Holdings in American Literature: The center has endeavored to acquire all books by black authors; significant literary works about blacks have been collected. Juvenile literature has not been regularly acquired because of the existence of the James Weldon Johnson collection of books for children about the black experience located in the Countee Cullen Regional Branch, 104 West 136th Street. Finely illustrated children's books and those containing matter of adult interest have been added to the Schomburg Center.

Many first editions and other rare materials are featured in the center. Phillis Wheatley's *Poems on Various Subjects* (1773) were written by an African-born slave taken to Boston around 1761. There are copies of the Almanac (1792 and 1793) compiled by Benjamin Banneker. Jupiter Hammon's *An Address to the Negroes in the State of New York* (1787) is an outstanding item, as is a copy of William Wells Brown's *Clotel, or the President's Daughter* (1852), considered to be the first novel written by an American Negro. More recent authors are available in numerous editions, inscribed presentation copies, and foreign translations.

Manuscripts in the Schomburg Center include the holograph original of the sermon *Universal Salvation* (1821) by Lemuel Haines, a Negro who served as pastor to the white congregation in Rutland, Vermont, for thirty years. There are also a number of manuscript sermons by Alexander Crummell. Literary correspondence includes more than 100 manuscript letters from Paul Laurence Dunbar to his publisher, most of them written in the early 1900s. Among additional manuscripts are Langston Hughes's "Weary Blues," a poem published in collected form in 1926, a typescript of Claude McKay's *Home to Harlem* (1927) with autograph corrections, and examples of the works of William S. Braithwaite, Countee Cullen, Booker T. Washington, and Richard Wright. A number of unpublished typescripts of plays produced by Negro playwrights, particularly those connected with the Harlem Showcase Theatre, are also noteworthy.

Related Materials: Carl Van Vechten's deep interest in the Negro's contributions to the intellectual life of the United States is reflected in the many items he presented to the library. First, second, and third manuscript drafts of *Nigger Heaven* (1926), and numerous published editions of that novel in English and in translation are in the Manuscripts and Archives Division, along with letters from James Weldon Johnson, Charles W. Chesnutt, Countee Cullen, and others, discussing Van Vechten's novel and other matters.

Holdings of Individuals

Washington Irving: Washington Irving was the first president of the Astor Library, now part of the New York Public Library, and it is fitting that the Research Libraries' collection of Irvingiana is particularly strong.[7] The Isaac N. Seligman collection was presented in 1925 by Seligman's widow. An important segment of this collection features some 42 manuscript journals for the

years 1804 to 1842, covering the author's travels in Europe and America. Manuscripts of Irving's books include *Oliver Goldsmith* (revised version, 1849), 15 sections of *Bracebridge Hall* (1822), and a portion of Volume V of the *Life of George Washington* (1855–59). There are approximately 100 letters written by Irving, many to his lifelong friend and adviser, Henry Brevoort. Among other items are original drawings for Irving publications by Felix Darley and a substantial run of first editions, some in elaborate bindings.[8] In 1929, George S. Hellman, a nephew of Seligman, presented his collection of Irvingiana. This includes manuscripts for two plays, English versions of stories from German operas: the *Wild Huntsman*, a tragedy; and *Abu Hassan*, a farce. Other items in the gift include first editions, prints, portraits, papers, and correspondence.[9] Both the Seligman and the Hellman gifts, administered by the Manuscripts and Archives Division, are on permanent display in the third floor north corridor of the library.

The Berg Collection's holdings for Irving equal those in the Seligman and Hellman collections. Added to a substantially complete run of first editions are 40 manuscripts (both fragmentary and complete) and some 70 letters. Among the manuscripts are a 394-page version of *Legends of the Conquest of Spain* and a 371-page version of *A Tour on the Prairies*, which complements the Seligman collection's 4 manuscript journals of American travels used in writing *A Tour on the Prairies* (1835).[10] Also complementing the Manuscripts and Archives Division holdings are 128 pages in manuscript and other notes and fragments of Volume V of the *Life of George Washington*. The Arents Collection of Books in Parts has 76 pages of the original manuscript of the *Life of George Washington*.

The Washington Irving papers and other collections in the Manuscripts and Archives Division contain further letters and manuscripts, the most important of which is the author's holograph of *Astoria* (1836), a total of 389 pages, consisting of seventeen complete and five incomplete chapters from Volume I. In the Duyckinck collection is a 12-page holograph of the preface to the revised edition of the *Knickerbocker History of New York*; the manuscript is dated 1848.

Sixteen manuscript pages of consular information written by Irving about 1842 are in the Arents Tobacco Collection. They relate to the American tobacco trade with Spain while Irving was ambassador there.

James Fenimore Cooper: The library's excellent Cooper holdings include a number of copies of the first German and French editions, which in some cases preceded the publication of the first English and American editions.[11] The manuscript hold-

---

Informal Social History, ed. by Roi Ottley and William J. Weatherby, with a preface by James Baldwin and a foreword by Jean Blackwell Hutson.

7. See Andrew Myers, "Washington Irving and the Astor Library," *BNYPL* 72 (1968): 378–99.

8. See "Catalogue of the Seligman Collection of Irvingiana," *BNYPL* 30 (1926): 83–109. Published separately by the library as *The Seligman Collection of Irvingiana*.

9. See "The Hellman Collection of Irvingiana," *BNYPL* 33 (1929): 207–19. Published separately by the library.

10. See H. L. Kleinfield, "A Census of Washington Irving Manuscripts," *BNYPL* 68 (1964): 13–32; and Lola L. Szladits, "New in the Berg Collection: 1962–1964," *BNYPL* 73 (1969): 227–28.

11. In 1929 the gift of the library of Rear-Admiral Franklin Hanford, USN, helped to build

ings of the Berg Collection are particularly strong; the outstanding item is the 364-page holograph of *The History of the Navy of the United States of America* (1839). Although incomplete, the holograph was used as a copy-text for what has been called the first scholarly history of the navy; there are also manuscript pages of the revision begun by Cooper in 1846. Among other manuscripts in the Berg Collection are *Wyandotté* (1843), and thirty chapters from *Afloat and Ashore* (1844) and *Homeward Bound* (for the English publication of 1838). The Manuscripts and Archives Division supplements the Berg Collection with a manuscript promptbook of *The Spy; A Tale of Neutral Ground* by Charles Powell Clinch, a dramatic romance in three acts based on Cooper's novel.

William Cullen Bryant: In addition to one of the Bryant family scrapbooks, most editions of the poet's works, and the printed proceedings of various Bryant festivals, the library possesses a number of separate collections devoted entirely to Bryant, or containing a large amount of closely related material.

The Berg Collection holds an outstanding group of Bryant first and early editions, including 2 copies of his first book, *The Embargo, or Sketches of the Times; A Satire. By a Youth of Thirteen* (1808). This is one of the rarest publications in American literature; fewer than 10 copies are known. Also in the Berg Collection are 20 manuscripts and 70 letters from the poet.

The Manuscripts and Archives Division houses the Bryant-Godwin collection, which consists of correspondence to and from the poet and material addressed to Parke Godwin, his son-in-law. More than 17 boxes of manuscripts include letters and notes from more than 700 correspondents. Approximately 1,000 pieces comprise the Bryant family papers; a majority of the letters are to and from the Illinois Bryant family. Miscellaneous papers include manuscript court dockets by Bryant and a manuscript version of "Among the Trees." On restricted deposit in the Manuscripts and Archives Division are microfilms of papers owned by the Bryant estate.

Ralph Waldo Emerson: Although the Manuscripts and Archives Division has a small group of Emerson letters, the library's strong holdings of Emerson materials are found in the Berg Collection, including copies of almost all his books in first or important editions, including such presentation copies of unusual interest as *Nature* (1849), inscribed to Nathaniel Hawthorne, and *Representative Men* (1850), inscribed to Henry David Thoreau. Absorbing examples of Emerson's methods of composition can be seen in the manuscripts of 20 poems published in his first collection, *Poems* (1847), and a 148-page manuscript of his essay "Immortality." Among the 110 autograph letters in the Berg Collection are many written to Thoreau and Carlyle. In addition is manuscript material by Whitman, Thoreau, and Sophia Peabody Hawthorne that casts added light on the Concord philosopher.[12]

Nathaniel Hawthorne: The library has strong collections of first and early editions of Hawthorne in its Rare Book Division and in the Berg Collection, including 2 copies of *Fanshawe; A Tale* (1828), a book much sought after by collectors, and *Twice-Told Tales* (1837), the first book to bear Hawthorne's name on the title page. The Berg Collection has a manuscript comprised of four pages of what is believed to be an early draft of *Dr. Grimshawe's Secret* (not used in Julian Hawthorne's version), along with two pages that were used by the younger Hawthorne in chapter XI of his 1883 version. There are 15 other manuscripts of minor importance in the Berg Collection, and a signed consular document in the Arents Tobacco Collection.

The Manuscripts and Archives Division contains a 32-page holograph of "The Old Manse" from *Mosses from an Old Manse* in its Duyckinck collection, and the division holds some 300 letters from Hawthorne, reinforced by hundreds of letters from Sophia Peabody Hawthorne to members of her family over the period 1829–68, now in the Berg Collection. Sketch books, account books, commonplace books, diaries, and journals are also included in this extensive Sophia Peabody Hawthorne archive.[13]

Edgar Allan Poe: The presence in the Berg Collection of two copies of *Tamerlane and Other Poems* (1827) gives particular distinction to the library's holdings of first and important Poe editions. There are only twelve known examples of this very rare item; one of the Berg copies is in its original tan paper wrappers. The Berg copy of *The Murders in the Rue Morgue, and The Man That Was Used Up* (1843) is one of ten copies known to exist. Also in the Berg Collection is Poe's presentation copy to his cousin of *Al Aaraaf, Tamerlane, and Minor Poems* (1829) in tan cloth, bearing an imprint date altered to 1820 and with manuscript alterations and compositor's marks.

The Manuscripts and Archives Division houses one of the finest extant specimens of a Poe "roll manuscript," separate narrow strips of paper fastened end to end with sealing wax. This is the manuscript of the tale "Thou Art the Man" printed in *Godey's Lady's Book* for November, 1844.[14] Another holograph in the division, the poem "Eulalie," was found in a copy-book used as an autograph album between 1845 and 1850.[15] In the division's Harkness collection is an original manuscript by Poe concerning Brooklyn. Other manuscript fragments are in the Berg Collection, which also holds twenty autograph letters. Nine Poe letters in the Manuscripts and Archives Division are addressed to Evert A. Duyckinck on personal and literary matters in 1845 and 1846.[16]

Henry David Thoreau: The substantial general collections of literary and critical material on this author are enhanced by the Berg Collection first editions of *A Week on the Concord and*

the library's holdings of Cooper first editions and works on the history and literature of the sea. See *BNYPL* 35 (1931): 841–46.

12. See John D. Gordan, "Ralph Waldo Emerson, 1803–1882; Catalogue of an Exhibition from the Berg Collection," *BNYPL* 57 (1953): 392–408 et seq. Published separately by the library.

13. See John D. Gordan, "Nathaniel Hawthorne, the Years of Fulfillment 1804–1853," *BNYPL* 59 (1955): 154–165 et seq. Published separately by the library.

14. See Thomas O. Mabbott, "A Poe Manuscript," *BNYPL* 28 (1924): 103–05.

15. See Victor Hugo Paltsits, "The Manuscript of Poe's 'Eulalie,'" *BNYPL* 18 (1914): 1461–63.

16. See John D. Gordan, "Edgar Allan Poe: An Exhibition from the Berg Collection," *BNYPL* 53 (1949): 471–91. Published separately by the library.

Merrimack Rivers (1849). Five presentation copies to Bryant, Emerson, Hawthorne, and others contain the author's manuscript corrections. The Berg holdings of *Walden* (1854) include variants with the April, May, June, and September advertisements. A handbill advertising Thoreau's engineering services may be his first signed publication.

Thoreau manuscripts include his holograph poems, nature notes, and the journal dated 1846.[17] Further items are an original pencil map of Walden Pond and several large collections of notes and observations of nature in a commonplace book dating from the 1830s or early 1840s. The holograph of "Night and Moonlight" in the Manuscripts and Archives Division is a draft for which the Berg Collection has seventy-five pages of rough holograph notes dated 1851–54.

Walt Whitman: For a Walt Whitman exhibition held at the library in 1925, there was "only an incomplete file of Whitman editions. . . . It was necessary, therefore, to invite the private collectors to aid the library, if a representative showing were to be made."[18] This was no longer the case in 1955, when a *Leaves of Grass* centenary exhibition was produced from the Oscar Lion Whitman collection and the Berg Collection.[19] Gifts and purchases have made the library rich in Whitmaniana. Oscar Lion presented a portion of his remarkable collection of over 500 pieces, including books, periodicals, pamphlets, and portraits, in May, 1953; the remainder of his collection was placed on deposit and title was gradually transferred. In 1960 the entire collection became the property of the library; it is administered by the Rare Book Division.[20] The gem of the collection is Whitman's personal copy of the second issue of *Leaves of Grass* (1855) in its original paper covers. Pasted and pinned to the blank flyleaves are seven different manuscript versions of introductions intended for American editions of the book. Another notable feature of the collection is a notebook of twelve pages containing first sketches and drafts for "Passage to India," and a later manuscript of the complete poem which falls in order between the sketch and the final printer's manuscript. Of greater celebrity is Whitman's heavily corrected and revised copy of the Boston (1860–61) *Leaves of Grass* in blue paper covers. Discovery of this "Blue Book" in Whitman's desk by Secretary of the Interior Harlan probably led to the poet's dismissal from the Department in June, 1865. The Lion collection also contains a group of 7 letters and documents relating to this incident and to Whitman's work in the departments of the Interior and the Treasury. The "Blue Book" has been published in facsimile by the library.[21]

A comprehensive sequence of various Whitman editions in the Lion collection includes presentation copies inscribed by the author, periodical articles, and many translations into languages as diverse as Catalan, Japanese, and Yiddish. The section of books and pamphlets about Whitman's life and poetry numbers almost 200 items.

The Berg Collection holds an almost complete set of Whitman editions, among which are bibliographical rarities and copies annotated and corrected by the author. Included is a copy of *Franklin Evans; or The Inebriate* (1842) by a "Popular American Author" in printed wrappers. A first edition, first issue of *Leaves of Grass* (1855), with the label of William Horsell, a London book dealer, represents one of the few copies that Whitman sent to England for sale in 1856.

Whitman correspondence in the Lion collection consists of 22 letters from the poet and about 80 letters and notes from his associates. Some 176 letters and 180 post cards from Whitman are in the Berg Collection; a great number of them are addressed to Ellen M. and William D. O'Connor. There are also fragmentary drafts of poems.

Herman Melville: The library's holdings of first and important Melville editions are substantially complete.[22] Other Melville holdings in the library center on material in the Manuscripts and Archives Division. The Gansevoort-Lansing collection, donated in 1919 by Victor Hugo Paltsits under the terms of the will of Catherine Gansevoort Lansing, is the largest of these holdings. The gift includes some 25,000 manuscript pieces and several hundred volumes covering the social, business, military, and political careers of members of the Gansevoort, Lansing, and related families during a period of 250 years. Herman Melville was of this ancestry, and he figures prominently in the collection.[23] Also included are notebooks, copy-books, and the personal and business correspondence of Allan Melville, father of the writer. The Duyckinck collection contains letters and books that were owned by Melville and his family. In 1951, Mrs. Abeel D. Osborne, granddaughter of the author, made a gift of 70 separate volumes from Melville's library, many bearing his notes and marginalia. These are shelved in the Manuscripts and Archives Division.

Samuel Langhorne Clemens (Mark Twain): The Berg Collection contains strong holdings of the first and important editions of Mark Twain; the few titles lacking are found in the Rare Book Division. A number of the more important items are present in many variants, and examples of first English and Canadian, as well as American,

---

17. His lecture/essay *Huckleberries* was published from the previously unpublished manuscript in the Berg Collection by the library and the Windhover Press in 1971.

18. See Emory Holloway, "The Walt Whitman Exhibition," *BNYPL* 29 (1925): 763.

19. See Lewis M. Stark and John D. Gordan, compilers, *Walt Whitman's Leaves of Grass: A Centenary Exhibition from the Lion Whitman Collection and the Berg Collection of The New York Public Library* (The New York Public Library, 1955).

20. See *Walt Whitman: The Oscar Lion Collection* (The New York Public Library, 1953). The Lion collection is on permanent display in the third floor south corridor. See also Edwin H. and Rosalind S. Miller, *Walt Whitman's Correspondence: A Checklist* (The New York Public Library, 1957).

21. *Walt Whitman's Blue Book; The 1860–61 Leaves of Grass Containing His Manuscript Additions and Revisions* (The New York Public Library, 1968) 2 vols., with textual analysis by Arthur Golden.

22. See Herbert Cahoon, "Herman Melville: A Check List of Books and Manuscripts in the Collections of The New York Public Library," *BNYPL* 55 (1951): 263–75 et seq.

23. See Victor Hugo Paltsits, "Family Correspondence of Herman Melville, 1830–1904; In the Gansevoort-Lansing Collection," *BNYPL* 33 (1929): 507–25 et seq.

editions are present. The Berg Collection also has a number of manuscripts, most notably *A Connecticut Yankee in King Arthur's Court* (1889) and *More Tramps Abroad* (1897), along with a quantity of related correspondence. The latter work was published in the United States as *Following the Equator* (1898), the typescript of which is in the collection. Other important Clemens manuscripts are *Tom Sawyer Abroad* (1894), *The Stolen White Elephant* (1882), and an unpublished satire on Theodore Roosevelt written in 1904.

A stock ledger in the Berg Collection of the American Publishing Company for the years 1867–79 furnishes information on the sales of the author's books during this period.[24] Other business papers and memoranda document the Mark Twain-George Cable readings in 1884–85 and in 1895. Approximately 500 letters, notes, postcards, and telegrams from the author to his publishers and associates during most of his creative life are also available. Supplementing this massive correspondence are letters from Olivia Clemens, the author's wife, and Clara Clemens, his daughter. In the Arents Tobacco Collection are 6 Clemens letters dating from 1872 to 1908, and the original autograph manuscript of a portion of chapter XXVIII of *A Tramp Abroad*. The Manuscripts and Archives Division has 18 unpublished autograph comments in the Harkness collection.

Edwin (Charles) Markham: The Berg Collection's holdings for this poet are remarkable. A substantial group of first editions includes most of the editions of "The Man with a Hoe" published in Markham's lifetime, including the first appearance of the poem as a supplement to the San Francisco *Examiner* for Sunday, January 5, 1889; another copy, in the Rare Book Division, is inscribed and contains textual alterations in Markham's hand. The Berg Collection has some 280 letters from the poet covering the period from 1896 to 1930. The preponderance of the letters are addressed to Robert and Leonora Mackay. There are also 77 drafts of poems in manuscript, a notebook, and numerous pages of fragments. Among the manuscripts is a copy of "A Man with a Hoe" dated September, 1911, and "Ballad of the Gallow's Bird," with a typescript of a revised draft.

The Manuscripts and Archives Division holds approximately 80 letters, as well as drafts of 14 poems, including "Third Wonder," "Right of Labor in Joy," and "Our Deathless Dead."

Edwin Arlington Robinson: In 1947 a noteworthy Edwin Arlington Robinson collection was given to the library by Mrs. Lewis M. Isaacs in memory of her husband. The collection includes 613 pages of working drafts or holographs in Robinson's characteristically minute handwriting. Among other items are original drafts of his longer poems *Captain Craig*, *The Glory of the Nightingales*, and *Amaranth*, and manuscripts of 19 sonnets printed as part of a larger collection in 1928. Many of the originals are accompanied by typed copies or galley proofs bearing revisions by the author. The collection of published works is comprehensive, including first editions of all works published in volume form in limited, special, or trade editions, a total of more than 60

items. Nearly all are inscribed or presentation copies.[25]

H. L. Mencken: In 1937, H. L. Mencken presented to the library 113 pieces from his collection of author's manuscripts, among which were typescripts by Bliss Carman, James Branch Cabell, Lord Dunsany, and others. The gift includes typescripts of Mencken's reviews and editorials which appeared principally in the *American Mercury*, and a holograph in pencil entitled "Appalachia," which appeared in the *Evening Sun* of Baltimore on August 8, 1927. There are also letters addressed to Mencken. A later donation by the editor added 111 of his letters to Isaac Goldberg and 96 to D. Louise Pound. The greater part of Mencken's correspondence is retained by the Manuscripts and Archives Division, and was opened to scholars in 1971.[26] It is an especially rich collection of about 30,000 letters, notes, postcards, and memoranda from about two thousand correspondents, including Joseph Conrad, Clarence Darrow, Scott Fitzgerald, Lillian Gish, Frank Harris, Kaiser Wilhelm II, and Richard Wright.

Carl Van Vechten: The library received the Carl Van Vechten collection of printed and manuscript material as a gift from the author; it contains substantially complete editions of books he inscribed, annotated, or revised, along with typescripts, manuscripts, notes, scrapbooks, portraits, and other material. Unusually comprehensive, the collection can be used to trace the work of this distinguished author from rough notes through manuscripts, typescripts, and proofs, to printed volumes. Van Vechten included a number of books and published criticisms about his literary production and career. The gift of material began in 1941 and continued over two decades; it has been retained as a unit under the administration of the Manuscripts and Archives Division.

Other gifts from Van Vechten include nearly 5,000 photographs taken by him and presented to the Manuscripts and Archives Division and the Theatre, Dance, and Berg Collections, and inscribed first editions from his personal library presented to the Berg Collection. Among the authors represented are Ronald Firbank, Somerset Maugham, Eugene O'Neill, and Sir Hugh Walpole.

Other Notable Collections

Theodore Dreiser is represented by holographs of *Sister Carrie* and *The Hand of the Potter* in the Manuscripts and Archives Division, a gift of H. L. Mencken to the library. A collection of 1,500 items by and about Frank Harris, presented by Mrs. Einar Lyngklip, consists of inscribed copies of books, magazines, pamphlets, letters, and portraits. An interesting feature is a group of books that have been marked to indicate references to Frank Harris; the books are otherwise unindexed. In addition are typescripts of the author's novels and stories, and autograph letters. The library's holdings of the work of Lafcadio Hearn include some 85 autograph letters, 70 of them written from Japan and addressed to Elwood

24. See Hamlin Hill, "Mark Twain's Book Sales, 1869–1879," *BNYPL* 65 (1961): 371–89.

25. See "Edwin Arlington Robinson; A Descriptive List of the Lewis M. Isaacs Collection of Robinsoniana," *BNYPL* 52 (1948): 211–33.

26. See *Man of Letters: A Census of the Correspondence of H. L. Mencken*, compiled by Betty Adler (Baltimore: Enoch Pratt Free Library, 1969); and "A Scout for the Scholars: H. L. Mencken," *BNYPL* 75 (1971): 63–65.

Hendrick. The author's manuscript in the Berg Collection of his first translation from Théophile Gautier, entitled "Avatar: A Most Fantastic Romance," bears many corrections.

The Harkness collection in the Manuscripts and Archives Division contains original manuscripts of Frances Hodgson Burnett, Poe, Whittier, and Thoreau, as well as letters of these and other authors. The Montague collection in the division has autographs of such authors as Ambrose Bierce, Stephen Crane, Bret Harte, Edward Everett Hale, Amy Lowell, Agnes Repplier, and manuscripts of James Fenimore Cooper and others.

It has been the policy of the Berg Collection to acquire the work of contemporaries. Next to the collection of James Russell Lowell's manuscripts and letters are manuscript poems by Robert Lowell. A massive collection of Gertrude Stein's printed works is followed by those of John Steinbeck. The early history of the Provincetown Playhouse is reflected in the archive of the two writers closely connected with its founding: George Cram Cook and Susan Glaspell. Typescripts of plays and original correspondence of Eugene O'Neill are available to students of the theatre both in the Berg Collection and in the Manuscripts and Archives Division. Among other holdings of twentieth-century figures in divisions of the library are manuscripts and papers of V. F. Calverton, Willa Cather, William Dean Howells, Randall Jarrell, Edgar Lee Masters, Upton Sinclair, Joel E. Spingarn, and Lincoln Steffens.

24

ENGLISH LITERATURE

English literature is collected on a comprehensive basis in all genres. Works from Australia, Canada, New Zealand, and South Africa are collected on a representative basis, as are those in Gaelic and Welsh; in fact, literary works in English are sought wherever they are published, and current material is being acquired from India, Jamaica, Japan, and Singapore.

The resources in English literature exceed those in American by some 40,000 volumes. A tabulation of the growth of the collections follows:[1]

1921	43,341 volumes
1930	56,192
1941	63,000
1966	100,000

Exceptional holdings of first and important editions, literary manuscripts, and authors' correspondence in the Berg Collection augment the general collections. Although the Manuscripts and Archives Division is not particularly rich in British literary materials, it has important holdings in Irish papers of the nineteenth and twentieth centuries. The Arents Collection of Books in Parts contains many literary editions first published in series, reflecting the great popularity of periodical publication in the nineteenth century. The Arents Tobacco Collection has acquired first editions, typescripts, holograph manuscripts, and letters and notes containing references to tobacco or smoking made by noted English authors. The Spencer Collection's holdings of illustrated books include many English literary classics.[2]

All important English literary bibliographies, dictionaries, and periodicals are held by the library. Periodical coverage includes literary publications of the seventeenth century such as *The Gentleman's Journal* and *The Athenian Gazette*; *The Tatler*, *The Spectator*, *The Guardian* and similar titles of the eighteenth century; and *Blackwood's*, *Edinburgh Magazine*, *The Edinburgh Review*, and others of the nineteenth century. In addition to files of important journals such as *Anglia* and *Review of English Studies*, there are the publications of the Chaucer Society, Spenser Society, English Dialect Society, and important sets such as *The Harleian Miscellany*. The library currently receives approximately thirty British literary periodicals.[3]

A valuable feature of the Public Catalog is the selective indexing of contributions appearing in serials. Literary form headings group all materials represented in the catalog under one alphabetical index by author under a heading for forms, such as "English Literature—Collected Works."

A fairly strong archive of ballads and songs includes printed collections and an extensive collection of broadside ballads. Related sources include a full collection of folk songs (generally with musical notation) in the Music Division, where they are indexed by title and first line.

Standard authors are well represented in collections arranged by literary forms; authors' works are found both in individual and collected editions. The latter are added if they contain new material, valuable criticism, or noteworthy illustrations. Although substantial holdings of first editions of the major authors of nineteenth-cen-

---

1. Astor Library figures, given for other literatures, have not been given here. Joseph Cogswell indicated only one figure of 3,400 volumes for the English literature holdings in 1854, by which it is assumed he meant literature in the English language. See Lydenberg, *History*, p. 30.

2. Reference to division holdings of the library may be obtained from the following publications of G. K. Hall & Co. of Boston: *Catalog of the Theatre and Drama Collections* (1967), 21 vols.; *Dictionary Catalog of the Henry W. and Albert*

A. Berg Collection of English and American Literature (1969), 5 vols.; *Dictionary Catalog of the Manuscript Division* (1967), 2 vols.; *Dictionary Catalog of the Rare Book Division* (1971), 21 vols.; and *Dictionary Catalog and Shelf List of the Spencer Collection of Illuminated Books and Manuscripts in Fine Bindings* (1970), 2 vols.

3. The general acquisition policy of the library is discussed in full in chapter 20.

tury fiction are found in the library, holdings of first editions of secondary novelists are not strong. Authors of recognized merit are usually represented by full collections of their works, and a selection is made from the work of less established authors.

SIGNIFICANT HOLDINGS IN ENGLISH LITERATURE

The Westmoreland Manuscript of the poems of John Donne in the Berg Collection is one of the most important sources for the textual study of Donne's poetry. In an unidentified hand, it may have been presented by the poet to his friend Rowland Woodward about 1619.

The Rare Book Division's first five editions of Izaak Walton's *The Compleat Angler* (initially printed in 1653) form part of an extensive collection of editions of the book published in England and the United States. The first four editions are available in the Berg Collection as well.

The Arents Tobacco Collection has examples of the first eight editions of Robert Burton's *Anatomy of Melancholy*; the collection's copy of the fifth edition (1638) is apparently the only extant copy with a printed and engraved title page. The larger part of the Burton holdings came from the Holbrook Jackson collection, together with a group of manuscripts, typescripts, and extracts from periodicals and booksellers' catalogs relating to the book which had been accumulated by Jackson.

The Arents Tobacco Collection contains the manuscripts of Acts I and II of Oscar Wilde's *The Importance of Being Earnest*, typescripts of Acts I, III, and IV, and a 74-page corrected typescript of the entire play. The marginal notes and corrections in Wilde's hand are of particular interest. A selection from these materials has been published in facsimile.[4]

Both the Harkness and Montague collections in the Manuscripts and Archives Division contain a number of literary autographs of English authors. Included are Matthew Arnold, Charlotte Brontë, the Brownings, Marie Corelli, Dickens, Austin Dobson, Kipling, D. H. Lawrence, Pope, and others, along with literary manuscripts of Carlyle and Thackeray.

Important English literary holdings found in the Berg Collection include an archive of Arnold Bennett printed and manuscript material;[5] the correspondence of the firm of Richard Bentley, amounting to more than 600 letters from Dickens, Wilkie Collins, Charles Reade, and others; a strong collection of Browning materials; extensive printed and manuscript holdings for Joseph Conrad; important editions and association copies of C. L. Dodgson (Lewis Carroll); Gissing materials including his diary for the years 1887–1902, literary manuscripts, and presentation copies of his works;[6] and an extensive John Masefield archive.[7]

The Edward Marsh papers, consisting of 5,600 letters and manuscripts from leading figures in English literary, artistic, music, drama, social, and political circles during the first half of this century, were acquired in 1957 by the Berg Collection.[8] Other figures represented include D. H. Lawrence, T. E. Lawrence, Mrs. Patrick Campbell, Noël Coward, Sir Jacob Epstein, the Sitwells, Thornton Wilder, H. W. Fowler, and Marcel Proust.

The Berg Collection owns the corrected typescript of T. S. Eliot's *The Waste Land* in 57 leaves with substantial revisions by Ezra Pound.[9] With this manuscript are 56 loose leaves and a bound notebook containing holograph and typescript poems dated from 1909 onward. These Eliot materials, which contain a sizable number of unpublished poems, came to the library as part of the John Quinn memorial collection.[10]

THE IRISH LITERARY RENAISSANCE

The purchase of Lady Gregory's papers by the Berg Collection in 1964 brought the library books, letters, photographs, and manuscripts from the personal archive of a central figure of the twentieth-century Irish literary revival. Lady Gregory's manuscript journal for the years 1915–32, in 45 volumes, holds a wealth of information on the political events of the day, as well as literary and artistic matters. There are 757 letters from Lady Gregory to William Butler Yeats, and hundreds of letters to other eminent figures in the arts, politics, and society.[11] First editions of the work of John Millington Synge, Sean O'Casey, George Moore, and Bernard Shaw are included in the archive; in addition are manuscripts, corrected typescripts, and proofs of Irish authors. Yeats is perhaps most notably represented; also included is the typescript of Synge's *Riders to the Sea*. Numerous fragments of *Diarmuid and Grania*, a projected collaboration of Yeats, George Moore, and Lady Gregory, are also included.

James Stephens was well represented in the Berg Collection even before the Lady Gregory purchase. Some 270 letters and a substantially complete run of first editions supplement numer-

---

4. Oscar Wilde, *The Importance of Being Earnest* (The New York Public Library, 1956), 2 vols.

5. See John D. Gordan, "Arnold Bennett; the Centenary of His Birth," *BNYPL* 72 (1968): 72–122. Published separately by the library.

6. See John D. Gordan, "George Gissing 1857–1903," *BNYPL* 58 (1954): 489–96 et seq., published separately by the library; and Jacob Korg, ed., "George Gissing's Commonplace Book," *BNYPL* 65 (1961): 417–34 et seq., published

separately by the library. See also Pierre Coustillas, ed., *The Letters of George Gissing to Gabrielle Fleury* (The New York Public Library, 1964).

7. See John D. Gordan, *John Masefield's Salt-Water Ballads* (The New York Public Library, 1952).

8. See John D. Gordan, "Letters to an Editor; *Georgian Poetry*, 1912–1922," *BNYPL* 71 (1967): 277–305. Published separately by the library.

9. See Donald Gallup, "The 'Lost' Manuscripts of T. S. Eliot," *BNYPL* 72 (1968): 641–55. A facsimile edition of *The Waste Land* was published by Harcourt Brace Jovanovich, New York, in 1971.

10. See Harvey Simmonds, "An Exhibition to Mark the Gift of The John Quinn Memorial Collection," *BNYPL* 72 (1968): 569–88. Published separately by the library.

11. See Daniel Murphy, ed., "Letters from Lady Gregory: A Record of Her Friendship with T. J. Kiernan," *BNYPL* 71 (1967): 621–61 et seq. See also Lola L. Szladits, "New in the Berg Collection: 1962–64," *BNYPL* 73 (1969): 227–52.

ous literary manuscripts, including the original holograph of *The Crock of Gold* in 6 notebooks.

The Sean O'Casey archive acquired by the Berg Collection in 1968 includes holograph notebooks, typescripts (almost all in a number of versions with a considerable amount of unpublished material), and corrected page and galley proofs.[12] Among the works represented are O'Casey's major plays, *The Silver Tassie, Within the Gates, The Star Turns Red, Red Roses for Me,* and *The Drums of Father Ned*; his one-act plays; 6 autobiographical books; and poetry, particularly for the volume *Windfalls*. There is also the manuscript of his unpublished and unproduced play *The Harvest Festival,* written in 1918–19.

The John Quinn memorial collection, presented to the Manuscripts and Archives Division of the library between 1962 and 1968, reflects Quinn's years of friendship with members of the Irish Literary Renaissance and the Irish Home Rule movement. In this gift are letters from Lady Gregory, George W. Russell, Douglas Hyde, William Butler Yeats and members of the Yeats family, James Joyce, and other important literary and political figures.

SIGNIFICANT AUTHOR COLLECTIONS

The following discussions are concerned with authors represented by collections of exceptional strength, and so attention is directed to the more unusual materials; the holdings of standard editions and critical material in the general collections are comprehensive.

WILLIAM SHAKESPEARE

Materials on Shakespeare, which are collected comprehensively, have been given the special class mark *NCI-*ND in the Billings Classification Schedules. Shakespearean holdings include many collected editions, among them the Rowe edition of 1709, those of Pope, Theobald, and Johnson, and modern textual editions. A great number of translations and critical studies in foreign languages are included. The Theatre Collection has many promptbooks and acting versions of the plays ranging in date from the late eighteenth through the twentieth centuries; included are Kemble's *Richard III* and Maurice Evans's *Richard II*. Also found in the collection are clippings and related material on the production of the plays. A special file in the Music Division identifies settings, incidental music, operas, and other music based on Shakespearean plots and music inspired by Shakespearean texts.

The library holds three first quartos: *The Merchant of Venice* (1600), *King Lear* (1608), and *Othello* (1622). There is a complete set of the Pavier Quartos (six Shakespearean plays and three incorrectly attributed to him published in 1619). The Rare Book Division contains five first folios, ten second folios, three third folios, and four fourth folios; in the Berg Collection are rebound copies of each of the first four folios.

The central core of the holdings is comprised of items from the Lenox Library.[13]

JOHN MILTON

Milton materials receive the special class mark *NC-*NCH in the Billings Classification Schedules. The collecting policy for works by and about the author is comprehensive.

James Lenox "undertook to bring into his net all the editions of Milton, and succeeded in acquiring it is believed nearly all the known editions, as well as many not previously recognized, of the early separate pieces in both prose and verse."[14] In consequence of his interest, the library's holdings are substantially complete both for the prose and the verse published in Milton's lifetime, and lack only minor appearances in print. The Lenox collection is described in No. 6 of the *Contributions to a Catalogue of the Lenox Library* (1881). The Rare Book Division and the Berg Collection have extensive sets of the many variant early editions of *Paradise Lost*. The Berg Collection has a first edition of the masque, *Comus* (1637), and many association copies, including volumes which once belonged to Pope, Landor, Stevenson, Hawthorne, and others.

The Beverly Chew collection of portraits of English authors, bequeathed in 1924 and housed in the Prints Division, includes more than 300 portraits of Milton, the earliest a likeness of the poet at ten years. A group in which Chew took much interest was the American portraits of Milton.[15] In the Manuscripts and Archives Division are two of the poet's letters and twelve papers relating to his estate.

JOHN BUNYAN

Bunyan materials receive the special class mark *NE-*NEN in the Billings Classification Schedules. The collecting policy is comprehensive.

Bunyan was a favorite author of James Lenox who "not only edited an edition of the 'Pilgrim's Progress,' but undertook to collect all editions and translations of it."[16] This early interest is still mirrored in the library's holdings: of the 970 editions of the author's works, some 800 are editions of *Pilgrim's Progress*. There are specimens of the work in forty languages, with an interesting group of prototypes and imitations.[17]

The Rare Book Division holds the first 20 editions of Part I of *Pilgrim's Progress* with the exception of the seventeenth (1710); copies of early Dutch, German, and Italian editions; and the first edition in French (1685). Of note is an edition in Hawaiian published in Honolulu in 1842. Other first editions include *The Holy War* (1682) and *The Life and Death of Mr. Badman*

---

12. See Ronald Ayling, "A Note on Sean O'Casey's Manuscripts and His Working Methods," *BNYPL* 73 (1969): 359–67; "O'Casey Papers Acquired," *BNYPL* 73 (1969): 357–58; and Lola L. Szladits, "New in the Berg Collection: 1965–1969," *BNYPL* 75 (1971): 9–29, published separately by the library, with additions.

13. See Lydenberg, *History*, p. 105. See also John D. Gordan, "The Bard and the Book; Editions of Shakespeare in the Seventeenth Century," *BNYPL* 68 (1964): 462–76. Published separately by the library.

14. Stevens, *Lenox*, p. 34.

15. See Ruth Shepard Grannis, "The Beverly Chew Collection of Milton Portraits," *BNYPL* 30 (1926): 3–6. Published separately by the library.

16. Stevens, *Lenox*, p. 33.

17. See Charles F. McCombs, "The Pilgrim's Progress; John Bunyan, His Life and Times, 1628–1928," *BNYPL* 32 (1928): 786–809.

(1680). There has been no attempt to build extensive collections of subsequent editions of these and other Bunyan titles. Although the library does not hold many editions of Bunyan's works prior to 1678, the Berg Collection has copies of *The Holy City* (1665) and *Differences in Judgement about Water-Baptism* (1673).

FRANCES BURNEY D'ARBLAY AND THE BURNEY FAMILY

Charles Burney, Sr., father of Frances Burney d'Arblay, is represented in the Berg Collection by the copy of his *A General History of Music* (1776–89) presented to Samuel Johnson and bearing manuscript corrections. Madame d'Arblay's *Memoirs of Doctor Burney* (1832) is also to be found in the Berg Collection, together with a twenty-six page holograph of "Characters extracted from various writings of my dearest father," a transcript made by her for inclusion in the *Memoirs*; much of the manuscript is in her father's hand.

The Berg Collection Fanny Burney holdings are exceptionally strong. There are manuscripts of *Evelina* (208 pages, incomplete), *Cecilia* (547 pages, incomplete), and *Camilla* (95 pages, incomplete). Another five-volume manuscript of *Camilla* is in the hand of the author's husband, General Alexandre d'Arblay, with corrections and additions in another hand. Of note is an early holograph of the play *Edwy and Elgiva*, with 58 pages of additional material in the hand of other members of the family. A juvenile journal from March 27, 1768 to July, 1777, with some periods missing, is continued by Madame d'Arblay's diary, 8 volumes in 10 boxes, which covers the period from March, 1778, to March 10, 1823; in addition are letters arranged and annotated by Charlotte Barrett. More than 900 letters from Madame d'Arblay form only part of an archive of over 2,000 letters from members of the Burney family.[18]

WILLIAM MAKEPEACE THACKERAY

The Berg Collection's holdings of Thackeray first and important editions, manuscripts, letters, drawings, and other materials, represent one of its greatest strengths. The resources include the author's contributions to periodicals, literary annuals, and to books by other writers. Many of the first editions are presentation copies, and numerous examples of each edition exist showing its variant states. Of the 300 drawings, sketches, and watercolors by Thackeray, about half are for his own books. Some represent early trials, as in the set of drawings for *The Kickleburys on the Rhine*, while others represent the final published illustrations; in addition are 5 sketch books.[19] The Spencer Collection has 6 original drawings for *The Paris Sketch Book* dated around 1840.

Some 300 autograph letters in the Berg Collection document the author's life. The most extensive of the literary manuscripts are those for portions of *The English Humourists of the Eighteenth Century*. In the Manuscripts and Archives Division are 3 short manuscripts dated about 1841: "An Essay on the French Nation," "Pumpernickle," and "An Essay on Louis Philippe," along with 3 letters. The Arents Collection of Books in Parts has a good representation of the works of Thackeray published in parts, together with some letters and manuscript material. The Arents Tobacco Collection owns proofs of chapters IV to VII of *The Adventures of Philip* containing numerous autograph corrections by the author, and 2 pages of manuscript. There are also several autograph letters.

CHARLES DICKENS

Among the numerous editions of Dickens's works in the library's general collections are many translations; some of his better-known works are available even in shorthand transcription. Although these collections contain almost all the standard texts, critical editions, and journals, it is to the Special Collections, particularly to the Berg Collection, that the researcher must turn for Dickens first and important editions and other rarities. The Berg Collection Dickens holdings are one of its greatest strengths.[20] For example, *Pickwick Papers* (1837) is represented by two of the very few known "prime Pickwicks" in parts. The substantially complete collection of first editions contains many presentation copies. Dickens developed twenty-one readings for public performance; of the twenty-one he used only sixteen. The Berg Collection owns twelve of the sixteen books used for the readings and three of the five prepared but not used: most are heavily corrected in black, blue, and red ink. Both *Mrs. Gamp* (adapted from *Martin Chuzzlewit*) and *A Christmas Carol* are among the treasures of the library.[21] Other examples of Dickens's interest in the theatre are copies of dramatizations of his stories and novels and playbills for commercially produced dramas and amateur theatricals in which the author performed.

There are some 500 autograph letters from Dickens in the Berg Collection, a great number of them addressed to the publisher Richard Bentley. Also included are business documents, agreements, and manuscript fragments. Drawings by illustrators associated with the novelist are well represented; most numerous are the pencil drawings and watercolors of Hablôt K. Browne ("Phiz"), some of them being unique sets of watercolors prepared from illustrations by the

18. See Joyce Hemlow, "Preparing a Catalogue of The Burney Family Correspondence 1749–1878," *BNYPL* 71 (1967): 486–95; and Joyce Hemlow, with Jeanne M. Burgess and Althea Douglas, *A Catalogue of the Burney Family Correspondence 1749–1878* (The New York Public Library and McGill–Queen's Univ. Press, 1971).

19. See Lola L. Szladits and Harvey Simmonds, *Pen & Brush: The Author as Artist* (The New York Public Library, 1969).

20. See Lola L. Szladits, *Charles Dickens 1812–1870; An Anthology . . . from Materials in the Berg Collection* (The New York Public Library and Arno Press, 1970); and Philip Collins, "The Text of Dickens' Readings," *BNYPL* 74 (1970): 360–80, and ". . . A Postscript," *BNYPL* 75 (1971): 63. See also John D. Gordan, "Reading for Profit: The Other Career of Charles Dickens," *BNYPL* 62 (1958): 425–42 et seq. Published separately by the library.

21. See *Mrs. Gamp by Charles Dickens; A Facsimile of the Author's Prompt Copy* (The New York Public Library, 1956) and *A Christmas Carol: The Public Reading Version* (The New York Public Library, 1971).

artist. George Cattermole, George Cruikshank, Marcus Stone and other illustrators of Dickens are also represented by drawings.

The Arents Collection of Books in Parts has additional specimens of these artists' work, both drawings and etched steel plates. Arents also has a "prime Pickwick" and a strong collection of Dickens first editions in parts, including some very rare American editions. The Manuscripts and Archives Division holds 32 letters of the author, some miscellaneous notes and other holograph material, and an original unsigned manuscript of "Out of Town" in eleven pages.

BERNARD SHAW

The Berg Collection houses a major Shaw archive, with many letters, corrected proofs, proof copies, and presentation copies as well as bound volumes with the author's manuscript corrections. Shaw's five novels are available in first editions. Among the literary manuscripts are a holograph of *Widowers' Houses* and the corrected typescript of *You Never Can Tell*. Reflecting the movie versions of Shaw's plays is a typescript scenario for *Arms and the Man*, adapted by Cecil Lewis and heavily corrected by Shaw, along with many small sketches showing suggested stage settings. A group of approximately 800 letters from Shaw includes over 530 to Siegfried Trebitsch, his German translator, covering the period 1902–46. There are also 50 letters from Charlotte Shaw addressed to Trebitsch.[22]

The Manuscripts and Archives Division has about 50 letters and notes by Shaw in thirteen collections; those in the Macmillan Company records are concerned with the publication of *Man and Superman*. An eight-page manuscript in the Maloney collection records notes of an interview between Shaw and Sir Roger Casement. In the Montague collection six sheets of typewritten questions, mainly on women's dress, bear fourteen lines of answers in Shaw's hand.

The Arents Tobacco Collection contains several Shavian manuscripts, notes, and letters, including a typescript of a portion of the preface of "Far Fetched Fables," with corrections and emendations in the hand of the author. Typescripts and promptbooks for performances of Shaw's plays in the western hemisphere are to be found in the Theatre Collection.

RUDYARD KIPLING

The Berg Collection houses the greatest concentration of important material on Kipling. A substantially complete set of first editions and first appearances in print includes such items as *Schoolboy Lyrics* (1881) with both variant wrappers, and *Echoes: By Two Writers* (1884) in which appeared early poems by Kipling and his sister. Among the literary manuscripts is a notebook entitled "Sundry Phansies" dated February, 1882, containing thirty-two holograph poems. Other notebooks preserve copies of his poetry made for Florence Garrard. There is a draft of "The Road Song of the Banderlog" from *The Jungle Book*.

In the Arents Collection of Books in Parts is a manuscript of *The War in the Mountains* consisting of five parts, one part of which is as yet unpublished. Five Kipling letters in the Arents Tobacco Collection have some connection with tobacco or smoking. They date from 1891 to 1921 and include one written to his cousin Stanley Baldwin, humorously signed "Erasmus Hogon Polwhale." An association item of unusual interest is the manuscript "My Greatest Adventure," written by Major General L. C. Dunsterville, the model for Stalky in *Stalky and Co.*

VIRGINIA WOOLF

In the Berg Collection is found the largest single collection of Virginia Woolf manuscripts, the larger part of the author's papers and notebooks, and her diary. The collection holds the manuscripts of many of her novels, among them *The Voyage Out, Jacob's Room, To the Lighthouse, The Waves, The Years,* and *Between the Acts,* as well as those of some of her short stories, and drafts of articles, essays, and reviews. The correspondence includes 409 letters written to Violet Dickinson during the years 1902 to 1936, and many letters written to Virginia Woolf from literary figures such as T. S. Eliot and E. M. Forster.[23]

ANGLO-SAXON, GAELIC, WELSH, CORNISH, AND MANX HOLDINGS

Anglo-Saxon and Anglo-Norman texts are generally represented in their best forms with adequate critical apparatus; classics of Irish, Scottish, Gaelic, and Welsh literatures are available in definitive editions. Modern literature in these languages is most extensive for materials published after 1949; holdings prior to 1949 are uneven, although substantial runs of scholarly periodicals are available. The library has a complete set of the Scottish Text Society publications (Scottish literature in English is not separately treated in this *Guide*). There is an extensive collection centering on James Macpherson's *Ossian* and the Ossianic controversy, with many translations, particularly into the German.[24] Welsh literature is represented by runs of the journals *Y Geninen, Cymru,* and *Y Llenor* and by critical editions of the classics in the language. Since the 1960s the library has acquired a substantial proportion of the output in that language, both literary and scientific, as well as writings in Cornish; there are also publications in Manx.

CANADIAN LITERATURE IN ENGLISH

General works of Canadian literature are well represented in the library's collections. The representative collection of Canadian literary periodicals

22. See John D. Gordan, "Bernard Shaw: 1856–1950; An Exhibition from the Berg Collection," *BNYPL* 61 (1957): 117–38 et seq. Published separately by the library.

23. See Lola L. Szladits, "New in the Berg Collection: 1962–1964," *BNYPL* 73 (1969): 227–52; and "New in the Berg Collection: 1965–1969," *BNYPL* 75 (1971): 9–29, published separately by the library, with additions; and "The Writer's Diary," *BNYPL* 75 (1971): 7.

24. See George F. Black, "Macpherson's Ossian and the Ossianic Controversy," *BNYPL* 30 (1926): 424–39 et seq.; and John J. Dunn, "Macpherson's Ossian and the Ossianic Controversy: A Supplementary Bibliography," *BNYPL* 75 (1971): 465–73.

includes one of the earliest, the late eighteenth-century *Nova-Scotia Magazine*. Among nineteenth-century periodicals are incomplete sets of the *Literary Garland, Canadian Magazine, Canadian Review*, and *Week*. Thirteen literary periodicals are currently received from Canada.

Holdings of Canadian belles-lettres are adequate, although usually without copies of first or early editions. Among the resources are the works of Stephen Leacock, the historical novels of John Richardson,[25] the comic stories of Thomas C. Haliburton, and the well-known novels of Mazo De La Roche. Poetry is well represented with examples of the work of Charles Heavysege, Isabella Crawford, William Kirby, Edwin J. Pratt, and Patrick Anderson, among many others.

The Berg Collection lists a number of Bliss Carman first editions, many of them presentation copies, and a typescript of his "Sappho Lyrics" with manuscript corrections. There are also thirteen letters dating from 1906 and 1907, most of them addressed to Hildegarde Hawthorne. Supplementing these are fifteen examples of privately printed or limited editions of Carman's works in the Rare Book Division.

AUSTRALIAN LITERATURE

The general collections of the library contain a good working collection of Australian literary criticism and bibliography, including most of the standard works issued during the last seventy years. Files of the earlier literary periodicals, although not complete, include the *Literary News* (1837–38) and the *Adelaide Miscellany of Useful and Entertaining Knowledge* (1848–49); also present are the *Bulletin* from volume 28, and some issues of *The New Triad* and *Bookfellow*. As of 1966 the library received eight Australian literary periodicals including *Meanjin, Southerly*, and the *Australian Quarterly*.

The leading figures in Australian literature can be studied in early editions; representative are W. C. Wentworth's *Australasia* (1823) and Marcus Clarke's *For the Term of His Natural Life* (1876); the adventure novels of Thomas A.

25. See David Beasley, "Tempestuous Major: The Canadian Don Quixote," *BNYPL* 74 (1970): 3–26 et seq.

Browne are also well represented. The Berg Collection has a set of first editions of the novels of Henry Handel Richardson, including a copy of the trilogy *The Fortunes of Richard Mahony*. A group of fifteen autograph letters in the Berg Collection dated from 1917 through 1923 are for the most part addressed to Carl Van Vechten.

Holdings of contemporary literature in the general collections are substantial, with special attention devoted to modern Australian poetry. The Rare Book Division houses publications from a number of the private presses in the country.

NEW ZEALAND LITERATURE

The collection of New Zealand literary criticism is not extensive; currently the library receives five literary magazines from New Zealand. Katherine Mansfield is perhaps the best-represented New Zealand writer. The Berg Collection has first editions of her works including *The Garden Party* (1922) and seventeen letters from her, among which fourteen (dated 1917 to 1919) are to Virginia Woolf. Also in the Berg Collection are letters relating to Katherine Mansfield from other English writers. Current acquisition policies ensure that copies of recent belles-lettres publications of New Zealand are received.

SOUTH AFRICAN LITERATURE IN ENGLISH

The library's holdings are comprehensive for major South African figures such as Olive Schreiner, Sarah Gertrude Millin, Pauline Smith, Stuart Cloete, Nadine Gordimer, and Alan Paton. The work of lesser-known writers of fiction is selectively held, including among others that of Douglas Blackburn, Bertram Mitford, and William C. Scully. Poetry ranges from the work of the early nineteenth-century poet Thomas Pringle to that of Roy Campbell and others of the present day.

Bibliographical coverage of the field is uneven, with most studies bearing on important individual authors. Literary criticism is found in *English Studies in Africa* (1960–) and elsewhere. The library's strong holdings of world literary and general periodicals provide good coverage for the contributions of South African authors and critical writers on their work.

25

EUROPEAN AND RELATED LITERATURES

The arrangement of this chapter has been determined by a combination of linguistic and geographical considerations; the reader should consult the Table of Contents for a detailed listing of the national literatures included. Following is a listing of the major chapter divisions: German; Scandinavian; Dutch; French; Italian; Hispanic; Rumanian; Balto-Slavic and other European literatures. Editions or translations of classical texts have been considered primarily in chapter 22 of this *Guide*; works in Hebrew, Yiddish, and related languages are discussed in chapter 26. The General Research and Humanities Division administers holdings in the European literatures, excepting those in the Slavonic and Jewish Divisions.

GERMAN LITERATURE

RESOURCES

In 1854, Joseph Cogswell wrote that German literature was a relatively "recent growth" of the Astor Library, and that "of the fourteen hundred volumes in this language of the class of *belles-*

lettres, certainly one thousand must be the productions of the present century, and not above one hundred anterior to the middle of the last."[1] An idea of the subsequent growth in this field may be obtained from the following tabulation:

1854	Astor Library	1,400 volumes
1921	New York Public Library	14,016
1930		20,075
1941		30,000
1966		42,000

Outstanding gifts and acquisitions which have enlarged the holdings include volumes from the Bancroft collection purchased by the library in 1894. First editions of Goethe, Schiller, and Lessing came from Alexander Maitland in 1896, and from Francis M. Weld in 1948. A number of German gift books and almanacs were given by Mrs. Henry Draper as part of a larger gift of the genre in other languages.

Collected editions of the major authors are an important feature of the working collection. Separate works are also present, but if a title is available in an author's collected edition, new editions are not acquired unless they contain important additional scholarly material. Literary criticism and biography are strongly represented. There are numerous analytic entries in the Public Catalog for articles in learned journals and periodicals not covered in the standard commercial indexes.

The continuity of the collections during both world wars was ensured by agreements concluded prior to each war, whereby German serial and monograph publications were sent to the library through a neutral country or held in storage until the war was over. After World War II, through a cooperative acquisitions project with the Library of Congress, the New York Public Library received at one time a vast number of wartime German publications in all disciplines.[2]

After 1959 the library began to receive current publications in belles-lettres on general order from the Federal Republic of Germany; these are supplemented by selections from bibliographic tools, with the result that the representation of modern authors is very extensive. Acquisition of materials from the German Democratic Republic is somewhat less satisfying because of difficulties in obtaining material, but the intention is to be comprehensive in belles-lettres. There is little autograph and manuscript material and, with the exception of occasional gifts, few first or other rare editions.

Although the general collecting policies of the library apply to German literature, certain special cases exist. For example, all translations into German of Dante, Shakespeare, Cervantes, Milton, and Bunyan are purchased as they appear. As in all literatures, German drama is collected exhaustively. The prompt-book and typescript holdings of the Theatre Collection are rich in translations and adaptations for American productions of plays by Grillparzer, Goethe, Kotzebue, Lessing, Schiller, and Brecht. Poetry holdings are also significant.

There are complete or substantially complete sets of the most important general periodicals, serials, and learned society publications in the field. Among others are *Deutsche Vierteljahrs-*

shrift für Literaturwissenschaft, Jahrbuch der Goethe-Gesellschaft, and Deutsche National-Litteratur.* The library presently receives many literary journals from both German republics. From the eighteenth and early nineteenth centuries, the holdings of "Musenalmanache" and "Taschenbücher" are interesting but lack many of the rarities mentioned in Pissin's *Alamanache der Romantik*. There is a file of the *Frauentaschenbuch*, edited by de La Motte Fouqué, and a number of volumes of F. A. Brockhaus' *Urania*.

Rarities

Literature in Old High German, with its ballads and folk songs, is well represented. Of note is the Spencer Collection's copy of Conrad Celtis' magnificently illustrated edition of the works of Hrosvitha of Gandersheim, *Opera Hrosvite Illustris Virginis* (1501). Celtis, according to his own account, discovered the manuscripts of the long-forgotten poems and dramas of Hrosvitha in a monastery. Although she wrote in Latin, she is considered to be the first German dramatist and poetess. The *Nibelungenlied* and other popular and courtly epics of Middle High German are available in many editions.

A group of fine illustrated books in the Spencer Collection from the Renaissance add lustre to the holdings for this period; the oldest example is *Das neue Narrenschiff* (1495), an unauthorized edition of *Das Narrenschiff* of Sebastian Brant, published the year before. The collection also holds a French translation entitled *La Nef dez Folz du Monde* (1497) with 115 colored woodcuts in the text, and Alexander Barclay's English translation *The Ship of Fools* (1509). The satiric illustrations of the work, sometimes attributed to Albrecht Dürer, were widely copied and contributed to its great popularity. Other Renaissance revivals of Medieval poetry are the *Heldenbuch* (1509) and *Die Mörin* of Hermann von Sachsenheim (the Spencer Collection copy is dated 1538).

Martin Luther's translation of the Bible gave Germany a new literary language. In the Lenox collection of the Rare Book Division are located the New Testament (1522), often called the "September Bibel," and the first edition of both Testaments issued in 1534. Both Bibles are illustrated with woodcuts; those of the 1534 Bible are colored by hand and illuminated. Another treasure of the Rare Book Division is Luther's beautiful *Geystliche Lieder* (1545).

Schiller is represented by a number of first editions in both the Rare Book Division and the Berg Collection. Indicative of nineteenth-century English interest in German literature is a first edition of Thomas Carlyle's *Life of Friedrich Schiller* (1825) and his *Translations from the German* (1858) in the Berg Collection.

Goethe

Forming a nucleus of the German literature collections for the late eighteenth and early nineteenth centuries are some 4,000 card catalog entries for the extensive Goethe holdings. The preponderance of the material is literary criticism. Three early collected editions of Goethe's work are available: *Schriften* (1787–90), and the Cotta editions of 1815–19 and 1827–42. Later standard editions include the Weimar edition in 142 volumes (1887–1919), the Cotta *Jubiläums-Ausgabe* (1902–07), and the recent Cotta edition (1949–63).

---

1. Lydenberg, *History*, p. 30.
2. See Robert B. Downs, "Wartime Co-operative Acquisitions," *Library Quarterly* 19 (1949): 157–65.

The group of Goethe first editions includes the very rare *Götz von Berlichingen* (1773). *Faust* is the best represented among Goethe's individual works. 180 entries in the catalog include a large number of translations. Both the Berg Collection and the Rare Book Division possess copies of the first edition of the first portion of the drama called *Faust. Ein Fragment* (1790);[3] the Rare Book Division also has the first edition of the whole of Part I (1808). The Berg Collection holds a first edition of both parts in original boards dated 1834. Many theatrical versions, several in typescript and unpublished, operatic versions, and theatrical versions in numerous languages are present. English translations are plentiful.

FRISIAN HOLDINGS

In 1937 the library acquired a collection of about 1,000 books in the Frisian language and on Frisian literature, thus making its collection outstanding. There are almost 200 volumes of poetry and fiction, about 50 children's books, and nearly 300 plays. The sets of important periodicals are generally complete; many are now very nearly unobtainable, the volumes before 1875 having been printed in limited numbers. Some of the interesting titles include Johannes Vliet's *Braedasche Almanac* (1664), one of the earliest examples of Frisian printing; Wiarda's *Asega-Buch* (1805), and M. de Haan Hettema's *Proeve van een Friesch en Nederlandsch Woordenboek* (1832), called the first attempt at a Frisian-Dutch dictionary. Periodicals of importance and rarity include *For Hûs en Heem* (1888–95), *Frisia* (1917–36), and *Fryslân* (1916–41). This important collection continues to grow.

GERMAN AMERICANA

German Americana received great collecting emphasis in the early years of this century and is still well represented in the library's holdings.[4] Works on many subjects are included, among them religion, Bibles, description and travel. Among the scarce items in the collection is a file of *Deutsch-amerikanische Dichtung* (1889–90), published in New York City; of lesser rarity is the standard *German American Annals*. Poetry is a strong feature of these holdings.

In addition, the library has a small but significant group of publications in the Pennsylvania Dutch dialect, including many critical works and later studies, with early editions of the works of Henry Harbaugh and Ezra Grumbine.

SCANDINAVIAN LITERATURE

Scandinavian literatures are currently collected comprehensively. The growth of the collections in this area may be seen in the following:

1854	Astor Library	809 volumes
1921	New York Public Library	7,365
1930		11,265
1941		15,000
1966		21,700

DANISH LITERATURE

There is a rich collection, numbering 6,500 volumes, for the study of Dano-Norwegian literature and philology. At one time the library added to its already valuable collection of early literary periodicals 21 titles covering the period 1720–1890, and later secured several more early Danish periodicals. Among the titles represented are the *Danske Magazin* (1794–), *Skandinavisk Museum ved et Selskab* (1798–1803), *Dansk Litteraturtidende* (1720–1837), and *Tilskueren* (1884–1939). The library currently receives 4 literary periodicals from Denmark, including *Perspektiv* (1953–), and *Bog-Anmelderen* (1945– , incomplete).

A work of world importance in Danish Medieval literature, the *Gesta Danorum* of Saxo Grammaticus, is in the library not only in its first printed edition (Paris, 1514) but in first editions of the translations into Italian, German, and English. Both Italian and German translations are also in the Spencer Collection.

Major Danish authors are held, for the most part, in collected editions, with many translations. In certain cases individual works are available in several separate translations, but appear only in a collected edition in the original Danish. The library has the first edition in Latin of Ludvig Holberg's *Nicolai Klemii Iter Subterraneum* (1741) and of the English translation entitled *A Journey to the World Under-ground* (1742). There are also many later editions of Holberg's plays, both in the original language and in translation, and vocal scores for operatic versions of his works. Hans Christian Andersen is abundantly represented in translations and in illustrated editions. There are also many scores, libretti, and prompt-books for musical and theatrical versions of his stories. Yiddish and Hebrew translations of Georg Brandes and Meïr Goldschmidt in the Jewish Division add to the general holdings in the original language and translations into Western European tongues.

FINNISH LITERATURE

The literature of Finland in Swedish and Finnish, both official languages of that country, is collected on a comprehensive basis; on the whole, works in Swedish are better represented, with translations into German and French. The collection of 3,250 volumes is uneven, however, the weakest holdings being for works published in the period from 1900 to 1925. General order arrangements enable the library to obtain all currently published materials in belles-lettres, and efforts have been made to fill gaps in the collections. The largest holdings are of fiction, with approximately 950 titles; there are 400 poetry and 230 drama titles.

Periodicals in both Finnish and Swedish are held in strength. Included are *Finsk Tidskrift för Vitterhet, Vetenskap, Konst och Politik* (1876–), and the more specialized *Kirjallisuudentutkijain Seuran Vuosikirja* (1929–), along with *Toimituksia* (1835– , incomplete), a publication of the Suomalaisen Kirjallisuuden Seura. As part of an extensive collection on the *Kalevala*,

---

3. These are probably not true separate editions, but remainder sheets from the collected edition of the same period assembled with a new title page.

4. See Richard E. Helbig, *German American Researches: The Growth of the German American Collection of The New York Public Library During 1906–1907* (Philadelphia: International Printing, 1908).

the *Kalevalaseuran Vuosikirja* (1921– , incomplete) is noteworthy.

In 1949 the Consul General of Finland presented to the library a 32-volume set of the *Suomen Kansan Vanhat Runot* (*Old Finnish Folklore*) published by the Finnish Literature Society. The work contains folklore material, including epic poetry, lyrics, songs and nursery rhymes, from all Finnish-speaking districts of northern Europe.

NORSE LITERATURE (including Icelandic and Faeroese)

Some 2,200 volumes are included in the collection of Norse literature and philology. The extensive collection of some 800 sagas and 300 eddas includes facsimiles and early editions of those texts, critical works, and translations dating from the seventeenth century to the present. A feature of the holdings is the group of collected works in Ejnar Munksgaard's monumental series *Corpus Codicum Islandicorum Medii Aevi*, Finnur Jonsson's *Norsk-isländske Skjaldedigtning*, and most of the publications of Det Arnamagnaeanske Legat. Periodicals in the field in the Library are *Félagsriten Gömlu* (1780–89, lacking the final volume), and complete files of *Ny Felagsrit* (1841–73), and *Safn Fraeðafjelagsins* (1922–43). Of interest among the English translations of the nineteenth century is *The Saga Library*, the joint work of William Morris and Eirikr Magnússon. In the Berg Collection is a holograph of "The Story of Magnus the Blind" with William Morris' corrections and additions, a part of *Heimskringla.*

Modern Icelandic literature after 1700 is not extensive, and the collection is not growing rapidly. There are some 200 fictional titles, with approximately 50 titles each in poetry and drama.

A small but significant collection of the literature of the Faeroe Islands reflects the revival of the language in the nineteenth century. There are some 20 poetry volumes, 10 volumes of drama, and 10 fiction titles. The periodical *Faeroensia* is available for the years 1945 onward.

NORWEGIAN LITERATURE

All periods of Norwegian literature and philology are represented in the library's collections, which number 3,250 volumes. Among important general periodical and society publications are the Memoires of the Kongelige nordiske Oldskrift-Selskab (1836–1933), various series of *Aarbøger*, and the *Skrifter* of the Kjeldeskriftfondet (1858–). The library currently receives 2 Norwegian literary periodicals: *Edda* (1914–), and *Samtiden* (1891–).

Authors are best represented in collected editions, with a few individual works in separate editions. For the major figures of Norwegian literature, including Henrik Ibsen, Bjørnstjerne Bjørnson, and Sigrid Undset, the holdings are more extensive with many critical works. Literary manuscripts and first editions are not collected. Fiction and drama are the strongest aspects of the resources, with approximately 900 volumes in each category. There are about 300 poetry titles.

Norwegian-American literature can be studied in the works of such authors as Waldemar Ager and Ole Rølvaag, both in Norwegian and in English translation. The library also holds the Norwegian-American periodical *Symra* (1905–14).

SWEDISH LITERATURE

The literature of Sweden is represented in a good collection, numbering 6,500 volumes; among histories and works of criticism few important titles are missing. Periodical and society publications are an important feature. Some of the more significant are the *Redogörelse* of the Kulturhistoriska Föreningen för Södra Sverige (1885–); the *Samlingar* of the Svenska Fornskrift-Sällskapet (1844–62); *Samlaren* (1880– , incomplete); *Svensk Litteraturtidskrift* (1938–), one of three complete files in the United States; and *Bonniers litterära magasin* (1932–). The library currently receives five literary periodicals from Sweden.

The library has the second edition of *Sveriges national-litteratur 1500–1920* (1921–22), in 30 volumes, among collected works. Holdings in drama and poetry are generally stronger than fiction, particularly for materials published before World War II. There has been no attempt to collect all editions of the individual works of major Swedish authors, the standard collected editions being considered sufficient. Literary criticism is adequate in all languages, although certain significant works of criticism are regrettably absent.

The library acquires all important translations of Swedish works into English. The most frequently translated classic is Esaias Tegnér's *Frithiof's Saga*; copies of some 28 separate versions in English include many presentation copies by American authors of the last century. "Children of the Lord's Supper," another translation from Tegnér by Henry Wadsworth Longfellow, is included in a presentation copy of his *Ballads and Other Poems* (1842) to William Cullen Bryant.

Holdings of Swedish-American authors are adequate, although not complete. Poetry is the strongest literary form among these works published in the United States during the late nineteenth and early twentieth centuries.

DUTCH, FLEMISH, AND AFRIKAANS LITERATURES

Dutch, Flemish, and Afrikaans literatures are collected on a comprehensive basis. The growth of the collections in these areas is indicated by the following:

1854 Astor Library	106 volumes
1921 New York Public Library	4,784
1930	5,050
1941	7,000
1966	11,300

Good working collections are available of Dutch, Flemish, and Afrikaans literature, particularly for the nineteenth and twentieth centuries; substantial material is also available in Walloon. A tabulation of the entries for poetry in the literary form headings catalog shows the following relative strengths: Dutch poetry, 2,070 entries; Flemish poetry, 330 entries; Afrikaans poetry, 140 entries; and Walloon poetry, 30 entries. Other literary forms follow a similar pattern of distribution with the exception of Walloon drama, in which the holdings are very strong for the late nineteenth and early twentieth centuries.

Drama and poetry are the genres held in greatest strength for these literatures, following the general pattern of the collections of the Research Libraries. Dutch, Flemish, and Afrikaans fiction are also strongly represented in late nineteenth- and twentieth-century materials. Authors' works are generally present in collected editions; single editions are acquired only if there is no collected edition or if the single edition contains scholarly matter not found elsewhere. Translations into English of Dutch, Flemish, or Afrikaans literary works are in the collections when those are available.

The collection of Dutch literature is particularly strong in belletristic pamphlets of the eighteenth and nineteenth centuries. Subject cards do not appear in the Public Catalog for much of this material; the more important titles may be found under an author entry, while others, principally dissertations, have been bound in volumes of the "n.c." category.

Periodicals are an important feature of the resources. Eighteenth-century Dutch periodicals are generally lacking; there are complete runs of *De Gids* (1837–1953), *De Nieuwe Gids* (1885–1943), and a substantial run of *Groot Nederland* (1911–44). The library currently receives nine literary periodicals from the Netherlands, including *Podium*. Flemish literary periodicals include a run of the *Vlaanderen: algemeen Vlaamsch maandschrift*, held by only three libraries in the United States, and the *Verslagen en mededeelingen* published by the Koninklijke Vlaamsche academie voor Taal-en Letterkunde, of Ghent. All literary periodicals published in South Africa are received by the library.

RARITIES

There are editions of the collected works of Jacob Cats, *Alle de Wercken*, dated 1658, 1700, 1712, and 1726, the last of these in the Spencer Collection; the engraved plates present a lively picture of Holland during that golden age of Dutch literature. Of special interest for an American library is the only known copy of a volume of poems by Jacob Steendam, the first poet in New Amsterdam, entitled *Zeede-sangen voor de Batavische-jonkheyt* (1671). Bernardus Freeman's *De Spiegel der Zelfskennis* (1720) is one of the earliest literary productions from Long Island. The Arents Tobacco Collection has verse satires and other seventeenth-century works about tobacco by Cats, Jan van Beverwijck, and others.

FRENCH LITERATURE

The literature of France is collected comprehensively, with the exception of drama, which is collected exhaustively. The growth of the collections is indicated by the following:

1854	Astor Library	3,101 volumes
1921	New York Public Library	23,120
1930		30,393
1941		40,000
1966		47,400

French belles-lettres have been a feature of the collections from the library's inception. In 1883, John Jacob Astor presented the Astor Library $15,000 for necessary additions in French literature. In 1884 the Lenox Library received the Felix Astoin collection of some 5,000 French works, which contained excellent editions of literary works and criticism, and was probably the most complete collection on French bibliography to be found in the United States at the time. The George Bancroft collection, which the Lenox Library secured in 1894, contained approximately 1,000 volumes of French and Italian literature.

The year 1928 was memorable for the gift by Edward S. Harkness, then a trustee of the Library,

of a mid-fifteenth-century manuscript of *Petit Artus de Bretaigne*. The George Blumenthal collection of first editions and manuscript material of Anatole France, with printed works by Lamartine, Loti, Gide, Valéry, and other French authors in bindings by Gruel, came to the library in 1937. Francis M. Weld presented in 1948 a fine set of the works of Jean Antoine de Baïf and early editions of Molière, Montaigne, and Corneille. Notable holdings of works both by and about Montesquieu are available.[5]

RESOURCES

In general, the resources in French literature in the Research Libraries may be described as a scholarly working collection, strong in bibliographies and critical works, with some rarities. Standard sets of periodicals and society publications are present, although some of the earlier journals of the seventeenth and eighteenth centuries are lacking. Holdings in French drama are exceptional; prompt-books in the Theatre Collection and scores and librettos in the Music Division augment the collections of monographs and periodicals.

Early periodical sets include *L'Année littéraire* (1754–61) and *Mercure de France* (1677–1820, incomplete). Of the 37 periodical titles in the Public Catalog, 11 are current from seven countries. These include *Revue d'histoire littéraire de la France* (1894–) and *Yale French Studies* (1948–). Almanacs include the *Almanach des Muses* (1765–1833) and the *Almanach des Dames* (1806–98, incomplete). Many of these were presented by Mrs. Henry Draper. The *Almanach des spectacles de Paris* (1752–1837), available in a complete run, is valuable for the study of French drama.

Critical texts are present in all languages, with many entries in the Public Catalog for articles in journals not usually indexed by the regularly available guides. There are numerous translations from French into English; in many cases there are more translations available for a work than there are editions in French. Only in the case of drama are there sizable numbers of translations from French into languages other than English.

To illustrate the nature of the resources in the various literary forms, individual authors have been singled out for analysis in the following sections. The representative author collections discussed are adequate for scholarly research.

Poetry

Among the illustrated books in the Spencer Collection are a number of sixteenth-century editions of *Roman de la Rose*. In the Rare Book Division and in the Spencer Collection are copies of a 1490 translation into Spanish of Guillaume de Deguilleville's influential *Pèlerinage de la vie humaine* (ca. 1320); a verse translation attributed to Hoccleve, "Pilgrimage of the Soul" (ca. 1430) is among the manuscripts in the Spencer Collection. The Rare Book Division also holds a fine untrimmed copy of *Les amours du bon vieux tems* (1756), which contains the first printing in book form of *Aucassin et Nicolette*; the library also holds the first printed example of that text in *Mercure de France* (1752). Augmenting rare

---

5. See David C. Cabeen, "Montesquieu: A Bibliography," *BNYPL* 51 (1947): 359–83 et seq.

holdings are standard modern editions of Medieval texts, such as *Classiques français du moyen age* and the publications of the Société des anciens textes français. Poetry of the French Renaissance, especially the work of the Pléiade poets, is present in significant printings, in addition to the standard modern editions and critical texts.

As an indication of the relative strength of resources in modern French poetry, there are some 140 entries in the Public Catalog for works by and about Paul Valéry. Included are the first edition of *La jeune Parque* and several presentation copies in fine bindings from the Blumenthal collection. Illustrated editions are in the Spencer Collection.

Drama

The literary form headings for French drama in the Public Catalog permit a reasonably accurate estimate of the size of the holdings. These number some 22,000 titles, approximately 4,000 of which are translations from French into twenty other languages, translations into English predominating.

Collections of plays are a strong feature of the resources, including items such as the *Répertoire du théâtre français* (1821–25) and the *Petite bibliothèque des théâtres* (1783–91). The library also has the Fall City microcard edition of *Three Centuries of French Drama*.

Molière holdings are extensive. In addition to standard modern editions of his plays, numerous translations are available, including Arabic, Turkish, Greek, and Slavic. Pictorial documentation of gala productions of *Les plaisirs de l'isle enchantée* and *Le malade imaginaire* at Versailles for Louis XIV is available in the engravings issued in the *Cabinet du Roi* (1679–1743), which is in the Prints Division. There are some 600 entries in the Public Catalog for works by Molière, and some 500 entries for criticism of the playwright.

Augustin Eugène Scribe is represented by more than 900 entries for editions in French and translations into other languages (including Russian and Serbo-Croatian), prompt-books, adaptations, librettos and opera scores.

Narrative

One of the treasures of the Spencer Collection is a chivalric romance in a manuscript from the mid-fifteenth century, *Petit Artus de Bretaigne*. On vellum and illuminated with thirty-two miniatures, the manuscript is believed to have been executed for Jacques d'Armagnac, duc de Nemours; it was presented to the library in 1928 by Edward S. Harkness.[6] Other rarities and manuscripts lend interest to holdings largely distinguished for collected editions of works. The George Blumenthal collection brought to the library first editions and some manuscripts of Anatole France. The Manuscripts and Archives Division has letters of Paul Bourget, Alexandre Dumas, and Guy de Maupassant, and eleven autograph letters of Emile Zola dated 1867 to 1896, some addressed to his brother. In the Montague collection are a thirteen-page manuscript of chapter XV of *Consuelo* and two letters by George Sand, and a Rousseau letter dated 1730 addressed to M. de Tilles.

Although the Berg Collection does not collect French literature, there are items of interest in its holdings such as a Rousseau letter dated 1765 to M. Guy and Zola's *Germinal* in galley proofs dated 1885, with the author's manuscript corrections.

Voltaire, whose work of course extends beyond narrative fiction, is represented in the Public Catalog by approximately 650 entries for works by him and some 600 for critical works about him. Collected editions include the "Kehl edition" (1785–89), among 17 others. The library has a file of *Studies on Voltaire and the Eighteenth Century* (1955–) and the monumental 107-volume edition of correspondence edited by Theodore Besterman (1953–65). In the Berg Collection is a 1759 *Candide*, apparently a trial edition, antedating the first Cramer edition; and interesting association copies such as Leigh Hunt's copy of the *Philosophical Dictionary* (1843) with Hunt's manuscript notes, and Hawthorne's copy of several volumes of a collected edition. In the Rare Book Division is George Washington's copy of the translated *Letters* of Voltaire (1770). Among other items in this division is *Le Ligue* (1723), later expanded into the epic *La Henriade*. Adaptations of Voltaire include the libretto of the musical version of *Candide* for which Lillian Hellman wrote the book. The Manuscripts and Archives Division has two autograph notes of Voltaire. There is even a purported nineteenth-century communication from the hereafter in Mrs. Elizabeth Sweet's *Voltaire in the Spirit World*.

The Blumenthal collection provided the library with an almost complete set of first editions of Anatole France's works, many of them presentation copies of special issues in uniform bindings of red and pink morocco by Gruel. The gift also includes the printer's copy of *L'Anneau d' améthyste* (1898), and the page proofs of *M. Bergeret à Paris* (1900) and *Le parti noir* (1903), all with the author's manuscript additions and corrections. The Spencer Collection holds illustrated editions in fine bindings, most notably *Thaïs* with illustrations by Paul-Albert Laurens in a unique copy printed for Albert Bélinac. The binding is by Henri Marius-Michel with the artist's original watercolors and various states of the engravings bound in.

African authors writing in French are discussed in chapter 26 of this *Guide*. The library also has material on French literature in Haiti, Réunion, and other localities.

Provençal Literature

Daniel Haskell, in his 1921 bibliography of Provençal literature and language, described the library's resources as "a fairly good collection of books of either the old Provençal or the modern revival."[7] The collecting policy has remained comprehensive since that time, making this description of the resources pertinent. There are currently some 400 separate titles. Of these 300 are poetry, approximately equally divided between old Provençal and modern. Drama numbers approximately 70 titles; there are 30 fiction titles. There are 20 periodicals in the field, with a

---

6. See Wilmer R. Leech, "Livre de Petit Artus," *BNYPL* 32 (1928): 391–96.

7. Daniel C. Haskell, "Provençal Literature and Language Including the Local History of Southern France," *BNYPL* 25 (1921): 372–400 et seq. Published separately by the library.

notable run of *Armana prouvençau* (1855–), the organ of the modern revival of interest in Provençal language and literature.

In 1916 and in the years following, Mrs. Thomas A. Janvier gave more than 500 works in Provençal, runs of periodicals, and other materials. In 1917 she presented a collection relating to Frédéric Mistral, part of which consisted of manuscripts ranging in date from 1895 to 1908. Among these are letters from Mistral to Mr. and Mrs. Janvier, and also from Felix Gras, Gaston Jourdanne, and Jules Ronjat. Subsequent purchases of manuscripts by Mistral include "Soulomi," "La terro d'Arle," "Lou bon viage," and "Lou cat que fai lume."

Among individual authors the greater number of works, some 240 entries in the Public Catalog, are by and about Frédéric Mistral. Theodore Aubanel is represented by about 30 original and critical titles. The troubadour poets Bertran de Born and Peire Vidal receive some 30 entries, including entries for journal articles and works of drama and fiction about them.

French-Canadian Literature

The holdings of French-Canadian literary works are not particularly strong. Most of the important critical works, bibliographies, and collected works of the best-known authors are present. The library receives eight French-Canadian literary periodicals; collections of earlier periodicals are not extensive. There are few first editions, and the overall coverage of authors is uneven. Occasionally there is a single representative work for an author who has published a number of titles, as in the case of Blanche Beauregard (Lamontagne). In other cases a substantial group omits certain works, making it unfeasible to use the collection for research in depth. There are translations for the major works in prose, such as Aubert de Gaspé's *Les anciens Canadienes* and Louis Hémon's *Maria Chapdelaine*. Translations occasionally outnumber the editions of the work in the original language.

ITALIAN LITERATURE

Italian belles-lettres are collected comprehensively. The growth of the collections in this area is indicated by the following:

1854	Astor Library	1,761 volumes
1921	New York Public Library	7,536
1930		9,953
1941		12,000
1966		19,600

The holdings of Italian literature form a good working collection, with historical and critical studies for all periods and an excellent representation of literary periodicals. Approximately one-third of the material consists of plays and works related to the drama. While the resources devoted to Dante and Petrarch do not compare in size to those for Shakespeare or Cervantes, they do include a good representation of early editions and translations into English, French, German, and other languages.

Most Italian Renaissance authors are held in later editions. The major figures of the seventeenth through the nineteenth centuries are well represented, even though no single author is collected exhaustively. Holdings from the 1920s are uneven, yet the recognized classics are generally available in reprints or new editions, if not in their first editions. Since 1960 the output of the major Italian publishers of belles-lettres has been acquired.

Among the journals in the collection are the early *Biblioteca italiana* (1816–39), and the *Giornale storico della litteratura italiana* (1883– , incomplete), *Nuova antologia* (1886– , incomplete), and *Lettere italiane* (1949–). The library currently receives approximately 20 Italian literary journals. Literary collections include *Classici italiani* (1802–18) and sets for the drama such as *Teatro italiano antico* and *Teatro italiano contemporaneo*.

Notable additions to the collections of Italian literature came with the George Bancroft library, acquired by the Lenox Library in 1894, which contained about 1,000 volumes relating to French and Italian literature. In 1901, L. E. Opdycke gave 29 editions of Castiglione's *Il libro del cortegiano*, published between 1528 and 1901.

TRANSLATIONS

Translations from other languages into Italian are not acquired. Certain exceptions to the policy indicate the type of decision made in special cases; for example, the library buys Italian translations of the work of Ezra Pound, and has a first edition of Boris Pasternak's *Dr. Zhivago*, first published in Italian translation. The Piccolo Teatro of Milan issues editions of the plays it produces, many in translation, and in this manner a number of Italian texts of plays from other languages enter the collections.

The Berg Collection contains several first editions of English translations of the Italian classics, among them the Fairefax translation of Tasso's *Godfrey of Bulloigne* (1600); an anonymous English translation, published by Iaggard, of Boccaccio's *The Decameron* (1620); Edward Dacres's translation of Machiavelli (1636); Leigh Hunt's version of Tasso's *Amyntas* (1820), with a 113-page holograph; and Longfellow's translation of *The Divine Comedy* (1867).

DANTE

The Dante collection is a strong one, including early editions and translations into many languages. Periodicals devoted to the poet include *Dante Studies*, *Deutsches Dantejahrbuch*, and *Studi Danteschi*.

Among the incunabula in the Spencer Collection are a copy of the first Florentine edition of the *Divina commedia* (1481) with the commentary of Christoforo Landino, and both the March and November 1491 Venetian editions. The 1502 Aldine printing of *Le terze rime* in the Rare Book Division is in the small format popular for sixteenth-century texts. Also in the Rare Book Division is a copy of the first edition of the *Vita nuova* (1576). An interesting association item is John Milton's copy of *L'amoroso convivio di Dante* (1529).[8]

MANUSCRIPTS

A manuscript held by the Manuscripts and Archives Division contains Petrarch's *Trionfi* and *Canzoniere*. It has eleven miniatures, including

---

8. See Maurice Kelley, "Milton's Dante-Della Casa-Varchi Volume," *BNYPL* 66 (1962): 499–504.

illustrations of the triumphs of Amor, Chastity, Death, Fame, and Eternity. The miniature for *Canzoniere* shows Petrarch standing near a laurel tree attended by two muses. Decorative designs and mottos in verse face the illustrations.

A number of Spencer Collection manuscripts relate to Boccaccio's *De claris mulieribus*. A fifteenth-century French illuminated manuscript entitled *Des clères et nobles femmes* contains seventy-six small miniatures. A South German manuscript has pen and wash illustrations based on the 1473 Ulm printed edition.

HISPANIC LITERATURES

The term Hispanic Literatures is here taken to include the literatures of Spain, the Spanish-speaking countries of Latin America, and Portugal and Brazil. Present resources exceed 36,000 volumes, excluding general literary periodicals. Separate statistics for the growth of the collections in Hispanic literatures are not available, but the following, which includes figures for less widely used Romance languages such as Rumanian, gives an indication of the rate of growth:

1921	15,796 volumes
1930	19,316
1940	24,500

These holdings may be characterized as a good working collection.

Peninsular Spanish Literature

Holdings of society and periodical publications are strong, with all major titles complete. Sets less commonly found include the publications of the Sociedad de Bibliófilos Españoles (incomplete), Sociedad de Bibliófilos Andaluces, *Cruz y raya*, *Razón y fe* and *Revista de ideas esteticas*.

General critical material provides the usual bibliographic tools, including those of Raymond L. Grismer, the Hispanic Society, and José Simón Díaz. The Public Catalog lists 400 general histories of the literature, among them such standard works as those of Ticknor, Menéndez y Pelayo, Mérimée, Fitzmaurice-Kelly, and Valbuena Prat. In addition, the collections contain works of criticism on specific periods, genres, and individual authors.

Drama

Dramatic literature has received more emphasis than other literary forms. Although the Research Libraries possess no early editions of *La Celestina*, the major dramatic work prior to the Golden Age, they do contain one of the 200 facsimile copies of the 1499 Burgos printing, along with standard editions, English translations, and a number of critical works on the masterpiece.

Holdings of individual dramatists are strongest for Lope de Vega. The signed holograph of *El Brasil restituido* (1625) came to the New York Public Library from the Lenox Library, where it formed part of the Obadiah Rich collection, acquired by James Lenox about 1848. The Rich collection also contains a nineteenth-century manuscript copy of the original. In the Research Libraries are several early editions of Lope; among these are *La hermosura de Angélica* (1605) and *Pastores de Belén* (1613). Also included are some 250 individual works, with translations into Dutch, English, French, German, Polish, and Russian. The Public Catalog provides over 200 references to biographical and critical works. There are the standard studies by Rennert, Morley, and Montesinos, and a number issued in connection with the third centenary of Lope's death in 1935; the majority have appeared within the last forty years.

Calderón de la Barca is also well represented, with approximately 425 individual works recorded in the Public Catalog, some of them eighteenth-century editions. There are a dozen editions of *La vida es sueño*, with translations into English, French, German, Polish, and Russian, and numerous critical studies are also available.

Extensive holdings of Spanish plays provide special strength. Plays from older periods are generally present in modern collected editions. Between 1909 and 1911 the library acquired several thousand modern Spanish plays in large purchases; under the policy of comprehensive collecting of dramatic literature constant additions have been made. Although there are a few *comedias sueltas* from the seventeenth and eighteenth centuries and some plays published in the first half of the nineteenth century, the great majority appeared after 1850. Important figures are represented, but the chief value of the collection is its inclusion of works by many minor playwrights.

For the major contemporary figures, Benavente, Martínez Sierra, the Quintero brothers, and others, resources include, in addition to collected works and critical studies, the original editions of individual plays, English translations, and prompt-books of a number of New York productions. The Public Catalog contains more than 100 entries for works by and about García Lorca (including poetry as well as dramatic works). There are translations into French, German, and Swedish as well as English.

A collection of one-act plays and material relating to the drama in Spain came to the library from the estate of John Garrett Underhill, translator of Benavente and other contemporary playwrights. Also worthy of mention in the Manuscripts and Archives Division are the papers of Miguel de Zárraga, playwright, novelist, and editor, which cover the period 1904–25, and include letters from Jacinto Benavente, Vicente Blasco Ibáñez, Manuel Linares Rivas, and Ramiro de Maeztu, as well as the manuscripts of 10 of Zárraga's plays. In all, the collections of the Research Libraries contain more than 16,000 texts of Spanish plays including duplicate issues and translations.

Cervantes

Fiction holdings are much less extensive than dramatic, with little strength in early editions. The Cervantes collection deserves special mention, however, because the library has continued to augment its holdings since receiving in 1893 a gift from Wendell Prime of 435 volumes of early editions and translations of *Don Quixote*. Resources now include the first and second editions (1605), as well as numerous other early editions from Valencia, Madrid, Milan, and Brussels. The library also holds the first edition of Part II (1615). There are approximately 100 editions in Spanish from the eighteenth century to the present.

The largest number of translations of *Don Quixote* are into English, beginning with the first edition of the first translation by Thomas Shelton in the Berg Collection (1612). The library has the 1706 edition of John Stevens's revision of the Shelton translation, and first editions of translations by John Motteux (1703), Charles Jarvis (1742), Tobias Smollet (1755), and Charles Henry Wilmot (1774), as well as those of later translators such as John Ormsby and Samuel Putnam. There are approximately 100 editions of *Don Quixote* in English and 40 French versions, of which the two earliest (both 1625) are the fourth edition of Oudin's translation of Part I and the third edition of Rosset's translation of Part II. There are 20 German and 7 Italian translations; among other languages represented are Albanian, Catalan, Croatian, Czech, Dutch, Gaelic, Greek, Hebrew, Latvian, Polish, Portuguese, Russian, and Swedish.

Worthy of mention is a group of finely printed and illustrated limited editions of *Don Quixote* in the Spencer Collection and the Rare Book Division. This includes the Ashendene and None-such Press editions, those illustrated by Daniel Vierge, Enric Ricart, Edy Legrand, and Salvador Dali, and a copy of the 1941 Basel edition with Imre Reiner wood engravings which has proofs of sixteen wood engravings and three original drawings bound in.

Holdings of other works by Cervantes are adequate. There are more than 20 editions (including English, French, and German translations) of the *Novelas exemplares*, of which the earliest is the Brussels 1614 edition. About 70 issues of individual tales supplement these collections. The library owns the eighth edition of *Persiles y Sigismunda*, published in Paris in the same year as the first edition (1617); although the first English translation (1619) of this work is not in the collections, the second (1741) and third (1854) are. The library does have the first edition (1784) of *La Numancia*. Standard modern editions of all Cervantes' works are naturally available.

The Research Libraries provide excellent critical material for the study of Cervantes and his works, including runs of the *Anales Cervantinos* and *Crónica Cervantina*. Some 700 entries in the Public Catalog list general biographical and critical studies and those on special topics such as Cervantes' characters, the influence of his work in other countries, his language and philosophy. The collection contains volumes issued for the third centenary of Cervantes' death (1916) and the fourth centenary of his birth (1947). An additional 500 entries refer to *Don Quixote* alone. The majority of these studies are in Spanish, but other languages, especially English and French, are well represented, and the library has acquired microfilm copies of a number of dissertations on topics related to Cervantes.

Fiction

Among resources for the study of modern writers are interesting materials relating to Vicente Blasco Ibáñez; more than 150 entries in the Public Catalog refer to works by and about him. In addition to his complete works and Spanish editions of individual novels are many translations into English, and a number into French, Italian, Lettish, and Esperanto. The library has a signed presentation copy of *The Four Horsemen of the Apocalypse* and the 1941 screen adaptation by Jo Swerling of *Blood and Sand*. The Manuscripts and Archives Division has signed manuscripts of two Ibáñez stories, "La pluma del caburé" and "La vieja del cineme."

Poetry

The library does not have strong collections in early editions of the classical Spanish poets; however, a good historical and critical collection includes studies by Julio Cejador y Frauca, José María de Cossío, Menéndez Pidal, Menéndez y Pelayo, Pedro Salinas, J. B. Trend, and Karl Vossler. The *cancioneros* are generally available in modern reprints or critical editions. The Public Catalog lists some 35 monographs on the Spanish ballad, including those by John G. Lockhart, S. G. Morley, and Menéndez Pidal. The earliest editions of Garcilaso de la Vega are from the late sixteenth century; of the Golden Age poets Góngora is best represented with the 1636 edition of *Soledades* and the 1654 edition of the *Obras*, as well as critical editions and modern studies resulting from the revival of interest occasioned by the tercentenary of his death in 1927. In general, the collection contains the standard editions of collected verse of major writers of the Golden Age and later, in addition to individual titles of nineteenth- and twentieth-century poets. Figures of secondary importance are less well represented.

Regional Literature

Catalan literature is well represented in the holdings of the Research Libraries. Among some 30 histories and critical works are those of Bertrand, Montoliu, and Riquer. For the earlier period the Public Catalog contains entries for various editions of the works of Ramón Lull, and some 80 entries for criticism of Lull.

Of the genres of Catalan literature, drama is predominant. The only recorded complete file of *El nostre teatre* (1934–38), each issue of which contains the text of a play, deserves mention. Included are 40 plays by Ángel Guimerà, with translations into Spanish and English. The poet Jacinto Verdaguer is represented by the *Obres*, various individual titles, and critical material which includes a full set of the *Biblioteca Verdagueriana*. Among other poets, Juan Maragall, Juan Alcover y Maspons, and Miguel Costa i Llobera figure importantly in the collections. Anthologies and 4 issues of the *Consistori dels jochs florals de Barcelona* are complemented in the Spencer Collection by "Romansos Catalans," 102 Catalan ballad chap-books published in the mid-nineteenth century.

The collection contains about a dozen literary histories of Galicia, along with Couceiro Freijomil's *Diccionario bio-bibliográfico de escritores*. Sets of *Biblioteca Gallega* and *Biblioteca Galicia*, both containing a number of literary works, supplement the holdings of individual titles. There are separate and collected editions of the poems of Rosalía Castro as well as several critical studies.

The library actively acquires the literature and criticism of Andalusia, Aragon, Valencia, and other Spanish regions.

MEXICO

Resources in the literature of Mexico include a good collection related to Sor Juana Inés de la Cruz. There are numerous early printings, notably the first editions of her complete works in 3 volumes, *Inundación castalida* (1689), *Segundo volumen de las obras* (1692), and *Fama y obras postumas* (1700). Also present are modern editions of individual works of Sor Juana, and the 4-volume *Obras* (1951–57). Some 50 critical and bibliographical titles, many of them issued at Sor Juana's tercentenary in 1951, provide information on Mexico's "Tenth Muse"; prominent among these are studies by Pedro Henríquez Ureña, Dorothy Schons, and Ermilo Abreu Gómez. The larger number of studies are by Mexican critics, although there are several from Spain, Argentina, and America.

Also well represented is the author and journalist José Joaquin Fernández de Lizardi. *El periquillo sarniento*, the first Mexican picaresque novel, is present in the fourth edition (1842); there are 2 additional nineteenth-century editions (1884 and 1897), several modern editions, and Katherine Anne Porter's translation, *The Itching Parrot* (1942). The collection contains early editions of other novels, including *Don Catrín de la Fachenda* (1832); *Noches tristes* (1819); and *La quijotita y su prima* (1842). There is a second edition of *Fábulas* (1832). Although the library possesses only scattered issues of the journal *El pensador mexicano*, it contains some 200 polemical pamphlets by and about Fernández de Lizardi. Dating between 1811 and 1826, these include *Chamorro y Dominquín*, *Segunda defensa de los Francmasones*, and several "dialogos de los muertos" and "sueños," the latter being favorite literary forms of "El Pensador." Critical materials include bibliographies by Paul Radin, a biography by Luis González Obregón, and numerous studies by Jefferson Rea Spell.

A good collection of fiction related to the Mexican Revolution is available. Holdings of novels by major figures such as Mariano Azuela, Martín Luis Guzmán, Gregorio López y Fuentes, José Mancisidor, and José Rubén Romero, are virtually complete, although the library does lack some early or privately-printed editions of those authors. Supplementing the works of these and secondary novelists are critical and bibliographical studies.

SPANISH AMERICAN LITERATURE

As with peninsular Spanish literature, the library has considerable strength in general literary periodicals of the Spanish-speaking Central and South American countries. It has also assembled more than 800 general histories and critical studies of these literatures (exclusive of those dealing with specific genres and individual writers) and has acquired the standard bibliographies originally issued in the 1930s by the Harvard Council on Hispano-American Studies. The library's participation in the Latin American Cooperative Acquisition Project (LACAP) since its inception in 1960 has contributed to strengthening resources of works published since the late 1950s.

The collections of the various national literatures vary considerably in size and scope. A count of titles for the major genres of drama, essays, fiction, letters, and poetry reveals most extensive holdings for Argentina (more than 3,500 titles), Mexico (more than 2,500 titles), and Chile (more than 1,600 titles), reflecting literary and publishing trends in Latin America. The next largest collections (some 1,000 titles each) are for two small countries, Cuba and Uruguay; they are from 20 to 50 percent larger than holdings for Colombia, Peru, and Venezuela. For the remaining republics resources of belles-lettres generally range from 50 to approximately 300 titles. In every case holdings of fiction and poetry account for an estimated three-quarters of the total number of titles; plays rank third, counter to the library's generally comprehensive coverage of dramatic literature. For Chile and Mexico more works of fiction than of poetry are present, but the situation is reversed for Cuba, Peru, and Venezuela; in the cases of Argentina, Colombia, and Uruguay a nearly equal distribution prevails.

Brief observations on certain features of the largest collections follow after a comment on holdings related to Latin America's most important literary movement, *modernismo*, which had spread to all countries by the end of the nineteenth century. Resources on *modernismo* are diversely located in material classed with Spanish American literature, in general periodicals from these countries, and in other locations; taken together these holdings form a substantial body of material. Discussions of the modernist movement as a whole, stylistic analyses, published lectures, and biographical studies are abundant. While only 25 percent of the principal poetic works of the most important writers (Julián del Casal, Rubén Darío, Enrique González Martínez, Manuel Gutiérrez Nájera, Leopoldo Lugones, Amado Nervo, and others) is available in first editions, later printings and collected works provide full access to the texts. Strong holdings of studies of major figures, both monographic and serial, supply excellent critical coverage.

The largest quantity of material concerns Rubén Darío; the Public Catalog contains approximately 250 entries for works by and about him. Two of Darío's most significant volumes, *Azul* (1888) and *Cantos de vida y esperanza* (1905), are present in first editions. Other prose and poetry appear in separate volumes or as part of Darío's *Obras completas*. The translations of Darío's poems by Thomas Walsh and Lysander Kemp are available. Examples of critical studies are those by Max Henríquez Ureña, Gustavo Alemán-Bolaños, Osvaldo Crispo Acosta, E. K. Mapes, Arturo Marasso Rocca, and Arturo Torres-Ríoseco. To these and the bibliographies by Henry Grattan Doyle and Julio Saavedra Molina numerous journal articles can be added; nevertheless, resources are best characterized as extensive rather than exhaustive.

Argentina

Holdings for Argentina form the largest block of materials for a single South American country, reflecting in part literary items contained in two gift collections: 464 volumes and 303 pamphlets were received in 1914 from President Theodore Roosevelt, and some 2,000 volumes displayed in the Argentine pavilion at the 1939–40 New York World's Fair were divided between the Branch and Research Libraries. Approximately 1,500 works of fiction are concentrated in the period since 1930, although important earlier writers like Gálvez, Güiraldes, Mallea and Wast are represented. There are some 40 original titles and translations of Argentina's most famous contemporary writer, Jorge Luis Borges, along with critical monographs.

Entries in the Public Catalog for works by and about Domingo Faustino Sarmiento, Argentinean author, educator, and president, exceed 200. Included in this collection are an *Obras* in 53 volumes, 10 editions of *La Vida de Juan Facundo Quiroga*, a bibliography of the Sarmiento collection at the National University of La Plata, numerous biographies, and studies of Sarmiento's educational and political ideas.

Literary works inspired by the gaucho compose an interesting group of more than 100 items, including epics, novels, plays, works of criticism, and studies of gaucho folklore. Although these publications deal chiefly with the Argentine gaucho, some relate to Uruguay and to the Brazilian province of Río Grande do Sul. Editions of José Hernández's *Martín Fierro* and studies of that novel constitute the largest unit within this group.

Chile

The best represented work of Chilean literature is Alonso de Ercilla y Zúñiga's *La Araucana*, the epic poem about the revolt of the Araucanian Indians. The Rare Book Division has the Hispanic Society facsimile of the first edition, and a number of early editions, including the first illustrated edition (1776). The Medina edition (1910–18) in five volumes is available, as are English and French translations. The contemporary poet Pablo Neruda is well represented; in addition to the *Obras* and translations into English there are many separate volumes of verse, and critical studied by Amado Alonso, Alfredo Cardona Peña, and others.

Chilean literature is represented by a working collection. Major authors such as Alberto Blest Gana and Eduardo Barrios have received good coverage, and an adequate collection of literary histories and critical essays is available.

Uruguay

The history and criticism of Uruguayan literature are documented in such works as Carlos Roxlo's *Historia crítica*, the *Historia sintética* issued by the Comisión Nacional del Centenario, as well as by various studies by Alberto Zum Felde. Collections of literary works include the Biblioteca de Escritores Uruguayos. The Public Catalog contains about 100 entries related to José Enrique Rodó; included are editions of *Ariel, Motivos de Proteo* and other writings, a 2-volume bibliography issued by the National Library in 1930, and articles and monographs about the man and his work. Also well represented by texts and critical material is the playwright Florencio Sánchez.

Cuba

Resources for Cuban literature are good. Numerous lectures given at the Academia Nacional de Artes y Letras from 1920 to the early 1950s supplement a full set of the Academia's *Anales*; other available sets are the Biblioteca Cubana, Grandes Periodistas Cubanos, and Universidad de la Habana series. J. M. Carbonell y Rivero's *Evolución de la cultura Cubana* and various studies by Juan N. José Remos y Rubio provide background.

Approximately 400 entries in the Public Catalog represent writings by and about José Martí. In addition to the 73 volume *Obras completas* (1936–53), several earlier collections are present. The constantly growing literature on Martí encompasses biographies, pamphlets and ephemera, microfilm copies of theses, a set of the *Archivo José Martí*, and numerous publications issued in Cuba and elsewhere in Latin America for Martí's centennial in 1953. The library has editions of several of Gertrudis Gómez de Avellaneda's plays,

the *Obras*, 1 of the 500 copies of her *Memorias inéditas* (1914), and a number of modern reprints. Contemporary criticism, including studies by Emilio Cotarelo y Mori and Edwin Bucher Williams, is available.

Portuguese Literature

Resources in Portuguese literature (more than 5,000 titles, excluding serials) constitute a good working collection. The library has complete sets of the *Boletim de filologia* and the *Revista da faculdade de letras* of the University of Lisbon (neither widely held in American libraries). There are approximately 100 titles of general literary history and criticism, including the standard works by A. F. G. Bell, Theophilo Braga, Fidelino de Figueiredo, Forjaz de Sampaio, and José Simões Dias.

The author most strongly represented is Luis de Camoens. The Research Libraries contain several editions of *Os Lusíadas*, the earliest of them dated 1597 (along with a facsimile reprint of the first edition, 1572). Although the collections lack the first English translation (1655), versions by William Julius Mickle, Richard Fanshawe, T. M. Musgrave, Leonard Bacon, William C. Atkinson and J. J. Aubertin are available; French, German, and Italian translations are held. The standard edition of Camoens' *Rimas*, edited by Costa Pimpão, may be consulted, and several editions of the *Obras* provide access to other works. About 100 entries in the Public Catalog refer to general monographic and serial publications about Camoens.

Eça de Queirós is represented by some 50 editions of individual works in addition to the *Obras*, and by some 100 publications about him, including not only Portuguese but also Brazilian and Spanish American criticism.

The library greatly enriched its resources by purchasing two collections of Portuguese drama in 1908 and 1910. This collection contains one-act plays, as well as full-length works. Although the plays range in date from the late eighteenth century to the present, nineteenth-century imprints compose approximately 90 percent of the total. Earlier playwrights are represented in a collection of material by and about Gil Vicente. Total holdings of plays number approximately 3,000 titles. Fiction and poetry are much less extensive, about 900 titles each.

A small number of novels and other works by such authors as Castro Soromenho, Fausto Duarte, and Manuel Lopes represents the literature which has developed in the Portuguese African colonies in the past twenty-five years.

Brazil

The Brazilian collection compares favorably in quantity with the important university collections, although it ranks well below that of the Library of Congress.[9] It possesses greater strength for the contemporary than for earlier periods. A good collection of literary history and criticism exceeds 100 titles, with numerous works by standard authors such as Manuel Bandeira, Afrânio Coutinho, José Lins do Rêgo, Samuel Putnam, and Sylvio Romero; older publications are not,

---

9. See William Vernon Jackson, *Library Guide for Brazilian Studies* (Pittsburgh: Univ. of Pittsburgh Press, 1964), p. 33.

however, always available. As an example of serial holdings there is a complete file of the *Revista da Academia paulista de letras*.

For individual authors the largest block, about 120 titles, contains works by and about Machado de Assis; this includes English translations of several novels. José de Alencar is represented in some 50 editions of different works.

The library holds more than 2,500 titles in Brazilian belles-lettres; of these, approximately 1,300 are fiction, 700 verse, 325 plays, and 175 essays. Holdings for the major writers Jorge Amado, Aluízio Azevedo, José Lins do Rêgo, Graciliano Ramos, Antônio de Castro Alves, and Erico Veríssimo are good, and the library has added available English translations to its copies of the originals. Numerous anthologies (several regional in scope) provide coverage for Brazilian poetry; there are several volumes of English, French, and Spanish translations. The compilations and critical studies by Manuel Bandeira deserve mention. Expansion of resources for the contemporary period in all genres is continuing on an active basis.

RUMANIAN LITERATURE

Rumanian literature is well represented. Since 1960 general order arrangements have enabled the library to obtain most of the current literary publications. The library does not collect Rumanian literature in the Cyrillic alphabet; resources instead are concentrated on works in the Roman alphabet from the late nineteenth century to the present, and are strongest for materials published after 1930.

Of the more than 600 titles 330 are fiction, 170 are poetry, and 120 are drama. These figures include a number of translations; in drama are translations both of Rumanian plays into other languages and foreign plays into Rumanian.

Publications of learned societies and institutions include the Academia Româna's *Din vieata popurului Roman* and its successor *Anuarul arhivei de folklore*, an incomplete file of the *Viata Romînească*, and *Langue et littérature*.

BALTO-SLAVIC LITERATURES

The Slavonic Division attempts to obtain the best available edition of the collected literary works of major and minor authors. This may be the most recent edition, but early editions of authors published before 1917 or editions published outside Russia are often found to be more textually accurate. Fiction is collected on a selective basis in all Balto-Slavic languages except Russian, Polish, and Czech and Slovak, discussed in the following sections. Poetry and drama collections are strong. Juvenile literature is acquired selectively in all languages.

The Slavonic Division regularly acquires translations, usually into Russian, of classic authors such as Homer and Dante. It maintains extensive English translations from the Balto-Slavic languages.[10] As the division's collecting responsi-

bility extends to minor languages, there are a number of translations from lesser languages into those more widely used, as in the case of translations from Bulgarian or Lithuanian into Russian. There are also a number of translations of Russian classics into the minor languages. The Jewish Division collects and retains the works of Russian authors translated into Yiddish.

RUSSIAN LITERATURE

Russian fiction is collected on a representative basis; poetry and drama are acquired comprehensively. Collected editions in belles-lettres are a feature of the Russian-language holdings of some 21,000 volumes; all collected editions of Russian authors published by learned institutions are acquired as a matter of policy. In certain cases major authors have not been published in collected editions (the Symbolists are an example); the division attempts to obtain works in any form, either as separate book publications, in photocopy, or on microfilm. Individual editions of an author's work are ordinarily purchased as they are needed, rather than as the result of a specific policy. Literary criticism and bibliography for Russian authors are well represented in all languages. The division also collects a sampling of current Russian science fiction.

Translations

Literary translations into Russian are acquired selectively, with the exception of world classics, all of which are available. Translations into Russian of texts in other Balto-Slavic languages are often purchased. The Slavonic Division collects translations of poetry into Russian on the theory that these translations have been made by poets and are themselves works of literary merit. In addition, translations from Russian into other languages are well represented. Also included are a number of first editions of translations into English of Turgenev, Chekhov, and Lermontov.

Periodical and Society Publications

The collecting policy for periodicals in Russian literature is representative; the policy for the journals of learned societies is comprehensive. Both categories form an outstanding feature of the resources.

The *Yezhemesyachnyye sochineniya* (1755–64), and the *Drevnyaya rossiĭskaya vivliofika* (1783–84) come from the eighteenth century. But the holdings reach their greatest strength with the golden age of Russian literature in the nineteenth century. Representative titles include *Sovremennik* (1848–65; incomplete), *Vestnik yevropy* (1803–26; 1866–1917), *Biblioteka dlya chteniya* (1834–65; incomplete), and *Otechestvennyya zapiski* (1839–84). Twentieth-century holdings include the periodicals *Apollon, Vesy*, and *Shipovnik* from the early years of the century, and the current *Oktyabr', Zvezda, Novyĭ mir* and *Yunost'*. Also of interest are the Russian-language periodicals published in other nations: from the United States come *Novyĭ zhurnal* and *Vozdushnyye puti*, from France *Sovremennyye zapiski* and *Vozrozhdeniye*,

---

10. See Richard C. Lewanski, compiler, *The Literatures of the World in English Translation: A Bibliography. Volume II: The Slavic Literatures* (New York: The New York Public Library and Frederick Ungar Publishing Co., 1967; second printing, with corrections, 1971); see also Rissa

---

Yachnin and David H. Stam, compilers, *Turgenev in English* (The New York Public Library, 1962).

and from Germany *Grani* and *Mosty*. The division currently receives 25 literary periodicals in Russian.

Individual Authors

A discussion of the holdings for several individual authors will afford an impression of the content and depth of the Russian literary resources. In each case a large number of the catalog card entries refer to original or critical material published in journals.

Fiodor M. Dostoyevski is represented by 300 titles, for the most part later editions. Featured are collected works and numerous translations into English, Hebrew, Italian, German, Latvian, Hungarian, and other languages. Another feature of the Dostoyevski holdings is the presence of periodicals containing the first appearances of many of his works, including *Epokha* and *Vremya* (of which Dostoyevski was joint editor). Critical works number 800 titles, more than half of which are in languages other than Russian.

Translations compose the greater part of the 260 items by Nikolai V. Gogol. The larger number are works published after the author's death. A further 470 titles represent critical, bibliographical, and biographical works. The Theatre Collection holds typescripts for American performances of Gogol plays and a great amount of material relating to international productions of his plays dating from the late nineteenth century to the present.

Anton P. Chekhov holdings number some 330 entries for original titles and approximately the same number for critical material. Typescripts, acting versions, and production material for Chekhov plays are found in the Theatre Collection.

Rare Books

First and early editions of literary works are not a feature of the collections, with the exception of certain collected editions. Lermontov's *Geroi nashevo vremeni* (*A Hero of Our Time*) dated 1840, some first and early editions of Gogol and Pushkin, and seventeen plays by Catherine II which appear in *Rossiĭski teatr* (1786–87) are among noteworthy items.

Belorussian Literature

Belorussian literary periodical and society publications are collected comprehensively; fiction is collected selectively; and other materials are collected representatively. The holdings of belles-lettres number approximately 500 volumes.

Several rare volumes in the Slavonic Division represent the beginning of printing in Belorussia. Notable among them is a copy of *Chetveroyevangeliye* (The New Testament), dated 1575.

The nineteenth century is represented by several pamphlets published in Cracow and London around 1870. The holdings from 1905 to 1920 are uneven; when possible, gaps are filled with photocopies. From 1920 to the early 1930s the holdings are fairly strong in belles-lettres. Representation is very uneven in all fields for the period from 1935 to 1955. After 1960 the collections are good for publications from both the BSSR and western (Polish) Belorussia.

As is the case with most of the national republics of the Soviet Union, the Slavonic Division has received all of the publications of the various academies of science in the BSSR. As the division has been largely unable to obtain national catalogs or bibliographies, it has been difficult to determine what other materials have been published. The library receives émigré material published in the United States, Germany, France, and Great Britain, including the important émigré literary periodical *Polymya*.

Bulgarian Literature

A holding of approximately 1,200 volumes emphasizes Bulgarian publications of the late nineteenth and early twentieth centuries. Currently both monograph and serial publications are acquired on a representative basis. Serial files include *Ezik* (1946–, incomplete) and the *Izvestiya* (1961–) of the Bǔlgarska Akademiya Na Naukite. The division currently receives 5 literary publications in Bulgarian.

Collected works and the history and criticism of literature are the strongest aspects of the collection. Ivan Vazov is the Bulgarian author best represented, with approximately 40 entries for works by him; included are 2 translations into English and an opera score based on his works, along with some 20 entries for works about him. There are 12 titles by Pencho Slaveykov and a similar number about him. The humorous novel *Bay-Ganyu* by Aleko Konstantinov is present in 5 editions, the earliest dated 1895.

Church Slavonic

Because of its close relationship with Old Church Slavonic, the oldest known form of the Slavic language, Church Slavonic is of great interest to the Slavonic Division. The division catalog holds approximately 200 entries for dictionaries, grammars, and other philological works, and about 250 entries representing texts and translations. Although the language is no longer written, the division acquires all new editions of standard texts when they are published. The collecting policy is comprehensive.

One of the library's treasures is the *Triod' tzvetnaya* (1491), a printed liturgical work in Church Slavonic. The Manuscripts and Archives Division has an illuminated lectionary of the Acts of the Apostles on vellum from the late fourteenth century. In the Spencer Collection is a group of manuscripts in the language, on paper and illustrated, dating from the fifteenth to the eighteenth centuries and including the Four Gospels, Canticles, a "Ladder" of St. John Climachus, and other works.

Czech and Slovak Literatures

History, criticism, and bibliography of Czechoslovakian literature are collected comprehensively; literary works are collected on a representative basis. The collection of 2,800 volumes is strong in all aspects for the eighteenth and nineteenth centuries and the division acquires all contemporary literary material, both original and critical.

Collected works of authors are well represented; editions of individual works are acquired only if they are not found in collected works, or if they contain important critical or textual material. Translations into Czech are seldom purchased except for major authors; in accordance with a standard library policy, however, translations into English or other languages more widely known than the original are acquired.

Literary periodicals and society publications are collected on a representative basis. Among the nineteenth-century titles are *Wlastimi* (1840–42) and *Květy* (1879–1915); twentieth-century titles include *Plamen* (1959–) and *Česká literatura* (1953–). The Slavonic Division currently receives ten literary periodicals from Czechoslovakia.

There are sixty cards for works by the Czech author Karel Čapek in the Slavonic Division catalog, and a similar number for works about him. Prompt-books and typescripts of his plays, particularly *R. U. R.* and *The Robber* are held by the Theatre Collection. The Czech poet Karel Mácha is represented by nine catalog entries for works by him, and fifteen for works about him. There are five entries for Slovak author L'udovit Štúr and eight entries for works about him.

LATVIAN LITERATURE

Literature forms a strong part of the Latvian holdings, constituting some two-thirds of the total 3,500 volumes. Other strong subjects are linguistics, archaeology, history, political science, economics, and ethnography, with folklore, and particularly folk songs, an important feature of the latter. The Latvian collection is substantially complete for items published in Latvia itself; there is a fair collection of material published outside the country. The Slavonic Division endeavors to develop the resources in the latter category.

Bibliographical control of the literature is provided from 1587 to the present by copies of the bibliographies of Karl Napiersky and Janis Misins, the *Latvijas Valsts bibliotekas biletens*, and the *Latvijas PSR preses hronika*. Outside Latvia, the exile bibliographies of Benjamin Jegers and Janis Velde give similar coverage. Dictionaries of the language in the library include G. F. Stender's *Lettisches lexicon* (1789–91) in a first edition, and a copy of the monumental publication of Karlis Muelenbachs and J. Endzelīns entitled *Latviešu valodas vārdnīca* (1923–56). Folk song holdings center around the exhaustive K. Barons *Latwju dainas* (first edition 1915; second edition 1922) which lists 35,789 basic songs and 182,000 variations.

Collected works of major authors are a feature of the literature collections, together with all standard works in literary criticism. Rudolfs Blaumanis is represented by approximately 50 titles, and there are 3 critical works about him. The division holds first editions of his novels *Andriksons, Naves ena*, and *Salna pavasari*, all published in 1899. Jānis Pliekšans (known as J. Rainis) is represented by approximately 50 titles including collected works and 12 translations into Esperanto, English, Russian, and other languages. The author himself translated the works of Dumas, Goethe, and Schiller into Latvian; all are in the Slavonic Division collections. There are some 6 books of criticism on Rainis.

Of the exiled writers the Research Libraries have a good collection of the works of Zenta Maurina in both Lettish and German, as well as her translations from the English, French, and Swedish. There are complete holdings of the poetry of Veronika Strēlerte, Zinaīda Lazda, and Klāra Zāle; and of the fiction and drama of Anšlavs Eglitis.

Latvian journals received include *Karogs* (1946–), perhaps the outstanding literary periodical; among the literary periodicals published outside Latvia are *Akademiska dzive* (Indianapolis), *Jaunā gaita* (Ann Arbor), and *Universitas* (Stuttgart).

LITHUANIAN LITERATURE

The collecting policy in this area is representative for both monographs and periodical and society publications. Most Soviet Lithuanian academic publications are received on exchange, but little else in received. Only a small proportion of the substantial number of books in Lithuanian published outside the Soviet Union comes to the division. Although the library endeavors to acquire these materials they remain very difficult to obtain. A number of pamphlets in Lithuanian are in the "n.c." classmark (materials not separately cataloged). The library currently receives three Lithuanian literary periodical and society publications.

MACEDONIAN LITERATURE

The Macedonian literature holdings of approximately 50 volumes compose a substantial representation of a new literary language; the entire resources in Macedonian are limited to 100 volumes. The division's collecting policy is representative for this literature. The establishment of exchange relationships with other libraries and the purchase of material from dealers continues to build the collection.

POLISH LITERATURE

The history, criticism, and bibliography of Polish literature are collected comprehensively, while poetry, fiction, and drama are collected on a representative basis. Fiction is the genre held most extensively, with an approximate total of 4,700 volumes.

The library currently receives 10 periodical titles related to the literature of Poland. Included are *Wiadomości literackie* both in the original Polish publication and the London continuation, and *Kultura*.

Translations of works of Polish literature into English are acquired as a matter of policy. Other translations are purchased sparingly, as in the case of translations from Polish into more widely used languages. More than 25 works of Henryk Sienkiewicz are present in languages other than Polish, including *Quo Vadis*, which is held in 6 separate English translations, and also as a play and a libretto.

First or early editions are not a strong feature of the holdings; a notable exception is Adam Mickiewicz's epic *Pan Tadeusz* (1834). When possible the division obtains collected editions of major authors; if a collected edition is available, editions of individual works are not acquired unless they contain new critical material. An author of the stature of Mickiewicz is represented by some 150 entries in the Public Catalog, and by some 290 additional entries for works concerning him, including the *Mickiewicz-Blätter* (1956–). The Slavonic Division adds to its holdings of Polish imprints before 1600 and other rare materials as funds become available.

SERBO-CROATIAN LITERATURE

Serbian (which employs the Cyrillic alphabet) and Croatian (which employs the Roman alphabet) literatures are acquired on a representative basis. Fiction is acquired selectively. Of the larger language units of the Slavonic Division, the Serbo-Croatian with its 1,800 volumes has shown the greatest growth: 400 percent from 1945 to 1966. Literary holdings commence with the second half of the nineteenth century, and include the major works of Borisav Stanković, Stevan Sremac, August Šenoa, Ivo Vojnović, Vladimir Nazor, and Ivo Andrić. Each author is generally represented by a collected edition and several separate editions of individual works; there are few translations, with the exception of the works of Ivo Vojnović and Ivo Andrić. First or early editions are generally limited to authors of the nineteenth century. Literary journals include the publications of the Matica Srpska, and the periodical *Život* issued by the Jugoslovenska Akademja.

SLOVENIAN LITERATURE

Although this is a small collection of some 100 volumes, it is considered to be strong in the field, and is growing rapidly. The collecting policy is representative except for fiction, which is acquired selectively. The classic writers Ivan Cankar and France Prešeran are held in twentieth-century editions.

SORBIAN (LUSATIAN) LITERATURE

The division seeks to build up its holdings of some 120 volumes by acquiring all available items published in Sorbian, the language of the 500,000 Slavs remaining in Germany. Most of the material obtained is in the fields of literature and philology, with scientific material confined for the most part to folklore and ethnology. Literary material is largely of the twentieth century, although there are dictionaries and works of individual authors from the nineteenth century in the collection.[11] Perhaps the most significant item is the first grammar of the language, Georg Matthaei's *Wendische Grammatica* (1721). The Institut za Serbski Ludospyt's *Spisy* has been received by the library since 1954.

UKRAINIAN LITERATURE

Although periodical and society publications in Ukrainian are collected comprehensively, other literature is acquired on a representative basis. This means that periodicals are perhaps the strongest feature of the holdings of some 2,000 volumes. The most important pre-Revolutionary periodical, *Kiyevskaya starina*, is held in a nearly complete run. A rare group of periodicals published during the politically turbulent 1920s, among them *Zhytta i revolyutziya*, *Chervonyi shlyakh*, and *Visti*, has been preserved. Works of individual authors of the same period are equally rare, as in the case of Mykola Khvyl'ovyi. The library currently receives 7 periodicals in Ukrainian literature, one of the most important being *Zapysky naukovoho tovarystva*.

Fiction and poetry are a stronger aspect of this literature than drama. The division obtains a good selection of the émigré publications from areas in the United States, Canada, and Germany, as well as the publications of the USSR. Taras Shevchenko is the most fully represented Ukrainian author with 90 titles, including collected works and individual editions, the larger part twentieth-century printings. Critical works about Shevchenko are more numerous, totaling more than 300 entries. A second great Ukrainian author, Ivan Franko, is represented by 80 original titles (including the 20-volume jubilee edition of 1956), and a similar number of critical works and bibliographies. The Slavonic Division has a first edition of his work on Ukrainian proverbs (1901–10).

NON-INDO-EUROPEAN LANGUAGES

The library also selectively obtains materials in the non-Indo-European languages of the Soviet Union.[12] Of current publications only materials in the Finno-Ugric languages (Cheremis, Mordvins, Votyak, and Zyrian) employing the Cyrillic alphabet are collected. Printed matter in the Paleo-Asiatic languages of extreme northern Siberia is virtually unobtainable.

The Oriental Division maintains a large collection of materials from the 1920s and 1930s in the Altaic languages (Turkic), as well as a large collection of Georgian literature with some material in the other Caucasian tongues. The largest collection is in pamphlet form under the "n.c." classmark (materials not separately cataloged); the largest single group in this category consists of 70 volumes of Turkic pamphlets.

OTHER EUROPEAN LITERATURES

ALBANIAN LITERATURE

Albanian literature is collected on a representative basis, but the holdings are not extensive. They are strongest from 1960 onward: general order arrangements which insured that the library received all publications in belles-lettres were in effect from 1960 to 1965; since that time only periodical publications have been supplied in this way. Monographs are now selected from available bibliographical tools. The library currently receives the literary periodical *Nëndori*.

Problems in cataloging affect the reader's use of Albanian publications. Unless a catalog card is available from the Library of Congress the book is put into a deferred cataloging category until it can be processed; no record appears in the Public Catalog for a considerable number of books in Albanian literature which are in the library's possession but temporarily unobtainable.

BASQUE LANGUAGE AND LITERATURE

Entries in the Public Catalog under this heading number approximately 300, including index entries to articles in journals. The collecting policy is comprehensive, but much of the material receives deferred cataloging and is not immediately available to the public. All types of literature are represented, especially drama and fiction. Also available are historical, critical, and philological works in the various dialects of the Basque language. Periodical holdings include the *Revue internationale des études basques* (1907–36) and *Eusko-Jakintza* (1947–52).

Andrés de Poza's *Dela antigua lengua, poblaciones, y comarcas de las Españas* (1587) is in

---

11. See Richard C. Lewanski, "The Lusatians; A Bibliography of Dictionaries," *BNYPL* 63 (1959): 242–46.

12. See Edward Allworth, "Central Asian Publishing and the Rise of Nationalism," *BNYPL* 69 (1965): 493–522. Published separately by the library, with a list of publications in the library added.

the Rare Book Division. A number of early translations of the Bible into Basque, many of them in the Bonaparte collection, have been given the class mark RAEC. This group of valuable materials acquired by the Lenox Library consists of works published by Louis Lucien Bonaparte in English and continental European languages and dialects, the larger proportion Basque with many Bibles, but also including maps and works on philology.

The library has examples of standard Basque dictionaries and grammars, including Resurrección Maria de Azkue's *Diccionario vasco-español-francés* (1905–06) and Arturo Campión y Jaime-Bon's *Gramática de los cuatro dialectos de la lengua euskara* (1884). Also of importance are the works in the Ekin series (Biblioteca de cultura vasca) published in Buenos Aires during the 1940s and 1950s.

ESTONIAN LITERATURE

Estonian literature is collected on a comprehensive basis. Although not large, the collection has interesting features. For the period before 1917 the library's holdings may be considered good for Estonian learned society publications, generally in German. University publications after 1918 are well represented, but there are no substantial holdings of literary material published in the Estonian language. There is no general order arrangement for the supply of literary publications from this area. The holdings of some 600 volumes include approximately 240 titles in fiction, 140 in poetry, and 40 in drama, including translations from other languages.[13] The library currently receives the literary periodicals *Keel ja kirjandus* (1958–   ) and *Looming* (1957–   ).

The Andrew Pranspill papers, presented to the Manuscripts and Archives Division in 1958 and 1966, consist of correspondence from the leading Estonian writers of the twentieth century. Also included are 3 holograph poems by Vallak, Vis-

13. See Ants Oras, "Estonian Poetry," *BNYPL* 61 (1957): 595–603. Published separately by the library.

nagran, and Vogust, a holograph of an unpublished magazine article by Artur Adson, newspaper clippings, photographs, and other items. The 185 pieces are dated from 1923 to 1955. Among the writers included are A. H. Tammsaare, Marie Under, Bernard Kangro, A. Kitzberg, and Artur Adson.

HUNGARIAN LITERATURE

Hungarian literature is collected on a comprehensive basis. Bibliographical tools allow a careful selection of the best works published in the country. New editions of older works are generally acquired as they are issued in preference to original editions, which are difficult to locate. The resources in Hungarian literature, numbering some 5,280 volumes, emphasize historical and critical works, periodicals, collected editions, and general literature; they are strongest in publications of the nineteenth century and for the period after 1930. The greatest expansion of the collections has taken place in the last decade.

Among the resources useful for studying the history of Hungarian literature are Antal Szerb's *A Világirodalom története* (1957) and Klaniczay, Szauder, and Szabolcsi's *History of Hungarian Literature* (1964). The library's holdings of periodicals include one of the two reported substantial runs of *Nyugat* (1908–41), and *Irodalomtörténet* (1924–62). Four periodical titles in literature are currently received from Hungary, among them *Helikon* and *Kritika*. Collections range from *Deliciae poetarum Hungaricorum* (1619) to the collected works of Mikszáth, Jókai, and others.

Fiction is the most fully represented genre, with editions of the works of Nemeth, Móricz, and other contemporary authors. In drama are numerous works by Herczeg, Fodor, and others. In the Manuscripts and Archives Division are notes, outlines, and early versions of plays by Ferenc Molnár presented by the author in memory of Wanda Bartha in 1947; included are *Esküvö* (Wedding Day), *A Cukrászne* (Delicate Story), *Szivdobogás* (Game of Hearts), and *A Csaszár* (The Emperor). Hungarian poetry is held from the sixteenth- and seventeenth-century poets Balassi and Zrinyi through Ady and other contemporary poets.

26

LITERATURES OF AFRICA, THE NEAR EAST, AND THE FAR EAST

The library's collections of the literatures of Africa, the Near East, and the Far East augment important holdings in history, religion, philosophy, and archaeology. Arabic is the best represented literature both in number of volumes and in range of coverage, although since 1950 holdings in Japanese and Korean literature have been considerably strengthened. The Spencer Collection's rare illustrated Japanese books and scrolls, many of which are literary in nature, augment the resources. The Armenian, Georgian, and Central Asian literatures have benefited from increased acquisitions since

1950: the Armenian collection, while not large numerically, represents a great proportion of the available published works. The Oriental Division acquires only a sampling of current popular literature from the Near East and Far East.

Among the research tools available for locating materials mentioned in this chapter are the *Dictionary Catalog of the Oriental Collection* in sixteen volumes (1960) and the *Dictionary Catalog of the Slavonic Collection* in forty-four volumes (1974), both of which were published by G. K. Hall & Company of Boston.

AFRICAN LITERATURES

The African literatures considered in this section are those of nations south of the Sahara Desert, with the exception of the literature of South Africa. The responsibility for acquiring material in African languages which employ or once employed the Arabic alphabet (such as Fula, Hausa, Somali, and Swahili) lies with the Oriental Division; other African languages are the responsibility of the General Research and Humanities Division. The collecting policies in both areas are representative.

The interest in acquiring literature in the African vernaculars is one of long standing, although prior to World War II there was a small amount of such materials available. For example, there are some twenty-five items in Zulu vernacular, excluding translations from other languages, and approximately half that number in Swahili. Much material formerly came from missionary stations and was, therefore, primarily religious in nature. With the development of the countries there has been a growth of creative literature, which is being acquired through the aid of new bibliographical publications. African writing in the Western European languages, most notably English, French, and Portuguese, is collected on the same basis as other materials in those languages.

The Schomburg Center

The Schomburg Center is devoted to the acquisition and preservation of materials relating to persons of African descent, and contains rarities not available in the general collections of the Research Libraries. Among unique materials is a copy of the Latin verse of Juan Latino, printed in Granada in 1573; another rarity is Bakary Diallo's *Force-bonté*, considered to be the first novel produced by a French West African.

The Schomburg Center has especially interesting holdings on the histories of the ancient African kingdoms and on Portuguese Africa and Madagascar. There is a good representation of the contemporary literature of Senegal, Uganda, Nigeria, Ghana, and other countries, which includes the work of Moussa Travélé, Léopold Sédar Senghor, Antoine Bolamba, Gaddiel R. Acquaah, and other authors. The center is also acquiring examples of one of the livelier manifestations of the modern African creative spirit, popular fiction, poetry, and drama published in paperbound format. Written primarily in English and for the most part in Nigeria, the material is the production of the younger African writers. A proportion of the literature produced in vernacular African languages reaches the Schomburg Center, but current creative work is principally written in English and French.

A *Dictionary Catalog of the Schomburg Collection of Negro Literature and History* in nine volumes was published by G. K. Hall & Company of Boston in 1962. Five-year Cumulation Supplements are to be issued; the first appeared in 1967, the second in 1972.

HEBREW AND YIDDISH LITERATURE

The Jewish Division has the responsibility for collecting Hebrew and Yiddish literature, as well as literature in Jewish languages and dialects such as Ladino and Judeo-Arabic. Works of sociological, ethnological, and linguistic importance relating to the Jewish experience are collected along with Hebrew and Yiddish belles-lettres.

Hebrew and Yiddish fiction, poetry, drama, and essays are acquired comprehensively. Contemporary translations into Hebrew and Yiddish are acquired selectively, with a comprehensive attempt to collect nineteenth-century translations. The Jewish Division collects all anthologies of Hebrew and Yiddish literature translated into languages other than English.

A *Dictionary Catalog of the Jewish Collection* in fourteen volumes, including a three-volume title catalog of works in Hebrew and Yiddish, was published in 1960 by G. K. Hall & Company of Boston.

Hebrew Literature

The 4,000 volumes of Hebrew literature represent 12 percent of the total holdings in the Hebrew language, as compared to Yiddish literature, which represents about 40 percent of the total holdings in the Yiddish language. These proportions are somewhat misleading, due to the fact that so much material of a literary nature in Hebrew is classified as "religion," "Bibles," or "philosophy."

Strong resources in Hebrew literature include important early literary periodicals such as *ha-Me'asef* (1784–1811) and *Bikure ha-'Itim* (1820–31), as well as modern examples such as *Moznayim* (1929–) and *ha-Do'ar* (1921–). Hebrew literature of the Middle Ages is represented primarily by modern printed texts. Among the approximately forty incunabula in the division are Immanuel ben Solomon's *Sefer ha-mahbarot* ("Book of Poems") (1491) and Solomon ibn Gabirol's *Mivḥar ha-peninim* ("Maxims") (1484). Other rare texts include Ephraim Luzzatto's *Eleh bene ha-ne'urim* (Poems) of 1766, and Moses Chayyim Luzzatto's play *la-Yesharim tehilah* (1743). A number of first editions of the nineteenth century are worthy of note. The novel *ha-Avot veha-banim* (1868) by Shalom Jacob Abramowitsch (Mendele Mokher Sforim), the grandfather of modern Hebrew and Yiddish literature, and his first story, *Limdu hetev* (1862), are both in the division. Judah Loeb Gordon's play *Mishle Yehudah* (1859) is also present. Poland, Israel, and the United States were the leading centers of publication in Hebrew before World War II; after the war Israel assumed leadership in this field. The Jewish Division has obtained almost all the significant publications from the major areas of Hebrew book production. There is complete coverage of materials published in Israel since 1964. Most of the Hebrew literary manuscripts held in the Jewish Division date from the twentieth century, together with several hundred letters written by Hebrew literary figures. An older manuscript of outstanding importance is the 1640 copy of the first play in Hebrew by Leone Sommo de Portaleone.

Yiddish Literature

Approximately 6,500 volumes in Yiddish literature are administered by the Jewish Division. The division also has rich holdings in manuscripts of Yiddish drama (some 460 items); 300 plays and prompt-books were donated by the family of Boris Thomashefsky, and cover his career on the New York stage from the end of the nineteenth century to the 1930s. The division holds an additional 150 plays, parts of plays, and scenarios which were performed in the New York Yiddish theatre from the last decades of the nineteenth century to 1920. Works of the classic Yiddish literary authors are present in the collections, with Shalom Jacob Abramowitsch (Mendele Mokher Sforim), Isaac Loeb Perez, and Sholom Aleichem (Shalom Rabinowitz) best represented. The division presently receives everything of significance published in Israel, the United States, Argentina, and France, as well as from countries with less ambitious publishing programs.

Among rare items in the division are first editions of nineteenth-century Yiddish authors. Works of Shalom Jacob Abramowitsch, Israel Axenfeld, and Abraham Goldfaden are particularly worthy of mention.

LADINO (JUDEO-SPANISH) LITERATURE

A small collection of material in Ladino consists primarily of translations of ethical and Kabbalistic works, commentaries on the Bible, and translations of popular literature from French and Spanish. The first printed original work in the language, Moses ben Baruch Almosnino's *Regimento de la vida* (1564) is outstanding among the holdings. The division has files of four major newspapers published in Ladino.

JUDEO-ARABIC LITERATURE

Judeo-Arabic is the dialect spoken by the native Jews of Tunisia, Morocco, Iraq, and other Oriental countries; it is written in Hebrew characters. Resources in this area include approximately 100 volumes published in a village on the island of Jerba off the Tunisian coast, among those liturgical works, rabbinical texts, biblical commentaries, and biographies of religious leaders. Some 50 paperback romances, translations for the most part, were published in Tunis and in the town of Sousse. *Sefunot*, published annually by the Ben-Zvi Institute of Hebrew University, is devoted to gathering documents, stimulating research, and encouraging publication of studies bearing on Oriental Jewish communities.

ARABIC LITERATURE

The 2,000 volumes of literary materials in the Arabic languages, including translations and criticism, form a strong archive of the Oriental Division. Arabian poetry is collected comprehensively; other genres are collected on a representative basis. Translations from the European languages into Arabic are acquired selectively.

There are 720 volumes of Arabian poetry, 634 volumes of Adab, fables, romances, and drama, 96 volumes of proverbs and sayings, and 440 volumes related to the *Arabian Nights*. There are more than 250 Arabic manuscripts in the Oriental Division, 36 in the Manuscripts and Archives Division, and 12 in the Spencer Collection. The greater number pertain to fields other than literature, such as law, medicine, religion, and philology.

Texts of the *Arabian Nights* number 440 volumes. Arabic texts include the Calcutta II edition, dated 1839–42, edited by Macnaghten, and the Breslau edition of 1825–43, edited by Habicht. Most of the standard translations into Western European languages are present, from Galland to Burton, Payne, and Mardrus.

INDIC LITERATURES

SANSKRIT LITERATURE

The collecting policy is representative for Sanskrit literature. Many of the epics, dramas, and fables in Sanskrit are contained in the library's rich holdings of some 720 volumes. Epics number approximately 400 volumes, with numerous editions of the *Mahābhārata* and the *Rāmāyana* both in Sanskrit and in translation. The drama holdings, 120 volumes, feature many editions of Kālidāsa's *Sakuntala*. Somadeva's *Kathāsarit-sāgara* (Ocean of Story), both in the original and in the Tawney translation of 1924–28, is among some 200 volumes in the Sanskrit fiction section. There are also editions of *Pañcatantra* (Five Chapters on Wisdom) and the *Hitopadesa* (Good Counsel). The Spencer Collection has fine illustrated editions of Sanskrit fables. Some of the 13 manuscripts in Sanskrit in the Manuscripts and Archives Division contain verse; all of these are Indian, and they date from the sixteenth to the nineteenth century.

MODERN INDIAN LITERATURE

Before 1950 few libraries in the United States had extensive material in the modern Indic languages. Since that time the library has acquired Hindi, Urdu, Gujarati, Tamil, and Marathi publications. The collecting policy is selective. There are approximately 600 volumes related to Hindic languages and literature, and some 1,400 volumes related to the modern languages of India, Pakistan, and Ceylon. The great backlog of materials acquired under the PL-480 Program must also be taken into consideration: this amounts to more than 14,000 pieces for India and Pakistan, many of them literary in nature.

Of note is a small group of holograph poems in English by Sir Rabindranath Tagore, including a 65-page typescript of "Gitanjali" with corrections in the hand of W. B. Yeats, in the Berg Collection.

OTHER LITERATURES

ALTAIC LITERATURES

The collection policy is representative for literatures in the Altaic languages. Materials received before 1940 are maintained in the Slavonic Division, for the most part designated by the "n.c." classmark (materials preserved but not separately cataloged); materials received since that time are administered by the Oriental Division.

In 1965 it was estimated that the library held 810 books and pamphlets and 24 magazines published before 1946 in Kazakh, Uzbek, Kirghiz, Turkoman, Karakalpak, and Uigur.[1] These rare publications range from Uzbek Muslim poetry to Kazakh Communist Party reports, and from material on education among the Kirghiz to the planning and utilization of the Turkistanian cotton crop. The larger part of the material in the collection is printed in the simplified Arabic script, although material currently received is in modified Cyrillic scripts.

ARMENIAN LITERATURE

This is considered one of the best collections of Armenian literature in the United States, and

---

1. See Edward Allworth, "Central Asian Publishing and the Rise of Nationalism," *BNYPL* 69 (1965): 493–522. Published separately by the library, with a list of publications in the library added.

contains some 720 volumes. Material is acquired on a representative basis. The periodical holdings are strong; there are runs of *Gotchnag* (New York, 1910–) and *Hayrenik* (Boston, 1901–), and literary and popular journals from Armenia as well as the daily newspaper, *Sovetakar Hayasdan*. Some 100 items by Armenians in the United States represent the remarkable literary production of a small ethnic group; other holdings emphasize Bibles and saints' lives.

CHINESE, JAPANESE, AND KOREAN LITERATURES

The library's collection of the literatures of China, Japan, and Korea are not exceptionally strong. The literature of each nation is acquired on a representative basis. Material published before 1912 has generally not been acquired, and a great percentage of the material published since 1912, especially in Japan, is scientific and technical.

Two literary periodicals are currently received from the People's Republic of China, *Renmin wenxue* and *Ju ben*; from Nationalist China comes *Sinica*. Approximately 900 books in Chinese literature include 250 volumes of poetry and some 640 volumes of fiction, drama, and essays. There are editions of major works in Chinese, with many translations into English and other European languages. Collected works and standard texts are not a feature of the holdings.

Japanese literature is represented by some 200 volumes of poetry and 760 of fiction, drama, and essays. Among Japanese literary periodicals currently received is *Ashibi*. Editions of individual works are more often found than collected editions; there are a great number of translations into English and other European languages. Drama, and especially the Noh drama, is well represented.

The extensive collection of manuscripts and printed books from Japan in the Spencer Collection adds strength in this area. Some 350 printed books range from the *Ise monogatari* of 1608, considered the earliest Japanese story book printed from movable wooden type, to early nineteenth-century first editions of the novels of Bakin. There are a number of editions of the *Genji monogatari emaki* by Lady Murasaki (the earliest dated 1650) as well as novels, plays, and ghost stories. There is an equally rich collection of some 235 Japanese manuscripts, a large number of which are literary. Of great interest is the *Matsukase murasame emaki* (Love-drama of Matsukase and Murasame), one of the earliest Noh scrolls in existence, dated 1520, a 1554 manuscript of *Genji monogatari emaki*, and the original manuscript of Bakin's *Mukashi gatari shichiya no kura*, which was published in 1810.

The collection of Korean literature is currently growing at a rapid pace. Modern collected editions of both classic and modern authors are a feature of this group of approximately 260 volumes.

Manchu Literature

The collecting policy in this instance is exhaustive. As little material is available, the holdings are small but adequate, and predominantly historical. Included are editions of the Manchu Shih and the regulations for the Eight Banners or divisions of the Imperial Army. The Oriental Division holds 52 reels of microfilm from the Tenri collection of the Manchu books in Manchu

characters, consisting of dictionaries, grammars, and readers, in all numbering some 43,000 pages. A small group of manuscripts are in the Manuscripts and Archives Division; these are official texts and decrees of the Ch'ing dynasty, the oldest dated 1661.[2]

GEORGIAN LITERATURE

Although the collecting policy is representative in the Georgian language, the holdings were minimal before 1950. The collection has since grown to some 300 volumes, with particular strength in the fields of linguistics and belles-lettres, although scientific material is also collected. Georgian émigré literature is acquired when available. Editions of Shot'ha Rusthaveli's epic *The Knight in the Tiger Skin*, both in the original and in translation, are a feature of the resources. Additional materials in Georgian received in the 1920s and 1930s are found in the "n.c." classmark (material preserved but not separately cataloged) in the Slavonic Division.

PERSIAN LITERATURE

Three aspects of Persian literature are collected comprehensively: Avestan and Pahlevi works (which are predominantly liturgical rather than literary); Persian poetry, from the time of Firdausī; and works relating to the *Rubáiyát* of Omar Khayyām. Other literary works are acquired on a representative basis. There is an approximate total of 840 volumes in the collection.

Persian poetry in the Oriental Division commences with the classical writers such as Firdausī, Rumī, Sa'di, and Hāfiz. In the Oriental Division catalog there are some 50 entries devoted to Firdausī; 50 for Hāfiz; 25 for Rumī; and 70 for Sa'di. These entries represent the collected and individual works of the poets in Persian, numerous translations into European languages, critical works, and articles in periodicals. Thirteen manuscripts of the works of these poets in the Manuscripts and Archives Division date from the sixteenth to the eighteenth century. A group of 24 illustrated manuscripts in the Spencer Collection includes a 1614 copy of the *Shāhnāmāh* (Book of Kings); another *Shāhnāmāh* is a 1550 translation into Turkish with more than 100 miniatures.[3]

The *Rubáiyát* of Omar Khayyām is present in some 150 volumes, for the most part translations into English and other European languages. In the Berg Collection are copies of the first 4 editions of the Edward Fitzgerald translation, and also copies of his earlier translation of Jāmī's *Salámán and Absál* (1856).

SOUTHEAST ASIAN LITERATURES

The resources in the literatures of various southeast Asian nations are not strong. Such ma-

2. See John L. Mish, "A Manchu-Chinese Scroll," *BNYPL* 52 (1948): 143–44.
3. See Richard Gottheil, "The Shahnámeh in Turkish," *BNYPL* 36 (1932): 9–10; and "The Shahnámeh in Persian," *BNYPL* 36 (1932): 543–54.

terials are acquired on a representative basis. Participation in the PL-480 Program since 1964 brought Indonesian materials to the library for several years. Critical materials in the Western languages are relatively abundant, particularly in periodical format.

Six Burmese, forty-nine Thai, and three Indonesian manuscripts in the Spencer Collection are for the most part religious in nature.

Spanish and English are represented in the collection of Philippine literature, in addition to works in the native languages. Works by and about José Rizal y Alonso include *Noli me tángere* (Berlin, 1887) and *Mi último pensamiento* (Hong Kong, 1897).

TURKISH LITERATURE

Turkish literature is acquired on a representative basis. General literature, including translations of the Bible, is perhaps the strongest category with some 200 volumes; poetry and drama are represented by 120 volumes; there are 120 volumes of fables, among which editions of the fables of Nasr-al-Din are the most numerous. Translations of Turkish literature into the Western European languages are not plentiful in the collections. The shortage of qualified catalogers has produced a backlog of Turkish literature not presently available to the public.

27

LINGUISTICS

COLLECTING POLICY

The Research Libraries have always been strong in materials relating to linguistics, and now contain 52,000 manuscripts, volumes, and maps related to this field. Although the resources are substantially complete in all languages where there are published works, they are perhaps most noteworthy in American Indian languages and the languages of Africa and Polynesia, with a number of works on the universal languages (e.g., Esperanto, Volapük). In 1941 it was estimated that there were resources in the collections for the study of fourteen hundred languages; currently the Research Libraries have at least a specimen of almost every written language. Minor languages have always been the New York Public Library's special domain.

In its current acquisitions, considerable selectivity is exercised, although an effort is made to obtain everything of importance in the English language published both here and abroad. For the classical languages and modern foreign tongues, dictionaries and glossaries of languages and dialects, as well as the standard general treatises on grammar and philology are secured. An extensive file of journals is also maintained. In minor languages the Research Libraries continue to collect both critical writings and printed textual examples. Routine materials and many unusual imprints have been gathered.

The collecting policy in Greek and most languages using the Roman alphabet is comprehensive, except for the pedagogic aspects of the subject, including textbooks, grammars, and readers, which are collected on a selective basis. Some Romance languages such as Rhaeto-Romanic, Dalmatian, Catalan, Rumanian (and also Albanian) are acquired on a representative basis.

Most Oriental languages are collected comprehensively in the field of linguistics, with the following notable exceptions, which are collected representatively: African languages which use or formerly used the Arabic script (Fulah, Hausa, Somali, Swahili, etc.); the Middle Indian language Prakrit; the languages of the Malay Archipelago (except Indonesia, Malay, and Malaya); and the languages of Indo-China.

Balto-Slavic languages are acquired comprehensively by the Slavonic Division, but the non-Indo-European languages of the USSR are collected only selectively.

The Jewish Division acquires works in Hebrew, Yiddish, and Jewish dialectal linguistics comprehensively with the exception of Aramaic and Biblical Hebrew, which are acquired on a representative basis. In accordance with its policy in Yiddish literature, the division acquires exhaustively all available material in Yiddish linguistics, including grammars, textbooks, and other pedagogical items.

A brief tabulation reveals the growth of the linguistics collections:

1921 New York Public Library	14,098 volumes
1930	19,500
1966[1]	40,500

In 1966 the distribution of linguistic materials by language area was approximately as follows:

General works	6,660 volumes
International languages	2,000
Greek and Latin	8,900
Italian	1,260
French	4,270
Spanish	2,265
Portuguese	570
Other Romance languages	480
General Teutonic languages	1,350
German	2,830
Dutch	915
Scandinavian	1,200

---

1. These statistical figures do not include 6,000 volumes in the linguistics collection of the Oriental Division, 1,400 volumes in the Slavonic Division, and 5,200 volumes in the American History Division representing American Indian languages. Additional adjustments in the areas of Scandinavian and international languages in the distribution table have been made in order to represent the extent of the linguistic resources in the Research Libraries more accurately than is possible through the statistical figures based on the Billings Classification Schedule.

English	7,580
Minor European	1,350
African	830
Oceanic	300
American Indian	5,200
Hebrew and Yiddish	1,900
Oriental languages	6,000
Balto-Slavic languages	1,400

HISTORICAL SURVEY

As early as 1851, Dr. Cogswell, in his Annual Report for the Astor Library, considered the collection in linguistics "approaching towards a full apparatus of grammars, vocabularies, dictionaries, and other facilities for acquiring the various languages of the earth." In 1854 he declared the collection "would do credit to a much older institution," having "grammars and dictionaries of one hundred and four different languages, and numerous vocabularies of the rude unwritten ones" as well as "chrestomathies, and other useful facilities for studying them. All the families and branches of European languages, and a greater part of those of Asia and Africa, are represented in the collection. It contains the best works on the Egyptian hieroglyphics, the cuneiform inscriptions, and the other curious records of the ancient nations of the East. It has also the best of the vocabularies of the ancient dialects of the Mexican and South American Indians, which were collected and published by the early Spanish missionary priests."[2] The Lenox Library, while it could boast no extensive collection in this field, had some early, rare materials, such as Molina's *Aquí comiença un vocabulario enla lengua castellana y mexicana* (1555) and the *Doctrina Christiana* (1578).

The Ford collection, given in 1899, contained much manuscript material relating to the lexicographer Noah Webster; it was strengthened by a gift from Mrs. Theodore Bailey in 1954. In 1908 Wilberforce Eames gave a large collection of volumes in the African languages, continuing other gifts of similar material. In 1916, Mrs. Thomas A. Janvier gave about 500 works on Provence, including material on the Provençal language.[3] In 1932 a collection gathered by the American Board of Commissioners for Foreign Missions was acquired, a collection made up of materials printed in the native languages of those locales where the board had its stations. The collection contained over 5,000 volumes of catechisms, tracts, portions of the Gospels, the whole Bible, and other religious books, in native dialects of India, Africa, and other parts of the world. In 1936 the Research Libraries purchased two collections of interest in this field. The first was the C. P. G. Scott library, consisting almost entirely of standard linguistic works; its particular feature being an important group in the Malay languages. The other was portions of the Starr collection, of interest principally to anthropology but containing imprints in minor languages as widely scattered as those of the Philippine Islands, East Africa, and Mexico. Gifts over the years have helped to form the collection of materials in

2. See Lydenberg, *History*, p. 29.
3. See Daniel C. Haskell, "Provençal Literature and Language Including the Local History of Southern France," *BNYPL* 25 (1921): 372–400 et seq. Published separately by the library in 1925.

Esperanto and Volapük; the Mrs. Dave H. Morris gift in 1948 and 1949 added notably to materials in Esperanto and Ido.

RESOURCES

Few of the important European or American studies relating either to comparison of languages or individual tongues are wanting. Included are dictionaries and glossaries, formal treatises, periodicals, essays, and a variety of manuals (grammars, rhetorics, "easy method" textbooks for learning foreign languages). Current school textbooks are not usually acquired; there is, however, an interesting collection of earlier examples.

The Research Libraries have an unusually good collection of dictionaries, composed not only of current and standard publications but including many others of historic interest. There are good representations of earlier editions of French, German, and particularly English works. Many of these were of secondary importance and are consequently more difficult for the scholar to locate. Additional copies of authoritative works are added if they seem to be useful; earlier editions of important works and secondary works not in the collection are also added, but no attempt is made to keep variant imprints or issues of any but rare works in this field. Abridgements are not ordinarily added to the collections.

Two collections of dictionaries are accessible. The Main Reading Room collection is designed to meet all ordinary needs of the public; the reference collection of works in linguistics maintained by the Preparation Services is adapted to staff needs. These latter works are available in the reading rooms on request. Modern language dictionaries kept in the special reading rooms (the Jewish Division, the Oriental Division, etc.) are generally duplicates of works in the reference collections mentioned or the stack collection, and are available for readers in those rooms only. Copies needed for desk use elsewhere may be secured from the stacks.

Dictionaries and glossaries of subjects include standard works. Their extent depends upon the strength of the subject in the collections. Important scientific and technical dictionaries, for example, are usually present but no exhaustive holding is maintained; similarly, medical dictionaries have been updated since the end of World War II, particularly those with foreign and English language equivalents, but no attempt is made to achieve full coverage in this field.

PERIODICALS

An outstanding feature of the collection is its periodicals, with long files of such journals as the *American Journal of Philology, Archiv für das Studium der neueren Sprachen und Literaturen, Nordisk Tidsskrift for Filologi og Paedagogik, Revue de linguistique et de philologie comparée, Language: Journal of the Linguistic Society of America,* and the *Transactions of the Philological Society, London.* Serial publications devoted to individual languages are equally representative, and the files are as substantial as those of the general titles.

The indexing of serial publications for philological contributions has long been a special feature of the Public Catalog. For the minor tongues, including dialects, the indexing is extensive. Included are not only linguistic publications but those of academies and learned societies and periodicals in such other subject fields as local history.

INTERNATIONAL LANGUAGES

The collection relating to international (or universal) languages is of considerable interest. Materials relating to Esperanto and Volapük include the writings of their inventors, L. Zamenhof and J. M. Schleyer, as well as of detractors and enthusiasts. Serial publications, including those of societies and congresses, are held in strength. The Esperanto collection, represented by some 2,000 entries in the Public Catalog, contains an unusual representation of books in the language. There are also printed works in Volapük. Materials on other universal languages are less extensive. Philological journals make some contribution to this special field, and the publications of certain groups that have advocated international languages offer unindexed sources.

The Mrs. Dave H. Morris artificial language collection was given in 1948–49. It consists of some 1,500 items, the larger part in Esperanto with some in Ido and other international auxiliary languages. All types of writings are found in the collection, including juvenile books, essays, reports of congresses, conferences, grammars, readers, and belles-lettres.

AFRICAN LANGUAGES

The collection relating to African languages is good. Some 3,300 cards in the Public Catalog represent more than 600 African languages and dialects. These include references ranging from a single title to substantial representations for such languages as Bantu, Ewe, Fulah, Hausa, Kongo, Swahili, Yoruba, Zulu, and others; the Berber languages have an even greater number of citations, as do the Ethiopic language and its tongues. The extensive number of references for African languages is due in part to close indexing of journals and other serials. There are, however, numerous separate studies and many printed examples of these tongues. Bibles and religious manuals often provide the principal printed texts; English, French, and German linguistic studies predominate.

Students of the African languages will find especially valuable resources in the Schomburg Center. There are notable holdings in some 60 indigenous languages as diverse as Adangme, Nyanja, Sotho, Swahili, and Zulu: the language held in most strength (59 works) is Xhosa. More than 140 African languages and dialects are documented by dictionaries, grammars, and general studies in English and the European languages (the largest number of these in French). Among extensive phonodisc holdings in the center, the important *Sound of Africa* series contains 3,000 items in 128 languages which are of linguistic as well as musical significance.

OCEANIC LANGUAGES

This area is one of considerable strength; it is estimated that some 210 Oceanic and 320 Australian languages and dialects are now represented. Unusual Hawaiian materials in the Rare Book Division include alphabets, grammars, phrasebooks, textbooks in the sciences, New Testaments, the first Hawaiian hymn book, royal statutes, and other material published in Honolulu or the islands in the first half of the nineteenth century.

The library attempts to complement these materials by extensive acquisition of modern Hawaiian language texts and those in Polynesian languages related to Hawaiian.

AMERICAN INDIAN LANGUAGES

There are some 5,200 references to American Indian languages in the Public Catalog. Approximately 600 languages of North, Central, and South American Indians are covered. There are substantial groups relating to the following tongues: Algonquin, Chippewa, Choctaw, Cree, Creek, Eskimo, Massachuset, Mexican Indian, Mohawk, Quechua, Santee, and Tupi-Guarani. Rare works from the seventeenth, eighteenth, and the first half of the nineteenth centuries are to be found in the Rare Book Division. Among them are many works by John Eliot in the Massachuset Indian language, including his *The Indian Grammar Begun* (1666), and his famous translations of the New Testament (1661) and the Bible (1663). Roger Williams's *A Key into the Languages of America* (1643) is also present.

BALTO-SLAVIC LANGUAGES

As in other areas, a comprehensive attempt is made in acquisitions, except where practical considerations intervene. From the establishment of the Slavonic Division everything available to the Western world has been collected, with resulting holdings of some 1,400 volumes. The collection of Balto-Slavic linguistic journals is unusually complete. Grammars and textbooks are normally purchased only when they are of importance to scholarship; ordinary textbooks are not acquired unless they are in one of the non-Indo-European languages of the USSR, in which case everything available is obtained. The Slavonic Division card catalog contains index entries for articles in linguistics from learned journals.

HEBREW AND YIDDISH LANGUAGES

The Hebrew and Yiddish holdings in the Jewish Division represent a scholar's collection, with some material in Ladino and other Jewish dialects. The division is careful to fill gaps in the collections as well as to acquire new works as they appear. Incunabula in Hebrew linguistics find a place in the Jewish Division: David Kimhi's *Sefer Ha-shorashim* in two editions printed in Naples in 1490 and in 1491. Sixteenth-century editions include the works of Moses Kimchi and Elijah Levita, and those of the Christian Hebraists of the period: Johannes Böschenstein, Johann Reuchlin, and Sebastian Münster.

ORIENTAL LANGUAGES

Holdings in the linguistics of Oriental languages total some 6,000 volumes, or about one-tenth of the total holdings of the Oriental Division. The collections include materials in or about some 200 Asiatic tongues; in addition, about 100 tongues in the Malayan group are represented. The areas of greatest numerical strength are Arabic, Japanese, the modern Indic languages, Chinese, and Sanskrit, in the order given. As the collecting policy for modern Indic languages is representative, future acquisitions cannot be expected to parallel those of the past. Other languages of smaller speech communities have been given considerable attention, such as Armenian, Manchu,

Tibetan, and the non-Slavic languages of the Central Asian republics of the USSR.[4] There is good and steadily increasing coverage in the Caucasian languages; in 1966 more than half the materials were in Georgian, but collections in other Caucasian languages are being developed.

A number of rarities in the Oriental Division include the first grammar in Kanarese by John McKerrell, entitled *A Grammar of the Carnataca Language* (Madras, 1820), a work which no longer exists in the original in the South Indian home of this Dravidian language. The linguistic survey of India made by the Indian government from 1903 to 1928 is another rare and valuable item.

NOAH WEBSTER

The Webster collection is remarkable not only in bulk of material but in its significance; many of the volumes were Webster's own or have other association value.[5] Possession of the major portion of Webster's personal and business papers makes the holdings outstanding. The strength of the collection is based on the gifts of Worthington Chauncey Ford and Paul Leicester Ford in 1899, and further additions made by their sister Mrs. Emily Ellsworth Ford Skeel. The Noah Webster materials in the Ford collection in the Manuscripts and Archives Division include about 1,500 pieces of correspondence, Webster's diaries for the years 1784–1820, and lexicographical materials, in addition to the papers of Noah Webster's son William Greenleaf Webster. The extensive collection of early dictionaries and school books by Webster in the Rare Book Division was strengthened by a gift in 1954 from Mrs. Theodore L. Bailey, presented as a tribute to her aunt, Emily Skeel. This brought editions of Webster's speller and other works not hitherto available in the Research Libraries, most notably a first edition of *A Grammatical Institute, of the English Language* . . . (1783).[6]

---

4. See Edward Allworth, "Central Asian Publishing and the Rise of Nationalism," *BNYPL* 69 (1965): 493–522; republished as the introduction to *Central Asian Publishing and the Rise of Nationalism; An Essay and a List of Publications in The New York Public Library* (The New York Public Library, 1965).

5. See Emily Ellsworth Ford Skeel, *A Bibliography of the Writings of Noah Webster* ed. by Edwin H. Carpenter, Jr. (The New York Public Library, 1958). Reprinted by Arno Press and the library, 1971.

6. See Lewis M. Stark, "Mrs. Theodore L. Bailey's Gift to the Noah Webster Collection," *BNYPL* 58 (1954): 476–77.

PART THREE

28

ART AND ARCHITECTURE DIVISION AND GENERAL FINE ARTS RESOURCES

The Art and Architecture Division contains a reference collection of 125,000 volumes. The portions of the classmark in the Billings Classification Schedule assigned to the Art and Architecture Division include the plastic arts in general: painting, drawing, sculpture, architecture, and the minor, decorative, or applied arts. The collection on these topics is intended to be comprehensive, regardless of period, nationality, or language, for bibliography, biography, history, and theory. It generally includes the same topics found in more familiar classification schemes such as the Dewey Decimal 700–750 numbers and the Library of Congress "Class N" Schedule, and makes many of the same distinctions, such as between architecture and formal design (in this division) and the technical aspects of architectural practice (classed as Building, Engineering, etc., in the Science and Technology Research Center). Handbooks, manuals of practice, and similar works are collected selectively both for their pertinence to present practice among artists and designers, and for their historic interest. The books and pamphlets in the Art and Architecture Division range from rare works to currently published materials.[1]

An extensive collection of periodicals, journals, and bulletins covers the fine arts, antiques, architecture, design, furniture, and interior decoration. Periodicals are held in the Periodicals Section until cumulative volumes are bound. In addition are scrapbooks and clippings kept in vertical files which supplement, but not often duplicate, information found in the book collection. There are bound volumes of engravings, aquatints, watercolor drawings, and other materials on costume and similar aspects of the decorative arts. Most of these items represent gifts from individuals

---

1. See Mary W. Chamberlin, *Guide to Art Reference Books* (Chicago: American Library Association, 1959). Of the 67 "Original Sources and Early Works" listed on pages 269–79, about half are available either in the Art and Architecture Division, the Rare Book Division, or the Spencer Collection in first or early editions; the remainder of the material is for the most part available in later editions.

interested in particular subjects; they are cataloged under headings such as "Costumes of Religious Orders" or "Collection of Chinese Drawings on Rice Paper." Ephemera, including exhibition notices, fact sheets about artists and people connected with the arts, and newspaper clippings bring up to date the published record for contemporary artists: these ephemera provide a key to past information otherwise difficult to locate. A selective file of illustrations of the works of artists is incorporated into the clipping files.

Mechanical reproduction and industrial applications in the minor arts, physical properties of materials, and technical processes are largely covered by the Science and Technology Research Center. But though most works on optics, pigments, spectroscopy, and similar topics are located there, the Art and Architecture Division does collect some technical works on a variety of topics such as color theory, artists' materials, bronze casting, and ceramic glazes.

Holdings of books reproducing examples of artists' works or styles range from representative to very selective, particularly for picture books of familiar works already illustrated elsewhere in the library's collections, and books with a brief text of no critical or biographic interest.

The arts of all peoples and periods are generally held in the Art and Architecture Division, with the major exception of American Indian art, which is collected by the American History Division, along with the library's notable collection on other aspects of American Indian cultures and languages. Other exceptions include arms and armor, theatrical and military costume, stage scenery, and a variety of special-purpose structures such as concert halls, theatres, schools, libraries, hospitals, fortifications, and bridges. In the periodicals classed in themselves under arts or architecture there is, of course, a considerable body of information on all the exceptions noted above.

Works dealing with engraving (including woodcuts) and lithography are in the Prints Division, as is material on book illustration. Other book arts (including handwriting, printing, book illumination, and bookbinding) are under the jurisdiction of the General Research and Humanities Division, examples being of course represented in the Special Collections. Folk art of the European peoples in the Americas is in the Art and Architecture Division. Archaeology as such is not collected by the division, although materials on the arts of ancient cultures are.

The division does not collect slides or reproductions and illustrations as such, although it does selectively acquire illustrations of the works of individual artists for its clipping files. The library's largest pictorial archive is the Picture Collection, a unit of the Branch Libraries. There pictorial material is arranged by subject or by artist and is sourced so that users may locate and consult the book, journal, or other publication containing the picture.

Correspondence, journals, diaries, and sketchbooks of artists, architects, and others are held by the Manuscripts and Archives Division. Among those represented are such figures as Alexander Jackson Davis, Asher B. Durand, Charles F. McKim, and James Abbot McNeil Whistler.

Additional resources in art, costume, stage design, and related fields are found in the Theatre and Dance Collections of the Performing Arts Research Center.

HISTORICAL SURVEY

The library's art and architecture collection is built upon the foundation of its predecessor libraries. Two of the three original collections, the Astor Library and the Tilden collection, contained noteworthy material. In the annual report of the Astor Library for 1854, Dr. Cogswell mentioned a complete set of Piranesi's *Antiquities*, Raphael's *Loggia of the Vatican* engraved by Volpato and colored by hand, Gruner's *Fresco Decorations of Italy*, also colored by hand, and Lepsius's *Denkmäler aus Ægypten*, among important titles present.[2] The Lenox Library originally had little, with the exception of galleries of plate books and other finely illustrated books. In the Astoin, Stuart, and Duyckinck collections, however, it gained some very good materials, and when the Tilden collection was added, it could boast an excellent representation of works devoted to the fine arts.

During the early years of the twentieth century Mrs. Henry Draper gave the library thousands of books, many of them relating to art. She also established memorial funds, and at her death the library received bequests of both books and funds. Of the latter, the income from the John S. Billings Memorial Fund in part provides for the purchase of finely illustrated art books.[3] One of Mrs. Draper's gifts was the Vinkhuizen collection of military costume. The collection, presented in 1911, is the foundation of the Research Libraries' strong holdings on military costume, which are administered by the General Research and Humanities Division.

In 1930, Mrs. Helen Hastings gave the professional library of her husband, Thomas Hastings of the firm of Carrère & Hastings, the architect generally responsible for the design of the library's Central Building. This collection consisted of approximately 1,500 books, pamphlets, and scrapbooks, 3,000 plates, and some personal material, devoted mainly to classical French and Italian architecture. In 1948 the Helen and Thomas Hastings Book Fund was established on the framework of an earlier bequest by Mrs. Hastings, the income to be devoted to support of the work of the Research Libraries in art and architecture.

Under the will of Mrs. Lathrop Colgate Harper, four funds were established, one of which is used for the purchase of books on jewelry and precious stones.

DIVISION CATALOG AND SPECIAL INDEXES AND FILES

The extensive Art and Architecture Division catalog is intended to locate material pertinent to its subjects regardless of location in the Research Libraries. It contains some 500,000 references by author, editor, and subject; title entries are rare. Works on art printed in the Hebrew, Chinese, Japanese, and Cyrillic alphabets are included, regardless of whether the book is located in the Art and Architecture Division. Works located elsewhere can be found through the catalog; for example, works on the history of a region which appear only under place name in the Public Cata-

---

2. Lydenberg, *History*, pp. 28–29.
3. See "The Draper Bequests," *BNYPL* 19 (1915): 419–22.

log often have references under "Art," "Architecture," or "Monuments" in the Art Division catalog.

For periodicals literature the division catalog and files must be used in conjunction with the *Art Index* for currently published periodicals indexed there. The *Répertoire d'art et d'archéologie* also provides references to a wide selection of art periodicals and, in addition, includes those of historical, literary, and archaeological societies, a large percentage of which are in the library, although not necessarily in the Art and Architecture Division. Back files of many of these periodicals, up to the point of their inclusion in published indexes, have been indexed by the library into the Art and Architecture Division catalog.

The following special indexes and files index only information not to be found in published sources such as *Art Index*.

CARD FILES

Inside File

This file is an index to illustrations and textual material in fields which concern the division (active, limited, 115 drawers). The field of interest is inclusive. It is primarily a subject file, with such entries as "Children—Costume;" "Costume;" "Fashion Designers;" and "Saints" (by name). Miscellaneous information found in sources to which there is no routine approach is included. Many reproductions of artists' works are indexed by name.

Architecture File

In this index to illustrations and textual materials on architects and buildings the cards for illustrations of buildings are grouped by classes (Clubs, Hotels, Public Buildings, etc.) (active, limited, 27 drawers). The file is kept up to date for certain often-requested information and for the specifically emphasized materials on architects and buildings of New York.

VERTICAL FILES

Artists' Files

A collection of clippings about artists, architects, art collectors, and other persons prominent in the art world, this file includes obituaries, reproductions, sales records, and biographical information (active, 157 large file trays). The material is sourced. The file supplements book and other cataloged material entered in the Art Division catalog and includes thousands of persons not indexed elsewhere.

Museums, Art Organizations, Galleries File

In this file are collected ephemera (announcements, prospectuses, news releases, etc.) pertaining to museums, galleries, and other art organizations (active, 16 trays). The file is primarily for United States organizations, with coverage of selected foreign institutions. Outdated material is periodically discarded.

Vertical File

The file could equally be called semi-moribund or active (4 trays). Where it is active or of any value lies in the retention of certain topical materials, such as the peace symbol and current art movements, cases where there is public interest but few or fugitive sources of information.

Scrapbooks

A collection of mounted miscellaneous clippings with such titles as "Costume," "Homer [Winslow Homer]," "Jewelry," "Mythological Subjects," and "Stairways" (inactive since 1946, 600 scrapbooks). About 50 of the scrapbooks have the subject title "Costume" with appropriate subtitles added. There is an index to the scrapbooks for the use of the division staff.

RESOURCES

DRAWING, PAINTING, AND RELATED GENERAL FIELDS

Most areas of the fine arts are collected on a comprehensive basis. Works on art clubs, associations, and art education in schools are not emphasized; books on children as artists are collected comprehensively. Works on collectors and collecting, public collections, and general works on art sales are acquired comprehensively; other exhibition, sales, auction, and dealers' catalogs are collected on a selective basis. Works on painting are collected comprehensively except for technical books, which are acquired selectively. There are 27,500 volumes in the subject area of drawing and painting.

Although the collections are predominantly in the European languages, policy changes in the 1960s have brought into the division works in the Cyrillic alphabet and in Oriental languages, originally the responsibility of the Slavonic and Oriental Divisions. Periodicals and society publications are extensive on an international basis: all of the 250 outstanding titles for art research given by Mary Chamberlin are available in the Research Libraries.[4]

Printed catalogs of private collections are another strong feature of the holdings. Emphasis is given to guidebooks and catalogs to the public collections of art of the world. This collection extends back to the early nineteenth century for institutions such as the British Museum and the Louvre.

Although holdings of exhibition catalogs are largest in twentieth-century materials for American and European galleries and dealers, the division's holdings of nineteenth-century catalogs form one of the strongest collections in the United States. The catalogs are arranged by institution or firm and held for ready access while they are of current interest. After two years they are examined and, if format permits, may be bound and collectively cataloged as exhibition catalogs of a particular gallery for the given period. Certain important individual catalogs are bound and cataloged as books; the remainder are clipped or eventually discarded. Of the more ephemeral catalogs (which are retained for the period of their greatest usefulness), those on artists are put in the Artists' Files; those on group or thematic exhibitions, in the institutional file.

Auction catalogs form one of the unusual sec-

4. Chamberlin, *Guide to Art Reference Books*, pp. 291–326.

tions of the library's general collections.[5] Auction catalogs are arranged by number or in chronological order. Catalogs for the Parke-Bernet Galleries (and its predecessors), Sotheby's, and Christies are available in almost complete sets; other auction catalogs are less emphasized. The Art and Architecture Division has the standard published indexes to art auction and sale records.

Few important titles are wanting from the collection of materials relating to drawing and painting, and there is a good general representation in these fields.[6] The division has copies of Leonardo da Vinci's *Trattato della pittura* ranging from the Paris 1651 edition to a modern facsimile edition and translation into English. The Spencer Collection has a number of drawing books, including some of the sixteenth century, which have been collected for their fine illustrations; among them is Lucas's *Progressive Drawing Book* (Baltimore, 1827). The Prints Division regularly augments the collection of drawing books acquired primarily as examples of fine prints or of book art. Among other important acquisitions are Alexander Browne's *Ars Pictoria* (1675), David Cox's *A Treatise on Landscape Painting* (1814), and two American drawing books: John Hill's *Hill Drawing Book* (Charleston, South Carolina, 1821), and William Strickland's *The Art of Drawing, Colouring and Painting Landscapes* (Baltimore, 1815). Because so much modern material of this nature is published, the Art and Architecture Division does not attempt to collect more than a representative sampling, although the collection ranges from instruction books in the fine arts to those on simple handicrafts and places particular emphasis on the latest techniques and media. There are also many books on Chinese and Japanese painting and calligraphy.

Books on anatomical studies for artists in the Research Libraries include several sixteenth-century editions of Dürer's classic work, *Hjeriñ sind begriffen vier Bücher von menschlicher Proportion*; the earliest (Nurenberg, 1528) is in the Rare Book Division. Other works in the Art Division include Peter Paul Rubens' *Théorie de figure humaine* in an edition of 1773, J. Fau's *Anatomy of the External Forms of Man* (London, 1849), and among modern works Jeno Barcsay's *Anatomy for the Artist* (1955). In a related field Eadweard Muybridge's *Animal Locomotion* (1887), in eleven volumes of photographic studies, is an extremely rare and useful source of figure studies for the artist. The Research Libraries do not systematically collect books on medical anatomy; there is, however, a small group of such works, among which the rarest are perhaps a Joannes de Ketham (Venice, 1493) in the Spencer Collection, and a 1568 Vesalius in the Rare Book Division.

DANCE OF DEATH

Works on the Dance of Death are collected comprehensively; there are approximately 100 entries in the division's card catalog including entries for articles in learned journals, facsimiles

of incunabula, representations of examples once painted on the churchyard and cemetery walls of Europe, and other forms. The Spencer Collection owns a copy of Hans Holbein the Younger's famous woodcuts in their first printed edition, *Les Simulachres & historiees faces de la mort* (Lyon, 1538), as well as the first known appearance of John Lydgate's *Daunce of Machabree* in his translation of Boccaccio's *Fall of Princes* (London, 1554). Supplementing other library holdings of Mattaeus Merian's engravings of the Dance of Death at Basle is the eighteenth-century manuscript in the Spencer Collection on paper with 40 original watercolor drawings after the engravings of the 1744 edition. There are several examples of William Combe's *English Dance of Death* (1814–16) in the library: in the Arents Collection of Books in Parts are 9 original drawings for the work, including 2 that are unpublished. The Spencer Collection has another set of 33 original watercolor drawings by Thomas Rowlandson, only 26 of which were engraved and published.[7]

EMBLEM BOOKS

Materials for bibliographical and critical study of emblem books are found in the Prints Division. The library has a representative collection of some 250 emblem books in the general collections and in the Rare Book Division, including rarities of the sixteenth and seventeenth centuries. Books by Andrea Alciati are numerous, including German, French, and Italian editions as well as those in the original Latin. The earliest edition of Alciati's *Emblematum Libellus* (1534) is in the Spencer Collection. In the Berg Collection is a copy of Francis Quarles's *Emblems* (1635). The Arents Tobacco Collection has a second corrected edition of the work issued in the same year, and a fifth edition (1658), as well as an attractive and extremely rare emblem book, *Symbolica in Thermas et Acidulas Reflexio* (Munich, seventeenth century). This volume consists of a set of emblematic engravings illustrating the medical and social aspects of thermal springs and bathing establishments in Germany, with explanatory verses in Latin, German, and French; from the library of Robert Hoe, it appears to be the only known copy.

SCULPTURE AND ENGRAVED GEMS

The collecting policy for the plastic arts is generally comprehensive, with the exception of works on engraved gems, which are collected exhaustively.

The rich holdings of eighteenth- and nineteenth-century works on engraved gems in the general collections is continually augmented through purchases made possible by the Mrs. Lathrop Colgate Harper Fund. In 1954 a remarkable collection of wax impressions of antique legal seals was given in part, and in part placed on deposit, by Mortimer and Anna Neinken. Consisting of almost 14,000 impressions, the collection is housed in the Manuscripts and Archives Division and contains specimens of the seals of royal

---

5. See Harold Lancour, "American Art Auction Catalogues, 1785–1942; A Union List," *BNYPL* 47 (1943): 3–43 et seq. Published separately by the library in 1944.

6. See Carl W. Drepperd, "American Drawing Books; A Contribution toward a Bibliography," *BNYPL* 49 (1945): 795–812.

7. The Spencer Collection drawings are listed, and many of them illustrated, in Robert R. Wark's *Rowlandson's Drawings for the English Dance of Death* (San Marino, California: The Huntington Library, 1966).

and noble houses of Europe, together with a representation of ecclesiastical and guild seals of the seventeenth, eighteenth, and nineteenth centuries.[8]

Some 34,000 volumes make up the Art and Architecture Division's holdings on sculpture, including important collections of monographs on individual sculptors. There is much additional material in that part of the collection devoted to architecture dealing with types of structures of which sculpture is ordinarily a part.

A large body of literature relating to classical Greek and Roman sculpture is supplemented by the collection of archaeological works; though under the jurisdiction of the General Research and Humanities Division, it is represented in the catalog of the Art and Architecture Division by entries of interest to the student of sculpture. The Jewish, Slavonic, and Oriental Division also have materials of interest, particularly those in the Oriental Division dealing with Egyptian and Indian sculpture. The special indexes, clipping files, and scrapbooks of the Art and Architecture Division complement the monographic resources for the study of sculpture.

NUMISMATICS

Only dictionaries of numismatics are collected comprehensively by the General Research and Humanities Division; other aspects of the subject receive selective treatment. The collections in this area contain several notable features, including finely illustrated works produced during the eighteenth and nineteenth centuries, strong holdings in English and foreign-language periodicals, and museum and dealers' catalogs. The collection of books is augmented by approximately 1,000 cataloged pamphlets and hundreds of pieces of more fugitive material in volumes listed by subject. The literature relating to ancient and classical coins is particularly extensive and rich.

Other types of material supplement the literature in this field. National and local history, archaeology (particularly the strong collection of periodicals), and the publications of learned societies and institutions are all important. With the catalogs may be associated the more general art catalogs of museums and other institutions having permanent collections of coins, and of dealers' and auction catalogs. Other divisions having material of interest include the Jewish, Oriental, and Slavonic Divisions.

The library is not an art gallery or a museum, but it has occasionally received coins, medals, tokens, and other similar objects, the more notable being those originally in the Lenox Library and those received in the Emmet and Draper collections. Such material is generally kept in the Rare Book Division. The collection of American and European coins is small. Among the tokens and medals are several collections worth notice: European medals of honor, Kings of France, Kings of England, British victories, copper and brass tokens of the Civil War, and the early American works by C. C. Wright.

The library has an unusual collection of early American, Confederate, and foreign paper money. With the Myers collection came 8 folio volumes with the special title "A Complete Series of the Paper Money Issued by the Continental Congress during the Revolution, with Specimens of Colonial and State Issues," containing some 270 pieces. In 1902, Charles K. Needham gave a small collection of mid-nineteenth-century American paper money. In 1913, Howard Townsend contributed his collection of early American materials containing paper money for the period 1815–37. Dr. Frank P. O'Brien gave 20 pieces of colonial paper money printed by Hall and Sellers of Philadelphia and Mr. T. Green of New London in the years 1773, 1775, and 1776. Another unusual collection consists of German and Austrian "Notgeld" issued after World War I. All of the paper money mentioned is housed in the Rare Book Division, as is a Chinese banknote on mulberry bark paper of the Ming Dynasty dated about 1375.[9] The Prints Division has a collection of engraved bank note vignettes, some arranged under "American Bank Note Company," and others under the name of the engraver. Other mounted bank notes in this division are the work of mid-nineteenth-century engravers.

DECORATIVE ART

The collections under this general heading are extremely good; the collecting policy is comprehensive, with the exception of popular technical manuals. Periodicals are a strong feature. The literature of some of the subclasses under the general subject is outstanding, particularly in interior design and decoration, the materials describing period interiors being especially strong.[10] Festival decoration, processions, signs and signboards, and lettering are well represented. The excellent collection of festival books in the Spencer Collection adds strength to these resources. A group of Japanese pattern books of the nineteenth and early twentieth centuries is of particular interest.

The special indexes and files of the Art Division contain much related material; the book materials on all subjects in the field of decorative art are supplemented by special scrapbooks of pictorial material arranged by subject.

ADVERTISING ART

Since the 1940s the holdings in advertising art and layout have been strengthened to include the major periodicals in Western European languages as well as monographs. Advertising and marketing is one of the subject strengths of the Economic and Public Affairs Division; this collection stresses the economic aspects of advertising, but contains much of related interest. Early advertisements may be studied in the holdings of journals and newspapers.

COSTUME

The Art and Architecture Division is responsible for collecting works describing or representing national and folk costumes, and the General Research and Humanities Division is responsible for acquiring similar works on military

8. See Gerald D. McDonald, "The Mortimer and Anna Neinken Collection of Antique Seals," *BNYPL* 58 (1954): 159–61.

9. See Benjamin Schwartz, "A Chinese Paper Bank Note," *BNYPL* 42 (1938): 750–51.

10. See Gertrud Lackschewitz, *Interior Design and Decoration; A Bibliography* (The New York Public Library, 1961). A supplement is in preparation.

and naval uniforms. The responsibility for theatrical costume is divided between the Theatre and Dance Collections. The collecting policy is comprehensive for these areas. In addition, the library contains a great body of material on subjects relating to costume, as for example works on textile manufacture or hairdressing, which is housed in other divisions. Illustrated books and prints in the Arents Collections, the Spencer Collection, and the Prints and Music Divisions should also be consulted by the serious researcher.

Periodicals are a strong feature of the collections of materials on costume. The Art Division holdings, while notable for texts in Western European languages, also include works in other languages, such as books on Japanese costume. A feature of the division's holdings is a number of late eighteenth- and early nineteenth-century ladies' fashion magazines: journals, bound collections of prints from them, and the actual watercolor drawings for many of the plates in Ackermann's *Repository of Arts, Literature, Fashion, etc.* (1809–29). Important titles include the *Ladies' Pocket Magazine*, *Journal des dames*, and the *Gallery of Fashion* (1794–1803), of which the division's file lacks only the years 1802–03. Among other early nineteenth-century books which are of less importance as sources but which retain their artistic interest are Alexander's *The Costume of the Russian Empire* (1803) and George Henry Mason's books on Chinese costume and punishments. A number of bound and accessioned collections, gifts to the division, represent a collector's interest in accumulating watercolor drawings, aquatints, or engravings of ecclesiastical costume, Swiss costume, and other special subject groups.

Several of the special indexes and files in the Art Division are particularly useful to the student of costume. The Inside File indexes costume plates in miscellaneous sources—illustrated travel books, examples of portraits and genre painting, etc.—in which costume detail is emphasized. Indexes have been prepared for volumes of costume plates which lack such keys. Scrapbooks of various sorts include one of over thirty volumes which covers many minor nationalities whose costumes are not easily available in pictorial material. Another series is composed of plates from fashion periodicals of the period 1797–1870. A third contains reproductions of portraits in which costume is a prominent feature.

The Spencer Collection contains a substantial number of books on costume, including the first printed costume book with text and illustrations, written by François Deserpz and published in 1562, and some of the earliest costume books representing France, Germany, and Italy, dating from the second half of the sixteenth century. These include Hans Weigel's *Habitus Praecipuorum Populorum* (1577) and Cesare Vecellio's *Degli habiti antichi, et moderni* (1590). There are books of costume drawings for China, Japan, Peru, and other countries. The Spencer Collection's rich resources in festival books and the Dance of Death provide many representations of costumes of the period illustrated.

Theatrical costume can be studied in books in the Theatre Collection, and in thousands of original stage and screen costume designs, photographs, engravings, and other representational forms. Materials on the French and English theatre from the seventeenth century to the present and for the American theatre from 1860 are most fully represented. Important gifts of

designers' work include material by Aline Bernstein, John Boyt, Bonnie Cashin, David Ffolkes, Nat Karson, and the Motleys, and items in the R. H. Burnside collection.

The Dance Collection has a great number of drawings, prints, and photographs of dance costume throughout the ages, particularly in the Lincoln Kirstein and Cia Fornaroli collections. In addition are original designs by such artists as Alexandre Bénois, Leon Bakst, Mitislav Doboujinski, and Nathalia Gontcharova. Photographs in the Roger Pryor Dodge gifts, and photographs and drawings in the Isadora Duncan collection, the Denishawn collection, and others document costumes used in the dance in modern times in the United States and other parts of the world.

The Jewish, Slavonic, and Oriental Divisions have works of interest to the student of costume in their respective literatures. The Rare Book Division also has many works of supplementary interest for various nationalities, particularly the American Indian. Much called for by readers are the De Bry *Voyages*, and the Prinz von Wied-Neuwied's *Travels in the Interior of North America* with the magnificent Bodmer illustrations. A collection of 326 watercolors by Fiodor Gripor'yevich Solntzev entitled *Costumes of the Russian State* was executed between 1820 and 1879. It is contained in a red morocco case with the bookplate of Czar Nicholas II and housed in the Rare Book Division. The Schatzki collection of children's books, which has the special class mark 8-NASZ, offers unusual pictorial resources for later eighteenth- and early nineteenth-century children's costume, particularly in Germany. The Arents Collection of Books in Parts includes several rare books on costume that were first issued in parts, and also original watercolor and pen-and-ink sketches for many of the English nineteenth-century books in the collection. The Arents Tobacco Collection contains drawings, engravings, and other pictorial material on costume documenting the period from 1507 to the present.

MILITARY AND NAVAL UNIFORMS

The Art and Architecture Division is not responsible for the collection of material on military and naval uniforms. There is, however, a very extensive collection of such material under the jurisdiction of the General Research and Humanities Division. Scrapbooks are not actively collected and no separate index is maintained. The collecting policy is comprehensive.

Unusual strength is given to the resources by the Vinkhuizen collection on military costume presented by Mrs. Henry Draper in 1911. Described by experts as the best public collection on military uniforms in the United States, it consists of 32,236 plates, cut from books on uniforms and other sources, supplemented by original watercolor drawings, in numbered scrapbooks arranged chronologically by country. Most of the countries of Europe, Great Britain and its former colonies, Russia, Turkey, Egypt, and some South American countries are covered, but not the United States. Among the most extensive groups are those on France and its former colonies (with particular emphasis on the Napoleonic period), Italy, and the Netherlands. In most cases the coverage is from the earliest periods to about 1909.

In 1938 the library received from the estate of General DeWitt Clinton Falls a collection of scrapbooks of pictures, drawings, photographs, and other representations of military uniforms and insignia, with particularly valuable coverage of United States uniforms. The collection is most useful for the period beginning with the Spanish-American War and continuing through World War I.[11]

Additional resources for the study of military and naval uniforms in the Research Libraries are extensive, including well-illustrated works and many of the dress regulations manuals of armies and navies. Other rich collections in the sections on military art and science, nautical art and science, and naval history supplement these resources. Regimental histories are especially valuable for the army, as are the illustrations in such publications as those of the Society for Army Historical Research.

APPLIED ART

The Mrs. Lathrop Colgate Harper Fund enables the library to collect exhaustively in the field of jewelry and precious stones. Materials on goldsmithing and silversmithing, jewelry (including trade papers), ivories, and jades are also collected.

Jeweler's workbooks, consisting of collections of drawings, engravings, lithographs, and other material with notes on stones, prices, and similar details include the workbook of an unidentified Italian jeweler of 1690 to 1702, and seven workbooks of art nouveau jewelry dated 1900 to 1910 from the Paris firm of Basset et Moreau. The General Research and Humanities Division collects works dealing with engraved gems; the mineralogical or technological aspects of precious stones (excepting those set as jewelry) are comprehensively collected by the Science and Technology Research Center.

Works on pewter, lacquers, textile design, carpets and rugs, tapestry, embroidery, art needlework, and lace are collected comprehensively. Other forms of the applied arts are collected on a representative basis. Policy dictates that works addressed to the craftsman and artist are purchased rather than those which might appeal to the hobbyist. The division carefully adds to its collections works containing up-to-date information or descriptions of the latest techniques.

The Art and Architecture Division has maintained scrapbooks for the applied arts; the series relating to furniture is the largest, being fifteen volumes. The collection of trade journals on jewelry and furniture is extensive. American periodicals of the late nineteenth and twentieth centuries are best represented, although there are such important foreign-language periodicals as *Die Goldschmiede-Kunst*. Included are extensive files of such journals as the *Jewelers' Circular*, the *Keystone*, the *Manufacturing Jeweler*, and others, and among furniture periodicals, the *American Carpet and Upholstery Journal*, *Decorative Furnisher*, and the *Upholsterer*. In addition are long files of directories of jewelry, furniture, and allied manufacturers, generally issued by the journals.

Among fine illustrated books on jewels and jewelry in the division are items such as H. R. Bishop's *The Bishop Collection: Investigations and Studies in Jade*, Stanley C. Nott's *Chinese Jade Carvings in the Collection of Mrs. Georg Vetlesen*, G. P. Baker's *Calico Painting and Printing in the East Indies*, the Österreichisches

Handelsmuseum's *Oriental Carpets* and the supplement *Ancient Oriental Carpets*, the Manchoukuo National Museum's *Tapestries and Embroideries of the Sung Yuan, Ming, and Ch'ing Dynasties*, S. E. Lucas's *The Catalogue of Sassoon Chinese Ivories*, and the Morgan catalogs, especially those on watches and jewels.

Most of the technological aspects of the applied arts are the collecting responsibility of the Science and Technology Research Center or other divisions. The demarcation is not always distinct but may be used as a guide. Thus, textile design books and some general handweaving works are in the Art and Architecture Division, while more technical books on handweaving and materials on textiles and fibres are in the Science and Technology Research Center. A like division holds for carpets and lace, with works on design in the Art and Architecture Division and technological works in the Science and Technology Research Center. There is also a useful collection of books on the sewing aspects of needlework and lace under the jurisdiction of the General Research and Humanities Division.

CERAMICS AND GLASS

This subject field is collected comprehensively by the Art and Architecture Division. In keeping with the scope of the division, the materials are devoted mainly to design or the artist's involvement with the craft; works on the commercial manufacture of pottery and glass and the technical processes involved are to be found in the Science and Technology Research Center.

There is an excellent working collection of materials on pottery: histories, handbooks, catalogs of collections, etc. There is also a strong collection of books on marks and monograms. Some 3,400 entries in the Art and Architecture Division card catalog are devoted to regional references, with such entries as "Pottery, German—Dresden," "Pottery, Chinese—Collections—Private—[Name of Collector]." There are a number of index entries to articles in periodicals and journals. While all countries are well represented, the classical and the Oriental holdings are perhaps the most extensive, with a good representation of finely illustrated volumes ranging from the engravings of the collection of Greek vases belonging to Sir William Hamilton to current works. Among others are the *Corpus Vasorum Antiquorum*, Furtwängler and Reichhold's *Griechische Vasenmalerei*, Eumorfopoulos's *The George Eumorfopoulos Collection; Catalogue of the Chinese, Korean, and Persian Pottery and Porcelain*, W. T. Walter's *Oriental Ceramic Art*, and the catalog of porcelain in the National Palace Museum in Taichung, Taiwan.

The Art and Architecture Division has some 3,000 general materials covering ornamental glass (cut, embossed, sandblasted, etc.) and ornamental glass used in buildings; and a good collection on bottles, drinking vessels, paperweights, etc. English and American works are strongest numerically. Stained and painted glass are well covered; the rich collection of materials on ecclesiastical architecture in the division has much supplementary material, particularly in illustrations.

Both ceramics and glass have allied materials in other library divisions. Periodicals, for the most part technical, are in the Science and Technology Research Center; these are represented by entries in the Art and Architecture Division catalog. There are supplementary materials in Oriental

---

11. See Karl Brown, "Military Costume and General Falls," *BNYPL* 42 (1938): 425–27.

languages and in the Cyrillic alphabet in the Oriental and Slavonic Divisions. Those in the Slavonic Division are notable, particularly materials on pottery; some 200 catalog card entries are arranged to provide geographical access by region and by country.

The contributions on ceramics and glass from publications in local history and archaeology journals and in publications of learned societies and institutions are also of importance, particularly for pottery. In many instances there are index cards for these contributions in the Art and Architecture Division card catalog, particularly for archaeological items, which are not the collecting responsibility of the division.

Ceramics and glass are represented in the general scrapbooks and special indexes and files maintained by the division.

ARCHITECTURE

The collecting policy is comprehensive for most areas of architecture, with 25,000 entries in the division's card catalog for works on architecture. Related holdings in the Research Libraries include material on engineering, building, building materials, and legal regulations in the Science and Technology Research Center, and materials on the sociological or economic aspects of urban planning in the Economic and Public Affairs Division. Many works on individual cathedrals, castles, châteaux, and other public buildings provide additional background description and historical material; they are to be found in the local history collections. Important contributions found in the publications of learned societies and institutions, and the studies and illustrations of earlier periods in the archaeology collections, are also useful to the student of architecture. Index cards for much of this material are to be found in the Art and Architecture Division catalog, with the notable exception of materials on city planning. These are divided between the Economic and Public Affairs Division (sociological and economic aspects in government documents and other publications), the Science and Technology Research Center (technical aspects), and the General Research and Humanities Division (other aspects of the subject). The reader should consult the Public Catalog.

The collection of international architectural journals is substantial. There are some 600 entries in the Art and Architecture Division catalog representing periodical and society publications in the arts; the largest number are from the United States (96 titles), Germany (56 titles) and Great Britain (48 titles); the holdings for both older and current serials are in most cases complete. Currently the Research Libraries receive 120 titles in architecture from all over the world.

The architecture collection serves as an adequate working collection for the specialist as well as the general public. A number of the classic works are present in the Art Division, Rare Book Division, and Spencer Collection, but the library does not stress acquiring such materials, since the scholarly community in the area of New York City has access to the facilities of the Avery Architectural Library. Among the older materials Americana is perhaps most noteworthy. Though the library is on occasion able to add rare works, the Art and Architecture Division primarily obtains significant texts in reprint editions.

Some of the rarities in the division are Robert Adam's *Ruins of the Palace of the Emperor*

Diocletian at Spalatro (1764), several eighteenth-century editions of Palladio in English translation, and a first edition of C. N. Ledoux's *L'Architecture* (1804), with the Daniel Ramée supplemental volume of 1847. In the Rare Book Division are editions of Palladio (Venice, 1581), Serlio (Venice, 1569), and Vitruvius (Venice, 1567). The Spencer Collection owns a first edition of Palladio (Venice, 1570), a number of first and early editions of Vitruvius in French, Italian, and German, Ferdinando Galli da Bibiena's *L'Architettura civile* (Parma, 1711), and other notable items including 53 lithographs of Chicago before the great fire, issued in installments during the years 1866–67 as *Chicago Illustrated*.

Architecture holdings in the special language divisions should not be overlooked. In the Petrine collection of the Slavonic Division are 2 works on fortifications translated from the Dutch of Menno baron van Coehoorn (1710) and from the French of François Blondel (1711). Over 1,000 card entries in the division's catalog are devoted to architecture of Eastern European countries. There are about 50 files of architectural periodicals. The Oriental Division's holdings, although not extensive, contain interesting items, such as the exquisitely produced 1925 edition of Li Chieh's *Ying Tsao Fa Shih*, originally published in the Sung Dynasty, which is one of the few surviving early works on Chinese architecture.

A Chinese carpenters' pattern book in the Manuscripts and Archives Division, consisting of 14 volumes of drawings, is also noteworthy,[12] as well as the approximately 40,000 pictures of architecture and ornament in the James Layng Mills collection of the Picture Collection.

MANUSCRIPT RESOURCES IN ART

Materials on American art and artists in the Manuscripts and Archives Division come from a variety of sources. Among the Bryant-Godwin papers are 71 letters from artists and writers on the arts, dating from 1828 to 1900. An additional 3,800 pieces are in the *Century Magazine* papers, the Duyckinck collection, and the papers of John Durand, editor of the *Crayon*, a nineteenth-century art magazine published in New York. These represent for the most part letters from painters, sculptors, and critics of the nineteenth and early twentieth centuries. The papers of Gordon Lester Ford contain 400 letters from mid-nineteenth-century American painters and include the records of the Brooklyn Art Association.

Artists whose correspondence and papers form part of the collection include Asher B. Durand (900 pieces: correspondence, diaries, etc.), John Trumbull (300 items: chiefly correspondence), and James Abbot McNeill Whistler (3 volumes: letters, telegrams, clippings, etc.). Among other Whistler family items is the journal of Anna Mathilda Whistler, mother of the artist.[13]

Also included are 38 letters from John Ruskin to H. S. Marks dated from 1877 to 1887, and a volume of letters to Dora Thomas for the period

---

12. See Daniel Sheets Dye, *A Grammar of Chinese Lattice* (Cambridge: Harvard University Press, 1937), 2 vols.

13. See "A Preliminary Guide to the Collections of the Archives of American Art," *Archives of American Art Journal*, vol. 5, no. 1 (January 1965): 1–19. Most of the material described has been filmed by the Archives.

1877–83. These items are in the Harkness collection, as is a 26-page George Cruikshank manuscript, *A Pop-Gun Fired Off by George Cruikshank in Defense of the British Volunteers*, bound with a copy of the printed pamphlet. In addition are over 2,000 items representing correspondence and miscellaneous documents of American artists and writers on art, chiefly of the nineteenth century. Among them are Audubon, Bierstadt, Mary Cassatt, Eastman Johnson, Gilbert Stuart, and Thomas Sully. The collection also includes the correspondence (1888–1942) of Frank W. Weitenkampf, chief of the New York Public Library Prints Division for many years.

The John Quinn memorial collection in the Manuscripts and Archives Division contains letters to and from Quinn and his associates and friends among the art dealers and artists of his day. John Quinn's interest in modern art intensified in about 1909 and continued until his untimely death in 1924. During this period he helped to organize the 1913 Armory Show, from which he was the largest private buyer. Quinn established one of the finest private collections of modern art of his time, particularly strong in works from the School of Paris. This collection was dispersed within three years of his death. Included in the archive are letters to and from art dealers during the period 1902 to 1924 filling approximately 7 letter-file boxes. Associated with this group are Quinn's correspondence with Henri-Pierre Roché, who acted as his adviser in France (183 items from Roché), and with Walter Pach, who acted in the same capacity in the United States (156 items from Pach). Among French artists there are letters from Jules Pascin, André Dunoyer de Segonzac, Georges Rouault, Raoul Dufy, Marcel Duchamps, and the sculptor Constantin Brancusi. The most notable accumulations of letters from English artists are those from Augustus John, Gwen John, and Jacob Epstein, but there are also letters from Charles Shannon, Jack Yeats, members of the Vorticist School, and other artists in England and Ireland. Letters from American artists include those from Maurice and Charles Prendergast, John Sloan, Walt Kuhn, and Ernest Lawson.

The most sizeable collections of papers of architects in the Manuscripts and Archives Division are those of the Americans, Alexander J. Davis (6 boxes, and 8 volumes: architectural specifications, diaries, correspondence, etc.), Charles F. McKim (3 boxes: letters and diaries), and Harold Van Buren Magonigle (11 boxes).

Correspondence of English literary figures who were also prominent in the arts is found in the Berg Collection. There are 90 letters from Dante Gabriel Rossetti and members of his circle, and 75 John Ruskin letters which complement those in the Manuscripts and Archives Division. In addition are manuscript materials and drawings of George Cruikshank and other well-known nineteenth-century illustrators.

The Arents Collections contain miscellaneous drawings and letters of the eighteenth- and nineteenth-century artists and illustrators, both English and American.

FINE ARTS RESOURCES

Although impressive portrait holdings are present in various divisions of the library, notably the Theatre and Dance Collections of the Performing Arts Research Center and the Prints Division (see chapter 55 of this *Guide*), since 1912 it has not been library policy to increase its collections of paintings and statuary. A file cabinet and index maintained in the Art and Architecture Division locates, identifies, and provides provenance information for the statuary and paintings located in the various divisions of the library. Among the treasures on view to the public in the Central Building are Asher B. Durand's "Kindred Spirits" (W. C. Bryant and Thomas Cole), in the third-floor corridor, and a collection of portraits on permanent display in an exhibition gallery (Room 318), among which are representative paintings of Gilbert Stuart, John Singleton Copley, Sir Henry Raeburn, and Samuel F. B. Morse. The Schomburg Center for Research in Black Culture has a particularly fine collection of paintings and sculpture by black artists, some donated to the center and others on indefinite loan; there are also artistically significant holdings of African artifacts.

29

PICTORIAL RESOURCES

PHOTOGRAPHY

COLLECTING POLICY

The strong collections on general photography are administered by the General Research and Humanities Division. Technical works on optics, light, and other subjects are the collecting responsibility of the Science and Technology Research Center. Works on the production of motion pictures form part of the Theatre Collection and are discussed with the resources of that collection. There are three main categories of materials in the field: (1) books and periodicals on all phases of the subject; (2) collections of single photographs usually arranged by subject; and (3) personal papers, diaries, etc., of photographers. The

policy governing the acquisition of materials varies for each of the categories.

1. Books and periodicals are acquired comprehensively. This includes works on motion pictures and their production.
2. Individual photographs (and such other pictorial material as photographs, reproductions, technical drawings, plans, blueprints, etc.) are acquired for the Research Libraries only for those collections already established:

    American Indians (American History Division, Rare Book Division)

    American views, particularly New York (American History Division, Manuscripts and Archives Division, Prints Division)

Black culture (Schomburg Center for Research in Black Culture)

Dance iconography (Dance Collection)

Fine arts, including iconography and works of named artists and craftsmen not otherwise covered (Art and Architecture Division)

Music iconography (Music Division, Theatre Collection)

Portraits (American History Division, Dance Collection, Music Division, Prints Division, Theatre Collection)

Stage iconography (Theatre Collection)

Tobacco iconography (Arents Collections)

Transportation (Science and Technology Research Center)[1]

3. Personal papers of American photographers are acquired by the Manuscripts and Archives Division, particularly those in some way related to New York City or New York State.

RESOURCES

Books and Periodicals

With over 7,000 entries devoted to photography in all its aspects, the Public Catalog constitutes a useful bibliography of the subject. Included are references to important contributions in the publications of learned and scientific societies and institutions. The Public Catalog is less thorough in citing articles in photographic journals which are treated by such current abstracting services as the *Abstracts of Photographic Science and Engineering Literature* (1962–) and its predecessors, the *Monthly Abstract Bulletin* and *Ansco Abstracts, Science, technique & industrie photographiques*, and *Résumés des travaux des laboratoires de recherches Kodak*.

Periodicals of the collections are an important feature; journals, society and club publications, house organs, and other serials, both American and foreign, are represented. Among the nineteenth-century journals of short duration is *La Camera obscura* (Milan, 1863–67); the library has a complete file of the publication. Of the 28 photographic journals from photography's first decade listed by Helmut Gernsheim, 13 are in the Research Libraries, including 2 long-lived journals, the *Photographic Journal* (formerly *Journal of the Photographic Society of London*) (1853–), and the *Bulletin* of the Société française de photographie (1854–).[2] Long runs of the camera journals edited by Alfred Stieglitz, *Camera Notes* (1897–1903) and *Camera Work* (1903–17), are also present. Currently the library receives 46 photographic journals from all over the world as well as related journals in microphotography and document reproduction.

The acquisition in 1937 of a collection of approximately 50 books, pamphlets, and specimens of the earliest photographic experiments of Fox Talbot and the French school of Daguerre provided the library with many of the early works

in the history of photography. The collection had come from the library of Hippolyte Louis Fizeau, himself a pioneer of photography. Among the books are rare works such as L. J. M. Daguerre's *Historique et description des procédés du Daguerréotype et du diorama* (1839) and its first English translation (1840) by J. S. Memes, as well as copies of Talbot's *The Pencil of Nature* (1844), said to be the first book with actual photographic illustrations. Other books illustrated with early photographs have been classified according to their subject. Examples of this kind of material are Nathaniel Hawthorne's *Transformation* (Leipzig, 1860) extra-illustrated with 37 mounted photographs, and Eadweard Muybridge's *Animal Locomotion* (1887) with 781 photoengravings.

Among the library's general materials are approximately 1,000 cataloged pamphlets and many others in the "n.c." classmark (material not separately cataloged), together with such fugitive works as Dagron's *Traité de photographie microscopique* (1864), the first important description of the process of microphotography.

Individual Photographs

The library generally acquires the work of individual photographers only in book form—commercial publications, annuals of photography, exhibition catalogs, etc. Single photographic prints as an art form are not collected. Individual examples of photography have been collected primarily for subject interest or as examples of early photography. Photographs of the period 1838–52 include a set of original photographs by Fox Talbot, an original colored photograph by Charles Cros, and a number of daguerreotypes. They are from the Fizeau collection. Two photographic transparencies of the moon taken by Professor Henry Draper, the American astronomer, are also of note. Two giant portfolios of photographic views of the Yosemite Valley were presented to the library in 1952 by Albert Boni. They represent the work of C. E. Watkins (1861) and Charles L. Weed (1859), probably the first photographers in the Valley.[3]

The American History Division maintains a small collection of photographs and other pictorial material relating to subjects within its collecting field: some of the material consists of outsize photographs of such items as fairs and centennials, New York City views, historical views, etc. An extensive group of 30,000 pictures came largely from the Robert Dennis collection. Arranged by state, most of the slides are views, but there are some humorous items and portraits of presidents and other personalities.

The Local History and Genealogy Division has 49 cabinet drawers of photographic views of the five boroughs of New York City, the earliest dating from the late nineteenth century, but the larger number taken in the 1920s and 1930s by Percy Loomis Sperr, who was commissioned by the library to take photographs of buildings soon to be demolished in the New York metropolitan area. The Lewis Wickes Hine photographs document social conditions in New York City from 1905 to 1939. The Armbruster collection of 14,000 photographs of old buildings and their surroundings in Long Island, New York City, and

---

1. Pictorial separates in this category are acquired on a very selective basis in the following categories only: ships and shipbuilding (excluding fighting ships); locomotives and cars; aeroplanes, aerodromes, astronautics (including fighting planes); automobiles.

2. See Helmut Gernsheim, *The History of Photography* (London: Oxford University Press, 1955), pp. 380–81.

3. See Gerald D. McDonald, "Photographs of Yosemite," *BNYPL* 56 (1952): 374–75.

Westchester County during the period 1890–1930 was acquired in 1934, but is unindexed and only partially available.

The Schomburg Center for Research in Black Culture maintains a photograph collection of many thousands in its field of research, over 15,000 of them indexed. These include materials from the "Harlem on My Mind" Exhibition and picture files from several organizations (the National Urban League, the New York *Amsterdam News*, etc.).

Photographs made by Carl Van Vechten of his friends have been distributed by subject between the Berg Collection (literary figures), the Dance Collection (dancers), the Theatre Collection (theatrical personalities), and the Manuscripts and Archives Division (all other portraits). In addition, the Dance Collection holds numerous examples of the work of prominent photographers who have portrayed the dance or dancers, including Walter Owen, George Platt Lynes, Wilbur Stephan, Albert Kahn, and others.

In the Theatre Collection a vast archive of pictorial documentation of the theatre, motion pictures, and the circus numbers in the hundreds of thousands of items. More detailed information on this archive is given in connection with the discussion of the Theatre Collection. However, certain extensive groups should be mentioned here, particularly the Francis Bruguiere collection of 2,000 photographic plates made during the period 1918–27 of the principal theatrical productions of that period, and the Florence Vandamm collection of photographs and negatives of New York stage productions from 1920 until 1962. Also notable are the photographs in the G. Maillard Kesslere collection, the Universal Studios "still books" (for which the collection is a depository), and the White Studio "key books" of theatrical photographs for a period of approximately two decades, ending in 1935.

An extraordinary group of photographs of Russian subjects is in the Kennan collection in the Manuscripts and Archives Division. The library's News Bureau office has a cabinet of photographic negatives and slides of the library's Central Building, the old site (Croton Reservoir), and the library's branches, gathered by the late E. W. Gaillard. In connection with this group is the collection of official photographs, now in the Art and Architecture Division, consisting of scrapbook volumes and single photographs devoted to the Astor and Lenox libraries, the Central Building from the beginning of its construction to the present, the buildings of the Branch Libraries, other pictures of library interest, portraits of trustees, officers, and staff, etc. Other material including single photographs of staff members, group pictures, etc., is available in the general collections of the General Research and Humanities Division.

Picture Collection of the Branch Libraries: The Picture Collection includes among its subject files photographs which are available for circulation to the public. In addition are several noncirculating collections of photographs for reference use within the collection:

1. Franziska Gay Schacht memorial collection (1,500 items). Emphasizing photography as a fine art, this collection contains the prints of distinguished American photographers as well as the work of many photographers made while they were still unknown. Among those represented are Berenice Abbott, Elizabeth Buehr-

mann, Lewis Wickes Hines, Dorothea Lange, Helen Levitt, and Ben Shahn.

2. An extensive collection of photographs made in the United States during the Depression. These fall into two large groups: (a) Federal Art Project "Changing New York" (1,500 items). This project was under the supervision of Berenice Abbott. The Picture Collection has a substantially complete collection of prints made at the time from the original negatives (now in the Museum of the City of New York). The prints are closely classified and located by street number. (b) Farm Security Administration Photographic Project (300,000 items). This extensive collection is arranged by state and covers most of the states in the Union. There is also a subject file.

Manuscript Materials: Among the holdings of the Manuscripts and Archives Division are the papers of Peter Henry Van der Weyde, covering the period from 1844 to 1894, valuable for the history of photography. The diaries of William Henry Jackson, given by Mrs. Clarence Jackson in 1942 and 1947, document the life of a pioneer American photographer. They extend from 1862, when Jackson was a Union soldier, until 1942, and cover his daily life as photographer and painter, as well as his travels. There are also letters and sketch books. The register books of Mathew B. Brady from 1863 to 1865 list the persons for whom photographs were made by Brady during the Civil War period and include the autograph signatures of many distinguished persons. The correspondence of Professor Henry Draper with astronomers and other scientists throughout the world, dating from 1869 through 1882, relates in part to Professor Draper's principal contribution to science: valuable spectrum photographs made after 1871, through which sufficient data had been accumulated in 1877 to prove the presence of oxygen in the sun. The papers of Robert Hobart Davis, Elizabeth Buehrmann, and Harry Godfrey also contain material of interest in the study of photography.

POSTERS

The Research Libraries do not collect posters except in a very limited manner for certain established collections such as dance and stage iconography, fine arts, and tobacco. Posters offer special problems in handling because of their size and fragility, and those specimens that are in the library have not been stored in a uniform manner. Some posters have been placed in large print cabinets in the Prints Division and the Theatre Collection; others have been mounted on sheets and bound in portfolio volumes in the Art and Architecture Division; still others have been mounted in oversize bound volumes. Single posters are usually cataloged separately, but bound collections are given collective subject treatment in the Public Catalog. There remain in the Research Libraries the following large categories of posters: theatrical posters, art posters, and advertising posters, including tobacco advertising.

Beginning in 1914 the library began to actively acquire posters related to World War I. By 1919 over 3,000 posters had been accumulated. Photographs of more than two-thirds of these were bound into five large volumes. In 1974, however, the library donated its original posters from World War I, formerly housed in the general collections, to the Hoover Institution on War, Revolution and Peace. The bound volumes of photographs were retained in the stack collections. There is also in the Slavonic Division a one-volume collection of posters, public notices, and decrees collected by John Reed in Russia during the period 1917–18. Election and presidential campaign posters are in the American History Division. Broadsides are a featured holding in the Rare Book Division; a group of broadsides from Lowville, New York, includes twenty-nine Civil War enlistment posters of various sizes.

A collection of hundreds of original posters in the Theatre Collection is strongest for stage materials, with the cinema and the circus represented in smaller numbers. The material ranges in date from the later nineteenth century to the present. The coverage is international, with items from the United States predominating. Posters vary in size from window cards to very large pieces in twelve sheets. Among them are several Alfons Mucha posters of Sarah Bernhardt. Presently in process of being rearranged, many of the posters will be kept in groups by name of artist or play. Cinema posters include many from Sweden and Russia of the 1930s and 1940s; circus posters include those of Wild West shows. The Dance Collection retains about 500 posters and broadsides on the dance from the late eighteenth century to modern times.

Although the Prints Division does not collect posters as a form, it does have examples that represent an integral part of the oeuvre of an artist, as in the case of Bonnard or Toulouse-Lautrec. These posters are classified under the name of the artist.

The Art and Architecture Division has mounted and bound in two portfolio volumes a number of advertising posters, many for books, magazines, and newspapers, made by American artists during the period 1893–1924 and held for their artistic merit. The work of Edward Penfield, Charles H. Wright, and others is included. Additional examples are found in the bound volumes of lithographic publisher's proofs of the publications of L. Prang & Company, 1888.

Other advertising posters of artistic interest collected as specimens of tobacco advertising are in the Arents Collections. About sixty American and a small group of Japanese posters illustrate brands of cigarettes and tobacco of the late nineteenth century.

Books on posters are collected comprehensively by the library. Approximately 350 card entries in the Public Catalog refer to the subject in American, English, and Western European sources; a great number of these are index entries for periodical articles.

The Picture Collection, a unit of the Branch Libraries, has several hundred roughly-classified posters in nineteen boxes. Although there is general coverage of a number of subjects, the concentration is upon the 1940s and World War II, with posters from the United States, Russia, China, England, and other countries. There are also a number of World War I posters, including material on recruiting, the Red Cross, and other subjects.

PICTURE COLLECTION

The Picture Collection, a unit of the Branch Libraries of the New York Public Library, is an indexed and organized collection of picture documents for fact-finding use, historical research,

comparison, display, and study. The collection contains over 2,000,000 pictures classified under approximately 8,000 major subject headings. It includes all types of pictorial representation— photographs, postcards, prints, posters, clippings from books and magazines— and covers the entire panorama of world history, architecture, science, apparel, sports, news events, and the contemporary scene. Although there is full coverage in all subjects, the collection is particularly strong in pictures of flora and fauna, furniture, costumes, interiors, geographic and historic views, and portraits. The pictures are available for free circulation to the public but are not available for classroom use by teachers or students, other than art students.

Established in 1915, the resources of the collection had grown by 1930 to 150,000 items. Under the curatorship of Romana Javitz the file was expanded, specifically classified, indexed, and sourced, and serves as a model for other libraries and collectors.

The Franziska Gay Schacht collection also began in the 1930s, was augmented by gifts and purchases, and was established as a memorial in 1963. Consisting of 1,500 prints by distinguished American photographers, this is a noncirculating part of the Picture Collection and must be used in the room. The Farm Security Administration Photographic Project collection, numbering 300,000 pieces, and covering most of the states in the Union, was presented in the early 1940s. These collections are described further in the section on photography earlier in this chapter.

SPECIAL INDEXES AND FILES

The Picture Collection does not have a regular catalog of its holdings; the card indexes and files described below are of importance for an understanding of the collections. The Subject Index, Alewyn Flora and Fauna Index, and Personality Index are primarily for staff use.

Source Catalog

Each book, periodical, or group of pictures which comes into the Picture Collection is given an identifying number or symbol (books and groups of separate pictures are given numbers; periodicals are given letter symbols). A full bibliographic record of the source is placed on a catalog card and filed in numerical or alphabetical sequence (16 card drawers). A borrower wishing to know the source of a picture may then obtain full information from the Source Catalog by referring to the number or symbol on the mount.

Subject Index

The card index of subject headings used by the Picture Collection contains extensive cross-references to alternative headings which might suggest themselves for particular subjects (30 card drawers).

Alewyn Flora and Fauna Index

An alphabetical index by common name of plants and animals with cross-references from other common ways of referring to them, for example "Flowers and Plants, Heartsease see Flowers and Plants, Pansy"; "Animals, Mountain Lion see Animals, Puma." Latin names, while indicated on the cards, are not used as filing headings (4 card drawers).

Geographical Names Index

An index of the folder location of small geographic or ethnographic units which do not have individual folders, this file places such entities as the African Masai under the references "Kenyan Life" and "Tanzanian Life" (4 card drawers).

Personality Index

This index gives the filing name under which a personality usually known by a nickname or pseudonym may be found in the Picture Collection (17 card drawers). Examples are "Mark Twain see Clemens, Samuel L."; "Minnesota Fats, Billiards Champion see Wanderone, Rudolf."

30

PRINTS DIVISION AND GENERAL PRINTS RESOURCES

The purpose of the Prints Division, determined at the time of its establishment in 1900 with the donation of the S. P. Avery collection, is to acquire representative examples of original prints and to provide books and other materials useful to the study of prints. The print collection ranges from the fifteenth century to the present, and includes some 150,000 prints and 12,000 books and pamphlets. It is open to the public upon presentation of an admission card obtained from the Research Libraries Administrative Office.

Prints are arranged by print maker within his nationality and period. Notable exceptions to this arrangement are found in the special subject collections, such as the I. N. Phelps Stokes collection of Americana, the Eno New York views, the South Sea Bubble caricatures, peep show prints, American political caricatures, and bookplates. There are also many original drawings in the collection. The division has developed a number of indexes which are of use in answering questions related to its well-rounded and representative collection of fine prints.

The collection of reference materials in the division is extensive. It consists of three parts:

1. A comprehensive group of reference books consisting of historical and technical works on printmaking, biographies of printmakers and catalogs of their work, bibliographies of prints, and the like. Periodicals devoted exclusively to prints and printmaking are also available.
2. A selective group of illustrated books containing original graphic work.
3. A large collection of clippings and ephemeral material relating to individual artists. Reproductions of the works of such artists as Nast and Keppler have been bound in scrapbooks, and frequently provide information not found in published works.

There is, in addition, a small collection of printmaker's tools (original metal plates, lithographic stones, wood blocks, etc.), and a collection of mounted original bookplates arranged by name of owner or designer.

COLLECTING POLICY

Prints are acquired selectively as examples of the work of individual artists or for subject interest. Drawings of American views, political caricatures, and book illustrations are accepted as gifts on a selective basis. The division does not purchase drawings.[1] Books on printmaking are collected comprehensively, as are all oeuvre catalogs, prints bibliographies, and other reference works useful for work within the print collection; periodicals in the field are also collected comprehensively, although few periodicals are specifically devoted to the subject. Books on printmaking techniques are acquired on a representative basis; the division collects elementary works only in rare instances. Descriptive works on book illustration and caricature are collected comprehensively, but the division adds to its holdings of illustrated books only items containing original graphic work (woodcuts, engravings, etc.), on a very selective basis. Fine illustrated books are collected by the Spencer Collection. Other book arts (bookbinding, calligraphy, illumination, printing, etc.) are collected by the General Research and Humanities Division, and are discussed in chapter 8 of this *Guide*.

NOTABLE ACQUISITIONS

The library had a collection of prints before the establishment of a special division for their administration. Two of the predecessor libraries had notable materials: the Lenox Library housed a general collection, and the Tilden collection included an extraordinary group of caricatures by Gillray. Prints had been received as early gifts from the Duyckinck and Stuart collections given to the Lenox Library, and from the Emmet and Ford collections presented to the library after the consolidation of the Astor, Lenox and Tilden foundations.

Samuel P. Avery, an art dealer and a trustee of the New York Public Library, donated his

---

1. The Spencer Collection collects original drawings for books in its resources; the Arents Collection of Books in Parts buys drawings for the illustrated books in parts in its holdings; the Arents Tobacco Collection acquires drawings related to tobacco; there are drawings on the dance, music, and theatre in those subject collections; the Berg Collection, although it does not collect drawings, has numerous items by Thackeray and other nineteenth-century English illustrators.

personal collection of prints in 1900.[2] Consisting of 14,890 items, which with variant states number 17,557 pieces, the Avery collection is primarily composed of the etchings of nineteenth-century European artists and lithographs from the time of Senefelder.

In 1901, Charles Stewart Smith donated 1,700 Japanese woodcuts which had been collected by Captain F. Brinkley. Included were the work of such important artists as Harunobu, Shunshō, and particularly Utamaro.[3] In 1903, John Bigelow gave caricatures and posters issued in Paris during the Siege and Commune; in 1908, Mrs. Cyrus Lawrence gave 621 prints, including a large number of lithographs by Daumier. During the same year Joseph Pennell gave 1,006 lithographs which had been featured in the centenary exhibition of 1898 at the South Kensington Museum in London, and which had also been the basis for his *Lithography and Lithographers*. The material presented included many rare items from the earliest Senefelder prints to contemporaneous specimens, with particularly good representation of Bonington, Raffet, and Charlet, as well as early English works, and a number of Pennell's own lithographs. In 1909 the Hon. J. L. Cadwalader gave 145 German, French, and Italian line engravings of the early nineteenth century; later he added to the collection and left as bequests his collections of engravings, mainly English stipple and mezzotints of the eighteenth and early nineteenth centuries, along with a fund to be used primarily for the purchase of old prints.[4]

During the period 1911–15, Mrs. Henry Draper gave many prints to the library, including original woodblocks and metal plates by or relating to George Cruikshank, John Leech, Hablôt K. Browne ("Phiz"), and other English illustrators of the nineteenth century; in 1915 she bequeathed her library, including a collection of prints.[5] In 1912, Samuel Arlent Edwards gave examples of his mezzotints in several states; this gift was followed by an additional one in 1936 of mezzotints by the artist made after famous paintings. Two collections were given by Edward G. Kennedy in 1912: one of etchings and engravings, another of etchings by English artists made in the 1860s. Kennedy continued his gifts through the 1920s.[6] In 1915 the library received 14,000 prints from the estate of David McNeely Stauffer, a group especially rich in examples of American work of the eighteenth and early nineteenth centuries.[7] This gift was subsequently supplemented by Stauffer's widow, Mrs. Oscar H. Rogers.

An important collection of 477 New York views from the seventeenth through the nineteenth century was received in 1922 from Amos F. Eno.[8]

The Beverly Chew collection of portraits, featuring those of Milton and Pope, was bequeathed to the library in 1925.[9] In 1926, W. O. C. Kiene gave a collection of material relating to American caricature as exemplified by Joseph Keppler, founder and chief cartoonist of *Puck* (St. Louis), and by other artists associated with him. This gift was continued in 1938 when Keppler gave a large collection of original drawings for *Puck*, including his own and examples of the work of F. Graetz, F. Opper, G. Kühn, and others. In 1930 the Phelps Stokes collection of American historical prints and early views of American cities came to the library as a gift of I. N. Phelps Stokes. It is known as the Phelps Stokes collection, in memory of Anson Phelps Stokes and Helen L. Phelps Stokes. It includes nearly 800 watercolors, drawings, engravings, lithographs, and a few paintings produced over a period of four centuries, from the earliest European discoveries of the West Indian islands through the nineteenth century. The collection is composed primarily of views of towns and historical scenes. Selections are always exhibited in the third floor corridor of the Fifth Avenue building.[10]

In 1942, Dr. Herman T. Radin presented his collection of more than 3,000 bookplates by distinguished contemporary European artists, as well as books relating to bookplate artists. In the same year the Charles Williston McAlpin collection of portraits of George Washington came to the library as a gift. It contains over 1,700 engraved portraits, primarily after the paintings of Stuart, Peale, Trumbull, and Savage, along with many fictitious Washington portraits—prints based on no known painting or likeness. The collection contains portraits in other media including lithographs, textiles, and embroideries.

In addition to historical and literary material, the 1950 bequest of Mary Stillman Harkness contained drawings by Rowlandson, Cruikshank, Hablôt K. Browne ("Phiz"), F. O. C. Darley, Walter Crane, Arthur Rackham, and others.[11] In 1959 a gouache on vellum was given to the library by the estate of James Hazen Hyde. The work of Jacques Le Moynes de Morgues, it depicts American Indians and Huguenot settlers of Florida in 1564, and is the earliest known European representation of Indians on their native ground.[12] During the 1950s, Mortimer and Anna Neinken made valuable additions to the holdings of peep show prints in the division. Other important gifts include 85 etchings by James McBey, given by Mrs. McBey in 1963, and an extensive collection of the graphic work of Reginald Marsh, given by Mrs. Marsh.

2. See *A Handbook of the S. P. Avery Collection of Prints and Art Books in The New York Public Library* (New York: DeVinne Press, 1901). See also supplement, *BNYPL* 24 (1920): 719–36, and notes on gifts by the Misses Welcher *BNYPL* 25 (1921): 533; 26 (1922): 256. See also Lydenberg, *History*, pp. 381–84, and *BNYPL* 14 (1910): 89–96.

3. See *BNYPL* 5 (1901): 39–40; 40 (1936): 3–8.

4. See *BNYPL* 18 (1914): 344.

5. See *BNYPL* 19 (1915): 421.

6. See *BNYPL* 30 (1926): 928–29.

7. See *BNYPL* 20 (1916): 335–37.

8. See *BNYPL* 29 (1925): 327–54 et seq.; published separately by the library.

9. For a listing of the Beverly Chew portraits, see *Catalogue of an Exhibition Commemorative of the Tercentenary of the Birth of John Milton* (New York: Grolier Club, 1908); *An Exhibition of the First Editions of the Works of Alexander Pope* (New York: Grolier Club, 1911); and *BNYPL* 30 (1926): 3–6.

10. See I. N. Phelps and Daniel C. Haskell, *American Historical Prints, Early Views of American Cities, etc., from the Phelps Stokes and Other Collections* (The New York Public Library, 1933). Reprinted with additions and corrections from *BNYPL* (1931–32); a new edition is in preparation.

11. See *BNYPL* 55 (1951): 213–24.

12. See *BNYPL* 64 (1960): 243–44.

SPECIAL INDEXES AND FILES

The holdings of prints by established artists are indicated by notations in standard oeuvre catalogs, so that in most cases there is only a form card in the division's catalog indicating the presence of such material. In addition to the regular catalog, there are numerous card indexes which analyze the collection. Vertical files supplement book and print holdings with clippings from diverse sources and printed ephemera.

Author's Works Illustrated Index

A card file arranged alphabetically under main entry (author or title) of the work illustrated (active, 1 card drawer). The index indicates the form of the illustration, the title, and the name of the illustrator. A large part of the file is taken up by cards for illustrations of the Bible arranged by the names of the books of the Bible and subdivided under special topics.

Book Illustrators Index

A file arranged alphabetically under the name of the illustrator of the book (active, 60 card drawers). It indexes mainly illustrated books shelved elsewhere in the library and does not include magazine or comic strip illustrators.

Bookplates Index

A card file arranged alphabetically by name of the owners of bookplates included in books throughout the Research Libraries (active, 14 card drawers).

Caricatures

An index of single prints of caricatures (primarily American and political) in the Prints Division arranged chronologically by country (1 card drawer). This index is not a complete list of the division's holdings; in those cases where there is a published checklist, the division's holdings are checked there.

Illustrated Books Index

A highly selective file arranged alphabetically by country, then chronologically (active, 6 card drawers). It primarily indexes illustrated books shelved elsewhere in the library.

Original Drawings Index

A catalog of original drawings in the Prints Division and to book illustrations in the Spencer Collection, arranged alphabetically by artist (active, 2 card drawers). The information given includes artist, title, date if known, size, and possible attribution to other artists.

Prints after Painters Index

An index arranged alphabetically by name of painter after whose work the print was made (active, 3 card drawers). The cards also give the name of the engraver and other pertinent information if known. The file is not complete.

Print Makers (Engravers, Etchers, etc.) Index

A catalog of original single prints in the Prints Division, arranged under name of printmaker (active, 41 card drawers). Cards for some of the plate books in the division are filed in this catalog under the name of the engraver of the plates; books with original plates shelved elsewhere in the Research Libraries are occasionally listed.

Saints Index

An index to a collection of twelve albums of mounted engravings of saints ranging from the sixteenth to the eighteenth century (inactive, 1 card drawer).

SUBJECT INDEXES TO ORIGINAL SINGLE PRINTS

This file is in three groups as follows:

Subjects

All except the subjects "Portraits" and "Views" are included. This is a highly selective index to subject (active, 6 card drawers).

Subjects: Portraits

This index is an aid to locating portrait prints as well as those bound or incorporated in books (active, 6 card drawers). The arrangement is alphabetical by sitter. Portraits of print makers are separately filed.

Subjects: Views

The views are arranged alphabetically by town or geographic locality (as for Delaware Water Gap, Niagara Falls) (active, 6 card drawers). Views of New York City are subdivided by subject group (for example, churches, hotels, museums, parks, public buildings, schools, theatres), and then by named and numbered streets and avenues.

SUBJECT INDEXES TO ORIGINAL SINGLE PRINTS ELSEWHERE IN THE RESEARCH LIBRARIES

This file is divided into two groups as follows:

Portraits

A card index to engraved portraits in selected books which are shelved elsewhere in the Research Libraries (active, 24 card drawers). It indexes portraits in extra-illustrated books administered by the Rare Book Division and in the Emmet collection in the Manuscripts and Archives Division.

Views

A card index to foreign views in books shelved elsewhere in the Research Libraries which are of special interest because of engraver, etcher, etc. (active, 5 card drawers). The arrangement is alphabetical by town and occasionally by locality.

VERTICAL FILES

Print Makers File

All sorts of ephemera, reproductions of works, exhibition notices, reviews, obituaries, and the like, arranged in envelopes by name of print maker (125 linear feet). There is a form card in the Prints Division card catalog indicating that material is available for particular artists.

Print Collections

Miscellaneous information regarding print rooms in museums and libraries, print dealers, print clubs, etc., is arranged in envelopes by name of organization (18 linear feet).

Clipping File of Illustrations from Dealers' Catalogs

A vertical file of illustrations clipped from dealers' catalogs (25 file boxes). The file is arranged by country (then by town) of publication; for larger centers of population (for example, Paris, London, Venice), by date of publication grouped in five-year periods.

Portraits

The portraits are arranged by sitter (200 file boxes). They are engravings for the most part, although photographs and half-tone reproductions are interfiled.

RESOURCES

This description of the prints resources is primarily concerned with single prints (rather than collections of prints, or prints with text) found in the Prints Division, the major repository of such material in the Research Libraries. In cases where significant holdings of prints are found in other divisions, the location of the material is indicated. It should be noted that the Schomburg Center for Research in Black Culture, the Theatre and Dance Collections, and the Music Division contain prints associated with their special fields,[13] and that the Arents Tobacco Collection acquires prints depicting tobacco and its uses.

FIFTEENTH AND SIXTEENTH CENTURIES

The Prints Division holds a representative collection of single prints of these centuries, particularly extensive in German works, including those of the "little masters" H. S. Beham, Aldegrever, Altdorfer, Pencz, and others. The collection is strongest in the engravings of Albrecht Dürer.[14] In the Spencer Collection are found fine copies of this artist's three "great books" of woodcuts with text (the *Apocalypse*, the *Life of the Virgin*, and the *Great Passion*). A recent purchase from the Destailleur collection brought to the Prints Division an almost complete set of the engravings of Étienne Delaune bound in two volumes. Among other artists and engravers of the period represented in the division are Cranach, Schongauer, Lautensack, De Bry, Goltzius, Van Leyden, and Raimondi. There are more than 100 chiaroscuro prints in the Prints Division.[15]

SEVENTEENTH AND EIGHTEENTH CENTURIES

Among the most important groups of prints by single artists of this period are the division's holdings of the work of Stefano Della Bella; two albums of mounted prints give an almost complete representation of his work, together with eight festival books in the Spencer Collection carrying his illustrations. There are four albums of mounted prints by Jean Le Pautre and numerous works by Abraham Bosse. Other seventeenth-century works include those of Hollar, Ostade, Backhuysen, Waterloo, Van Vliet, Potter, Callot, Jegher, Van Dyck, Vorsterman, Rembrandt, and others. Among portrait artists, there is the work of William Faithorne and Nanteuil, Mellan, Morin, Edelinck, and others of the French school.

Eighteenth-century works include English mezzotints (from the Cadwalader gift), two albums of the work of John Smith, and French line engravings (including some illustrated books), among which is a collection of engravings by and after Cochin. There are three albums of mounted prints in various states by William Hogarth, and also etchings of Chodowiecki; chiaroscuro prints by Lesueur, Jackson, and Kirkall; and several sets of Piranesi's etchings. Fine sets of the work of Rowlandson and Gillray are noted in the discussion of caricatures. Among the eighteenth-century Japanese prints in the division those of Utamaro are outstanding,[16] but there are many examples of the work of other print masters of the "pictures of the floating world." An interesting eighteenth-century reprint (Vienna, 1799) is the "Triumphal Arch of Maximillian" by Albrecht Dürer and others, on permanent exhibition in the main corridor of the Central Building; it was presented to the library in 1910 by Atherton Curtis.

NINETEENTH AND TWENTIETH CENTURIES

European

The Avery collection of nineteenth-century French materials has such nearly-complete representations of the work of some artists as to be almost unique. Avery attempted to secure at least one example of the work of every contemporary artist whom he had met or of whom he had heard. Avery added to the collection during his lifetime and his family did thereafter; his son, Samuel Palmer Avery, established a fund for the purchase of modern foreign prints.

The 226 pieces which comprise the Turner holdings center on the "Liber Studiorum," and consist of rare outline etchings, first states of published and unpublished mezzotints, and photographs of original drawings. The Goya holdings are also strong and contain a lithograph (Delteil 272) of which only two other impressions are known. The representation of Meryon is good; there is a nearly complete set of Haden's works, a fine collection of Whistler, and a special collection of work by women. Manet is represented by more than eighty items, including a watercolor and an original drawing for a frontispiece to a collection of his etchings.[17] There is a good set

13. See *Dancing in Prints 1634–1870* (The New York Public Library, 1964); Lillian Moore, *Images of the Dance* (The New York Public Library, 1965); Sydney Beck and Elizabeth Roth, *Music in Prints* (The New York Public Library, 1965).

14. See "Fifteenth and Sixteenth Century Prints in the Collection of The New York Public Library," *BNYPL* 38 (1934): 919–33 et seq.

15. See "Chiaroscuro Prints," *BNYPL* 20 (1916): 493–98. A scarce print in the collections is described in Henry Meier's "Giulio Campagnola's 'Woman Reclining in a Landscape' and Its Technique," *BNYPL* 46 (1942): 735–38.

16. See *Catalogue of the Work of Kitagawa Utamaro, 1753–1806, in the Collections of The New York Public Library* (The New York Public Library, 1950).

17. See Theodore Reff, "Manet's Frontispiece Etchings," *BNYPL* 66 (1962): 143–48.

of the graphic work of Mary Cassatt, along with two original drawings and some letters housed in the Prints Division. Also noteworthy is the graphic work of Delacroix, including a copy of his *Faust* (1828) in the original wrappers.

The collection of twentieth-century European prints, while it contains a fair representation of all schools and modern trends, is strongest in the work of Liebermann and the German Expressionists, including Beckmann, Nolde, Pechstein, Slevogt, and others. The Käthe Kollwitz holdings are good. Gifts from Joseph Pennell and others, along with division acquisitions, have established a strong and representative collection of lithographs.

American

The David McNeely Stauffer gift is strong in eighteenth- and nineteenth-century American print makers, although other nationalities are represented from the sixteenth century onward. Other important holdings in the division are those for A. B. Durand, James Smillie, Burt, Jones, J. W. Spenceley, and Timothy Cole. The work of twentieth-century artists includes that of S. Arlent Edwards, Anthony, John Taylor Arms, Cadwallader Washburn, and firm resources in the so-called "middle period" of American printmaking from 1900 through 1930 with such artists as Hassam, A. B. Davis, Sloan, Marsh, Biddle, and Fritz Eichenberg.

SCHOMBURG CENTER FOR RESEARCH IN BLACK CULTURE

The Schomburg Center has an extensive collection of prints in its field of research. There were 2,000 etchings, lithographs, engravings, and watercolors by black artists or about black subjects which became part of its resources when the personal library of Arthur A. Schomburg was added in 1926. These have been augmented by line illustrations and other items from the Picture Collection. Gathered from diverse sources, the prints in the center represent the habits and customs of black people in Guinea, the Congo, Ethiopia, Ghana, the West Indies, and the United States. There are etchings and engravings by Albert Smith, W. E. Braxton, and Patrick Henry Reason (other engravings by Reason are in the Prints Division).

CARICATURES AND CARTOONS

The caricatures and cartoons in the Prints Division should be divided into two groups for study: political and social.

Political Cartoons: The division is actively building its resources in this field; an example is the recent purchase of late eighteenth-century Italian political caricatures. There is a good collection of nineteenth-century French cartoons, and some Russian cartoons from the Napoleonic period. The almost complete collection of Gillray prints (along with many drawings) was started with the bequest of Samuel Jones Tilden of a group of 137 caricatures. There are also fine holdings of South Sea Bubble caricatures. The strong Daumier holdings contain much political caricature.

It is in American political caricature that the collections have the greatest breadth.[18] Substantial

holdings of the work of Thomas Nast are reinforced by 40 original drawings and a sketchbook of a Fourth of July picnic attended by the artist in 1859. The Kiene gift included materials relating to Joseph Keppler and other artists associated with him on the magazine *Puck*. In the general collection are proofs of political cartoons by Rollin Kirby in the *World*, the *New York World-Telegram*, and the *New York Post* from 1930 to 1942, and by Daniel R. Fitzpatrick in the *St. Louis Post Dispatch* for the period from 1939 to 1958. A collection of 35 original caricatures by Harry Hopkins was presented by Mrs. Hopkins in 1951.

Social Cartoons: Examples of the Prints Division's holdings in this category include the etchings of Rowlandson and George Cruikshank, more thoroughly treated in the discussion of book arts, chapter 8. Daumier and Garvani are exceptionally well represented, as are other French cartoonists of their period. The James Wright Brown cartoon collection was a centennial Christmas gift to the library in 1948. It consists of 809 original editorial cartoons, many with captions: included are Johnny Anderson, Charles Dana Gibson, Gee Tee Maxwell, Louis A. Paige, John Walbridge, and others. Social cartoons are found in other divisions of the Research Libraries, particularly in the Theatre and Dance Collections and in the Music Division, where they have been acquired for their subject interest. Notable are a group of caricatures of Paganini in the Muller collection in the Music Division. The Theatre Collection received in 1966, as a gift from the widow of Alfred J. ("Al") Frueh, more than 400 original drawings by Frueh, including theatrical caricatures for the *New Yorker* and other magazines and newspapers from the early 1900s onward.[19] There is also a collection of over 970 sketches and caricatures by Alex Gard.

Many examples of humorous pictures are to be found elsewhere in the collections; political cartoons are generally classified with history, and such humorous publications as *Punch*, *Life*, *Fliegende Blätter*, the *New Yorker* and many lesser known publications, of which the library has long files, are general collection materials.

BOOKPLATES

A rich collection of bookplates in the Prints Division is arranged by owner or by artist. The holdings are notable for the work of contemporary American and European artists (mainly from the collection given by Herman T. Radin), but extend backward in time to the Buxheim bookplate (ca. 1480) and the earliest Swiss bookplate, that of Balthasar Brennwald, dated 1502. A bookplates index in the division lists bookplates by name of the owners of the bookplates in books located throughout the library.

IMAGERIES POPULAIRES

Prints produced for the populace are a special interest of the Prints Division. The largest national collections are those for France, Italy,

---

18. See Frank Weitenkampf, *Political Caricature in the United States in Separate Published*

Cartoons: An Annotated List (The New York Public Library, 1953; reprinted by the library and Arno Press, 1971).

19. See Maxwell Silverman, comp., *Frueh on the Theatre: Theatrical Caricatures 1906–1962* (The New York Public Library, 1972).

Russia, Spain, and China, although there are examples of the production of other nations. The Italian prints range from the sixteenth to the nineteenth centuries. A recent acquisition has increased the number of Italian popular prints of the seventeenth and eighteenth centuries to more than 100. Most of these are by the house of Remondini of Bassano and illustrate such subjects as the five senses, meals of the day, and biblical scenes, with stencil coloring which is preserved in its original freshness. There are 6 albums of mounted popular song sheets illustrated with woodcuts, which include late nineteenth-century Florentine *canzonette*, *romanze d'amore*, and the like. Bound collections of nineteenth-century Russian *lubki* in the Prints and Slavonic Divisions often represent variants of a prototype, although each division attempts to avoid duplication of the other's holdings. Spanish materials are for the most part religious in nature and date from the nineteenth century; however, there are several bound collections of secular woodcuts produced by printing firms over a period of years. A collection made by Carl Schuster of 250 Chinese popular prints of the early twentieth century from various provinces of China was acquired by the library in 1954. These gaily colored woodcuts representing Chinese household gods served as a starting point for a library exhibition of the world's *imageries populaires*. Some 50 additions have been made to the collection.

Other materials in the Research Libraries associated with *imageries populaires* are handbills, broadsides, and chapbooks in the Rare Book Division, many of which are illustrated, and the *rappresentazione* in the Spencer Collection.

DRAWINGS

The holdings of drawings in the Research Libraries are discussed by location. Certain groups of drawings are largely excluded from the following discussion: original cartoons and caricatures were considered earlier in this chapter; drawings made for book illustration receive their fullest treatment in chapter 8 of this *Guide*.

Prints Division

Although the Prints Division does not purchase drawings, it has accepted as gifts over the years many European and American works dating from the seventeenth century to the present. Among the European drawings are many once in the van Suchtelen collection, which came as a gift to the Astor Library. The major part of this gift consists of Dutch drawings of the seventeenth century, but also includes some French and Italian, as well as German, drawings ranging in date from the seventeenth to the mid-nineteenth century. By bequest of Mrs. Mary Stillman Harkness the Prints Division received several albums with mounted drawings and watercolors, chiefly by English artists of the nineteenth century, including Thomas Rowlandson and Kate Greenaway. Drawings by Maria and Richard Cosway were presented by Francis Peabody in 1952, together with a collection of engravings after their work. In the superb collection of Gillray caricatures from the Tilden library are many preparatory drawings. Original drawings by Bracquemond, Manet, Meryon, Pissarro, Seymour Haden, Charles Keene, Whistler, Mary Cassatt, and many more, are included in the S. P. Avery collection of prints.

Drawings and watercolors are found in the I. N. Phelps Stokes collection of American views, including several by J. W. Hill. Thomas K. Wharton is represented by more than 50 drawings, apart from his illustrated diaries in the Manuscripts and Archives Division. In addition to a bound volume containing 90 pen-and-ink drawings by Asher B. Durand designed for banknote vignettes, there are other drawings by this artist in the collection.

A large proportion of the drawings in the Prints Division were made for book illustrations, such as those by William Denslow for Baum's *The Wizard of Oz*, and all those by Reginald Marsh, a gift from Mrs. Marsh in 1969. The bulk of the collection of drawings, however, consists of political and social caricatures and cartoons, including many by Joseph Keppler, Thomas Nast, Charles Dana Gibson, and others. Civil War drawings by staff artists of *Leslie's Weekly* are another important group. A card index locates original drawings in the Prints Division, as well as those in the Spencer Collection.

Manuscripts and Archives Division

Drawings found in the Manuscripts and Archives Division relate directly to the manuscripts or are a part of them. There are also numerous sketches in the extensive collection of diaries. The large collections of author's typescripts often contain specimens of the book designer's art, typographer's designs, or other matter placed with the final script or the galley proofs. An architect's drawings are considered to be part of his personal papers and are found in the Manuscripts and Archives Division.

Examples of these types of drawings include a sketch book with the diaries of Thomas K. Wharton, which is illustrated with pen-and-ink landscapes of Ohio, New Orleans, New England, and other places where the architect lived or which he visited during the mid-nineteenth century; this is complemented by 50 additional Wharton drawings, for the most part Ohio views made in the 1830s, held in the Prints Division. Architectural drawings are in the papers of Alexander Jackson Davis of the firm of Town, Davis, Dakin of New York; and in the correspondence of Richard Upjohn and Richard Michell Upjohn. There is a 14-volume collection of drawings for Chinese lattice.

A number of drawings by Robert Fulton are included in the important holdings of the papers of Robert Fulton in the Parsons collection and the Gilbert H. Montague collection of Robert Fulton manuscripts. Those in the Parsons collection are the more important, consisting of drawings for the submarine, submarine bombs, and mode of attack executed and signed by Fulton in 1804.[20] Drawings in the Montague collection include a group illustrating the mode of using the sleeping torpedo.

The Harkness collection contains sketches by Alfred Crowquill, David Maclise, George Du Maurier, and others, many in letters, although there are original drawings by Hablôt K. Browne ("Phiz") made to illustrate "The Goblins and the Sexton" in the *Pickwick Papers*. Particular interest is centered in the Shirley Brooks album in the collection which contains many sketches by Leech,

---

20. Reproduced in William B. Parsons, *Robert Fulton and the Submarine* (New York: Columbia Univ. Press, 1922).

Thackeray, Tenniel, Edward Linley Sambourne, and others, most of them in letters to Brooks, who was the second editor of *Punch*. The Montague collection contains similar materials.

Berg Collection

The collection's not inconsiderable holdings of drawings are connected with literary figures or are examples of book illustration. There are 300 drawings and sketches by Thackeray, over 100 by Kipling, and a great number by the artists who illustrated Dickens. Among the illustrators of children's books, Kate Greenaway is represented by about one hundred drawings, watercolors, and designs. A number of the manuscript journals of Arnold Bennett include pen and watercolor drawings.[21]

Spencer Collection

The Spencer Collection's special interest in the illustrated book has prompted the acquisition of drawings; these are more fully discussed in chapter 8 of this *Guide*. Interesting drawings in the collection include a series of 104 pencil drawings of male and female heads, copies of a collection of Leonardo da Vinci caricature heads. They are bound in an edition of the works of Rabelais (Rouen, 1669) and may have been done by Wenceslaus Hollar.[22] Fifty-four drawings represent views of American scenes made by Archibald Robertson, later Lieutenant-General of the Royal Engineers, during the Revolutionary period. They were purchased together with his diaries for the same period, and are supplemented by other library holdings which include 6 manuscript maps probably in Robertson's hand.[23]

Arents Collections

The Arents Tobacco Collection has a high ratio of illustrated materials in proportion to its total holdings; among these are a number of original drawings. Herbals, sketchbooks, and other items from the seventeenth century to the present are illustrated with drawings and watercolors depicting the history and production of tobacco. There is an interesting group of original drawings for cigar box labels by German artists of the nineteenth century. There are examples of the work of Woodward, Cruikshank, Thackeray, and others. The collection also has an original drawing by Thomas Nast of Santa Claus holding a pipe, a

representation which standardized the modern image of that jovial figure. Two of the Arents Publications contain reproductions of original drawings held in the collection. *A Few Words About Pipes Smoking and Tobacco* (1947) is a first edition of Alfred H. Forrester's illustrated manuscript. A republication of John Bain's *Tobacco in Song and Story* (1953) reproduces a copy of the original edition (1896) which had been enlarged by a collector who employed artists of the day to draw illustrative sketches in the margins. Mr. Arents in turn commissioned Rube Goldberg to add illustrations to a copy of the republication.

The Arents Collection of Books in Parts is equally rich in original drawings, including original sketches and working drawings of the great English illustrators from Rowlandson to Caldecott.[24] They are discussed more fully in chapter 8 of this *Guide*.

Rare Book Division

The division has an album of drawings of the Sioux Indians in pencil and watercolor made by Francis B. Mayer during the mid-nineteenth century. An album of 167 leaves of pencil drawings made for *Souvenir of North American Indians* (London, 1850–53) is signed by the author, George Catlin. An elaborate set of costumes of the Russian state by Solntzev consists of 326 watercolors.

Performing Arts Research Center

The Dance Collection's strong holdings of pictorial material on the dance include a number of original drawings and sketches. There are stage and costume designs by such artists as Alexandre Bénois, Eugene Berman, Giorgio de Chirico, Cecil Beaton, Rouben Ter-Arutunian, Léon Bakst, Mitislav Doboujinsky, Nathalia Gontcharova, Leonor Fini, and others. The important Isadora Duncan holdings contain original drawings of the dancer by Rodin, Bourdell, and Grand'jouan.

In the Theatre Collection are thousands of original scene designs, costume sketches, and caricatures for all types of theatrical performances. Artists represented include Léon and André Bakst, Simon Lissim, Nathalia Gontcharova, Ludolfs Liberts, Robert Edmond Jones, Norman Bel Geddes, Donald Oenslager, David Ffolkes, Lucinda Ballard, Erté, Marcel Vertès, Aline Bernstein, John Boyt, Bonnie Cashin, Nat Karson, the Motleys, Cecil Beaton, Lee Simonson, and Howard Bay. There are drawings documenting the history of French and English theatre from the seventeenth century to the present, and the American theatre from 1860 onward.

The large collection of portraits of figures in the musical world, held by the Special Collections of the Music Division, contains a number of original drawings.

---

21. See Lola L. Szladits and Harvey Simmonds, *Pen & Brush* (The New York Public Library, 1969).

22. See A. H. Scott-Elliot, "Caricature Heads after Leonardo da Vinci in the Spencer Collection," *BNYPL* 62 (1958): 279–99.

23. See Harry M. Lydenberg, ed., *Archibald Robertson; His Diaries & Sketches in America, 1762–1780* (The New York Public Library, 1930). Reprinted *BNYPL* 37 (1933): 7–37 et seq. Published separately by the library; reprinted by the library and Arno Press, 1971.

24. See Hellmut Lehmann-Haupt, "English Illustrators in the Collection of George Arents," *The Colophon*, n. g. s. 1 (1940): [23–46].

PART FOUR

31

MUSIC DIVISION AND GENERAL
MUSIC RESOURCES

HISTORICAL SURVEY

The richness of music resources of the New York Public Library effectively dates from the 1888 gift to the Lenox Library of the private collection of Joseph W. Drexel, which is now an important part of the Music Division. Numbering 5,542 volumes and 766 pamphlets, the Drexel collection contains several incunabula, most notably Franchino Gaffurio's *Theorica Musica* (1492). From the sixteenth century are 12 volumes, including a copy of Baltazarini da Belgiojoso's *Balet comique de la Royne* (1582), which formerly belonged to Ben Jonson and Horace Walpole. The 48 seventeenth-century books are particularly interesting to the historian of English vocal and instrumental music; included is the unique copy of *Parthenia In-Violata* (ca. 1625).[1] Among the 483 items from the eighteenth century are many specimens of English vocal music, and several volumes of broadsides of theater and concert songs; ballad operas are well represented. The remainder of the collection consists of nineteenth-century books and music issued before 1888. The books included in the original Drexel collection were listed in a short-title inventory published by the Lenox Library in 1899 (No. 11). In 1918, Drexel's daughter, Katharine Drexel Penrose, bequeathed $10,000, the income from which was designated to augment the Drexel collection "by the acquisition of books and musical compositions which shall be of the same general character as those now constituting the Library and which shall have been originally published since the year 1888."[2]

The origins of the Music Division may also be traced in the Astor Library, which as early as 1883 had designated a portion of a gift of $15,000 for needed titles in music, through which such items as the *Paléographie Musicale* and some of the publications of the Plainsong and Mediaeval Music Society were purchased. In 1896 the Astor Library acquired a collection of Italian opera librettos, a few of which date from the seventeenth century. The Astor and Lenox collections were united in the Lenox Building in 1898, and were transferred to the new building at Fifth Avenue and Forty-second street in 1911. Since that date the library has continued to develop its music collection by the addition of books, periodicals, scores, and other materials on an international basis. Only acquisitions of particular interest and importance will be mentioned here.

In 1921 a number of friends purchased the library of the critic James G. Huneker and gave it to the Music Division as a memorial. Two years later, through the efforts of Edward Ziegler and other friends, the library received the collection of Henry Edward Krehbiel, consisting of 2,000 books and pamphlets and a large assortment of sheet music. Funds for new purchases were scanty during this period, but in 1928 a decision was reached to strengthen music holdings by acquiring materials at auction from the library of Dr. Werner Wolffheim of Berlin, and 450 lots from the sale were secured with funds provided by the Beethoven Association, the Carnegie Corporation, Harry Harkness Flagler, and the Juilliard Musical Foundation. The oldest documents obtained were early vellum fragments dating from the tenth to the sixteenth centuries. The purchase contained a fine representation of works from the Palestrina period in the sixteenth and early seventeenth centuries, as well as a number of early lute books, the rarest of which is Jean Baptiste Besard's *Novus Partus Sive Concertationes Musicae* (1617). Seventy-five volumes of literature of the early French song, and a number of important English song books and collections of instrumental music of the eighteenth century further strengthened the Music Division.

In 1932 a magnificent collection of musical manuscripts was presented to the library in memory of Miss Lizzie Bliss and Dr. Christian A. Herter by their families. It included holograph scores of cantatas by Bach, Handel, Haydn, and Mozart, and compositions by Schubert and Schumann, in addition to autograph letters of figures in the musical world. The same year, through the generosity of Harry Harkness Flagler, the library received a holograph page of Haydn's first notes for *The Creation*. In 1938 as a memorial to Dr. Henry Hadley a growing collection of American musical scores was placed on permanent deposit by the National Association for American Composers and Conductors, of which Hadley was founder.

A collection of musical portraits came to the library in 1939 as the gift of Joseph Muller, an Americana specialist on the staff of the Music Division. Portraits, manuscripts, musical drawings, and musical Americana are found in this collection. The library of the Beethoven Association, New York, was presented to the Music Division in 1940; in addition to books the gift consisted of music, pictures, manuscripts, musical instruments, statues, copyrights, and contract rights.

A large number of the manuscripts of Louis Moreau Gottschalk and George Frederick Bristow were purchased in 1948. These form an important part of the Music Division's Americana Collection, which grew to importance under John Tasker Howard; appropriately a number of his manuscripts have been placed there.[3] 1956 was

---

1. See a facsimile edition, *Parthenia In-Violata* (The New York Public Library, 1961).
2. Lydenburg, *History*, pp. 118–19.

3. Among published library resources in American music is *The Piano Works of Louis Moreau Gottschalk*, edited by Vera Brodsky Lawrence

notable for the purchase of the Shapiro collection of early American sheet music. The division acquired a collection of Felix Mendelssohn Bartholdy family letters in 1960. Having established a comprehensive collection of Percy Grainger's published works, the division was especially happy to receive a number of this composer's manuscripts from his widow in 1962. In the same year Paul Wittgenstein, the Viennese pianist, left to the library his holdings of musical manuscripts, which included 7 important Brahms items. Wittgenstein, having lost his right arm in World War I, had commissioned well-known composers to write concertos for the left hand. Manuscripts of these formed part of the bequest.

In 1963 the Music Division was fortunate to receive from Sol Rozman 2,000 pieces of sheet music, the majority in first printed editions, representing virtually every composer in nineteenth-century Vienna. The Music Division acquired in 1967 as a gift of Eugene List, the pianist, 2 manuscripts of the works of Louis Moreau Gottschalk. In 1968 the division received a bequest from Dr. Otto Kinkeldey, the income from which has been used to augment and improve the collection of the Research Libraries in the wide field of musicology, and to raise its quality as an institution for scholarly study and research. Jazz manuscripts are always rare; the 1968 gift by Duke Ellington of his "Sacred Concert" is of exceptional interest and importance.

When in 1968 the National Orchestral Association placed on deposit with the Music Division Mozart's 57 page autograph score for the *Haffner* Symphony, K. 385, this great work became available for study by qualified researchers for the first time since its completion and public performance in 1783.

In 1965 the Music Division, Dance Collection, and Theatre Collection were relocated in what is now called the Performing Arts Research Center in the New York Public Library at Lincoln Center. The new quarters made space available for the separate housing of the Drexel collection. The Americana Collection has been given an area for the storage and administration of books on American music and music in America, folk songs, and the Henry Hadley library of American musical scores. This section also controls the holdings of manuscripts of American composers, and the Elliott Shapiro collection of American sheet music.

The music listening facilities of the Library & Museum of the Performing Arts, the New York Public Library at Lincoln Center opened the 110,000 recordings in the Rodgers and Hammerstein Archives of Recorded Sound to the public. In 1965 the Toscanini Memorial Archives in the Special Collections of the Music Division were dedicated. A microfilm collection of autograph musical manuscripts, the archives make available for consultation more than 1,000 scores gathered from public and private collections from around the world.

(New York: Arno Press, 1969), 5 vols. Significant library publications include *The Collected Works of Scott Joplin*, edited by Vera Brodsky Lawrence with the assistance of Richard Jackson (The New York Public Library, 1972), 2 vols., and *Some Twentieth Century American Composers: A Selective Bibliography*, by John Edmunds and Gordon Boelzner (The New York Public Library, 1960), 2 vols.

The Children's Library of the General Library of the Performing Arts, a unit of the Branch Libraries, contains a reading-room collection of sheet music, books, and musical and nonmusical phonodiscs and cassettes by or for children.

SPECIAL INDEXES AND FILES

A 33 volume *Dictionary Catalog of the Music Collection* was published by G. K. Hall & Company of Boston in 1964; a supplement was published in 1966, and in 1973 a final supplement was published cumulating material cataloged in the earlier supplement with new material acquired through 1971, after which new works are being covered by the *Dictionary Catalog* of the Research Libraries. Also published in 1966 was the enlarged second edition of Music Subject Headings (1959); unlike the library's general subject headings, music subject headings have undergone systematic revision. The *Dictionary Catalog of the Music Collection* does not contain entries for all manuscripts and manuscript scores, some of which are listed in Appendix III of the comercially-published catalog of the Manuscripts and Archives Division.

A detailed description of the special indexes and files in the Music Division follows:

Biographical Index

Entries in this index refer to miscellaneous biographical information about musicians (189 card drawers). It consists of blue slips which duplicate authority cards in the library's Official Catalog, along with manila cards which refer to a selected number of clippings, obituary notices, and similar material. In addition, subject heading cards contain entries which refer to published material including Festschriften, yearbooks, essay collections, and serials which are not analyzed in the main catalog.

First Performance and Program Notes Index

This is a card file documenting first performances (world premieres, first American performances, first New York performances, etc.) of operatic or orchestral works (32 card drawers). Also contained are indexes to program notes, primarily on symphonic music, published by United States orchestras and other musical organizations.

Instrumental Index

Cards for instrumental works with distinctive titles are arranged alphabetically in this file (23 card drawers). If the title is given in more than one language, there is an individual entry for each language.

Song Index

One of the Music Division's principal indexes, this is a title and first line index to published folk, art, and popular songs (575 card drawers).

Clipping File

Each day the *New York Times* and other New York newspapers are clipped for items related to music (132 vertical file trays). Clippings are filed by composer's or performer's name and by general topic.

Other files include a Poet File (7 card drawers), a Shakespeare File (8 card drawers), Composer File (2 file trays), and smaller files and indexes pertaining to libretti since 1830, popular songs adapted from classical melodies, and an index to pseudonyms and nicknames. In addition, the Music Division maintains files of catalogs of colleges and universities with music programs, music publishers' catalogs, and concert programs for United States and foreign performances. A Sample File is maintained for periodicals too slight to bind and catalog.

Separate files kept by the various units of the Music Division are described below:

SPECIAL COLLECTIONS READING ROOM

Muller Portrait Index

A card index of the Joseph Muller collection of musicians' portraits, giving subject, birth and death dates, and engraver's name (10 card drawers).

Iconography Index

This index provides reference to pictorial materials held by the division's Special Collections (11 card drawers). Cards are arranged alphabetically by subject.

Plate Number File

Although sheet music is not always dated, it usually carries a publisher's serial number or plate number (15 card drawers). This file is arranged by name of music publisher, with the plate numbers for each publisher.

Toscanini Memorial Archives File

Arranged by composer, this file gives information about the location of autograph manuscripts of the great composers (7 card drawers). A file is also arranged according to location.

Facsimile Index

An index to all facsimiles of musical manuscripts owned by the library: this refers to sketches, fragments, and parts of compositions, as well as to complete compositions (2 card drawers).

AMERICANA COLLECTION

Americana Catalog and Shelf List

Included are cards for all music materials cataloged by the library's Preparation Services with "Amer" or "U.S." in the classmarks (27 card drawers). A main entry catalog for material cataloged in 1964 or after is designed to supplement the division's commercially published catalog.

Americana Medium and Subject Files

Cards for material by American composers located anywhere in the Music Division, cataloged or uncataloged, are included (72 card drawers). Most sections of the Medium File are subdivided into three periods (to 1831; 1831–70; and 1870–). Many headings in the Medium File duplicate the Public Catalog in content, if not in form. The subject index includes entries for the same material as the Medium File, primarily under subject

headings (as with "Boat songs," "Boyhood"), but also under some series cards ("Carr's musical miscellany, no. 19") and medium and quasi-medium cards ("Bugle music," "Campaign songs").

Musical Comedies and Movies Index

This index consists of three files, arranged by composer, by title of musical comedy or movie, and by date (to 1956) (10 card drawers).

Nineteenth-Century Musical Activity Index

An index to musical performances (1800–31) is arranged by date, with two subdivisions for each year: General Concerts and Theatrical (42 card drawers). The index is comprised of transcripts and newspaper accounts taken mainly from the *New York Evening Post* and the *New York Commercial Advertiser*; when the contents of a concert were listed, each item has been analyzed. An index to music published between 1800 and 1830 is arranged by title. This index refers to not only material in the New York Public Library, but also at the Library of Congress and some Boston libraries, along with information gleaned from newspaper advertisements.

Other Americana indexes provide information on broadsides; the Gauthier collection of vocal music; the Henry Hadley memorial library; and poets whose works were set to music (where the poet or the composer was American).

RESOURCES

A survey of Music Division resources presents special problems due to the variety of materials to be found on its shelves, including books and manuscripts about music, music scores, manuscript scores and composition sketches, music programmes, dealers' catalogs, music periodicals, recordings, iconographies of music, and other material. Most of the holdings are found in the general collections of the division, but specialized items are housed as follows:

Special Collections Reading Room: Drexel collection, all music manuscripts and printed material before 1800 (including Americana), Toscanini Memorial Archives, and other valuable items.

Americana Collection: All books on music in America, American folk songs, scores and manuscripts of American composers, the Elliott Shapiro collection of American sheet music, the American popular song collection, the George Goodwin collection, and the Henry Hadley memorial library.

Rodgers and Hammerstein Archives of Recorded Sound: All phonodiscs and tapes; printed material relating to phonorecords except discographies of special subjects and technical publications; antique phonographs.

In this description, books and manuscripts about music have been treated apart from music scores, music manuscripts, and sketches. For example, all biographical materials about Beethoven, whether printed or manuscript, are described as a unit; all music, whether printed or manuscript, is treated as a separate unit.

The Music Division contains approximately 225,000 volumes. In addition to the holdings described below are a number of objects representing types of materials no longer collected, such as Clara Schumann's pencil, a collection of portrait medallions, pictures, statues, and musical instruments.

PERIODICALS

The real strength of the library's periodical collection begins with nineteenth-century holdings. Among the important musical journals of that period in complete sets are the *Allgemeine musikalische Zeitung* (1798–1848), the *Revista musicale italiana* (1894–), the *Neujarhrsblatt der allgemeinen Musikgesellschaft in Zürich* (1813–), and the *Musical Quarterly* (1915–). Two important Scandinavian musical journals are also held in full runs: *Svensk Tidskrift för Musikforskning* (1919–) and the *Norsk Musikkgranskning* (1937–). There are broken runs, lacking earlier issues, of *Musical World* (1836–76), *Musical Times* (1844–), *Etude* (1883–1957) and *Musician* (1897–). In *A Check-list of Publications in Music*,[4] Anna H. Heyer lists principal musical periodicals together with a union list of library holdings; the library now has complete or substantial holdings of each of these. Although Russian musical journals are perhaps less well represented in United States libraries than those of Western Europe, the Music Division has available the most complete of three sets of the *Russkaya muzykalnaya gazeta* (1894–1916) presently reported in this country. Recently a microfilm reproduction of *Muzyka i Peniye* (1895–1917) has been acquired to complete the file in the New York Public Library. Substantial runs of Latin American periodicals are to be found in the division, with a strong representation from Argentina and Brazil. The library also has the only reported copy of such Argentine periodicals as *Correo musical sud-americano* (1915) and *Crótalos* (1933–38).

Although the library's resources in eighteenth-century musical periodicals are uneven, the Drexel collection contains one volume of the *New Musical and Universal Magazine* (1774–75), described as the first step toward real musical journalism in England. Of interest because of its rarity is the March 1759 issue of *L'Echo; ou, Journal de musique Françoise, italienne,* which while containing no text, does print the music and words of current arias, songs, and dance tunes. The Americana Collection possesses an interesting group of American periodicals of the same type. The earliest of these is Benjamin Carr's *Musical Journal* (1799–1802) followed by the *Musical Magazine* (1836–37).

It is the Music Division's current policy to acquire by gift, purchase, or exchange every musical periodical appearing in those countries with substantial numbers of publications. From areas where little is published, such as China, Africa, or the Balkan countries, the library tries to obtain either the best available musical periodical or some representation of what is published. The library currently receives about 550 music periodicals, approximately half of which are publications of the United States or Canada, with the larger part of the remaining half published in Western Europe. Only a handful of Latin American journals are received; also collected are 7 from Australia, 3 from India, and 4 from Africa. Periodicals on phonorecording are the most numerous, with musicology and current events next

in number. Church music, music education, and voice receive approximately equal emphasis. The collection of jazz periodicals is steadily growing.

BIBLIOGRAPHIES, THEMATIC CATALOGS, DEALERS' CATALOGS, PROGRAMMES

Due to the importance of music bibliographies and thematic catalogs to the music researcher, the division is required to maintain complete holdings of these valuable works. This task is simplified by the modern procedure that calls for the reprinting of many out-of-print titles. Most thematic catalogs are kept on the open shelves, readily available to the public. All dealers' catalogs received are retained either in vertical files or on the open shelves, although holdings for the period 1940–66 are limited. The programme collection, on the other hand, is substantially complete for the major musical organizations in New York City and in the United States: the Metropolitan Opera, the New York Philharmonic Orchestra, the Los Angeles Philharmonic and similar institutions. European musical associations are represented by only a sampling of programmes. The index to first performances and programme notes compiled from the programme collection and other sources is one of the major special files of the division.

BIOGRAPHY

The biography collection of 8,400 titles is comprehensive, regardless of the importance of the artist or composer. Book material is augmented by aids such as the Muller portrait collection and other iconography, the extensive clipping files, scrapbooks of biographical material (many of them on microfilm), and autograph and facsimile manuscripts.

The nearly 300 volumes of biographical material about Mozart include works on his composition and style, fictional works about his life, and iconography of the composer.

The collection of musical literature about Beethoven is the division's most extensive biographical resource, in large part the result of a major gift from the Beethoven Association. About 900 titles, the larger number in English and German, include biographical and critical studies, along with some 70 titles devoted to the composer's letters. A portrait of the composer as a young man hangs in the Special Collections Reading Room, a contemporary copy of the original by W. J. Mohler, and the Music Division holds five Beethoven holograph letters.

Next in size and importance is the collection of some 570 books about Richard Wagner. Included are a number of works on Wagner's relations to the philosophic currents of his time, along with studies of his operas and editions of his philosophic and critical works. There is also a broken run of Bayreuth Festspiele programmes starting with 1927, and a number of books about Wagner at Bayreuth.

A collection of 700 family letters of Felix Mendelssohn Bartholdy, which narrowly escaped destruction in the bombing of Dresden in 1945, was acquired in 1960 by the library; it begins with his twelfth year and ends ten days before his death in 1847. Included in the composer's correspondence with contemporary musicians are Hector Berlioz, Robert Schumann, Richard Wagner, Louis Spohr, F. Fétis, Ferdinand Hiller, Frédéric Chopin, Franz Liszt, Giacomo Meyerbeer, Luigi Cherubini, Jenny Lind, and Moritz

---

4. Ann Arbor, School of Music, University of Michigan [1944].

Hauptmann; the letters, together with a collection of books pertaining to Mendelssohn and his circle, provide a rich resource for the study of European music circles of the time.[5]

Particular interest is centered in the library's holdings of Paganiniana. The Joseph Muller collection of portraits contains sketches, engravings, drawings, and caricatures of Nicolò Paganini, in addition to 22 holographs, including 15 letters as well as briefs and contracts or contract drafts.[6] Documentary material for the lives and careers of Walter Damrosch, Eva Gauthier, Charles T. Griffes, and others is found in the Americana Collection. The American tours of John Philip Sousa and the orchestra of Eduard Strauss are documented in the business correspondence of David Blakely.[7] The Americana Collection's resources in the biography of jazz musicians complements the substantial material on musicians in the Schomburg Center for Research in Black Culture. The center, for example, also holds the personal papers of Lawrence Brown, a widely acknowledged musician and composer who was for many years accompanist to Paul Robeson and Roland Hayes.

HISTORY, THEORY, AND INSTRUCTION

The collection of approximately 2,000 titles in music history includes several editions of the standard works on the subject in both the original languages and English translation, with the greatest concentration in English, German, and French. All aspects of music history are covered. The resources for the study of Oriental and Slavonic music are good in Western languages, although little music literature in the non-Roman alphabet is found; since 1966 an attempt has been made to fill this deficiency.

Earlier and rarer features of the library's resources in the history and theory of music include a selection of manuscript fragments bearing early notation. From the Drexel collection come incunabula dealing with the theory of music, among them Franchino Gaffurio's *Theorica Musice* (1492) and *Practica musice* (1496). A helpful reference work is the *Syntagma Musicum* (1615–20) of Michael Praetorius, which contains plates showing contemporaneous instruments drawn to scale. Representative of the seventeenth-century Spanish school of music theory is Pedro Cerone's *El Melopeo y maestro* (1613). The Music Division is fortunate in having a copy of this rare work, since all but thirteen copies were supposedly lost in a shipwreck. Marin Mersenne's *Traité de l'harmonie universelle* (1627) is another early history of music found in the division. Also present are copies of the two best-known eighteenth-century English histories of music: Sir John Hawkins's *A General History of the Science and Practice of Music* (1776) and Charles Burney's *A General History of Music* (1776–89). More recent works include A. W. Ambros's *Geschichte*

der Musik (1862–78), works by H. Riemann, G. Adler's *Handbuch der Musikgeschichte* (1924), the *Oxford History of Music* (1901–29), and the *New Oxford History of Music* (1954–   ).

The library's manuscript collections often provide unique insights to a musical period of a nature not available through printed texts. This is true of such collections as the Beethoven and Mendelssohn papers, and also of those typified by the Francesco Finelli collection of letters, calling cards, signed pictures, clippings, and miscellany relating to Italian musical life in the late nineteenth century.

Of the special types of music, resources in folk music are notable. Oriental and Slavonic holdings are stronger than in other fields of music literature. The number of books on folk music is small (approximately 350 titles), but the introductions to collections of folk music and song and the international journals of music provide a great deal of additional information. The Music Division's policy has been to acquire representative scholarly works published on folk music in all countries.

Some 700 books on dramatic music stress opera, particularly the development of the great opera companies of Western Europe and the United States. As New York City is the home of the Metropolitan Opera and the center of the musical comedy theatre, it is appropriate that the library should have important collections of materials on dramatic music.

A number of early and rare items are found among the more than 3,000 titles on music instruction. The Music Division does not collect exercise or technique books, or material published for the musical education of the young, the beginner, or the self-taught, but does attempt to have at least one authoritative text for the study of the method and technique of every instrument.

INSTRUMENTS, VOICE

Several fine fourteenth- and fifteenth-century manuscripts in the library contain illuminations which document the use of musical instruments and performance practices in the Middle Ages. Music Division holdings are supplemented by those of the Spencer Collection, among them the *Tickhill Psalter* (ca. 1310), a *Psalter* from Naples (ca. 1450), the *Wingfield Hours and Psalter* (ca. 1450), and *Le Livre du petit Artus* (fifteenth century).[8] In the Prints Division a series of nine woodcuts attributed to the Swiss artist Tobias Stimmer bridges the gap between the crudely-proportioned illustrations of instruments in early printed books and the more accurately-calibrated representations of instruments in the works of Praetorius.[9] *Music in Prints* (1965) by Sydney Beck and Elizabeth Roth, a library publication, documents the history and use of musical instruments from medieval to modern times with materials from the Prints Division.

The piano, violin, and organ are most extensively treated in the Music Division's 3,400 titles devoted to musical instruments. Whereas the 750

5. See Eric Werner, "The Family Letters of Felix Mendelssohn Bartholdy," *BNYPL* 65 (1961): 5–20.

6. See Albert Mell, "Paganiniana in the Muller Collection," *Musical Quarterly* 39 (1953): 1–25.

7. See Margaret L. Brown, "David Blakely, Manager of Sousa's Band," *BNYPL* 65 (1961): 313–32 et seq.; and "David Blakely, Manager of the First American Tour of Eduard Strauss," *BNYPL* 66 (1962): 215–35 et seq.

8. See Edmund Bowles, "Musical Instruments in Illuminated Manuscripts," *BNYPL* 70 (1966): 86–92.

9. See Jan La Rue and Jeanette B. Holland, "Stimmer's Women Musicians: A Unique Series of Woodcuts," *BNYPL* 64 (1960): 9–28.

books on the piano center on theory and instruction, a great number of the 450 books on the violin describe the manufacture of that instrument and its bows and varnishes. This is also true of some 350 books on the organ which deal not only with theory and instruction, but also with the history and manufacture of the instrument, including modern electronic organs. Storrs H. Seeley's gift of 13 ring binders of notes, photographs, clippings, and other information on bells of all kinds, from dinner bells to carillons, makes a valuable collection of source material on this ancient instrument.

Adding to the strong collection of literature on dramatic scores and libretti are the division's 1,200 titles on voice technique, singing, singers, and histories of song literature. The collection is particularly strong for America, Great Britain, and Germany, although the library has a policy of comprehensive collecting in this field.

SCORES

Manuscripts of the great composers add distinction to the holdings of published scores and compositions. Vellum fragments from the tenth to sixteenth centuries provide early examples of musical notation, but the oldest complete musical manuscript owned by the library, now in the Manuscripts and Archives Division, is a gradual on vellum completed in 1494. Another valuable antiphonary of 1695 once belonged to Charles X of France. The Drexel collection is particularly strong in early English instrumental music; among other manuscripts are 3 important books of virginal music, one believed to have been written at least in part by Orlando Gibbons. A collection of sacred and secular compositions of the sixteenth century is to be found in the holograph volume entitled *Francis Sambrooke His Booke*, an early seventeenth-century anthology of anthems, motets, and madrigals. Some of the pages are damaged by sea water, but more than 300 compositions by Lasso, Byrd, Coperario, and others are intact.[10] There is, in addition, a fragmentary manuscript of Coperario's "Fancies for Two Voices and Bass." *Parthenia In-Violata or Mayden-Musicke for the Virginalls and Bass Viol* (ca. 1625) is a unique copy of Robert Hole's second collection of instrumental music. Somewhat earlier is one of two copies known to exist of John Farmer's *Divers and Sundry Waies . . .* (1591). The treble viol part of Thomas Morley's *First Booke of Consort Lessons . . . For Sixe Instruments* (1611), also in the Drexel collection, led to a search for the missing parts. The reconstructed score illustrates the close relationship of consort music to the theatre of the time.[11] Song books of the period are represented by John Playford's *Catch That Catch Can* (1667); Thomas Weelkes's *Ayeres or Phantasticke Spirites For Three Voices* (1608) is to be found in the Arents Tobacco Collection. A copy of the first book printed in the New World to contain music, the *Missale Romanum Ordinarium* (1561), is in the Rare Book Division. In the Spencer Collection

are three hymnals acquired for their illustrations but of great interest for their music as well: the earliest is Johann Leisentritt's *Geistliche Lieder und Psalmen*, published in Budissin in 1567, the first Catholic song book printed in Protestant Silesia. From a church famous for its music comes the *Pjsne Duchownj Ewangelistské (Hymn Book of the Moravian Brethren)* (Kralice, 1581); an eighteenth-century canticle and hymnal of the Russian Orthodox Church is of unknown provenance but beautifully illuminated in Russian folkart style.

As performers become increasingly aware of the usefulness of consulting a composer's manuscript as a guide to interpretation, the library's collection of holograph music grows in significance. The special collections section of the Music Division houses the holograph scores of Bach's cantata "In allen meinen Taten" dated 1734, and Handel's coronation anthem for George II, "My Heart Is Inditing." A manuscript copy of Haydn's *Oxford* Symphony bears the endorsement of the composer, and is of additional interest as the adagio and finale differ from those in the composer's autograph at the Bibliothèque Nationale. The division also holds the manuscript score of Haydn's F Minor Variations (1793), and a sketch for *The Creation*. The 22-page holograph of Mozart's G Major Symphony, K. 318 (1779), is one of the library's great treasures. In 1968 the original autograph score of the composer's *Haffner* Symphony was placed on deposit by the National Orchestral Association. Among other Mozart autographs in the library's collections are the Sonata for Piano and Violin, K. 296, and a sketch for an aria from the *Schauspieldirektor*.

Beethoven holographs include the finale of the string quartet Op. 18 no. 2, sketches for the piano trio Op. 97, the *Archduke*, and "Clärchenlieder," "Die Trommel Gerühret," and "Freudvoll und Leidvoll" from *Egmont*. There are three Schubert songs in holograph: "Labetrank der Liebe," "Leiden der Trennung," and "Skolie." In addition to the autograph "Herzeleid" by Schumann are Franz Liszt's score of a male chorus, "Jeder Frevler heisset Feind," his "Zweite Elegie" for piano and violin, and a signed manuscript of his song "Le Vieux Vagabond." The collection of Paganiniana includes the original manuscript of "Perpetual Motion," dated Geneva, April 6, 1835.

The Music Division contains a number of full orchestral scores for early nineteenth-century operas in manuscript, among them Johann Simon Mayr's *Medea in Corinto* and Ferdinando Paër's *L'Agnese*. Of greater significance are the manuscripts of Rossini's *Aureliano in Palmira* (1820?), *Ricciardo e Zoraide* (1820?), and a manuscript of Act I of *The Barber of Seville*. Wagner, Verdi, and Gounod are present in holograph fragments. An incomplete holograph of an unidentified work by Jacques Offenbach and a polka-mazurka from the *Gypsy Baron* by Johann Strauss represent the light opera compositions of the nineteenth century.

Among the important collections of Brahms manuscripts given to the library by Paul Wittgenstein are a full score of the "Alto Rhapsody," his "Paganini Variations," songs, and piano pieces. Igor Stravinsky's "Capriccio for Piano and Orchestra," the vocal score for *Symphonie de Psaumes*, and the *Symphony in 3 Movements*, are prominent in the manuscript holdings for modern European composers.

Manuscripts of American composers include a large number of George Frederick Bristow and Louis Moreau Gottschalk scores. A gift of seven

---

10. See *English Instrumental Music of the 16th and 17th Centuries from Manuscripts in the . . . Library* (The New York Public Library, 1947), 2 vols.

11. See Sydney Beck, ed., *The First Book of Consort Lessons* (The New York Public Library, 1959).

Gottschalk manuscripts in 1968 included his *Second Symphony* (*A Montevideo*) and *Escenas Campestres*. This acquisition in conjunction with the Gottschalk manuscripts purchased in 1948, gives the Research Libraries almost every known holograph of this composer's works. Charles Tomlinson Griffes, Percy Grainger, and Edward MacDowell are also well represented in the collection of American musical manuscripts. Duke Ellington's "Sacred Concert" is a work in fourteen sections, prepared for and performed at the Cathedral Church of St. John the Divine in 1968 by invitation of the Protestant Episcopal Bishop of New York; the manuscript was presented to the library by the composer.

Supplementing the holograph scores are a number of facsimiles, along with microfilms and photographic reproductions of autograph music manuscripts in the Toscanini Memorial Archives. The growing resources of the archives make available to the scholar reproductions of scores and sketches of the master composers acquired from collections all over the world.

About 60 percent of the volumes on the division's shelves are devoted to printed music scores, with first or standard editions of the instrumental works of major composers for single instruments, ensembles, and orchestras. In all there are approximately 135,000 volumes. Generally the division retains only the original version of a work rather than attempting to collect arrangements or adaptations.

Opera's origins are found in the sumptuous theatre of the sixteenth and seventeenth centuries, and some sense of the magnificent public presentations of the period may be gained from the Spencer Collection copy of a festival book, *La Magnifica et Triumphale Entrata del Christianiss [imo] Re di Francia*, which records a state visit of Henry II and his queen, Catherine de Médicis, to Lyon in 1648. Of the same period is Belgiojoso's *Balet comique de la Royne* (1582) in the Music Division's Drexel collection, which describes a *ballet de cour* organized to celebrate the wedding of the Duke de Joyeux to Mlle. de Vaudemont, sister to the queen of France. Many theatrical designs by Giacomo Torelli remarkable for their startling sense of distance are found in the Prints Division. Seventeenth-century theatrical design is well illustrated in the Spencer Collection copy of Moniglia's libretto for *L'Hipermestra* printed in Florence in 1658. The ballad operas of the eighteenth century are well represented in the Drexel collection and material subsequently acquired. The larger part of the strong collection of approximately 6,100 operatic scores are piano-vocal arrangements, but many full orchestral scores are also included. Special emphasis is given to operas and musical comedies produced in New York City. European librettos are held in the original language with a copy in English translation if available; the collection numbers more than 2,800 titles.

The holdings of scores for voice (other than dramatic music) are particularly full for vocal ensembles, especially duos, as well as voice with chamber ensemble and other instrumental accompaniment.

The division's American popular music collection is substantial, amounting to over 300,000 individual titles. The George Goodwin collection acquired in 1966 consists of some 200,000 pieces of popular sheet music, predominantly American, ranging in date from the late nineteenth century to the 1960s. The resources are indexed in the Song Index card catalog. There is a representative collection of foreign popular music.

Another division strength is its collection of folk music. The more than 3,000 titles form a large and authoritative international source. Associated holdings of folk songs and ballads in other parts of the Research Libraries include the Rare Book Division's bound collections of English and Irish street ballads of the nineteenth century and American ballad sheets, with an important group of Civil War materials. The latter supplement some 500 American broadsides of the same period in the Music Division. In the Spencer Collection are two especially fine collections of Spanish chapbooks with interesting holdings of ballads.

The Henry Hadley memorial library in the Music Division contains scores of the first American grand operas and symphonic works by Bristow, Fry, Paine, and their contemporaries, along with the latest compositions of Copland, Hovhaness, Cage, and Babbitt. The National Association of American Composers and Conductors regularly adds scores by composer members, as does the Composers' Forum.

In 1956 the purchase of the Elliott Shapiro collection of early American sheet music, amounting to 7,500 items, coupled with previously existing resources, gave the library one of the best collections of musical Americana in the United States.[12] The Shapiro collection includes music dating from the mid-eighteenth century to 1889; one of the finest pieces is a first American printing of "Yankee Doodle" in the *Federal Overture* by Benjamin Carr (1795), especially as the library's copy is believed to be the only one in existence. Other outstanding items are a first edition of "Hail, Columbia" and 22 early editions of "The Star Spangled Banner," including a copy of the 1814 amended edition published by J. Carr which is considered to be even rarer than the first edition, as well as 55 later editions (up to 1870). Excluded from this purchase was perhaps the most valuable of all American sheet music, a first edition of the Francis Scott Key anthem; the library has owned its copy since 1938. The Shapiro collection also maintains a large number of Confederate imprints; almost every edition of "Dixie" is included, in addition to a manuscript in the hand of its composer Daniel D. Emmett, the famous minstrel. Negro songs are to be found dating as far back as 1795, together with compositions relating to the war with Tripoli and contemporaneous songs about George Washington.

RODGERS AND HAMMERSTEIN ARCHIVES OF RECORDED SOUND

Although these Archives form a new research facility at the Performing Arts Research Center of the New York Public Library at Lincoln Center, the collection of 110,000 phonodiscs and tapes has been built up over many years. The first major gift came in 1937, when Columbia Records began to deposit review copies of its new issues. Other record companies followed Columbia's lead, along with private collectors. A bequest to the archives by Alphonse Giarizzo in 1963 helped to fill gaps in the collection of Italian

12. The library's holdings and those of other major libraries are indicated in Richard J. Wolfe, *Secular Music in America 1801–1825: A Bibliography* (The New York Public Library, 1964), 3 vols.

operatic performances. Recently local radio stations, among them WNEW, WQXR, and WCBS, have given large numbers of recordings to the library.

Foundation help has been of great assistance. A generous grant from the Rodgers and Hammerstein Foundation made it possible to organize and catalog the collection and thus offer service to the public in the Performing Arts Research Center. A foundation grant enabled the archives to purchase the Jan Holcman collection of piano recordings dating from the beginnings of recording through the 1960s. Still another grant, from the Avalon Foundation, has enabled the archives to equip a recording laboratory devoted to the preservation of all forms of recorded sound.

The major gifts have extended and strengthened the holdings of the archives in related fields. In 1967, Jerome Lawrence and Robert E. Lee, the producer-playwrights, presented material which included a large number of sound recordings. Notable among these is a complete set of the "Railroad Hour" radio adaptations of theatrical musicals. In 1969, Lauder Greenway, chairman of the board of the Metropolitan Opera Association, presented some 9,000 historical vocal recordings documenting the art of singing from the earliest Pathé vertical-cut discs and Edison cylinders to the 78 rpm electrical recordings of the 1940s.

Most of the major recording companies now deposit current releases with the archives. A number of companies have arranged to donate not only current releases but their entire back catalog to the archives. These gifts indicate the significance of the Rodgers and Hammerstein Archives as a permanent deposit of information and materials dealing with the growth and production of the record industry in America.

The special indexes and files included in the Rodgers and Hammerstein Archives of Recorded Sound are listed below:

Main Catalog

A dictionary catalog to all officially cataloged records (130 card drawers). Uncataloged discs and new acquisitions are indexed in an additional 50 card drawers.

78 Catalog

A file with one main entry and an added entry (usually for performer) for 78 rpm records cataloged prior to 1963 (39 card drawers).

Record Number Files

A listing of 78 rpm and LP records arranged by manufacturer's name and number (67 card drawers). New acquisitions and uncataloged records are included in this file.

WNEW Catalog

Performer and title cards for a collection of popular 78 and 45 rpm records (109 card drawers).

Audio Cardalog

A commercial cataloging service (no longer published) for nonmusic recordings, including readings from the drama, poetry, and belles-lettres (6 card drawers).

Matrix Number Files

Files of the matrix numbers (the number stamped on the record, as opposed to the manufacturer's or catalog number) of 78 rpm and LP records in the collection (7 card drawers). The arrangement is by manufacturer's name and matrix number.

Other Rodgers and Hammerstein Archives files include the Information File, Tape Check List, Liner Note Files, Song Index, and a checklist of 16-inch pressings and acetate recordings. Clipping files in the archives represent material related to phono-material transferred from the Music Division clipping files.

MUSIC RECORDINGS

All phono-material in the Research Libraries, both musical and nonmusical, is housed in the Rodgers and Hammerstein Archives as a matter of general policy; classical music recordings form the core of the collection. However, the Schomburg Center for Research in Black Culture has a strong collection of both tape and phonograph recordings in its field of research. Among the earliest classical recordings in the Rodgers and Hammerstein Archives are the wax cylinder recordings made by Lionel Mapleson during actual performances at the Metropolitan Opera House in 1901–03. Of even greater importance is the presence in the archives of the only complete set of the Columbia Grand Opera Records of 1903, which provides unique documentation of the beginning of celebrity recordings. Both sets have been reissued on modern discs: a number of the Mapleson cylinders by the International Record Collectors' Club, and the Grand Opera Series by Columbia Records. The archives are rich in privately made tapes and recordings of historically important live performances from the turn of the century to the present day. They are a depository for tapes of work by contemporary composers commissioned by the American International Music Fund.

A small but highly selective library of folk music recordings purchased from Harry Smith provides the archives with many of the rarest and best examples of sacred folk singing, hillbilly, and other popular ballads. Among the performers represented are Blind Lemon Jefferson, Uncle Dave Macon, and Bessie Tucker. A good representation of commercial recordings in this field documents the musical achievements of most of the world's ethnic groups, but field recordings, which form the backbone of a strong collection of this kind, are few in number.

The Schomburg Center contains a collection of 3,000 musical items in 128 African languages entitled *The Sound of Africa*. Edited by Hugh Tracey for the International Library of African Music, the 210 LP records have complete indexing and descriptive notes. Also in the Schomburg Center are recordings of works of all kinds composed or performed by blacks, including spirituals, operas, African and West Indian folk music, rock and roll, and "Soul Music," with some on-the-spot recordings of singing by street-corner groups.

The 37,000 discs in the WNEW collection in the archives document the popular music of the 1930s, 1940s, and 1950s. A particularly valuable feature of this collection is a title and performer card catalog. This important collection gives depth to the archives' holdings in a field too often neglected. The archives do not make a concentrated effort to obtain foreign popular music recordings unless such recordings are issued in the United States.

NONMUSICAL RECORDINGS

The theatre is represented by original cast recordings of Broadway plays, as well as film sound tracks and recordings of outstanding performances by important actors and repertory companies. Noteworthy is a unique set of recordings featuring John Barrymore's readings of scenes from Shakespeare and Rostand. A more recent gift of several 5-inch acetate disc recordings made privately by Tennessee Williams forms a valuable addition to the archival holdings of the playwright's commercially produced readings from his poetry and plays. Other recordings of poets reading their poetry are included. The dance is documented by recordings of ballet scores, music for ethnic and modern dance, recorded dance instruction, and taped interviews with important dancers, choreographers, and dance critics and historians.

The archives are developing the documentary aspects of the collection with particular emphasis on historical and political material. Radio Free Europe has presented a set of documentary narrative accounts of events in Poland from 1918 to 1940 and of major Polish figures such as Paderewski, and the Israel Broadcasting Service has given the archives a series entitled "Vistas of Israel" presenting aspects of the cultural life of the country. The Schomburg Center for Research in Black Culture has both tape and phonograph recordings of poetry readings, lecture series, speeches, musical programs, interviews, and documentary productions.

In addition to the wide range of subjects to be found in the Rodgers and Hammerstein Archives, every form of recording to which the industry has given its attention is present, from the Edison cylinder recordings and the Berliner discs of the 1890s to the most recent stereophonic recordings. Included in this array of materials are piano rolls, hill-and-dale recordings, tapes, transcription records, and music-box discs.

PRINTED AND MANUSCRIPT MATERIALS

The Rodgers and Hammerstein Archives collection of printed and manuscript materials relating to recordings is one of the most extensive in the world. In addition to many complete runs of periodicals in all languages devoted to recordings, the archives have an important collection of manufacturers' catalogs. Long catalog runs of the major companies (RCA Victor, Columbia Records, the Gramophone Company Ltd., etc.) are supplemented by a number of rarities. Among these is a large group of the Polydore Company monthly supplements from the 1930s, early Zonophone catalogs, and a Bettini catalog of the nineteenth century. The history of recording is further documented by dealers' and equipment catalogs from all periods.

Current recordings are listed in the trade and national discographies in the collection. Among these are the *Phonolog Reports*, which lists all records currently available in the United States, and the *Schwann Long Playing Record Catalog*, which lists all 33.3 rpm records in "print" in the United States. Important, too, is the *Audio Cardolog*, a commercial card indexing service that covered nonmusical recordings to the end of the 1960s. The trade catalogs of other countries add to archive resources; among them are *Bielefelder Katalog* and *Der grosse deutsche Schallplatten-Katalog* from Germany and *Gramophone Long Playing Record Catalog* from Great Britain.

Other aspects of recorded sound covered by the archives include books on record selection, catalogs of libraries and archives of recorded sound, books devoted to historical records and rarities, and discographies of jazz and folk music. Among the unusual tools available for research are a typescript index to *Record Research*, a jazz magazine of major significance, and a microfilm of Bernard Lebow's *American Record Index*. This work, a discography of American recordings from 1897 to 1949, was never completely published. Its presence in the archives is of unusual interest to those studying the history of American sound recordings.

32

DANCE COLLECTION AND GENERAL DANCE RESOURCES

DANCE COLLECTION

HISTORICAL SURVEY

The aim of the Dance Collection is to be genuinely comprehensive: to include ethnic, primitive, and folk dance; social forms as various as the minuet and the cha-cha; and the many theatrical modes, among them ballet and modern dance. Although the collection first developed its strength in twentieth-century American dance, the gifts of splendid private collections have made it a treasure house of historical material for many periods and countries. Books form a numerically small percentage of the Dance Collection; pictorial material is important and extensive.

The Dance Collection contains 28,000 volumes; 8,000 librettos; 6,000 prints, original drawings, costume and stage designs; 4,500 playbills and posters; 70,000 programmes; 150,000 photographs; 350,000 newspaper and magazine clippings; 80,000 manuscripts and letters; more than 1,250,000 running feet (2,200 reels) of motion picture film and videotape; microfilms; and 95 dance notation scores.

In 1895, when the Astor and the Lenox Libraries and the Tilden Trust were consolidated, only a few rare books and contemporary newspaper accounts representing the dance were included. By 1933 the field had been defined and the monographs placed in the Music Division. With the gift of the Roger Pryor Dodge collection of Nijinsky photographs in 1937 and the purchase of the Walter B. Graham collection of dance books in 1938, the collection began to take shape; by 1944 there was an informal dance section containing monographs, clippings, and photographs under the jurisdiction of a Music Division librarian. By 1947 the collection required the full-time attention of a librarian. During the first phase of the collection's development, this librarian sought out collections on the dance in America, organized dance lectures, and mounted exhibits.

The next twenty years witnessed rapid growth in the collection's resources. A keystone of the American dance holdings came in 1951 when Ted Shawn and Ruth St. Denis presented the Denishawn collection of material, documenting their joint careers. At the same time the gift of the Humphrey-Weidman collection and that of Hanya Holm augmented the history of the twentieth-century American dance. But it was in 1955 with the gift by Walter Toscanini of his great dance library of historical materials in memory of his wife, Cia Fornaroli, that the Dance Collection became an internationally important historical archive.

In the 1940s the Museum of Modern Art dance archives ceased functioning as a special unit, and in 1956 the museum transferred its holdings to the New York Public Library (250 books, 30 boxes of clippings, photographs, etc.). This material, which had been acquired prior to 1940, strengthened the resources of the Dance Collection for the two decades preceding its establishment. To commemorate the thirtieth anniversary of Isadora Duncan's death, her adopted daughter Irma Duncan presented in 1957 books, drawings, manuscripts, letters, and other objects which had belonged to Miss Duncan or pertained to her. This gift was augmented by gifts from other associates of the dancer. Further documentation on the history of the dance in the United States came in 1960 with the collection given in memory of Irving Deakin, and in 1964 there was a bequest of similar material from Louis Horst. Horst had been a composer, editor, and long-time accompanist and friend to Martha Graham, and had started his career as conductor of the Denishawn Company orchestra. In 1961 the holdings were greatly enriched by the historical collection on the dance in the eighteenth and nineteenth centuries given by Lincoln Kirstein. He has continued his interest in the development of the archive with extensive gifts of prints, original stage and costume designs, drawings, manuscripts, rare books, and films.

Gifts from photographers have greatly aided the development of the picture files. Significant gifts were received from Walter Owen in 1955 and Carl Van Vechten in 1956; the latter is established as the Fania Marinoff collection in honor of Mrs. Van Vechten. The gifts of George Platt Lynes (1958), Wilbur Stephan (1954), and Frederick Melton (1961) brought a total of more than 10,000 negatives. In 1962, Robert W. Dowling presented 6,000 negatives of photographs of Galina Ulanova taken by Albert Kahn.

Because of its growth in size and public service, and because of its position in the field, the Dance Collection was raised to the status of a division in 1964; in 1965 it moved into expanded new quarters in what is now called the Performing Arts Research Center of the New York Public Library at Lincoln Center. Two organizations have been of vital importance in the development

of the collection: the Committee for the Dance Collection formed in April 1957 and the Friends of the Dance Collection established in the spring of 1958.

The collection is now developing the cinematic method of preserving the dance, the recording of this fleeting medium of expression on motion picture film. The American choreographer Jerome Robbins has said, "We must be able to observe works in their original state and be able to watch the specific, subtle and elusive qualities of performance and performers which are outside of the actual choreography itself, and which no system of dance notation or verbal description is ever able to realize."[1] Robbins has given substantial aid to this project, and the collection of films has been named the Jerome Robbins film archive.

The library has published a number of volumes as part of a continuing program designed to make widely available the unique visual treasures of the Dance Collection; especially important are *Dancing in Prints* with a commentary by Marian Eames (1964) and Lillian Moore's *Images of the Dance* (1965). Exhibitions on the dance have always been a collection feature: in 1962 there were two notable exhibitions, including photographs of the great Soviet ballerina Galina Ulanova (negatives of the photographs were presented to the library by Robert W. Dowling), and an exhibition entitled "Stravinsky and the Dance" in honor of the composer's eightieth birthday. The Committee for the Dance Collection and the staff collaborated in locating material in public and private collections all over the world.[2]

SPECIAL INDEXES AND FILES

Dance Collection Catalog

The Dance Collection has never possessed its own integrated card catalog. Cards for books on the dance were originally filed in the Music Division catalog, while the Dance Collection maintained a number of special files (e.g., dance steps, titles of dances, dance iconography) for nonbook and analytical materials. In 1965 the library received a grant from the Ford Foundation to create a catalog for the collection. The use of a computer has made it possible to combine the special files (with the exception of the three indexes described below). The catalog was published in ten volumes by the library and G. K. Hall & Company of Boston in 1974. Entries under established headings will be arranged by the form of the material, for example books and magazine articles, visual material, music, and audio material.

The scope of coverage is broad. Entries for individual dance titles cover professional theatrical performances and note the first performance, the first performance in the United States, the first performance in New York, the first performance

---

1. Jerome Robbins, quoted in "Prospectus for the Development of the Film Resources in the Dance Collection, The New York Public Library." (Typescript in the Dance Collection.)

2. See *Stravinsky and the Dance; A Survey of Ballet Productions 1910–1962* (The New York Public Library, 1962) and the companion volume *Stravinsky and the Theatre; A Catalogue of Decor and Costume Designs for Stage Productions of His Works* (The New York Public Library, 1963).

by a major company other than the original, and also performances with new or revised staging or choreography. Entries for visual material serve to index illustrations of dance subjects found in other parts of the library, as well as the photographs in the Dance Collection; those for music provide references to music written for the ballet.

Index of Dance Material in Nondance Sources

This file represents an index of information on the dance located in sources not ordinarily connected with the field held by institutional libraries in greater New York City; works on anthropology, ethnology, and comparative religion are included (30 card drawers). Although started and brought to fruition as a WPA project and no longer actively maintained, this file supplies much valuable information.

New York Clipper Index

A project to index the *New York Clipper*, an entertainment newspaper published from 1853 to 1924, began in 1964. A selective index to the early issues of the paper is to appear in book form and will cover sports, music, and theatre as well as the dance.

Vertical File

The Dance Collection staff regularly clips the *New York Times* and other pertinent sources of information for material on dancers, dance companies, and dance subjects. This file of 63 trays contains approximately 350,000 clippings. Scrapbooks and clippings given to the Dance Collection by Ruth St. Denis, Ted Shawn, Doris Humphrey, Charles Weidman, and others, although separately maintained, supplement the Vertical File.

RESOURCES

Bibliographies, Dictionaries, Periodicals

The collection attempts to be exhaustive in all reference works on the dance. Bibliographies and dictionaries number some 75 titles, the earliest dating from 1802. Among modern tools is Anatole Chujoy's *Dance Encyclopedia* (1967); all phases of the dance are covered in the *Enciclopedia dello spettacolo* (1954–62). Alfonso J. Sheafe's *A Dictionary of the Dance* (1937?) in typescript has proved a valuable reference source. The collection has 41 volumes of this 42-volume set. Two standard bibliographies of the dance frequently consulted are Cyril W. Beaumont's *A Bibliography of Dancing* (1929) and Paul D. Magriel's work of the same title (1936).

Approximately 60 periodicals are currently received by the Dance Collection. About half are United States publications, with the balance coming from England and Western Europe. Of significance are complete runs of: *Ballet* (London, 1939–52), *Dance News* (*London,* 1949–), *Dance Observer* (1934–), *Dance Perspectives* (1959–), and *Dancing Times* (1910– , lacking n. s. vol. I). Also of research value are runs of nineteenth-century theatrical publications which contain much about the dance, particularly *Teatri arte e letteratura* (1824–57). Of interest for a study of the Russian ballet is the *Annals of the Imperial Theatres* (St. Petersburg, 1890–1915, incomplete).

Programmes and Posters

The collection retains comprehensive sets of programmes from American dance companies, including their foreign tours; foreign companies are represented primarily by programmes for their American tours. New York programmes are most strongly represented. Souvenir programmes of special performances of dance companies are collected when possible. The library has good collections of the programmes of the Anna Pavlova Ballet, the Ballets Russes de Dyagilev, the Bolshoi Ballet, and the Royal Ballet (Covent Garden), most of them received as gifts. Files of other foreign ballet company programmes are incomplete but sufficiently extensive to show production trends. The Dance Collection generally acquires programmes for ethnic dance performances in New York and has limited holdings for performances in other cities. As a general policy the collection keeps fliers of dance events that have taken place, rather than announcements of future events which may fail to materialize.

A group of some 4,500 posters and playbills relating to the dance date from the late eighteenth century to the present. Holdings include such items as a colorful poster showing how the Maggio Musicale Fiorentino introduced the New York City Ballet to Italian audiences and a poster for the performance of Isadora Duncan dancing the bacchanal in *Tannhäuser* at Bayreuth.

History of the Dance

The collection's resources on the history of the dance, including social dancing and stage dancing other than ballet, are composed as follows:

Published Materials: A collection of more than 200 books on the history of the dance forms a core around which is massed a much larger collection of manuscripts, prints, photographs, clippings, and other material. A manuscript dated about 1460 by Giorgio e del Giudeo is one of 5 extant examples by Renaissance Jewish dance masters, 4 of them in European libraries. This collection of choreographed dances is not a presentation copy made by a professional scribe or master penman, but a working copy made by the dancing master for his own use. Second only to the Siena copy in number of dances described (23 and 32, respectively), it contains 3 dances not found in any other copy, including several choreographed by Lorenzo de Medici. Additional sources for the documentation of the dance in the Renaissance are found in a second early sixteenth-century manuscript of 15 dances by Giovannino il Papa and in facsimile reproductions: *Le Manuscript dit des basses danses* from the Bibliothèque de Bourgogne, and the Robert Copland translation from an unknown French source, *The Manner to Dance Bace Dances*. These were published in limited editions and are themselves rarities. Also in the collection is a 1670 edition of Antoine d'Arena's *Ad Suos Compagnones Studiantes Qui Sunt de Persona Friantes, Bassas Dansas. . . .*

Perhaps the most curious record of the dance in medieval Europe, the Dance of Death, is represented in the library's Spencer Collection by a copy of the earliest known edition of 41 woodcuts from Hans Holbein the Younger's drawings entitled *Les Simulachres & histoirees faces de la morte* (Lyons, 1538). One of the celebrated books of dance literature finds a place in the library in both of its early editions: Cesare Negri's *Le gratie d'amore* (1602) in the Dance Collection and his

Nuove inventioni di balli (1604) in the Dance Collection and in the Spencer Collection. Equally rare is Fabrizio Caroso's *Il ballarino* (Venice, 1581), a classic early history of the dance in the Spencer Collection, remarkable for fine engravings by Giacomo Franco. Claude F. Menestrier's *Des ballets anciens et modernes selon les règles du théâtre* (Paris, 1682), described as the first printed history of the dance, is represented in the collection, as is John Weaver's *Essays Towards an History of Dancing* (1712), the first historical book on the dance in the English language. From the seventeenth century, John Playford's *The Dancing Master*, published in 17 editions between 1651 and 1728, is available in the Dance Collection in a twelfth edition dated 1703; other editions are available on microfilm. All examples of this book are rare; as a practical book giving music and instruction for country dances, copies were literally worn out. A book by a famous dancing master of the first half of the eighteenth century, Pierre Rameau's *Le Maître à Danser*, is present in both its original 1725 edition and in a later edition of 1734.

The most famous work of Carlo Blasis is *Code complet de la danse* (1830), but his *Traité élémentaire, théorique et pratique de l'art de la danse* (1820) was an attempt to reduce the art of the dance to fixed principles for the first time. However, Blasis considered *L'Uomo fisico, intellettuale e morale* his most important book. Each of these, with copious annotations in the hand of Walter Toscanini, is in the collection; the *Traité élémentaire* is also found in the Drexel collection of the Music Division. Strong holdings of work by and about Blasis include translations and biographical material.[3] Three of the 4 volumes of S. N. Khudekov's history of the dance (St. Petersburg, 1915) are held by the Dance Collection. All but a few copies of the fourth volume of this monumental history were burned in the Russian Revolution; the Dance Collection has an electrostatic copy of the fourth volume. Among the holdings of modern histories of the dance are Gaston Vuillier's *La Danse* (1898) and the standard *Eine Weltgeschichte des Tanzes* (1933) by Curt Sachs, both available in English translation.

Approximately 450 books on the biography of dancers emphasize the lives of such great ballet dancers as Nijinsky and Pavlova. There are some 25 books on Isadora Duncan, many in foreign translations. Published items on the lives of Ted Shawn, Ruth St. Denis, and Filippo Taglioni reinforce the mass of primary material available in the Dance Collection. The preponderance of the biography holdings are in English or Western European languages.

Dancing as a part of opera, musical comedy, or revues is documented in book materials in the Dance Collection, particularly in its vertical file. Specific information on dancers and dance sequences can be found in the collection, but readers are also referred to the Theatre Collection and to the Music Division for general background information.

Primary Source Material: Primary source material on the dance throughout the world comes from the collections honoring Louise Branch and

relating to the Dance International, a month-long festival of continuous film showings, performances, and exhibitions directed by Miss Branch and sponsored by Anne Morgan in 1937. More than 7,000 items (photographs, letters, programmes, and press cuttings) document every phase of this enormous enterprise and are a descriptive index to the dance personalities and companies, both ethnic and theatrical, of the time. The Hanya Holm collection, a gift of the dancer in 1952, documents the history of European modern dance, especially the careers of Mary Wigman and Miss Holm in America. New material is added each year to this collection.

The history of the American dance, one of the main strengths of the Dance Collection, can be traced through the mass of primary source material acquired by gift and purchase. A very important holding of material devoted to Isadora Duncan includes her early journals written in Paris in 1901, her letters to Edward Gordon Craig from 1904 to 1920, her letters to Irma Duncan, and manuscript notes and papers of some of her biographers; much of it is from the collection given by Irma Duncan.[4] There are albums of photographs, original drawings by various artists (Rodin, Bourdelle, Grand'jouan, and others) and more than 400 letters and programmes. Several major gifts focus on the activities of Ruth St. Denis and Ted Shawn: the Denishawn collection, the personal papers of Ruth St. Denis and the personal papers of Ted Shawn. They contain 8,000 photographs, 15,000 clippings and programmes, and 4,000 letters and manuscripts. Coverage begins with the first performance of Miss St. Denis and extends over the early careers of Martha Graham, Doris Humphrey and Charles Weidman, the men's group formed by Ted Shawn which toured from 1933 to 1940, and the organization and development of Jacob's Pillow. The photographs represent work by many noted modern photographers.[5]

Following the work of Doris Humphrey and Charles Weidman after they left Denishawn in 1928, the Humphrey-Weidman collection of more than 800 photographs, 30 volumes of press clippings, 200 programmes, set designs, playbills, and other miscellaneous items mirrors the dance of the 1930s. It gives valuable information about the early professional activities of Sybil Shearer,

---

3. See Marian Eames, "When All the World Was Dancing; Rare and Curious Books from The Cia Fornaroli Collection," *BNYPL* 61 (1957): 383–95, esp. 389–92. Published separately by the library.

4. See Irma Duncan, "Isadora Duncan, Pioneer in the Art of Dance," *BNYPL* 62 (1958): 228–40. Published separately by the library. See also the register of the Craig-Duncan Collection, *BNYPL* 76 (1972): 181–98; letters from this collection form the basis of *Your Isadora* published by the library and Random House in 1974.

5. See Christena L. Schlundt, "A Chronology of the Professional Appearances of the American Dancers Ruth St. Denis and Ted Shawn 1906–1932," *BNYPL* 66 (1962): 7–30 et seq. Published separately with an index as *The Professional Appearances of Ruth St Denis & Ted Shawn* (1962). See also her "A Chronology of the Professional Appearances of Ted Shawn and His Men Dancers," *BNYPL* 70 (1966): 505–27, 586–605, 647–62. Published separately with an index as *The Professional Appearances of Ted Shawn and His Men Dancers* (1967). Among other publications which have drawn upon the resources of the Dance Collection are Professor Schlundt's *Tamiris: A Chronicle of Her Dance Career 1927–1955* (The New York Public Library, 1972).

Katherine Litz, and José Limón. The Doris Humphrey Committee, organized after the dancer's death, has provided funds for augmenting the collection; additions include films, notated scores, and tapes. Charles Woodford, the dancer's son, has presented photographic and manuscript materials which include more than 6,000 letters.[6]

The growth of the Dance Collection depends heavily on gifts from dancers and companies. Yearly deposits of clippings, programmes, and photographs come from the regional ballet companies and university workshops in the United States. In addition is a concentrated effort to document the careers of individual dancers. Among those superbly represented through gifts of material are Nora Kaye, Agnes de Mille, Catherine Littlefield, and members of the Philadelphia Ballet Company. A collection of 150 press books compiled in Sol Hurok's office from 1930 to 1960 covers all phases of the dance and provides a detailed history of performance for those artists and companies under his management. The Deakin collection consists of 2,700 photographs, the manuscripts of Deakin's books, and typescripts and tapes of the author's interview programs on radio station WQXR from 1937 to 1943. Of especial interest is the correspondence relating to the organization of the Ballet Theatre during the years 1939 to 1940.

Dance Notation

For at least five centuries the problem of preserving the art of the dance has occupied dancers and dance scholars. The dance has no basic record for most of the great works in its repertory that can compare with musical scores. Among some 60 volumes dealing with this problem, one of the pioneer attempts is Jehan Tabourot's (Thoinot Arbeau) *Orchésographie*, first published in 1588; an edition dated 1596 is in the Drexel collection of the Music Division. The Dance Collection possesses a copy of Raoul Auger Feuillet's *Chorégraphie, ou l'art de décrire la dance* (1700) and a 1706 translation of this work by John Weaver. Later attempts to notate the dance by Rameau, Saint-Léon, and others are to be found in the collection, together with the standard work by Rudolf von Laban, *Schrifttanz* (1928). Labanotation is probably the most finely differentiated of the modern systems of dance notation. It is equally applicable in recording sports and the theatre as it provides symbols used in combination to depict movements of the body as well as the relation of the body to other bodies and objects. In 1953 the library began to collect dance scores marked in the Labanotation method; at that time it was able to borrow and microfilm scores held by the Dance Notation Bureau in New York City. There are more than 16 notated microfilm scores, including Balanchine's "Symphonie Concertante" and Doris Humphrey's "Day on Earth." The Dance Collection, with the cooperation of the Doris Humphrey Committee, has commissioned notated scores of the choreographer's works, including "Ritmo Jondo." From the Dance Notation Bureau, the Dance Collection has recently received electrostatic copies of its entire library of notation holdings, including 95 scores in various stages of completion. Among these are Helen Tamiris's "Negro Spirituals," José Limón's "Chaconne," Anna Sokolow's "Session for Six," and Balanchine's "Agon."

---

6. A register of the collection was published in *BNYPL* 77 (1973): 80–142.

Jerome Robbins Film Archive

In looking beyond the Labanotation method of preserving the dance, the collection has in its Jerome Robbins film archive approximately 2,200 reels of film of dances available for reference and research purposes. Approximately 1,250,000 running feet of 16mm and 35mm dance film and videotape in black and white and color are available; the Dance Collection is actively adding new materials both through gifts and by purchase. This includes both commercial and privately produced films of past and current productions of dance companies and artists from the United States and abroad. Gifts continue to expand the archive, which is projected as a fully cataloged collection of dance films and kinescopes plus important dance sequences in nondance films, and a film record of works in the current ballet, modern, and ethnic dance repertories. Two of the most important collections are gifts of Ted Shawn. The Jacob's Pillow collection consists of some 150 reels, documenting the performances of the world's greatest dance artists at the Jacob's Pillow Dance Festival in the 1950s and 1960s. The Ted Shawn collection of more than 100 reels is primarily devoted to the activities of the Denishawn Company before 1930 and to Ted Shawn and His Men Dancers.

Equally significant is a unique collection of films documenting virtually the entire creative output of Leonide Massine; 267 reels, in black and white and for the most part silent, represent Massine's choreographic legacy from 1920 to 1968. The archive contains not only the original Massine masterpieces of *Le Beau Danube, Le Tricorne, Gaieté Parisienne*, and *La Boutique Fantasque*, but also several versions filmed decades apart. Also in the archive are his choreographic ventures in abstraction, from the first abstract ballets to the symphonic scores of Beethoven, Brahms, and Berlioz. Massine, an admirer of the choreographer Michael Fokine, also filmed 9 of the latter's ballets dating from the 1930s: *Le Carnaval, Les Elfes, Prince Igor, Les Sylphides, Don Juan, Petrouchka, Les Éléments, L'Épreuve d'amour* and *Schéhérazade*, all of which are now preserved in the archive.

The gifts from professional artists have included works of Agnes de Mille, Pearl Lang, Merce Cunningham, Ruth Page, Jacques d'Amboise, and Portia Mansfield. Films commissioned by special archive funds, added to by generous gifts, have insured the preservation of works by the companies of Murray Louis, Alvin Ailey, the New York City Ballet, the City Center Joffrey Ballet, and the American Ballet Theatre.

A special significance of most of the films in the archive is that they are unavailable in other agencies. Three which are of wide interest to the professional dance world and are among those most requested and viewed by dance researchers are a commercially produced film of *Giselle* (Alicia Alonso and Azari Plisetzki), a television excerpt of *La Sylphide* (Carla Fracci and Erik Bruhn), and a nine-hour series of technical training films of the Kirov Ballet in Leningrad.

Selected films were purchased by the archive from commercial distributors. The biographical film *Galina Ulanova* supplied memorable footage of this great dancer. Ted Shawn, certainly one of the Dance Collection's greatest benefactors, helped the archive to obtain a copy of the film *The First Lady of the American Dance: Ruth St. Denis*. Also purchased was the award-winning *Pas de*

154

Deux, a startlingly effective multiple-image dance film by Norman McLaren. Of great interest is a group of short motion pictures created during the early years of the American film industry.

Oral Tape Archive

The oral tape archive was formally begun in 1965, although taping in an informal fashion began in the late 1950s. It consists of two groups of materials: taped lectures, classes, radio interviews and the like; and oral history tapes using the same techniques employed by the Oral History Collection at Columbia University and elsewhere. These interviews, usually a series of in-depth sessions of recall, provide information and detail not found in published sources; they will be a repository of dance information usually found in past decades in letters and diaries. The archive will furnish original source materials from which future books can be written.

At the present time interviews with about 180 dance personalities are in the archive with a master index of references. The tapes represent gifts, purchases, and copies of other tapes hitherto in the hands of private individuals, institutions, and broadcasting concerns. Some of them will not be open to use for fifty years from the date of taping, but others are now available to qualified dance researchers.

The archive now holds more than 450 tapes, including 125 tapes of radio sessions entitled, "The World of the Dance"; classes in choreography conducted by Doris Humphrey; and 27 hours of taping sessions made with Charles Weidman in the summer of 1967. (This tape is not now available to the public.)

The Ballet

The collection of materials on ballet is one of the strongest holdings of the Dance Collection. More than 600 books cover the history and development of the form in many countries of the world. Perhaps the most complete coverage (some 50 titles) is given to Russian imperial and Soviet ballet. The collection includes one of the most lavishly produced modern texts, Boris Kochno's *Le Ballet* (1954); there are also a number of books by Cyril W. Beaumont, including his *A Manual of the Theory and Practice of Classical Theatrical Dancing (Cecchetti Method)* (1922), written with Stanislas Idzikowski.

The holdings of ballet librettos include some 8,000 in the Dance Collection, and 300 in the Music Division and Spencer Collection. These range from the early seventeenth century to the present day, but the best coverage is in Italian productions of the period 1700–1900. A recent gift of some 80 librettos increases the Dance Collection's documentation of French court and academic ballet from 1659 to 1813. Three early Italian titles, *Il mondo festiggiante* (1651), *Medea vendicativa* (1662), and *l'idea di tutte le perfezioni* (1690), are lavishly illustrated with plates depicting the presentations. Notable also for its illustrations is a group in the Spencer Collection dating from the seventeenth century and including *Gverra d'amore* (1615) with illustrations by Jacques Callot and *Die triumphirende Liebe* (1653) with etchings by Konrad Bruno and August John.

The 2,500 ballet scores in the Music Division include about 100 scores published before 1800. The Music Division's Drexel collection also houses the original libretto of the celebrated *Balet comique de la royne* (1582), a seminal work for the study of the beginnings of the ballet in the Renaissance. Most of the earlier scores are fully orchestrated, and only after 1800 do a number of piano reductions and arrangements appear.

Pictorial Documentation: From the Lincoln Kirstein collection, the Cia Fornaroli collection, and through other gifts and purchases, the library has acquired a group of drawings, lithographs, engravings, photographs, and other pictorial material that exceeds in numerical quality the book and manuscript items. A predominant part of this material depicts the ballet, both in representations of famous dancers, such as the Focosi lithograph of Marie Taglioni dancing in "La Gitana," and in designs for costumes and scenery, such as a recent gift of 150 cut-outs by Isamu Noguchi for a 1948 production of the ballet "Orpheus." The Cia Fornaroli collection is particularly rich in prints of Fanny Cerrito, Marie Taglioni, and other nineteenth-century dancers. In addition the Dance Collection possesses original stage and costume designs by such artists as Boris Anisfeldt, Alexandre Bénois, Eugene Berman, Giorgio de Chirico, Cecil Beaton, Rouben Ter-Arutunian, Léon Bakst, Mstislav Doboujinsky, Nathalia Gontcharova, Leonor Fini, Marc Chagall, and others.

The Roger Pryor Dodge gift of 500 photographs of Vaslav Nijinsky covers most of his great roles, among them "L'Après-Midi d'un Faune," "Petrouchka," and "Schéhérazade," as well as personal photographs taken offstage. Among the dancers pictured with him are Karsavina and Pavlova. Ballet in America is documented by the George Platt Lynes collection of 2,000 photographs and an equal number of negatives; the Constantine collection, donated by the photographer in 1964, portrays the American Ballet Russe in the 1940s and 1950s. The Fania Marinoff collection, a visual record of some 3,000 photographs of dancers of all styles who appeared in New York City between 1931 and 1962, was initiated by Carl Van Vechten in 1956. A varied collection, it is especially rich in photographs of the ballerina Alicia Markova and such luminaries as tap dancer Bill Robinson. The Kahn collection of photographs of Galina Ulanova, given by Robert W. Dowling in 1962, presents a comprehensive account of the dancer's performances and her daily professional activities; there are more than 6,000 negatives with their contact prints, as well as 300 exhibition prints.

The library's Prints Division provides some pictorial documentation of the early history of the dance. Stefano della Bella is particularly well represented by a collector's album of 890 mounted prints including, among other subjects, depictions of horse ballets and stage settings for theatrical performances. There is also a collector's album of engravings after Jean Bérain for ballets of the time of Louis XIV. The Prints Division has an edition of the *Cabinet du roi* (1679–1743), volumes X and XI of which depict the carrousel, or horse ballet of the king, performed in the Place du Carrousel, to which it gave its name; *Les Plaisirs de l'ile enchantée* illustrates the fêtes of Versailles. The Lincoln Kirstein collection brought to the Dance Collection *Il mondo festeggiante* (1661) portraying a *balletto a cavallo*, and Claude Menestrier's "Recueil des devises et des poésies." The latter is a fragile volume containing a collection of the small publications on the fêtes, horse ballets, carriage processionals, and ceremonials of Menestrier's day, with descriptions of the decorations and edifices built for each. Interleaved and bound with the publications are handwritten notes, letters, and pages in manuscript on which the author has added further observations and reminiscences. In the eighteenth century Jean G. Noverre, called the "Shakespeare of the dance," set forth his revolutionary ideas on transforming the classic ballet into something approaching its modern form. His *Lettres sur la danse et sur les ballets* (1760) is one of the treasures of the Dance Collection. The collection has all the editions of Noverre's work, including the famous St. Petersburg edition of 1804.

Notable Gifts and Purchases: The Cia Fornaroli collection, the gift of Walter Toscanini in 1955, consists of more than 4,500 prints, 3,300 books, 2,000 librettos, 850 pieces of music, 1,000 letters and manuscripts, and 15,000 clippings, photographs, and playbills. The music includes ballet scores (principally of the nineteenth century), solo dances, ballet excerpts from operas, original manuscript scores, and autograph scores of dances created for specific ballerinas, among other material. The larger portion of the clippings are from European newspapers and are a valuable supplement to the collection's files, which primarily contain cuttings from American newspapers. The collection is particularly strong in Italian materials of the nineteenth century, with special attention being given to the choreographers Gasparo Angiolini and Salvatore Viganò, and the teacher and theorist Carlo Blasis. Toscanini's research on the career of Salvatore Viganò led to the collecting of a wealth of scores, librettos, stage designs, etc. Of special interest is the material related to the ballet "Prometheus" with music that Viganò commissioned from Beethoven.

Another fascinating item is the two-volume compilation made by the choreographer Salvatore Taglioni of librettos, production notes, drawings, and other documentary material relating to his career. A more recent manuscript of considerable interest is the manual of exercises and technical studies in Enrico Cecchetti's hand, written in 1894 in St. Petersburg, where he taught Pavlova, Nijinsky, and other great Russian dancers of the first decades of the present century. The variations and class music used by Cecchetti when he taught at Warsaw are also present in a holograph copy.[7]

In 1959 the library, aided by the Committee for the Dance Collection, purchased the Gabriel Astruc archive of more than 1,300 documents relating to the formation and early years of Dyagilev's Russian Opera and Ballet in Paris, 1909–16.[8] This manuscript collection of letters, telegrams, contracts, and other papers comprised the working files of the impresario who organized Dyagilev's activities. Complementing this are the materials given by the estate of Tatiana Chamié in 1953, permitting the study of the late Dyagilev period of the Ballets Russes, 1923–29, the René Blum period, and the beginnings of the De Basil and

the American Ballet Russe era. The collection includes more than 100 programmes, 600 photographs, and miscellaneous clippings, letters, diaries, and other memorabilia. Especially generous manuscript gifts have brought the Dance Collection some 200 letters to Serge Dyagilev from dancers, admirers, and others, in the Lincoln Kirstein collection; a growing collection of the letters and papers of Agnes de Mille covering various phases of her career, manuscripts of her writings, scripts, and related materials; and the personal letters, papers, and writings of Lillian Moore, as well as a number of rare manuscripts and letters relating to dancers of the past.

Folk and Ethnic Dance

The resources on international ethnic and folk dance in the collection include some 800 volumes, but coverage is uneven. Works on Oriental dance in Oriental languages, most notably in Chinese and Japanese, are not held in strength. Material published in the Cyrillic alphabet is not extensive, with the exception of publications acquired for their ethnological interest. A consideration of American Negro dancing and American Indian dancing would require research not only in the Dance Collection but the Schomburg Center and the American History Division of the Research Libraries, where material of ethnological value has been collected.

The Cia Fornaroli collection has a body of original material on Italian folk and national dance arranged by province, the result of field work done by the dancer and her husband, Walter Toscanini. Also in the collection is a booklet by Louis Puccinelli entitled *Souvenir de la tarantella napolitaine* (Naples, 1840?) describing the dance with charming, hand-colored lithographs. A manuscript in the collection is perhaps an original draft for or a copy from a work on the tarantella published in Naples in 1834.

Holdings of prints, both in the Dance Collection and the Prints Division, reinforce book holdings on folk and ethnic dance, particularly of the late eighteenth and early nineteenth centuries.

Social Dancing

The earlier aspects of social dancing are discussed in the section of this chapter (above) concerned with the history of the dance. Most standard contemporary works, such as Lady Lilly Grove Frazer's *Dancing* (1895) and Philip J. S. Richardson's *A History of English Ballroom Dancing* (1946), are available. The majority of titles on social dancing are books of instruction, many including music, as in the case of Gladys B. Crozier's *The Tango* (1913); the collection of nineteenth- and twentieth-century manuals is outstanding in its completeness. Additional information may be found in the clipping files.

Prints illustrating social dancing, while present in the library's collections from the earliest days of printmaking, are of the greatest assistance in documenting the dance in the eighteenth century. A number of early nineteenth-century popular aquatints and etchings satirically illustrate the social dance of the period. The Dance Collection also holds original watercolor drawings of the early nineteenth century. The iconography of social dancing in photographs and reproductions is most easily located by a search under the names of dancers who specialized in a particular dance.

---

7. See Marian Eames, "When All the World Was Dancing; Rare and Curious Books from The Cia Fornaroli Collection," *BNYPL* 61 (1957): 383–95. Published separately by the library.

8. See Nicki N. Ostrom, "The Papers of Gabriel Astruc (1864–1938): A Register," *BNYPL* 75 (1971): 357–70. For later gifts and purchases related to this period and to all aspects of the history of the dance, see [Lincoln Kirstein], *A Decade of Acquisitions: The Dance Collection 1964–1973* (The New York Public Library, 1973).

33

THEATRE COLLECTION AND GENERAL
THEATRICAL RESOURCES

THEATRE COLLECTION

One of the earliest working theatre libraries in the United States, the Theatre Collection has served as a model for many theatre archives in this country. Exhibitions are regularly mounted, and the resources of the collection have formed the basis of a large number of books and articles. The Theatre Collection exhaustively collects all types of material concerned with the various phases of the theatrical arts. It is international in scope with emphasis on the New York scene. Its primary concern is with the theatre, motion pictures, radio and television, the circus, magic, night clubs, carnivals, fairs, vaudeville, minstrel shows, and theatrical "haunts" (clubs, hotels, and restaurants). The Theatre Collection does share responsibilities in some areas with the Music Division and the Dance Collection. The Theatre Collection acquires materials on music in the theatrical media and on musical performers when their work is done in these forms. The collection has material on dancers whose careers are centered in musical comedies, motion pictures, night clubs, and similar areas, in addition to having a fairly complete record of the dance as an aspect of the theatre, motion pictures, and television.

The principal resources of the Theatre Collection are nonbook materials: approximately 1,000,000 playbills and programmes; over 200,000 photographs; prints and engravings; several million clippings from newspapers and magazines; thousands of original scene and costume designs; several thousand scrapbooks and press books covering the production records of American managers; more than 1,000,000 motion picture stills, and several thousand photographs of radio and television personalities. Book materials number over 24,000 volumes, including bound periodicals; published plays are not held in the Theatre Collection but are a collecting responsibility of the General Research and Humanities Division. The collection receives nearly 400 theatrical periodicals and newspapers.

A number of individual collections in the Theatre Collection contain letters, contracts, and other autograph material mounted in scrapbooks, in addition to unmounted letters and autographs of theatrical celebrities. The Theatre Collection has always been responsible for the collection and retention of promptbooks and actor's parts, even though they may have annotations or may be entirely in manuscript. In such cases the library considers the primary importance of the work to be theatrical. In the case of manuscripts which show the creative processes of the author and are primarily literary, the material generally is held in the Manuscripts and Archives Division.

HISTORICAL SURVEY

On September 1, 1931, the New York Public Library established its Theatre Collection as a separate unit, but more than twenty-five years had gone into the development of this section of the library's service. The donation of George Becks's collection of promptbooks in 1905 served as a beginning. This collection consists of promptbooks and holograph scripts of plays produced in England and the United States, primarily during the eighteenth and nineteenth centuries.[1] Impressed by the existence of this core collection, the Dramatists' Guild of the Authors' League of America in 1932 passed a resolution urging its members to deposit typescripts and prompt-copies of their unpublished plays in the library. Since then more than 5,000 scripts have been added.[2]

The nucleus of the Theatre Collection, the Robinson Locke collection of dramatic scrapbooks, came in 1925.[3] Representing Locke's lifetime devotion to the stage, this archive, collected by the owner of the *Toledo Blade*, covers the American stage and screen from 1870 to 1920. There are 800 bound and sourced volumes and over 2,500 portfolios of loose clippings, programmes, holograph letters, and unmounted photographs. Among the artists represented are Maude Adams (8 volumes), Theda Bara (2 volumes), Sarah Bernhardt (11 volumes), Geraldine Farrar (6 volumes), Henry Irving (6 volumes), Richard Mansfield (8 volumes), Ignace Jan Paderewski (2 volumes), and Lillian Russell (6 volumes).

The impetus to establish the Theatre Collection as a separate service unit came in 1931, when the executors of the David Belasco estate offered the papers in the Belasco Theatre, with the proviso that this material be made available to the public immediately after cataloging. The library agreed to these terms and established a separate Theatre Collection. The Belasco gift consisted of 2,999 volumes, 8,432 pamphlets, 15,759 photographs, scrapbooks and clippings, reviews of plays, sketches of scenery and costumes for a number of the Belasco productions, sheet music, orchestral pieces, and theatrical programmes.

Immediately after this third major gift, the Provincetown Playhouse collection was presented through the interest of Helen Deutsch and Stella Hanau. Then in the winter of 1932–1933, the library acquired the Hiram Stead collection devoted to the English theatre from 1672 to 1932. It contains 600 portfolios which include letters, autographs, and written copies of leases and documents relating to theatrical litigation, along with a vast file of playbills and portraits.

The Winthrop Ames memorial collection, presented in 1932, includes typescripts, prompt scripts, production notes, and lecture notes relating to Ames's career in the Boston and New York theatres between 1905 and 1932. The Paul Kester

---

1. See "Catalogue of the Becks Collection of Prompt Books in The New York Public Library," *BNYPL* 10 (1906): 100–148.
2. Some of the unpublished typescripts are listed in Paul C. Sherr, "Bibliography: Libretti of American Musical Productions of the 1930s," *BNYPL* 70 (1966): 318–24.
3. See "The Robinson Locke Dramatic Collection," *BNYPL* 29 (1925): 307–22.

collection, acquired in 1933, contains 20,000 letters written to Kester, a playwright of international reputation, from 1890 to 1933. Many important English and American authors are represented. In 1934, the Hénin collection of French stage material was purchased. It concerns the Parisian stage, primarily during the period of the eighteenth and nineteenth centuries, although some material dates back to the beginning of the seventeenth century. The chief treasures are unpublished original drawings for costumes and scenery. The collection is in 38 volumes and includes playbills, prints, original drawings, autographs, and other material.

The Oliver M. Sayler collection, donated over a period of years, contains photographs and press material relating to the Moscow Art Theatre during the 1920s. Sayler served as press agent for Morris Gest, who brought the Moscow Art Theatre to this country. The library also has a large collection of books, pamphlets, periodicals, and photographs from the Gest estate, given by his widow in 1942. Oliver Sayler established the Ray Henderson Memorial collection in 1937 in memory of the former president of the Association of Theatrical Press Agents and Managers (ATPAM). This collection contains press material—posters, programmes, clippings, etc.—on the theatre in New York. Members of ATPAM continued to add to this gift during the 1940s.

Francis Brugiére, a leading stage photographer, gave 2,000 of his photographic plates made from 1918 to 1927. The gift, which came in 1935, covers the principal theatres and companies of the period with the exception of the Theatre Guild; photographs of Guild productions were retained by that organization. In 1943 Carl Van Vechten presented 314 mounted photographs, 284 of which are of theatrical personalities and European theatres. This gift was augmented by Mrs. Van Vechten (Fania Marinoff) with material covering her own career and with additional material about her husband. In 1944 the Players collection of more than 600 portfolios, each devoted to a single important player of the American, English, French, and Italian stage, came to the library.

In 1945 the Theatre Collection was elevated to the status of a full division of the Research Libraries. By 1951 the documentation of the work of Alice and Irene Lewisohn at their Neighborhood Playhouse was a part of the collection; Actors' Equity had turned over its scrapbooks and records of the years 1919 to 1942, documenting labor relations in the theatre; and notable material had been given by William Morris, Jr., of the William Morris Agency, establishing a record of the work of his father and of the organization founded in the early twentieth century. In 1954 the Joe Laurie collection of hundreds of joke books and other materials was added.

Gift material continued to expand the Theatre Collection during the 1960s. Furnishing a valuable record of the workings of a theatrical agency from 1910 to 1961, the archives of the Chamberlain and Lyman Brown Theatrical Agency were given in 1961. The Vandamm collection of photographic prints and negatives was purchased by the library in the same year. Florence Vandamm and her husband were leading theatrical photographers in New York City, and during the period 1925 to 1950 photographed over 2,000 professional theatre productions. The Vandamm collection includes positive photographs of about 1,200 productions, each represented by an average of 25 different scenes and many individual portraits; in addition are approximately 50,000 negatives and key-sheets for individual productions. The collection provides a photographic history of four decades of the New York stage and is indexed by name of actors and actresses and by production title. The library reproduces prints from the negatives, on which it owns reproduction rights, for a modest fee. Other important archives of theatrical photographs in the Theatre Collection are those of the White Studios, Inc., 31 indexed volumes of positives and key books, given in 1957, and the Alfredo Valente collection of stage photographs, given in 1967.

In 1964, Mrs. Hallie Flanagan Davis, director of the Federal Theatre during the late 1930s, donated her theatrical and professional papers and books. The gift includes annotated plays and scripts (among them a number by Eugene O'Neill), lectures, administrative papers, and published articles and books which thoroughly document the Federal Theatre Project, among others.

Sixty-five cartons of play manuscripts, programmes, playbills, radio transcriptions, tapes, recordings, screenplays, photographs, correspondence, notes and other source materials representing a twenty-year collaboration of the noted playwriting team of Jerome Lawrence and Robert E. Lee came to the library as a gift in 1967.

The gift collections described are only a selection from the wealth of material which has come to the Theatre Collection by donation. Gifts in the more specialized theatre-related fields are described following this general survey of the Theatre Collection. In addition to these, the collection has records of the following theatrical institutions which have come by gift: Actors' Fund of America; American Educational Theatre Association; American Theatre Wing, War Service, Inc.; Gates and Morange; Group Theatre; Jones and Green; Klaw and Erlanger; the Living Theatre; Playwrights' Company; Theatre Guild; USO; Stuart Walker; and others. Among the records of professional careers are those of Viola Allen, Brooks Atkinson, William A. Brady, Earl Carroll, Katharine Cornell, Cheryl Crawford, Edward Eager, Maurice Evans, Gilbert Gabriel, Crosby Gaige, Max Gordon, Helen Hayes, Burl Ives, G. Maillard Kesslere, Gertrude Lawrence, Joshua Logan, Richard Mansfield and Mrs. Mansfield (Beatrice Cameron), Guthrie McClintic, Gilbert Miller, Paul Muni, Brock Pemberton, Vernon Rice, Oliver Sayler, Sophie Tucker, and Weber and Fields. The collection also has the original designs for costumes and scenery for productions of Howard Bay, Aline Bernstein, Bonnie Cashin, Tom Adrian Cracraft, H. M. Crayon, Mstislav Doboujinsky, Erté, David Ffolkes, Robert Edmond Jones, and others. There is also a large collection of theatrical caricatures (original drawings) by Frueh.[4]

THEATRE COLLECTION CATALOG

The catalog of the Theatre Collection is primarily a subject catalog; author and title entries are not always included. Many of the subject headings differ from those used in the Public Catalog of the Research Libraries. Theatre Collection headings must be more specific and exact to pinpoint areas for professional and scholarly use. These subject headings were published in

---

4. See Maxwell Silverman, comp., *Frueh on the Theatre: Theatrical Caricatures 1906–1962* (The New York Public Library, 1972).

book form by G. K. Hall & Company in 1960 under the title *Theatre Subject Headings*, with a second edition appearing in 1966.

The card catalog of the Theatre Collection is divided into two parts:

Book Materials

The arrangement is primarily by subject. The materials (including books, scripts, periodicals) are for the most part concerned with production; plays are not included except in the form of promptbooks or typescripts listed under the subject heading "Drama—Promptbooks." The catalog is prepared and maintained by the Preparation Services of the Research Libraries.

Nonbook Materials

Again the approach is primarily by subject, under which are indicated the types and forms of materials available (including reviews, photographs, programmes, clippings, scrapbooks, etc.). A major characteristic of this file is that available items on a play are listed under the name of the play as subject and not under the name of the author: materials on *Romeo and Juliet* are listed under *Romeo and Juliet*, not under Shakespeare. Under Shakespeare are found materials relating to Shakespeare's personality, Shakespeare collections, etc. This catalog is prepared and maintained by the staff of the Theatre Collection.

Theatrical manuscripts, autographed photographs, letters, theatrical postage stamps, theatrical Christmas cards, golden anniversary performance tickets, and other rarities are kept in file cabinets with restricted access. In the staff area is a Cage File or card index to these materials which are not recorded in the public catalogs of the collection.

Book catalogs of holdings of parts of the Theatre Collection have been published in fifteen volumes by G. K. Hall & Company of Boston. The *Catalog of the Theatre and Drama Collections: The New York Public Library* appeared in 1967 in two parts. *Part I: Drama Collection* (6 volumes) lists more than 120,000 plays in the Research Libraries written in the Roman and Greek alphabets. Most of these plays are in the general collections of the library, but the Theatre Collection retains a large collection of more than 10,000 promptbooks and typescripts. *Part II: Books on the Theatre* (9 volumes) lists approximately 23,500 books on 121,000 cards on all phases of theatrical art covered in the Theatre Collection. The vast holdings of fugitive materials in the Nonbook Materials catalog of the collection do not appear in these book catalogs, nor do the manuscripts and rarities held in the restricted-access file cabinets.

SPECIAL INDEXES AND FILES

In addition to its regular card catalogs, the Theatre Collection maintains a number of special indexes and files. All files are active unless otherwise indicated.

Official Subject Authority Files for Theatre Headings

The official catalog for the established form of subjects (other than personal and corporate names and place names) (6 card drawers). A duplicate of the file is maintained as one of the Preparation Services's official files. This catalog has been published in book form as *Theatre Subject Headings* (Boston: G. K. Hall & Company, 1960; 2nd ed. 1966).

Cage File

A card file containing subject and personality entries for the manuscripts, autographed photographs, theatrical memorabilia, and other rarities in the collection (9 card drawers). This material is available to qualified researchers.

City Theatre File

An inactive card file arranged (1) alphabetically under the names of the cities in the United States and elsewhere in the world, (2) under cities alphabetically by names of theatres in each city, and (3) under names of theatres chronologically by year, listing alphabetically under each year the titles of plays or cinemas produced in that year (5 card drawers). This file is complete from June 15, 1933 to January 1, 1939, except for New York City, which is complete through September 15, 1939. Cinemas are listed only through 1937.

Play Statistics

Three separate files give the following information: title, press agent, photographs received, programmes, script, date of opening, date of closing, number of performances, theatre (4 card drawers). The three files are made up of (1) cards for the current season arranged alphabetically by title, (2) cards for other than the current season arranged alphabetically by title, and (3) cards for seasons chronologically arranged, beginning with the 1958–59 season. Under each season the arrangement is by title.

Press Agent Files

Two card files arranged alphabetically under names of press agents, noting the plays for which each agent acted and the production date of each play (1 file box). One file is current and periodically interfiled in the Play Statistics file. The second file covers the period from July 1, 1936, to January 1, 1939, except for New York City which is covered through September 15, 1939.

Cinema Credits File

Reviews or other capsule listings from journals are clipped and pasted on catalog cards to form this file (17 card drawers). Such vital information about each film as director, cast, date of release, etc., is thus quickly obtainable. The listing is in alphabetical order by name of film.

Motion-Picture Stills Catalog

This index to stills transferred from the Picture Collection of the Branch Libraries is arranged in two parts (13 card drawers). The first is an alphabetical arrangement by title of the motion picture giving the producing company, director, the cast, and other information. The second is an alphabetical arrangement by subject. Each subject card bears on the particular subject; for example, under the heading "Army, Confederate States of America" are listed *Gone with the Wind, Operator 13, So Red the Rose*, and others.

Index to Vandamm Collection

A card file of theatrical personalities appearing in the Vandamm collection of photographs (6 card drawers).

Toy Theatre Index

This is an alphabetical file of titles, with a notation of author and/or actors (1 card drawer).

Research in Progress File

An informal card file which indicates the subjects of research in progress in the Theatre Collection (1 card drawer). From this file the student or scholar can learn if a particular subject is being investigated, enabling him to compare notes or initiate research in a different field.

Vertical Files

Clipping/Obituary/Programme File. A very extensive file, which includes pictures as well as reviews, programmes, obituaries, and other printed materials (254 file cabinets). The collection regularly clips New York newspapers as well as those from other theatre centers. *Variety* is clipped in great detail. Reviews of the New York stage from 1917 and of the cinema from 1930 have been mounted and bound. When a sufficient number of programmes have been accumulated for individual productions they are sorted, exact duplicates are discarded, and the material is bound. Cards for each programme are prepared for the Nonbook Materials Catalog. The same procedure is followed with clippings, although the bound volume receives a single entry, such as "Clippings on Sarah Bernhardt." Obituaries, since there are usually only a few for each personality, are retained uncataloged in the vertical files.

Photograph Files. Theatrical photographs of all kinds are retained in this file, including those of personalities, productions, theatre buildings, cinema, studios, television studios, night clubs, theatrical restaurants, and Academy Award dinners. The photographs are placed in folders and arranged in three categories according to size. Cabinet-size photographs are placed in the (A) category; those approximately eight and one-half by eleven are placed in the (B) category; and oversize photographs are filed in (C). Although at one time photographs of a theatrical subject were bound in volumes, this practice has been discontinued and existing volumes are being unbound. The collection's large photographic archives which are separately cataloged and housed include the Vandamm, Brugiére, Kesslere, White, and Valente collections. The bound volumes of Universal Pictures motion-picture stills are also separately shelved.

RESOURCES

THE STAGE

The stage, or legitimate theatre, is one of the primary concerns of the Theatre Collection. The collecting policy is exhaustive for both book and nonbook materials. Although coverage is international, there is particular strength in materials covering New York City and the United States.

Notable gifts of stage materials are described in some detail in the historical survey of the Theatre Collection.

Periodicals

The Theatre Collection currently receives nearly 400 periodicals and newspapers on all phases of theatrical art. In addition, the collection receives 20 nontheatrical newspapers for clipping. Periodicals relating to the stage are an outstanding feature of the holdings. They include both annuals and journals ranging from the eighteenth to the twentieth centuries. Among the annuals are the *Deutsches bühnen Jahrbuch*, the *Annuaires du théâtre*, the *Spotlight* (London), *Player's Guide*, *Radio Annual*, and others useful in biographical research. The collection owns one of several complete sets of the eighteenth-century French *Almanac des spectacles* in the Research Libraries. Other important titles with substantial, if not complete runs, include *Theatre World*, *Billboard*, *Drama* (both the American and English publications), *Era*, the *S. A.* [*South African*] *Pictorial*, *Play Pictorial*, *Dramatic Times*, *Variety*, *New York Dramatic Mirror*, and other English language titles of long and short duration. Among the French publications are *Annuaire dramatique*, *Revue d'art dramatique*, *Bravo*, *Comaedia illustré*, and *Le Théâtre*. German titles include *Charivari*, *Die Scene*, *Das Theater*; the Italian *Scenario* is received; and there are unusual titles such as the Czech *Loutkár* and the Finnish *Työväen näyttämotaide*. Many other periodicals in the Research Libraries contain theatrical information and may be considered related materials; for example the sporting journals *New York Clipper* and *Spirit of the Times*. A project to microfilm and index the *New York Clipper* began in 1964; the index, covering music, sports, and dance as well as the theatre, will appear in book form.

The Slavonic Division receives a number of theatrical periodicals, including the Soviet *Teatr* and *Teatral'naya zhizh'*, *Divadlo* from Czechoslovakia, and the Polish *Teatr*. Of note also are the older Russian dramatic periodicals, including a run of *Yezhegodniki imperatorskikh Teatrov* (1890–1919).

Book Material

There are approximately 17,000 volumes on the stage in all its aspects, including bound periodicals and prompt-books, which form a nucleus around which a much larger collection of nonbook material coalesces. In various special fields, the collection is extensive. Technical works dealing with producing, scenery-making, and acting (addressed mainly to the amateur), are more than adequate. Lesser subjects, such as marionettes, puppets, and pageants are well covered.

Puppetry as a subject is being developed with particular attention. Holdings of the Czech puppet periodical *Loutkár* have already been noted; in addition are earlier items such as Edward Gordon Craig's *The Marionette* (1918) now on microfilm in the library. Approximately 300 entries for puppet plays in the Public Catalog cover American, English, French, German, and Italian puppet plays with a representation from other languages; there are few translations into English. The Slavonic Division holds Russian, Czech, and Polish material; there are books on Oriental puppetry and puppet plays (primarily Japanese) in the Oriental Division; these are supplemented by index entries for articles on puppetry in journals. Standard works on the subject in all countries are to be found in the Theatre Collection.

The collection of histories of the theatre is more than adequate for practical research purposes, both in older works and current publications; all countries in which the theatre has been or is notable are covered. The histories of individual theatres in the United States, as well as those in Berlin, Paris, Stockholm, Moscow, and other centers, may be followed in detail. Included are such standard works as Karl Mantzius's *A History of the Theatrical Art* (1903), *A History of the Theatre* (3rd rev. ed., 1968) by George Freedley and John A. Reeves, and more specialized works such as William Dunlap's *History of the American Theatre* (1832), T. Allston Brown's *A History of the New York Stage* (1903), and George Odell's *Annals of the New York Stage* (1927–49).

Theatrical biographies number more than 3,500 volumes. Although studies in English of American and English artists predominate, there is also material on such world figures as the Chinese Mei Lan-fang, the Russian Konstantin Stanislavski (with much material in the Cyrillic alphabet), and the Austrian Max Reinhardt.

Material on stage architecture, costume, and scenery is present in the Theatre Collection, but for extended research the holdings of the Art and Architecture Division must also be consulted. Resources include works such as Adolphe Appia's *Die Musik und die Inscenierung* (1899), Edward Gordon Craig's *On the Art of Theatre* (1911), and Martinet's *Petit galérie dramatique* (1796–1870) and *Galérie dramatique* (1844–70). The splendid collection of festival books in the Spencer Collection should not be overlooked.

The Oriental Division has material on the theatre in the Orient and texts of Sanskrit, Chinese, as well as Japanese plays in the original and in translation. The Slavonic Division, in addition to strong holdings of the collected works of dramatists, holds theatrical biography, histories of the theatre and of theatre groups, and stage periodicals. Materials on the Yiddish Art Theatre of New York and similar organizations are available in the Theatre Collection; however, some of the conventional printed materials are in the Jewish Division, as are such journals as the *Jewish Theatrical News*.

The magnificent resources of the Picture Collection, administered by the Branch Libraries of the New York Public Library, include iconography of every aspect of the theatre as well as some motion picture stills (by subject). The Schomburg Center for Research in Black Culture of the Research Libraries contains important materials on the stage and dramatic literature.

Drama as a literary form has always been collected exhaustively by the Research Libraries for its general collections. There are over 120,000 titles represented in the Roman and Greek alphabets; these holdings are discussed more fully in chapter 20. Manuscripts, first, and significant editions of the work of English and American playwrights are held by the Berg Collection of English and American Literature, which is particularly notable for Bernard Shaw materials and the work of the Irish Literary Renaissance. The Berg Collection also houses typescripts of works by American dramatists of greater literary stature. This collection of over 2,000 typescripts comes from the files of the American Play Company, dramatists' agents, purchased by the library in 1967.

The remainder of the archive is held by the Theatre Collection. Included are the works of the Americans Maxwell Anderson, George M. Cohan, Rachel Crothers, Clyde Fitch, Lillian Hellman, Langston Hughes, Eugene O'Neill, and Edward Sheldon, as well as scripts by William Archer, Guy Bolton, W. Somerset Maugham, Ferenc Molnar, and Victorien Sardou.

In 1952 the R. H. Burnside collection was added to the Theatre Collection; it consists of about 4,000 annotated play scripts in English, French, and German for productions of Charles Frohman or the New York Hippodrome.[5] Burnside was associated with the Hippodrome in the early part of this century, first under the Shuberts and then under Charles Dillingham, and also with Charles Frohman. Included are typescripts of plays by Oscar Wilde, Arthur Wing Pinero, and W. Somerset Maugham, among many others.

Excluding the American Play Company scripts, the Theatre Collection holds over 5,000 bound and cataloged promptbooks. The material is in English and consists of plays produced in England and the United States. The original George Becks gift to the library consisted of approximately 1,400 prompt-books representing nineteenth-century performances; it has been added to by the Dramatists' Guild. More than 400 of the prompt-books are from productions of Shakespearean plays. The collection also has prompt-book librettos for operettas and musical comedies by Victor Herbert, Rudolf Friml, and the librettist Oscar Hammerstein. The Music Division also holds librettos for operas, operettas, and musical comedies, as well as complete sheet music for musical comedies.

Nonbook materials

Through its nonbook materials, the Theatre Collection can locate at least a partial record of any major or minor play produced in New York City in the past century; holdings are nearly as strong for Washington, D.C., Boston, Toledo, Chicago, and other major cities. These materials also document the lives and careers of most performers on the American stage and a great number on the English stage. Through its extensive holdings of programmes, the collection records the productions of individual theatres.

The English stage is comprehensively represented from 1673 to 1932 in the Hiram Stead collection of scrapbooks, portfolios of playbills, programmes, prints, photographs, critiques, biographical articles, box office statements, and memorabilia. The Hénin collection on the French stage is strong for the eighteenth and nineteenth centuries. The Russian stage in the twentieth century is covered in pictures, programmes, and scrapbooks in the Oliver Sayler collection.

The Robinson Locke collection documents the American stage from 1870 to 1920 and is arranged under the name of individual artists. Extensive gifts from theatrical artists themselves supplement and update the Locke collection, as do donations by theatrical agencies of scrapbooks, press books, personal memorabilia, letters, contracts, photographs, etc. These materials are augmented by

---

5. See Avi Wortis, "The Burnside Mystery," *BNYPL* 75 (1971): 371–409, for an essay and check list on this collection.

the Clipping/Obituary/Programme File in 254 file cabinets.

Archives of theatrical photographs are highlighted by the Vandamm collection of photographic prints and negatives of professional theatre productions in New York City during the period 1925 to 1950. The White, Valente, and Van Vechten collections are also worthy of note.

The Prints Division does not actively collect theatrical portraits; it does, however, have two volumes of theatrical caricatures, and its resources in prints ranging from the fifteenth century to the present day provide research material for stage and costume design. Theatrical prints and engravings are found throughout the files and scrapbooks of the Theatre Collection.

Thousands of original scene and costume designs in the Theatre Collection include work by such artists as Howard Bay, Aline Bernstein, Tom Adrian Cracraft, H. M. Crayon, Mstislav Doboujinsky, Erté, David Ffolkes, Robert Edmond Jones, and others. Related drawings and designs in the Dance Collection and musical portraits in the Music Division supplement these holdings.

The collection of theatrical posters in the Theatre Collection numbers several hundred pieces. International in scope, it ranges from the late nineteenth century to the present and includes a wide variety of forms.

The Theatre Collection maintains a newspaper clipping collection of dramatic criticism in 275 bound volumes dating from 1917 to the present. The clippings concern the New York City stage only, but including Broadway, off-Broadway, and off-off-Broadway productions. The reviews cover a wide range of sources and are arranged alphabetically by play title under each theatrical season. A supplementary tool is the Theatre Scrapbook File maintained by the General Research and Humanities Division in the Central Building, a card file alphabetically arranged by title, itemizing and locating reviews.

Manuscripts

Prompt-books, many with manuscript notations and additions, are retained in the Theatre Collection, instead of the Manuscripts and Archives Division. This is also true of the correspondence and papers of such theatrical figures as managers, producers, and impresarios. The Manuscripts and Archives Division, however, holds the manuscripts, correspondence, and papers of many dramatists notable principally for their literary, rather than theatrical, values. Extensive holdings of manuscripts of American and English playwrights are also found in the Berg Collection, and some few items in the Arents Collections.

The Theatre Collection holds the diaries, correspondence, and personal papers of such theatrical figures as Winthrop Ames, John Anderson, Brooks Atkinson, Robert H. Burnside, Jacob Charash, Mady Christians, Charles B. Dillingham, Charles Frohman, Paul Kester, Lillie Langtry, Gertrude Lawrence, Richard Mansfield, Edward Hugh Sothern and Julia Marlowe, and Sophie Tucker. The scrapbooks and press books contain occasional autographs, notes, letters, and other material; for example, there are letters of Edmund Kean in the Maynard Morris papers. The Children's Library of the General Library of the Performing Arts, a unit of the Branch Libraries, holds manuscripts and memorabilia of the Broadway child-star Elsie Leslie in its reading room

collection, as well as material relating to children's theatre.

Other manuscripts relating to theatrical activities held in the Manuscripts and Archives Division include records of the American Dramatic Fund Association of New York (1819–1903), the Olympic Theatre of New York City (1864–69), the New York Theatre Company (1885–94),[6] the Drama League of America, and the American Educational Theatre Association. Also included is an autograph file of German theatrical correspondence (1853–1917). Literary manuscripts in the division represent many nations: the United States (William Inge and Edward Sheldon); England (John Van Druten); Ireland (Dion Boucicault and Tyrone Power); Hungary (Ferenc Molnar); Spain (Lope de Vega and Miguel de Zarraga); the USSR (B. Lavrenev and V. Volovyov) and others.

The Eugene O'Neill holdings are of particular interest. In the Manuscripts and Archives Division are typescripts with manuscript revisions of *Ah! Wilderness, Days Without End*, and *Strange Interlude*, a typescript of *Mourning Becomes Electra*, and correspondence, clippings, and articles about the plays. In the Rare Book Division are found the corrected galley proofs of *Strange Interlude*, and the Theatre Collection holds prompt-books of many O'Neill plays. Additional materials in the Berg Collection include variant typescripts of *Lazarus Laughed* and a collection of his letters (1914–16) to Beatrice Ashe which give a picture of his early work and hopes.

THE CINEMA

The collection numbers some 8,600 volumes of book material: 6,100 bound volumes of periodicals, 1,500 monographs, and 1,000 movie scripts. Nonbook materials form the largest body of materials relating to the cinema; included are over 1,000,000 movie stills, 125 volumes of clipped reviews, 800 bound scrapbooks, over 1,000 press books now on microfilm, and a vast number of clippings on the cinema in all its aspects.

The Theatre Collection acquires materials on the commercial and artistic aspects of motion pictures; it also has a selection of materials on the technology and use of cinema equipment. The scientific principles involved in the making of cinema equipment are found in the Science and Technology Research Center. The Economic and Public Affairs Division covers financial aspects of the cinema industry, but does not have strong holdings in this field. The Slavonic Division has important materials on the cinema in its collections.

Historical Survey

Fifty years ago the New York Public Library laid the foundation for what is now one of the largest book and periodical collections relating to the cinema in any public institution. In 1907 the library subscribed to the *Moving Picture World*, now the *Motion Picture Herald*. Before that year, the library had bought available books on the popular but still embryonic art of the cinema. Chief among these was the *History of the Kine-*

---

6. See H. L. Kleinfield, "Theatre as Business; The Minute Book of the New York Theatre Company," *BNYPL* 63 (1959): 379–92.

matograph, Kinetoscope, and the Kineto-Phono-graph by William Kennedy and others, published in 1895. It was ten years before the industry had a periodical of its own. The library was one of the earliest subscribers to this periodical, and from that day to the present the printed annals of the motion picture have been actively collected.

The Robinson Locke collection of dramatic scrapbooks contains hundreds of portfolios on the film. There are volumes relating to the early careers of Mary Pickford, Charles Chaplin, Douglas Fairbanks, Theda Bara, and those operatic and stage artists who also had film careers: Mary Garden, Jane Cowl, Ethel Barrymore, and Geraldine Farrar among them. George Kleine, a pioneer with Edison and the first great importer of foreign films, presented his account books, business papers, scrapbooks, and press sheets in 1928–29. These represent a complete picture of his activities in the field and give a clear impression of business conditions in the early period of film production. Through the good offices of the late Frank J. Wilstach and the Motion Picture Producers and Distributors of America, the major film companies began in 1928 to present stills and press books of their current pictures. Paramount Picture Corporation assembled for the library a full set of press books dating from 1919, and have continued to deposit these important records. More than 1,000 press books on microfilm represent an outstanding collection covering the periods 1909–15 and 1927 to date.

In 1933, Universal Pictures began to deposit in the Theatre Collection its books of stills which now number more than 2,100 volumes. Each volume represents a single motion picture. A full set of scrapbooks and stills for Inspiration Pictures contains a record of many of the films of Richard Barthelmess and Lillian and Dorothy Gish; these include The White Sister, Romola, The Bright Shawl, and Tol'able David. In 1939, Metro-Goldwyn-Mayer donated a set of continuities or synopses for its films released since January 1, 1928. This has been a continuing gift, with scripts released to the library after they have been held for three years. There are also scrapbooks from the Capitol Theatre and Loew's, Inc. Many other film companies have generously contributed to these holdings, finding the Theatre Collection a convenient repository and reliable custodian.

Cinema Periodicals

The library's collection of periodicals related to the cinema range from the fan magazine to the serious review, from the rating sheet to the trade journal and house organ. About 125 periodicals in the Roman alphabet are received from all over the world. Examples of these strong holdings include, from the United States, Films in Review, Film Library Quarterly, Film Culture, Film Quarterly and the recently launched Making Films in New York; from Argentina Tiempo de cine; from Chile Ecran; from England Films and Filming and Movie; from France L'Avant scène du cinema, Cahiers du cinema, and Image et son; from Germany Film; from India Film World; from Italy Cinema y film, Cinema nuovo, and Bianco y nero; from Portugal Celuloide; and from Sweden Chaplin. Older files in the collection include Motion Picture Herald (1907– , under varying titles), Bioscope (1912–20), Photoplay (1913–), Close Up (1927–33), Movie Classic (1931–37), Box Office (1932–), and the all-encompassing Variety

(1905–). East European titles in the Cyrillic alphabet are in the Slavonic Division: the Soviet Iskusstvo kino, and Sovetski film; the Polish Film; the Bulgarian Kinoiszkustvo, etc. The Oriental Division receives the Japanese film magazine Engekikai; through the PL-480 Program acquisitions have been received from Indonesia, India, and the United Arab Republic.

Reflecting the library's interest in sociological matters are a number of serials on the censorship and classification of the cinema. The collection holds an extensive file of the Green Sheet (the Film Board of National Organizations film reports), Reviews and Ratings of Current Films (Protestant Motion Picture Council) and publications of the National Catholic Office for Motion Pictures. House organs of the motion picture companies include the early Edison Kinetogram (1909–16) and the Kalem Kalendar (1914–15) of the Kalem Company, the Fox News, Paramount News, etc.

Book Materials, Movie Scripts, Manuscripts, and Other Items

Book materials in the field of cinema are more than adequate. The library attempts to preserve both books and pamphlets in this field, even those of slight interest. Amateur moving pictures and the technique of writing for films are covered by substantial holdings. The body of separate works relating to the photographic and engineering phases of the cinema was comparatively small until the advent of the talking picture. Continuing accessions since that time, together with contributions which have appeared in the general scientific journals (in the Science and Technology Research Center), provide an adequate library on the subject. History of the cinema is also well represented, with holdings which include such works as Terry Ramsaye's A Million and One Nights (1926), Benjamin B. Hampton's A History of the Movies (1931), Marcel La Pierre's Les Cent visages du cinéma (1948), and Paul Rotha's The Film Till Now (1949).

The collection of approximately 1,000 bound movie scripts represents the productions of American companies from the 1920s to the present. Included are such films as Flirtation Walk (1934), The Informer (1935), Across the Pacific (1942), and Splendor in the Grass (1959). There are also approximately 100 shorter treatments, synopses, and similar forms, bound in pamphlet volumes, and a collection of Metro-Goldwyn-Mayer film continuities, plot summaries used in the editing process. A number of movie scripts were acquired with the archive of the American Play Company. The Theatre Collection acquires published scripts of commercial films; the Slavonic Division holds a number of these from the USSR.

The press books of American film companies number approximately 1,000 volumes; also included are more than 1,000,000 movie stills, the core group being 2,100 volumes of Universal Pictures stills covering the period from the mid-1920s to the present. Other stills are incorporated into the iconography files of the Theatre Collection. The 600,000 stills originally in the library's Picture Collection complement and supplement these resources; in this collection American films are best represented, but excellent holdings of materials on the cinema in Russia (Artkino, Amkino), France, (Société de Films), England (Eagle-Lion, Gaumont-British), and Germany

(Ufa) are also available. A subject index to the pictorial content of these stills is of great value to artists and researchers.

The collection of scrapbooks and clipping files of the Theatre Collection are mainly in English, although some items in Western European languages are included. Through them a researcher can document the lives and careers of virtually all major and minor American cinema artists, and many foreign ones too, particularly those whose careers have touched the American consciousness. These files document cinemas, movie theatres, companies, premières, and all other phases of the industry in the United States, Europe, and Asia. They include not only clippings, but programmes, photographs, announcements, and all sorts of ephemera as well. More valuable and important ephemera and curiosities are kept with the manuscripts in the collection's cage file, including such items as academy award citations, early patent applications for cinematic equipment, contracts, letters, theatrical and cinematic postage stamps, and other valuable material—even the Oscar awarded to Burl Ives.

The Theatre Collection maintains a collection of newspaper clippings of moving picture criticisms dating from 1930. Now consisting of 125 bound volumes, this archive contains each year's reviews from New York City newspapers; at present four newspapers are clipped: the *New York Times*, the *Daily News*, the *New York Post*, and the *Village Voice*. This service is up to date, and reviews are available to the public within a week of the performance.

Manuscript material on the cinema is present in the Theatre Collection in the papers of Paul Muni, Montgomery Clift, Burl Ives, and others. The diaries and papers of L[egaré] Rogers Lytton in the Manuscripts and Archives Division deal in part with the actor's association with the Vitagraph Company of America in the early years of this century.

Motion Picture Films

The Research Libraries collect motion picture films, videotapes, and filmstrips in subject areas of the performing arts such as music, theatre, and the dance; in subject areas where the collections are unusually strong, the Research Libraries collect documentary films. The Dance Collection has acquired in its Jerome Robbins dance film archive approximately 1,250,000 feet (2,200 reels) of motion picture film and videotape illustrating the work of dance companies and artists from the United States and abroad. These represent both commercial and privately produced films.

The Film Library at Donnell Library Center, administered by the Branch Libraries, has a collection of 16mm documentary sound films on a wide variety of subjects available for borrowing by individuals or nonprofit organizations for free showing. A catalog is issued periodically by the library.[7] The Film Library also maintains a reference collection of books, magazines, distributors' catalogs, producers' catalogs, subject lists, and film evaluations.

An Archive of Black Films is projected for the Schomburg Center which will document the contribution to and involvement of black people in the motion picture industry.

THE CIRCUS

The library's circus collection—photographs, reviews, posters, broadsides, and programmes—contains materials documenting this form as early as the eighteenth century in England. Special periodicals on the subject include *Circus Scrap Book* (1923–31) and a good file of *White Tops* (1928–). Other periodicals in the holdings such as *Billboard, New York Dramatic Mirror*, and *Variety* contain circus information. Circus route books furnish a valuable and often unique record of the tours of various troupes including Barnum and Bailey (dating from 1886), Great Floto, Forepaugh-Sells, Ringling, Tom Mix, Cole Brothers, and others, as well as programmes for these and for Wild West shows such as those of Pawnee Bill and the celebrated Buffalo Bill. Most of this material relates to American circuses, although some English tours are included. There are a few route books and programmes for continental circuses, including that of Hagenbeck-Wallace. Much circus material came to the library with the Townsend Walsh collection.

Standard reference works on the circus include general studies, biographical works, and regional surveys. Here as in other areas of the Theatre Collection much vital information, particularly for contemporary figures, can be found in scrapbooks and clipping and iconography files where, for example, are stored clippings, programmes, and photographs of the famous circus clowns Felix Adler, Poodles Hanneford, Emmett Kelly, and Grock; and, from the last century, Joseph Grimaldi, whose career is documented in the Hiram Stead collection with engravings, including portraits and playbills. There is a variety of ephemeral material in the vertical files, such as tickets, route cards, advertising material, handbills, and publicity material. A representative selection of circus posters is available for consultation.

Manuscript material relating to the circus is not extensive in the Research Libraries. Perhaps the most notable archive consists of seventeen letters on show business from Phineus T. Barnum to Moses Kimball in the Manuscripts and Archives Division, dated 1846 to 1876. With them are issues of Southern newspapers of 1843 containing articles about Barnum's exhibition of his "mermaid."

VAUDEVILLE, NIGHT CLUBS, ACTORS' RENDEZVOUS

The resources in this area, although extensive, consist primarily of nonbook materials: clippings, programmes, photographs, and ephemera. Vaudeville coverage is best for the United States from the late nineteenth century to the present. There is reasonable coverage for England during the same period and some continental European material is also present. The William Morris gift provides a record of the clients of the William Morris Agency and includes route books, correspondence, contracts, scrapbooks, and similar material from the early twentieth century through the heyday of vaudeville. A feature of the Robinson Locke collection is individual scrapbooks for notable performers; the Townsend Walsh collection is particularly strong in programmes of theatrical and vaudeville performances; the Joe

---

7. *Films; A Catalog of the Film Collection in The New York Public Library* (The New York Public Library, 1972).

Laurie, Jr. collection preserves many photographs of vaudeville performers and acts. Holdings are strongest for the New York City area with material on Koster and Bial's Music Hall, Tony Pastor's, the Palace, and other theatres across the country to San Francisco's Orpheum. Reviews of vaudeville performances are present and the lives and careers of performers, including burlesque dancers, are well documented.

Nonbook material documenting night clubs and cabarets consists of clippings, souvenir programmes, reviews of acts, menus, and similar ephemera. The range is international, with professional dancing and dancers featured. Theatrical rendezvous as a subject of interest in the Theatre Collection includes not only clubs such as the Lambs and Players, but meeting places of theatrical folk in many countries, among them Sardi's and the Algonquin in New York City, Romanoff's in Los Angeles, Maxim's in Paris, Sacher's in Vienna, and the Savoy in London. The collection has a number of the theatrical caricatures of Alex Gard, whose work covers the walls of Sardi's Restaurant.

RADIO AND TELEVISION

The importance of radio became nationally known with the broadcast of election returns in November, 1920; soon afterward the library began collecting books and periodicals on the subject. Since 1931 newspapers and trade papers have been clipped for reviews, biographical matter, current trends, and other related topics. Broadcasting companies, as well as local stations, have supplied press material, programmes, and scripts. Only the entertainment and educational aspects of radio and television are discussed here. Extensive technical resources are considered as aspects of communications and technology (see chapter 56).

The library currently receives thirteen periodical titles dealing with radio broadcasting and television, including the *Radio Times* (1939–   ), *Radio and Television Weekly* (1916–   ), *Radio and Television* (Prague, 1960–   ), *Television Age* (1953–   ); the long-lived *Billboard* (1894–1960) is now on microfilm in the library.

Radio scripts in bound volumes furnish a valuable record of the industry. The collection holds, among others, scripts of the series "Moonshine and Honeysuckle" (1930–33); the "Cavalcade of America" (1935–53); the Orson Welles adaptations of classics for the Campbell Playhouse in 1938 and 1939, among them *Arrowsmith* and *A Farewell to Arms*; the Gilbert Seldes series "Americans All—Immigrants All" prepared for the United States Office of Education in 1939; and "The Eternal Light" (1951–   ). Hector Chevigny, at one time president of the Radio Writers' Guild, presented a large number of his radio scripts to the library, among them those for the show "The Second Mrs. Burton." Other scripts in the Manuscripts and Archives Division represent broadcasts made in 1940 on international affairs; they preserve the political climate of pre-World War II days, and are by Elmer Davis, Arthur Hale, and H. V. Kaltenborn, accompanied by related correspondence.

Standard book material in the field is generally available. There are extensive holdings on the educational uses of radio and television, including a number of government publications.

As television has become one of the nation's foremost communications media, efforts are made to collect television scripts as well as books, magazines, photographs, and clippings on the subject. The library is the official repository for the American Television Society, which undertakes to collect pertinent material for the Theatre Collection. Scripts for television productions have been added, including several of the Hallmark Hall of Fame productions and those of the NBC Matinee Theatre.

The Rodgers and Hammerstein Archives of Recorded Sound house several thousand 16-inch vinyl acetate transcripts of radio programs of the 1930s and 1940s. These, although including documentary and popular programmes, are primarily recordings of the NBC Symphony Orchestra, Boston Symphony, and other major American orchestras. In addition, many tapes of the post-World War II period carry complete opera performances, primarily foreign, but including a full sequence of the Metropolitan Opera Broadcasts since the 1965 season.

MAGIC

An outstanding collection is concerned with stage magic and professional stage magicians. Other divisions of the Research Libraries contain strong collections of material on the occult sciences (the General Research and Humanities Division; see chapter 1) and on the Kabbala (the Jewish Division; see chapter 10). Some sorcerer's and fortune-teller's handbooks from Thailand in the Spencer Collection are also noteworthy. Only the Theatre Collection holdings in manipulative magic are discussed here. These consist of several thousand books and pamphlets in various languages from the seventeenth to the twentieth century. Periodical runs, programmes of stage performances of magic, catalogs of magic supply houses, scrapbooks, and material in the extensive clipping and iconography files of the collection supplement this archive.

In 1910, Mrs. Henry Draper purchased and presented to the library the collection of 664 volumes and 433 scrapbooks gathered by Dr. Saram R. Ellison. Ellison continued building the collection of printed materials and reimbursed the library for the purchase price of the original collection in order that it might be known as his gift. Of interest are the press books of Howard Thurston, and 25 volumes of manuscript letters, articles, and clippings for the period 1855–1909, gathered by Ellison, relating to magic, hypnotism, spiritualism, legerdemain, ventriloquism, etc.[8]

Attracted by the accession of the Ellison collection, the Society of American Magicians, through the efforts of John Mulholland, designated the library as the depository of its materials, with the exception of apparatus. Since then both the society and its individual members have contributed books, pamphlets, and periodicals (some of great rarity, including a perfect copy of *Will Goldston's Exclusive Magical Secrets*), photographs, scrapbooks, and other ephemeral items, as well as material related to the proceedings of the society: programmes, playbills, menus, and various publications. The collection is now, as a result, extensive.

---

8. See "Behind the Magician's Curtain; An Exhibition of Books and Prints Relating to Conjuring and Magic," *BNYPL* 32 (1928): 83–87.

Materials are treated in various ways. According to an agreement reached with the Society of American Magicians, there are four categories for magic: (1) materials duly cataloged and available to the general reader, (2) materials for which author cards only appear in the Public Catalog, (3) materials for which both cards and books are in "8-" class mark and made available only to members of the society, and (4) materials with cards in the Official Catalog only (the working catalog of the library) which is not available for a period of ten years after its accession; and then made available only to members of the society.

In 1929, Dr. Samuel Cox Hooker began making gifts, including rare works, which culminated in 1936, after his death, in the presentation from his estate of his library on magic, consisting of over 900 books and pamphlets. Harry Miller Lydenberg, former director of the library, took particular interest in gathering books on magic for the collection.[9]

Periodical holdings include a long and scarce run of *M.U.M: Magic, Unity, Might* (1911– , with interruptions and changes of title), the official organ of the Society of American Magicians. Other runs are the *Linking Ring* (1923–29), *Goodliffe's Abracadabra* (1923–59), and a very early title, Wiegleb's *Natürliche Magie* (1782–1805). The earliest among a small number of books in the Rare Book Division is Richard Argentine's *De Praestigiis et Incantationibus Daemonum et Necromanticorum* (1568). In the Manuscripts and Archives Division is a curious "D. Johannis Faustens Miracul Kunstund Wunder-Buch" (1612), "Magical Memorandums" by Angelo Lewis, and items from the Hooker and Society of American Magicians collections.

---

9. See John Mulholland, "Magic in Books," *BNYPL* 55 (1951): 107–11.

SECTION

III

THE SOCIAL SCIENCES

PART ONE

34

ECONOMIC AND PUBLIC AFFAIRS DIVISION

Of the several subject collections of the Research Libraries, the Economic and Public Affairs Division has the largest collection, with over one million volumes and ten thousand serials. A division of social sciences, it includes economics, business, sociology, demography, political science, and international relations among its fields of collecting interest. Resources in the specific subjects will be described in the following chapters. In almost every case the division attempts to acquire on a comprehensive basis the essential materials in its fields of interest without regard to language, place, date, or form of publication.

HISTORICAL SURVEY

While the Astor Library did not attempt to purchase much now considered essential to the special business library, it did have standard works in the field of economics and, for the time, an unusual collection of public documents from various countries relating to public finance. In 1897, Dr. Billings enlarged the library's list of periodicals in commerce, finance, trade, industry, and technology, and commenced the systematic indexing of these titles in the library's card catalog. The Lenox Library was virtually without resources in this field, except where its history collection, particularly American, offered allied materials. Samuel Tilden's library contained important works on banking (including 225 scarce English tracts, one of which was a treatise on bank credit printed in 1683), and on taxation and finance. There were also long files of leading economic journals. In 1899 the accession of the Ford collection strengthened general materials in the writings of American, English, French, German, and Italian economists, and added special features, such as editions of Adam Smith, works on the West Indian Trade, the Bullion Report, the Bank Act of 1844, the Repeal of the Corn Laws, and American writings on tariff legislation, taxation, and currency.

SPECIAL INDEXES AND FILES

The majority of cards in the dictionary catalog of the Economic and Public Affairs Division duplicate those prepared for the Public Catalog. A small percentage of cards, however, represent selective indexing by subject of articles in journals, and are present only in the division. The division is the center for information on the government publications in the collections of the library. (The terms "government publication" and "public document" are used interchangeably in this *Guide.*) The key to these extensive holdings is the division's Catalog of Government Publications, certainly one of the most important of its kind in the world.[1] A fuller description of the catalog is found in chapter 36.

The special indexes and files of the Economic and Public Affairs Division are:

Censuses Index

A card index of recent official census publications on population, housing, agriculture, business, etc. (active, 2 card drawers). The cards are arranged alphabetically under country, listing publications ordered or in process.

Directories Index

An index to the directories in the Research Libraries of interest to the Economic and Public Affairs Division, arranged under such broad subjects as banks and banking, commerce, labor, securities (active, 9 card drawers). The information given for each title includes the issues available in the library and the library classmark.

General Newspaper Clippings and Pamphlet File

A file of current pamphlets and newspaper clippings (active, 32 vertical file trays). Subject headings generally follow those used in the *Public Affairs Information Service Bulletin.*

Government Reports by Popular Names

A finding list on cards arranged by name of chairman or other identifying term for reports of official committees and commissions of the United States and other governments (active, 1 card drawer). An entry such as "Beveridge Report" represents the catalog entry "Gt. Britain. Interdepartmental committee on social insurance and allied services. *Report.* 1942."

---

1. The *Catalog of Government Publications in The Research Libraries* was published in book form in 40 volumes by G. K. Hall & Co. of Boston in 1972; the catalog is primarily a corporate-author listing.

Index of Current United States Congressional Committee Prints

As there is no convenient finding list for Congressional "committee prints," the Economic and Public Affairs Division assigns numbers to them as they are received and files them accordingly in a vertical file (active, 2 file trays). The number of any item in this temporary location is found by referring to a card file where the prints are listed first by committee and then alphabetically by title. After each Congress, the prints receive regular cataloging and are added to the permanent collections.

Market Surveys Vertical File

Current market surveys are arranged by subject in this file under such headings as "Market Surveys—Automobile Ownership," "Market Surveys—Boston" (active, 3 file trays).

Periodicals File

A listing on cards of the periodicals currently received in the Economic and Public Affairs Division arranged by country of origin (active, 3 card drawers). In cases where many periodicals are received from a single country there is a subdivision by subject.

Reference Questions File

A card file made up of information found in answering reference questions and stored for future use (active, 2 card drawers). It is arranged alphabetically under general subjects.

Soils Survey Index

A geographical index, using a state-county approach, to the U.S. Soils Bureau's *Field Operations* (1899–1922) and to the U.S. Plant Industry Bureau's *Soil Surveys* from 1923 to the late 1950s (inactive, 1 card drawer).

RESOURCES

A general description of the extent of the resources in the division by form of material follows.

BOOKS

The book collection is intended to contain all the principal works in the fields of division interest from every country, and as much useful secondary subject material as can be discovered and acquired. Included are the publications of such bodies as the National Bureau of Economic Research, the Brookings Institution, the Royal Institute of International Affairs, the Council on Foreign Relations, and their counterparts in other countries, as well as market surveys and special reports of trade missions and chambers of commerce.

Among the outstanding aspects of this collection are the holdings on regional and city planning, foreign trade, banking and finance, corporation history, railroad history, labor, and political science. When Sir John Clapham's *The Bank of England, A History* was published in 1944, an examination of his citations revealed only two published items which could not be found in the library; the others were, for the most part, present in first editions from the late seventeenth century onward.

PERIODICALS

The division attempts to obtain all important general periodicals issued more frequently than once a year in its fields in addition to a representative selection in special subjects. These include the journals of the central banks; chambers of commerce; trade associations; learned societies; professional associations; labor, research, and charitable organizations; and financial, tax, and news services. Room is available for the current issues of only some 2,000 of these titles; approximately 3,000 other periodicals of interest to the division are shelved in the Periodicals Section.

NONCURRENT SERIALS

Examples of serials issued once a year or less frequently are stock exchange manuals; bank and corporation reports; trade directories; proceedings of professional, trade, and labor organizations; yearbooks relating to housing, legislation, international law, transportation, municipal and state government; and monographs issued in series by societies, universities, and other research agencies. The holdings are comprehensive.

GOVERNMENT PUBLICATIONS

The Economic and Public Affairs Division has one of the world's great collections of government publications. It is a depository for United States public documents, receives all federal official publications issued by the Queen's Printer, Ottawa, as well as those issued by many other government agencies throughout the world. Files are usually available from the earliest periods.

An attempt is made by the division to acquire essential official documents from every country, including official gazettes; parliamentary proceedings and papers; annual legislation; foreign correspondence and treaties; departmental reports; censuses; and statistical reports, both current and annual.

In this collection are many outstanding files; a few may be cited. Official gazettes form a strong group and provide a detailed current record of executive and legislative activity; through its Gazettes Acquisition and Microfilming Program, the library now has on film files dating from the late 1950s for most of the world's official gazettes, and is working to complete filming of its retrospective holdings.[2]

The collection of British Parliamentary Papers and similar files for the British Commonwealth of Nations are notable for their completeness. They include the collected papers of the independent states and dependent territories, as well as of many provincial and state legislatures.

The holdings of census reports, foreign trade statistics, treaties, and foreign office reports and correspondence represent a large proportion of the materials published in most of the countries of the world.

STATE, PROVINCIAL, AND MUNICIPAL PUBLICATIONS

The collection is excellent for the United States and the British Commonwealth; the library is a

2. See James Wood Henderson, "The Acquisition and Preservation of Foreign Official Gazettes," *Farmington Plan Newsletter* 31 (1970): 1–24.

depository for the state publications of New York, Washington, and California, and also receives most New Jersey publications. Holdings are not particularly strong for other localities. In general the division attempts to acquire the municipal publications of all cities in the United States with a 1970 population of 400,000 or more. It also acquires the municipal publications of Canadian, Central, and South American cities with a population of 250,000 or more; and the publications of the cities of Europe, Africa, and Asia with populations of 500,000 or more. If a city is a national capital, or has some other special significance, its municipal publications will be sought by the division regardless of its size.

PUBLICATIONS OF INTERNATIONAL ORGANIZATIONS

The library served as a depository for League of Nations documents, and maintains the same relationship with the United Nations and such affiliated agencies as the International Labor Office, the International Court, and the International Bank. The library is also a depository for the publications of the European Economic Community and the Organization for Economic Co-operation and Development. The proceedings and papers of a great number of international congresses have also been acquired.

MICROFORMS

A growing number of publications are being produced in microfilm. The division receives many of these, including the Readex Microprint series of United States government publications listed in the *Monthly Catalog* from 1953 onward, and the *Human Relations Area File* microfiles. The division is also responsible for acquiring and collating the titles included in the Gazettes Acquisition and Microfilming Program of the Research Libraries.

35

GENERAL RESOURCES IN ECONOMICS AND BUSINESS ADMINISTRATION

Resources in economics and business administration (including those on transportation and communication) have for many years formed a significant proportion of the total holdings of the Research Libraries, as shown by the following statistics:

1921	93,778 volumes
1931	153,857
1941	231,000
1966	455,800

These figures provide a conservative estimate of holdings in the area, excluding large numbers of government publications shelved with the general collection of public documents, items housed in the Jewish, Slavonic, and Oriental Divisions, and recent acquisitions of microform sets (such as the annual reports of all companies listed on major United States and Canadian exchanges).

The library collects comprehensively in most areas within economics and business administration. The field is such that many publications dealing primarily with the local, rather than the national, scene in foreign countries do not find their way into the collections. Similarly, less material is available on the economies of smaller states outside the northeastern region of the United States than on New York and surrounding states. As research in this field emphasizes the use of recent publications, the library gives higher priority to their acquisition than to that of older imprints, although it makes an exception to this policy in the case of already established special collections. The library does attempt to obtain a very high percentage of all publications of research value for certain areas within the field: economic history, banking, industrial relations, accounting, and advertising.

The collection of reference material is strong; the library orders almost all such publications in all languages. The policy is especially true in regard to bibliographies, indexes, and other bibliographic tools, extending to the published catalogs and accession lists of libraries with important resources in the field.

A large collection of serials embraces titles from all over the world, with generally complete files of major journals and a good representation (although not always beginning with the first volume) of those of lesser importance. The fact that the *Union List of Serials* can locate but few copies of some journals in other libraries indicates the library's strength in the more unusual publications; not infrequently the library's set may be one of as few as five available in this country. Older foreign titles present in complete sets, for example, include the *Revue économique et financière, Der National-Oekonom Jahrbücher für Nationalökonomie und Statistik, Swedish Journal of Economics, Giornale degli economisti,* and *Revista de ciencias económicas* (Argentina). Among the more recently established journals are *Australian Economic History Review, Actividade económica de Angola, Economia internazionale, Estudios económicos, Ekonomska politika* (Yugoslavia), *Royal Nepal Economist,* and *La Tunisie économique.*

University monograph series in economics and related fields constitute another strong portion of the resources. These files, usually complete, represent the publications of departments, faculties, or institutes of economics from such universities or institutions as Bordeaux, Buenos Aires, Catholic University (Santiago, Chile), Central University of Venezuela, Columbia, Halle, Jena, Kobe, Oxford, University of the East (Manila), Stellenbosch, and Wisconsin. A related group consists of the publications of American university schools of commerce and business administration.

ECONOMIC HISTORY

Resources in economic history are excellent. Holdings of rare and early books on economics and business, while not matching in extent the Kress Library at Harvard University, form a sizeable block of material; for some years the library has been acquiring items in the published catalogs of the Kress collection which it lacked, and has also added some titles not listed there. The full extent of these resources cannot be readily determined, however, because they are merged with the general collection of rare books; no separate catalog or checklist is available. The collection of seventeenth- and eighteenth-century English and French pamphlets is excellent.

For major economists the library has not only standard editions and extensive critical material, but also many first, early, and unusual editions and some translations of key works into major European languages. The mercantilists and physiocrats, for example, are represented in first editions of Thomas Mun, Sir William Petty, Charles Davenant, Richard Cantillon, Ferdinando Galiani, Anne Robert Jacques Turgot, and François Quesnay.

The library has notable resources on Adam Smith, especially editions of *The Wealth of Nations*. These include not only the first editions published in England and Ireland, but also the rare first American edition (Philadelphia, 1789) and that published in Switzerland in 1791. Among later editions of importance are those edited by David Buchanan (1814), John Ramsay McCulloch (1828), and J. E. T. Rogers (1869); a curious item is the 1809 volume with the cover title *Enfield's Wealth of Nations*, a paraphrase of Smith's treatise. In all, the library holds approximately 50 English-language editions published between 1776 and the end of the nineteenth century, and numerous modern reprints and extracts, as well as the first translations into French, Italian, and Spanish, and an early edition in German. More recent translations include those into Czech, Finnish, and Polish, and additional versions in the languages already mentioned. While lacking equal strength in Smith's other writings, the library's collections contain first editions of his first important work, *The Theory of Moral Sentiments* (1759), of *Essays on Philosophical Subjects* (1795), and of his *Works* (1811–12), and the Public Catalog has about 300 references to books and journal articles by and about him. Material on Smith—in Dutch, French, German, Italian, Polish, and Spanish as well as English—consists of such varied forms as biographies, contributions to periodicals, studies of his ideas and their influence, doctoral dissertations, and curiosities (such as the proceedings of the London dinner held on the hundredth anniversary of the publication of *The Wealth of Nations*).

Thomas Malthus is represented by *An Essay on the Principle of Population* in the first edition, the 1803 revision, and more than a dozen later editions, as well as other works; the Public Catalog contains approximately 100 entries on Malthus, most dealing with his theory of population. Extensive holdings are also available on David Ricardo (130 Public Catalog entries for works by and about him); included are the first 3 and several later editions of his *Principles of Political Economy and Taxation*, a number of pamphlets in early editions, and critical studies. Also well represented are the works of such critics of the classical economists as Jean Charles Sismondi, Adam Müller, and Friedrich List.

Among later figures, the library's most extensive holdings are centered on Henry George and his theories. His daughter, Anna George de Mille, presented to the library the books and papers in her possession relating to her father in 1925; in subsequent years she added a number of items. Her daughter, Mrs. Agnes de Mille Prude, has continued to add to the collection. Numerous forms of material are represented. Manuscripts include Henry George's correspondence (1854–97); his diary (1855–96 with some intermissions); text and notes of lectures; the original draft of *Progress and Poverty*; and miscellaneous items. Correspondence received by Mrs. Henry George, the manuscripts (1881–1916) of Henry George, Jr., and some letters to Anna George de Mille supplement these papers. The largest holdings of published works are editions of *Progress and Poverty*: the first copy in print is present in the form of stereotype plate proofs of the first five books, pasted by the author into a municipal report. An interleaved copy of the book bears George's manuscript notes; there are numerous later editions and translations into Chinese, Dutch, Finnish, French, German, Italian, Norwegian, Russian, Spanish, and Swedish. First and later editions of George's other works are present, as well as some translations. Clippings from newspapers and periodicals fill 29 volumes (4 of them devoted to the New York mayoralty campaign of 1886); photographs and daguerreotypes show Henry George at various ages.

Although the library has also assembled an extensive amount of critical material (indicated by more than 150 entries on George in the Public Catalog, exclusive of those specifically on *Progress and Poverty*), it lacks some publications which would add significantly to the value of the resources: for example, the number of single tax publications is small, and files are generally incomplete.[1]

Extensive resources dealing with the economic history of individual countries are available; the number of cards in the Public Catalog under the heading "Economic history" with geographical subdivisions exceeds 28,000. The following entry count provides an indication of the quantity of material assembled on some major nations: Brazil—500, Canada—450, China—400, France—1,200, Germany—2,600, Great Britain—1,850, India—850, Indonesia—175, Italy—1,125, Japan—375, Mexico—375, Poland—375, Russia—1,600, Sweden—200, and the United States—5,400. Even the smaller and more recently developing states (for example, the Cameroons, Laos, and Uruguay) have between 10 and 50 references.

Among the newer phases of economics the Research Libraries have assembled a good collection on national planning for economic and social development; the exact nature of resources and

---

1. See Rollin Alger Sawyer, "Henry George and the Single Tax; A List of References to Material in The New York Public Library," *BNYPL* 30 (1926): 481–503 et seq. Published separately by the library. See also "Henry George Exhibition," *BNYPL* 31 (1927): 899–903.

their full extent is difficult to ascertain, because material is entered under several headings in the Public Catalog, all of which list other types of publications as well. Two such headings are "Cities—Plans" (many publications entered here deal primarily with planning on the local level) and "Regional Planning," but the bulk of material appears under the heading "Economic Policy." Important source materials are the texts of national development plans, most of them projections for goals to be reached in the five or ten years following their release (from about 1955 through the early 1980s); among the countries represented are Burma, Ecuador, Egypt, Guatemala, Jamaica, India, Kenya, Pakistan, Peru, Singapore, the Soviet Union, Trans-Jordan, Trinidad and Tobago, Turkey, and Yugoslavia. Under the same heading are found the reports of the missions of the International Bank for Reconstruction and Development, and the reports of such private consulting firms as Arthur D. Little, Inc., Robert R. Nathan Associates, Inc., and Development and Resources Corporation; supplementing these resources are several hundred studies, reports, and documents from AID (U. S. Agency for International Development) missions in specific countries, publications of the Inter-American Development Bank (IDB), and similar items appearing in the Public Catalog under the heading "Economic and Technical Assistance, American." The library's files of the journals devoted to this specialized area— among them *Planning and Development in the Netherlands*—are generally complete.

BANKING AND FINANCE, INCLUDING TAXATION AND INSURANCE

General materials on money, coins, and currency form a significant group, embracing early publications on and historical studies of money and prices in various countries, complete sets of the reports of the American and British mints, and proceedings of various monetary conferences. The library's collection of works on coins and paper currency and resources for the study of numismatics are discussed in chapter 28 of this *Guide*. There is a strong collection on prices, including comparative price indexes over the years and material on prices in foreign countries (chiefly European). More than 1,800 entries in the Public Catalog form an unusual index to information on prices by commodity or product— agricultural products, automobiles, books, gold, oranges, painting, paper, securities, etc. Entries under such headings as "Exchange, Foreign" and "Inflation and Deflation" locate related material.

The collection on banks and banking is excellent, with notable holdings in certain areas. Banking in the United States is well covered, with extensive files of journals which include, among others, *American Bank Reporter, Banking*, the publications of many state banking associations, and the reviews of business conditions issued by the twelve Federal Reserve banks. The history of commercial banking is also well documented, for the early years as well as the period since 1863 and the development of the Federal Reserve Banking System. The collection contains long files of the reports of state agencies which supervise banks, extending back over a century for such states as Connecticut, New Jersey, New York, Pennsylvania, and Rhode Island, and to the turn of the century for many others. However, the library has followed a highly selective policy

in acquiring material on individual banks; resources are generally limited to the annual reports of major New York and Chicago banks and of a few other institutions (for example, the Bank of America) principally for the postwar period, and published histories and miscellaneous titles appearing under the imprints of individual banks.

The Public Catalog lists approximately 4,500 titles on banks and banking in specific foreign countries. Especially notable in this area are the files (in most cases complete) of the bulletins and annual reports of foreign central banks and of the reports of national development banks in such countries as India, the Netherlands, Niger, Paraguay, the Philippines, and Tunisia. Holdings of general foreign serials are also good, with some titles existing in few other American libraries. Since 1945 the library has collected extensively the reports of individual foreign banks.

In recent years holdings in the field of international banking have expanded greatly. These include all publications of and significant items about the International Monetary Fund, the International Bank for Reconstruction and Development, the Bank for International Settlements, and regional development banks (e.g., African Development Bank, Central American Bank for Economic Integration, and Inter-American Development Bank). For such important current questions as the gold crisis, international liquidity, actions of the "Group of Ten," and Euro-dollars, the library attempts to secure all types and forms of publications wherever issued.

The Public Catalog contains more than 1,100 entries under the subject heading "Banks and Banking, Savings." They represent, in addition to general monographic works, such items as reports of state agencies dealing with savings banks, publications of the National Association of Mutual Savings Banks, and reports of state associations. Material about individual states is most abundant for New York and Massachusetts. A good collection of periodicals includes titles such as *World Thrift* and *The Savings Bank Journal*. Literature on savings banks abroad is most extensive for Australia, Germany, and Great Britain; an unusual group consists of the commemorative histories of approximately fifty Norwegian savings banks, the majority of which were issued for centennial observances.

Material on building and loan associations, while less extensive (500 entries in the Public Catalog), is comprised of publications of the United States Savings and Loan League and leagues in such states as New York, Illinois, Colorado, Montana, and Pennsylvania, and reports of state agencies which supervise these associations. Coverage of states in the latter category is selective. For foreign countries material is most extensive for Great Britain, as exemplified by a full set of the *Building Societies Year Book*.

The Economic and Public Affairs Division has not systematically collected specialized material relating to the financial structure of corporations (organization and reorganization plans, bylaws, indentures, mortgages, deeds, reports to the Securities and Exchange Commission, proxy statements, notices of annual and special meetings, registration statements, letters to stockholders, and the like) and maintains no special files of such material. However, the classified collection does contain annual reports (with some gaps) of major American corporations, generally from the 1920s through the mid-1950s; since 1956 the library has subscribed to the microform editions of the reports of all corporations listed on the major United States and (more recently) Canadian stock exchanges. In the past several years the library has also begun to acquire microform editions of annual reports of unlisted American and Canadian corporations. There is a large group of histories of individual business organizations, including a great many of the published versions of addresses given at the American Branch of the Newcomen Society.

Additional material on corporate finance includes Poor's and Moody's investment manuals (complete sets) and their foreign equivalents (extensive holdings). The collection of popular books on personal investing in securities is large, although most add little to existing knowledge in the field. General investment periodicals such as *Barron's, Financial World, Forbes*, and the *Magazine of Wall Street* are present and complete, but the high cost of investment advisory services has made it necessary for the library to subscribe only to some of the major ones: *Moody's Stock Survey* and *Bond Survey, The Outlook, United Business Service, Value Line Investment Survey*, and others of this type.

Holdings on government regulation of business are notable, embracing not only general monographs on actions against monopolies, cartels, and trusts, but also the decisions and reports of such regulatory agencies as the Federal Power Commission and Federal Trade Commission (for publications of the Interstate Commerce Commission and Civil Aeronautics Board, see chapter 37 of this *Guide*). Files of many state public utilities commissions reports are available and usually are complete or lack few numbers.

The Public Catalog contains over 1,200 entries on the subject of stock exchanges (in addition, the publications of individual exchanges are listed under specific names). Best covered, of course, is the New York Stock Exchange, for which files of the successive editions of the constitution and by-laws, the *Directory, Fact Book, Listing Statements* (beginning 1884), and *Report* are virtually complete; in all, there are more than 100 publications issued by the exchange itself. Similar titles are present for the American Stock Exchange, but the set of *Listing Applications* is incomplete. Less material is available on the regional exchanges. Holdings on the prices of American securities are very extensive. The library has assembled a nearly complete group of Securities and Exchange Commission publications, including its *Decisions and Reports* from the first issue.

The largest body of resources on foreign exchanges deals with London and Paris, but others represented include Amsterdam, Berlin, Bogotá, Buenos Aires, Copenhagen, Geneva, Hong Kong, Johannesburg, Madrid, Melbourne, Montreal, St. Petersburg (prior to 1917), Tokyo, Toronto, and Vienna. Material on stock prices makes it possible to furnish stock exchange quotations for many countries, in some cases (e.g., Belgium, France, Germany, India) on a daily basis, in others on a weekly or monthly basis.

Resources on American investment companies include Speaker's *The Investment Trust* (the first book published in the United States on the subject), other studies, and the numerous magazine articles which have appeared from the height of the popularity of trusts in the 1920s to the present. Also in the holdings are the hearings and reports of the Securities and Exchange Commission's investigations, the annual surveys compiled by Arthur Wiesenberger and Company, and the *Annual Report* and other publications of the Investment Company Institute, as well as the reports of the investment companies themselves. There is also material on foreign investment companies, especially British.[2]

The collection contains strong resources on public finance and taxation. A particularly notable feature consists of the financial reports of nearly all of the world's national governments and American states, generally for long spans of years. Sets for the United States federal government include the reports and other serials issued by the General Accounting Office, the Comptroller General, the Internal Revenue Service, and the Department of the Treasury. Holdings for political subdivisions outside the United States (provinces, states, cantons, etc.) are limited, with the best coverage given to Canadian provinces. Municipal finance is discussed in the political science section of the chapter on sociology.

The Public Catalog shows extensive holdings on the general subject of taxation: over 3,000 entries related to the United States and individual states, and over 3,500 related to specific foreign countries. Notable are historical publications, especially for such nations as France, Great Britain, the Netherlands, and the United States. Additional material appears under the entries on specific forms of taxation (e.g., some 1,800 entries on income tax and 3,300 entries on tariff); the library also catalogs materials on taxation as a subdivision under the subject taxed; for example, advertising, bread, church property, corporations, insurance, libraries, and water supply. Coverage of organizations dealing with taxes and tax questions is excellent; included are the publications of the National Tax Association, Tax Institute of America, Tax Foundation, and International Bureau of Fiscal Documentation, as well as those of current research programs, such as the Harvard Law School International Program in Taxation and the Joint Tax Program of the Organization of American States and the Inter-American Development Bank. The library has also assembled some special material, including fiscal codes, tariff statistics, several of the Commerce Clearing House tax services, and the reports and studies of state tax commissions and state equalization boards. The Manuscripts and Archives Division holds the papers of the American Free Trade League (1916–33).

Entries in the Public Catalog reveal substantial holdings on the general topic of insurance and for such subdivisions as agents, finance, government control, rates, risks, and taxation. In addition, approximately 7,600 references deal with special types of insurance, such as accident, bank depositors, burial, disability, disaster, fire, health, library, life, marine, mortgage, surety and fidelity, unemployment, and workmen's. Of these, the most extensively represented are health, life, and unemployment insurance. With some exceptions there is an adequate collection of material on insurance in various foreign countries.

Reference materials include such standard tools as *Insurance Periodicals Index, Insurance Almanac, Who's Who in Insurance*, and the various

---

2. See Gilbert A. Cam, "A Survey of the Literature on Investment Companies 1864–1957," *BNYPL* 62 (1958): 57–74. Published separately by the library, and reprinted 1964.

publications of the Best Company. Serial publications, both periodicals and the reports and proceedings of organizations, are well covered; for example, *Local Agent, National Underwriter*, and *Moniteur des assurances* (one of three sets in the United States), as well as publications from the American Association of University Teachers of Insurance, Institute of Life Insurance, and National Association of Insurance Commissioners are available. The library currently receives about 90 periodicals in the field. An interesting group consists of complete files of the proceedings and journals of such actuarial groups as the Institute of Actuaries, Faculty of Actuaries in Scotland, and the Institut des Actuaires Français, along with *Skandinavisk aktuarietidskrift*. The reports of state insurance departments are a notable feature; for a substantial majority of the states (the exceptions generally being in the south and west) the sets are complete or lack only a few early years.

The life insurance field includes material on such subjects as agents, finance, government control, investments, and rates, as well as popular books on buying life insurance. The published histories of individual companies are present, but their annual reports have not been collected extensively. On the whole there is little material about the industry in countries other than the United States. The resources on health insurance encompass a substantial block (both pro and con) on socialized medicine, in addition to official publications from countries and other political units having government-sponsored health plans, such as Saskatchewan and Great Britain.

INDUSTRIAL RELATIONS

The rich holdings on industrial relations embrace all those relationships evolving from the state of employment. In this area the collecting policy has long been comprehensive. Total holdings probably exceed 75,000 volumes, although the dispersion of resources makes it impossible to obtain a precise count. For bibliographic aids the library has acquired virtually every significant publication, including abstracts, bibliographies, guides to the literature, surveys and catalogs of library collections, and the like; for example, *International Labor Documentation* of the International Labor Office and its other bibliographies, the published catalog of the New York State School of Labor and Industrial Relations Library, the *Selected List of Recent Additions* to the U.S. Department of Labor Library, and the publications of the Committee of University Industrial Relations Librarians are all available. In addition, the library has acquired the bibliographic series issued by such university units as the New York State School of Industrial and Labor Relations at Cornell, the Institute of Industrial Relations at the University of California at Los Angeles, the A. B. Bush Library of the Industrial Relations Center at the University of Chicago, and the Institute of Labor and Industrial Relations at the University of Illinois.

The collection of general monographs contains nearly all standard and classic treatises—by such authors as Frank Tracy Carlton, John R. Commons, Samuel P. Orth and Selig Perlman—usually in the first edition and in every important subsequent edition. Journal files are also extensive and usually complete from the first volume; they include *Industrial and Labor Relations Review, Plebs, Revue française du travail* and *Sosialt arbeid*. The library also receives such services as the *Labor Relations Reporter* of the Bureau of National Affairs, *Government Employee Relations Report*, and *White Collar Report*.

The annual reports of U.S., state, and foreign departments and bureaus of labor form the most important element in the holdings of government publications in industrial relations, but also present are the findings of special labor commissions and other ad hoc investigations, the hearings and reports of legislative committees, decisions on arbitration and workmen's compensation, and texts of labor laws. On the whole, publications of the labor departments of the United States government, European national governments, and New York and other northeastern states are very well represented; those of other jurisdictions are covered selectively.

Holdings of material on labor issued by international organizations are substantial. The International Labor Organization is represented by more than 1,000 entries in the Public Catalog, comprised of numerous monographic studies and conference reports, full sets of periodicals such as *Industry and Labour* and *Industrial Safety Surveys*, the *Studies and Reports* (original and new series) and the *Reports* made to many individual countries under the Expanded Programme of Technical Assistance. These make up one of the largest collections of ILO documents in existence. Other organizations of this type which are strongly represented are the International Confederation of Free Trade Unions (ICFTU) and the Confederación de trabajadores de América latina (CTAL).

Resources for the study of labor unions form the strongest segment of this area of economics material, as indicated quantitatively by the fact that the Public Catalog contains over 8,500 entries under the heading "Trade Unions," of which about 3,700 refer to unions in specific industries and 2,500 to unions in various countries and states. Chronologically the collection begins with seventeenth-century publications from the European craftsman guilds. American holdings begin in the middle of the nineteenth century, with some of the earliest items from the National Labor Union, Knights of Labor, Cigar Makers International Union, and International Typographical Union. Particularly important as primary source materials are the official journals and convention proceedings of unions. Of the former the library possesses an extensive collection (approximately 600 different titles); many files cover a long span of years, but relatively few are complete. Examples of sets complete or lacking only a few early years include *The International Teamster, Graphic Arts Unionist, American Federationist, Railway Carmen's Journal*, and *UAW Solidarity*. Coverage of current journals is excellent; at present the library receives nearly all those issued (about 100 titles) by AFL/CIO unions, exclusive of those from state and local central bodies and joint councils. Holdings of convention proceedings cover many organizations (about 200 different unions), but gaps are present in the files, even when taking into account the fact that such proceedings are often printed in journals, rather than issued separately. Among the complete or nearly complete collections are those for the Amalgamated Clothing Workers, Congress of Industrial Organizations, International Association of Fire Fighters, National Maritime Union, Transport Workers Union, United Furniture Workers, and United Hatters, Cap, and Millinery Workers International Union. Still another important type of publication is the labor contract, which the library has selectively collected since 1955 for many industries and groups, among them actors, aircraft workers, atomic energy workers, bricklayers, civil service employees, department store employees, journalists, telephone employees, and television artists. Entries in the Public Catalog under the heading "Labor Contracts" subdivided by groups or industries provide a convenient listing of these resources. Although about 700 series appear there, the sets do not generally include all successive contracts between a company and a given union; in some cases the file consists of a single agreement, now superseded.

The Manuscripts and Archives Division has a large collection of memorabilia of Samuel Gompers, presented by the American Federation of Labor in 1925. Consisting primarily of scrapbook volumes, these resources include addresses, magazine articles, press statements, and biographical sketches. The period from 1917 to Gompers's death in December 1924 is especially full. Sixty-two volumes contain letters and telegrams addressed to Gompers on special occasions during his life; 3 volumes contain invitations and souvenirs; 27 scrapbook volumes contain newspaper clippings relating to the last few months of his life. More than 500 photographs document his life.

While the Research Libraries do not undertake to collect material about foreign trade unions on the comprehensive basis assumed for domestic organizations, they have assembled publications covering more than 50 foreign countries. The most extensive holdings deal with France, Germany, Great Britain, and the USSR. Recent acquisitions greatly augment resources on the twentieth-century labor movement in Japan; about 60 items, some of them issued to commemorate the tenth or fifteenth anniversary of the founding of a union, provide historical material on unions in such industries as electrical manufacturing, mining, paper, railroads, and steel, in addition to covering the union activities of civil servants.

The literature by and about employers and their activities in the area of industrial relations is not as extensive as that by and about labor groups; nonetheless the Research Libraries are strong in this field. Among early publications are several issued by the Manufacturers' and Business Men's Association of New York and the Providence Association of Mechanics and Manufacturers. Perhaps most important are the publications relating to the National Association of Manufacturers, well represented in the collections. They include not only such general items as the *Directory* and *Report*, but also the studies from such general units as the Government Economy Department. Industrial Relations Department, Money and Credit Committee, and Research Department. Also included are a few publications from state and local employers' associations.

In addition to the material described, the holdings in certain other phases of the field of industrial relations are also strong. Material on laborers —their wages, working conditions, industrial safety, housing, and the cost of living—is well represented. For instance, there are extensive resources relating to social security (about 1,600 entries in the Public Catalog under the heading "Insurance, Workmen's") and similar benefits; they encompass specialized periodicals, papers and proceedings of international congresses on social security, and the reports and other publications

of government agencies responsible in various countries for the administration of social security systems. Another substantial block of material treats the processes through which employees determine the conditions of employment. Although this embraces all phases of the collective bargaining process, holdings on industrial arbitration and conciliation are especially notable. There are files of such serials as *Arbitration News* and the *Proceedings* of the National Academy of Arbitrators, and publications of the National Labor Relations Board and of state boards of arbitration and mediation. Among the resources on arbitration abroad are particularly long runs of arbitration reports for Australia and New Zealand.

Significant manuscripts include the papers of the National Civic Federation, 1876–1948, which contain correspondence, financial records, material relating to the federation's annual meetings and to the activities of various "departments" of the NCF, and miscellaneous subject files. The Manuscripts and Archives Division also houses the records of the Society of Shipwrights and Caulkers of New York City, 1815–27, including the roll of members, constitution and bylaws, minutes, and financial data. A third interesting group consists of eleven volumes of handwritten minutes of meetings held from 1870 to 1917 by the New York Typographical Union No. 6, the oldest continuous union in the City. Two collections pertain to the International Ladies' Garment Workers Union: the papers (1919–62) of Fannia Cohn and those of Rose Pesotta, which cover the years 1922 to 1965. The former group (nineteen boxes) consists of correspondence, notes, writings, speeches, and other material relating to Miss Cohn's activities as a vice-president of the ILGWU and secretary of its Educational Department. Miss Pesotta's papers include letters, manuscripts of her published books, diaries for the years 1934 to 1949, reports, correspondence, and other material relating to the labor movement in general and specifically to the ILGWU, of which she was a vice-president. In addition, the personal papers of leading political figures and lawyers often provide information on industrial relations; the papers of Frank P. Walsh, for instance, bear on his work as chairman of the U.S. Commission on Industrial Relations from 1913 to 1915 (including correspondence by board members, reports by special investigators, testimony of witnesses, etc.), as well as on his work as lawyer for many labor unions, and his legal activities in regard to child labor. The papers of Norman Thomas (fully described in chapter 14 of this *Guide*) and of Gino Speranza, the lawyer and author, also provide useful insights to industrial relations. In the Schomburg Center are the archival records of the International Labor Defense and the National Negro Congress and its affiliates, including the Negro Industrial League and the Negro Labor Victory Committee.

COMMERCE

Extensive resources on commerce form a strong collection, including good holdings of publications on business abroad, as indicated by the fact that the Public Catalog contains about 900 entries under the heading "Commerce, Foreign" and more than 23,000 under "Commerce," subdivided by country. Of the latter group approximately 2,400 refer to Great Britain and 6,400 to the United States. General materials include large collections of publications of organizations such as the Committee for Economic Development and the National Industrial Conference Board. Several types of special material strengthen the resources in this area. Chamber of commerce publications form one such group: American and foreign organizations, chiefly those in cities of commercial importance, are represented, although the sets of titles discontinued a number of years ago are now chiefly of historical interest. Among the cities abroad for which the library has especially full files are Adelaide, Algiers, Bombay, Le Havre, London and Zurich; many additional cities are represented for shorter time spans. The collection also includes publications of American chambers of commerce in such foreign countries as Brazil, France, Japan, the Philippines, and Spain, and of foreign organizations in other countries such as the British Chamber of Commerce in Argentina and the Swiss Chamber of Commerce in France.

Holdings of house organs compose another important group. The collection contains about 1,600 titles, of which approximately 400 are currently received. The fact that many house organs ceased publication during the depression or war years explains, in part, the difference between the two figures. The library attempts to obtain only those publications containing material of substantive value; it does not collect those dealing chiefly or exclusively with news of company personnel. On the whole, the sets which are complete from the first volume and which extend over many years represent large American corporations in a variety of industries, among them the Chase Manhattan Bank, Chicago *Tribune*, Kaiser Aluminum, Norfolk and Western Railroad, and U.S. Steel; in some instances the collections contain the publications of more than one division—DuPont, Eastman Kodak, and General Electric are examples. Perhaps 10 or 15 percent of the total titles come from foreign companies, chiefly British, although there is a small number of magazines from Germany and Japan and one or two from each of a dozen other countries.

The publications of university schools of commerce and business administration, both serial and monographic, form another important class of materials in the resources on commerce. Examples of institutions represented include Harvard, Illinois, Kentucky, Michigan, Minnesota, Northwestern, Ohio State, Pennsylvania, and Stanford. The publications encompass studies from bureaus or institutes of business research, lecture series, entrepreneurial histories, proceedings and papers of conferences and symposia, and bibliographical compilations. Finally, long files of trade and commercial directories, both domestic and foreign, constitute another valuable holding. An interesting collection is a complete set of the catalogs of Sears, Roebuck and Company.

Resources on the South Sea Company form a substantial block of material, although they do not rival in extent the Bancroft collection at Harvard University's Kress Library.[3] About 250 entries in the Public Catalog represent both eighteenth-century and later publications. More than 130 items compose the former group, which begins in 1711

with such titles as Daniel Defoe's *True State of the Case between the Government, and the Creditors of the Navy*, Herman Moll's *View of the Coasts, Countries and Islands within the Limits of the South-Sea-Company*, and *A True State of The South-Sea-Scheme*. Holdings are well distributed over the remainder of the century, and for several titles the library possesses one of only a few known copies. Of modern publications are monographs like John Carswell's *The South Sea Bubble* (1960) and articles which have appeared in such serials as *Journal of Economic and Business History, Political Science Quarterly*, and *Hispanic American Historical Review*. The Prints Division has a collection of over 100 caricatures and broadsides dealing with the South Sea and Mississippi Companies. The largest number are Dutch, followed by English and French materials; many date from 1710 to 1720. The Research Libraries contain more than 200 publications by and about the Hudson's Bay Company. They include its annual report since the turn of the century (with some gaps), published documents from the British Colonial Office, legal materials on the boundaries of Ontario, and accounts of early life in northern Canada.

Of the special phases of business literature not already mentioned, accounting has probably received most attention. The Research Libraries have acquired the standard bibliographies and indexes and some foreign, as well as the most important American, journals on the topic. The publications of the American Institute of Certified Public Accountants and of some state societies are present, while a group of early American accounting and bookkeeping titles forms a small but interesting historical assemblage. Publications on auditing, cost accounting, depreciation, and accounting for special industries (e.g., agriculture, automobiles, corporations, hotels, petroleum) are also available.

For other phases of business and commerce the Research Libraries collect more selectively. In the area of sales literature substantial holdings on special fields such as real estate or retail trade complement general publications on salesmanship and the psychology of selling; also included are many titles of the self-help variety, but on the whole little foreign language material. Resources on personnel cover not only current domestic and foreign practices but are also useful in tracing their evolution. There has been no attempt to assemble a strong collection on business education, but some publications on this subject are held.

Although the Manuscripts and Archives Division does not actively collect records of modern corporations, it has a considerable amount of material on the merchants and entrepreneurs of the eighteenth and nineteenth centuries. Among the manuscript groups of substantial size are the following: 18 mercantile account books relating mainly to the general business affairs of the Van Cortlandts and other merchants and ranging in date between 1700 and 1839; a large quantity of land papers, ledgers, account books, and other material from about 1780 to the late nineteenth century from various members of the Gansevoort family;[4] papers, account books, and shipping papers (1774–1803) of William Constable, Revolutionary War officer, merchant, and land pro-

3. See John G. Sperling, *The South Sea Company; An Historical Essay and Bibliographical Finding List* (Boston: Baker Library, Harvard Graduate School of Business Administration, 1962).

4. See *BNYPL* 24 (1920): 125.

moter (25 volumes and 31 boxes);[5] papers, letters, accounts, land papers, maps, memoranda, etc. of Isaac Bronson (1760–1838) and of his sons, Arthur, Fredric, and Oliver on their business activities in banking, land speculation and promotion of westward expansion from about 1796 to 1868 (207 boxes); personal and mercantile account books, (1830–70) of William E. Dodge (2 boxes), and papers (1818–59) of Phelps and Peck—later Phelps, Dodge and Company (30 boxes); papers, ledgers, and other financial records of Moses Taylor, of his firm, Moses Taylor and Company, and of other commercial undertakings with which he was associated, covering the period from 1832 to 1888 (approximately 1,100 volumes and 200 cartons of unbound papers);[6] and a great many additional letters, order books, and financial records (usually in small quantities for individual merchants and their firms) from the end of the eighteenth to the twentieth century from such New York City organizations as Brown Brothers,[7] Gouverneur and Kemble, Hill and Ogden, Willets and Seamans, Seth Low and Company, Lott and Troup, Nevins and Company, and Fisher, Blashfield and Company. In addition, the Manuscripts and Archives Division keeps together account books of individual merchants and firms which are unrelated to larger manuscript groups (the majority of such holdings date from the nineteenth century). Among them the Virginia group (approximately 81 volumes) consists of the records (1770–1877) of the general merchants successively known as Hooe, Stone and Company, Jenifer and Hooe, Hooe and Harrison, Robert T. Hooe and Company, Lawrason and Fowle, and William Fowle and Son. There are numerous account books from New York, but such other states as California, Illinois, Indiana, and Massachusetts are also represented.[8] Additional materials are noted in the description of Manuscripts and Archives Division resources.

ADVERTISING

The collection is strong in the history of advertising, with standard works by such writers as Henry Rush Boss, Edgar Robert Jones, Frank

Spencer Presbrey, Henry Sampson, and Playsted Wood, and the reminiscences of Leo Burnett, Claude C. Hopkins, Albert D. Lasker, David Ogilvy, James Webb Young, and others. Documentary materials for the study of actual advertisements go back to the seventeenth century with files of *The London Gazette* and *The Athenian Mercury*[9] and continue to the present; useful for a study of the second decade of the century is a *Collection of Advertising Pages from American Magazines*, the contents coming from such periodicals as *American Magazine, Century, Harper's, Literary Digest, Review of Reviews, Scribner's,* and *Woman's Home Companion* for the years 1911 to 1921.

General materials include the publications of such organizations as the American Marketing Association, Advertising Council, Advertising Federation of America, Advertising Research Foundation, and Association of National Advertisers. Also present are the proceedings and other publications of the American Association of Advertising Agencies. Numerous texts cover the basic and advanced theory of advertising (including case materials), as well as advertising psychology. An interesting group consists of more than 800 titles on advertising individual products and services; for example, alcoholic drinks, automobiles, banks, drugs, hotels and restaurants, libraries, petroleum, and the tourist industry.

Periodical resources are also strong; basic titles such as *Advertising Agency, Journal of Marketing, Mediascope, Printers' Ink*, and *Tide* are complete, as are many serving special segments of the profession, such as *Journal of Retailing, Reporter of Direct Mail Advertising*, and *Sponsor*. Currently the Research Libraries subscribe to 84 periodicals in the field, including titles from Canada, Great Britain, France, Germany, and the Netherlands, and to such services as *Leading National Advertisers, Standard Rate and Data*, and the *Standard Directory of Advertisers*.

The Research Libraries collect all kinds of general consumer market surveys made by newspapers, magazines, and other media, but subscribe to only some of the specialized services offered by firms which undertake market analysis research. Current issues of some general surveys are housed in the Vertical File of the Economic and Public Affairs Division; a selection of useful but superseded studies is retained and added to the cataloged collection.

---

5. See *BNYPL* 47 (1943): 93; 48 (1944): 402.
6. See Wilmer R. Leech, "The Moses Taylor Papers," *BNYPL* 35 (1931): 259–61.
7. See Victor Hugo Paltsits, "Business Records of Brown Brothers & Co., New York—1825–1880," *BNYPL* 40 (1936): 495–98.
8. For a complete listing see the *Dictionary Catalog of the Manuscript Division*, 2 vols. (Boston: G. K. Hall & Co., 1967) 1: 1–9.

---

9. See Harold C. Whitford, "Expos'd to Sale; The Marketing of Goods and Services in Seventeenth-Century England," *BNYPL* 71 (1967): 496–515 et seq.

36

GOVERNMENT PUBLICATIONS

HISTORICAL SURVEY

Government publications (or public documents; the terms are used interchangeably throughout this *Guide*) have always been an outstanding feature of the library's collections. Their importance

as sources of many kinds of information was recognized from the beginning. That part of the collection of public documents not specifically classed by subject numbers 350,000 volumes. Administered by the Economic and Public Affairs Division, it has been assigned the class mark *S in the Billings Classification Schedule. There are, in addition, many other volumes of public documents in the collections which have been classified in nearly every subject area of the library. Several of these areas are extensive: law, with its long files of session laws; the Patents Collection, made up almost entirely of official government publications; and the extremely important and extensive collection of official census and statistical reports. A conservative calculation of the number of public documents outside the *S class mark is in excess of 700,000 volumes, twice the number to be found within the class mark.

The Research Libraries attempt to collect and retain permanently all important publications in their subject fields of interest issued by international governmental agencies, and by the national, state, and provincial governments of all countries. Municipal documents are collected with limitations described in a following paragraph. Certain categories of public documents are not usually acquired:

1. Intra-agency documents of importance only for internal operations and management.
2. Press releases (except those of the White House and a few other agencies of the United States; and of the Governor of New York State).
3. Minor educational materials, or other items of temporary use or ephemeral nature.
4. Documents having security classifications.

Book counts and estimates taken by the library have always included only those public documents within the *S class mark. The following tabulation of the library's document holdings, therefore, gives only a partial picture of the growth of the holdings since 1897, when a public documents collection was first organized:

1897	10,000*
1921	86,802**
1930	120,331**
1941	162,000*
1966	350,000**

(*Estimated figure; **Census figure)

Dr. Cogswell of the Astor Library predicted the value of public documents in supplying current information, as well as historical data. His point of view may have resulted from the necessity of meeting the interests of the New York public which the Astor Library served—the pressure of finding information about conditions both here and abroad for commercial, industrial, and cultural uses—but whatever the cause, as early as 1851 he observed, in his Annual Report, the "great number of important and costly scientific, statistical and historical works . . . which we might have gratuitously. . . . " from various governments.[1]

In the same year Cogswell recorded the receipt of copies of all volumes on hand of documentary history published by the British Record Commission, and of important statistical works issued by the Danish government. By 1879 it was routinely stated that the Astor Library had received British documents relating to India and official publications from New Zealand, New South Wales, Canada, France, Italy, and Prussia.

American public documents were not neglected by either of the foundation libraries. Early legislative publications were collected primarily during 1893 and 1894, when the Lenox Library made extensive purchases of American law and legislative journals from the library of Dr. George H. Moore. The Astor Library also had some early and rare materials in this field, notably in the Ford collection. But previous to this Cogswell had started seeking contemporary publications as well. In 1854, Albany contributed an extensive selection of New York state documents, and the Maine legislature passed a resolution directing the Secretary of State to forward complete sets of state documents. Massachusetts took similar action in 1856. These were the beginnings of the library's ordered plan to secure important material as it appeared, and by 1902 the documents from these states and from New Jersey, Indiana, and Pennsylvania were complete.

In the library's 1909 Annual Report is an excellent survey of public documents. Much of the general information provided is applicable today, since the library has kept well abreast in this field.

The major subject areas in which the library now collects government publications comprehensively are business, the social sciences (with special emphasis on economics, government, and international affairs), and the physical, chemical, and engineering sciences. Few public documents in the medical and natural sciences are collected, since the library does not specialize in these fields. Originally legal literature was considered primarily of interest to the law student and to the lawyer, and was accordingly left to the university and the special law library for cultivation. The realization that law is not a thing apart but a definite aspect of the social and historical picture of any political unit has resulted in the strengthening of the collections bearing on statutory law. The Research Libraries also selectively collect the law reports or court decisions of U.S. federal courts and New York State courts of record. The library's resources and acquisition policy in the field of law are more fully discussed in chapter 37 of this Guide.

The library's holdings of official gazettes or newspapers have always been of exceptional strength for most countries of the world. In 1956 the library began to preserve its files on microfilm, and by 1969 had been successful in acquiring and filming current issues of most titles. Relatively little has been accomplished, however, in the attempt to preserve holdings prior to the late 1950s.

The library is a depository for the publications of the United Nations and other international agencies and for the federal government publications of the United States and Canada. In addition, the library is a depository for the state publications of New York, California, and Washington. There is a vast collection of public documents, federal, state, and to a lesser degree municipal, received by the library from most of the countries of the world.

CATALOGS

At present all government publications retained by the library are fully cataloged, with the exception of very minor material. Many important documents are given author and subject entries as well as serial entries. In recent years, however,

---

1. It should be noted, in passing, that the proportion of government publications received free of charge has been decreasing steadily since 1945.

more and more reliance has been placed on published indexes for a subject approach to documents. There are some cards for government publications in most division catalogs, but filing rules are not the same everywhere. Therefore the reader is advised to ascertain that he understands the rules for the catalog he is using; if he does not, he is urged to seek the aid of the reference librarians.

The main listing for government publications in the Research Libraries is found in the Catalog of Government Publications located in the Economic and Public Affairs Division and in book form. This is basically a corporate-author file with no cards for subjects or personal names. The listings for serials and nonserials (monographs) are separated under each corporate entry. First are the serials, arranged in alphabetical order by title, followed by the nonserials, chronologically arranged by date of publication. This arrangement is considered an aid to ready reference, for a preponderance of the titles begin with commonplace words or form phrases which would necessitate a tedious search through a strictly alphabetical arrangement.

RESOURCES IN GOVERNMENT PUBLICATIONS

There are in actuality two collections of government publications in the Research Libraries. The first consists of administrative publications, legislative proceedings, sessional papers, government directories, etc. of various nations, states, and cities, and such general materials as are not easily classifiable by subject. This collection is classed as *S in the Billings Classification Schedule and is administered by the Economic and Public Affairs Division. Although current practice is to classify an increasingly large percentage of government publications elsewhere, this class mark covers some 350,000 volumes and remains important.

The second group of public documents includes census reports, patents, session laws, and other materials identified by subject, such as geological surveys, meteorological reports, etc. This group of over 700,000 volumes is located in the various divisions and collections of the library. In the following analysis of the public document resources of the library, reference will be made only to those portions of the *S class mark which are in active use at the time of this writing, and certain rarities primarily in the Rare Book Division (*K class mark).

BIBLIOGRAPHY

Bibliographical materials classed in *S consist only of publications originating from governmental agencies, and consequently do not include much material dealing with public documents but classed under subject. All Library of Congress bibliographical publications are included. Official records of material published, such as the Library of Congress *Official Catalog of Publications* and similar publications from other national agencies, form a second class of bibliographical tool. A third is catalogs of accessions of governmental agencies; notable examples are the catalogs of the Canadian Parliament from 1862 and the Danish Kongelige Bibliothek from 1901. This class of materials includes some accession records of the Library of Congress and the state libraries.

ARCHIVES

Only material about archives is included: dissertations, indexes, lists, etc. Typical of the latter are the *Lists and Indexes* of the British Public Record Office and the *Press List of Ancient Documents* of the India Record Department. Reprinted archives are classed with subject materials.

OFFICIAL GAZETTES (Government Newspapers)

This is an exceptionally strong feature of the holdings; the importance of government newspapers in establishing the historical record of any country cannot be overestimated. The Gazettes Microfilming Project, started in 1956, continues.[2] Unfortunately, gazettes are usually printed on the cheapest paper stock and, unless an effort at preservation is quickly made, they rapidly deteriorate. The library's Gazettes Microfilming Project attempts to record these materials on microfilm as they become available. The following titles serve merely as examples; in no case should it be assumed that the file is complete, as for the most part, they are not. But among those cited, the representation is substantial.

The *London Gazette* is complete from its beginning as the *Oxford Gazette* in 1665. The files of the *Dublin Gazette*—continued by the *Belfast Gazette* and by the *Iris oifigiuil*—and of the *Edinburgh Gazette* both commence about the turn of the century.

Continental European countries are well represented. The French *Journal officiel* commences in 1789; the Spanish *Gaceta de Madrid*, in 1808; the Italian *Gazzetta ufficiale*, in 1861; the German *Reichs-Anzeiger*, in 1875. Among smaller countries, the Netherlands *Staats-Courant* begins in 1813; the Belgian *Moniteur Belge*, in 1831; the Swiss *Bundesblatt*, in 1848; the Rumanian *Monitorul oficial*, in 1896. Russian, Greek, and Bulgarian gazettes are included. The smaller French and German districts and states are well represented.

Asiatic materials include the *Gazette of India*, which commences in 1912, and strong holdings for the individual Indian states. Among other Asian gazettes are the Hong Kong *Government Gazette* from 1909; the Straits Settlements *Government Gazette* from 1909 (continued by the Singapore *Government Gazette* from 1958); and the Federated Malay States *Government Gazette* from 1909 (continued by the Malaysia *His Majesty's Government Gazette* from 1963). Other titles include the Goa *Boletim oficial* from 1906 (continued by the Goa, Daman, and Diu *Government Gazette; Boletim oficial* from 1961), the Macao *Boletim oficial* from 1930, and the French Indo-China *Journal officiel* from 1889 (continued in part by the Viet Nam *Công-Báo Viet-Nam Công-Hoa* from 1955). China is represented by *King Paon* (in Chinese) from 1885 to 1899, and the *Translation of the Peking Gazette* (1872–99).

The library has always recognized the political importance of Africa. There is unusual strength in the gazettes of the former colonial governments of that continent. Although repeated attempts have been made to obtain complete files

---

2. See James W. Henderson, "The Acquisition and Preservation of Foreign Official Gazettes," *Farmington Plan Newsletter* 31 (May, 1970): 1–24.

of the gazettes of the newly independent states, there has been only varying success (many of these are held by the Schomburg Center in microfilm copies). The Belgian Congo *Bulletin administratif* begins in 1912, while the *Bulletin officiel* of the Congo is nearly complete from 1855. They are succeeded by the *Moniteur congolais* (Kinshasa, 1960–) and the *Journal officiel de la République du Congo* (Brazzaville, 1958–). The library's holdings of the gazettes of former British colonies are of exceptional completeness up to the time of independence; after independence they are as complete as it has been possible to make them. The Portuguese Mozambique *Boletim oficial* begins in 1921, and the Guinea *Journal officiel* from 1906; both are continued by the gazettes of the newly independent nations. South Africa is equally well represented from 1910 by the *Government Gazette* under the Union and the *Staatskoerant* under the Republic. An unusual title in this field is the gazette of the British administration of the Transvaal (1878–79) before it was returned to the Dutch.

The American continents are well covered. The *Canadian Gazette* commences in 1881; most of the provinces have excellent files. The Mexican official newspaper, under various titles, is more or less continuous from 1805; those of the Mexican states vary. South American republics have, in some instances, good representations at the national level (for example the Argentine *Boletín oficial* from 1899, and the Brazil *Diário oficial* from 1900) but relatively little for smaller political subdivisions.

OFFICIAL AND NONOFFICIAL DIRECTORIES

This is another strong group. Among the longer sets United States directories and registers are substantially complete; those of the states are held in strength. Such directories and manuals as have been issued by cities are also present, as far as the library has been able to collect them—the Boston *Municipal Register*, from 1840; the Newark (N.J.) *Manual*, from 1872; and others.

For the rest of the world, a few outstanding titles issued by nations, provinces, and cities will perhaps be suggestive: Australia's *Yearbook of Australia*, from 1885; Belgium's *Almanach royal officiel*, from 1841; the Canadian *Parliamentary Companion* (later, *Guide*), from 1867; the Netherland East Indies *Regeering Almanak*, from 1822; France's *Almanach national* (previously *royal*), from 1708; Great Britain's *Colonial List*, from 1879, and the India Office's *India List*, from 1813; Jamaica's *Handbook*, from 1882; the Netherlands *Jaarboekje*, from 1833; Prague's *Almanach hlavního mesta Prahy*, from 1898; Sardinia's *Calendario generale*, from 1824–47; the Swedish *Sveriges och Norriges Calender*, from 1779. Though many of these files are incomplete, most of them are substantial and lack few numbers.

NATIONAL AND STATE GOVERNMENT PUBLICATIONS

In the following description, as elsewhere in this *Guide*, specific titles are mentioned; they are intended to be suggestive of types of material present, rather than to emphasize the importance of those particular titles. Throughout the discussion the commencing date of the library's file is provided, seldom with any indication if the file is absolutely complete or whether it is current; files cited are generally very substantial, if

not complete. Only original publications are taken into account. In many instances where these are lacking—particularly the early volumes—there are compilations, reprints, etc., which the library generally has; it would be incorrect to assume that the library does not have the legislative proceedings of any given country if the date noted in this description happens to be later than the initial volume.

United States: Federal, State, and Colonial

This is one of the finest collections in the library, and detailed description is unnecessary. As a depository library for U.S. federal government publications since 1884, the library has received materials so distributed. The library also has been receiving the Readex Microprint edition (opaque microforms) of all nondepository items listed in the Monthly Catalog of U.S. Government Publications since 1953 and all depository items listed since 1956. The library is a depository library for the state publications of New York, California, and Washington. There is a strong representation of the publications of other states; the federal district; and the outlying territories and areas from the earliest periods of publication.

Rare materials in the Rare Book Division include documents published by the federal government through the first fourteen congresses, those of the thirteen original states through 1800, and those of territories to the date of admission as states. The collection of contemporaneously printed federal documents from 1789 to 1817, while not bibliographically complete, is nevertheless of major importance. There is also a notable group of documents published by the Confederate States of America and by the separate states of the Confederacy.

The British Commonwealth of Nations

This is another extensive collection. The library's set of *Parliamentary Papers* for the years 1731 to 1800 (slightly incomplete for the earlier years) is one of a small number of sets in the United States.[3] The files of *Parliamentary Debates* are complete. Publications common to former crown colonies—*Gazette*, *Bluebook*, Legislative Council *Minutes and Debates*, and the various reports in collected or separate form—are a notable feature; the library's files of the "Bluebooks" usually commence about the turn of the century. Dominion publications, as well as those of their component states, and *Debates* are held in strength. Special mention may be given India and Pakistan, as the library has substantial runs of the administrative reports of the various states, under both English and native rule, and there are substantial files of the legislative proceedings of the states. *Selections from the Records* of the various Indic states is noteworthy.

Other European Countries

These form an excellent representation. The library has made a particular effort to obtain the

---

3. See "British Parliamentary Papers: Catalogues and Indexes," and H. H. Bellot, "Parliamentary Printing, 1660–1837," *Bulletin* of the Institute of Historical Research, London University 11 (1933): 24–30, 85–98.

documents of new countries emerging in the aftermath of World Wars I and II. The legislative proceedings of France are virtually complete, as are those of Germany. Following are a few other important series: the Spanish Cortes *Diario*, from 1810, and that of the Diputados, from 1834–35; the Norwegian Stortinget *Forhandlinger* is complete from 1814, and the Danish Rigsdagen *Forhandlinger*, from 1850. The Netherlands Staaten-General *Verslag* commences with 1814–15. The Swiss Bundesrath *Bericht* commences in 1864. The various publications of the Finnish Eduskunta make an almost continuous file from 1809. The Czechoslovakian parliamentary proceedings and documents are complete, as is the Stenographic Report of the Polish Parliament. European state and provincial documents vary in their representation considerably. Those of the French departments and the German state legislative proceedings are comparatively negligible; the Italian provincial publications, on the other hand, are an outstanding feature, as are those of the Netherlands—*Verslag van den toestand, Notulen*, and *Provincialblad* (common to all Dutch provincial governments)—usually commencing with the printing. The Zeeland *Notulen* dates from 1590.

Asia

This is not a large group; it is most notable for strong holdings of gazettes, mentioned in an earlier paragraph.

Latin America

Although less systematic than those of other countries, the collections of legislative proceedings and reports from this area of the world are, on the whole, good. It has proved most difficult to secure publications from the countries to the south. A few of the longer files include the Mexican *Diario*, from 1793; the Argentine *Diario de sesiones*, from 1854; the Brazil *Annaes*, from 1849–50; the Chile *Boletin*, from 1866; the Paraguay *Registro oficial*, from 1869–75; and the Uruguay *Diario*, from 1830. The collections also include much material in reprint; thus, the Bolivian *Redactor del H. Congreso nacional* commences with 1825. The Schomburg Center Kurt Fisher collection contains strong holdings of Haitian documents, including presidential proclamations and numerous other printed and manuscript records, from the time of the French Revolution.

MUNICIPAL DOCUMENTS

These constitute one of the unusual collections of the library, relating both to government and local history. Municipal documents are such a highly specialized type of material that any extended description of the content of this class would become a catalog. An outline of the present collecting policy in this field follows:

1. Cities of the United States: The Research Libraries attempt to collect and permanently retain all current publications in the subject fields of their interest that are issued by the governments of cities in the United States: (a) with populations of 400,000 or more; (b) with populations of less than 400,000 but having some special significance for geographical or other reasons, e.g., Anchor-age, Alaska; and (c) with populations of 50,000 or more in New York state, New Jersey and Connecticut.

   Materials in the following categories are to be excluded: (a) intra-agency documents of importance only for internal operations and management; (b) press releases (except those of the Mayor of New York City); (c) minor educational materials or other items of temporary use or ephemeral nature; and (d) legislative bills (but legislative bills for New York City are acquired and added to the permanent collections).

2. Cities outside the United States: The Research Libraries attempt to collect and permanently retain publications of research value in the subject fields of their interest that are issued by the following groups of cities: (a) for cities in Canada, and Central and South America with populations of 250,000; (b) for all cities with populations of 500,000 or more in other parts of the world; and (c) for smaller cities which have some special significance by virtue of being the capital or the largest city in a small country or for other reasons, as determined by the Documents Librarian. These include proceedings of legislative bodies, reports of executive agencies, periodicals, and significant monographs and reports of special surveys or commissions.

3. Inter-city agencies: The Research Libraries attempt to collect and permanently retain publications of research value in the subject fields of their interest that are issued by inter-county and inter-city authorities or agencies involving cities with populations of one million or more.

The present collecting policy for municipal documents varies in some respects from the policy as it has developed over the years. It should be noted that in 1941 the collecting policy for municipal documents called for the acquisition of materials from American and Canadian cities of 30,000 population or more, and from foreign cities of 200,000 or more. New York state municipal documents are unusually strong; those of New York City constitute a rich collection. Other than New York, the library's first effort has been to secure the "collected documents," though few cities outside the New England area now issue such publications. The proceedings of the council or similar legislative body, the ordinances, and the municipal gazette (if published) are sought. To name but a few files of proceedings of more important cities are those of Baltimore, from 1869; Boston, from 1853; Chicago, from 1870; Cleveland, from 1874; Indianapolis, from 1891; Philadelphia, from 1857; and St. Louis, from 1859.

The library's collection of American municipal charters is of unusual importance.[4] County documents are collected in the fields of the library's interest issued by counties in New York State, New Jersey, Connecticut, and a few of the largest metropolitan areas across the nation. The supervisors' journals of New York state counties constitute a very strong feature. Although not ac-

---

4. "List of City Charters, Ordinances, and Collected Documents in The New York Public Library," *BNYPL* 16 (1912): 631–719 et seq. American and foreign municipalities are included.

tively collected, the representations from many New England counties and towns are interesting.

European municipalities are well represented, especially larger ones such as London, Paris, Berlin, Vienna, and Rome. There is a variation in the resources by country. German cities have long files of *Verwaltungsberichte, Haushaltspläne,* as well as some of the *Verhandlungen* of the local Rat. French municipalities are well represented. The older files of Italian cities are good, but recent material is often lacking. Swiss and Dutch series are strong. Outside Madrid, Spanish materials are weak; the Scandinavian holdings are irregular.

37

TRANSPORTATION AND COMMUNICATION

TRANSPORTATION

Responsibility for the subject of transportation —which is collected comprehensively—is shared primarily by the Science and Technology Research Center and the Economic and Public Affairs Division. There is a particularly strong collection of periodicals and related government publications from most countries; the total book resources number approximately 115,600 items. These are supplemented by index entries in the catalogs for periodical articles; this practice is at present limited to those periodicals not included in the standard commercial indexes. A collection of pictorial material on transportation is mounted in scrapbooks in the Science and Technology Research Center; reference should also be made to the resources of prints, photographs, drawings, and other pictorial materials in various locations in the Research Libraries. Under the broad heading of transportation, railways are perhaps the category most fully covered.

BICYCLES

Bicycles are adequately covered as a subject, with emphasis on periodicals. There is also material on motorcycles and motorcycle racing. An extensive collection on bicycling made by Luther H. Porter was given to the library by the Newark Public Library in 1924.

AUTOMOBILES

The resources on the automobile include an extensive collection of manufacturers' catalogs and price lists numbering in excess of 8,000 pieces, and covering the first three decades of this century. Most American and many foreign makes are represented. This archive is in the Science and Technology Research Center; a listing of available materials is held at the center's inquiry desk. The tremendous proliferation of these catalogs after the 1930s precluded further acquisition by the center, which now relies upon commercial publications and manuals to furnish required information. Resources for the study of the technological aspects of the automobile are further discussed in the mechanical engineering section of chapter 57 of this *Guide.*

RAILROADS

Numbering over 50,000 volumes, this subject is one of the rich resources of the library with good world coverage and considerable depth. Particular emphasis has been placed upon the great age of the railroads in the United States from their beginnings to the end of World War I.[1] The preponderance of material is in the general collections, with some technical works in the Science and Technology Research Center.

Railroads are a subject long of interest to the library. Some materials came to the library with the Tilden collection; in 1906 Dr. Billings reported that the library was strong in official statistical reports in this field. Gifts of materials from the various railroad companies and from private individuals have enriched the holdings. The Parsons collection in the Science and Technology Research Center contains railroad materials including a set of early Bradshaws.[2] The William John Wilgus collection is made up of books, scrapbooks, and other material on engineering subjects including transportation; it is housed in the Science and Technology Research Center.[3] The papers of Bion J. Arnold, William Barclay Parsons, Frank Julian Sprague, Timothy Shaler Williams, and others in the Manuscripts and Archives Division include documentation on the AEF Transportation Corps in World War I, the New York Central Railroad, the Rapid Transit Commission in New York City, the electric trolley, the electrification of railroads, and other related subjects. The papers of Robert Brewster Stanton consist in part of his survey of the Grand Canyon made for the Denver, Colorado Cañon and Pacific Railroad from 1889 to 1890.[4]

Serial publications on railroads are strong, with substantial if not complete files of important journals from many countries, and good historical coverage. There are such titles as *Zeitschrift für Eisenbahnen und Dampfschiffahrt der österreichisch-ungarischen Monarchie* (1888–97), the French *Journal des chemins de fers* (1842–

---

1. See "Check List of Works Relating to Street Railways, Rapid Transit, etc., in the City of New York in The New York Public Library," *BNYPL* 5 (1901): 160–62; "List of Works in The New York Public Library Relating to Government Control of Railroads, Rates, Regulation, etc.," *BNYPL* 10 (1906): 184–209, published separately by the library.

2. See "Catalogue of the William Barclay Parsons Collection," *BNYPL* 45 (1941): 95–108 et seq. Published separately by the library.

3. See *BNYPL* 42 (1938): 40.

4. See Victor Hugo Paltsits, "Robert Brewster Stanton, Engineer, and His Work on the Colorado River," *BNYPL* 38 (1934): 991–93.

1940) and *Chemins de fer* (1951–); the German *Organ für die Fortschritte des Eisenbahnwesens* (1846–1944) and *ETR; Eisenbahntechnische Rundschau* (1952–); the British *Railway Times* (1838–1914) and *Railway Gazette* (1906–); and the *American Railway Review* (1859–62) and *Railway Age Gazette* (1870–); as well as others which commenced in the 1870s and 1880s. Other short files of periodicals that appeared in earlier decades beginning with the 1840s are also present. Another type of administrative and technical serial publication, the proceedings of unions, associations, congresses, etc., is very well represented, as are railway employees' magazines. The official publications of federal, state, and municipal governments also constitute a strong feature. The file of the *Official Guide of the Railways and Steam Navigation Lines of the United States, Porto Rico and Mexico and Cuba* is virtually complete. Annual reports of railroad companies, especially those in the United States, are noteworthy if not always complete. Since 1956 the Economic and Public Affairs Division has made available on opaque microforms the annual reports of those railroad companies whose stocks are listed on the major American and Canadian exchanges.

All aspects of the railroad, including the financial and technical, are covered in the library's holdings. Headings in the Public Catalog range from "Railways—Abandonment—U.S." to "Railways—Yearbooks." The resources for electric railways include contract specifications for construction for the New York City Transportation Board. A splendid exhibition mounted by the Science and Technology Research Center in 1967, entitled "The Rise and Fall of the Elevated Railroad 1867–1967," displayed the library's wealth of printed and pictorial resources. In 1968 the donation of the Walter Weichsel transfer collection added an extensive array of bus and streetcar transfers, ferry and toll tickets, passes, etc., for the United States and the larger nations of the world.

One of the most significant aspects of this collection is the vast amount of pamphlet material, much of which might be considered ephemeral. This includes reports of legal cases involving railroads, indentures, mortgages, manuals of operation, promotional and tourist materials, and labor contracts, among other items. The greater part of this material is American, issued prior to World War II.

MERCHANT MARINE

This is a generally strong section. The collection of books and pamphlets is extensive and particularly interesting for its early material. Important features include long files of serial publications, both journals and shipping registers, and a strong representation of government reports on shipping from all parts of the world. The current years of such important registers as *Lloyd's Register of Shipping* (1842/43–), *Bureau veritas* (1905–), and *Record of the American Bureau of Shipping* (1870–) are kept in the Main Reading Room; back issues form part of the general collections. Most of the material is entered in the Public Catalog under the subject heading "Shipping" and its subdivisions.

The Science and Technology Research Center holds technical material on shipbuilding and can provide information on the sources of illustra-

tions of ships and portraits of ships' captains through its Ships Index card file. Related materials appear in various other subject classes in the library, the most important, perhaps, being the rich collection of coast pilots and sailing directions described in chapter 44 of this *Guide*. Laws and official reports and regulations are supplemented by the strong collections classed with law materials and public documents. Materials classed with nautical art and science are also valuable.

The Manuscripts and Archives Division's Robert Fulton collection contains much material relating to the development of shipping in the United States, as do the papers of American merchants engaged in foreign trade with China and other countries.

CANALS AND INLAND NAVIGATION

The collection is strong and includes a large representation of books and pamphlets of the nineteenth and twentieth centuries. An important feature consists of the publications of waterway associations and companies, as well as journals. National and state government reports are held in strength.

The library attempts to cover adequately canals of all countries with emphasis on American canals, particularly the Panama Canal. The more technical aspects of the subject are covered by materials in the Parsons collection in the Science and Technology Research Center, among them eighteenth- and early nineteenth-century works on specific canals in the United States and England,[5] and in the Schuyler papers in the Manuscripts and Archives Division which relate to the construction and operation of canals in New York State from 1792 to 1803. The John Bigelow papers in the division deal with the selection of the route for and construction of the Panama Canal. Pictorial material on canals is also available in the I. N. Phelps Stokes collection of American historical prints in the Prints Division.

Various other subject classes supplement the materials specifically devoted to canals, such as the works classed with coast pilots and sailing directions, which include inland waterways; specific public documents; and items dealing with the legal aspects of canal building and operation, classed with materials on law.

AVIATION

Aviation is considered here in both its economic and technical aspects, including the various activities on which flying depends (e.g., maintenance and operation of aircraft and airports), and the field of astronautics. The acquisition policy for this subject, as for other sciences, stresses the development of holdings of basic scholarly texts, serials, and government documents rather than publications of a popular nature. Not actively collected are the near-print publications which characterize certain phases of the literature. The resources are, in general, strong for research in both historical and current topics, with the technical aspects receiving more attention than the economic at the present time. Although it is not possible to estimate the present extent of holdings in all aspects of the field, as early as 1936 the library enumerated 5,574 refer-

---

5. See note 2 above.

ences to books and journal articles in its collections on the history of aeronautics alone.[6] In 1967 it was estimated that there were 6,565 volumes on aviation, exclusive of serial items, which in the Science and Technology Research Center are not shelved by subject.

Holdings of bibliographical and other reference tools are strong, including a good group of bilingual and polyglot dictionaries. There is a large collection of serials, both general titles and those specializing in one or more phases of the field; about 700 different files are present, of which the most important are either complete or lack only a few early issues. Included are publications as diverse as *Air revue* (Brussels), *Aviation Week and Space Technology*, *Canadian Aeronautics and Space Journal*, *Esso Air World*, *Journal of the Royal Aeronautical Society*, *New Zealand Aviation*, and *Western Aviation, Missiles and Space*. The library currently receives about 150 periodicals in the field from many countries.

The library has assembled a strong collection of the publications, both serial and monographic, of federal agencies concerned with aviation, notably the Federal Aviation Agency (and its predecessors), the Civil Aeronautics Board, the National Advisory Committee for Aeronautics, and the National Aeronautics and Space Administration. While not all series of technical reports are complete, holdings in most cases encompass a high proportion of the numbers issued. Reports of state aeronautics commissions are available only for some states, chiefly those of the Northeast and Middlewest.

Very good holdings on the history of aeronautics include items on balloons and dirigibles as well as heavier-than-air craft, military aviation, individual flights, and jurisprudence. Included are such works as John Wise's *A System of Aeronautics* (1850), John Jeffries's *A Narrative of the Two Aerial Voyages* (1786), Barthélemy Faujas de Saint-Fond's *Description des expériences de la machine aérostatique de MM. de Montgolfier* (1783) and Kratzenstein's *L'art de naviguer dans l'air* (1784). Of more than 550 publications dealing with the general subject of aeronautics in specific countries, histories tracing national developments form a sizeable group; holdings are substantial for France, Germany, and Great Britain.

There are over 500 entries under the heading "Aeronautics—Ascensions, Flights, etc." in the Public Catalog, many of which relate to such epochal long-distance trips as Amsterdam-Batavia, Cape-Cairo, Rome-Brazil, and round-the-world flights, or have to do with reminiscences of aviation pioneers. There are entries for works by and about the Wright brothers and Santos Dumont, and a wealth of additional biographical material about Amelia Earhart, Hugo Eckener, Charles A. Lindbergh, August Picard, and other figures, both American and foreign. Although the Manuscripts and Archives Division does not house any large collections related to aeronautics, the papers (1913–47) of Major August Post, an early flyer, and the correspondence (1923–27)

of Edward P. Warner, a professor of aeronautics at the Massachusetts Institute of Technology, provide material of limited scope on the development of aviation.

The library collects comprehensively in the general area of aeronautical engineering. The Public Catalog contains about 600 entries under "Aerodynamics," with additional material appearing under such related headings as "Aerofoils," "Air Flow," "Air Resistance," "Skin Friction (Aerodynamics)," and "Wind Tunnels." There is a large collection of material on the airplane; about 2,700 cards in the Public Catalog represent not only general publications but also those on control, design, maintenance and repair, manufacture, stability, and testing of aircraft. The subdivision "Type" (approximately 200 entries) enables the reader to locate pertinent data on specific kinds of aircraft, for example, the B-29, Caravelle, Comet, DC-3, and Spitfire; the set of *Jane's All the World's Aircraft* is virtually complete from the first issue in 1909. There are also significant holdings of publications pertaining to instruments, motors (both piston and jet), and construction materials.

About 500 titles in the holdings deal with the construction and operation of airports. In addition to general material are studies and reports of major commercial fields, particularly those serving the New York metropolitan area.

Although the library collects in the field of medicine only on a limited scale, about 100 publications on the medical aspects of aviation have been acquired, including files of two specialized journals, *Aerospace Medicine* and *Revue de médecine aéronautique*. There is material on the medical problems of military aviation during World Wars I and II and, more recently, on space medicine. Special publications on flight safety include the reports of the Flight Safety Foundation and the accident reports of the Civil Aeronautics Board and the British Ministry of Aviation.

There is a good working collection on the air transport industry, as indicated by approximately 900 entries in the Public Catalog for "Aeronautics, Commercial." Publications on air transport in individual countries compose about half the material; the remainder centers on such topics as costs, fares, finance, routes, traffic, and operational procedures of airlines. A nearly complete set of the *Official Airline Guide* (various editions) since 1944 provides the historical timetable information for studies of service and competition. The publications of the Air Transport Association of America and of the International Air Transport Association are available. There is a large block of serial and monographic publications of the International Civil Aviation Organization, although files of its *Bulletin*, *Circular*, and *Documents* are incomplete. The collections contain complete sets of the *Report*, economic decisions, and various statistical series of carriers' traffic and finance issued by the Civil Aeronautics Board, but the Research Libraries have not collected the briefs and exhibits presented to the board in connection with applications for new routes. Resources on individual airline companies are good for domestic trunk lines and fair for other carriers. Domestic trunk lines and Pan American World Airways are represented by annual reports for recent years (in some cases for a longer period) either as issued or in microform, some labor contracts, and a few company histories, house organs, and miscellaneous publi-

---

6. See William B. Gamble, comp., "History of Aeronautics: A Selected List of References to Material in The New York Public Library," *BNYPL* 40 (1936): 27–48 et seq. Published separately by the library; reprinted by the library and Arno Press, 1971.

cations. Relatively little is present for local services, territorial companies, or foreign airlines, with the exception of recent annual reports for Air Canada, Air France, Air India, BOAC, BEA, and KLM. The set of *The Airline Pilot*, issued by the Airline Pilots Association, International, is complete as is *Airways International*, issued by the International Federation of Airline Pilots Associations; the journals of pilots' associations in several foreign countries including France, Great Britain, Italy, and Pakistan are available for recent years. Other than publications on passenger service, the collections contain relatively few publications specifically on airmail service (chiefly histories of the service in the United States and in other countries) and on airfreight (much of it on the potential for transporting cargo by air). Most of the material about flight equipment and finances of airlines appears respectively in publications on airplanes and on air transport as an industry in the corporate finance area.

Most of the material on military and naval aviation deals with the United States and Great Britain. It includes histories of the U.S. and Royal Air Forces and publications on the role of the airplane in World Wars I and II, strategic bombing, and the U.S. Military Air Transport Service.

The library currently pursues a policy of extensive acquisition in the field of aeronautics. There is a comprehensive collection of the reports and technical publications of the National Aeronautics and Space Administration. Full sets of *Astronautics and Aerospace Engineering, International Aerospace Abstracts*, and other publications of the Institute of the Aeronautical Sciences are present. There are more than 500 entries in the catalog of the Science and Technology Research Center under "Rockets," including publications of the American Rocket Society, the British Interplanetary Society, and the Rocket Research Center at the Massachusetts Institute of Technology. The library currently receives 27 periodicals in the field. This material, and related items under the heading "Satellites, Artificial," provide both English and foreign-language publications on rockets, missiles, and space exploration. In addition, the library collects both popular and scholarly publications on flying saucers. Holdings amount to more than 75 monographs in English and several foreign languages; in this field the library currently subscribes to 14 periodicals from Australia, the Netherlands, and Great Britain as well as from the United States.

COMMUNICATION

This is, on the whole, a very strong collection covering telegraph, radio, telephone, pneumatic tubes, and other methods of communication, and television and radio in both their economic and social aspects. The collecting policy is generally comprehensive; a number of exceptions are noted in the following discussion. The holdings are divided between the economic and social aspects of communication, held in the general collections; and the technical aspects, located in the Science and Technology Research Center.

Excellent collections of books and pamphlets cover the economic and social aspects of the subject for the nineteenth and twentieth centuries. Other features include extensive files of periodicals and journals, and a large collection of government reports, particularly of bureaus of communication, from virtually every country in the world. Files are not always complete but in most cases are extensive. The publications of the International Telecommunication Bureau, Bern (before October 1, 1947, the International Telegraph Bureau, Bern) are virtually complete.

The technical literature is also strong, both in older and current works; works on lasers, microwaves, radar, and other modern aspects of the subject are present, as are works on the telegraph and early radio. The library has gathered a noteworthy collection on the laying of the first Atlantic cable. Bibliographic works are actively collected when available.

As is the case with many subjects, various classes of material in the Research Libraries contribute to the communications holdings. Radio and television as entertainment are excellently covered in the Theatre Collection of the library's Performing Arts Research Center at Lincoln Center. The Picture Collection of the Branch Libraries provides extensive pictorial documentation in the field. Additional coverage appears in the library's legal and public document resources.

POSTAL SERVICE

Only bibliography and history of the subject are collected comprehensively; this is, however, a generally adequate section with a variety of materials—books, pamphlets, and a good selection of periodicals. Among those materials relating strictly to postal service, the reports of national post office departments are unusually strong, and postal guides are numerous. To supplement its historical works the library indexes important magazine articles, particularly those on early postal service; this indexing is not so extensive as it previously was because of the number and excellence of standard commercial indexing services.

Materials on philately form an adequate if not strong collection. There is an extensive group of philatelic periodicals and journals, but many of the files are incomplete. Stamp catalogs and handbooks of stamp collecting are numerous and the subject is kept up to date with current publications.

The library does not collect postage stamps but has retained gifts received in previous years. The Miller collection of United States stamps is considered to be one of the outstanding collections of its kind in the country. Benjamin Kurtz Miller of Minneapolis donated his collection to the library in 1925 and until his death in 1928 continued to increase its scope. The collection covers the period 1845 to 1926 and is on permanent display in the Fifth Avenue lobby of the Central Building.[7] In the Manuscripts and Archives Division are the account books and notebooks of Benjamin Miller giving the description, source, and price paid for the various items in his collection, with other items relating to postal service, including way-bills of the California and Oregon United States Mail Line operated by the Oregon State Company during 1866 and 1867.

---

7. See Charles J. Phillips, "The Miller Collection of United States Postage Stamps," *BNYPL* 40 (1936): 421–26.

38

LAW

The New York Public Library's criterion for acquiring law materials was first set by the Astor Library in 1854. Rather than enter into wasteful competition with the specialized collections of neighboring colleges and bar associations, it was decided to provide works rarely found in New York and not attempt to form a complete law library. Now numbering about 83,700 volumes, the collection reflects this original policy as modified over the years to make available such resources as the general public, in contrast to the practicing lawyer or legal specialist, might reasonably expect to find in a large research library. As a result the collection is rich in works on the bibliographic, historical, sociological, and economic aspects of law, but contains few practitioners' manuals, legal textbooks, or other items of professional literature. There are few legal digest services, and court reports in general are left to the responsibility of the local law libraries. The library does, however, make available the reports of the U.S. Supreme Court, the U.S. Court of Claims, the U.S. Court of Customs and Patent Appeals, and the federal district courts in the New York area. The reports of New York state courts of record also are acquired. Because this material is difficult to use, most of it is on the open shelves of the Main Reading Room where some ready assistance can be provided.

In recent years the library has been adding to its files of legal periodicals, because much of what is now being published in these journals is closely related to other subject areas in the social sciences.

The acquisition policy for international law and diplomacy has been comprehensive from the beginning, and holdings in these fields are excellent. The collection of treaties is especially strong.

Statute law has been collected widely, not so much for the lawyer as for the social historian. The files of session laws for the United States and the individual states have few gaps. The files of session laws of national governments other than the United States are also strong. Codes of law for the United States and other countries are not collected widely, but are well represented.

HISTORICAL SURVEY

The basic law collection of the library came from the Astor Library. In 1854, Dr. Cogswell stated, "The collection is good on the civil law, embracing various editions of the Corpus Juris, and commentaries upon it; it contains also, all the codes of Scandinavia, and of other parts of Europe, during the middle ages; the system of jurisprudence as now practised in Italy, Portugal, Germany, Denmark and Sweden; the Fuerosa siete Partidas, and Recopilaciones of Spain, together with the digests and commentaries of the Musselman, Hindoo, Gentoo and Chinese laws. In French law, the Library is really rich, beginning with the Ordonances des Reis, and coming down to the very latest volume of the Journal du Palais. The selection for the English common law was made by two of the most eminent jurists in

the country; it is not large, but very choice."[1]

Mr. Brevoort, in his Annual Report for the Astor Library in 1877, stated, "As there are, however, several libraries in the city especially devoted to the departments of theology, jurisprudence, medicine, natural history and geography, I have considered it advisable to direct the chief expenditure towards the completion of other important subjects."[2] This policy was somewhat revised when a part of $12,000 given by J. J. Astor in 1882 was used to fill gaps in foreign jurisprudence, and a portion of $15,000 given by him in 1883 was allocated for general law materials.

With the Lenox Library came a notable collection of American laws and legislative journals printed before 1800 from the library of Dr. George H. Moore, purchased in 1894. A few law books came with the Tilden Trust, but Tilden's unusual law library went elsewhere.

A brief table shows the growth of the collections over the last hundred years:

1854 Astor Library		3,107 volumes
1921 New York Public Library	30,492	
1930		43,032
1941		60,000
1966		83,700

RESOURCES IN LAW

PERIODICALS

While it is true that the library acquires law journals dealing principally with social, economic, or industrial problems, it also has a fair collection of general law periodicals. The collection is representative of the field rather than comprehensive. It includes files of some of the leading American law journals, the more important English and continental European titles, and the conference proceedings of some state bar associations. Among these are the *American Bar Association Journal* (1915–), the *Canadian Bar Journal* (1964–), *Harvard Law Review* (1891–), *Current Legal Bibliography* (1960–), *Index to Foreign Legal Periodicals* (1960–), and *Tijdschrift voor Rechtsgeschiedenis* (1918–). About 60 titles are currently received.

INTERNATIONAL LAW

This strong collection is one of the principal resources for the texts of treaties in this country. There are essentially complete runs of the publications of both the League of Nations and the United Nations. The library is currently a depository for all the publications of the United Nations. Also included in the collection are a large number of treatises on international law and works on diplomatic relations.

Periodicals in the field of international law reflect the strength of the resources: of 27 serials listed in *Ulrich's International Periodicals Direc-*

---

1. Lydenberg, *History*, p. 26.
2. Ibid., pp. 64–65.

tory (11th ed.) the library has 23 (of which 6 titles are not entirely complete), including all the United States journals; 4 from France; 3 from Germany; 2 each from Great Britain, Italy, and Belgium; and 1 each from Peru, the U.A.R., Denmark, and Sweden.

General collections of treaties include such series as Martens's *Nouveau recueil général de traités*, the League of Nations *Treaty Series*, the United Nations *Treaty Series*, and others. Those national in scope are represented by the British "Rymer Foedera," and the *Treaty Series* of the Foreign Office; D. H. Miller's *Treaties and Other International Acts* of the United States; and similar compilations for other countries. Officially published collections of diplomatic correspondence appearing from year to year are typified by the French "Yellow Book" (*Documents diplomatiques*), the German *Weissbuch*, and others from the principal nations of the world, constituting one of the best representations in this country. Also present are the large sets of diplomatic papers, such as the *British and Foreign State Papers, Staatsarchiv*, and *Archives diplomatiques*. There is also a good collection of miscellaneous administrative publications and annual reports of various foreign offices. A special feature of this last type consists of the "Memorias" of South American countries, which are present in large numbers. Series in this field are usually complete.

Of less importance, perhaps, although unusual in extent, is the collection of single treaties. Those of the sixteenth and seventeenth centuries are of particular interest, especially the treaty for the Pacification of Ghent (1576) and the first treaty published by authority in England, between that country and Spain in 1604.[3] The holdings of Indian treaties gain additional importance when considered in conjunction with the library's great collection on the Indians of North America. Contemporary eighteenth-century printings of treaties between the colonies of Pennsylvania, Virginia, New York, Massachusetts, etc. and various Indian tribes are in the Rare Book Division. Of the 13 known treaties printed by Benjamin Franklin between 1736 and 1762, the library has 8 (the earliest dated 1742), all collected by James Lenox.[4] Another group of 75 Indian treaties, presented by Charles Eberstadt, date from the mid-nineteenth century. There are numerous Indian treaties in the resources, in their original form or in reprinted editions.

Other subject classes in the library should be associated with the collection on international law, particularly history and public documents, the latter containing extensive files of the legislative proceedings of most of the nations of the world.

LAW REPORTS, TRIALS

Law reports form a relatively weak collection, those of the major United States federal courts and of the New York state courts of record constituting the principal part. There are relatively good collections from neighboring states, but the files are incomplete; other states are represented by only fragmentary holdings. The library has a fair representation of reports of English courts. Most of the current reporting services are not acquired.

Trials, while not an extensive subject in the library's resources, do represent an important feature of the collections as a whole. There is a rich representation of reports of American and English trials, most of which are listed under the heading "Criminology" in the catalogs. Early reports, because of their interest as imprints, are usually kept in the Rare Book Division; there are also shorthand transcripts of some trials in the Manuscripts and Archives Division.

LAW TEXTS, SESSION LAWS, COMPILED CODES, DIGESTS, ETC.

This is an area of decided strength. Among the historical materials for the United States is an extensive collection of session laws and compilations covering British colonial America and the early federal and state governments. The Rare Book Division houses an outstanding collection of American public documents, most of them printed before 1801, among which are session laws, collected statutes, etc. There is a related collection of Confederate public documents. When the library does not have original printings, it attempts to secure reprints or photostat copies. Current materials include all session laws of the individual states, with a good representation of compilations (civil and penal codes, etc.). In addition, the library maintains files of the House and Senate bills of the United States Congress (fragmentary from 1804, but extensive since 1891) and of the New York State Legislature since 1830.

The collections for Great Britain and its Commonwealth associates are also strong. The *Statutes of the Realm* (the most comprehensive official edition of British statutes from the Conquest to the reign of Queen Anne) is complete. The library also has occasional printed session laws in original editions for the period 1543–1691 and a practically complete collection covering the years 1691–1806.[5] The period 1806–66 is covered by other editions; from 1866 to date, the texts are complete in official form. Counterparts of the *Statutes of the Realm* are present for Scotland and Ireland. The sets of session laws of the former British dominions and their provinces are notably comprehensive but the compilations are not so well represented. The files of the session laws of the former crown colonies are also extensive, with less numerous compilations.

Holdings of session laws for European countries are good. There are complete files of the Italian *Raccolta ufficiale delle leggi e dei decreti* from 1861. With this set may be associated similar series for the kingdoms now a part of Italy, among them *Raccolta degli atti del governo di sua Maestà il Re di Sardegna*, complete from 1814 to 1861, and *Collezione delle leggi e dei decreti reali del Regno delle Due Sicilie*, also complete. In 1937 the library purchased a collection of about 1,400 broadsides and pamphlets, including decrees and proclamations issued in Tuscany from 1729 to 1841. The richness of the

---

3. See *BNYPL* 14 (1910): 84–85.
4. See *Indian Treaties Printed by Benjamin Franklin* 1736–1762 (Philadelphia: The Historical Society of Pennsylvania, 1938).

5. See Rollin A. Sawyer, "From Cuckfield Park to Bryant Park; A Set of English Session Laws," *BNYPL* 41 (1937): 3–7.

French law collection was increased in 1937, when an outstanding group of 15,000 royal French ordinances, edicts, and decrees from the late seventeenth to the late nineteenth century was acquired. The holdings were further augmented when after World War II an additional several thousand royal acts were purchased. A checklist of these items is in the course of preparation. The French *lois annotées* and *coutumes* are other significant aspects of the resources. The holdings of *Gezetzblatts* of Germany and Austria and of many of their component states are substantial. The *Svensk Forfättningssamling* is complete from 1825; the Norwegian laws almost complete from 1814; the Danish, from 1871. The library has a full representation of the session laws of the nations created after World War I in Europe—Lithuania, Poland, Czechoslovakia, Finland, etc.—up to the outbreak of World War II. After that time, session laws for Czechoslovakia and Poland are perhaps the most complete, with representative holdings for the other countries of Eastern Europe. For imperial Russia, the Slavonic Division has statutory law as it appeared in the Government Gazette from 1869 to 1917 and in the proceedings of the Senat and the Duma. Soviet session laws are found in the *Sobraniye postanovlenii i rasporyazhenii pravitel'stva* (1924–   ) and in various compiled codes of law as they are published; codes are also available for the member states of the Union.

The holdings of the session laws of Cuba, Haiti, and the Dominican Republic are strong. The Mexican collection, although consisting of many sets, is not exceptional. South American countries are well represented. There are extensive files of session laws for Brazil, Peru, Paraguay, Bolivia, Uruguay, and the Argentine Republic. An important compilation entitled *Codigo braziliense* is made up of original statutes, decrees, treaties, etc., printed in Rio de Janeiro during the period 1808 to 1821. Other holdings, particularly those for Venezuela and Colombia, are less strong both in session laws and in compilations, and Ecuador and Chile are poorly represented. These defects in the collections are due in part to administrative policy and in part to inaccessibility of materials. The library purchases compilations only selectively; many session laws are extremely difficult to acquire because of poor methods of distribution, and often the quality of the paper is so poor that it is almost impossible to preserve them. The library's preeminent collection of official gazettes supplements the holdings for those countries in which session laws are published in this source.

ORIENTAL LAW

Muhammadan (Islamic) law is especially well covered in the Oriental Division; the holdings number some 900 titles in both Eastern and Western languages and include materials on such various schools as the Hanafite, Malikite, and Shafiite. Index entries for articles in learned journals, particularly for the period before World War II, are a feature of the Oriental Division card catalog. Many of the Arabic, Persian, and Turkish manuscripts in the division are treatises on law.

After Muhammadan law, Indian law is perhaps most fully represented, including works on the law of Manu, Dharmasatra, etc. Indian government publications in the Economic and Public Affairs Division also contain much legal material; the provincial gazettes of the country are an example. Additions made possible under Public Law 480 have enriched the Indic holdings in all areas since 1962.

JEWISH LAW

Virtually all the great editions of the standard codes of Jewish law and their commentaries are available in the Jewish Division. The division also has an outstanding collection of rabbinical decisions and responsa, that is, written opinions and decisions by eminent Hebrew authorities in various lands and in all periods of Jewish history. This collection numbers almost 2,000 volumes. Statutes and session laws are received regularly from Israel.

39

SOCIOLOGY, STATISTICS, POLITICAL SCIENCE

The subjects classed under sociology in the Billings Classification Schedule reflect the broader interpretation of the term current in the early 1900s. These subjects (with economics, history, anthropology, and associated fields) are now considered subdivisions of the social sciences. The sociology subgroups in the Billings Classification Schedule are:

General materials
Statistics
Political science
Socialism

Poverty
Providence (insurance, savings, pensions, etc.)
Societies and associations
Crime and punishment
Woman and children
Public health

The approximately 215,000 volumes in these fields form one of the stronger collections of the Research Libraries. The collecting policy has been comprehensive from the beginning. As early as 1877, James Carson Brevoort, in his annual report for the Astor Library, stated that sociology (or the social sciences) was a field of knowledge upon which the library should make one of its chief expenditures.[1] Since that time rich historical materials have been gathered and extensive files of current publications have been maintained.

The holdings of journals and other publications of social organizations and institutions are outstanding, but most important are such source materials as public documents (national, state, and municipal) and the reports of nongovernmental institutions here and abroad.

The subjects represented vary in strength. In part this reflects the selection policy of the library. For example, the holdings on public health are comparatively strong in their sociological aspects, but are inadequate for certain types of extensive research because of the lack of works on medicine. Of the special language materials, those in the Slavonic Division are the most important: both books and periodical literature relating to social theory and tendencies are held in strength.

The inclusion in the card catalog of index entries for periodical articles on sociological subjects, long an important feature of the library's resources, is now of less importance because of the increase in the number of published indexes which cover specific aspects of the field. After 1965 indexing became very selective.

Many of the important collections have come to the library by gift. Among these are various manuscript collections treating the subject of women, among the most important being the Schwimmer-Lloyd collection portraying the progress of the feminist movement during the first forty years of this century as represented in letters, files of source documents, leaflets, pamphlets, and books. The library also received the papers and books of Mrs. Carrie Chapman Catt. The William Jay Gaynor memorial collection fund is one of the funds used for the purchase of books on sociology, economics, and the science of government.[2] The library has notable book and manuscript materials on Mayor Gaynor and his epoch.

The Economic and Public Affairs Division has the major responsibility for collecting in the field of sociology, although the greater part of the materials are shelved with the general collections. The Economic and Public Affairs Division gives reference service in this field, but limitations in shelf space and seating accommodations dictate that many questions must be handled by the General Research and Humanities Division. Books in this class are extensively consulted in the Main Reading Room, where they are supplemented by general treatises and reference works held on the open shelves. The distinction made in the reference work of the two divisions is not so much one of subject as of the nature of particular inquiries. A request for one or several books on a subject, or an inquiry which can be answered from sources on hand or from the Public Catalog, is generally handled by the General Research and Humanities Division; a question that requires specialized resources or guided research is ordinarily referred to the Economic and Public Affairs Division.

1. See Lydenberg, *History*, pp. 64–65.
2. See *Outlook* 107 (1914): 583; 108 (1914): 443–44 et seq.

GENERAL RESOURCES

The collection covering general works on sociology is strong for research in historical and current materials. Bibliographical works and series include not only American and English publications, but such continental European compilations as Grandin's *Bibliographie générale*, the *Bibliography of Social Sciences* of the Hungarian Sociological Institute (1926–   ), *Rassegna bibliografica della scienze giuridiche, sociali e politiche* (1926–37), and *Übersicht der gesammten staats- und rechtswissenschaftlichen Litteratur* (1869–1914), with other important keys to the library's rich collections.

Periodicals, publications of societies and institutions, and other serials of a general nature are especially fully represented, usually by complete files for important titles. These include American, English, and continental European materials, with particular emphasis on French, German, and Italian publications.

General treatises including histories, works on the theory of social organization, and essays, both American and foreign, are often represented by various editions. For historical study the holdings of publications covering the latter half of the nineteenth century are strong. The sociology collection held on the open shelves of the Main Reading Room is confined to general treatises and reference works.

Other topics of note represented by substantial holdings are the history of social conditions in various places, manners and customs, and etiquette. In addition to works specifically classed with these subjects there are notable supplementary resources in the local history collections. The very extensive collection of national, state, and municipal public documents adds significant source materials.

Manuals of etiquette are of particular importance to the resources, providing research materials both for scholars studying manners and customs from an historical point of view, and members of the reading public seeking information on questions of current practice. The file is dated in the Public Catalog (for example, "Etiquette—Manuals, U.S. 1868") and extends from Italian courtesy books of the sixteenth century to materials of the present day. The earliest American item is a book on juvenile etiquette, *The School of Good Manners* (Boston, 1794); also included are many editions of Emily Post's famous standard work. Under the representative collecting policy the General Research and Humanities Division attempts to provide a current book on etiquette in each major language.

STATISTICS: POPULATION (Demography)

This extensive collection constitutes one of the strong subject holdings of the library. Statistics are acquired comprehensively in all languages and in every area of human activity, including such diverse fields as industry, business, education, finance, labor, transportation, and agriculture; special aspects such as cultural and criminal statistics are also covered. The holdings in the main classmark for materials of this type number about 45,800 volumes, the preponderance being official publications of the countries of the world. There are in addition related statistical materials classed with the public document collections of the library and still others classed under subject.

Systematic collecting in this field began about the turn of the century. Dr. Billings, in his annual report for 1906, noted the important resources in statistical material on population, finance, taxation, railroads, commerce, and trade; and in his report for 1910 he commented on the library's attempts to collect publications of the various federal, state, and municipal bureaus.[3] Since that time the library has added older files, completed many others, and maintained current series. General works in the field, collected works, essays, and miscellanies are not emphasized.

Two types of materials are of outstanding importance. The first, periodicals and society publications, is an unusually extensive collection. Included are proceedings of international statistical congresses, some dating from the middle of the nineteenth century, and complete files of most important journals, such as *Sankhya; The Indian Journal of Statistics, Revista brasileira de estatistica, Revista italiana di economia, demografia e statistica,* and the *Australian Journal of Statistics.*

The second particularly important type of material is composed of publications of international governmental agencies, along with reports of the national, state, and municipal levels. The section containing population statistics and general series is strong. The national materials composed of census publications, numbered series of official statistical reports, and statistical yearbooks and periodicals published by governmental agencies are noteworthy: the census publications are virtually complete for many countries. States and cities do not publish separate statistical reports as extensively, but the library has an excellent representation of these materials. Municipal publications are actively solicited from cities in the New York metropolitan area with populations of 50,000 or more, from other American cities with populations of 400,000 or more, and from foreign cities with populations of 250,000 or more.

Other sources for statistical information include strong collections of official handbooks and manuals of governments (principally national and state). Compilations and series relating to specific subjects other than demography are usually classified with other subject materials: for example, publications relating to crop production are classed with agriculture.

The library fully catalogs its statistical materials and files cards under appropriate subject headings in the Public Catalog and in the various special catalogs of the divisions.

The collecting policy of the Research Libraries in the field of population statistics and studies long anticipated the great current interest in demography. In addition to the files of serial publications, governmental and private, there are also extensive holdings of early monographs. Among the most noteworthy of these are John Graunt's *Natural and Political Observations . . . Made Upon the Bills of Mortality* (1662), the first and early editions of the works of Sir William Petty, and copies of the first eight editions of Malthus's *An Essay on the Principle of Population.*

POLITICAL SCIENCE

The collection of some 25,000 books and pamphlets relating to political science per se is strong; taken in conjunction with related materials in other subject classes it may be characterized as very strong. While this subject did not receive attention as early as some others, J. J. Astor's gift of $12,000 in 1882 was used in part to fill important gaps. The library has continued to add historical and current materials.

Periodicals of the late nineteenth and the twentieth century are very well represented. Included are such titles as the *Egyptian Political Science Review* (1962–), the Polish *Odnowa* (1959–61, incomplete), *Political Science Quarterly* (1886–), *Zeitschrift für Politik* (1907– , incomplete), and many others. Holdings of bibliographical serials include such publications as *Bibliographie der Sozialwissenschaften (Bibliographie der Staats–und Wirtschaftswissenschaften)* (1905–), *International Bibliography of Political Science* (1952–), and *Bulletin analytique de documentation politique, economique et sociale contemporaine* (1946–).

Monographic publications are available from the very earliest periods. Subject entries in the public catalogs are dated; under such entries as "Political Science, 1500–1600" will be found books first written or published during that period. The library is rich in first and early editions of the classics in this field, including the works of Jean Bodin, Robert Filmer, Hobbes, Spinoza, and Montesquieu, among others. There are many copies of the works of Thomas Paine, among them a number of early editions of his famous pamphlet *Common Sense,* first issued in Philadelphia in 1776 and passing immediately through many printings. The Rare Book Division has the first edition, first issue and also the first edition in German, published in Philadelphia during the same year.

Later editions of these and other rarities are added to the collections if they contain additional scholarship. New works on all aspects of the subject are collected comprehensively. A study made at the University of Chicago some years ago revealed that of a list of books on political science judged by experts as necessary in the collection of a great library, the New York Public Library had approximately 90 percent. Another study made at the same university showed that of the books on political science published throughout the world, the library had more than the five largest Chicago libraries combined.[4]

Various manuscript collections furnish additional coverage to the very strong holdings of book materials in such areas as socialism, anarchism, and communism. The Kennan collection includes the letters of Catherine Brehkovskaya, known as the Grandmother (Babushka) of the Russian Revolution, among other materials;[5] the papers of Norman Thomas, Emma Goldman, William Frey, and others also contain much of importance.

The archives of the American Civil Liberties Union of New York, formerly deposited with the Manuscripts and Archives Division, were transferred to Princeton University in 1950; the library has retained a microfilm file, and has in addition

3. See *BNYPL* 10 (1906): 351; 15 (1911): 67.

4. See Andrew J. Eaton, "Current Political Science Publications in Five Chicago Libraries: A Study of Coverage, Duplication, and Omission," *Library Quarterly* 15 (1945): 187–212.

5. See Avrahm Yarmolinsky, "The Kennan Collection," *BNYPL* 25 (1921): 71–80.

the papers (1896–1938) of Frank P. Walsh, who was active in the Union for many years.

Government as an area of study is another important feature of the library's collections, with an extensive representation of older works. Materials on parliamentary procedure include not only the early editions of the classics (Robert's *Rules of Order,* Cushing's *Parliamentary Practice,* Dodd's *Parliamentary Companion,* etc.), but recent manuals as well. There is also a good collection of the official manuals of nations and the smaller units of government throughout the world.

Holdings on suffrage include specific materials (histories, and works on theory) as well as vast resources of historical works in the general collections. Additional rich source materials may be found in the holdings of public documents. Woman suffrage is discussed more fully in the section of this chapter dealing with woman as a subject.

SLAVERY

Resources

This subject is strongly represented in the Research Libraries; the collecting policy is comprehensive. Over 5,000 entries in the Public Catalog relate to slavery with many other headings for associated topics. An important section deals with the abolition of slavery and controversial literature on the subject: for the United States alone there are about 1,600 entries. Some 1,000 pamphlets from many countries are often of additional importance as examples of the earliest imprints from the towns or countries in which they were published. Other subject headings leading to relevant information are "African Slave Trade," "Slave Trade," and the names of individual slave ships: under "Amistad (Schooner)" 15 entries include both contemporary pamphlets and index entries for later periodical articles. More than 60 entries are found under "Captivities, Barbary States," ranging in date from the late seventeenth to the mid-nineteenth century. References are also made to the Las Casas tracts published in 1552 and 1553 dealing with South American Indian slavery, to be found in the Rare Book Division. Other related subjects with extensive representations include indentured servants in colonial America, coolie labor, and the padrone system.

The collections include early abolitionist periodicals, among them the *Anti-Slavery Reporter* (1825–32) and the *Reports of the Directors* (1807–25) of the African Institution, London. Recent materials on civil liberties and civil rights are available, including *Civil Liberties* (1949–) and the *Civil Rights News Letter* (1956–) of the Civil Rights League of Cape Town.

The Schomburg Center has a strong collection on slavery represented by about 5,000 card entries in its dictionary catalog covering such diverse aspects of the subject as fiction, fugitive slaves, insurrections, law, periodicals, poetry, and the like. Among these may be noted slave narratives, including those of Gustavus Vassa, born in Benin in 1746 and carried into slavery at the age of twelve, and manuscript poems and early editions of the works of Phillis Wheatley, a slave girl. Additional information is found under such related headings as "Slave Trade," and "Slavery and the Bible." The Schomburg Center also has actual slave certificates of registration and bills of sale for the purchase of slaves.

Manuscripts

In addition to the noted Schomburg Center holdings, the Ford, Myers, and Bancroft collections of the Manuscripts and Archives Division contain important materials on slavery. Other items include logs and journal books of ships engaged in the slave trade, and of American and British naval vessels cruising off the coasts of Africa and South America in search of slave ships. The division holds the minutes of the executive committee of the Dutchess County (New York) Anti-Slavery Society for 1838 to 1840. There are also the letters of Elizabeth L. Van Lew (1818–1900), who was an abolitionist as well as an agent of the United States Secret Service at Richmond, Virginia, during the Civil War; and other diaries, accounts of slave insurrections, appraisals of property including slaves, etc. In 1903 Georgina Schuyler presented several thousand letters relating to Pierre Toussaint, the Santo Domingo slave who was freed by his émigré owners, and became a hairdresser in New York. He was an intimate of prominent citizens and a guide and adviser to persons of his own race until his death in 1849. From South America a "Discursos sobre el Estado y pobreza en que se halla El Nuevo Reyno de Granada" by Juan de Sologuren, accountant of the Royal Treasury, is dated July 24, 1630 to October 28, 1632. Sologuren urges the importation of African slaves to replace Indians in the mines of New Granada.

In the Arents Tobacco Collection a large group of eighteenth- and nineteenth-century manuscript documents from Frederick County, Maryland, includes slave bills and other materials concerning slavery.

CIVIL SERVICE

This is an extensive and noteworthy collection. For the United States the publications adequately cover federal, state, and city groups, with particular emphasis on materials related to New York state and New York City. Foreign materials include the publications of Great Britain and the British Commonwealth of Nations, and less extensively, those of continental European countries which have civil service. The publications are both official and unofficial, although the former are more fully represented. Registers and rosters of civil service employees are not located in the civil service classification: registers of countries, states, and cities are classed with government documents, while works pertaining to a special subject are classed with that subject. Pension materials, for example, including those relating to special classes of civil servants, are classed under the subject "Pensions, Civil, Military, and Naval."

MUNICIPAL AFFAIRS

Lengthy files of periodicals and numerous reports of surveys and studies are noteworthy features of this collection. These include not only routine commercial publications but also those of official bureaus and departments of municipalities, as well as others from civic clubs and organizations whose purpose is to improve municipal affairs. The collection of city and regional planning reports is very good. Special emphasis is also given to materials on American cities, particularly New York. The holdings on city planning, of such importance in recent years and promising to be of increasing concern in the future, are located in several divisions of the library. Sociological and economic aspects of the subject covered in public documents and other publications are in the Economic and Public Affairs Division; the technical aspects are in the Science and Technology Research Center; most other aspects of the subject are administered by the General Research and Humanities Division, with the major exception of artistic and architectural materials, which are in the Art and Architecture Division.

COLONIZATION, IMMIGRATION, EMIGRATION

This strong collection is documented under several subject headings in the Public Catalog of the library. Under "Colonies and Colonization," for example, are approximately 4,400 entries covering such aspects of the subject as bibliographies, guides for immigrants, law, proceedings of congresses, etc. Former British colonies are fully covered with 1,100 entries (an additional 300 appear under the heading "Commonwealth of Nations"); colonies and former colonies of Portugal, France, and Germany are well represented.

Periodicals are a strong feature of the resources in this subject area, ranging from the early *African Repository* (1825–92) and publications of the Aborigines' Protection Society to some 20 titles currently received including *Civilisations* (1951–), *Congo* (Brussels, 1920–), *Tropiques* (Paris, 1948–), *Venture; Journal of the Fabian Colonial Bureau* (1949–), and others.

The subject heading "Emigration and Immigration" in the Public Catalog locates much of interest. Most of the works relating to the United States are classed here, including 1,100 card entries arranged in geographical sequence by states of the Union. More specialized information on immigration into the United States is found in the Local History and Genealogy Division and concerns persons, families, and national groups who have come to this country since the sixteenth century.[6] Representative of periodicals is the *Scottish Genealogist*, largely devoted to research on families of Scottish descent in America. The library holds the serial and monographic publications of the Immigration Restriction League of Boston.

Information on the Zionist movement is to be found in the Jewish Division, located under the catalog entry "Palestine—Colonization" for early titles and "Emigration and Immigration—Israel" for titles published after the establishment of the state of Israel. There is also much material on the Youth Aliyah Office.

SOCIALISM

This subject is of great interest to the Research Libraries and is collected comprehensively. A statement of collecting policy made in the Report of the Director for 1935 reflects the library's policy governing the acquisition of material on controversial questions:

Selecting books, like providing ventilation, is a constant effort to reconcile irreconcilables.

. . . The Library strives wholeheartedly to furnish its readers with books on all sides of all questions. It sets its wares before the readers for the gratification of their prejudices, for the opening of new points of view, for the questioning or confirming of long held beliefs. It seeks no converts, wants to prevent no new findings. . . . it seeks liberal and conservative expression of opinion . . . assuring each of a welcome, warning each that acceptance of the one can not be deemed to mean rejection of the other, asking nothing more than the privilege of urging, Hear the other side.[7]

About 15,000 entries in the Public Catalog fall under the subject heading "Socialism," covering both comprehensive works and those relating to specific countries. Numerous additional headings provide access to such specific topics as "Diggers," "Fourierism," and "Saint-Simonism."

Further analysis of the cards in the Public Catalog reveals that Bolshevism is extremely well represented with over 7,600 entries for works in languages using the Roman alphabet and many others (listed in the Slavonic Division catalog) in the Cyrillic script. It should be noted that works on Bolshevism are subdivided in the library's catalogs by language of the text, e.g., "Bolshevism. English" or "Bolshevism—Russia. English." The library's breadth of coverage was demonstrated in a survey of the literature on the Communist International and its front organizations; the New York Public Library ranks second among world institutions with 602 items out of a total of 2,300 works listed.[8]

Extensive holdings of the writings of various revolutionaries are held in both the original languages and in translation. There are approximately 550 entries in the Public Catalog for works by Karl Marx and some 1,000 for works specifically about him in the Roman alphabet; an additional 200 entries by him and 350 works about him in the Cyrillic script are entered in the Slavonic Division card catalog. The papers of F. A. Sorge in the Manuscripts and Archives Division include more than 30 letters addressed to Sorge by Karl Marx, Friedrich Engels, Johann Philip Becker, Joseph Dietzgen, and others during the period 1867 to 1895; they relate to labor, political, and socialistic movements of that period in Europe and America. The papers of Emma Goldman cover the period 1906 to 1940.

Substantial files of periodicals strengthen the collection. Representative publications of most of the sociopolitical ideologies are received from various parts of the world; anti-socialist periodicals are included. Bibliographical holdings are also strong, ranging from such current materials as the *Annali* (1958–) of the Instituto Giangiacomo Feltrinelli at Milan to earlier materials, such as *Guide to Books for Socialists* published by the Fabian Society in London in 1907. The library has extensive holdings of the Fabian Society tracts and other publications in the general collections; relevant writings of notable English and American authors are to be found in the Berg Collection.

---

6. See Harold Lancour, *A Bibliography of Ship Passenger Lists, 1538–1825; Being a Guide to Published Lists of Early Immigrants to North America*. 3rd ed. rev. by Richard J. Wolfe (The New York Public Library, 1963; 2nd, corrected printing, 1966).

7. *BNYPL* 40 (1936): 183.

8. See Witold S. Sworakowski, *The Communist International and its Front Organizations. A Research Guide and Checklist of Holdings in American and European Libraries* (Stanford University, Hoover Institution, 1965), pp. 11–13.

The library has unusual materials relating to communities and sects which have embodied various socialistic principles in their government, including the Mormons,[9] the Shakers, and the Icarian and Oneida communities, among others.

Utopias are of particular interest to the library, which continues to add unusual or rare editions of books in all languages on the concept of an ideal state. The Berg Collection holds the original edition in Latin (1516) of Sir Thomas More's famous prototype, as well as the first English edition of 1551. In the Rare Book Division is to be found Campanella's "Civitas solis" printed in his *Realis Philosophiae Epilogisticae Pàrtes Quatuor* (Frankfurt, 1623) and in the Economic and Public Affairs Division is found the *Free State of Noland* (1701), which may have been written by Daniel Defoe. Other books, pamphlets, and manuscripts in the library relating to the attempts to found ideal communities in the United States are of additional interest as Americana; among these is the Brook Farm experiment, for which first and early editions, as well as manuscripts in the Berg Collection, add primary source materials to holdings in the general collections. Similar experiments covered by materials in the library are the Icarian community near Corning, Iowa, founded by Etienne Cabet; the Oneida community of New York; and the settlement of La Réunion, Texas, by Victor Considérant.

In the Manuscripts and Archives Division the papers of George and Richard Lichtenberger and of Liberty D. Brooks, together with a ledger kept by Robert Dale Owen and additional items, document the community of New Harmony, Indiana, for the period 1837 to 1894. The Norman Thomas papers cover the life work and interests of this American socialist leader, and much pertinent material is to be found in the Horace Greeley papers. The Berg Collection documents socialism as it was reflected in the lives and works of nineteenth- and twentieth-century American and English authors.

POVERTY (Welfare, the Poor, Charities, etc.)

Works on poverty and plans, programs, and institutions designed to ameliorate the condition are acquired comprehensively. Among the 21,000 volumes classed here are most of the significant bibliographies, histories, and statistical studies published throughout the world. Other important works may be found in the resources for the study of religion and local history.

The international representation of periodicals and the publications of associations, conferences, and congresses is good. Many of the older works, now of historical interest, appear in various editions and languages. Primary source materials of several kinds are perhaps the most important feature of the collections. The official publications of American and foreign nations, states, and cities are strongly represented. Almost every important government report on poverty issued by Great Britain and the Commonwealth Nations may be found in the parliamentary papers series of these countries (Billings class mark *S). The publications of private welfare institutions include the reports of charitable funds and foundations, settlement houses, and other institutions for the underprivileged. The earlier materials are particularly strong; although many of the series of reports are incomplete, the files are representative. American cities are most fully covered.

There is a great deal of material in the library on related aspects of the subject. For example, approximately 2,500 entries on unemployment and the unemployed are found in the Public Catalog, with a dated arrangement for works after 1929. Materials published by or about the Works Progress Administration of the United States are also well represented, with about 3,500 entries. Photographs from the Farm Security Administration Photographic Project collection in the Picture Collection, a unit of the Branch Libraries, cover most of the states of the Union with an extensive and interesting file on the black American. Glass slides in the Local History and Genealogy Division document tenement life of the east side of Manhattan around the turn of the century. The library's Prints Division has a wealth of material ranging from sixteenth- and seventeenth-century representations of the seven acts of mercy to the work of present-day artists.

PROVIDENCE (Insurance, Savings, Pensions, etc.)

This is a strong feature in the library, represented by about 30,000 volumes excluding government publications. Most aspects of the subject are collected comprehensively, including material on mutual benefit associations; life, accident, and other insurance; savings and savings banks; building and loan associations; and pensions. Most of the material is from the United States. The substantial resources on health insurance include negative and affirmative arguments on socialized medicine, complemented by official publications from countries and other units having government-sponsored health plans.

A special feature of the holdings is the large number of compilations of laws and national and state reports. Of even greater importance are the reports and separate works issued by organizations in the field. The publications of fraternal orders and benevolent organizations are also noteworthy.

SOCIETIES AND ASSOCIATIONS

RESOURCES

Approximately 20,000 volumes in the Research Libraries relate to this topic. Most of the general materials are assigned the subject heading "Societies" in the Public Catalog with numerous additional references to names of particular social and political clubs, fraternal orders, secret societies, and the like. The holdings are adequate; the library collects comprehensively only general works, histories, bibliographies, directories and materials on New York City clubs.

City, country, and other social clubs are represented in the holdings, together with religious auxiliaries which have secular purposes, and other types including such organizations as German-American clubs. Fraternal orders receive adequate coverage with particular attention paid to the Freemasons and Odd Fellows. The holdings of material on American collegiate Greek letter societies are discussed in chapter 42 of this

---

9. See "List of Works in The New York Public Library Relating to Mormons," *BNYPL* 13 (1909): 183–239.

Guide. The American History Division has a collection of books and pamphlets on the Ku Klux Klan; there are also works on secret societies and cults in the Near East, India, and the Far East in the Oriental Division.

FREEMASONS

Of all the collections classed under societies, the most extensive group (some 5,000 titles) relates to Freemasons and Freemasonry. This is a nonacademic subject and therefore might not be collected by college or university libraries. For this reason, and because Freemasons have been important in the history of the United States, Great Britain, and Western Europe, the library once collected extensively in this subject field. With the development of libraries specializing in Masonic materials, however, the New York Public Library no longer undertakes to acquire items that might be duplicated in nearby libraries. The Library and Museum of the Grand Lodge of New York, located at 71 West 23rd Street in Manhattan, permits the general public to use its facilities upon request.

In addition to general works, histories and bibliographies, the holdings of the Research Libraries are composed, for the most part, of the proceedings and transactions of the grand lodges of most of the states in the United States, some of the provinces of Canada and the states of Australia, and other countries of the world including Costa Rica, Cuba, Germany, and Great Britain. Files extend from the early nineteenth century, although in some cases they are far from complete. The publications of local lodges or chapters are not usually collected, with the exception of such materials as centennial histories. Among the book and pamphlet materials are a number of the earliest imprints of American cities and towns. The Rare Book Division houses a group of eighteenth-century addresses and discourses on Freemasonry with some anti-Masonic tracts. The Williamson Masonic collection on black Freemasons in the Schomburg Center includes about 270 titles, both monographs and serials, covering both the York and Scottish rites. Cards for this collection are filed in the Public Catalog.

CRIME AND PUNISHMENT

About 25,000 volumes comprise the holdings in this subject field. The collecting policy is generally comprehensive.

The holdings of journals, publications of associations, and reports of congresses are outstanding; most important files, both American and European, are substantially complete. This is especially true of English, German, and Italian language publications. These materials range from scholarly studies of the criminal nature to radical reform programs of little-known organizations.

There is a fairly extensive collection of periodicals, with a wide geographical range, although it is difficult to estimate the full extent of the holdings, since material is classed under many different headings: criminology, criminal law, criminals, juvenile prisons, police, etc. General magazines received include the *International Review of Criminal Policy* (1952–), the *Revue internationale de criminologie et de police technique* (Geneva, 1953–), the *Revista penal y penitenciaria* (Buenos Aires, 1936–), and the *Archiv*

für Kriminologie (1898–). A number of titles relate to police forces—perhaps the most extensive run is that of the well-known *National Police Gazette* (1845– , incomplete); the library also has the New York City *Spring 3100; A Monthly Magazine of-by-for New York's Finest* (1930–) and from Canada the *Royal Mounted Police Quarterly* (Ottawa, 1933–) with journals from England, India, Italy, Poland, Sweden, and other countries. Convict publications are also received from institutions in the United States, among them the *Rikers Review* (1937–) from the New York State Penitentiary at Rikers Island.

Holdings related to juvenile delinquency and female criminals are strong. The first group is supplemented by materials on children (Billings class mark SO), and the second by materials on prostitution (Billings class mark SNY).

Special materials include a large collection of separately published reports of national, state, and municipal bureaus dealing with criminals. Compilations of laws and criminal codes are strong and are supplemented by associated resources in law and public documents. Statistical reports on crime are comprehensive. A good collection of printed criminal trials is included, the nucleus of which came with the Tilden collection. The library of A. Oakley Hall, district attorney and mayor of New York City, was given by his daughter, Miss Josephine B. Hall, in 1924. It includes the original error books and argument copies used by the district attorney in trials which he prosecuted.[10] In 1938 the library purchased the Edmund L. Pearson collection of about 2,000 volumes, of which some 1,200 were devoted to crime, criminology, trials, detective stories, and similar subjects. The George Kennan collection of books, pamphlets, and manuscripts refers to the Russian penal system of the latter nineteenth century, especially in Siberia.[11]

WOMAN AND CHILDREN

WOMAN

This is a strong subject in the Research Libraries, with particular strengths in certain aspects. At present only the following topics are collected comprehensively: the history, bibliography, and biography of woman; anthropology; marriage; woman suffrage; and prostitution. The library's holdings document thoroughly the progress of the feminist movement from its beginnings, especially in this country, and include a number of important manuscript collections.

The Economic and Public Affairs Division and the General Research and Humanities Division share collecting responsibility: the history, bibliography, biography, and anatomy of woman are covered by the General Research and Humanities Division; economic, legal, and sociological aspects are the responsibility of the Economic and Public Affairs Division. There are some 12,000 entries under "Woman" in the Public Catalog, with many subheadings which identify works on women as authors, athletes, artists, mothers, spinsters, and widows; their role in the professions; and their place in the societies of various countries of the

---

10. See "Books From the Library of A. Oakley Hall," *BNYPL* 28 (1924): 550–51.

11. See Avrahm Yarmolinsky, "The Kennan Collection," *BNYPL* 25 (1921): 71–80.

world, etc. The file has a chronological arrangement for general works and for those dealing with specific regions, for example, "Woman, to 1750," and "Woman—Great Britain, to 1500." Only Ancient Egypt, France, Germany, Great Britain, Russia, and the United States are chronologically subdivided.

Extensive files of general periodicals and journals are supplemented by those in such special fields as fashions. The indexing of periodical contributions on women are now largely restricted to biographical articles, although in former years the coverage was extensive. A feature of considerable interest is the large collection of publications issued by women's clubs and associations of various kinds. The library actively collects these materials, which relate both to sociology and to local history. Since 1961 the New York State Daughters of the American Revolution have deposited their publications concerning cemetery, town, and family records with the Local History and Genealogy Division.

Woman suffrage is represented by an unusually good collection of materials in the Research Libraries, not only of books and pamphlets but also of fugitive pieces. The library holds the office collections and correspondence of the National American Woman Suffrage Association, New York, of which Mrs. Carrie Chapman Catt was president. In 1947 the library received from the estate of Mrs. Catt 23 folders of manuscript materials and miscellaneous volumes, pamphlets, and scrapbooks, including a set of volumes 1 through 4 of *The Revolution*, the woman's rights paper published in New York from 1868 to 1872. The Stanton papers in the Manuscripts and Archives Division document the personality of Elizabeth Cady Stanton, another leader in the battle for the right of women to vote. The division has in addition a number of letters of Lucy Stone (Blackwell), remembered chiefly as a staunch advocate of a woman's right to retain her own name and legal identity in marriage.

The feminist, peace, and world government movements of modern times are substantially documented in manuscripts and in printed matter in the 1,777 boxes and 420 linear feet of shelved material of the Schwimmer-Lloyd collection of the Manuscripts and Archives Division, which includes the correspondence and papers of Rosika Schwimmer (1877–1948), Hungarian feminist and pacifist, and Lola Maverick Lloyd (1875–1944), American suffragist and pacifist. Access to the collection was restricted until January 1, 1974.[12]

The papers of other well-known women include those of Emma Catharine Embury, noted author; Helen Kendrick Johnson, author, editor, and lecturer; Elizabeth L. Van Lew, abolitionist and agent of the United States Secret Service at Richmond during the Civil War; Mary Hannah Hunt, educator and temperance reformer; Emma Goldman, noted American anarchist; Lilliam D. Wald, social worker; and others. Significant archives of manuscripts and books are in the Theatre Collection; the Dance Collection (including a superb collection on Isadora Duncan); and the Berg Collection (first editions, letters, and manuscripts, of such authors as Fanny Burney, the Brontë sisters, Elizabeth Barrett Browning, Lady Gregory, and Virginia Woolf).

---

12. See Robert W. Hill, "The Schwimmer-Lloyd Collection," *BNYPL* 47 (1943): 307–09.

CHILDREN

About 4,000 entries in the Public Catalog refer to the subject of children. Although the collecting policy is selective, certain areas of the holdings are of considerable strength. The Economic and Public Affairs Division is building an extensive collection of materials on juvenile delinquency, containing books and pamphlets from all countries. Charity for children is another strong feature of the resources. A small group of materials devoted to the Boy Scouts, Girl Scouts, and similar young people's organizations, is of interest. (Juvenile literature is discussed in a separate chapter.)

Among other holdings the following are notable:

Children's Asylums and Homes

Reports of institutions and societies which have local historical, as well as sociological, interest are included. Those for New York City organizations are particularly strong, although there is a good representation from other sections of this country and considerable material from abroad. Allied materials from religious asylums are classified under religion.

Child Labor

This subject is covered in depth, with supporting materials, in the official reports of various units of government in the public documents collection. Additional resources are to be found in the statutory law holdings.

Child Study

Adequate materials are supplemented by those classified under child training and the education of children.

Children's Games

The collection is adequate, although no effort is made to specialize in directed play activities and similar educational phases of the subject.

Children's Hospitals

The collection is particularly strong in reports and similar publications. The library does not collect material on the therapeutic aspects of the subject, or on children's diseases.

Public Care and Hygiene

Official publications issued by various units of government are a strong feature of this collection. Although the medical treatises are seldom acquired, the public health reports supply useful information.

PUBLIC HEALTH

This is one of the exceptionally strong collections of the library, numbering over 17,000 volumes. It represents the sociological, rather than the medical, aspects of the subject. Strong in standard works, histories, and primary materials, the resources do not include much secondary material such as textbooks.

The holdings of serials, including journals and the publications of health organizations, congresses, and special bureaus, are unusually extensive. Generally complete files of the more important titles are supplemented by an interesting representation of those which are secondary.

Another feature of great importance because of its extent and completeness is the collection of reports and other publications of national, state, and especially municipal health departments. The library's collecting policy is comprehensive for the publications of United States federal agencies, and those of New York State and City. United States resources are the most complete, but there is a very good representation of foreign materials.

The collections on such special topics as smoke regulation, working conditions, and disposal of the dead range from adequate to strong. Works on the purely medical aspects of public health are not extensive. Vital statistics, on the other hand, are thoroughly covered as a subject; hygiene of school buildings is adequately represented. Materials on food adulteration are held in strength. The library comprehensively acquires materials on the social and economic implications of air, water, and soil pollution. Those phases of public health which concern engineering are well documented.

Sanitation has long been a subject of interest. Notable early accessions were received in 1878, when the United States Sanitary Commission deposited its papers with the Astor Library, and in 1882 with a gift of $12,000 from J. J. Astor used in part to fill important needs in the collections dealing with sanitary science.

40

ANTHROPOLOGY AND ETHNOLOGY, AND FOLKLORE

Subdivisions of anthropology and ethnology are collected and maintained by the General Research and Humanities Division, the American History Division, and the Science and Technology Research Center. The anthropological resources are strong; those relating to ethnology and ethnography are particularly strong. There are about 16,400 volumes classified specifically under these subjects, with many additional works classed with history and sociology. Each of the special language divisions makes important contributions to the total holdings. While studies of all the races of the world are present, the resources are strongest for the African Negro,[1] the American Indian, the Australian aborigine,[2] the Gypsy,[3] and the natives of Oceania; there is a small but notable group of materials on the Ainu.

Although anthropology is the collecting responsibility of the General Research and Humanities Division, American Indian anthropology, which includes the Indians of all the Americas, is collected by the American History Division (Billings class mark HB). Genetics and evolution in a general sense are administered by the Science and Technology Research Center. Since this center does not stress the biological sciences, its collections are not remarkable; however, a strong core of basic reference works in the biological sciences is being acquired. Evolution as it applies to man is housed in the general stack collections with the holdings on such related topics as eugenics.

There is substantial bibliographical coverage of anthropology in the library extending from the comprehensive *International Bibliography of Social and Cultural Anthropology* (1955–) to such bibliographies covering more specialized areas as the *Boletín bibliográfico de antropología americano* (Mexico, 1937–); monographic bibliographies; and earlier attempts at coverage in the *American Anthropologist* (1888–).

Over 130 periodical titles on the general subject of anthropology are found in the library, of which some 25 are current. These include such journals as the *Bulletins et mémoires* (1860–) of the Société d'Anthropologie, the *Journal* (1871–) of the Royal Anthropological Institute of Great Britain and Ireland, the *Journal* (1886–) of the Anthropological Society of Bombay, and *Ethnographia* (Budapest, 1890–). The proceedings of international congresses of anthropology held since the late nineteenth century are present. Holdings of periodicals in the more specialized areas of both physical and cultural anthropology are substantial. The series publications of such bodies as the Wenner Gren Foundation for Anthropological Research (formerly the Viking Fund Publications in Anthropology), the Chicago Natural History Museum, and the American Anthropological Association are all available. General learned society publications relating to the Near and Far East in the Oriental Division include a great deal of anthropological information. Index entries for significant journal articles on anthropology appear in the Public Catalog.

Eugenics and evolution are among those topics for which materials are held in strength. There are many editions of Darwin's *On the Origin of Species* and *The Descent of Man*, and a host of works about him and his discoveries and their implications under such diverse subject headings as "Evolution and the Bible" and "Evolution and Religion."

1. The holdings of the Schomburg Center should particularly be consulted.
2. See "List of Works in The New York Public Library Relating to the Aborigines of Australia and Tasmania," *BNYPL* 17 (1913): 876–929.
3. See "List of Works in The New York Public Library Relating to Gypsies," *BNYPL* 10 (1906): 358–67.

Description and travel to Oceania and Australia, a subject represented by strong holdings from the sixteenth century to the present, contains a great deal of anthropological interest. Many specialized headings aid the researcher in his use of the catalog; for example, the resources on the Australian aborigine are subdivided by tribal names.

During the period 1943 to 1947, the library was given the Kamchadal and Asiatic Eskimo linguistic and ethnographic materials recorded by Waldemar Jochelson as a member of the Ryabushinski expeditions to Kamchatka in 1909–11. These include a description of the area and its people, their language and religion, with photographs and the texts of 40 folk tales. A catalog of the material is held with the collection in the Manuscripts and Archives Division.[4]

About 500 titles on Gypsies in the library include fictional and dramatic treatments and the *Journal* (1888/89–91/92, 1898–) of the Gypsy Lore Society. Three boxes of the manuscripts of Albert Thomas Sinclair consist of articles, extracts from printed works, letters, and other materials.[5] A small but noteworthy collection on the Gypsy language includes grammars, dictionaries, and studies of the dialects in various countries, as well as folk songs and poems in the tongue. This collection is classed with the Indic language materials of the Oriental Division.

FOLKLORE

COLLECTING POLICY

Folklore is one of the strong features of the library's collection, with holdings of 6,650 volumes. The collecting policy is comprehensive in all areas except in Oriental languages, which are collected on a representative basis. The collection of periodicals, including society publications, is good, with generally complete files in many languages. The Research Libraries currently receive approximately 40 periodical titles from the United States, England, and both Western and Eastern Europe dealing directly with folklore. Most of the important works on the subject which have appeared since the 1870s are in the holdings, as are a number of others of secondary importance. Related materials are found in the resources of such fields as dance, music (folk songs), juvenile literature, and philosophy (with works on occultism, witchcraft,[6] etc.).

A collection of about 450 volumes in the American History Division (Billings class mark HABR) contains material on Indian folklore of tribes of the Americas. It reflects the awakening of interest in American folklore just after World War II, and covers folk tales, folk dances, and folk songs. Periodicals include the *Journal of American Folklore* (1888–) and many other journals of a regional nature. The division selectively collects folklore written for children.

Most of the library's Oriental folklore holdings are in Western European languages, with the exception of rare illustrated books, manuscripts, and scrolls in the Spencer Collection and reprints of original texts in the collections of the Oriental Division. Other material in this division includes Henri Doré's *Recherches sur les superstitions en Chine* (1911–38), published first as part of *Variétés sinologiques*, also in the division, both in French and in English translation, and the works of Verrier Elwin on Indian folk tales and folk lore.

A folklore collection of about 1,500 titles in the Balto-Slavic languages in the Slavonic Division emphasizes folk tales and folk songs. The collecting policy is comprehensive, with the exception of materials in the Uralic and Altaic languages, which are selectively collected.

The Jewish Division holdings in folklore, numbering about 700 volumes, are strong in editions of the *Aggadah*. There are many editions of Jacob ibn Habib's anthology of the aggadic sections of the Talmud, *Ein Yaakov* (1460–1516). There is a good collection of modern periodicals and books on Jewish folklore.

CHAPBOOKS

The collection of English, Scottish, American, Italian, and other European chapbooks in the Research Libraries numbers 2,650 pieces, ranging from the fifteenth century to about 1850, and provides strong supplementary materials for the study of folklore and folk traditions.[7] Chapbooks include anything from broadsides to full-sized books sold by chapmen, peddlers, hawkers, or flying-stationers. Many chapbooks were designed for children. The Spencer Collection has over the years acquired a strong collection of Italian *rappresentazione* and other popular tracts of the fifteenth and sixteenth centuries. *Rappresentazione* are chapbooks, usually of four to six leaves, reproducing miracle and other sacred plays given on certain saint's days. The contemporary popular tracts consist of *frottola*, *noveli*, romances, etc. illustrated with woodcuts. About 150 items of this nature join the other rich holdings of material in the Rare Book Division and the Central Children's Room of the Branch Libraries. An alphabetical card catalog of all single chapbooks in the Rare Book Division is located there; other items in the Research Libraries are entered under the heading "Chapbooks," with geographical designations, in the Rare Book Division public catalog. Since 1935 the collections have been substantially augmented by gifts and purchases.

OTHER FOLKLORE-RELATED MATERIALS

The Spencer Collection's holdings of Oriental books, manuscripts, and scrolls contain a wealth of folklore-related material from China, Japan,

---

4. See Avrahm Yarmolinsky, "Kamchadal and Asiatic Eskimo Manuscript Collections," *BNYPL* 51 (1947): 659–69.

5. See Albert Thomas Sinclair, "An American-Romani Vocabulary," *BNYPL* 19 (1915): 727–38; "Avesta and Romani," Ibid. 955–57; and "Gypsies in Carniola and Carinthia," *BNYPL* 21 (1917): 15–18. See also George F. Black, "Romani and Dard," *BNYPL* 20 (1916): 451–54; and Lewis Bond, "The Gypsies of Monastir," Ibid. 839–42.

6. See George F. Black, "A List of Works Relating to Lycanthropy," *BNYPL* 23 (1919): 811–15.

7. See Harry B. Weiss, "A Catalogue of the American, English, and Foreign Chapbooks in The New York Public Library," *BNYPL* 39 (1935): 3–34 et seq. Published separately by the library with corrections, 1936.

India, Arabia, and other countries. The Indian materials dating from the sixteenth to the nineteenth centuries are written in Sanskrit or Hindi, and finely illustrated by artists of the Rajasthani, Punjabi, Kangra, and other schools. Japanese scrolls, books, and manuscripts in the collection excel in imaginative folklore; examples are a 1587 scroll entitled *Zegaibō emaki*, illustrated with impressionistic and humorous sketches of a Tengu (a dweller of the forest, winged, beaked, and clawed, belonging neither to heaven nor to hell), a printed version of *The Story of the Fox* of 1650, and a seventeenth-century scroll of demons roaming the streets at night.

The Prints Division has always emphasized *imagerie populaire*. A colorful group of Chinese New Year's pictures of ethnographic significance hail from many different provinces.

41

SPORTS AND GAMES

COLLECTING POLICY

The collection of 45,800 volumes and numerous manuscripts covers all sports and amusements with the exception of the theatre, dance, and music. Among the strong features are the holdings on fishing, with a fine collection of Izaak Walton's *Compleat Angler*; the chess materials centering on the Pfeiffer chess collection; and the baseball resources including the Spalding, Swales, and Goulston collections. These illustrate how individual gifts have enriched and strengthened the Research Libraries; much of the growth in this area since 1941, when the resources numbered 15,000 volumes, can be attributed to donations of specialized collections.

The collecting policy of the Research Libraries calls for comprehensive treatment of bibliography, history, and general works on sports and games; and for all materials relating to specific sports, including baseball, American football, horses and horse racing, fishing, hunting (particularly hunting in Africa and America), hawking and falconry, and among the indoor games, chess. Holdings of American sporting books published before 1860 are generally strong.[1]

Periodical holdings are strongest for early sporting titles, primarily in English; but files are not always complete. Among these are *Sporting Magazine* (1792–1860), *Annals of Sporting* (1822–27), *Badminton Magazine* (1895–1923), and *Baily's Magazine* (1860–1926). The library attempts to acquire only a representation of the more significant international titles from the great number of modern periodicals dealing with sports and games, including such publications as *Field and Stream* (1898–) and *Sports Illustrated* (1954–). In addition is a large number of sporting club periodicals, yearbooks, and other publications.

Material on the Olympic Games is chiefly made up of official accounts, accounts of the United States Olympic committees, personal accounts, and programmes.

In the special language divisions, the Slavonic Division collects comprehensively in chess and in hunting, and the Oriental Division has much of interest for the study of sports and games in the Near and Far East. Materials in this division include a number of books on *ma-ch'iao* (Mah-Jongg) dating from the early 1920s, when the game became popular in the United States.

Other classes of materials contribute to this subject, the most obvious being works on description and travel and works on ethnography. A small collection bearing directly on sports and games is included in the section of philosophy which contains materials on the ethical aspects of betting, gambling, and lotteries.

The following alphabetical arrangement describes those collections of materials on sports and games in which the holdings of the Library are strongest.

ARCHERY

Although this collection does not appear to be extensive from a count of entries in the Public Catalog, additional material listed under such headings as "Arms and Armor," "Arrow Heads," and "Cross Bow" lends strength to the subject. In addition to entries for books are many index entries for articles in periodicals and learned journals. In 1946 the library acquired the Paul H. Gordon collection of books on archery, which included periodicals and pamphlets; the material in the collection covers the period from the late 1600s to 1946. After that date materials have been added on a representative basis.

BASEBALL

The holdings are of considerable importance for a study of this national sport up to approximately the 1930s. They center around three large gifts: the Spalding, Swales, and Goulston collections. Currently the library acquires such periodicals as *The Sporting News* (1887–), *Amateur Baseball News* (1960–), and publications of the National League of Professional Base Ball Clubs. Baseball yearbooks are also present, such as *Baseball Blue Book* (1915–), *Little Red Book* (1926–), and *National League Green Book* (1935–).

The personal collection of A. G. Spalding came to the library in 1921 as a gift of his widow. Consisting of over 3,000 books and pamphlets, 102 periodicals, more than 560 photographs, and 30 original drawings (17 by Homer Davenport) the collection documents the history of baseball

---

1. See a partial listing in Robert W. Henderson, comp., *Early American Sport: A Checklist of Books by American and Foreign Authors Published in America Prior to 1860* (New York: A. S. Barnes, 1953).

from 1845 to about 1914. It contains much material on other sports, such as cricket, most of it in pamphlet form. Spalding had acquired and incorporated the Harry Wright and Henry Chadwick libraries, in themselves notable; the three collections contain extensive manuscript materials.[2]

In 1929, Mrs. Bradshaw Hall Swales presented the baseball collection formed by her husband, the noted ornithologist.[3] The collection is remarkable for its manuscript rosters of the various leagues dating from 1880 to 1926, and for score records and biographical data. With the collection is a twelve-drawer card file arranged alphabetically by name of player giving vital statistics, batting averages, etc. This file is in the general collections, the rosters and other biographical data are in the Manuscripts and Archives Division.

Leopold Morse Goulston presented his collection in memory of Leo J. Bondy, vice-president and treasurer of the New York Giants, in 1946. The collection is largely pictorial but contains a number of early books that make a contribution to a history of the sport, such as *By-Laws and Rules of Order* of the Takewambait Base Ball Club of Natick, Massachusetts (1858). Most of the 1,000 portraits of baseball players and pictures of old teams are advertisements inserted in cigarette packages of the late 1800s. There are also silver annual passes designed by Charles Dana Gibson and issued by the New York Giants in 1930 and 1931. Some 20 original drawings are by artists who contributed to the early *Life* and *Puck*; prints are included, among them some by Currier and Ives.[4]

BOXING

Among the items presented by Herbert Bayard Swope in 1951 are early works on boxing, including extremely rare *The Fancy; Or True Sportsman's Guide* (1826), in two volumes, Pierce Egan's *Boxiana* (1812–29), and *Pancratia: Or A History of Pugilism* (1812).[5]

BULLFIGHTING

A fair collection on this sport is perhaps most remarkable for its sets of scarce periodicals, such as *La lidia* (Mexico, 1943–), *El ruedo* (Madrid, 1944–), *El eco taurino* (Mexico, 1928–32), and *La fiesta brava* (Barcelona, 1926–36).

CARDS

This section of the library's holdings contains a number of old and modern editions of Hoyle. A strong group of materials on card tricks is to be found in the Ellison and Hooker collections, described fully in chapter 33. Materials on playing card design and history are in the Prints

Division and in the general collections. Sets of playing cards in the library, most of which came as gifts, are primarily held in the Rare Book Division. Both the Prints Division and the Spencer Collection have examples of the engravings of Stefano della Bella for Jean Desmarets de Saint Solin's *Jeux historiques des rois de France*. . . . The Prints Division has four sets mounted in its della Bella scrapbooks; the Spencer Collection has only the *rois* and *reines*. Also in the Prints Division are the sixteenth-century engravings by Ladenspelder made from Italian tarocchi cards. Two sets of playing cards engraved with engineering and mechanical instruments made in early eighteenth-century London are in the Parsons collection in the Science and Technology Research Center.

CHESS AND OTHER BOARD GAMES

There are about 2,500 entries relating to chess in the Public Catalog, representing an unusually good collection. Significant aspects of the game are chronologically categorized by date of publication. These categories include general books on chess (800 entries), chess problems (280 entries), and chess tournaments (330 entries). The purchase of the Prayer-Goldwater collection of tournament books in the late 1950s strengthened the resources in this area, which now include the following records: London, 1851 and 1862; Hastings, 1895; San Sebastian, 1911 and 1912; and New York, 1924. Books by chess masters and authorities are numerous, including works by Ruy Lopez de Sigura, Philidor (in many editions and translations), William Lewis, and Howard Staunton. Approximately 120 periodical titles cover the nineteenth and twentieth centuries. About 15 titles are currently received from 9 countries, including the *Deutsche Schachzeitung* (1846–), *British Chess Magazine* (1881–), and *Chess Review* (1933–).

Gifts by Gustavus A. Pfeiffer were most important in the development of the chess collection. The first gift, consisting of 590 volumes and 185 pamphlets, came in 1932; it is named in honor of Frank J. Marshall. This group primarily includes works published in the nineteenth century and reprints of earlier titles; chess Americana in the collection is worthy of note. An additional gift of 161 items came the following year. Upon his death in 1953, Pfeiffer made a further bequest of 700 manuscripts, books, scrapbooks, and periodicals, together with funds to be used in developing the chess collection. This final gift included 2 editions of Damiano of Odemira's *Libro da imparare giocare a scacchi* (Rome, 1525 and Venice, 1564); an anonymous Latin manuscript, probably of the fifteenth century, that contains 132 diagrams of chess problems of which 15 are completed; and about 100 letters of chess masters such as Frank Marshall (10 postcards, 2 letters), Emanuel Lasker (6 letters), William Steinitz (7 letters), and others. Additional chess rarities in the library include 4 fifteenth-century editions of Jacobus de Cessolis, including Caxton's translation *The Game and Playe of the Chesse* (Bruges, 1476), the second book printed in the English language. Cessolis's work is not a treatise on chess itself, but rather an essay on the moral virtues, with the different pieces used in the game symbolizing the various conditions of life.

The Oriental Division receives 2 periodicals on Chinese chess, *Wei Ch'i* (Shanghai, 1962–) and *Hsiang Ch'i* (Canton, 1963–) in addition to a

---

2. See "The Albert G. Spalding Collection," *BNYPL* 25 (1921): 635; "The Spalding Baseball Collection," *BNYPL* 26 (1922): 86–127. Published separately by the library.

3. See "The Swales Baseball Collection," *BNYPL* 33 (1929): 653–54.

4. See Robert W. Henderson, "Leopold Morse Goulston Baseball Collection in Memory of Leo J. Bondy," *BNYPL* 50 (1946): 663–64.

5. See Paul Magriel, "Bibliography of Boxing," *BNYPL* 52 (1948): 263–88. Published separately by the library.

Japanese periodical for the board game of *go*, the *Go Monthly Review* (1961–). Further book materials in the division refer to these and other Oriental games.

FENCING

Books of a general nature are included in this collection, as well as books of instruction and books on such related topics as the bayonet, sword exercise, stage fencing, etc. Although there are a number of files of older fencing periodicals in the holdings, only one title is received currently, *American Fencing* (1954–), in film reproduction. Perhaps most significant in the holdings on fencing are a number of early books of the sixteenth and seventeenth centuries in the Spencer Collection and the Rare Book Division by Salvatore Fabris, Henry de Saint Didier, Angelo Vizani, and others. A related collection on dueling is made up of over 500 volumes ranging from the sixteenth century to the present and including notable seventeenth- to nineteenth-century ordinances, court decisions, laws, and proclamations against dueling in England, Europe, Mexico, and Argentina.

FISHING

The rich collection on angling in the Research Libraries numbers approximately 2,500 entries in the Public Catalog, with strong sections on bibliography, handbooks, and game laws going back to the earliest periods of American, English, and European history. Fishing periodicals include such standard titles as *Field and Stream* (1898–), *Rod and Gun* (1902–), and *Skin Diver* (1952–).

Early books on fishing are a feature of the holdings; they include the first 5 editions of Izaak Walton's *Compleat Angler* issued during the author's lifetime (there are about 150 English language editions of this classic in the library) as well as examples of other books which exist in only a few copies, such as John Whitney's *Genteel Recreation* (1700) and Constantine S. Rafinesque's *Ichthyologia Ohiensis* (Lexington, Kentucky, 1820). Most of these items came from the Lenox Library and are listed in *Contributions to a Catalogue of the Lenox Library* no. 7 (1893). The Lenox collection, which included the library of Thomas Westwood,[6] numbered about 500 volumes. From 1897 to 1902 the Hon. John L. Cadwalader gave important collections relating to fishing and outdoor sports.[7] In 1937 the library received from the Misses Carolyn C. and Louise DeForest Haynes a collection of nearly 100 volumes on salmon fishing, given in memory of their brother.

Related collections in the holdings are described in chapter 62 of this *Guide*.

FOOTBALL

Originally the Football heading was used in the catalog of the library to include all games of this type, including Rugby and soccer. At present an attempt is made to separate these games under their individual headings, reserving "Football" for American football. The holdings are strongest for American football, but all types of the game are represented. Histories of the sport and of football clubs, associations, and leagues are included. No particular attempt is made to acquire periodicals. In 1937, Edward Kimball Hall, chairman of the Football Rules Committee of the National Collegiate Athletic Association, gave to the library reports of the committee, rules, letters and telegrams, and typescripts of periodical articles, contained in 3 boxes in the Manuscripts and Archives Division.

HORSES, HORSE RACING, AND HORSE BREEDING

This rich collection is covered by about 4,000 entries in the Public Catalog, including long files of studbooks, racing guides, and periodicals, with many early works on equitation, farriery, and similar subjects from the United States and other countries. In 1951, Herbert Bayard Swope presented a valuable collection of 217 volumes, the larger number pertaining to horse racing in America and horse breeding. This gift contains an exceptionally long set of *Racing Form; Charts of American Racing* (1896–1941) supplemented by *Daily Racing Form Chart Books* (1942–51), a continuation of which the library currently maintains. In addition are 14 periodicals concerning horses, horse racing, and horsemanship, including *El caballo* (Buenos Aires, 1935–), *Quarter Horse Journal* (1953–), *Western Horseman* (1936–), and *Blood Horse* (1938–). Studbooks include *American Stud Book* (1873–), *American Morgan Horse Register* (1894–), and *Arab Horse Stud Book* (1919–).

Early works on horses and horsemanship include a number published in sixteenth-century Venice, as well as early English and American items in the Rare Book Division. In the Spencer Collection is George Engelhard von Löhneyss's *Della Caualleria* (1624), a work on harnesses and saddles, Hans Creutzberger's *Eygentliche, wolgerissene Contrafactur und Formen de Gebisz* (1591), and other works on horse ballets and related matters in the collection of festival books. The Prints Division has numerous representations of horses and riding by such artists as Dürer, Delacroix, Géricault, and others; also the duke of Newcastle's *A General System of Horsemanship* (1743).

The papers of Robert Bonner in the Manuscripts and Archives Division relate to the breeding, development, and shoeing of trotting horses between the years 1860 and 1899. Several manuscript stud records include those of Seely's American Star and Eclipse, son of Marske.

HUNTING

The library has a very good collection of material on hunting in general and accounts of particular hunting expeditions;[8] there is particular interest in hunting in Africa and in America. As a matter of policy, the library does not collect the finely-illustrated hunting books of the past unless they can be acquired for the Prints Division or the Spencer Collection. In the Arents Collection of Books in Parts are some nineteenth-

---

6. See the catalog of J. W. Bouton, the bookseller, incorporated as no. 8 of the *Contributions*.
7. See "List of Works in The New York Public Library Relating to Fishing and Fish Culture," *BNYPL* 13 (1909): 259–307.

---

8. "List of Works in The New York Public Library on Sport in General and on Shooting in Particular," *BNYPL* 7 (1903): 164–86, 201–34.

century English sporting books and original drawings of hunting scenes by Henry Alken, John Leech, and others. Important related materials appear under such headings as "Ordnance," "Firearms," and "Munitions."

TENNIS

Lawn tennis materials are the most extensive. For the older games of court tennis and racquets, the library has contemporary works.[9]

9. See Robert W. Henderson, "How Old Is the Game of Racquets?" *BNYPL* 40 (1936): 403–10.

YACHTS AND YACHTING

This collection is particularly strong in periodicals; more than 35 titles are held, including 11 currently received from the United States, England, France, and New Zealand. Among these are *A.Y.R.S. Publication* (1955–), *Les Cahiers du yachting* (1967–), *The Rudder* (1891–), and *Sea Spray* (1945–). Monographic holdings include sections on yacht cruises and yacht racing.

42

EDUCATION

Although the Lenox Library's annual report (for 1894) mentions the acquisition of some early educational works from the libraries of Dr. George H. Moore and George Livermore, the field of education is not one in which the New York Public Library has endeavored to build strong resources. Over the years, however, it has assembled a sizeable collection; by 1941 the library's holdings amounted to 68,500 volumes; by 1966 they had increased to 97,800 volumes.

The Research Libraries have concentrated acquisition efforts in the areas of educational theory, education and society, history of education, and the education of individuals and groups outside the systems of formal schooling. The strongest features are the administrative reports of departments of education for various countries and for American states and large cities, material on colleges and universities, and resources on college fraternities; holdings in this field, on the whole, are stronger in materials published before 1930 than for the subsequent period. Such aspects of education as school administration and teaching methods, along with intensive collecting of textbooks, are left to the History and Social Science Department of the Mid-Manhattan Library (a unit of the Branch Libraries), to Teachers College, and to other libraries in the city specializing in the subject. Reflecting this informal division of responsibility for resources, the current collecting policy is selective for most areas in this field; exceptions include general history and bibliography and education for the culturally disadvantaged, which are collected comprehensively, and general works on education in the United States and administrative reports from other countries, which are collected representatively.

BIBLIOGRAPHY AND SERIALS

A good collection of bibliographies and indexes includes not only such tools as *Education Index* and *British Education Index*, but many bibliographies issued by the United States Office of Education. The Public Catalog lists a total of more than 200 bibliographies for the field.

The more important periodicals in the English language are generally complete and include *Catholic Educational Review, Educational Forum, Educational Record, Harvard Educational Review, Jewish Education, Journal of Educational Sociology, Journal of Experimental Education, Peabody Journal of Education, Review of Educational Research, School and Society,* and *Teachers College Record.* There are some state journals of education, but relatively few foreign titles. The Research Libraries currently receive more than 100 periodicals in the field.

Holdings of the publications of major associations are good. The Public Catalog contains about 500 entries for the National Education Association, including titles from its departments of Adult Education, Audio-Visual Instruction, Business Education, and Classroom Teachers, and its Research Division; also represented are various commissions, committees, and projects. There are about 400 entries for the American Council on Education, embracing its reports and surveys of individual institutions, such series as "American Youth Commission," and titles prepared by special committees and commissions. About 1,300 entries represent publications of the United States Office of Education. In addition to the *Report of the Commissioner* since 1867, the collection contains the *Directory*, and *Biennial Survey* in a complete run. Files of the *Circular* and *Bulletin* lack relatively few numbers. There are many miscellaneous publications. Examples of other organizations whose publications are held include Kappa Delta Pi and Phi Delta Kappa, as well as the World Confederation of Organizations of the Teaching Profession.

Administrative reports of ministries and departments of education form an important feature of the collection. The file for most American states is extensive, although not necessarily complete; in some cases few recent issues are present. British Commonwealth and Latin American countries are also well represented, but with more numerous lacunae in the files. For most other countries holdings are weak, with few reports for foreign political subdivisions such as provinces or states.

Reports of the boards of education of American cities are held in strength. The library no longer attempts to maintain files from cities with populations of less than 250,000 (with the exception of those in the metropolitan New York area), although the collection contains many late nineteenth- and early twentieth-century reports from smaller communities. Minutes and proceedings of boards of education are generally available only for the largest cities (e.g., New York, Chicago, Philadelphia, Boston, Cincinnati, St. Louis). Perhaps a dozen Canadian cities and an equal number in other Commonwealth countries are represented by reports.

HISTORY

The collection contains a representative selection of histories of education, expositions of educational theory, and works by major educators. There are, for example, 125 entries in the Public Catalog for publications by and about Johann Heinrich Pestalozzi, including his works in German and in English translation. More than 250 cards represent works by and about John Dewey, including critical studies in a number of foreign languages.

Although the library has not generally collected works of applied pedagogy, it does have some interesting examples of textbooks. For the United States these consist of readers, spellers (particularly Webster's spellers, many editions of which are held in the Rare Book Division), arithmetics, and other school books from the eighteenth century. There are also examples from later periods, including a group of schoolbooks issued in the South during the 1860s and 1870s. In the 1930s the library began to collect modern foreign schoolbooks for the political and social ideas they reflect, and acquired several hundred such publications before discontinuing the program. About 400 volumes came from Spain: 350 in Spanish, issued between 1900 and 1936, and 45 in Catalan, issued between 1920 and 1936. Both groups have readers (sometimes an entire series for the first through sixth grades), literary anthologies, books of religious instruction, and social studies texts; the Catalan items include some geographies and histories of the region. Other Spanish-language material includes 37 titles issued in Argentina during the 1930s. Another group of 200 items appeared in Germany between 1925 and 1936; some of the social science texts show the propaganda of the early years of Hitler's regime. There are 10 Italian readers and grammars from this period. The classified collections contain some primers and other textbooks in minor Asian and African languages, collected as representative publications from areas with small publishing outputs, and as examples of less widely known languages.

HIGHER EDUCATION

The library holds strong resources on higher education, both in the United States and abroad. Files of *Index Generalis, Minerva,* and *The World of Learning* are complete. A good collection of society publications includes those of the American Association of Collegiate Registrars, Association of American Colleges, Association of American Universities, Association of Graduate Schools, College Entrance Examination Board, and the International Association of Universities. Extensive holdings on the history and development of higher education embrace surveys, works on academic freedom, and material on the role of philanthropy in education, as well as general treatises. The most notable feature of these resources consists of long files of the publications of American and foreign colleges and universities. The Research Libraries attempt to secure catalogs and announcements of courses for American undergraduate, graduate, and professional schools (excluding law, medicine, and veterinary medicine) and to maintain files of superseded issues for historical research. For some institutions (e.g., Bowdoin, Brown, Dartmouth, Yale) the retrospective files begin as early as the 1820s and 1830s, while for other important universities the collection now covers approximately a century— in both cases there are occasional gaps.

Administrative reports, chiefly those of presidents and treasurers, are also noteworthy. Relatively few sets are complete; the period 1920–40 offering the richest representation. The Research Libraries generally acquire certain types of unofficial publications (histories, collections of photographs, reminiscences); other types are generally excluded (alumni bulletins, class reports, yearbooks and other student publications, song books). There are, however, alumni magazines for some Eastern institutions (e.g., Brown, Dartmouth, Princeton, Smith, and Williams) and fewer for other institutions not in the East (e.g., the Universities of Chicago, Michigan). Alumni directories are acquired for their value as biographical reference works.

Two collections in the Manuscripts and Archives Division contribute to the history of higher education: a portfolio of correspondence (1873–85) from Cornelius Vanderbilt and his son, William Henry Vanderbilt, with Bishop H. N. McTyeire on the founding of Vanderbilt University; and the extensive personal papers of John Houston Finley. Covering the period 1900–40, the Finley papers include correspondence, writings, reports, and diaries relating to Finley's editorial work with *McClure's Magazine* and the *New York Times,* his association with Grover Cleveland, and his service as Commissioner of Education of the State of New York. The collection is housed in 90 boxes, 2 volumes, and 39 steel cases.

An unusually large and complete group of publications deals with Harvard University, embracing a nearly unbroken file of catalogs and announcements from the nineteenth century to date, together with the reports of the president, treasurer, and departments of the University. Included are *Harvard Alumni Bulletin, Harvard Lampoon,* more than 400 class reports, and a number of books about the institution. Not classified with these general titles are monographic series and other publications of individual faculties, institutes, and centers, which are shelved with appropriate subjects. The Public Catalog contains about 4,000 entries for the university. There are similar but less extensive holdings for Columbia, Princeton, and Yale. Other major universities are represented by smaller files.

Material on overseas universities is strongest for Australian, British, Canadian, and other British Commonwealth institutions. The sets of *Calendars* for major universities in these countries extend back many years, but holdings of administrative reports are less extensive than those for American institutions. The *Commonwealth Universities Yearbook,* of which the library possesses a complete set, provides basic information. A much smaller collection covers other continental, Asian, African, and Latin American institutions. There are publications from nearly all major universities, but in many cases files are incomplete and not current.

Two other types of university publications, monograph series and doctoral dissertations, require special comment. In the subjects of collecting interest the Research Libraries have assembled extensive holdings of monograph series published by universities which are usually classified under subject. Only general series (for example, studies in the humanities) are classed with university publications; these form a very limited portion of the total monographic publications issued from major universities.

The Research Libraries actively collected American and foreign doctoral dissertations before 1940; when the custom of publishing American theses ceased and the War made most foreign studies unavailable their acquisition decreased markedly. Since the 1960s the Research Libraries have acquired certain American titles (almost exclusively on microfilm) and some foreign works listed in national bibliographies, selected as publications of value to scholarly users. The collection contains the volumes of summaries of doctoral dissertations that major American universities commonly issued until expanded coverage in *Dissertation Abstracts* led to their discontinuance. The annex houses a collection of more than 750 bound volumes of foreign dissertations not fully cataloged. The majority of these are from German universities (Berlin, Bonn, Breslau, Erlangen, Jena, etc.); there is a small representation from Swiss, Dutch, and Swedish institutions. The greater number are from the period 1920 to 1940, although a few are as early as the seventeenth century.

There are more than 5,000 volumes on Greek letter societies; the nucleus of which (1,300 items) dates from 1921, when Beta Theta Pi deposited the William Raimond Baird collection. Long runs of the periodicals published by individual fraternities and sororities constitute the most notable feature of these resources and account for as many as 80 percent of the volumes. The library has files of the magazines of Alpha Chi Omega, Alpha Tau Omega, Kappa Alpha Theta, Kappa Kappa Gamma, Lambda Chi Alpha, Sigma Chi, and Sigma Nu; many runs lack only a few early volumes. Additional publications include yearbooks, manuals, song books, and national and local directories of individual fraternities. The Manuscripts and Archives Division holds the records and documents of Delta Upsilon Fraternity and its constituent chapters from the 1880s to the 1930s, housed in 50 boxes and various volumes of minute books; some of the chapter records date from as early as the 1840s. The set of *Baird's Manual of American College Fraternities* is complete from 1879, and *Banta's Greek Exchange* and *Yearbook of the National Interfraternity Conference* are complete from the first volumes. Despite the strong emphasis on social fraternities, the holdings encompass some material relating to the history of Phi Beta Kappa and of Sigma Xi; for the former the Research Libraries have acquired a number of directories and histories of individual chapters. There is little about other Greek letter honor societies, although the publications of some (e.g., Sigma Delta Chi) are available.

Information on many other aspects of educational conditions and school life in the United States from the late eighteenth century to the present appears in a number of collections in the Manuscripts and Archives Division. Diaries, correspondence, composition and exercise books, and other material contribute to studies of elementary and secondary, as well as higher education. A full listing appears in the division's published catalog (Boston: G. K. Hall & Company, 1957, 1: 265–70).

EDUCATION OF SPECIAL GROUPS

In accordance with its policy of building resources on education for persons not served by traditional school systems, the Research Libraries have strong holdings on industrial and technical education, adult education, and education of the culturally disadvantaged and physically handicapped.

The Public Catalog contains about 3,400 entries under the heading "Education, Industrial and Technical"; a sizeable number of these relate to individual institutions in various countries (e.g., Denmark, France, Great Britain, Greece, Mexico, and the United States). There is a considerable amount of material on the German Technische Hochschule.

Specialized resources on adult education include long runs of such periodicals as *International Journal of Adult and Youth Education*, *Continuous Learning*, and *Journal of Adult Education*. There are about 700 entries in the Public Catalog, many of them dealing with adult education in individual American localities and in foreign countries having active movements (e.g., Finland, Germany, Great Britain, India, Poland, the Soviet Union, and Sweden). Catalogs and other publications from American institutions offering extension and home-study courses are present. Long files of periodicals greatly strengthen the collection of material on the Chautauqua Institution and the Chautauqua system. There are early files of the *Chatauquan Daily* (from 1876), *Weekly*, and *Quarterly*; while the sets lack some numbers, they are very extensive. The gifts of Arthur E. Bestor in 1934 (1,477 items) and Rebecca Richmond in 1948 substantially enlarged the holdings of Chautauqua materials.

The Manuscripts and Archives Division houses material from two organizations in the field of adult education: the correspondence of the American Association for Adult Education (1939–40); and the records of The People's Institute, including general correspondence, scrapbooks of clippings and memorabilia, financial records, and printed programs and publications (1883–1932; 36 linear feet). Another relevant group consists of 16 boxes and 2 volumes of the letters, lectures, sermons, notebooks, and scrapbooks (1886–1917) of Henry Marcus Leipziger, long associated with the New York City Board of Education.

The Research Libraries have made special efforts to collect in the field of education for the culturally disadvantaged. This includes material on such topics as prejudice in education, intergroup relations, and the treatment of foreign peoples and cultures in textbooks. Related to this are more than 100 publications listed in the Public Catalog under the heading "Discrimination in Education, Racial and Religious."

Education of certain minority groups receives good coverage. For the topic as it relates to black Americans are such serial publications as *Expanding Opportunities* and *Journal of Negro Education*, and the catalogs, reports, and other publications of such individual Negro schools and colleges as Hampton and Tuskegee Institutes. The Public Catalog has approximately 75 entries for works by and about Booker T. Washington. General works on the education of American Indians (about 200 entries in the Public Catalog) include both monographs and serial titles, some of which are complete from the first issue (*Indian Education* and *Journal of American Indian Education*). An interesting group of publications, including several eighteenth-century imprints, deals with Eleaza Wheelock's Indian Charity School in Lebanon, Connecticut; with the Indian Industrial School in Carlisle, Pennsylvania; and with various other special schools for Indians.

The most significant feature of holdings on the education of the physically handicapped consists of the reports of institutions and associations, foreign as well as domestic, which work with these groups. The period from the late nineteenth century to World War II is best covered, although the file of reports from the Perkins School is complete from 1832 and that from the American Printing House for the Blind from 1869 (with

some gaps). While the majority of these reports come from individual institutions in various states, there is some representation from foreign countries, including Australia, Argentina, Canada, China, France, Germany, Great Britain, Ireland, and Sweden. Files of specialized periodicals such as *The New Beacon*, *American Annals of the Deaf*, and *Volta Review* are generally complete. Two interesting groups deserve mention: a number of publications on Frenchmen handicapped as a result of injuries received in the two World Wars; and approximately 50 publications by and about Helen Keller, including translations of several titles into French and German. An unusual item in the Rare Book Division is a copy of the autobiographical *Midstream* (1929), with the author's inscription to Mrs. Andrew Carnegie and the autograph of Anne Sullivan Macy.

PART TWO

43

MAP DIVISION AND GENERAL MAP RESOURCES

COLLECTING POLICY

The Map Division contains approximately 300,000 sheet maps, 6,000 atlases, and 11,000 volumes on cartography and the techniques of map making; a sample of almost every type of map available is included. The primary aim of the division is to secure maps, atlases, and works in the field of cartography of use to the reading public. The division collects sheet maps and atlases on a universal basis, irrespective of date, country of origin, size, or rarity; large-scale maps are preferred. Particular emphasis is placed on maps of New York City and New York State.

The collecting policy follows the tabulation given below:

Comprehensive acquisition:
  Astronomical or celestial maps and charts
  New York City assembly district maps
  U.S. county atlases and New York City property atlases
  U.S. Army Map Service (now U.S. Army Topographic Command) collections
  U.S. Coast and Geodetic Survey charts
  U.S. Geological Survey quadrangles
  U.S. Department of Agriculture soil survey maps

Representative acquisition:
  World, regional, national, and thematic (historical, geological, real estate, lunar, and pictorial) sheet maps and atlases
  Foreign street plans
  U.S. city (population of 10,000 and above) maps
  U.S. Hydrographic Office (now U.S. Naval Oceanographic Office), Great Lakes Survey, and Mississippi River Commission charts

Selective acquisition:
  Current files of U.S. road maps published by oil companies or state highway depart-

ments. A retrospective file of road maps is retained.
  Weather charts

The Research Libraries do not collect in the following categories:
  Aerial photographs
  Aeronautical landing charts
  Pilot charts (except those published by the U.S. Naval Oceanographic Office)
  Puzzle maps
  Relief models
  Roller maps

The 6,000 atlases now in the Map Division date from the seventeenth century to the present. Atlases and separate maps published prior to 1600 in Europe and before 1800 in the United States are housed in the Rare Book Division; the Map Division maintains a growing collection of facsimiles of early atlases and maps. Manuscript maps are generally held in the Manuscripts and Archives Division; there are many rare atlases and maps in the Spencer Collection, the Prints Division, and in other divisions of the Research Libraries (discussed in later paragraphs).

The Map Division catalog includes entries for these items with analytic entries for maps in atlases published before 1800; it is a union list for all maps in the Research Libraries. The 11,000 volumes in the division form an outstanding collection on the history of cartography and the techniques of map making.

HISTORICAL SURVEY

The map collection began as a dual heritage of the Astor and Lenox Libraries. Because the Astor Library served as the reference library of New York City it secured the best atlases and maps of the period in keeping with Dr. Cogswell's intention to provide standard and authoritative works in all branches of knowledge. Although there is no indication that Cogswell emphasized rare maps and ancient atlases, his voluminous collecting of geographical works, accounts of voyages and explorations, and rare works of travel literature brought many notable maps into the Astor Library.

The Lenox Library was definitely a collector's library of rare and unusual works. Lenox's securing of accounts of voyages and travels and early Americana brought to his collection a great number of facsimiles of famous maps as well as certain rarities. There were few ancient maps of consequence not present in the Lenox collection in some form. After Lenox's death in 1894, separate maps were acquired from the George H. Moore and the Livermore library sales.

Dr. Billings, the first director of the consolidated Astor, Lenox and Tilden foundations, reported that during his European trip of 1896 he had purchased a valuable collection of early atlases and maps. Alexander Maitland's gifts of rare Americana in 1898 and of $20,000 for the purchase of Americana and early cartography in 1907 added unusual materials. At the time of the move from the Astor Library to the Fifth Avenue building in 1911, holdings of 1,200 atlases and about 7,000 sheet maps were placed in the Map Room.

By 1930 the collections had expanded to 25,000 sheet maps. In that year Louis C. Karpinski gave the library a collection of photostats of early maps of the Americas from the originals in French, Spanish, and Portuguese libraries.[1] In 1933 the library published the first English translation of the *Geography* of Claudius Ptolemy.[2] Prince Yūsuf Kamāl began to donate volumes of his *Monumenta Cartographica Africae et Aegypti* (1926–51) in 1938; there is now a complete set in the library. The map collection became a division of the library in 1941. At the end of World War II, the U.S. Army Map Service began to deposit surplus maps; until 1949, when the program was temporarily deactivated, the Map Division received thousands of items, including sets of captured war maps from Germany and other countries. The program was reactivated in 1957 and continues to enrich the collections immeasurably.

The number of maps in the collections reached 180,000 by 1949. In that year the first two volumes of *Monumenta Cartographica Vaticana* (1944–55) with reproductions of treasures in the Vatican Library were acquired; the set of four volumes is now complete. In 1956 the division purchased 213 insurance atlases and 1,789 insurance sheet maps published by the Sanborn Map Company, for the most part covering New York City and New York State from 1884 to the 1930s. In 1962 the division received as a gift of the Portuguese government Armando Cortesão and Avelino Teixeira da Mota's *Portugaliae Monumenta Cartographica* (1960).

SPECIAL INDEXES AND FILES

The Map Division catalog contains cards not only for the maps and other cartographic publications in the division but also for manuscript maps in the Manuscripts and Archives Division, early printed maps in the Rare Book Division, and maps in the Phelps Stokes collection of American historical prints in the Prints Division. The catalog is a dictionary listing, with entries under author's name; place entries (the most extensive type); subject entries (for such topics as geology and pictorial maps); and title entries for some books. The catalog of the Map Division was published in book form in ten volumes by G. K. Hall & Company of Boston in 1971.

The following special files are in the Map Division:

Bibliography File

This is a card file arranged first by map subject (globes, braille maps, etc.) and then alphabetically by author under these subjects (active, 9 card drawers). The file refers to books and periodicals containing information on maps and cartography.

Clipping File

The Map Division clips from newspapers and other sources information on maps and cartography (active, 10 folders). Clippings are mounted on sheets arranged by geographical area in file folders. The material is not cataloged.

Vertical File

The division retains maps in unusual format (such as those used in advertising, on dust jackets, on Christmas cards, or on place mats) arranged in folders by broad subject or form (active, 1 file drawer). This material is not cataloged.

The American History Division maintains the following file relating to maps:

American Historical Maps

This is a card index to historical maps found in the older books in the American History Division (inactive, 1 card drawer). It includes primarily maps of the United States and does not index historical maps in the Map Division or in other divisions of the library.

MAP RESOURCES

This discussion is composed of two sections, the first relating to the resources of the Map Division, and the second the maps and atlases located elsewhere in the library, for the most part works printed before 1600, manuscripts, and other rarities. It should be noted that the holdings in geography, administered by the General Research and Humanities Division, are considered in chapter 44 of this *Guide*.

Map Division

The division's holdings number approximately 300,000 sheet maps, 6,000 atlases, and 11,000 volumes on the history of cartography and the techniques of map making. Although the rarest treasures are shelved elsewhere, the atlas collection dates from the beginning of the seventeenth century and includes the works of most of the outstanding masters of cartographic art of this period. There are editions of Mercator (1616,

---

1. See Louis C. Karpinski, "Manuscript Maps of American European Archives," *Michigan History Magazine* 14 (1930): 5–14.

2. See Edward Luther Stevenson, trans. and ed., *Geography of Claudius Ptolemy* (The New York Public Library, 1932).

1623, 1638), Blaeu (1659, 1664), Jansson (1652–75), Groos (1672), de Wit (1690?), and Jaillot (1695). There is also a representative and fairly complete collection of atlases of the eighteenth and nineteenth centuries, including editions of Moll, Vandermaelen, Jeffreys, and Faden. The division has 3 copies of Des Barres's *Atlantic Neptune*, including both folio and narrow folio examples; with the 8 *Atlantic Neptune* views in the Phelps Stokes collection of the Prints Division there are 167 different plates in the collections.[3] For the nineteenth and twentieth centuries there are a number of detailed atlases of various counties of the United States, as well as insurance and real estate atlases for New York City and other American regions. Modern world atlases include the standard works of Stieler, Andree, Philips, Bartholomew, the Italian Touring Club, Rand-McNally, and Hammond, as well as Soviet atlases. More detailed atlases cover individual continents and countries.

Facsimile atlases and books on the history of cartography are useful in studying the development of map making. Scholars frequently refer to Karpinski's collection of photostats of early maps of America from originals in French, Spanish, and Portuguese libraries. There is also an outstanding collection of books dealing with the technical problems of cartography and map interpretation.

The rich and varied collection of miscellaneous sheet maps includes some of the best efforts of private and governmental cartographers dating back to the earliest printed maps. Especially noteworthy is the group of nineteenth-century American maps. There are several thousand maps of New York City and New York State.[4] Another useful and growing collection is that of modern plans of American and foreign cities. The growth of American cities, which are more fully represented, can be traced by plans in the division from the time of their founding to the present day. Foreign cities, particularly those of Western Europe, are documented from early periods; for example, Venice from the sixteenth century, Cuzco from 1606, Tokyo from 1845, and Shanghai from the 1880s. Road maps and automobile guidebooks for all states and for many foreign countries are available. Included are some editions dating from the early years of motoring and a number of bicycle guides from the 1890s. The collection of several hundred modern pictorial and animated maps is of considerable interest.

More specialized types include complete sets of the topographic maps of the U.S. Geological Survey, National Forest Service maps, and RFD maps of the Post Office Department. Charts of the U.S. Coast and Geodetic Survey, the Great Lakes Survey, the U.S. Hydrographic Office (now the U.S. Naval Oceanographic Office), and the Mississippi River Commission are held in strength.

Also available in the Map Division are the sheets issued to date of the International Map of the World on the scale of 1:1,000,000, as well as

the Army Map Service (now the U.S. Army Topographic Command) collections. There are excellent holdings of topographic maps covering parts of all the continents. Included is the complete set of Cassini's "Carte Géométrique de la France" (1789), the first of the detailed national surveys.

The division receives approximately 20 current periodical titles, including such items as *Globen* (1922–62, 1964–), *Cartactual* (1965–), and *Map Collectors' Circle* (1963–).

RESOURCES ELSEWHERE IN THE COLLECTIONS

The Rare Book Division has an outstanding representation of early geographies and atlases, most of which came from the Lenox Library. Among them is an almost complete collection of the various editions of Ptolemy's *Geography*; forty-six editions of the work range from the first printing of 1475 to 1730.[5] The Ulm 1482 Ptolemy in the Spencer Collection is printed on vellum, and was once owned by Prince Eugene of Savoy. The earliest and rarest of the Ptolemys is the Ebner Codex (de Ricci 97), purchased in 1892. Now in the Manuscripts and Archives Division, it was edited in northern Italy about 1460 by Nicolaus Germanus. Its twenty-seven exquisitely colored maps were the main source of those in the Roman editions of Ptolemy.[6] In 1932 the library published the first English translation of the *Geography*, with reproductions of the maps in the codex.[7] Another edition, the so-called German Ptolemy in the Rare Book Division, is the only known complete copy containing both text and hand-colored world map of a work printed about 1493 by George Stuchs in Nuremberg.[8]

One of the greatest rarities in the collections of the library, the Hunt-Lenox globe in the Rare Book Division, is perhaps the oldest extant globe.[9] Dating probably from the first decade of the sixteenth century, it is a hollow copper ball about five inches in diameter, engraved to show the orb of the earth with the four continents. Holes at its polar points suggest that it was originally fixed on a rod, possibly as part of an astronomical clock. In 1937 the globe was mounted by the library in a bronze armillary sphere. Richard Morris Hunt, architect of the Lenox Library, first brought the globe to this

---

3. See Robert Lingel, "The Atlantic Neptune," *BNYPL* 40 (1936): 571–603.

4. See "Check List of Maps and Atlases Relating to the City of New York in The New York Public Library," *BNYPL* 5 (1901): 60–73; "Check List of Maps in The New York Public Library Relating to the City of Brooklyn and to Kings County," *BNYPL* 6 (1902): 84–88.

5. See Charles E. Armstrong, "Copies of Ptolemy's Geography in American Libraries," *BNYPL* 66 (1962): 105–14.

6. See Walter W. Ristow, "The Western Hemisphere," *BNYPL* 46 (1942): 419–44. See also Joseph Fischer, "An Important Ptolemy Manuscript with Maps in The New York Public Library," *Historical Records and Studies* 6 (1913): 216–34.

7. See Edward Luther Stevenson, trans. and ed., *Geography of Claudius Ptolemy* (The New York Public Library, 1932). See also Victor Hugo Paltsits, "First English Translation of the Geography of Claudius Ptolemy," *BNYPL* 37 (1933): 255–57.

8. See Erwin Rosenthal, "The German Ptolemy and Its World Map," *BNYPL* 48 (1944): 135–47.

9. See Frederick J. Pohl, "The Fourth Continent on the Lenox Globe," *BNYPL* 67 (1963): 465–69; and also Edward Luther Stevenson, *Terrestrial and Celestial Globes* (New Haven: Yale Univ. Press, 1921).

country in 1855; he gave it to James Lenox between 1870 and 1880.[10]

Globe gores of the first half of the sixteenth century in the collections include the Boulengier gores, to which the library has assigned a date of ca. 1518; a set of gores possibly made at Nuremberg about 1530 which indicate the course of Magellan's voyage; and the De Mongenet gores of 1552.

Among map first editions in the Rare Book Division is one of two known copies of Mercator's first published double cordiform map of the world, *Orbis Imago* (1538), and the first American map, engraved by John Foster in William Hubbard's *A Narrative of the Troubles with the Indians in New-England* (1677), the so-called White Hills map. The division also owns a copy of the White Hills map appearing in the London 1677 edition of this work. There is a good representation of Ortelius's *Theatrum Orbis Terrarum*, including the first issue, dated May 20, 1570; a copy of the *Epitome of Ortelius* (1602) bound in contemporary vellum bears the gilt badge of Queen Elizabeth I. One of the most important maps of modern times, the Wright Molyneux map from Hakluyt's *Principall Navigations* (1598–1600) represents the practical exposition of the theory and method by which Wright made the Mercator system of projection practicable for the use of mariners.

In the Spencer Collection is an illuminated Portolan atlas of great beauty assigned to the third period of Agnese's atlases, or about 1552. Purchased by the collection in 1920, it is in its original binding of red morocco.[11] Also to be noted is a hand-colored example of Joan Blaeu's *Geographia* (1662).

Of the maps and charts in the Phelps Stokes collection housed in the Prints Division, the following may be mentioned as among the most important: the Virginia Company chart of circa 1606–08, a manuscript map drawn in gold and colors on vellum and mounted on a roller; Blaeu's

"First Paskaart" of 1617; one of five known impressions of the earliest issue of Smith's map of New England made in 1614; the rare early issues of the N. J. Visscher and Danckers maps of New Netherland (ca. 1647–51, 1651–55 respectively); and a group of maps recording the birth of the United States in 1783. This last group includes the earliest known impression of the important Abel Buell maps, the first maps of the country engraved within its borders. Of the plans in the Phelps Stokes collection, the most important are the first and fourth issues of the Bonner maps of Boston issued in 1722 and 1743, and the best of three known impressions of the Bradford map or Lyne Survey of New York, depicting the city in 1730. Other items include early engraved surveys and plans of Philadelphia, Baltimore, Washington, and other cities.[12]

In addition to the famous Ebner Codex the Manuscripts and Archives Division houses Nicholas Comberford's celebrated "Manuscript Map of the South Part of Virginia," an original colored drawing with the artist's signature mounted on hinged oak boards and dated 1657.[13] Two fifteenth-century manuscripts of Leonardo Dati's *La Sfera* (de Ricci 109, 110) are in Italian verse, both of them delightful in their colored maps, diagrams, views, and real or fanciful pictures of actual buildings. Other manuscript maps in the division relate to the American Revolution, and to estates and properties, roads, and city plans of eighteenth- and nineteenth-century America; the individual maps in the division are cataloged in geographical groupings. A "Mapa de la Sierra Gorda" on vellum (ca. 1763) shows the towns and missions established in Mexico by José de Escandon.

---

10. See Robert W. Hill, "The Lenox Globe," *BNYPL* 41 (1937): 523–25.

11. See Henry R. Wagner, "The Manuscript Atlases of Battista Agnese," *PBSA* 25 (1931): 1–110.

12. See I. N. Phelps Stokes and Daniel C. Haskell, *American Historical Prints, Early Views of American Cities, Etc., from the Phelps Stokes and Other Collections* (The New York Public Library, 1933). Reprinted with additions and corrections from *BNYPL* (1931–32); a new edition is in preparation.

13. See W. P. Cumming, "The Earliest Permanent Settlement in Carolina: Nathaniel Batts and the Comberford Map," *American Historical Review* 45 (1939): 82–89.

44

GEOGRAPHY

Geography has been an important subject in the Research Libraries since their inception. Both the Astor and Lenox Libraries contained rich holdings of the literature of exploration and travel. As early as 1851, Dr. Cogswell expressed interest in securing accounts of voyages and travels for the collections of the Astor Library. James Lenox's biographer Henry Stevens remarked that "his first absorbing penchant was for collecting early editions of the Bible and parts thereof in all languages. Then he took to books relating to North and South America, including

all the great collections of voyages and travels, as well as the prior or original editions of which they were composed. This soon led to collecting everything pertaining to the great 'Age of Discovery,' whether in Spanish, Portuguese, English, French, Dutch, Italian or German. In this way he soon had more pet-lambs than he could well watch, such as De Bry, Hulsius, Ramusio, Purchas, Thévenot, Haertgerts, Saeghman, etc."[1]

---

1. Stevens, *Lenox*, p. 33.

Voyages and travels, including early documentation on the search for a Northwest Passage, are very well represented. Geographical periodical holdings are of great importance. Some aspects of geographical literature, including early imprints and rare works, are noted in the sections of this *Guide* dealing with history; maps and atlases in the Map Division and elsewhere in the Research Libraries are treated in chapter 43.

The following table illustrates the growth of the resources in geography:

1921	12,333 volumes
1930	17,469
1966	39,300

GEOGRAPHICAL RESOURCES

BIBLIOGRAPHY

A small group of bibliographical works, mainly of historical interest, is held in the general collections; this includes such early publications as J. G. Hager's *Geographischer Büchersaal* (1764–78). There are other working lists in the reference collections throughout the library; compilations of bibliographic interest are also to be found in the Rare Book Division.

SERIALS

The holdings of geographical serials are extremely strong. They include the periodicals of geographical societies such as the *Geographical Review* (1916–) of the American Geographical Society, the *Geographical Journal* and its predecessors (1893–) of the Royal Geographical Society, *Boletín* (1839–) of the Sociedad Mexicana de Geografía y Estadística, *Izvestiia* (1865–) of the Vsesoiuznoe Geograficheskoe Obshchestvo of Leningrad, and others. There are also the proceedings of geographical congresses, including those of the International Geographical Congress (1871–), of the Deutscher Geographentag (1881–), and of the Congresso Geografico Italiano (1892–). Additional materials include the periodicals published by independent geographical societies such as the Petermanns Mitteilungen aus Justus Perthes's Geographischer Anstalt; annals such as the *Annals of the Association of American Geographers* (1911–) and the *Publication of the Institute of British Geographers* (1935–); and periodicals issued by associations of teachers of geography such as *Journal of Geography* (1902–). Holdings in the scholarly series published by universities are extensive. Specialized geographical serial bibliographies are well represented.

The rich international collection of publications of the geographical divisions of learned societies and institutions in other fields should be associated with these titles. Additional important sources of geographical literature are the publications of local history societies, especially those of North America and Western Europe. Serial articles on those aspects of geography of particular interest to the library are indexed in the Public Catalog and in appropriate division catalogs. For general purposes published subject bibliographies and cumulated serial indexes should be consulted.

RARITIES

There is a strong collection of early imprints in the Rare Book Division. The Ptolemy and Ortelius holdings and other notable map resources are treated in detail in chapter 43. Apianus and other geographers of the sixteenth and seventeenth centuries are well represented. The library has four fifteenth-century editions of one of the most celebrated ancient works on geography, Pomponius Mela's *De Situ Orbis*, as well as many sixteenth-century editions.

HISTORY OF GEOGRAPHY, COAST PILOTS, AND RELATED MATERIALS

A large and interesting section on the history of geography includes formal studies of the subject in addition to works, such as Strabo's *Geography*, which are important historically.

Coast pilots and similar mariners' guides constitute a significant feature of this general collection. The United States, England, and Germany are the most comprehensively represented; the library has long files of "Notices to Mariners" and similar series from these countries. There are also publications from most of the other countries which issue such material. Publications of the U.S. Hydrographic Office (now U.S. Naval Oceanographic Office), Coast and Geodetic Survey,[2] and Light House Service are extensively represented. Significant current series of most countries are received. Since 1929 the library has made a particular effort to complete its files of the English-language classics in this field. An outstanding collection includes various editions of Bowditch's *The New American Practical Navigator*, W. N. Brady's *The Kedge-Anchor*, Darcy Lever's *The Young Sea Officer's Sheet Anchor*, Joseph Blunt's *The Merchant's and Shipmaster's Assistant*, and *The American Coast Pilot*. Systematic works include strong holdings in imprints of the eighteenth, nineteenth, and twentieth centuries; many of the earlier works are historically interesting. There are several thousand pamphlets and a number of volumes in the "n.c." classmark (material retained but not individually cataloged), the majority of which are pamphlet guides and ephemeral publicity materials of the nineteenth and twentieth centuries. These relate to various localities and are of historical as well as geographical interest. A dated file of textbooks contains examples from 1784 in the United States, 1757 in France, and 1630 in England.

PLACE NAMES

A large and rapidly growing section relates to geographical onomastics, the study of place names. More than 3,300 entries in the Public Catalog show extensive coverage for the United States and Europe, although all areas of the world are represented. Many entries are index references to periodical articles on such different aspects of the subject as dictionaries, studies of origin, pronunciation, and etymologies. Periodicals include complete holdings of *Onoma* (1950–) and proceedings of most of the international congresses on onomastic sciences.

The collection on place names is to be found in several locations in the Research Libraries. The larger part of the holdings is in the general collections, but the gazetteers of the United States Geographical Names Board are in the Map Divi-

---

2. The Science and Technology Research Center maintains an index to the more important serial publications of this agency.

sion; there is much information in the local histories of the United States and England in the Local History and Genealogy Division.

VOYAGES AND TRAVEL

The material described in this section documents travels that cover a number of countries; voyages to or travel within single countries are described in the chapters of this *Guide* dealing with the history of specific countries. Periodicals include the older *Tour du Monde* (1860–1914) and such current publications as *Hotel Monthly* and *Holiday*. Collections of travels from the earliest dates are available in various editions. Society publications include those of the Hakluyt Society, the Linschoten Vereeniging, and others.

Dr. Cogswell of the Astor Library and James Lenox established remarkable pioneer collections of voyage and travel literature. The Lenox Library's collection of the De Bry "Great Voyages" to the West Indies and America and "Small Voyages" to the East Indies is among the finest in existence; in addition to numerous variant copies and editions, it contains a set with the extremely rare *Elenchus* of 1634.[3] Other copies of the "Great Voyages" are in the Arents Tobacco Collection. There are remarkable sets of the collections of travels made by Hakluyt, Hulsius, Purchas, Prévost, Thévenot, and others. The library has all the known editions of James Cook's voyages and a number of those of William Dampier.

The very rich and extensive literature of American exploration includes one of the finest collections of the contemporaneous editions of the letters of Columbus, more fully described in chapter 52, and important groups such as the sixteenth- to eighteenth-century accounts of European voyages in search of the Northwest Passage. Many works generally related to the New World have more general relevance; for example, the "Jesuit Relations" and the accounts of De Bry also relate to the Far East.

Notable among the volumes of travel literature bearing upon the Far East is a first edition of Marco Polo's *De . . . orientalium regionum* (ca. 1484) which is bound in with Ludolphus de Suchen's *Iter ad terram sanctam*; associated with these works, and possibly published at the same time, is Mandeville's *Itinerarium*. Five fifteenth-century editions of Mandeville are in the Rare Book Division and the Spencer Collection, and there are many later editions. Of great rarity are two 1614 printings of Fernão Mendes Pinto's *Peregrinacam*.

Voyages Around the World

Some 1,400 entries in the Public Catalog provide a dated guide to ancient as well as modern world voyages. Early accounts present in the Rare Book Division include the first account of Magellan's voyage around the world in Antonio Pigafetta's *Le Voyage et navigation faict par les Epaignolz es isles de Mollucques* (ca. 1526), Oliver van Noort's *Beschryvinghe van de voyagie* (1601), Willem Schouten's *Australische Navigation* (1619), Sir Francis Drake's *World Encom-*

3. See "Catalogue of the De Bry Collection of Voyages in The New York Public Library," *BNYPL* 8 (1904): 230–43. Published separately by the library.

passed (1628), and voyages of later centuries including those of Laperouse, Krusensten, Kotzebue, Langsdorff, and many others.

Polar Exploration

The very extensive arctic holdings are recorded by some 1,400 dated entries in the Public Catalog. Under the heading "Arctic Expeditions" is found the library's copy of Dionyse Settle's *A True Reporte of the Laste Voyage . . . by Capteine Frobisher* (1577). Arctic voyages of this period made in search of a Northwest Passage to Cathay include the voyages of Gerrit de Veer, William Barendz, Jan Huygen van Linschoten, Hessel Gerritsz, and Luke Fox. The chronicle of the search continues through the eighteenth and nineteenth centuries in the descriptions of the voyages of Vancouver, Sir John Franklin, and others. Modern arctic exploration is equally well covered; there is much documentation of the Peary expedition to the North Pole and the controversy that surrounded it, as well as accounts of flights over the pole by Amundsen, Ellsworth, and others. There are extensive holdings of the publications of bodies such as the Arctic Institute of North America, the Expéditions Polaires Françaises, and the Arkticheski i Antarkticheski Nauchnoissledovatel'ski Institut of Leningrad.

Antarctic exploration, beginning with the voyage of Captain Cook in the eighteenth century, is covered by more than 500 entries in the Public Catalog. The library has one of the most complete files in existence of the reports of the United States Exploring Expedition to the South Pacific and Antarctica, and a set of the scientific reports (1897–99) of the Commission de la "Belgica," published between 1901 and 1938. An excellent scrapbook series and the commercially produced editions of the *Little America Times* (1933–35) document the various expeditions of R. E. Byrd. A similar edition of the *South Polar Times* (1902–03, 1911) relates to the Scott expeditions.

GUIDEBOOKS

Guidebooks and similar publications are a significant feature of the geographical resources. Up-to-date editions of guidebooks for many countries are available in the Research Libraries collections to provide current information for the traveler. The main value of the library's holdings, however, is historical. The reader using the Public Catalog and division catalogs should be aware that "Guidebooks" is used as a subheading under the name of a country, for example, "England—Guidebooks." Under this general heading are found guidebooks that describe all of England; guidebooks for a specific area or county, such as Yorkshire, are cataloged under "Yorkshire—Guidebooks." Entries for guidebooks form a dated file (such as "New York City—Guidebooks, 1846").

The Local History and Genealogy Division maintains the major holdings of local guidebooks, both cataloged and uncataloged and including vertical file material, for the United States and England. Material for the United States emphasizes national parks and monuments and other notable areas as well as the larger cities. New York City is exceptionally well represented with more than 300 catalog entries from 1807 to the present. At the Information Desk in Room 315 an additional group of historic and current New York City guidebooks is kept for ready reference.

Guidebook material for England emphasizes historical places, abbeys, castles, and the larger cities, especially London.

There is a complete set of the WPA Federal Writers' Project American Guide Series in the Main Reading Room; another complete set is held in the American History Division, where studies including guidebooks for the United States, Canada, and Latin American countries are also kept. Materials in the general collections are of considerable historical importance and cover all countries. The holdings are extensive from the period since the early nineteenth century and include series such as Baedeker, Appleton, Murray, and Guide Bleu. United States materials, particularly those for New York State, are more complete.

About 100 of the latest guidebooks are held at the reference desk in the south hall of the Main Reading Room for public reference use. The larger number of the books cover whole countries rather than small areas, although some are devoted to major cities and such important geographical sections as the Riviera. The present policy of the General Research and Humanities Division is to purchase standard guides for each country or area at five-year intervals. A particular attempt is made to include exotic or out-of-the-way places.

The Art and Architecture Division has a small group of older guidebooks from all countries, particularly Baedekers of the late nineteenth and early twentieth centuries, retained for information on the art treasures of the world.

MANUSCRIPTS

In the Manuscripts and Archives Division materials related to the subject of geography include a vellum copy of Ptolemy's *Geographia*, dated 1460,[4] "An account of the different geographical systems taught in Hindoo writings" by Roy Radhaprusal (1838), and explorers' correspondence in the papers (1899–1939) of Constance Lindsay Skinner. Accounts of travel from the eighteenth century to the present are found in the division's collection of diaries. Examples of

such materials are the diary of Fred C. Bond[5] and the diaries of Fred G. Blakeslee kept during the period of his world travels (1931–38) made to collect materials for his books on costumes and uniforms of the world. Further examples may be cited in the Seligman collection of Washington Irving materials, which includes Irving's manuscript journals covering his travels in Europe and the United States between 1804 and 1842.[6]

ADDITIONAL RESOURCES

Geographical literature on Central Asia is strong; a set of the *District Gazetteers of the Provinces* of India is of interest. One of the most extensive sections of geographical materials is devoted to Europe. Besides guidebooks there is much miscellaneous material of interest in geographical studies of the United States, such as the Massachusetts Harbor and Land Commission publications. The collections on the Middle and Far West of this country contain important titles.

Publications on legendary and mythical geography are acquired comprehensively by the General Research and Humanities Division; there is much material on Atlantis, Lemuria, and other mythical regions.

The collections provide strong resources for the study of modern developments in geography such as economic geography, economic zoning, industrial surveys, market surveys, and physical geography; material on the science of geopolitics is best located under headings such as "Imperialism" and "Territorial Expansion" in the Public Catalog. Among current periodical titles covering this topic are *Geopolitica* (1939–41) and *Zeitschrift für Geopolitik* (1924–43, 1951–68, incomplete).

Other related materials include the extensive collection of maps in the Map Division and in other parts of the library. Much material in the science class marks such as scientific expedition reports, or studies of mountaineering, applies to the study of geography.

---

4. See Edward Luther Stevenson, ed. and tr., *Geography of Claudius Ptolemy* (The New York Public Library, 1932).

5. See "Flatboating on the Yellowstone, 1877," *BNYPL* 28 (1924): 783–94 et seq. Published separately by the library.

6. See "Catalogue of the Seligman Collection of Irvingiana," *BNYPL* 30 (1926): 83–109. Published separately by the library.

45

ARCHAEOLOGY

The library's rich collection of archaeological works reflects a comprehensive collecting policy. The acquisition of works stresses the artistic, architectural, historical, anthropological, and ethnological aspects of the subject. Archaeology is not the collecting responsibility of any single division of the library. Cataloging of nonclassical archaeology is generally by geographical area rather than by subject: a work on British archaeology appears under the subject heading "Great

Britain—Archaeology" in contrast to a work on British art, which is cataloged as "Art, Great Britain." It should be noted that important holdings on Roman Britain appear under headings such as "Great Britain—Archaeology—Roman Remains" and that a large proportion of the resources on the archaeology of the Americas is classed with American Indian materials.

In addition to standard works, handbooks, museum catalogs, and such material, the collection has two noteworthy features. There are numerous finely illustrated folios, many of which came from the Astor Library, among them Piranesi's *Antiquities*, and Lepsius's *Denkmaeler aus Aegypten und Aethiopien*. The Tilden collection contained a number of the now famous "galleries" relating to art and archaeology. The Stuart collection brought rarities such as the Spencer-Stanhope *Olympia* (1824) and Lord Kingsborough's *Antiquities of Mexico* (1831–48).

The second important aspect of the archaeological holdings consists of the extensive files of archaeological journals, many of them substantially complete. Among these are the *Acta archaeologica* (1930–), *Antiquity* (1927–), and *Revue archéologique* (1844–). Institutional and society publications are represented by imprints such as the Föreningen Urd, Upsala, the Münchener Altertums-Verein, and the Archaeological Institute of America. There is a good representation of the proceedings of archaeological congresses. Among many museum and other institutional publications are those of the Rijksmuseum van Oudheden te Leiden, the Reale Istituto d'Archaeologia e Storia dell'Arte, the Archaeologiai Értesito, and Johns Hopkins University.

The library has a rich collection of society publications relating to Greece and Rome, among them those of the Deutsches archäologisches Institut, the Osterreichisches archäologisches Institut of Vienna, and the Accademia Nazionale dei Lincei at Rome.

Related materials occur within many other subject areas in the library. Archaeological contributions, both monographic and serial, are often indexed in the library's catalogs.

DIVISION HOLDINGS

AMERICAN HISTORY DIVISION

The extensive collection relating to the archaeology of the Americas and the American Indian includes the publications of local societies and museums. The dictionary catalog in the division contains references not only to books in the collection but also to articles in American historical journals and other varieties of material. The Picture Index maintained by the division is of particular value for various aspects of Indian archaeology. Travel books and the personal narratives of members of exploratory or scientific expeditions included in the holdings of the division often contain archaeological and ethnological observations.

ART AND ARCHITECTURE DIVISION

Archaeology as a subject discipline is not a collecting responsibility of the division. As materials on the arts of all ancient cultures are collected, however, the division offers considerable archaeological resources.

JEWISH DIVISION

The Jewish Division collects materials covering ancient Jewish archaeology and modern excavations in Biblical countries.

The subject of Biblical archaeology relates to the ancient domestic, civil, and religious institutions of the Near East, especially those of Palestine. Jewish Division holdings document the history of the Jewish people from the earliest period

to the fall of Jerusalem in A.D. 70 and beyond, and include comprehensive studies on the Oriental, especially Semitic, civilizations; closely associated with these are works on the civilizations of Assyria, Babylonia, and Egypt in the Research Libraries.

The archaeology of Palestine covering the period of the Second Commonwealth is intimately connected with the social and economic life of the Jews during the time of Christ. The literature dealing with the archaeology of the Talmud, although forming a separate section, is closely related to this period.

The library's rich collection of general surveys contains a fine group of sixteenth- and seventeenth-century Latin works by authorities such as the Buxtorfs, Arias Montano, John Selden, Fabricius, Thomas Godwin, Johannes Leusden, and others. Modern works are equally well represented. The division's files of the publications of learned societies and institutions concerned with promotion of archaeological study in Biblical lands is virtually complete.

Special sections in the holdings deal with inscriptions, numismatics, metrology, sacred antiquities, sacrifices, the priesthood, and secular archaeology. The Picture Index, although no longer active, includes illustrations of subjects related to Biblical archaeology.

LOCAL HISTORY AND GENEALOGY DIVISION

A wealth of archaeological information on early English cultures, including Celtic and Roman Britain, is available in the collection of British county archaeological and historical journals administered by the Local History and Genealogy Division.[1] Entries for the more significant articles in these journals appear in the Public Catalog. Among these titles are *Archaeologia* (1773–) published by the Society of Antiquaries of London, and *Archaeological Journal* (1844–) of the Royal Archaeological Institute of Great Britain and Ireland. The initial volume of each county history in the "Victoria County Histories" contains archaeological information. Some of the town and county histories of the United States include archaeological information.

ORIENTAL DIVISION

The resources for ancient Egyptian, Assyrian, and Babylonian archaeology are very extensive, with a particular concentration on publications available before 1941.[2] Materials on Egypt in-

---

1. See "List of Works in The New York Public Library Relating to British Genealogy and Local History," *BNYPL* 14 (1910): 355–99 et seq.
2. See Ida A. Pratt, comp., "Ancient Egypt: A List of References to Material in The New York Public Library," *BNYPL* 27 (1923): 723–66 et seq. (published separately by the library, with additions and index, 1925); "Ancient Egypt: 1925–1941; A Supplement," *BNYPL* 45 (1941): 791–820 et seq. (published separately by the library); and "Modern Egypt: A List of References to Material in The New York Public Library," *BNYPL* 32 (1928): 589–634 et seq. (published separately by the library, 1929). The volumes have been reprinted as *Ancient Egypt* and *Modern Egypt* (New York: Kraus Reprint Co., 1969).

clude works such as the studies conducted during Napoleon's expedition, the researches of Lepsius, and the many publications of the nineteenth and twentieth centuries. An item of seminal importance is Jean François Champollion's *Lettre à M. Dacier* (1822) in which are established the principles for deciphering hieroglyphics; the library has, in addition, examples of the earlier attempts at interpretation by Horapollo and Athanasius Kircher.

Related to the holdings of the Oriental Division is a fine set of Egyptian archaeological maps in the Map Division, along with 624 Sumerian and Babylonian clay and stone inscriptions housed in the Manuscripts and Archives Division.[3]

---

3. See Leo A. Oppenheim, *Catalogue of the Cuneiform Tablets of the Wilberforce Eames*

SLAVONIC DIVISION

Russian materials are strong, with an extensive collection of serial publications of Czarist archaeological societies, the Russian Archaeological Commission, and the Academy for History of Material Culture, along with finely illustrated works. There are important materials relating to the Caucasus and the ancient Hellenic and Scythian cultures of southern Russia. More recent works include reports on the Soviet excavations at Pazyryk in Siberia and the sites of Iranian cultures of Central Asia.

Collection in The New York Public Library: Tablets of the Time of the Third Dynasty of Ur (New Haven: American Oriental Society, 1948).

46

GENERAL HISTORY

The collection of materials for the study of history in the Research Libraries numbers some 567,000 books and pamphlets. The holdings of printed materials and manuscripts relating to the Americas, among the strongest in the Research Libraries, include an outstanding collection of early Americana in the Rare Book Division. Materials on English local history are also of importance, as are those on the history of the Negro (with strong resources in both the Central Building and the Schomburg Center). Historical periods with exceptional documentation are the Age of Discovery and World Wars I and II.[1] Manuscript resources are strongest for the American Revolution. The collecting policy is generally comprehensive for all aspects of history.

Library participation in the Farmington Plan after World War II has helped to augment already strong resources and build those areas of the collections that were previously weak.[2] The New York Public Library has collecting responsibility for the following areas of history and topography: general and universal history; Eu-

---

1. Catalogs of the collections of the Research Libraries published by G. K. Hall & Co. of Boston include *Dictionary Catalog of the History of the Americas Collection*, 28 volumes (1961); *Catalog of Government Publications in The Research Libraries*, 40 volumes (1972); *Dictionary Catalog of the Schomburg Collection of Negro Literature and History*, 9 volumes (1962), *First and Second Supplement*, 4 volumes (1972); and *Subject Catalog of the World War I Collection*, 4 volumes (1961). A *Dictionary Catalog of the Local History and Genealogy Division*, in 18 volumes, was published in 1974.

2. The Farmington Plan is a voluntary agreement under which a number of leading American research libraries have accepted specific collecting responsibilities for publications from most foreign countries.

rope; The British Isles; general works on the Commonwealth of Nations; Algeria, Carthage, Egypt, Eritrea, Ethiopia, Morocco, Rio de Oro, Somaliland, the Sudan, and Tunisia; Latin America; West Indies; general history of South America and the following individual countries or colonies: Argentina, Guyana, Surinam or Dutch Guiana, the Falkland Islands, French Guiana, South Georgia, Uruguay, and Venezuela.

The growth of the collections in history is indicated by the following:

1854 Astor Library	23,350 volumes
1921 New York Public Library	188,700
1930	251,900
1940	300,000*
1966	567,000

(*Estimated figure)

RESOURCES IN HISTORY

The resources for the study of history derive strength from ancillary subjects in which the library has developed strong holdings. Material on description and travel, for example, has become a most important aspect of the collections; works of description and travel within a particular country or continent are classified with history; other accounts of world travel, including travel in the Arctic and Antarctic regions, are classified with geography, as are guidebooks. Publications on hunting trips are classified with materials on sports and games and are discussed with that subject. Views, another important supportive resource for historical research, are more fully discussed below. Diplomacy in the theoretical sense, international arbitration, and general treaties are assigned to the law class marks. History as a division of the library's scheme of classification includes politics, foreign relations, constitutional history, and constitutional law. Economic history is classed with economics. The library attempts to acquire all bibliographical tools relating to history.

Subject materials on history are held in the general collections, with certain exceptions: general history of the Americas is administered by the American History Division, and United States and English local history at a town or county level is administered by the Local History and Genealogy Division. Historical materials in the Cyrillic alphabet are held in the Slavonic Division; those in Oriental languages are the responsibility of the Oriental Division. The Jewish Division collects and administers materials on the history of the Jewish people and publications from or about Israel. Early and rare printed materials are kept in the Rare Book Division.

The General Research and Humanities Division provides assistance on reference and research subjects relating to universal and national history, but not history of the Americas or English local history. A collection of standard works suitable for international historical reference is kept on the open shelves of the Main Reading Room. Author and subject catalogs for the entire Main Reading Room collections are at the reference desk in the south hall of the Main Reading Room and at the Information Desk in Room 315.

No statement of numbers of volumes or description of books specifically classified as historical gives an adequate idea of the resources of the Research Libraries for historical study. The literary, political, social, and biographical contributions of the various subject and special collections in the library are apparent. Various types of material merit particular attention. Newspapers and periodicals, of which the library has extensive collections beginning with the late seventeenth century, offer sources for contemporaneous accounts and expressions of public opinion. Public documents are important primary sources; there are more than 352,000 volumes of this material published in various countries by federal, local, and municipal governments. These include, in addition to routine reports, much material concerning economics, sociology, and international affairs. The collection of government gazettes is unusually complete. The publications of learned societies, often more germane to historical study on the local rather than national level, along with the manuscript and map collections, are important resources for scholars of history.

Travel materials are held in strength and are supplemented by holdings in geography and anthropology; the subject of travel may be considered sufficiently well-covered for research in the literature of all countries. Special emphasis has been given to early Latin, English, and French works, and to early Oriental travels, particularly in India.

General and Universal History

The holdings in this field numbered 11,500 volumes in 1941, and had increased to 19,400 volumes by 1966. Entries for general works on history are arranged chronologically in the Public Catalog under headings such as "History, General—17th century." The broad range extends from editions of Ranulf Higden's *Polycronicon* printed by Caxton (ca. 1482) and four copies of Hartmann Schedel's *Das Buch der Chroniken* ["Nuremberg chronicle"] (1493) through editions of the works of writers such as Sabellico, Bossuet, Ranke, Laviss, and others. More popular works include Mme. de Genlis's *Annales de la vertu* (1781) and many printings of Samuel Griswold Goodrich's *Peter Parley's Universal History.*

Among the more famous modern universal histories, H. G. Wells's *Outline of History* is represented not only by numerous editions in the general collections, but also by four sets of the twenty-four parts as originally issued in 1919–20: one set in the Rare Book Division; another in the Arents Collection of Books in Parts; and two sets in the Berg Collection, one with the author's and Gilbert Murray's manuscript corrections and with inserted typewritten additions. Other studies of history by writers such as Spengler and Toynbee are available in the collections both in the original and in translation, along with many critical works about them. A small collection of these and other standard reference works is maintained on the open shelves of the Main Reading Room.

Another interesting section covers in depth the subject of historical chronology. Eusebius's *Chronicon* (1483) is one of the earliest works held; a large number of sixteenth-century publications in the Rare Book Division contain early references to America. Thomas Prince's *A Chronological History of New-England* (1736) is also in the division. More recent works are held in the general collections.

Oriental historians are not neglected, and the holdings of Arabic works in the Oriental Division include many editions of the Ibn Khaldūn in the original and in translation. Special class marks in the Billings Schedule provide for the ancient historians, among them Herodotus, Diodorus, and Polybius.

Periodicals and society publications range from *The Historical Register* (1717–39) to *Current History* (1914–), *Foreign Affairs* (1922–), *Documents on International Affairs* (1928–), and *Saeculum* (1950–).

Of particular interest are the sets of annual contemporary surveys beginning with the seventeenth-century *Mercure français* (1605–44), continuing with the eighteenth-century *Annual Register* (1758–), *Magazin für die neue Historie und Geographie* (1769–93), and others, including the nineteenth-century *Statesman's Yearbook* (1864–). The quarto and folio sets of many of the historical collections contain illustrations of artistic, archaeological, or historical interest.

Views

The large collection of views provides an important supplementary source for the student of history. There are two categories of topographic views in the Research Libraries, the collecting policy for which differs slightly. Commercially produced books of views with or without text and without special artistic or other interest are acquired by the General Research and Humanities Division on a selective basis at four- or five-year intervals. This policy reflects conditions occasioned by the vast number of such books currently produced, which are often repetitive in nature or simultaneously issued in a number of different languages. This policy does not apply to older materials; the holdings contain a wealth of items from woodcut delineations through aquatint, lithographic, and photographic depictions. The outstanding exception is in the field of American views, and especially those of the New York City metropolitan area. The Local History and Genealogy and American History Divisions collect comprehensively in this area, building on a strong and extensive collection. The Slavonic Division acquires books of views with texts in the Cyrillic alphabet; the Jewish Division seeks to obtain all views of Israel. Books of special artistic, archaeological, geologic, and other interest which include topographic views are excluded from the general policy; such materials are purchased and classified primarily as subject material.

The second category of topographic views includes those in loose pictorial form, such as prints, drawings, photographs, and stereoscopic slides. The Phelps Stokes and Eno collections of American historical prints in the Prints Division and the vast archive of New York City photographic views in the Local History and Genealogy Division are examples of this class of material. For the most part the library acquires views in loose pictorial form only for American scenes, and especially for the New York City metropolitan area. Collections of other views have come as parts of larger gifts, or in the oeuvre of an artist collected by the Prints Division.

Materials may be most readily secured by consulting place headings in the Public Catalog with the subhead "Views": "England—Views," or "Paris—Views." Despite the richness of this material it is not easy to use; the Public Catalog cards seldom contain notes and cannot serve as guides if a particular street, building, or object is desired: for this type of research the collections of guidebooks should be consulted.

Significant Collections

Both the Lenox Library and Tilden collection contained important prints holdings which included views. The Emmet collection, received in 1896, was rich in maps, scenes, and views, some in manuscript, some engraved.[3] The Rare Book Division holds early books containing views, such as the "Nuremberg Chronicle" and works by Matthaeus Merian, Zeiler, and Braun and Hogenberg. The Spencer Collection has some books of views, including the twenty-eight plates of *Scenographia Americana* (1768), as well as fifty-four sepia drawings done by Archibald Robertson during the American Revolution.[4]

American History Division

The American History Division has a large collection of stereopticon views in 1,200 boxes, which derives largely from the Robert Dennis collection. Representations of Niagara Falls are especially plentiful among the American views, and of Central Park among the scenes of New York City. There are also "comics," and other subject collections of views, such as those on the United States Navy. Collector's treasures in this archive include glass views of the period 1854 to 1862. A supplementary collection of postcard views of the United States and other countries numbers thousands of pieces. Check lists and inventories of these two collections are held at the reference desk of the American History Division. A picture index refers to views of American interest, among other items.

---

3. See *Calendar of the Emmet Collection of Manuscripts, etc., Relating to American History* (The New York Public Library, 1900; reprinted by the library, with additions, 1959).

4. See Harry Miller Lydenberg, ed., "Archibald Robertson, Lieutenant-General Royal Engineers; His Diary and Sketches in America 1762–1780," *BNYPL* 37 (1933): 7–37 et seq. Published separately by the library; reprinted by the library and Arno Press, 1971.

Art and Architecture Division

Views to be found in this division are primarily architectural and pictorial. In addition to monograph materials are scrapbooks of pictures on subjects such as monuments, palaces, and military buildings. The Architecture File in the division indexes illustrations and textual materials on architects and buildings, with special emphasis given to those of New York.

Jewish Division

The division has an inactive card file Picture Index indexing pictures in books shelved in the division. The subjects include archaeology of the Holy Land, portraits, and history.

Local History and Genealogy Division

Mounted photographs of views of the five boroughs of New York City fill 49 cabinet drawers in the division. Dating from the late nineteenth century, these are arranged by street name and number. The Armbruster collection of 14,000 photographs of buildings and their surroundings in Long Island, greater New York City, and Westchester County made during the period 1890 to 1930 is also in the division. The division has, in addition, thousands of contemporary views of New York City arranged by subject, and maintains a card index to New York City views arranged by subject groups, such as hotels or schools.

Prints Division

Here are found the two major collections of prints and drawings of views in the Research Libraries: the Eno collection of prints and other material relating to New York City from the seventeenth to the nineteenth centuries, and the Phelps Stokes collection of American historical prints, which includes early views of American cities. The division maintains a subject index to single prints of views in the Prints Divison arranged by town or geographic locality; this contains references to a large number of views of New York City subdivided by subject groups, such as churches or hotels. Another subject index in the division locates foreign views in books shelved elsewhere in the Research Libraries.

Theatre Collection

The Theatre Collection has views of theatre buildings, opera houses, and related structures, both in its vertical files and in its iconography files. Such material, consisting of prints, drawings, photographs, and reproductions, is located by consulting the Nonbook Materials Catalog of the collection under headings such as "Theatres—U.S.—New York—Vivian Beaumont." In addition are views of theatre buildings as illustrations in books on the theatre, which are not, however, indexed in the card catalogs but must be located in the books themselves.

The Picture Collection of the Branch Libraries

This is an excellent source for views of all kinds. The pictures in the collection are arranged by subject. This resource is discussed at length in chapter 29 of this *Guide*.

DIRECTORIES

The library comprehensively acquires the directories, governmental and nongovernmental, of international agencies, and of national, state, and provincial governments, as well as of capitals and large cities of the world (cities of 100,000 or more population in the United States, and 200,000 or more abroad). The library has a representative collection of the directories of national and international banks and other businesses, and at least one directory for each large professional, religious, or other group. Domestic and foreign telephone directories are generally acquired from those listed in the *Bell System Telephone Directory Price List*. The library has acquired on a selective basis United States city directories, the social registers of major cities in all countries, and alumni directories for major universities and senior colleges in the United States.

City Directories

In addition to the city directories of selected major cities of the United States (46 at present), there is an exceptionally complete collection of United States city directories from the earliest periods up through 1869 in the Local History and Genealogy Division. New York City directories for the years 1786–1933/34 are available on microfilm for public use. The collection of city directories after 1870 is kept in the Research Libraries Annex at 521 West 43rd Street. The General Research and Humanities Division administers a representative current group of United States city directories in the Main Reading Room.

Special Indexes and Files

There are three special indexes and files to the directories in the Research Libraries. The most complete file, in the General Research and Humanities Division (Room 315), contains approximately 12,000 cards covering all the divisions of the Research Libraries including those at Lincoln Center. The Economic and Public Affairs Division keeps a file for directories of economic, sociological, and governmental interest (approximately 8,000 cards) and the Science and Technology Research Center keeps a file for directories of scientific or technological interest (approximately 3,500 cards).

47

WORLD WARS I AND II

WORLD WAR I, 1914–1918

Approximately 35,000 volumes concerned with World War I make this one of the major collections on the subject. The collection is strong in periodicals, bibliographies, formal and informal histories, printed archives, military (including regimental) histories, monographs on the economic aspects of the European war of 1914–18, and pamphlet material. A *Subject Catalog of the World War I Collection*, in four volumes, was published in 1961 by G. K. Hall & Company of Boston.

Approximately 61,000 cards in the Public Catalog refer to World War I; some 58,000 entries are found under the main heading "European War, 1914–1918," with approximately 1,000 subdivisions running from "Addresses, Sermons, etc." through "Women's Work." Another 3,000 entries are for important related subjects such as "League of Nations," "Neutrality," "Peace Conference, Paris, 1919," and "United States Army, AEF, 1917–1919." There are geographic and other subdivisions. The causes of the war receive about 2,200 references; naval history receives 2,000, including some 350 relating to the submarine. Territorial questions have 2,250 entries, and regional and national histories devoted to the war about 5,000. These figures represent both book titles and entries for important periodical articles.

Related collections in the Research Libraries include that of the Slavonic Division (about 4,000 catalog entries) and the Jewish Division (about 500 entries). In the Slavonic Division are book and pamphlet materials in the Cyrillic script on the war; index references to articles in periodicals are included in the catalog. An associated collection of great strength in the Slavonic Division documents the Russian Revolution and is located in the catalog under the heading "Russia—History, 1917–1923," and similar headings. The Jewish Division collection is much less extensive but contains interesting items on Palestine during the war, on the Jewish legion (under the heading "Great Britain. Infantry—Royal Fusiliers—38th Battalion"), and other topics.

World War I and its controversial political nature generated a wealth of historical studies and printed archival materials. The library has secured many of the documents essential to a detailed study of the war. Personal accounts—letters, diaries, and other private records—have appeared in the thousands, and those available in print make an extensive collection of some 3,500 titles. These materials, with a great number of pamphlets (11,000 titles, many of them propaganda), pictorial material, and other holdings make this a very strong collection. Both ephemeral and permanent materials are included and a wide range of points of view are represented.

The library's classification schedule which covers materials on World War I indicates the scope of the collections; letter symbols indicate Billings class marks:

General (BTZE)
Bibliography (BTZF)
Sermons, addresses, speeches (BTZG)
Poetry, drama (BTZI)
Fiction (BTZK)
Economic Aspects, finances, food supplies (BTZO)
Peace terms (BTZP)

Treaties (BTZQ)
American participation in the war (BTZS)
Reconstruction (BTZT)
Influence and results (BTZV)
Hospitals, charities, Red Cross, YMCA, Knights of Columbus, Salvation Army, etc.; medical and sanitary affairs (BTZW)
Aeronautics, aerial operations (BTZY)
Newspapers, periodicals, etc., on trench and camp; camp publications, camp activities, camp life (BTZZ)

The library collects comprehensively in each of these categories with the exception of sermons, addresses, speeches; fiction; and hospitals, charities, etc., which are selectively collected.

The general classification covers personal narratives and regimental histories of the war. The biographical aspects of these narratives relate them to the biographical and genealogical sections of the resources of the library. An attempt has been made to gather everything of importance regarding the bibliography of the war. Sermons, addresses, and speeches do not constitute an important group of materials. Poetry, drama, and fiction, the belles-lettres of the war, are strongly represented; these subclasses do not, however, contain all of the pertinent material available in the library. During the war they were used consistently, but it was later decided to place in them only material primarily interesting as a depiction of the war. The holdings of literary autographs, manuscripts, and first and significant editions of English and American authors in the Berg Collection contain the works of many wartime figures.

Economic aspects of the war, finances, and food supplies are extensively covered. These phases of the subject are under the reference supervision of the Economic and Public Affairs Division, although this literature is not directly related to the economics collections. In addition to numerous unofficial writings about these matters are important official reports, such as that of the Canadian War Purchasing Commission, the *Guide pratique à l'usage des Français* issued by the Office des Biens et Intérêts Privés, and the *Volkswirtschaftliche Abteilung* of the German Wirtschaftsministerium. Belgium is represented by the *Handausgabe des Gesetz- und Verordnungsblattes*, among other publications; the German *Mitteilungen* of the Kriegsausschuss des Deutschen Industrie documents a marshalling of industry typical of many countries. Some of the publications were restricted in circulation when issued, such as the *Notes* of the Transfer Committee of the Reparations Commission, and the British *History of the Ministry of Munitions*. The problem of food supply is represented by many publications of the United States Food Administration, and works such as the *Rapport général sur le fonctionnement et les opérations* of the Comité National de Secours et d'Alimentation in Brussels. Food conservation and war cookery are included in the strong collections on food and cooking.

The subclasses for peace terms and treaties contain important titles which include the *Hungarian Peace Negotiations* and the *Recueil des décisions des tribunaux arbitraux mixtes institués par les traités de paix*. Publications of the Reparations Commission are found here and in other subclasses. The library also has one of forty published copies of D. H. Miller's *My Diary of the Conference of Paris, with Documents*; also in the holdings is a copy of *La Paix de Versailles*,

the findings of the Paris Peace Conference. There are, in addition, important materials in the holdings on law and public documents, classed with materials on war and peace.

The section of materials on American participation in the War is large and varied, containing important documentary materials such as *Papers Relating to the Foreign Relations of the United States*, issued by the Department of State. Important works deal with military history and include regimental histories. There is a good collection of publications relating to the American Legion. The papers of the American Civil Liberties Union of New York contain important related materials, including sixteen volumes of correspondence dealing with the rights of a free press, free speech, peaceful assembly, and liberty of conscience during the period 1917–18. The original materials were transferred to Princeton University in 1950; the library retains a microfilm of the collection.

Newspapers, periodicals, and other publications on armed forces life form a notable collection containing such titles as the original *Stars and Stripes* and other ephemeral publications from the war period. The library has an almost complete collection on microfilm of *Stars and Stripes* not only in its single World War I Paris edition, but also in some 30 editions published during World War II. Other titles include the 171 numbers of *La Libre Belgique*, published surreptitiously by the Belgians during the German occupation of their country. There are also composite volumes in the collection of trench and camp newspapers which contain examples of publications of which the library does not have established files.

Another group of materials includes the various "green," "yellow," and "white" books in which governments stated their points of view. These items are not listed under a generic heading in the Public Catalog but must be located through individual titles. Map materials are to be found in the Map Division and in the Manuscripts and Archives Division; there are also English General Staff maps in the Parsons collection in the Science and Technology Research Center.[1]

PERIODICALS

Pictorial weeklies and other pictorial publications issued at intervals form a substantial group. There is a bound file of *l'Illustration* for the war

---

1. Lists of holdings published by the library still of some interest include:

"Catalogue of a Collection of Books Relating to Emperor William II of Germany, Presented to The New York Public Library by Dr. John A. Mandel," *BNYPL* 17 (1913): 869–75.

"Economic and Social Aspects of War; A Selected List of References," *BNYPL* 19 (1915): 167–78.

"The Polish Question Since the War; A List of References in The New York Public Library," *BNYPL* 20 (1916): 585–94.

"Diplomatic History of the European War; A List of References in The New York Public Library," *BNYPL* 21 (1917): 413–31.

"War Taxation, 1914–1917; List of References to Material in The New York Public Library," *BNYPL* 21 (1917): 459–70.

"War Memorials; A List of References in The New York Public Library," *BNYPL* 23 (1919): 499–506.

years. The *Illustrated London News* published the weekly *Illustrated War News*, and the *New-Yorker Staats-Zeitung* published the weekly *Kriegs-Album*, which was entirely pictorial. *The War Illustrated* contains, in addition to photographs and drawings, articles on aspects of the war. *Wachtfeuer*, Berlin, features caricatures. No adequate index to this material exists.

The nonpictorial serials are of varying sorts. The *Deutsche Warschauer Zeitung*, a German periodical published in Poland, presented propaganda as news. In England, the weekly *The Great War* contained news and illustrations and in Germany *Der grosse Krieg; ein Chronik von Tag zu Tag* furnished similar war coverage. *La Grande guerre: la vie en Lorraine* covered a limited region. To these may be added the illustrated supplement of *Der Tag* (1914–19).

Pages d'histoire, with its monthly reprint of "Les communiqués officiels" and a semi-annual "Chronologie de la guerre," resembles the weekly review but contains, in addition, feature articles by scholars, military authorities, and others. *Pages actuelles* is devoted mainly to philosophical studies of social and political problems arising in the war, while periodicals such as *Les Archives de la guerre* and *Das Forum* are essentially literary, although not fictional. Serials of which each number generally contained a monograph include *Collezione italiana di diari, memorie, studi e documenti per servire alla storia della guerra del mondo*, *Der deutsche Krieg*, and *Le pagine dell' ora*. Periodicals containing retrospective studies which arrive at adjusted viewpoints include *Kriegsschuldfrage* and *Revue d'histoire de la guerre mondiale*; discussion of the causes of the war forms a substantial part of the content, and the contributions are international.

Index entries for important periodical articles on the war appear in the Public Catalog.

HISTORIES

The importance of documentary sources in historical research gives particular value to the large number of printed archives which the library holds. Certain periodicals, particularly continental publications, contain archival materials; to them may be added the *Diario della guerra d'Italia raccolta dei bullettini ufficiali*, which appeared serially. Outstanding compilations in book form include the German Reichsarchiv's *Der Weltkrieg 1914 bis 1918*. The French *Guerre de 1914: documents officiels, textes législatifs et réglementaires* is representative of more general collections, and the *Amtliche Aktenstuecke zur Geschichte der europäische Politik 1885–1914* of the Ministère des Affaires Étrangères of Belgium covers more specifically the questions of causes, for which there are additional compilations, and also original printed materials in the public documents collections of the Economic and Public Affairs Division, particularly useful in the study of diplomatic relations and international affairs.

A vast amount of controversial material is present, including the publications of the German Untersuchungsausschuss über die Weltkriegsverantwortlichkeit, principally concerned with causes of the war. Belgian publications are typical of this sort of material: *Réponse au livre blanc allemand du 10 mai 1915* of the Ministère de la Guerre de 1914–16 or *Violations des règles du droit des gens, des lois et des coutumes de la guerre* of the Commission d'Enquête.

There were also contemporaneous accounts of the war which appeared in parts and were generally illustrated and inexpensive; in France these include Joseph Reinach's *La Guerre de 1914–1918*, composed of digested news material; Maurice Schwob's *Pendant la bataille*, reprinted from *Phare*; and the *Histoire illustrée de la guerre de 1914* of Gabriel Hanotaux. In Germany there were *Der Krieg 1914–1918 in Wort und Bild* and Karl Aspern's *Illustrierte Geschichte des europäischen Krieges 1914–1918*; in Italy, *La guerra delle nazioni 1914–1918*.

Reprinted laws and commentaries are varied and abundant. The *Relazioni* of the Italian Reale Commissione d'Inchiesta sulle Violazioni del Diritto delle Genti Commesse dal Nemico deals primarily with international law. There are also conventional compilations, such as the German *Sämtliche Krieges-Gesetze, Verordnungen und -Bekanntmachungen* and the Italian *Raccolta di disposizioni legislative e regolamentari duranti l'attuale conflitto internazionale*. Translations such as the *German Legislation for the Occupied Territories of Belgium* are also present. While most of this material is available in other sources, the compilations make it more accessible for research.

The collection contains all of the major unofficial histories with documentary and archival materials and a good selection of all such works. Official histories are represented by works such as the Austrian *Osterreich- Ungarns letzter Krieg 1914–1918* and *History of the Great War Based on Official Documents*, issued by the Imperial Defense Committee of Great Britain. The library can present to the researcher not only contemporary material written during the war, giving current points of view, but also official statements of position, and the host of critical studies which are based on these earlier sources.

Among the military histories are works such as *Les campagnes coloniales belges* by the Section Historique of the Belgian General Staff and *Les armées françaises dans la grande guerre* by the Section Historique of the French General Staff. J. Kooiman's *De Nederlandsche Strijdmacht* describes the activities of the Dutch army.

Regimental histories are strongly represented in this collection. The substantial holdings of American regimental histories, many of them privately printed, include rosters published by states, such as the *Official Roster of Ohio Soldiers, Sailors and Marines* issued by the Adjutant General's Office of Ohio. An interesting group relates to the American Expeditionary Forces and includes two mimeographed publications made by members of the AEF under the supervision of the Historical Section of the Army War College: *World War Records; First Division, A.E.F., Regular* in twenty-five volumes, and the *German Documents* in four volumes, containing translated war diaries from German units opposing the First Division. The strong collections of regimental histories for all periods, more fully discussed in the chapter on military science, includes holdings of exceptional importance for the United States, England, Canada, Australia, and New Zealand.

English regimental histories have generally appeared as separate works for individual military units, but some of the continental histories appear in long series, such as the *Erinnerungsblätter deutscher Regimenter, Aus Deutschlands grosser Zeit; Heldentaten deutscher Regimenter*, and *Die Württembergischen Regimenter im Weltkrieg 1914–1918*. The Italian War Ministry's *Riassunti storici dei corpi e comandi nella guerra, 1915–*

1918 may also be cited. While these volumes generally contain lists of those killed, and other materials, there are separate lists, such as the Italian War Ministry's *Militari caduti nella guerra nazionale 1914–1918* and *Ireland's Memorial Records, 1914–1918.* In addition are publications such as the British War Office's *Soldiers Died in the Great War, 1914–1919,* its *Weekly Casualty List,* and the Austrian, Bavarian, and Prussian *Verlustlisten.*

Regional histories, which often contain lists of local residents participating in World War I, are found in both the American History Division and the Local History and Genealogy Division. Another source of service lists and obituaries is the large collection of memorial volumes published by colleges and similar organizations.

PICTORIAL MATERIALS; PAPER MONEY

Pictorial material is found in strength in the pictorial weeklies discussed with periodicals. This material ranges from photographs to sketches and, particularly in German publications, includes cartoons. There are also compilations such as *L'Album de la guerre,* reproduced from *L'Illustration.* Relevant prints held by the Prints Division must be located through the name of individual artists, such as Otto Dix, Kerr Eby, and Louis Raemaekers.[2] The Art and Architecture Division holds a collection of pictures relating to war memorials.

Beginning in 1914 the library began to actively acquire posters related to World War I; by 1919 there were over 3,000 posters. In 1974 the poster collection was given to the Hoover Institution on War, Revolution and Peace. In the Slavonic Division is a collection of posters, public notices, and decrees made by John Reed in Russia during 1917 and 1918.

A very large collection of *Notgeld,* German and Austrian paper money, is administered by the Rare Book Division. Included is a series of Reichsbank notes commencing with 1913; a set called *Amtliche Dokumente als Erinnerungszeichen an Deutschlands schwerste Zeit* (1918–23); and notes issued by almost every local governing body in Germany during the rapid post-war decline of the mark.

SIGNIFICANT COLLECTIONS

Part of the William Barclay Parsons collection in the Science and Technology Research Center contains works on military engineering, mainly of World War I, and a set of English General Staff maps.[3]

The Theatre Collection of the Research Libraries has material on theatrical productions pertaining to the period of the war, including clippings, programmes, and reviews, as well as materials on the activities of stage and screen personalities.

The Arents Tobacco Collection has a scrapbook containing miscellaneous items relating to gifts of tobacco to men in the armed forces during the war; there are also a number of tobacco posters from the war period.

In the Americana Collection of the Music Division are several bound volumes of sheet music for World War I songs; the individual songs appear in the Song Index of the division.

MANUSCRIPTS

The Manuscripts and Archives Division holds the letters, reports, and other material of the American Fund for French Wounded (1915–19). The Victory Hall Association deposited its card index and other files of material relating to persons from New York who died during the war; this collection includes 3,549 photographs, 2,953 biographies, and 5 books of clippings concerning war memorials and the proposed Victory Hall. Of special note is the gift made by Col. Robert C. Richardson, Jr., of a map showing the order of battle on the western front on November 11, 1918, when the Armistice was declared; it is a pen-and-ink drawing on a French topographical map, prepared in the Map Room of General Headquarters.

In 1939 the library received the William John Wilgus papers; a large section of these relates to the transportation of the AEF, and includes letters, orders, and reports on the organization, personnel, port facilities, and schedules.

WORLD WAR II, 1939–1945

Acquisition problems considerably affected the building of resources for the study of World War II. During the war period, no country, with the exception of those of the British Commonwealth and Central and South America, was able to send its publications regularly. Access to works from the USSR improved after 1957; by this date, however, Soviet wartime publications were no longer readily available.

Although during the war period special attention was directed toward gathering ephemeral material, with the exception of pamphlets, press releases, periodicals, and newspapers of underground movements and governments in exile, few forms of ephemera were available through established channels; the generosity of interested friends brought much material of this kind into the collections.

After the war the library, through a cooperative acquisition program with the Library of Congress, received a vast number of German publications for the war period in all disciplines.[4] The Army Map Service during the period from 1945 to 1949 sent to the Map Division thousands of items, including sets of captured war maps from Germany and other countries.

The strong collection of materials relating to World War II is composed of approximately 21,600 volumes. The Public Catalog has some 37,000 entries under "The World War, 1939–45," representing materials in the Roman alphabet; there is a wider range of material on the European theatre of the war. The entries are arranged under some 250 main headings, from "Abrasive Industry" and "Addresses, Sermons, etc." to "Women's Work." Some of the larger groups of materials are found under "Campaigns" with geographical subdivisions (2,800 entries), "Free and Resistance Movements" (1,400 entries),

2. See Frank Weitenkampf, "The War Zone in Graphic Art," *BNYPL* 22 (1918): 619–21.

3. See "Catalogue of the William Barclay Parsons Collection," *BNYPL* 45 (1941): 95–108 et seq. Published separately by the library.

4. See Robert B. Downs, "Wartime Co-operative Acquisitions," *The Library Quarterly,* 19 (1949): 157–65.

"Personal Narratives" (3,400 entries), and "Regimental Histories" (more than 2,000 entries). Under the literary form headings, fictional treatment of the war is covered by some 1,300 entries; poetry by 500 entries; and drama by 300; materials include typescripts, radio, and movie scripts. Index entries for periodical articles on World War II are less thorough than those for World War I because of the increased number of periodical indexes containing this information.

The Slavonic Division catalog has approximately 5,500 entries for items in the Cyrillic alphabet. Strong subjects in this collection are "Free and Resistance Movements," "Personal Narratives," and "Campaigns." Fictional treatment of the war is represented by 400 entries. There are approximately 1,600 entries relating to World War II in the Jewish Division catalog for materials in Hebrew, Yiddish, and other languages, relating to the Jewish people. Significant aspects are covered by approximately 250 card entries under "Atrocities" and a like number for "Personal Narratives"; war poetry in Hebrew and Yiddish is represented by some 100 entries.

Certain significant features of the holdings of World War II literature may be mentioned. Although the library has the official records and reports of the war crimes trials at Nuremberg and Tokyo, the major collection of documents, records, and exhibits is available at the Columbia University International Law Library; there is another fine collection at the New York State Library at Albany. Materials for the International Military Tribunal for the Far East are housed at the Columbia University East Asian Library. The great preponderance of materials listed in the Public Catalog under the heading "Prisoners and Prisons" is related to Germany and German concentration camps. Propaganda and psychological warfare are reflected in a small group of leaflets distributed from planes over Greece, the Philippines, and other countries, some of which are kept in the Rare Book Division. Another section of materials relates to prophecies connected with the war, including those of Nostradamus.

Although the Science and Technology Research Center does not generally collect material on the practical application of scientific principles to war, it does house certain items of significance, for example the National Nuclear Energy Series published by the Manhattan Project Technical Section. In the reference collection of the General Research and Humanities Division and in the general collections the reader will find adequate documentation of those aspects of World War II which represent the newer aspects of warfare, such as radar, submarine warfare, amphibious operations, and the like.

Extensive holdings of the Theatre Collection bear on World War II. A continuing gift from the USO documents wartime activities, as does a similar donation from the American Theatre Wing, War Service, Inc. In addition, the Theatre Collection has files of clippings, photographs, contemporary newspapers, and other materials which show both the service rendered by the theatre during the war and the war as it was reflected in the theatre, radio, cinema, vaudeville, and other forms of entertainment. Volumes of popular songs of World War II are in the Americana Collection of the Music Division.

Manuscripts, maps, music, and prints related to the war are found through the appropriate division catalogs. The Berg Collection holds first and significant editions, letters, and manuscripts of American and English literary figures active during wartime.

PERIODICALS AND NEWSPAPERS

Some 200 periodical holdings relate specifically to World War II. These fall into a great variety of categories; there is an outstanding group of periodicals published by free and resistance movements. The library lacks only a few of the 20 most significant German anti-Nazi periodicals for the period 1933 to 1945; the files include titles as notable as *Das Wort* edited in Moscow by Bertolt Brecht, Lion Feuchtwanger, and Willi Bredel, *Die Deutsche Revolution* edited by Otto Strasser in Berlin and Prague, and *Mass und Wert* edited by Thomas Mann and Konrad Falke in Zurich. Periodicals of the French resistance movement are a strong feature.

In addition to collaborationist periodicals, such as the official gazette of the Vichy government, the publications of governments in exile are held in strength. Those issued by the Comité Français de la Libération Nationale (Free French) include not only its London edition, *France: Liberté, Egalité, Fraternité*, but also publications of various associated groups in Mexico, New Delhi, Algiers, and elsewhere. The library also has a complete file of the Free French *Journal officiel*.

A substantial group of periodical publications is made up of the press releases of various government information services. Perhaps the largest holdings are the foreign broadcasts of the U.S. Central Intelligence Group during the period 1942 to 1947; there are also many publications of the British Information Services and other countries. Other types of publications include those of veteran's organizations; general historical journals, such as *The Second Great War* edited by Sir Charles Gwynn and Sir John Hammerton; and prisoner-of-war magazines. Conscientious objectors' magazines include *The Reporter*, the journal of the National Service Board for Religious Objectors. Outstanding among the library's holdings of newspapers for World War II are files of editions of the two United States armed forces newspapers *Stars and Stripes* and *Yank*.[5] The almost complete holdings of *Stars and Stripes*, comprising 30 editions published during World War II (along with the World War I edition), as well as many editions of *Yank*, are now on microfilm.

The war in the Pacific is well represented by Western materials. Perhaps most useful of the general studies are governmental publications such as *Radio Report on the Far East* (1942–45) published by the U.S. Central Intelligence Group's Foreign Broadcast Information Branch; or the U.S. War Department Pamphlets (1944).

The extensive holdings of the publications of free and resistance movements and clandestine publications include newspapers. Another very extensive collection on microfilm is that of German post-World War II papers, papers published in German-occupied countries, and papers pub-

---

5. See C. E. Dornbusch, "Stars and Stripes: Check List of the Several Editions," *BNYPL* 52 (1948): 331–40; 53 (1949): 335–38. Published separately by the library. See also his "Yank, the Army Weekly; A Check List," *BNYPL* 54 (1950): 272–79. Published separately by the library.

lished by the Allied occupational forces. 600 separate titles cover the period 1945 to 1949 and include such an item as *Le Canard enchaîné* from Paris, as well as titles from Italy, Guatemala, and Japan.

HISTORIES

Official histories form an extensive group which ranges from those published during the war by the German War Office to the records of the Allied forces published after the war, such as the *American Forces in Action* series published by the Historical Division of the Department of the Army, and similar publications of the Netherlands, India, Norway, England, New Zealand, and other nations. There are published works of scholarship such as Samuel Eliot Morison's *History of U.S. Naval Operations in World War II* (1947–62) and primary source material such as the hearings before the Joint Committee of Congress on the Pearl Harbor attack. The public documents collections of the library provide access to numerous other materials of a similar nature. Under the heading "Business Histories," for example, are found the accounts of surveys made by the Strategic Bombing Survey to provide surveys of targets to determine the effects of bombing, etc. Another category relates to the official state histories of the conflict such as New York's *Empire State at War*, by Karl Drew Hartzell. An interesting feature of the holdings are contemporary German accounts, both official and unofficial.

Shortly after the war a decision was made to collect records of the conflict as written and illustrated by men who were in combat and close to service operations. By 1950 more than 1,000 titles had been acquired from all branches of the services of the U.S. Army, Navy, Air Force, and Marines, consisting of regimental and unit histories, pictorial logs, yearbooks, and the like. Additional collecting was undertaken for other countries, primarily England, Canada, Australia, and New Zealand. Included are many scarce items published in the field and usually issued for the members of the service unit only. Over 2,000 entries in the Public Catalog cover the subject; Australia receives 50, Canada 100, France 70, Germany 100, England (including India) 300, New Zealand 24, and the United States 1,300. Regimental histories for the USSR are almost nonexistent in the holdings, although there are some for Polish, Czechoslovakian, and other national regiments from Eastern Europe. The American histories have been listed in bibliographies based on the library's holdings.[6]

6. See the following compilations by Charles E. Dornbusch: *Unit Histories of World War II, United States Army, Air Force, Marines, Navy* (Washington, D.C.: Office of the Chief of Military History, 1950; Supplement, 1950).

Histories of American Army Units, World Wars I and II and Korean Conflict with Some Earlier Histories (Washington, D.C.: Department of the Army, 1956); revised as *Histories, Personal Narratives, United States Army: A Checklist* (Cornwallville, N.Y.: Hope Farm Press, 1967).

Unit Histories of the United States Air Forces (Hampton Bays, N.Y.: Hampton Books, 1958).

Post-war Souvenir Books and Unit Histories of the Navy, Marine Corps, and Construction Bat-

Personal narratives of the war are unusually extensive. There are approximately 3,300 entries in the Public Catalog under this heading, of which 400 to 500 each pertain to American, French, and German accounts; there are 660 English accounts, and about 200 Polish personal narratives. The range is extensive, from descriptions by such high commanders as Churchill, Eisenhower, and Guderian to the "G.I. Joes."

Casualty lists are also represented, such as the records of the Imperial War Graves Commission of Great Britain and the *Honor List of Dead and Missing* issued by the U.S. War Department. Town and county histories are important sources for more specific lists of local inhabitants engaged in the war; in some cases separate lists covering a United States community have been published. These are usually located in the American History Division or the Local History and Genealogy Division. Additional sources of service lists and obituaries are the memorial volumes of colleges and other institutions.

In the official histories of the war published by the United States, Great Britain, Australia, New Zealand, and other countries, all of which are in the holdings, there is additional material related to the Pacific Theatre. The *China Handbook* (1937–43) published by the Chinese Ministry of Information gives a comprehensive survey of the major developments in China during six years of war. To cite a few other examples, the regimental histories of most European countries, Great Britain, Canada, Australia, the United States, and other countries are an excellent source of information. There are, however, few regimental histories from Asian countries, except for those of a few Indian regiments. Personal narratives of the war, again, are mostly those of Westerners, although there are some post-war accounts in the Asian languages, as in *Haruka naru sanga ni* ("In distant climes"; Tokyo, 1948), which contains the diaries of Tokyo University students who fell in battle.

Under the heading "China—History—Invasion of, 1937–1945" are found some 400 entries covering all aspects of that conflict including aerial operations, most of these materials in Western languages. Among the standard accounts by Edgar Snow, Theodore H. White, General Joseph Stilwell, Freda Utley, Chiang Kai-shek, and others in English or in translation, are a few studies in the Chinese language such as Chang Sha Kai's *True Account of the Changsha Campaign* (Kweilin, 1940).

PICTORIAL MATERIALS

The library's collection of materials for World War II is not so strong as that for World War I. Books of views and scenes of the war are well represented in the holdings, but there are no major collections of bound photographs; only a limited amount of poster material is available in the Picture Collection, which is a unit of the Branch Libraries. In the Prints Division the proofs of political cartoons of Rollin Kirby for the New York *Post* cover the early years of the war, and those of Daniel R. Fitzpatrick for the St. Louis *Post-Dispatch* document the entire conflict. There are original caricatures by Harry Hopkins, a key political figure for many years. Other pictorial

talions (Washington, D.C.: Office of Naval History, 1953).

materials in the division may be located under the name of artist or print maker.

MANUSCRIPTS

At one time, letters from American servicemen were a collecting interest of the library.[7] Other

---

7. See Glenn G. Clift, "A Letter from Salerno," *BNYPL* 47 (1943): 867–71; George Barnes, "Prisoner of War; A Letter from a Liberated Soldier," *BNYPL* 49 (1945): 427–31.

items include typescripts of wartime reminiscences of Benedetto Croce, and a holograph manuscript describing the flight from his home in Sorrento in 1943 to escape seizure by the German soldiers. Material related to World War II is found in the papers of Norman Thomas, Elizabeth H. Bennett, Ward Morehouse, Alexander N. Sack, Carl Van Vechten, and the Gaffney-Ahearn family, held in the Manuscripts and Archives Division.

48

HISTORY OF AFRICA, ASIA, AND OCEANIA

HISTORY OF AFRICA

Approximately 19,000 volumes form the basic collection on African history, which was estimated to contain 8,000 volumes in 1941. Supplementing this collection are massive resources in public documents and extensive materials on related subjects. The library's interests in the African continent have led to the building of strong collections of materials relating to Egypt and North Africa (the Oriental Division has traditionally collected in this subject area), slavery, the interrelation of American and African history, and colonial matters. More general subjects which supplement the historical holdings deal with native languages, anthropology, discovery, and travel.

Specific strengths of the African history collections include: Ethiopian history, Medieval through modern, with many rare book materials; Arabic materials from North Africa and modern material from the United Arab Republic (Egypt); Egyptian archaeological materials, comprehensive from the earliest periods to the mid-1930s and representative after that period; government documents from British and other colonial powers with extensive material on the former Belgian Congo and the Republic of South Africa; maps of Africa from all periods; African voyages and travel in all periods. Under the Farmington Plan the library is responsible for acquiring publications issued in Algeria, Eritrea, Ethiopia, Morocco, Somalia, Somaliland, Spanish Sahara, Sudan, and Tunisia; the history of these countries, as well as that of Egypt and Carthage; the general history of African civilization and culture; and African languages. Through the PL-480 Project the library receives current publications from the United Arab Republic and will receive materials from other countries in the future. The holdings of the Schomburg Center include well over 20,000 volumes on all aspects of African life and culture, and recordings, original artifacts, and the extensive series of historical television films "Black Heritage" as well; these are discussed below and in chapter 13.

PERIODICALS

A strong section of political and social periodicals (commencing about 1900), and a large num-

ber of the publications of museums and institutions relate to the study of the life and customs of African peoples. Approximately 300 titles are currently received in the Periodicals Section from or about Africa, including many valuable scholarly journals from all parts of the continent with highly specialized publications in the fields of economics and technology. Among the titles related to history are the *Bulletin of News* (1957–) and the *Journal* (1956–) of the Historical Society of Nigeria, the *Journal* (1901–) of the Royal African Society, which changed its title to *African Affairs* in 1944, the Boston University *Papers in African History* (1964–), and the *Bulletin* of the Afrika-Instituut of Pretoria (1963–). Much valuable African material in the older English and European scholarly journals dating from the late nineteenth century has been indexed in the Public Catalog. Among the periodicals regularly received by the Schomburg Center are *Jeune Afrique*, *Africa*, and *A Current Bibliography on African Affairs*. African newspapers, such as the *Evening News* (Ghana), are now available on microfilm. Resources in this area are described more fully in chapter 13.

MONOGRAPHS

The African history classifications contain both histories and the accounts of exploration and travel. All nationalities are well represented, but the Dutch accounts merit special attention. In the notable group of early accounts of Ethiopia are Portuguese descriptions of what was then believed to be the land of the legendary Prester John, among them Francisco Alvares's *Ho Preste Ioam das Indies* in the first edition of 1540 and several other sixteenth-century editions in French, German, and Spanish, and Damião de Goes's *Fides, Religio, Moresque Aethiopum* (1540). The Rare Book Division has other books by Arab scholars and travelers of the Middle Ages who explored Ethiopia, together with religious writings, dictionaries, and other materials.[1] A small

---

1. See David C. Haskell, "Ethiopia, and the Italo-Ethiopian Conflict, 1928–1935; A Selected List of References," *BNYPL* 40 (1936): 13–20; Published separately by the library. See also

group of Ethiopic liturgical manuscripts in the Spencer Collection and in the Manuscripts and Archives Division date from the eighteenth and nineteenth centuries.

The full range of Egyptian history is documented, including materials in the Arabic language from the collections of the Oriental Division and rarities such as the *Courier de l'Egypte* (Cairo, 1798–1801), published during the French occupation of Egypt.[2] Among more recent materials are those noted in 55 entries in the Public Catalog which refer to the Anglo-French intervention of 1956. Works on Liberia are augmented by material on the American Colonization Society and some manuscript material.[3] Materials on South Africa are also important. Emphasis is placed on the Boer War; the library has an extensive collection which includes not only retrospective historical studies but also controversial contemporaneous literature.[4] Resources in the Schomburg Center, discussed below and in chapter 13, include histories of the ancient African kingdoms.

PUBLIC DOCUMENTS

The collection of public documents relating to Africa includes not only the publications of the colonial offices of governments which formerly exercised authority, but also those issued by the colonial governments themselves and by the newly independent nations. It is one of the most important collections of such material in the United States. In addition to the Central Building holdings, the Schomburg Center has microfilm copies of the official legislative gazettes of a number of African countries.

The material issued by the former colonial offices is important, and the collection is strong for all colonies. The depth of holdings in African government publications varies. In general those of the French and Portuguese colonies and former colonies and the independent nations formed from them are weak; of the Italian and Belgian, adequate; and of the English, very strong.

The strongest feature of the collection is government gazettes and legislative proceedings. Among scarce sets is the *Transvaal Government Gazette* (1878–79). Other important sets document the political life of an area despite changes of government: for example, the official gazette of the Congo Independent State runs without break from 1885 to 1908; the file from the subsequent Belgian Congo is complete; and the *Moniteur congolais*, issued at Léopoldville from 1960 by the reorganized Republic of Congo, continues the documentation from the area. For the Republic of South Africa the series include not only those of the Union government but also those of the self-governing colonies preceding the Union. Documentary material from the provinces of the Union is held in strength, including current publications, and there are also municipal documents from the larger cities.

Closely related to the legislative proceedings are the compiled laws and session laws. The collections relating to former British colonies and the independent nations formed from them is the strongest group. Documents other than legislative series are also numerous. One important group consists of the "Blue Books" issued by each government, giving annual reviews of economic conditions, social and political life, and additional information. Another is composed of the combined annual reports of each colony, made up of the reports of individual departments, which are valuable sources of information on agricultural, educational, and other specialized governmental activities.

MANUSCRIPTS

The Manuscripts and Archives Division contains materials dealing with the Boer War and the Ethiopian War of 1935, several nineteenth-century journals of Americans traveling in Egypt, and several diaries kept by travelers in other parts of Africa. Other important items are the account books (1826–30) of Jeremiah Evarts, secretary of the American Board of Commissioners for Foreign Missions; and the papers (1904–11) of Emil Gribeschock, which include correspondence concerning the establishment of trade with Ethiopia. The papers of Charles P. Daly (1829–99) include material on American interests in Africa, particularly the Congo. The papers (1860–1911) of Alice Donlevy contain material on the Boer War, including items relating to Miss Donlevy and Jessie Fara, her associate in the Women's South African League and the Woman's Auxiliary League of the Boer Relief Fund. Materials relating to the island of Bourbon (Réunion) include transcripts of early eighteenth-century documents from the archives of the Ministry of Colonies in Paris, as well as original documents from the period of the administration of Sieur Jean Baptiste de Villers, governor under the Compagnie des Indes Orientales de France from 1707 to 1710.[5]

THE SCHOMBURG CENTER

Approximately half of the collection of 58,000 volumes in the Schomburg Center concerns people on the African continent. The collection contains many rarities; Hiob Ludolf's *History of Ethiopia* (1681–93) in Latin, English, and French,

George F. Black, "Ethiopica and Amharica; A List of Works in The New York Public Library," *BNYPL* 32 (1928): 443–81 et seq. Published separately by the library.

2. See Ida A. Pratt, "Ancient Egypt; A List of References to Material in The New York Public Library," *BNYPL* 27 (1923): 723–66 et seq. Published separately by the library, with additions and index, 1925. See also her "Ancient Egypt: 1925–1941; Supplement to: Ancient Egypt . . . New York, 1925," *BNYPL* 45 (1941): 791–820 et seq. Published separately by the library, 1942. See also her "Modern Egypt; A List of References to Material in The New York Public Library," *BNYPL* 32 (1928): 589–634 et seq. Published separately by the library, 1929. Reprinted in 2 vols. as *Ancient Egypt* and *Modern Egypt* (New York: Kraus Reprint Co., 1969).

3. See "List of Works Relating to the American Colonization Society, Liberia, Negro Colonization, Etc. in The New York Public Library," *BNYPL* 6 (1902): 265–69.

4. See "Works Relating to South Africa in The New York Public Library," *BNYPL* 3 (1899): 429–61; and "Supplementary List of Books and Magazine Articles Relating to South Africa, in The New York Public Library," *BNYPL* 3 (1899): 502–05.

5. See *BNYPL* 13 (1909): 7–63.

and Robert Sutherland Rattray's works on the Ashanti and the Gold Coast are examples. Ibn Batuta's *Travels in Asia and Africa* (1325–54) furnishes an eyewitness account of Medieval West African kingdoms at the height of their splendor. Māhmud Kāti's *Tarikh el-fettach* and 'Abd al Rahmān's *Tarikh es-Soudan* are books by indigenous African writers providing firsthand accounts and the histories of the royal houses and dynasties which ruled the western Sudan; these and other histories of ancient African kingdoms are of special interest.

The largest number of works in the Schomburg Center are in English, followed by works in French, German, and Spanish. Vertical file materials (clippings, magazine articles, programmes, and broadsides) supplement the monograph and periodical collection. The vertical file material is classified in detail on biographical, geographical, and other lines (9,000 subject headings). Files have been established for African personalities such as Tom Mboya, Sékou Touré, Félix Houphouët-Boigny, and Gamal Abdel Nasser, and on new countries such as Ghana, Nigeria, Togo, and Mali, as well as the French Community. Men such as Nkrumah and Azikiwe have been represented in the files for at least twenty years.

Among the major topics of interest to Africanists in the manuscript resources of the Schomburg Center are the slave trade, abolition movement, African congresses, Negro missionaries, Black Star Line, Liberia, Sierra Leone, and Nigeria. More than 500 letters and sermons of Alexander Crummell, who lived for many years in Liberia as a teacher and missionary, are valuable for mid-nineteenth-century religious and educational affairs. The John Edward Bruce collection of more than 400 editorials, letters, newspaper articles, and addresses includes some that refer to persons and events in Liberia, Sierra Leone, and Nigeria, and to the Garvey movement. Other miscellaneous papers dating from the eighteenth century deal with West Africa.[6]

A *Dictionary Catalog of the Schomburg Collection of Negro Literature and History*, in nine volumes, was published in 1962 by G. K. Hall & Company of Boston, a *First Supplement* in two volumes was issued in 1967, and a *Second Supplement* in four volumes in 1972. Further information on the resources of the Schomburg Center may be found in chapter 13 of this *Guide*, including descriptions of collections of African artifacts which are important primary resources for the study of African culture.

HISTORY OF ASIA

The holdings on the history of Asia are adequate. Estimated at 13,000 volumes in 1941, the holdings in the general collections presently total more than 30,000 volumes. There are, in addition, several thousand volumes on Asian history in the Oriental Division and a number in Cyrillic script in the Slavonic Division. An historically fascinating and rare collection of books and periodicals in Western-Turkistinian languages documents the social, cultural, and economic history of Central Asia, primarily from 1914 on.[7] These holdings are supplemented by the publications of learned societies and institutions and by the extensive collections of public documents in the Economic and Public Affairs Division.

The Oriental Division catalog contains entries for not only the works in the Oriental Division but also for material relating to the Orient shelved in other parts of the library. The Oriental Division catalog emphasizes geographic regions: here, for example, the form for subject entries is "India—Economic History," whereas the Public Catalog uses the form "Economic History—India." Books in Oriental languages or translated directly from Oriental languages are generally arranged by language in the catalog and then subdivided by broad topics; consequently books in Chinese or in direct translation dealing with history are entered under the subject heading "Chinese Literature—History" (such a heading covers books in Chinese or in direct translation not only on Chinese history, but also those dealing with topics such as European or American history). Similarly, books in Arabic or in direct translation on the social sciences would be entered under "Arabic Literature—Social Sciences."

PUBLIC DOCUMENTS

The holdings of government gazettes, particularly for India and the East Asian countries, are generally good. The *Gazette of India* commences in 1912 and similarly extensive files are found for the official gazettes of the Indian states of Bihar, Orissa, Madras, Bengal, the United Provinces of Agra, and Oudh, among others. Certain countries are represented by files spanning both their colonial and independent periods: the gazette for Vietnam is available under its different names from 1889, that for the Philippines from 1902, and for Malaysia from 1909; the gazettes of Hong Kong and Macao are available from 1909 and 1930 respectively. There are sparse holdings for Japan and China; the Korean official gazette is among recent acquisitions. The gazettes of Near Eastern countries are sparsely represented, with the exception of the United Arab Republic (Egypt) and Turkey, for which there are extensive files from 1834 to the present. These gazettes and others are included in the library's Gazettes Microfilming Project; most holdings for the past ten years are available for sale on film.

National documents from Asia show the same variety of coverage with a better representation for India and East Asian countries than for those of the Near East. The figures given here represent serial documents of a political, sociological, or economic nature received in the Economic and Public Affairs Division; other more specialized documents are located in the subject collections of the library and have not been included in the count. The library also receives the monographic publications of government agencies.

Among more than 100 Indian serial titles currently received in the Economic and Public Affairs Division are the debates of the Lok Sabha and the Rajya Sabha (the preceding Parliamentary

---

6. See the unpublished *Calendar of the Manuscripts of the Schomburg Collection of Negro Literature* of the Historical Records Survey, Work Projects Administration, completed in 1942 and available in the Schomburg Center.

---

7. See Edward Allworth, *Central Asian Publishing and the Rise of Nationalism*; An Essay and a List of Publications. . . (The New York Public Library, 1965).

debates dating from 1950 are also in the collections). The library receives the legislative council and assembly debates and other material, both historical and current, of a number of the Indian states. Except for isolated runs and certain individual titles little else is received from the provinces or municipalities of Asia. Some 30 titles are received from Japan and the Philippines, including the *Congressional Record* of the Philippines, which with its predecessors is available from 1926; 40 titles are received from Indonesia and 20 from Korea. Iran, Iraq, and Turkey are represented by no more than 5 titles each; 15 are received from the United Arab Republic. Israel is well represented by documents at both the national and municipal levels; the Economic and Public Affairs Division houses those publications in English (presently numbering about 15 titles) and those in Hebrew are the responsibility of the Jewish Division. Among them are the proceedings of the Knesset and the government gazette.

THE NEAR EAST

The extensive archaeological resources in the Oriental Division for the study of ancient Egypt, Assyria, and Babylonia are discussed in chapter 45 of this *Guide*. Remarkable acquisitions of classical Arabic literature in the period before 1930 made the division an outstanding center of study.[8] The manuscript materials purchased at that time are for the most part philological, legal, or medical, rather than historical. There are editions of the great Arabic historians such as al-Tabarī and al-Masūdī. The works of al-Makkarī and other historians of Moorish Spain are supplemented by those of Arabists such as Reinhart Dozy. Persian historians are adequately represented, as are those of Turkey and the Ottoman Empire;[9] a standard work in the field is Joseph von Hammer-Purgstall's *Geschichte des osmanischen Reiches* (1827–35). A fuller discussion of the holdings for the study of Turkey is found in the section on the history of other European countries in chapter 49.

The library is fortunate in possessing two copies of the rare subscriber's edition of T. E. Lawrence's *Seven Pillars of Wisdom* (1926). The copy in the Rare Book Division is bound in violet morocco; the copy in the Arents Tobacco Collection belonged to Mrs. George Bernard Shaw, and contains an unpublished critique by George Bernard Shaw. Among the papers presented to the library by Mrs. Thomas F. Burgess in 1939 are two series of letters written during the years 1827 to 1855 by the brothers Charles and Edward Burgess from Persia and the Near East.[10]

The history of the Jewish people in Palestine, of Zionism, and of the growth of the modern state of Israel are documented by the resources of the Jewish Division.

CHINA

Chinese history, covered by some 5,300 volumes, is one of the strongest features of the Oriental history collection. Histories in the Chinese language (approximately 1,500 volumes) are housed in the Oriental Division; a smaller group of histories in the Cyrillic alphabet are found in the Slavonic Division; the major holdings in western European languages are in the general collections, located under Public Catalog headings such as "China—History—Invasion, 1931–1933."

Histories in the Chinese language include the *Erh-Shih-Wu Shih* (Taipei, 1955–56) in a complete set, as well as other editions of individual works from the set with translations. Another source work, Kuang Ssu-ma's *Tzu-chih t'ung chien* ("Mirror of history") is available in its original form and in translations, including that by de Mailla made in the eighteenth century. The *Man-chou shih lu* in three languages (Manchu, Mongol, and Chinese) documents the Ch'ing dynasty.[11] A set of 24 pamphlets issued at Nanking by the Chinese insurgents (1852–61) relates to the Taiping Rebellion.

Histories and historical materials in other languages include the standard reference works in editions published from the sixteenth century onward, among them works such as *Memoires concernant l'histoire. . . . des Chinois* (1776–1814) and Otto Franke's *Geschichte des chinesischen Reiches* (1930–52). The political development of China from the beginning of this century is well covered; in addition to books are important reviews such as the *North China Herald* and directories such as the *Directory & Chronicle* published by the Hong Kong Daily Press (1879–1941). The strong holdings of Oriental society journals provide supplementary material.

Collections of travels into Central Asia and China are notable, from the earliest accounts of Giovanni di Plano Carpini, Ruy González de Clavijo, and others, through the embassies of Johan Nieuhof and Sir George Staunton, to modern accounts. The Oriental Division has the books of Sven Hedin and Sir Mark Aurel Stein describing their expeditions into Central Asia; Nicholas Roerich is also represented.[12] Although most complete for North America, the holdings of "Jesuit Relations" in the Rare Book Division are also strong for China and other countries of the Orient. The division also holds a block book in Chinese and Latin printed in Canton in 1671, entitled *Innocentia Victrix*, which tells of the clearing of the Jesuit missionaries of charges brought against them by the Chinese government. In the Prints Division is a fine set of engravings by Cochin entitled "Victoires et conquêtes de l'empereur de la Chine" (1767–74).

Among the materials in the Manuscripts and Archives Division are imperial scrolls bestowing honors: the oldest is dated 1661 and grants honors to the mother of a Manchu officer; a later scroll contains parts of the imperial decrees

8. See "List of Works in The New York Public Library Relating to Arabia and the Arabs, Arabic Philosophy, Science and Literature," *BNYPL* 15 (1911): 7–40 et seq. Published separately by the library.

9. See "List of Works in The New York Public Library Relating to Persia," *BNYPL* 19 (1915): 9–126. Published separately by the library.

10. See Mabel C. Weaks, "Gift of Anglo-Persian Papers," *BNYPL* 43 (1939): 484. See also Benjamin Schwartz, ed., "The Burgess Persian Letters," *BNYPL* 45 (1941): 351–62 et seq. Published separately by the library as *Letters from Persia.*

11. See John L. Mish, "The Manchus; A List of References in The New York Public Library," *BNYPL* 51 (1947): 635–39.

12. See Hugo Knoepfmacher, "Outer Mongolia: A Selection of References," *BNYPL* 48 (1944): 791–801.

for honors bestowed on the Grand Secretary Ortai in 1735 and 1738, and on his son Oyunggan in 1745.[13] Other manuscripts include the diary of Charles E. Blue describing incidents of a cruise to China, Loo Choo, and Japan on the U.S. Sloop of War *Vandalla* (1853–56); although of primary importance as describing Commodore Perry's reception in Japan, the narrative includes descriptions of incidents in Shanghai during the Taiping Rebellion. The correspondence of the Rev. Elihu Doty relates to China during the period from 1847 to 1865.

JAPAN

Works on Japanese history number approximately 2,800 volumes, including such items as editions of the *Kojiki* and the *Nihongi* as well as local histories of prefectures, among them those of Fukuoka-ken (Kyushu) and Nagasaki-shi. Standard histories in western European languages are also available. There is a great deal of contemporary material on the Russo-Japanese War, including picture histories and 280 Japanese prints (given in 1904 by Philip Schuyler). Perhaps the most important of the manuscripts relating to Japanese history in the library is the journal and logbook kept by John Redman Coxe Lewis on the expedition of Commodore Matthew Perry to Japan in 1854.[14] A scroll of watercolor sketches recording the scene on the first day after Perry's arrival at Uraga is in the Spencer Collection.[15] Ten letters from Townsend Harris describe his experiences and observations as the first United States diplomatic representative in Japan from 1856 to 1862.[16] The Japanese involvement in World War II is represented primarily by Western materials; the library, for example, holds the official records and reports of the war crimes trials in Tokyo.

KOREA

Monographs concerning Korea may be located in the Oriental Division and Public Catalog under headings such as "Korea—History" and "Korean War." In addition to printed materials, several manuscript collections relate to Korea. The George C. Foulk papers date from 1884 to 1887;[17] those of Dr. Horace Newton Allen from 1884 to 1905;[18] other manuscripts which cover

the activities of the mercantile firm of Frazar & Company in Korea and the Far East during the period 1883–1948 include the personal papers of Everett Frazar, Consul-General to the Kingdom of Korea in the United States.

THE PHILIPPINE ISLANDS

Historical materials on the Philippine Islands in the general collections are supplemented by related materials in the Spanish and American history classmarks, making this a strong area of the library's resources.[19] An example of the latter category is the Elihu Root collection of United States documents relating to the Philippine Islands (1898–1906) in 178 volumes. The holdings of the works of José Rizal contain many rarities. Manuscripts pertaining to the Philippines in the Obadiah Rich collection consist of transcripts, dated about 1800, of histories, descriptions, and accounts of voyages to the Islands, from the sixteenth and seventeenth centuries. Other collections in the Manuscripts and Archives Division include an eighteenth-century Spanish naval logbook, papers relating to the attack on the Philippines by the United States, the War of Independence of 1898 and 1899, and transcripts of the Acts of the Junta de Censura de Imprenta dating from 1866 to 1875.

SOUTHEAST ASIA

The collection relating to Southeast Asia is, on the whole, strong. The holdings in geography, anthropology, philology, and other subject classes also contribute research materials. Lengthy runs of the publications of learned societies add much to the value of the holdings, among them those of the École Française d'Extrême-Orient and the *Bijdragen tot de taal-, land-, en volkenkunde van Nederlandsch-Indië*, and others. Colonial documents of countries which have or have had possessions in Asia are important sources of political and historical information; the library has long runs of this documentary material, along with publications of the new states. Diverse materials from Indonesia include the addresses of Presidents Sukarno and Suharto and the decisions of the Madjelis permusjawaratan rakjat sementara. A standing order for Thai publications brings in a great deal of material; little is received from Burma. Items from both North and South Vietnam are received.

INDIA, PAKISTAN, AND CEYLON

As a result of the Research Libraries' participation in the PL-480 Program since 1961, comprehensive collections of current publications from Ceylon, India, Pakistan, and Nepal are being obtained. Among the first published books on the history of India is *De Ritu et Moribus Indorum* (1480) attributed to the legendary Prester John; also housed in the Rare Book Division are early accounts in the works of Barros, Maffei, Linschoten, and others of the sixteenth and seventeenth centuries. The Oriental Division holds the histories of Moslem writers written mostly in Persian, such as the *Ain-i Akbarī* of Abu al Fazl ibn Allāmī. These are available in the original lan-

13. See John L. Mish, "A Manchu-Chinese Scroll," *BNYPL* 52 (1948): 143–44. See also his "Grand Secretary Ortai," *BNYPL* 66 (1962): 535–38.
14. See Henry F. Graff, ed., "Bluejackets with Perry in Japan," *BNYPL* 54 (1950): 367–83 et seq. Published separately by the library.
15. See Harold A. Mattice, "Perry and Japan," *BNYPL* 46 (1942): 167–84.
16. See *BNYPL* 24 (1920): 213. See also "List of Works in The New York Public Library Relating to Japan," *BNYPL* 10 (1906): 383–423 et seq.; and "Japanese-American Relations: A List of Works in The New York Public Library," *BNYPL* 25 (1921): 47–54 et seq.
17. See *BNYPL* 5 (1901): 332.
18. See *BNYPL* 29 (1925): 208–09. See also Robin L. Winkler, *The Horace Allen Manuscript Collection at The New York Public Library* (Ypsilanti, Michigan: Korean Research Associates, 1950).

19. See "Works Relating to the Philippine Islands in The New York Public Library," *BNYPL* 4 (1900): 19–29.

guage and in translation; histories in English based wholly or in part on these works and shelved with them include Sir Henry M. Elliot's *History of India* and the *Cambridge History of India*. Voyages and travels to India are a strong feature of the resources.

British India is particularly well covered in the collections from the eighteenth century onward. In the Hardwicke collection in the Manuscripts and Archives Division are miscellaneous papers dating from 1750 to 1767 relating to the East India Company, including letters of Robert Clive to the directors. Fifty-seven holograph pages by Sir Philip Francis give his views on the government of India. Book materials include items such as the Punjab Record Office *Press lists of Old Records in the Punjab Civil Secretariat, 1806–68* (1915–33) and records of Madras from the late seventeenth century onward. Publications of the Archaeological Survey of India and a large group of district gazetteers (principally of the late nineteenth and early twentieth centuries) are also useful source material. Strong holdings of Indian public documents include a fine representation of state gazettes.

The independence movement in India is represented in the holdings by items such as the publications of the All-India Congress Committee from the 1930s onward; more than 550 entries in the Oriental Division catalog for works by and about Mohandas Karamchand Gandhi include D. Tendulkar's 8-volume *Mahatma* (1951–54). The Louis Fischer collection in the Manuscripts and Archives Division contains sources used for Fischer's *Life of Mahatma Gandhi* (1950) along with drafts of that work; 8 letters in the collection are addressed by Gandhi to his family and friends between 1914 and 1947. Since the founding of the Republic the holdings of the library have continued to be enriched with the products of new scholarship.

The history of Pakistan before 1947 is part of Indian history; since that time the library has regularly acquired published materials on the country as they have appeared.

Papers related to Sir Alexander Johnston, Chief Justice of Ceylon, are concerned with the history, government, and customs of that country in the early nineteenth century. These number about 1,000 pages, and include palm-leaf manuscripts with writing in Tamil and Telugu characters.

HISTORY OF OCEANIA

The islands of the South Pacific, Hawaii, Australia, New Zealand, and Tasmania are covered in this subject class. The collections are, on the whole, strong. The 2,500 volumes and pamphlets in this area of the resources are supplemented by works classed in geography, anthropology, philology, and elsewhere. The long interest of the library in the islands of the Pacific has resulted in remarkable holdings of materials in Oceanic and Australian languages and dialects. A strong feature of the subject area is the extensive collection of early voyages, which includes all known editions of the accounts of James Cook and a large number of those of William Dampier and others. Many of the important titles are located in the Rare Book Division.

The collection relating specifically to the history of Australia and New Zealand is strongest for the periods of discovery and exploration; it is supplemented by the extensive collection of docu-

mentary material in the public documents section, among which there are items covering both the federal and state constitutional proceedings of Australia dating from the late eighteenth through the nineteenth centuries.[20] Since the early twentieth century representative titles and works have been acquired, including periodicals and reviews.

There are approximately 160 catalog entries referring to Australian history, including serial publications such as *Journal and Proceedings* (1906–) of the Royal Australian Historical Society, and *Historical Studies* (1940–). Early immigrants' guides, among them one for Tasmania (1822) and another for Australia (1839), provide interesting insights. Individual states are well covered: there are some 60 entries for New South Wales including the serial publications of local historical societies; Victoria receives approximately 40 entries. There are about 170 catalog entries for New Zealand representing both early and current publications. General histories for Australia and New Zealand are held in strength for all periods; local histories are less well represented. Since World War II the library has built up a fine collection of Australian and New Zealand regimental histories and other military publications.

Australian government documents are strongly represented at both the national and state levels. From Canberra approximately 100 serial titles of a general political or economic nature are currently received; these include the parliamentary debates, the *Commonwealth of Australia Gazette*, and the publications of the Census and Statistics Bureau. Gazettes, parliamentary debates, and other serial documents are received from the states of Australia, but holdings of material from the large cities are uneven. About fifteen serial titles, including parliamentary debates, come regularly from New Zealand.

A topic of some importance for the South Pacific area relates to HMS *Bounty* and the celebrated mutiny which ended her voyage to gather breadfruit trees, and led to the settlement of Pitcairn and Norfolk Islands by the mutineers. Interest in the collection centers around the famous "Pitcairn Bible."[21] Material on Tahiti includes government publications from 1852 onward with several early imprints, among them a *Livre des lois*, dated from Papeete, 1845. In the Obadiah Rich collection of documents in the Manuscripts and Archives Division is an early holograph account in Spanish of a voyage made to the islands of Otaheite from Callao in 1774.

The material on Hawaii forms a strong collection. Much additional source material is to be found in United States government documents. Many of the early documents of the royal and republican period are housed in the Rare Book Division. In the Manuscripts and Archives Division are papers relating to the revolution in 1893.

The library receives the official gazettes and other material from French Polynesia, New Caledonia, and the New Hebrides.

---

20. See Adelaide R. Hasse, "List of Books and Some Articles . . . Relating to Political Rights, Constitutions and Constitutional Law, Part II, Foreign Constitutions. Australian Commonwealth," *BNYPL* 8 (1904): 53–58.

21. See "The Pitcairn Bible," *BNYPL* 28 (1924): 443–52; and "The Pitcairn Bible; Further Notes," *BNYPL* 28 (1924): 682–83.

HISTORY OF WESTERN EUROPE

This chapter is concerned with European history, and includes the history of Great Britain, France, Germany, Austria-Hungary, the Mediterranean and Iberian Peninsulas, and other European countries. The library holds approximately 300,000 books and pamphlets relating to the history of these nations; this estimate does not include public documents, works in such allied fields as sociology and archaeology, or manuscript materials. Table 2 indicates the growth of the collections in this area.

TABLE 2. GROWTH OF THE WESTERN EUROPEAN HISTORY COLLECTION

	1921	1930	1941	1966
General	6,672	9,326	9,500	31,600
World War I, 1914–18	16,421	23,489	30,000	35,000
World War II, 1939–45	—	—	—	21,600
Individual countries	69,706	93,240	140,000	210,700
Total	92,799	126,055	179,500	298,900

These totals exclude British local histories, which are included in the statistics for local history.

EUROPEAN HISTORY

This subject class does not constitute one of the library's areas of outstanding strength. It is a diverse collection which includes standard and systematic works, popular studies, serials and collections, and ephemeral and fugitive materials. It is the library's general practice to secure any edition of older or standard works that contains a revised text or new material. A selection of standard historical works in editions suitable for reference is kept on the open shelves of the Main Reading Room.

The collections are strengthened by the large holdings of serial publications. Contemporaneous surveys include the *Europische Mercurius* (1690–1756) and the *Diarium Europaeum* (1659–83), the latter sometimes characterized as one of the forerunners of the modern newspaper. Periodical holdings are extensive and are mentioned in the discussion of the resources for the study of general and universal history in chapter 46 of this *Guide*. Most European newspaper files begin early in the twentieth century, but notable exceptions are the London *Times* (1785–) and earlier English papers described in the section on the history of Great Britain, and the *Journal des débats politiques et littéraires* from Paris (1814–1942, incomplete). The Annex Section currently receives major European newspapers such as the *Manchester Guardian*, the London *Times*, *Figaro* and *Le Monde* from Paris, and *Le Soir* from Brussels.

The library has placed particular emphasis on the collecting of pamphlets. There are now more than 7,000 pamphlets cataloged under the heading of collections, essays, and miscellanies on European history; in 1941 the collections numbered 300 bound volumes of pamphlets estimated at 3,600 separate pieces. This group is particularly strong in eighteenth-century imprints. Among the more specialized collections, strong holdings of pamphlets, periodicals, and official documents of the French Revolution include more than 15,000 pamphlets.

General historical studies cover the full range of European history. There are good historical collections for the study of classical Greek and Roman history, although the most important works are more closely classified; for example, learned and society publications in this area are frequently located with materials on archaeology and philology. Materials for the study of Medieval and Renaissance history are held in strength, and include series such as *Monumenta Germaniae Historica*, *Rolls Series*, and the like. The Spencer Collection contains finely illustrated and bound books and manuscripts, many of which are important to historical research. The General Research and Humanities Division acquires facsimiles of early books and manuscripts interesting both for their historical and artistic content. Materials on heraldry are found in the Local History and Genealogy Division.

Materials for the study of modern European history are more than adequate, with much supplementary information in the strong holdings of public documents.

Public Documents

Official publications, issued by governments and international associations such as the League of Nations and the United Nations, form one of the extensive and important archives of the Research Libraries. Government publications may be divided into three categories: those concerning foreign relations, those relating to national affairs, and those devoted to local matters. Of particular importance in the study of general European history are those dealing with foreign relations.

This group includes diplomatic series; special mention may be made of the German *Weissbuch*, the French *Documents diplomatiques*, and the English *Diplomatic and Consular Reports*, most of these beginning in the nineteenth century. This material is indexed and fully analyzed in the library's catalogs. The various series corresponding to the English "Blue Books" for other European nations are also included. English, French, and German publications predominate, although the collections are strong for all countries and periods.

Resources for the study of international relations include an extensive collection of treaties. These are held in several locations but are brought together in the 3,600 entries under the subject heading "Treaties" in the Public Catalog. This number does not include treaties on certain subjects (for example, commercial treaties, for which there are 2,000 entries); separate treaties are in some cases classified under the name of the country concerned. The library has the important collected series of treaties, in addition to separate treaties from as early as the seventeenth century.

Manuscripts

The Bancroft and Hardwicke collections in the Manuscripts and Archives Division contain items of interest for the study of eighteenth-century Europe.[1] Collections related directly to the American Revolution, but also of importance to the study of European history, include the American Loyalist papers[2] and the Chalmers collection with transcripts of European archives and official records, and the Myers collection, notable for autographs of distinguished English, French, and Hessian officers.[3]

The Harkness collection contains a number of historical manuscripts ranging from Charles I to Edward VIII, including English, French, and other European figures.[4] Notable in the Montague collection is a fine group of more than 225 autograph letters of Henry, Viscount Bolingbroke, with 4 letter-books, for the years 1710 to 1714. Additional holographs include English royalty (37 letters and 8 signed documents of Queen Victoria) and other English, French, Italian, German, and Austrian figures. The Berg Collection has a variety of European documents of historical interest.[5]

HISTORY OF GREAT BRITAIN

The library's extensive collection of materials on the history of England, Scotland, Ireland, Wales, and the Isle of Man numbers approximately 52,100 volumes; it is rich in pamphlets, and supplemented by an outstanding collection of British public documents. Approximately 33,900 volumes representing British general and national history are located in the general collections; another 18,200 volumes in the Local History and Genealogy Division cover British local history at the county, city, or township level.

Both the Astor and Lenox Libraries had good collections relating to the subject. Dr. Cogswell of the Astor Library secured in 1851 a gift from the British Record Commission of all available volumes of its documentary publications. James Lenox made an extensive collection of old and valuable works relating to the great Age of Discovery. Mr. Tilden had in his private library books on English political history, English political parties and administration, parliament, and the constitution, as well as on English social life, antiquities, and biography. The library has continued to develop these subjects, emphasizing local history and topography, political history, and biography.

The estimated growth of the collections in this subject is indicated in table 3.

Serial publications form an important group which includes a large collection of British almanacs dating from 1665 to 1816. Early periodicals of historical interest range from seventeenth-century publications such as *Kingdomes Weekly*

TABLE 3. Growth of the History of Great Britain Collection

	1921	1930	1941	1966
British general and national history	19,231	20,404	24,525	33,900
British local history	9,810	13,590	15,000	18,200
Total	29,041	33,994	39,525	52,100

Intelligencer and *Mercurius Politicus* through *The Anti-Jacobin* and *Political Register and London Museum* of the eighteenth century to titles of the present day. Substantially complete runs of the publications of the Oxford Historical Society, the Pipe Roll Society, and the Surtees and Royal Historical societies are also available. Other items include the *Archaeological Journal* of the Royal Archaeological Institute of Great Britain and Ireland, and directories, among them *Dod's Parliamentary Companion* (1833–), *Thom's Official Directory* (1855–), and *Whitaker's Almanack* (1869–).

In 1948 the library purchased the Earl of Lonsdale's collection of seventeenth-century English "newsbooks," covering the period from 1646 to 1665, and bound in 22 volumes.[6] These provide a fine representation of newspapers published during the twenty years preceding the establishment of the official government newspaper, the *London Gazette*, of which the library has a complete file from its inception (1665). With the exception of the *London Chronicle*, which is fairly complete from 1757 to 1798, the newspaper holdings from the eighteenth century are uneven until the period of the American Revolution.

The collection of travel literature is extensive; of special interest are older illustrated works, such as Richard Ayton's *A Voyage Round Great Britain* (1814–25) with views by William Daniell. The holdings of geographical materials also contain books on topography, accompanied by a rich collection of guidebooks. Geological surveys are housed in the Science and Technology Research Center; atlases and maps, of which the library has an excellent collection including ordnance maps, are found in the Map Division. The strong collection of general systematic histories contains numerous editions of the works of the older historians.

Archives of early England, Scotland, Ireland, and Wales are present in printed form. The principal sources are the publications of the antiquarian societies and the various compilations of the Public Record Office, the Royal Commission on Historical Manuscripts, and the Royal Commission on Historical Monuments. Nearly all official archival publications of governmental bodies issued for public distribution are available.

Works on archaeology and antiquities are best represented in the local history collections. The publications of general British archaeological societies are classed with archaeology in the general collections; however, those of local historical and antiquarian societies are in the Local History and Genealogy Division, where they form a very important archive. Questions relating to the antiq-

1. See *BNYPL* 5 (1901): 303–36.
2. See *BNYPL* 3 (1899): 416.
3. See *BNYPL* 4 (1900): 112–14.
4. See Lewis M. Stark and Robert W. Hill, "The Bequest of Mary Stillman Harkness," *BNYPL* 55 (1951): 213–24.
5. See Lola L. Szladits, *Documents: Famous & Infamous* (The New York Public Library, 1972).

6. See Lewis M. Stark, "Lonsdale Collection of English Newspapers," *BNYPL* 52 (1948): 35–36.

uities and archaeology of Great Britain should be referred to this division.

Later periods of British history are well covered; particularly strong are the collections of materials related to the seventeenth century, when British history was closely involved with American exploration and settlement. These sections contain not only systematic works, but also memoirs, personal and official papers, etc. Printed materials for the study of parliamentary history are held in strength. New works and revised editions of older works on British history are acquired on a comprehensive basis.

Biography and history are closely related: the personal records of public men are generally classed with biography in the general collections. In the case of specialized materials, biographical works may be classed in the subject field; for example, naval biography is found with materials on naval science.

An interesting collection of biographies and other materials on monarchs has been established. Biographies of Mary, Queen of Scots, for example, (an extensive group), form a subdivision of the holdings in Scottish history. To augment its holdings on coronations, the library made a special attempt to acquire all available materials on the investiture of Queen Elizabeth II.

Historical portraits are described in chapter 55 of this *Guide*.

British local histories number some 18,200 volumes, and form one of the richest collections of printed materials in the library, supplemented by heraldic and genealogical archives.[7] The collections include town and county histories, parish registers, guidebooks to points of interest, publications of local history societies and patriotic associations, etc. Also included are most of the vast number of transcripts of records which have been published by the Public Record Office and its predecessor, the Record Commission. The city of London is represented by more than 2,500 histories and guides (excluding pamphlets), among which are the *Post Office London Directory* (1800–   , incomplete) and the *Anglo-American Year Book* (1913–61).

Related materials for the study of British history are found throughout the collections. They include such diverse items as the public documents housed in the Economic and Public Affairs Division, printed works on the American Loyalists during the American Revolution, an outstanding collection of Loyalist transcripts from the British Public Record Office, and British army lists which date from as early as 1754. The holdings which deal with the relationship of church and state are important for the study of British political history, and the special collections devoted to Bunyan, Milton, and Shakespeare include writings delineating sixteenth- and seventeenth-century English life and thought. The collections covering military and naval art and science also contain a great deal of British historical material in regimental histories and personal narratives.

Pamphlets

British history collections are very rich in ephemeral pamphlet material. In the general collections are more than 10,000 items in the larger groups alone: the group for the Hanoverian period numbers more than 3,000 items. In 1880, John Jacob Astor gave the Astor Library the William Hepworth Dixon collection of approximately 500 English pamphlets ranging in date from 1582 to the mid-eighteenth century, the majority of them published during the period of the English Civil War and the Protectorate.[8] Twenty-three English Civil War pamphlets, all published between 1642 and 1645, were added to this collection in 1944.

Manuscripts

Two major archives in the Manuscripts and Archives Division are important to the study of British history: a group centering on British and American Loyalist activities during the American Revolution, and British diplomatic papers of the eighteenth century in the Hardwicke collection. Transcripts of the manuscripts, books, and papers of the Commission of Enquiry into the Losses and Services of the American Loyalists during the Revolution, conducted from 1783 to 1790, make available copies of documents from the Audit Office Records of the Public Record Office in England. The Hardwicke collection of original materials and transcripts was formed during the eighteenth century by Philip, Lord Hardwicke, and his sons. It was given to the Astor Library in 1884 by John Jacob Astor. Included are the papers of Sir Luke Schaub, British diplomat and ambassador, dealing with state matters and diplomatic negotiations of the first half of the eighteenth century. Transcripts of sixteenth- and seventeenth-century historical letters and documents in British archives center on the reigns of Queen Elizabeth I and King James I.

British historical materials bearing on the American Revolution in the Myers collection include documents and autograph letters of British and Hessian officers who served in the war. Additional items are in the Montague and Harkness collections. Outstanding in the Montague collection is Sir Walter Raleigh's signed petition to the Lord High Chancellor requesting that a commission correct abuses relating to his royal authority for the retail sale of wines. There are two documents signed by Queen Elizabeth I and other royal autographs. Materials from the reign of Queen Victoria include thirty-seven letters from the Queen, most of them addressed to Sir Evelyn and Lady Wood, and eight documents with Victoria's signature. Among prominent Victorian figures represented by holographs in the collection are Disraeli, Gladstone, and Sir Robert Peel. The Harkness collection contains English historical autographs, including a letter of Mary, Queen of Scots, dated March 31, 1568. Additional royal autographs are to be found in the Arents Tobacco Collection and the Berg Collection.

Public Documents

The collection of British public documents is exceptionally large, and most of the important files are complete. The library secures nearly every British government publication; exceptions

---

7. For an early listing see "List of Works in The New York Public Library Relating to British Genealogy and Local History," *BNYPL* 14 (1910): 355–99 et seq. Published separately by the library.

8. See *Dixon Collection. A Collection of Pamphlets . . .* (New York: Astor Library, 1880?).

include minor materials such as amendments to regulations and other information that ordinarily appears in later revisions or compilations. Over a long period the *Parliamentary Papers* contained nearly all administrative and other reports of government offices and agencies; in some cases duplicate copies have been cataloged and classified according to subject classes. When subject files are incomplete, catalog cards locate items in the public documents set.

In the field of international relations—treaties, diplomatic papers, consular reports, and similar items—the library has made every effort to secure all published materials available for distribution.

The collection of publications national in scope is very rich. The *London Gazette* is complete from its beginning in 1665 as the *Oxford Gazette.* The *British Gazette*, published by the government during the general strike of May 1926, when other newspapers were forced to suspend publication, is also in the holdings. The files of the Belfast, Dublin, and Edinburgh gazettes begin about 1900. Parliamentary publications form another strong group, including a bound set of the *Parliamentary Papers* from 1731 onward. The set covering the years 1731 to 1800 (incomplete for the earlier years) is excessively rare, and at one time was the only known set in the United States; some numbers are missing for the period 1800 to 1830, but otherwise the run is complete. There are complete sets of the journals of the House of Lords, the House of Commons, and the *Parliamentary Debates.* Another important group is composed of proceedings and reports of royal commissions; the library has an extensive collection of these items.

The collection of laws is very strong.[9] It includes the compilations of the Record Commission, as well as the general acts; also included are the rare English session laws, 1690 to 1806, purchased in their original bindings in 1937.[10] There are good but incomplete files of *Statutory Rules and Orders* (from 1890), and *Local and Personal Acts* (from 1824); the latter is especially important as a record of British corporation legislation.

The administrative publications of Scotland, Ireland, and Wales form a strong group, as do the public documents of the Irish Free State and the Isle of Man.[11]

The collection of local documents is also extensive and important.[12] Representative publications for the larger English cities include the *Minutes* of the Town Councils, the *Abstracts of Accounts*, and the *Reports* of Medical Officers of Health. The collection of council reports and proceedings of the 28 boroughs of London, established in 1900, is especially notable. The collection is weak

in Scottish county government publications, but those relating to the municipal finance of Edinburgh and Glasgow are present, as are the Town Council *Proceedings* of these cities. There is also a good collection of municipal reports from Dublin and Belfast.

SCOTLAND

Printed materials concerning Scotland are extensive.[13] The collection of some 4,000 volumes is rich in printed records, systematic historical works, and special studies; it is divided almost equally between materials in the general collections and materials in the Local History and Genealogy Division. A large number of pamphlets dealing with Scotland are bound with others on British history. Resources include sets of the publications of such clubs as the Bannatyne, Maitland, and Spalding, and an exceptional collection of works on the popular subjects of clans and tartans. Other holdings in the Local History and Genealogy Division include the publications of the General Record Office at Edinburgh (among them *Register of Sasines* and *Register of Deeds*), along with rare items such as the *Inquisitionum* (1811; 1818) commissioned by George III of England, which records land inheritances in Scotland. The *Edinburgh Magazine and Literary Miscellany* (1739–1826) contains indexes of marriages, births, and preferments in each volume. Of considerable importance are the holdings of materials on Scottish church history, located with the holdings on religion in the general collections.

IRELAND

Approximately 3,000 volumes cover both the general and specialized history of Ireland.[14] Included are long runs of periodicals such as the *Analecta Hibernica* (1930–   ), published by the Irish Manuscript Commission, *Irish Historical Studies* (1938–   ), and the *Journal* (1849–   ) of the Royal Society of Antiquaries of Ireland. Local historical periodicals include the *Journal* (1892–   ) of the Cork Historical and Archaeological Society, the *Ulster Journal of Archaeology* (1853–   , incomplete), and other titles. Studies of Irish counties and towns are kept in the Local History and Genealogy Division. Among materials in the general collections are many pamphlets from the eighteenth century and some from the nineteenth and later, containing reports of trials, speeches, debates, arguments for union, and similar information. This group was augmented in 1967 by a purchase of 300 pamphlets, many having to do with the Land Question. Three folio volumes contain mounted political cartoons of the period from 1884 to 1886. Among materials in the Rare Book Division are such early histories of Ireland as Peter Lombard's *De Regno Hiberniae* (1632), and 65 political handbills, probably printed in Dublin in 1922, some in Gaelic.

---

9. See "A Check List of Works in The New York Public Library Relating to Corn Laws," *BNYPL* 6 (1902): 191–200. Published separately by the library.

10. See Rollin A. Sawyer, "From Cuckfield Park to Bryant Park; A Set of English Session Laws," *BNYPL* 41 (1937): 3–7.

11. See "List of Works in The New York Public Library Relating to the Isle of Man," *BNYPL* 15 (1911): 756–68.

12. See "List of City Charters, Ordinances, and Collected Documents in The New York Public Library," *BNYPL* 16 (1912): 631–719 et seq. Published separately by the library.

13. See "List of Works in The New York Public Library Relating to Scotland," *BNYPL* 18 (1914): 11–58 et seq. Published separately by the library in an expanded form and with an index, 1916.

14. See "List of Works in The New York Public Library Relating to Ireland, the Irish Language and Literature, etc." *BNYPL* 9 (1905): 90–104 et seq. Published separately by the library.

Modern Irish historical manuscripts in the library, especially those concerning the Irish revolutionary movement, are of major importance. The preponderance of this material came as the gift of William J. Maloney.[15] More than 2,000 pages of original material related to Sir Roger Casement include holograph letters, addresses, and memoranda for the period 1914 to 1916. Other key figures represented by substantial bodies of material are the Irish-Americans Joseph McGarrity and Jeremiah O'Donovan Rossa, and a great deal of material relating to Friends of Irish Freedom.

Two other groups of Irish manuscripts, principally of literary and artistic interest, also offer historical insight. The John Quinn collection reflects Quinn's years of association with members of the Irish Home Rule movement. The purchase of the papers of Lady Gregory by the Berg Collection in 1964 brought the library an archive of the greatest importance for the study of the Irish Literary Renaissance.

HISTORY OF FRANCE

A collection of 41,800 volumes, of which 9,800 volumes are devoted to local and colonial history, provides extensive coverage of all epochs of French history. Literature relating to the periods from Henry IV to Louis XIV is more than adequate; it is not, however, as strong as that for the eighteenth century and the Revolutionary and Napoleonic periods. The growth of the collection is illustrated by the following:

1920	17,362 volumes
1931	27,806
1941	36,500
1966	41,800

The resources are rich in printed source materials relating to general and local history.[16] Among important holdings are: *Recueil des historiens des Gaules et de la France* (1738–1904) edited by Martin Bouquet; *Les Classiques de l'histoire de France au moyen âge* (1923–   ); and *Collection de textes pour servir à l'étude et à l'enseignement de l'histoire* (1886–1929). New series are added to the collections as published. One such is the "Série in-8°" issued by the Section de Philologie et d'Histoire of the Comité des Travaux Historiques et Scientifiques. The library also has the monumental *Collection de documents inédits sur l'histoire de France*. Among important collections available are *Collection des mémoires relatifs à l'histoire de France*, annotated by François Guizot (1823–35), Michaud and Poujoulat's *Nouvelle collection des mémoires pour servir à l'histoire de France* (1851), and François Guizot's *Mémoires pour servir à l'histoire de mon temps* (1858–67).

Learned society publications include those of the Société de l'Histoire de France (1834–   ) and other long runs. Strong holdings in French general literary periodicals often contain much

of historical interest. Incomplete holdings of the *Almanach national* (previously *Almanach royal*) are available from 1708; a large group of French almanacs documents the period from 1880 to 1898.

Inventories of archives and manuscript depositories comprise another group of value for fundamental research, which includes the publications of the Commission Supérieure des Archives Nationales, Départementales, Communales et Hospitalières. The *Catalogue général des manuscrits des bibliothèques publiques de France* suggests indexes in other classes which serve as guides to French historical materials. Books of description, travel, and biographical studies are well represented.

Related subject classes contain noteworthy materials. Geography contributes works of importance: the literature of discovery and travel from James Lenox's collection, for example, includes French works on the Age of Discovery; there are also a large number of guidebooks and important topographical works. Source materials in the public documents collection form another rich and extensive archive. Notable materials for the study of French church history center on Jansenism, the Abbey of Port-Royal, and Gallicanism.

RESOURCES

Acts of French Royal Administration

This has always been one of the library's strong collections. Dr. Cogswell, reporting on the Astor Library in 1855, noted that "in French law, the library is really rich, beginning with the Ordonances des Reis, and coming down to the very latest volume of the Journal du Palais."[17] These and other French royal acts in the field of American interest formed part of a check list published in 1929 and 1930.[18] In 1937 an outstanding collection of 15,000 royal French ordinances, edicts, and decrees was purchased. These date from the late seventeenth to the late eighteenth centuries, and contain a wealth of material relating to America. Several thousand additional royal acts were purchased after World War II. The bulk of these later acquisitions (some 20,000 pieces) has not yet been fully cataloged. Preliminary research has revealed that the uncataloged materials contain several individual acts not noted in the *Actes royaux* of the Bibliothèque Nationale, together with a large number of variant editions which do not appear in that work. In addition, considerable strength is present in such categories as acts of the Conseil d'État, Chambre des Compts, and Cour de Parlement. The original dates of promulgation (as opposed to the dates of publication) of the acts in this uncataloged collection range from the middle of the thirteenth century to the Revolution.

Mazarinades

The collection of about 700 mazarinades (pamphlets in prose and verse published in France

15. The catalog of the collection is published as an appendix to the *Dictionary Catalog of the Manuscript Division* (Boston: G. K. Hall & Co., 1967) 2: 577–99.

16. Many titles of historical interest appear in "French Printing Through 1650: A Check List of Books in The New York Public Library," *BNYPL* 40 (1936): 87–96 et seq. Published separately by the library with additions, 1938.

17. See Lydenberg, *History*, p. 26.

18. "Acts of French Royal Administration Concerning Canada, Guiana, the West Indies and Louisiana, Prior to 1791," *BNYPL* 33 (1929): 789–800 et seq. Published separately by the library.

during the Fronde, or roughly in the period from 1648 to 1653) forms a counterpart to the collection of English pamphlets of the Civil War period.[19]

Revolutionary Pamphlets and Other Materials

In 1937 the library acquired a collection of pamphlets concerning the French Revolution that had formerly belonged to Charles Maurice de Talleyrand-Périgord (1754–1838). It is bound in 105 volumes and contains 2,027 titles. A wide variety of pamphlets—serious and facetious, official and unofficial—is included. There are nearly 100 *cahiers de doléances* and issues of various Revolutionary periodicals such as Marat's *L'Ami du peuple* (and imitations of it), *Journal universel*, and similar publications. All of the pamphlets, with the exception of a few of earlier date, were published between 1787 and September of 1791. The Talleyrand collection is especially strong in the following subjects: the financial crisis, the calling of the Estates General, the disorders in Brittany, the fall of the Bastille and the formation of the new government of Paris, and the disorders in Paris during the summer of 1789. The material is bound roughly in chronological order and supplements and strengthens the extensive pamphlet and periodical holdings relating to the early phases of the Revolution; the general pamphlet collection numbers some 2,200 pieces in 145 volumes.[20]

In 1948 the library purchased two large groups of French Revolutionary materials. The first was a collection of more than 13,000 pamphlets from the period 1787 to 1800, of which an estimated 20 percent are not held by the Bibliothèque Nationale. The second purchase brought 371 periodicals of the era, totaling 32,000 issues, providing documentation on all major and many minor issues of this intensely agitated historical period.

In addition to these large pamphlet and periodical holdings is a strong collection of other books and periodicals on the Revolution recorded in the Public Catalog. Approximately 4,800 references are arranged by chronological period. A number of broadsides printed at the time of the Revolution and the Directorate are in the Rare Book Division.

The Napoleonic Period

Almost 500 entries in the Public Catalog refer specifically to Napoleon and his campaigns; additional references refer to battles, personalities, and other aspects of his period. Items bearing on the private life of the Emperor are held in strength, but military campaigns have been given special attention. Related material is found in other subject areas; for example, many works on the Napoleonic period are classified with Spanish history materials.

Special mention should be made of important Slavonic Division holdings for the study of Napoleon. Most of this material is in the Cyrillic alphabet, and cards are found only in the Slavonic Division catalog. The library continues to make important additions to the collection, which includes contemporary works as well as formal studies of later dates. The collection is well provided with reprinted documents and archives, including such interesting compilations as a collection of public notices posted by the governor of Moscow, Count Rostopchin, during 1812. Secondary materials—collections, memoirs, and the like—are also present. Another interesting group is composed of finely bound contemporary pamphlets, primarily belles-lettres, which not only reflect the opinions of the period but also serve as examples of Russian bookmaking from the early nineteenth century.

Modern Materials

A small but important group of works relating to the Dreyfus case includes over 100 contemporary pamphlets. There is important material in the resources on France in World Wars I and II containing not only systematic histories but also collections of documents and archives; these are discussed in chapter 47 of this *Guide*.

French Local and Colonial History

The collection of materials for the study of French local history, numbering about 9,800 volumes, is stronger than similar collections for other foreign countries, with the exception of Great Britain, and is one of the most important features of the French historical section.

The number of periodicals and historical society publications is very large, with the majority of important sets complete. Serials in other areas important to the study of local history include general French periodicals, the publications of learned societies and institutions, and those of religious societies such as the *Bulletin historique et littéraire* of the Société de l'Histoire du Protestantisme Français. Many important contributions are indexed in the Public Catalog.

Printed archives appear in the publications of societies, but there are also separate compilations; of special importance are reprinted materials relating to the French Revolution. Additional material is suggested by the *Inventaire général des richesses d'art de la France*. A large number of cartularies have direct bearing on local and economic aspects of French history.

The holdings are rich for the histories of larger provinces and towns. Literature relating to Paris, Provence, and some of the cities of southern France (especially Avignon, Bordeaux, Marseilles, and Toulouse) is particularly extensive.[21] The notable holdings of works published during the eighteenth century devoted to description and topography are of importance both for their text and early plates and maps.

Associated materials include archaeological studies, both in the general collections and in the

---

19. See "A Check List of Mazarinades in The New York Public Library," *BNYPL* 41 (1937): 29–46. Published separately by the library with "French Printing Through 1650."

20. See "Pamphlets Relating to the French Revolution in The New York Public Library," *BNYPL* 2 (1898): 256–64. See also Horace E. Hayden, "French Revolutionary Pamphlets: A Check List of the Talleyrand and Other Collections," *BNYPL* 41 (1939): 3–18 et seq.

21. See Daniel C. Haskell, "Provençal Literature and Language, Including the Local History of Southern France: A List of References in The New York Public Library," *BNYPL* 25 (1921): 372–400 et seq. Published separately by the library with additions and index.

architectural resources of the Art and Architecture Division. Geography is another important allied class, with an extensive collection of guidebooks and such works as the *Dictionnaire topographique*. Biography is strongest in collective works, including the departmental biographies. The collection of numismatic works contains material of considerable interest.

The comparatively small group of items classed under French colonies and dependencies is largely composed of lengthy runs of learned society and governmental publications such as the *Comptes rendus* of the Académie des Sciences Coloniales and the *Bulletin* of the Office Colonial. Among older materials is a good deal on the Compagnie des Indes and the Compagnie d'Occident. With the independence of former French colonies, the library has continued to solicit and receive their official publications as well as studies about them. These may be located in the Public Catalog under the name of the country and under headings such as "The French in Brazil," "The French in Morocco," and "The French in the United States."[22]

Public Documents

Materials relating to French international affairs are held in strength. Reprints of important documents and many important historical works are present, together with treaties, diplomatic papers, and similar materials. The important "Livres jaunes" (*Documents diplomatiques*), commencing in 1860, are complete; earlier printed French royal acts are discussed above.

Extensive legislative series date from the eighteenth century. The library holds the *Archives parlementaires de 1787 à 1860* as far as the series has been published, as well as an incomplete set of the original proceedings. The *Annales* of the Senate and the Chamber of Deputies are present from their beginning (1870), preceded by a complete file of the *Annales du Sénat et du Corps législatif* (1861–70).

Laws form an important body of source materials. The *Recueil général des anciennes lois françaises depuis l'an 420 jusqu'à la révolution de 1789* is in the collection, as are the *Journal officiel* (beginning in 1789 as the *Gazette national*) and the *Bulletin de lois*. The *Recueil Sirey*, with its appendix, *Lois annotées*, begins in 1789, but is not entirely complete. The various "Collections" of the Assembly and the Convention are complete, as is the *Collection général des lois et des actes du Corps législatif et du Directoire exécutif*. There are other important series, with many private publications and reprints. An interesting feature of the French law materials is a number of "Coutumes."

In subject materials, the public documents collection is strong in budgetary and financial publications, statistical reports, and in other areas described in the section of this *Guide* dealing with economics.

Publications of the departments of France are not well represented. The *Procès-verbaux de Con-*

seil général and the *Rapport du préfet*, common to all the departments, are good for Manche, Oise, and Seine; good files of the *Annuaire* for Marne and Sarthe are also present. The best-represented municipal publications are those of Paris, Lyons, Marseilles, and Le Havre.

A group of related documents of some importance are the reprinted materials concerning the former French colonies in America which appear in Canadian public documents.

Manuscripts

An illuminated parchment scroll from the fifteenth century, a genealogy of the French kings containing 64 miniatures, was the gift of Mr. and Mrs. D. Jacques Benoliel and Mr. and Mrs. Somond Benoliel in 1945. The most significant manuscript materials relating to France cover French interest in America during the colonial period and French activities in the American Revolution, although there is representative material on territorial France.

The Hardwicke collection in the Manuscripts and Archives Division includes transcripts of the papers of French ministers in England during the reigns of Elizabeth I and James I. The Bancroft collection contains transcripts of the papers of Vergennes and Gérard, Marbois, Luzerne, and others on American affairs from 1776 to 1786. There are also transcripts of official correspondence on Louisiana, Pontiac's War (1754–65), and other matters. In the Ford collection approximately 1,200 transcripts record the correspondence of French ministers in the United States during the period 1791 to 1797. The Myers collection includes autographs of French officers who served in the American Revolution.

There are signed documents of Louis XIV, XV, and XVI, Robespierre, and others in the Montague collection, together with nine letters and three documents signed by Napoleon and letters of his family and marshals; there are also twenty-five Talleyrand letters. The Harkness collection includes letters of the Empress Marie Louise to her aunt during the period 1816 to 1821, with additional French royal and historical autographs.

Prints

The many portraits of French historical figures and events in the Prints Division must be located primarily through the name of the artist or printmaker, for the subject index is not inclusive. Among the periods particularly well represented are the French Revolution, the revolution of 1848, and the Franco-Prussian War. A sizable collection of pictorial material on the Commune, including caricatures, was in large part the gift of John Bigelow in 1903.

HISTORY OF GERMANY

The collection of printed materials relating to Germany (including the Holy Roman Empire) is strong, but less extensive than the collection relating to France. Perhaps the most remarkable feature of this area is its rapid growth in the period after 1941, as indicated by the following:

1921	8,563 volumes
1930	13,373
1941	15,000
1966	28,000

---

22. See Frank Monaghan, "French Travellers in the United States 1765–1931: A Bibliographical List," *BNYPL* 36 (1932): 163–89 et seq. Published separately by the library; reprinted with supplement by the Antiquarian Press (New York, 1961).

Much of this growth can be attributed to the vast number of publications received by the library immediately after World War II under the Cooperative Acquisition Project. Under this project the New York Public Library received more volumes than any American library other than the Library of Congress. Although most of the material received was nondocumentary, there are strong holdings on the Nationalsozialistische Deutsche Arbeiterpartei and the Third Reich, including a large number of serial titles rare in the United States. Approximately half of the total German history holdings, or some 14,000 volumes, concern local history.

Pamphlet holdings are less extensive than those for France, Great Britain, or Italy, but the several thousand items include many dissertations and reprints. There is a group of about 50 items published during the Thirty Years War in Paris and the Netherlands.

The historical collections relating to German tribes, the medieval empire, and modern Germany are numerous and important. They include such sets as the *Monumenta Germaniae Historica*, the contents of which have been fully cataloged by the library.

Among general materials is a large number of German historical periodicals. Approximately 40 titles are noted in the Public Catalog, including the eighteenth-century *Patriotisches Archiv für Deutschland* (1784–90) and the *Deutsches Archiv für Erforschung des Mittelalters* (varying title, 1937–). Publications relating to local history include those of the Historische Kommission für Niedersachsen with other publications on archaeology and antiquities, and reprints of documents and archives. Additional material is found in the publications of learned societies.

Systematic histories of Germany, the extensive collections of general literature devoted to politics, foreign relations, and diplomatic history, and primary materials in the public documents collection enrich the resources.

The literature of general travel is extensive. It is supplemented by material for the individual states of Germany. Although the works in geography are less numerous than for some other European countries, they form an important related group consisting of guidebooks, gazetteers, and other materials. There are representative collections for the study of early German colonial interests.

Biographical works relating to German rulers are an important feature of the resources; especially interesting is the literature pertaining to Frederick the Great, supplemented by several letters and documents in the Manuscripts and Archives Division, and to Kaiser Wilhelm II; the latter holdings are enriched by some 200 books and pamphlets presented by Professor John A. Mandel in 1913.[23] Holdings for Adolf Hitler include many editions of *Mein Kampf*; the Manuscripts and Archives Division has material on the early translations of the work into English.

Among materials in the Rare Book Division are *Cronica van Coellen* (1499), Hartmann Schedel's *Das Buch der Chroniken* ("The Nuremberg Chronicle," 1493), and early sixteenth-century printed statutes. The Spencer Collection has

Die güldin Bulle (1485), which concerns imperial election procedure and contains the 1356 decree of Charles IV with additions by the emperors Sigmund and Frederick. Works published in the eighteenth century form an interesting and rich collection. Not only are the systematic treatises present, but such older works as Moser's *Teutsches Staats-Recht* (1737–54) and Ludolf's *Electa Juris Publici* can be found as well.

Nineteenth-century printed materials include a large collection of contemporaneous books and pamphlets from the period of the 1848 revolution. The twentieth century is especially well represented. Materials relating to the world wars are described in chapter 47 of this *Guide*. The library began to collect material on Nazi Germany at an early date and acquired many ephemeral propagandistic publications. After World War II a great deal of material was received through the Cooperative Acquisition Project. Important related material is found in the Jewish Division.

A strong collection of books, periodicals, and other items on the Germans in America is administered by the American History Division.[24]

Public Documents

The strong collection of German public documents includes reprinted archives, diplomatic series, treatises, and similar materials. The file of the *Weissbuch* is complete, and other series, particularly those of reprinted documents, relating to World War I, are extensive.

Series national in scope are numerous and generally complete. The official gazette, *Deutscher Reichs- und preussischer Staats-Anzeiger*, begins in 1875 and continues to the outbreak of World War II, as does the *Stenographische Berichte* of the Reichstag (available on film from 1867–1937/38). The *Verhandlungen des Bundesrats* is essentially complete for the same period, as are publications of the various ministries of finance, posts and telegraphs, and the like, and the published reports of statistical bodies. Though some files of government publications are present for the years of World War II, coverage is uneven. There is a good representation of publications of the Control Council for all zones of Germany during the postwar period, including statutes and gazettes. The library currently receives publications of both the German Democratic Republic (East Germany) and the Federal Republic of Germany (West Germany). A larger proportion of materials comes from West Germany, with a strong representation of statistical publications. The official gazettes for both East and West Germany are complete.

Session laws, the *Reichsgesetzblatt*, are complete from 1871 to 1943. These are continued by the publications of the Control Council for the various zones of postwar Germany, and by the East German *Gesetzblatt* (1951–) and the West German *Bundesgesetzblatt* (1949–). Although the library has the standard works on the Nuremberg Trials, more extensive holdings of documents, records, and exhibits are to be found in the Columbia University International Law Library and the New York State Library at Albany.

---

23. See "Catalogue of a Collection of Books Relating Emperor William II of Germany, Presented to The New York Public Library by Dr. John A. Mandel," *BNYPL* 17 (1913): 869–75.

24. See Paul H. Baginsky, "German Works Relating to America," *BNYPL* 42 (1938): 909–18 et seq. Published separately by the library with revisions and corrections, 1942.

Of earlier materials, the collection contains such sets as the *Stenographischer Bericht über die Verhandlungen der deutschen constitutirenden, Nationalversammlung zu Frankfurt am Main* (1848–49).

For the North German Confederation, the library has a complete file of the session laws, the *Bundesgesetzblatt*, but its set of the *Verhandlungen des Reichstages des Norddeutschen Bundes* is incomplete. There are other important series.

Although holdings of the administrative documents, laws, and related materials of the German states are uneven, the collection as a whole is good. Some series are long, such as the *Gazette* of Hesse, or the *Gesetz-Sammlung für die Königlichen Preussischen Staaten*, which, commencing in 1810, continued until 1944. The collection is strongest for Baden, Prussia, Saxony, and Würtemberg.

The important collection of municipal documents includes some volumes of municipal statutes from the sixteenth to the eighteenth centuries. Municipal reports are numerous, series for the more important German cities being substantially complete with exceptions for the World War II and immediate postwar periods. In 1930 the library received as a gift a nearly complete set of publications for Bruchsal, Baden.

Manuscripts

With the exception of "Chronica der Stat Nuremberg" from 1348 to 1625, several letters and documents of Frederick the Great, and a body of eigtheenth-century diplomatic correspondence in the Hardwicke collection dealing with Hanover, Saxony, Prussia, and other states, the majority of German historical manuscripts pertain to international affairs during the American colonial period. The Anspach papers in the Bancroft collection are original documents concerning the troops furnished by the Margrave of Anspach-Brandenburg to the British government for service in America during the period 1776–85. There are also journals of German officers and German regimental histories of the American Revolution.

HISTORY OF AUSTRIA-HUNGARY

The Billings Classification Scheme, under which books on Austria and Hungary were classified until 1955, bears little resemblance to the present political alignment, but the materials located within .that scheme retain interest for a study of the old order (materials published after 1955 on the former political units are, of course, still being acquired). The holdings number approximately 5,000 volumes for Austrian history and 3,000 volumes for Hungarian (total holdings in 1941 were 2,500 volumes) with substantial additional materials in the Slavonic Division in Czech, Slovak, Serbo-Croatian, and other languages.

The collections in this area, while adequate, are not as distinctive as those for some of the larger European nations. Materials relating to Austria are stronger than those for Hungary. Such standard works of reference and source works as the *Fontes Rerum Austriacarum* and the *Monumenta Hungariae Historica* are present for both countries. Periodicals and society publications are held in extensive and generally complete runs from such early items as the *Archiv für Geschichte, Statistik, Literatur und Kunst* (1810–26) to the *Austrian History Yearbook* (1965–) and its predecessor the *Austrian History News-*

letter (1960–63). Serial publications provide important writings on general and local history, archaeology, and related subjects.

There are more than 400 entries in the Public Catalog for Bohemia (now part of Czechoslovakia). Included are source works such as the *Codex Diplomaticus et Epistolaris Regni Bohemiae* (1904–65), collections of maps in the *Monumenta Cartographica Bohemiae* (1938–[41]), and rarities such as a first edition (1552) of Bishop Jan Dubravius' *Historia Regni Boiemiae*. Government documents include original statutes in a collection of 188 *Artickel des allgemeinen Landtag* dated Prague, 1567 to 1823, supplemented by further collections in the *Zákonník Zemský Království Českého* (1850–1919), together with other studies both ancient and modern.

Transylvania (now part of Rumania) is represented by some 100 entries in the Public Catalog which cover the full range of its history. Included are early studies such as Ascanio Centorio degli Hortensi's *Commentarii della Guerra di Transilvania* (1565–70), and compilations such as the *Monumenta Comitialia Regni Transylvaniae* (1875–97).

Materials for the study of Austria and Hungary during the World Wars are extensive, with important resources located in the special collections. There is a notable collection on the Hungarian uprising of 1956, including microfilms of periodicals of the period such as the *Irodalmi Ujság*.

Public Documents

The collection of public documents, while uneven, is important. It includes extensive sets of parliamentary proceedings for Austria, Hungary, and various states of the Austro-Hungarian Empire from the latter half of the nineteenth century. Of special interest are the extensive holdings for Czechoslovakia, and the succeeding states which emerged after World War I.

The library currently receives the *Stenographische Protokolle* (1918/19–) of the Austrian Nationalrat, as well as statistical and other publications in substantial runs with gaps for the war years. From Hungary come the *Budapesti Közlöny* (1906–46, incomplete) and other publications. Law holdings are also extensive. Contemporary materials are supplemented by compilations, codes, and such materials, for earlier years.

The holdings of municipal administrative reports are uneven. Those of Austrian cities are generally adequate, with outstanding resources for Vienna and important groups for Budapest and Prague.

Manuscripts

In the Hardwicke collection of the Manuscripts and Archives Division are letters (for the most part rough drafts) of Sir Luke Schaub while he was British *chargé d'affaires* at Vienna during 1715 and 1716.[25] Transcripts of documents from the archives at Vienna for the period 1781 to 1783 are in the Bancroft collection.

HISTORY OF THE MEDITERRANEAN AND IBERIAN PENINSULAS

The library has good but not notable collections relating to the history of Greece (5,000

25. See *BNYPL* 5 (1901): 331, 332, 333.

volumes), Italy (15,000 volumes), Portugal (2,000 volumes), and Spain (7,000 volumes). Although in the past the library did not attempt to collect as extensively for these countries as for Great Britain and France, present Farmington Plan responsibilities in history require the same level of collection for all European countries. In addition to standard works and travel literature, the holdings include many of the collections of printed sources needed for research. These and related groups of materials mentioned below provide an adequate working collection. Among areas of particular strength are Spanish history during the American colonial and Revolutionary periods and during the Spanish Civil War of 1936 to 1939, and Italian provincial and local history publications.

Allied classes of material supplement the general collections. The collection of public documents is strong for Italy, Spain, and Portugal. Resources for the study of the classical periods of Greek and Roman history are enriched by extensive holdings relating to archaeology. The publications of academies and learned societies contribute materials important for both national and local historical study, along with some archaeological and biographical material.

In the field of foreign relations the publications of Italy, Spain, and Portugal are numerous, but those of Greece are not strongly represented. The most important diplomatic series are present—the Italian "Libri verdi" (*Documenti diplomatici*) from 1861 to date; the Spanish "Libros rojos" (*Documentos diplomáticos*) from 1865 to 1911 (incomplete); and the Portuguese "Livros brancos" (*Negócios estrangeiros*) from 1867 to date. Printed treaties of Italy, Spain, and Portugal also form an important group. Other diplomatic series and numerous single publications, together with the collections of reprinted documents, enrich the holdings in the field of international affairs.

GREECE

Approximately 5,000 volumes document the history of Greece; standard works and editions of the ancient and modern historians are present. The various series of the Akadēmia Athēnōn are held. Periodical publications include *Byzantinische Zeitschrift* (1892–), *Byzantion* (1924–), the *Epetēris* (1924–) of the Hetaireia Byzantinōn Spoudōn, *Journal of Hellenic Studies* (1880–), *Neos Hellēnomnēmōn* (1904–27), and many others.

Standard historians of classical Greece in the collections range from George Grote to John Bury. Among works more notable for literary or sociological than historical concerns are Oliver Goldsmith's *The History of Greece* and J. J. Barthélemy's *Voyage du jeune Anacharsis en Grèce*. The ancient historians are represented in a wide range of editions: for example, Curtius Rufus' life of Alexander is available in a variety of texts and translations dating from the seventeenth century, and Pausanias from *Atticae Descriptio* (Venice, 1500?) through the J. G. Frazer translation of 1898 to later editions.

Other works classified as general history supplement these resources. The principal allied literature is that of archaeology; the collection is particularly rich in older archaeological works and the publications of classical societies and institutions (such as the Archaeologisches Institut des Deutschen Reiches). The Art and Architecture Division collects materials on the arts of all ancient cultures. Works on Greek epigraphy include such items as the *Monumenta Asia Minoris Antiqua* of the American Society of Archaeological Research in Asia. Other works on Greek and Roman Egypt, and on Greek papyri, are in the Oriental Division.

Perhaps the outstanding item among the printed materials of the Byzantine period is the *Byzantinae Historiae Scriptores Varii* (1645–1702), a 1961 purchase which brought to the library this rare printing of the works of the Byzantine historians. It joins other collections of period writings, supplemented by important accounts and studies. The library subscribes to the current collection being published under the title *Corpus bruxellense historiae byzantinae*.

The collection of materials on the history of modern Greece includes publications of contemporary political bodies such as the Ethnikon Apeleutherotikon Metopōn, and the writing of such political figures as Metaxas, Venizelos, and Grivas. In addition are files of scholarly journals, among them the *Deltion* of the Historike kai Ethnologikē Heraireia tēs Hellados and the *Bulletin* of the Hetairia Diethnōn Meletōn. The extensive holdings of the publications of regional learned societies deal with a variety of historical topics and are well represented by *Balkan Studies, Kypriakai spoudai, Krētika chronica, Hetairia krētikōn historikōn meletōn*, and many others. Standard works in various European languages are present; there is a large number of travel books, including many of the elaborate plate books of the nineteenth century. Approximately 200 entries in the Public Catalog relate to the nineteenth-century War of Independence. An interesting group consists of contemporaneous pamphlets published in the United States, among them Daniel Webster's speech (1824) on the Greek Revolution. Greek underground movements during World War II are well documented.

The holdings of Greek public documents relating to international affairs are weak; the section relating to internal affairs, although incomplete, contains some important series. The *Ephemeres tes kuverneseos* (Daily Journal) of the Cabinet is complete from 1899. Serial publications in Greek and French of the Statistikon Graphieion, the majority of which commenced in the late 1930s, cover many commercial, financial, and social aspects of the country, providing adequate materials for the study of economics and certain related fields.

A group of books and indexed magazine articles on Crete and Mount Athos supply reference materials for these areas. Related holdings for the study of Mount Athos are to be found in the art and religion resources.

ITALY

Although the library's collection of 15,000 volumes is not outstanding, it is important for its substantial numbers of provincial and local historical publications, and for important material in related classes, including a large collection of public documents.

In addition to a great number of general works of history and travel are many editions of the great historians from Tacitus to Gibbon and other later writers. The library's practice is to secure any edition of a standard work containing material not included in those already in its collections. Among the general works are such collections of sources as Muratori's *Rerum italicarum scriptores.* Some of the folio histories and collections are notable for their illustrations. Of great interest and rarity is the Spencer Collection's Italian manuscript of the third decade of Livy's *De secundo bello punico*, dated circa 1475, and from the library of Matthias Corvinus, king of Hungary.[26]

Serial publications form another important group, providing materials for the study of both ancient and modern Italy. Included are files of such periodicals as the *Archivo storico italiano* (1842–), society publications as the *Risorgimento italiano* (1908–33), and academy publications, among them the *Bullettino* (1886–1953) of the Istituto Storico Italiano per il Medio Evo.

Closely allied materials include those works classed with general history which are devoted to the classical world, the Middle Ages, and the Renaissance. The collection of archaeological literature is rich in both older systematic works and the publications of learned societies and institutions.

Good collections of material are available for the study of later periods and the Italian states and provinces which preceded the Union in 1860. The period of the Risorgimento is represented by sizable holdings which include a number of broadsides. Interesting material related to the States of the Church includes a group of pamphlets and another of broadsides, *leggi*, and *regolamenti*. These are supplemented by those sections of the resources dealing with the Roman Catholic Church.

The literature relating to modern Italy forms an adequate reference collection, consisting of standard works in various languages, a representative selection of secondary materials, and a large number of books on travel, which includes a number of important nineteenth-century plate books. There is a good collection of material on Fascist Italy; works on the political aspects are to be found in the general collections and those dealing with economic factors in the Economic and Public Affairs Division. Italian underground and resistance movements of World War II are included in the library's generally strong holdings of this nature. Postwar political movements are well covered in the writings by and about such figures as Antonio Gramsci, Palmiro Togliatti (including a run of the periodical *Rinascita* edited by him between 1946 and 1962), and Pietro Nenni.

Approximately 6,000 volumes are devoted to the cities, provinces, colonies, and islands of Italy. This includes much of the material relating to the states and provinces which preceded the Union, and is important for the provincial literature which it contains. Here are found such publications as the *Atti e memorie* of almost all the provinces of Italy, the *Archivo storico lombardo*, and the *Archivio storico per le province napoletane*, most important for their biographical and local historical content. Local history of continental countries is not administered by the Local History and Genealogy Division, but is found with the general collections; works on genealogy and heraldry of Italian families and prominent individuals are, however, held in the Local History and Genealogy Division. These materials are supplemented by the public documents collections of the Economic and Public Affairs Division.

Public Documents

The important collection of public documents relating to Italian political affairs includes the *Atti* of the Italian Parliament (complete from 1848 to 1941), continued by the publications of the Camera dei Deputati. The *Gazzetta* is complete from its foundation in 1861 to the present.

Public documents of Italian provinces and former kingdoms are also held in strength. Among other files are the *Annali civili* (1833–60) of the Kingdom of the Two Sicilies, the *Gazzetta piemontese* of Sardinia from 1845 to 1860, and the *Gazzetta di Venezia* from 1848 to 1920. Gazettes are received from the regions of Sicily, Trentino-Alto Adige, and the Republic of San Marino. Most of the provinces are represented by the files of the *Atti* of the Consigli Provinciali.[27] Most of the series begin in the 1860s and are substantially complete through the first decade of this century. Files are continued by the Consigli Provinciali dell' Economia of many of the regions.

The important law holdings include the national *Raccolta ufficiale delle leggi e dei decreti* from its beginning in 1861 to 1951. There are also the laws of the Papal States, Sardinia, the Kingdom of the Two Sicilies, and Venice, with such reprints as the Cisalpine Republic's *Raccolta de' bandi, notificazioni, editti*. Statutes for the Republic of Italy are also well represented.

The holdings of municipal documents are particularly strong for the earlier periods, with volumes of municipal ordinances from the sixteenth through the eighteenth centuries, and long files of *Atti* of the various Consigli Communali. For various Italian cities are the files of the *Bollettino municipale mensile*, which contain statistical information pertinent to municipal affairs, as well as illustrated sections with articles on art, archaeology, local history, and biography. The collection on municipal finance is also good; there are files of the *Bilancio* and the *Conto consuntivo* of the important cities.

The Economic and Public Affairs Division acquires all Italian government documents that come to its attention through the standard bibliographies.

Manuscripts

Papers in the Manuscripts and Archives Division include Florentine records dating from 1575 to 1665 concerning the disposition of private property, and copies of orders of the Medici, Grand Dukes of Tuscany, concerning vessels and naval affairs from 1619 to 1735. A vellum manuscript dated 1647 sets forth privileges granted by the Duke of Venice to Jewish merchants. Among modern materials are travel diaries of the nineteenth and twentieth centuries, and a typed manuscript, corrected drafts, and other material related to Gilbert Seldes's study of Mussolini, *Sawdust Caesar* (1935).

---

26. See Walter Allen, Jr., "The Four Corvinus Manuscripts in the United States," *BNYPL* 42 (1938): 315–23; and Malcom E. Agnew, "The Affiliations of the Spencer Collection's Corvinus Livy," *BNYPL* 42 (1938): 324–26.

---

27. See *BNYPL* 14 (1910): 83.

PORTUGAL

The 2,000 volumes relating to the history of Portugal do not cover all periods with equal adequacy. Most of the larger standard historical works, related studies, and books of travel are in the holdings. Of particular supplementary importance is the set of reprints of the publications of the Academia das Ciências de Lisboa.

A distinctive feature of the collection is the presence of periodicals such as *O archeólogo português* (1895–1920) and *Revista portugueza colonial e marítima* (1897–1910), and recent publications such as *Studia* (1958–   ) and the *Luso-Brazilian Review* (1964–   ). Publications dealing with early maritime and colonial matters include the *Boletim* (1925–   ) of the Agência Geral do Ultramar, among others. The publications of the Portuguese government agencies for their overseas possessions are well represented.

Public documents include an extensive group of diplomatic papers with separate imprints, the *Diário do governo* from 1822, and many separately published decrees. Laws begin with compilations which extend back to 1446. In subject fields, statistics are held in strength.

In 1940 the library held an exhibition commemorating the eight-hundredth anniversary of the foundation of Portugal and the three-hundredth anniversary of the restoration of her independence. The catalog of this exhibition lists a number of the Portuguese rarities in the collections with emphasis on the Age of Discovery.[28]

SPAIN

Although the literature relating to the history of Spain, numbering some 7,000 volumes, does not cover all periods with equal adequacy, it is an interesting and important collection. Beginning in 1936 the library placed special emphasis on acquiring books and fugitive materials on the Spanish Civil War of 1936 to 1939; this fine collection is described below. Collections of printed sources include such works as the *Colección de documentos inéditos para España*; systematic histories are held in strength. Special periods are represented by such publications as the *Memoria* of the Junta Superior de Excavaciones y Antigüedades. There is an excellent collection of travel books, and large groups of biographies of monarchs.

An outstanding feature of the collection is the generally complete sets of periodicals devoted to history and social life, and the publications of societies and academies, such as those of the Real Academia de Historia.

The material dealing with Spanish history is relatively more important than some other, larger groups because of its relationship to such strongly represented subjects as early American history and the history of the Philippine Islands. Such collections as the *Colección de documentos inéditos relativos al descubrimiento, conquista y organización de las antiguas posesiones españolas de América y Oceanía* are closely related to early rarities in the field, a special interest of James Lenox, who collected many important works relating to the Age of Discovery. The holdings of Spanish materials are particularly strong through

the American Revolutionary period. Information on Spanish exploration and settlement may be found in the American History Division under such headings as "The Spanish in Cuba" and in the general collections through headings such as "The Spanish in Australia." Materials on the history of Moorish Spain are in the Oriental Division.

Spanish Civil War

There are approximately 1,400 entries in the Public Catalog under the heading "Spain—Civil War, 1936–1939," a figure which does not fully represent the resources. The library began to collect materials in 1936, but the most important part of the collection arrived in 1951. In this year the Veterans of the Abraham Lincoln Brigade began a continuing gift to be called the David McKelvy White collection in honor of a fallen comrade. When this collection was first acquired, much of it was given collective cataloging treatment (the separate materials were not individually cataloged but grouped together under headings such as "A Collection of Pamphlets about the Spanish Civil War"). Items in fragile condition were microfilmed: on film are collections of newspaper clippings, war posters, press releases, and speeches, along with incomplete files of 153 Spanish newspapers and periodicals of the period. In the latter group are files of *Solidaridad obrera* (Barcelona, 1933, 1936–38, 1947–49) and *La vanguardia* (Barcelona, 1936–39). Materials maintained in their original form include collected volumes of news bulletins, press releases on Spain dating from 1937 to 1947, press releases, radio addresses, memoranda, and other materials on Spain under Franco from 1928 to 1947; and a collection of pamphlets in 26 bound volumes. There are, in addition, book materials of all kinds.

Public Documents

The strong collection of public documents is important for the study of Spanish history. Materials relating to foreign affairs include the "Libros rojos" (*Documentos diplomáticos*) from 1865 to 1911 (incomplete), printed treaties, diplomatic series, and numerous single publications. For the study of internal affairs the collection contains an incomplete but substantial file of the *Gaceta de Madrid* (Boletín Oficial del Estado) from 1808, and the *Diario* of the Cortes from 1811, as well as the publications of all constitutional assemblies and a strong representation of administrative documents. The collection of published laws begins in 1814. There are many separate official publications for every reign from Philip II to the present government. In subject literature covered by public documents geology and statistics are more than adequate.

Manuscripts

Among the materials in the Manuscripts and Archives Division that came from the David McKelvy White collection are radio scripts from "Radio Madrid" from January 1937 to October 1938. There are also typescripts of works by Leland Stowe, and of Edwin Rolfe's *The Lincoln Battalion*. The papers of Frank P. Walsh contain material on Spanish affairs from 1937 to 1939. Ten boxes of correspondence relating to the Spanish Civil War were the gift of the American

---

28. See "Portugal: An Exhibition," *BNYPL* 45 (1941): 124–36. Published separately by the library.

Friends of Spanish Democracy. In the Berg Collection of English and American Literature are materials concerning Julian Bell and George Orwell and their connection with the Spanish Civil War.

Additional materials relating to Spain appear in the Ford, Bancroft, Hardwicke, and Rich collections; for detailed information on those collections, see chapter 14 of this *Guide*.

HISTORY OF OTHER EUROPEAN COUNTRIES

An approximate total of 31,000 volumes in the Roman alphabet and 1,200 volumes in the Cyrillic alphabet (in the Slavonic Division) cover this subject area. Table 4 illustrates the distribution and growth of the collections since 1941.

TABLE 4. GROWTH OF THE COLLECTIONS OF THE HISTORY OF OTHER EUROPEAN COUNTRIES

	1941	1966
Balkan States (as of 1904)		
Roman alphabet	1,400	2,585
Cyrillic alphabet	400	800
Belgium	1,700	4,860
Luxemburg	125	435
Netherlands	7,000	9,720
Scandinavian Countries	4,200	7,400
Switzerland	1,500	4,390
Turkey in Europe (as of 1904)		
Roman alphabet	1,200	1,805
Cyrillic alphabet	300	400

The 1899 Billings Classification Schedule is still used for Turkey in Europe and the Balkan States; as a consequence certain archaisms will be found in the sections dealing with the history of Eastern Europe, to which the twentieth century has brought such continued political change.

Materials relating to the countries considered here constitute good working collections. They are less noteworthy than those pertaining to Great Britain, France, or Germany.

It is important to note that only countries for which there are notable collections of materials are considered in the following descriptions.

The public document collections materially strengthen the holdings of general historical literature for each of the countries considered here. The printed historical collections of general and local documents and archives are strong for certain countries. Historical periodicals and society publications provide important related sources, as do geographical, archaeological, and other materials from various subject areas of collections.

The major resources for the study of those countries in which the Balto-Slavonic languages are used are found in the Slavonic Division. Although the holdings in the Cyrillic alphabet relating to Albanian, Greek, and Rumanian history are not strong, there are good resources in Cyrillic for Bulgarian history (500 volumes), Yugoslavian history (200 volumes), and Turkish history, with particular emphasis on the Russo-Turkish wars (400 volumes).

THE BALKAN STATES

Rumania

This strong collection of approximately 900 volumes contains a number of printed historical collections, such as the *Acte si documente relative la istoria renascerei României* (1888–1909) and Baron Hurmuzaki's *Documente privitore la istoria românilor* (1876–1938), as well as general works which have appeared since the last century. This historical literature is supplemented by the publications of the Academia Română, including its *Analele*.

Government documents held include the official gazette, *Buletinul oficial*, and statistical publications, in addition to publications of the Comitetul Geologic and other governmental institutes. Other Rumanian government publications are unevenly represented; they are perhaps most extensive for the period before World War II. The *Desbaterile* of the Senatul (1874–1932) and of the Adunarea Deputatilor are present. Refugee groups are represented by such publications as the *Cronica romaneasca* (1950–57) of the National Committee for a Free Europe.

Yugoslavia

Some 300 volumes in the Roman alphabet in the general collections deal with Yugoslavian history; these are supplemented by 1,000 volumes in the Slavonic Division in the Cyrillic alphabet covering all disciplines (some 200 being specifically historical), with a representation of the four languages of the country: Slovenian, Serbo-Croatian, Macedonian, and Albanian. Participation by the library in the PL-480 program for Yugoslavia for several years after 1968 has proved a valuable source of acquisitions in research materials of very high quality. Among other items are the publications of the Slovenska Akademija Znanosti in Umetnoski, Lublana, in various fields, including history.

Materials for the period before 1918 on the states and regions now part of Yugoslavia may be located in the card catalogs under such headings as "Croatia" and "Dalmatia." Other materials on the partisans, the government in exile, and similar topics are located under the heading "World War, 1939–1945—Free and Resistance Movements."

Government documents received from Yugoslavia are primarily statistical, although there is a strong run of the official gazette, *Službeni list*, under various titles since 1919. The *Zbornik dokumenata* of the Vojnoistoriski Institut of Belgrade is available in its various tomes.

BELGIUM

The collection relating to Belgium, numbering approximately 4,900 volumes, is not systematically complete, but may be used to good advantage in research. It includes general histories, a large group of printed historical collections, and a noteworthy collection of periodicals and society publications relating to general and local history. Reprinted archives and documents, and inventories of such materials, are well represented. Participation in the Farmington Plan has helped to strengthen the resources in all areas of Belgian history. For the period preceding Belgian independence in 1831 materials are found in the historical literature of the Netherlands and France.

The German occupation during World War I is covered in an extensive collection which includes the public documents issued at Le Havre, and a complete file of *La Libre Belgique* published surreptitiously during the war. There is also material on the German occupation of World

War II and the free and resistance movements. The library continues to collect comprehensively in Belgian history.

Materials for the study of local history appear primarily in periodicals and society publications; there are relatively few separate works. Certain important collections are present, such as the *Recueil des anciennes coutumes de la Belgique* issued under the auspices of the Commission Royale pour la Publication des Anciennes Lois et Ordonnances de la Belgique. Periodicals contain both historical studies and reprinted documents and archives and are supplemented by important holdings of cartularies. The publications of Belgian learned societies and academies often have sections devoted to the study of local history, archaeology, topography, and related topics.

There is a great deal of material both governmental and societal for the former Belgian Congo; see chapter 48 of this *Guide,*

Public Documents

The holdings of Belgian public documents are adequate, and include important files, among them a complete series of statutes. Holdings of treaties are incomplete; the official gazette *Moniteur belge* is fairly complete from 1831 to date; and the files of parliamentary proceedings of both chambers are good. There is also a substantial file of the *Almanach royal officiel* from 1840 to 1939.

A quarto volume of Belgian broadsides and other materials published at Liège from 1775 to 1823 relates to Belgian affairs and reflects the French Revolution and the Napoleonic period.

Holdings of provincial publications are generally weak. Municipal publications are fairly well represented, with a good collection for Antwerp after 1900. A bound volume in the Manuscripts and Archives Division records in Latin and French all the deeds (*chartes*) of Hainaut from 1200 to 1534 and of Mons from 1410 to 1483.

THE NETHERLANDS

This collection of approximately 9,700 volumes contains works of interest to the student of national and local history, but is of more importance for its relation to Dutch colonial history in America. It is rich in histories and other publications of the seventeenth and eighteenth centuries.

Large historical collections include publications such as *De Vrije Fries* of the Friesch Genootschap te Leeuwarden, and the *Algemene Geschiedenis der Nederlanden*. General histories and works of travel are well represented; periodical and society publications dealing with Dutch history and archaeology are also present. Annuals and yearbooks, including the eighteenth-century *Nieuwe Nederlandsche jaarboeken*, are an interesting feature. An important newspaper, the *Amsterdamsche Courant*, is present in a substantial file covering the years 1748 to 1881.

A collection of 20,000 Dutch pamphlets purchased in 1896, for the most part contemporaneous with the events which they describe, relate to the affairs of various European countries during the sixteenth and seventeenth centuries. As the Lowlands were the theatre of many wars—especially those of Louis XIV—the Dutch writers became important observers of international affairs at this period. The collection provides an especially rich source for Dutch history during the Wars of Independence, 1572 to 1648.

Archaeological publications include sets such as the *Publications* of the Société Historique et Archéologique dans le Duché de Limbourg; collections of documents and archives are represented by compilations such as the *Archives ou correspondance de la Maison d'Orange-Nassau* for the sixteenth and seventeenth centuries, and many works of a similar nature.

The library maintains this collection as a current research facility; there is much material on the German occupation of Holland during World War II, and on the postwar period.

The colonial interests of the Netherlands are well represented, with the collections reflecting the lessened importance of the subject in this century. Although the more specific items are entered in the card catalogs under headings established for the territories concerned ("East Indies, Dutch," "East India Company," "Curaçao"), much is also found under the general heading of Dutch history.

Materials for the study of Dutch local history appear in periodicals, local society publications, and separate works. Participation in the Farmington Plan has helped to strengthen this and other areas of Dutch history. The resources for Friesland are notable, especially in connection with the library's holdings in the Frisian language (principally linguistic and belletristic in nature), and an unusual collection in the Manuscripts and Archives Division of 106 bound volumes of the resolutions of the Frisian states from 1584 to 1793, together with scattered volumes from 1517 and registers for part of the period covered.

Public Documents

The collection of public documents is both rich and extensive. For international relations the file of treaties, *Recueil des traités et conventions*, is complete from 1813. Publications of national scope are generally complete and include the parliamentary proceedings, *Verslag der Handelingen* (1814/15–); the official gazette *Nederlandsche Staats-Courant* (1813–); and the session laws, *Staatsblad* (1813–). There are extensive files of departmental reports. In subject materials, statistical and meteorological publications are especially numerous.

The holdings include fifteen quarto volumes of Dutch broadsides published at Amsterdam covering part of the period of French domination (1795–1831), and collectively titled Amsterdam, *Staats-Publicatiën*. Although these items deal with Dutch affairs from the rise of the Batavian Republic to the beginnings of separation between Holland and Belgium, they are also interesting for their reflection of the French Revolution and the Napoleonic period.

Dutch provincial and local documents are outstanding. For the provinces, the *Notulen, Verslagen*, and *Provincialbladen* are particularly noteworthy; as an example, the *Notulen* of Zeeland, published yearly since 1587, is complete.

Manuscripts

Manuscripts useful in the study of Dutch history are of some importance, particularly for the period of American colonial history. There is much concerning the Netherlands in the papers of Dutch families of New York State, including patronship deeds, business papers, account books,

241

and signatures of such Dutch notables as Peter Minuit and Peter Stuyvesant. The Hardwicke collection contains transcripts of English diplomatic correspondence of the early seventeenth century relating to the Netherlands; the Bancroft collection contains similar material for the eighteenth century.

THE SCANDINAVIAN COUNTRIES

At one time this collection rivaled the more important university collections in the United States, and is still strong, especially in works in the Scandinavian languages. There are some 1,000 entries relating to Swedish history in the Public Catalog; Danish and Norwegian history each receive approximately 500 entries, and Finnish history 400; Iceland, which is classified with Denmark in the Billings schedules, receives 100 entries. In its selection of general works the library has, for the most part, chosen the important treatises, particularly the comprehensive historical works published during the late nineteenth and early twentieth centuries. Printed collections relating to Scandinavian history and to individual countries may be evaluated as follows: general works, excellent; Sweden and Iceland, very good; Denmark, Norway, and Finland, good.

Periodical and society publications are perhaps the most important feature of this subject area. Among them are the *Historisk Tidsskrift*, issued by the Danske Historiske Forening since 1840; the *Danske Magazin* (1794–); the *Mémoires* of the Société Royale des Antiquaires du Nord (Kongelige Nordiske Oldskrift Selskab), 1866 to date, and the various series of its *Aarbøger* from their commencement; the *Kulturen; en årsbok* of the Kulturhistoriska föreningen för södra Sverige, under various titles (1885–); the *Samlingar* of the Svenska fornskrift-Sällskapet (1844–); the *Skrifter* of the Norwegian Kjeldeskriftfondet (1858–1931); and the *Meddelanden* of the Swedish Riksarkivet (1875–). There are also the various publications of the Kungliga Vitterhets-, Historie- och Antikvitets-Akademien, Stockholm. The list might easily be extended by other general titles, as well as by those of national scope, and by still others relating to local history. In content these publications are varied. They contain reprinted archives and documents, historical and archaeological articles. The amount of historical writings in the publications of Scandinavian general learned societies and academies is small; science and natural history are the fields more often emphasized.

Description, travel, and social life as aspects of history are well covered; the holdings are strengthened by works classified with geographical materials. Royal biographies include interesting items relating to Gustavus Adolphus, Christina of Sweden, and other rulers.

Important subjects related to history include the Norman periods of invaded countries: works on this topic are usually classified with the history of the country, as in the case of England. Materials on Scandinavians in America are administered by the American History Division and located in the card catalogs under headings such as "Norwegians in the U.S.," and "New Sweden."[29] The Brooklyn newspaper *Nordisk Tidende*

at one time aided the library in collecting these materials; the holdings of this newspaper extend from 1925 to the present, with a scattered file before that time.

There is an interesting group of materials on the Vikings, although the library has not systematically collected literature on this subject; the excellent collection of materials relating to Iceland was substantially increased by purchase in 1934.

Public Documents

The holdings in this section are generally strong, with unusually strong subject holdings in statistics. The legislative proceedings—Sweden's from 1867, Norway's from 1814, Denmark's from 1849, Iceland's from 1845, and Finland's from 1809—are essentially complete. The official gazettes of Iceland, *Stjórnartidindi* (1875–), and of Denmark, *Statstidende* (1941–), are complete.

The collection is strong in the reports of legislative committees and commissions. Of special interest are the Greenland Commission reports currently received, and a number of items from the Faeroe Islands which add to the holdings in the Faeroese language.

Extensive holdings of law include the Swedish *Svensk författningssamling* from 1825; the Norwegian *Love* from 1814 (with a small break); and the Danish *Lovtidende* from 1871. These session laws are supplemented by a fair collection of compilations containing earlier laws, and by holdings of codes.

The collection contains excellent files of the publications of some Scandinavian cities, such as municipal council proceedings; among them are *Aarhus byraads forhandlinger* (1900–), *Göteborgs stadsfullmäktige handlingar* (1898–), and Bergen's *Innstillinger . . . med bystyrebeslutninger* (1876–1935). Copenhagen and Frederiksberg are strongly represented, with files generally dating from the 1860s. Holdings of the publications of Oslo and Stockholm are generally weak for the earlier periods; there are some series for the nineteenth century, but many important files commence only about 1920.

Manuscripts

The Hardwicke collection in the Manuscripts and Archives Division contains miscellaneous papers relating to Swedish history of the first half of the eighteenth century; the Bancroft collection includes transcripts of late eighteenth-century papers on Denmark from the Berlin archives.

SWITZERLAND

The collection relating to Switzerland is not systematically complete, but has a number of outstanding features. The printed historical collections relating to general history are exceptionally strong; those relating to local history are less numerous. There are important collections of printed archives relating to both general and local history. Inventories of documents and archives of the various cantons are present.

---

29. See Esther Elisabeth Larson, *Swedish Commentators on America, 1638–1865: An Annotated*

List of Selected Manuscript and Printed Materials (New York: The New York Public Library, in cooperation with the Swedish Pioneer Historical Society of Chicago, 1963).

Works of description and travel are numerous. There are extensive holdings of nineteenth-century publications; among other materials are some excellent folio volumes of aquatint views. The library continues to buy on a limited basis books of photographic views as they are published. A small but important group of nineteenth- and twentieth-century guidebooks are found in the geography collections.

Periodical and society publications form an extensive group, relating to both general and local history. General historical series include the *Bulletin helvetique* (1798–1800), the *Archiv für schweizerische Geschichte* (continued as the *Jahrbuch*), the *Anzeiger für schweizerische Altertumskunde*, and such current titles as the *Schweizerische Zeitschrift für Geschichte* and the *Mémoires et documents* of the Société d'Histoire de la Suisse Romande.

Local historical literature is not particularly strong in separate publications; the greater part of the material pertains to the cantons rather than to the municipalities, although there is a good collection relating to Zurich. For many cantons there are extensive files of periodicals and society publications, such as the *Archiv* of the Historischer Verein des Kantons Bern, *Revue historique vaudoise*, and *Musée neuchâtelois*.

Relatively little, other than travel literature, is found in other subject classes related to Swiss history. The publications of most of the academies and learned societies on general subjects are devoted to science and natural history.

Public Documents

The collection of public documents is not strong, although there are some important series. Treaties are well represented. Among administrative materials are the national and cantonal *Staats-Kalenders*. Holdings of such series as the parliamentary proceedings (the *Amtliches stenographisches bulletin* of the Bundesversammlung) and the official gazette (the *Bundesblatt*), while fragmentary for the nineteenth century, are generally complete following 1900. Laws, both of Switzerland and of the cantons, are held in strength.

Important holdings of administrative reports, especially of the cantons, are present, including the *Rechenschaftsbericht* and the *Staats-Rechnung*. The files are not all complete, although some of them comprise long runs—for example, Bern *Staats-Rechnung*, commencing in 1863, is incomplete until 1888, complete after that date.

Statistical publications are especially noteworthy.

TURKEY (IN EUROPE)

The Billings Classification Schedules locate materials for the study of eastern Turkey with Asian history; the stronger holdings are classified with European history and may be described as adequate. Materials in western languages and in Turkish are covered by some 1,200 references in the Oriental Division catalog, which unites the holdings; 400 volumes in the Cyrillic alphabet are found in the Slavonic Division. Among the western language holdings histories and works of travel predominate; a number of early works of the sixteenth and seventeenth centuries of particular interest are in the Rare Book Division. Reprinted Ottoman Turkish documents and archives are found in the learned society journals and series which form a strong feature of the Oriental Division; there are also facsimile documents published in Rumania and Hungary. Histories of Turkey written in Turkish, such as those by Jaudat, are found in the division catalog under the heading "Turkish Literature—History." Related subjects of importance include the Crimean War and the Turco-Russian War (both classified with Russian history). Materials on the Gallipoli campaign and other matters concerning Turkey are to be found in the library's strong World War I holdings. There is a small but good collection related to Istanbul.

The materials on the Eastern European question are both extensive and important; the library has from its early years sought to secure all available literature on international disputes.[30]

Most of the Turkish documents currently received are statistical, but there is a file of the Turkish government gazette, commencing in 1834. The treaties are principally those of the Ottoman Empire and include the *Recueil des traités de la Porte Ottomane avec les puissances étrangères* (1864–1911).

---

30. See "List of Works in The New York Public Library Relating to the Near Eastern Question and the Balkan States, including European Turkey and Modern Greece," *BNYPL* 14 (1910): 7–55 et seq. Published separately by the library.

50

HISTORY OF RUSSIA AND EASTERN EUROPE

This chapter is concerned with the library's collections on the history of Imperial Russia and the Baltic States, the USSR, Poland, and Czechoslovakia. The 1899 Billings Classification Schedule is still used for Russia and the USSR; as a consequence, certain anachronisms will be found in the sections dealing with the history of Eastern Europe, to which the twentieth century has brought continuing political change. An approximate total of 20,000 volumes documents the history of Imperial Russia, the USSR, Poland, and Czechoslovakia; materials in the Cyrillic alphabet are administered by the Slavonic Division, those in the Roman alphabet by the General Research and Humanities Division. The following presents the approximate number of volumes held by the library:

	1941	1966
Roman alphabet	5,100 volumes	8,000 volumes
Cyrillic alphabet	4,300	12,000

The Public Catalog records only materials in the Roman alphabet; the Slavonic Division dictionary catalog holds a complete record of historical materials in both the Cyrillic and Roman alphabets. Both catalogs should be consulted, however, since index entries for periodical articles are not duplicated in all cases.

The holdings in this area are of exceptional strength, with a splendid group of public documents from the pre-Revolutionary period. Soviet materials are characterized by a breadth of coverage in the many languages, including non-Indo-European, of the USSR.

HISTORY OF IMPERIAL RUSSIA AND THE BALTIC STATES

The holdings of standard and popular histories and books of travel and description published in the last century form an important group. Royal biographies are numerous; important collections relate to Peter the Great (including the collected edition of his letters and documents, *Pis'ma i bumagi imperatora Petra Velikago*), and to Catherine II.[1] The library has made an extensive collection of materials concerning the various rebellions in Russia; the conspiracy of 1825 and the revolution of 1905 are exceptionally well covered, as is the great Revolution of 1917.

Important holdings of periodical and society publications relating to Russia are available. Representative of the older, conventionally historical type is *Beiträge zur Kenntnis der russischen Reiches* (1839–1900). Of related interest is *Archiv für wissenschaftliche Kunde von Russland* which, while essentially scientific, contains some papers on historical, topographical, and geographical subjects. The Slavonic Division holds *Sbornik Russkago Istoricheskago Obshchestva* (collections of the Russian Historical Society) for 1867–1916. *Trudy* and other publications of the Akademiya Nauk Institut Istorii provide additional sources. *Free Russia* (1890–94) published in London, relates to other revolutionary material in the division.

While not large, the collections relating to the Baltic States contain important general histories and popular works, books of description and travel, and the like. Periodical and society publications, held in strength, include sets such as the *Sitzungsberichte* (1873–1914) of the Gesellschaft für Geschichte und Altertumskunde of Riga, and others. There are also collections such as *Monumenta Livoniae Antiquae*. *Acta et Commentationes* (1921–44) of Tartu University forms part of the growing collection of literature from Esthonia.

SIGNIFICANT COLLECTIONS

A number of major acquisitions, both gifts and purchases, lend unusual breadth to certain parts of the collections. The George Kennan collection was presented to the library in 1919 and 1920;

it consists of books, pamphlets, manuscripts, magazines, newspapers, and approximately 500 photographs and other pictures. The collection has information on political prison systems in Siberia, and documents the early phases of the revolutionary movement. Letters from political convicts and other people connected with the emancipatory movement include 40 from Catherine Breshkovskaya, known as the "Grandmother" (Babushka) of the Russian Revolution.[2]

The library holds 2,200 volumes once owned by Grand Duke Vladimir Alexandrovich.[3] It is most valuable for the dynastic, administrative, and military history of the empire, and contains many important government publications, including confidential reports. Court life for the years 1695 to 1815 is chronicled in the 143 volumes of the *Kamer fur'yerski tzeremonial'nyi zhurnal* (Journal of court functions). In addition, there are more than 250 manifestos issued during the nineteenth century to mark occasions such as births, baptisms, weddings, and deaths in the imperial family. The *Svod vysochaishikh otmetok* (Compilation of His Majesty's notations) is an annual publication of the notes written by Czars Alexander III and Nicholas II on the reports of provincial governors. Annual reports of the various government agencies and departments, some of them secret, are included in the collection. A large portion of the books and documents concern military affairs, including Russia's wars of the nineteenth century and the Russo-Japanese War. There are also regimental histories and materials on military schools and military costumes. A wealth of geographic, topographic, and statistical information on Russia's Asiatic possessions may be found in the publications of the General Staff entitled *Sbornik geograficheskikh, topograficheskikh i statisticheskikh materialov po Azii* (1883–1914) and the *Materialy* (Proceedings) of the Imperial Commission for the Study of Land Ownership in the Trans-Baikal region (1898).

An acquisition of 9,000 pieces of Slavonic literature, mainly from the nineteenth and twentieth centuries, resulted from a purchasing trip made by Avrahm Yarmolinsky and H. M. Lydenberg in Europe during 1923 and 1924. Some 1,000 volumes of history formed a prominent feature of these purchases, and included such source material as Novikov's *Drevnyaya Rossiiskaya vivliofika* (1788–91) and the *Polnoye sobraniye Russkikh letopisei* (1853–1922) published under the auspices of the Russian Archaeographic Commission. There were also family records in the archives of Prince Kurakin (1890–1912) and of the Counts Mordvinov (1901–03). Other materials included Skrebitzki's *Documents Relating to the Emancipation of the Serfs* (1867–68), special studies, local and municipal history, and substantial additions to the library's holdings on Peter the Great and the invasion of Russia by Napoleon.[4]

Preliminary Catalogue," *BNYPL* 73 (1969): 599–614; and Part II, *BNYPL* 75 (1971): 474–94.

2. See Avrahm Yarmolinsky, "The Kennan Collection," *BNYPL* 25 (1921): 71–80.

3. See Avrahm Yarmolinsky, "The Library of Grand Duke Vladimir Alexandrovich (1847–1909)," *BNYPL* 35 (1931): 779–82.

4. See Avrahm Yarmolinsky, "The Slavonic Division: Recent Growth," *BNYPL* 30 (1926): 71–79.

---

1. For this and other material on their period, see Edward Kasinec, "Eighteenth-Century Russian Publications in The New York Public Library: A

PUBLIC DOCUMENTS

Strong holdings in this area include a complete set of the thirteen sessions of the Imperial Duma, *Stenograficheskie otchety* (1906–17). There are complete collections of the laws of the Empire in the three series of the *Polnoye sobraniye zakonov Rossiiskoi imperii*, and in the *Svod zakonov Rossiiskoi imperii* (1857–1916) and its continuation (1906–14). Other significant items include a substantial file of the official gazette *Pravitel' stvennyi vestnik* (1869–1917) and of the official journals of the ministries of Education and the Interior. Other public documents were acquired with the library of the Grand Duke Vladimir Alexandrovich, described above in the section on significant collections.

MANUSCRIPTS

In addition to the manuscripts in the Kennan collection are approximately 100 letters from eminent Russians, including Tolstoi, Gorki, and Alla Nazimova, written to Isabel F. Hapgood and presented by her to the library. The Russian Historical Archives is a small collection of material principally related to Aleksandr V. Adiassewich, a petroleum engineer and writer on historical subjects, specifically in Armenia, Turkestan, and the Ukraine. Several travel diaries of the mid-nineteenth century describe regions of Russia; the unpublished Polish manuscript, completed about 1908, of Baron Gustav Manteuffel's "History of Livonia" is also included.

HISTORY OF THE USSR

The history of revolutionary movements, the Revolution of 1917, and the rise and progress of the Soviet Union are thoroughly covered in the library's holdings in materials in the Cyrillic and Roman alphabets. Every effort has been made to secure the important works of Russian émigrés and representative periodicals. Documentation is not restricted to books, but includes pamphlets, periodicals, clippings, and other ephemeral material. Such "n.c." (not separately cataloged) material is represented only by subject cards in the Public Catalog and division catalogs. The hundreds of uncataloged titles relating to the Soviet, such as leaflets and pamphlets in various languages, volumes of newspaper clippings, and an extensive though incomplete file of *Rosta*, the mimeographed bulletin of the Ryska Socialistika Federativa Sovjet-republikens Telegrambyrå of Stockholm, are of interest to the specialist. Works relating to the political theory of the USSR form a very rich collection. Complete holdings of the important *Krasnyi archiv: istoricheski zhurnal* (1922–41) exemplifies the periodical and society materials available in the collections.

The John Reed collection presented in 1935 consists of material published chiefly in 1917–18. Supplementing the letters of Catherine Breshkovskaya in the Kennan collection (described in the section on significant collections—above —in Imperial Russian history) are 174 letters from her to a Brooklyn resident (1923–34), discussing aid to Russian refugees. The papers of the social reformer and Positivist William Frey include correspondence with Russian liberals and revolutionaries, American communists, and others. The Emma Goldman collection (1917–28) and the Norman Thomas papers (1916–68) include material of interest to students of Soviet history.

PUBLIC DOCUMENTS

Holdings of public documents from the Soviet Union represent an accumulation of all materials available through normal channels of purchase, gift, and exchange. The library receives the *Stenograficheski otchet* (1939–) of the Supreme Soviet and the official gazette *Verkhovnyi sovet vedomosti* (1938–), among other materials. Statutes form a considerable if scattered group, consisting mostly of bound volumes of laws in specific fields such as labor accidents or criminal law.

Holdings of public documents for the member republics of the Soviet Union parallel those for the central government. The library receives the proceedings of the Verkhovna Rada of the Ukraine, for example, and also has a large number of individual statutes ranging in time from those published by the Ukrainian Revolutionary Committee in 1919 and 1920, through the laws of the German-occupied Ukraine during World War II, to those of the present. Materials relating to Armenia, Georgia, and the Altaic-speaking peoples of the USSR represent a particular collecting interest of the library. The library receives the official publications of the Communist Party and the local governments of most of the republics of the Soviet Union. Except for the Baltic countries, Belorussia, and the Ukraine, where these publications are in the vernacular, these gazettes are received in Russian-language versions. Particular strengths are noted below.

Esthonia

The file of the Estonian official gazette, *Riigi Teataja*, is complete from its beginning in 1918 until 1940. The library has received the party and government publication *Rahva Hääl* since 1959. The proceedings of the Constitutional Assembly, 1919–20, are complete; parliamentary proceedings commence with the second parliament, 1923, and run through 1940.

Latvia

The collection of Latvian public documents is very extensive until 1940. It includes the parliamentary proceedings from 1918; the legislative journal *Likumu un Ministru Kabineta Noteikumu* from the beginning (July, 1919), and the official gazette, *Valdibas Vestnesis* (1922–40, complete). Since 1957 the library has received the Latvian Communist Party and Council of Ministers publication *Cina*.

Lithuania

The official gazette, *Vyriausybes Žinios*, is complete from 1918 to 1940. The proceedings of Parliament (meeting as the Constitutional Assembly, 1920/22) are complete until 1927, when that body was dissolved. The library currently receives *Tiesa*, the Communist party publication.

HISTORY OF POLAND

The collection relating to the history of Poland includes more than 3,000 volumes. Accompanying the collections of works of the outstanding Polish historians of the nineteenth century (Lelewel, Kalinka, Szajnocha, Szujski among them), is a great number of the most important works of such modern historians as Korzon, Askenazy,

Halecki, Konopczynski, Limanowski, Kutrzeba, and Haiman. There is also a considerable number of memoirs, genealogies, and works of political leaders. Specimens of literature that appeared during the German occupation of the country during World War II, as well as selections of books and pamphlets produced by Polish émigrés and displaced persons, are also included in the collections. In 1952 the library received as a gift from the Polish Research and Information Service in New York City a collection of more than 2,000 post-World War II books, pamphlets, and periodicals which document recent trends in life in Poland. There are documentary recordings of interest to the student of twentieth-century Polish history in the Rodgers and Hammerstein Archives of Recorded Sound (described in chapter 31 of this *Guide*).

The small group of old Polish imprints in the library was considerably augmented by the acquisition in 1968 of some 300 pamphlets printed in Poland between 1590 and 1802, many of them at the Jesuit press at Wilno. Most of the pamphlets are panegyrics issued to commemorate such state events as royal weddings, declarations of war, or investitures of cardinals, and they contain a wealth of historical and genealogical information. Other early imprints include a rare first edition of Starowolski's *Reformacya obyczaiow Polskich* (1650?), Szymon Okólski's *Orbis Polonus* (1641), and Rudawski's *Historiarum Poloniae* (1755).

Important Polish periodicals and series are well represented. Among other titles are the *Monumenta Poloniae Historica* (1864–), *Akta grodzkie i ziemskie* (1868–1931), and the *Roczniki dziejów spoecznychi gospodarczych* (1931–).

PUBLIC DOCUMENTS

Documents for Poland include the *Sprawozdania stenograficzne* of the Sejm (1919–) and of the Senat (1922–38). The library currently receives the official gazette, *Monitor polski*. Statutes include early seventeenth-century and later examples continuing with the *Dziennik ustaw* (1939–); a separate set published by the government in London during the period from 1939 to 1945 is also available. Other documentary material is largely statistical in nature, although there is much from the Instytut Geologiczny. A few municipal documents, primarily statistical, come from Warsaw, Lodz, and other cities.

MANUSCRIPTS

The Hardwicke collection in the Manuscripts and Archives Division includes three volumes of official printed and manuscript documents relating to King Augustus II and other Polish matters during the years 1729 to 1731; two additional volumes in the Hardwicke collection contain letters and miscellaneous papers of Count Hoym, minister and diplomat during the same period. Other manuscript items include the official papers of domain councillor von Brause at Peterkau and Posen during the period from 1793 to 1800.

HISTORY OF CZECHOSLOVAKIA

Some 1,400 books and pamphlets document the history of Czechoslovakia. Periodical resources are extensive and are represented by publications such as the *Tschechoslovakische Quellen und Dokumente* (1931–) and *Slovakia* (1951–) published by the Slovak League of America.

Among standard histories are titles such as Josef Pekar's *Z duchovních dějin českých* (1941), Kamil Krofta's *Malé Dějiny československé* (1947), and Zdeněk Václav Tobolka's *Politické dějiny čéskoslovenské* (1932–37). Dealing specifically with Slovakia are František Bokes's *Dějiny Slovákov a Slovenska* (1946), *Slovenské dějiny* (1947), Joseph Mirkus's *Slovakia: A Political History 1918–1950* (1963), etc. Resources for the study of Bohemia, represented by more than 400 entries in the Public Catalog, include such titles as the *Acta Bohemicorum* (1621–22), *Archiv český* (1872–1921), and the *Fontes Rerum Bohemicarum* (1873–), in addition to such collections as the *Codex Diplomaticus et Epistolaris Regni Bohemiae* (1904–65) and *Monumenta Cartographica Bohemiae* (1930–36). Also present is a first edition (1552) of Bishop Jan Dubravius's history of Bohemia, and a collection of 188 original statutes published in Prague from 1567 to 1823.

Public documents include the *Těsnopisecké zprávy o schůzích* of both the Senate (1920–35) and the Chamber of Deputies (1925–38). The proceedings of the Národní Shromáždění are available as the *Exposé* from 1918/20 to 1932/33, and as the *Těsnopisecké zprávy* (1948/52–). The library receives the Czechoslovakian official gazette *Sbírka Zákonů*, which from 1962 has merged with the official statutes.

51

AMERICAN HISTORY DIVISION

The collection of approximately 100,000 volumes in the American History Division, in conjunction with allied resources of the library in this field, forms one of the strongest subject areas of the Research Libraries. The American History Division acquires and administers materials on the history of the Americas, along with the national and state histories of the United States.

Included in the holdings are works on the political, social, constitutional, military, and religious history of the Americas, as well as travel literature. Thousands of pictures, photographs, postcards, stereopticon views, and scrapbooks are an important part of the American History Division collection, as are other ephemeral materials, many of which never enter the normal channels of book distribution.[1] The division does not include works on economic history, which are to be found in the Economic and Public Affairs Division. Rare works of Americana are shelved in the Rare Book Division. American town and county histories are held in the Local History and Genealogy Division. Manuscript Americana is in the Manuscripts and Archives Division.

Outstanding aspects of this key division of the Research Libraries are noted in the following paragraphs; full discussions appear with the descriptions of particular fields. Pamphlets, political leaflets, and printed speeches are held in vast number, and there is an important collection of literature dealing with immigration and immigrant life in the United States. The group of state histories of the United States is extensive from the earliest periods. The Elihu Root collection of United States documents dated from 1896 to 1908 provides information on the rise of the United States to a position of international influence, with insular possessions and dependencies. Older materials on the Hawaiian Islands remain in the general collections. The American History Division assumed collecting responsibility for Hawaii only when it became the fiftieth state of the Union.

Holdings on the American Indian are outstanding, covering all phases of Indian history, archaeology, and anthropology, including works in over 300 languages. There is an extensive collection of works relating to the prehistory of America, including reports of expeditions in the Americas made by Europeans.

Of the Latin American countries, Mexico is currently the best represented, while the Cuban collection is the fastest growing. The Mexican materials include a good pamphlet collection relating to the independence movement and the period of Maximilian. Housed in the Economic and Public Affairs Division is a strong collection of Mexican federal and state public documents. There are extensive holdings of materials on South American revolutions.

Pictorial materials include 1,200 boxes of international stereopticon views which come largely from the Robert Dennis collection. In addition to views are files for such diverse subjects as comics, the navy, etc. A supplementary archive of postcard views of the United States and other countries numbers several thousand pieces. A checklist of the stereopticon collection, arranged by broad subject areas, is available at the Reference Desk of the division.

HISTORICAL SURVEY

Some idea of the growth of the holdings in American history may be gained from the following:

---

1. Listings of holdings of the American History Division and allied resources in the Research Libraries may be found in the following publications of G. K. Hall & Company of Boston: *Dictionary Catalog of the History of the Americas Collection* (1961), 28 vols.; *Dictionary Catalog of the Local History and Genealogy Division*, 18 vols. (1974); *Dictionary Catalog of the Schomburg Collection of Negro Literature and History* (1962), 9 vols., *First Supplement* (1967), 2 vols., *Second Supplement* (1972), 4 vols.; and *Subject Catalog of the World War I Collection* (1961), 4 vols.

1854	Astor Library	3,407 volumes
1911	New York Public Library	14,000
1921		57,229
1930		69,889
1941		86,500
1966		96,500

In the first Astor Library *Annual Report* (1854) it was noted that the American Historical Department was considered of primary importance and expected to grow toward a complete collection. James Lenox brought together in his library a collection of books relating to America in the fifteenth, sixteenth, and seventeenth centuries that attained a remarkable degree of completeness. This was increased by well-selected purchases in later years and by many gifts from Alexander Maitland.

The Bancroft, Emmet, and Myers collections included works relating to the ante- and post-Revolutionary periods. Materials on the latter part of the eighteenth and the nineteenth century came to the library with the Ford collection, which is rich in contemporaneous writings supporting or opposing the constitution of 1788, works relating to the first years of the Republic, later struggles over internal improvements, the United States Bank, slavery controversies, the Civil War, Reconstruction, and the protective tariffs.

The Tilden collection, the third of the library's foundation collections, contained a good selection of the important general works on American history, along with the chief publications relating to political parties, Congress, and political and constitutional conventions, especially those of New York State.

At the time of the opening of the Central Building at 42nd Street in 1911, the American History Division comprised not only 14,000 books on American state and national history, but also the library's collection of maps, manuscripts, and printed rarities which since that time have been organized as separate divisions.

The American History Division has always been sensitive to the contemporary spirit. Although the collecting policy remains comprehensive for all areas within its field, certain segments of the holdings have been acquired with special thoroughness: when folklore became a popular subject after World War II, the division's resources in American folklore grew in response to the public's enthusiasm for materials in that field; more recent special interests include Cuba and the Afro-American. The library collects heavily in the latter field, in response to a need for a strong collection on the Afro-American both in the Schomburg Center and in the Central Building.

SPECIAL INDEXES AND FILES

It should be noted that all cards in the official catalog of the American History Division are duplicated in the Public Catalog, with the exception of certain cards for periodical articles on the American Indian.

American Historical Maps

This is a card index to historical maps found in the older books in the American History Division (inactive, 1 card drawer). It includes primarily maps of the United States. It does not index historical maps held by the Map Division or other divisions of the library.

American Indian Design Index

Arranged by author and subject, the index is a working list of books and articles on Indian design found for the most part in the division (inactive, 1 card drawer). It includes materials on the Indians of North, Central, and South America.

Lincoln Quotations Index

The quotations are arranged by subject and catch word (inactive, 1 card drawer).

Military Rosters: Colonial and Foreign Wars, Revolution, War of 1812, Civil War, etc.

The coverage in this file is important up to the Civil War period; after that time few entries are found (inactive, limited, 9 card drawers). It includes payrolls, muster rolls, and the like, arranged for each war by name or number of military unit.

Picture (Illustrations) Index

This is the largest and most widely used of the card indexes (inactive, limited, 45 card drawers). The scope of the index is broad, covering both books and periodicals. It includes references to persons, places, events, and objects of American historical interest. Many references to North, Central, and South American Indians are incorporated.

Quotations and Slogans of United States History Interest Index

This is a card index of quotations and slogans primarily of interest for United States history (inactive, limited, 1 card drawer). It is arranged by catchwords and is supplemented by the separate index to Lincoln quotations.

52

GENERAL HISTORY OF THE AMERICAS

This chapter includes the history of the American Indians, Hispanic America, and Canada.

HISTORICAL SURVEY

The growth of the American history collection in the New York Public Library started when Joseph Green Cogswell began to assemble books for the Astor Library, and when James Lenox turned to the collecting of Americana, a field in which he was to become preeminent. Lenox was interested in the discovery, exploration, and early colonization of America; he emphasized the rare and often costly books through which the New World was first introduced to the Old. Most of the books acquired by Lenox are now in the library's Rare Book Division.

The Astor Library, under the guidance of Cogswell, was intent on bringing together all of the books on the Americas which had value for historical research. When the Astor Library building was opened in 1854, historical materials constituted a quarter of the holdings; a larger space was assigned to this collection than to any other, with the intention of making it the most complete. It was already strong in the early Spanish writers, the voyages, and the accounts of the first settlements, but in the collection of more modern works there were serious deficiencies.

These deficiencies were largely overcome through the acquisition of the library of the American historian George Bancroft, which was particularly strong in eighteenth-century United States history, and the Ford collection, a vast library notable for its many United States pamphlets of the eighteenth and nineteenth centuries. The library has continued to build its American history collections by gift and by the systematic purchase of current material and older material as it becomes available. Most areas of the subject

are collected comprehensively. Major exceptions to this policy are noted in the following discussions.

This large, well-rounded research collection reflects the development of the New World from the earliest times to the present. It is particularly strong in American Indian material, in pamphlets relating to political history, and in works dealing with discovery, exploration, and settlement. It also reflects the traditional concern of the library for ephemeral materials; the policy of book selection which gives emphasis to acquiring the old and the new; a belief that weeding would defeat the stated purposes of the collection; and a view of historical research which considers the history of British Columbia or Peru no less significant than that of the State of New York.

In 1961, G. K. Hall & Company published the *Dictionary Catalog of the History of the Americas Collection, The New York Public Library* in 28 volumes, reproducing 554,000 cards. The analytical cards are of particular importance, for the library early developed a useful reference aid by the indexing of important articles found in scholarly journals.

RESOURCES

The history of the Americas forms one of the strongest collections in the library. It covers the United States extensively, with national, state, and local histories, as well as the history of Canada and the countries of Central and South America. The entire holdings number far in excess of 300,000 volumes and 14,000 broadsides. The basic collections, classed under the library's Billings classifications H and I and located in the American History and the Local History and Genealogy Divisions, are works for the most part printed after 1800 covering the political, constitutional, military, religious, and other phases of the social history of the Americas. More than 74,400 volumes represent America excluding the United States (Billings class mark H); 129,600 volumes deal with the United States (Billings class mark I). Important holdings of Americana in the Rare Book Division are of materials printed prior to 1800; some 40,000 volumes and 10,000 broadsides relate to America excluding the United States, and 20,000 volumes and 4,000 broadsides deal with the United States, both before and after the Revolutionary War. Additional resources on the economic history of the Americas and a large collection of public documents are found in the Economic and Public Affairs Division.

Under the Farmington Plan, the library has been assigned the responsibility for collecting from the following areas: general history of Latin America; history of the West Indies in general and of all individual countries and islands; general history of South America and the following individual countries or colonies: Argentina, Guyana, Surinam or Dutch Guiana, the Falkland Islands, French Guiana, Uruguay, and Venezuela.

The books of interest to students of American history form two groups: those which because of value or rarity are segregated in the Rare Book Division (Billings class mark *K); and those in the American History and Local History and Genealogy Divisions (Billings class marks H and I). There follows a brief description of these book materials with a notation of related manuscripts, prints, public documents, and other resources.

EARLY IMPRINTS AND VALUABLE WORKS, RARE BOOK DIVISION (BILLINGS *K)

Many of the works available in the Rare Book Division are also available for general use in reprints, later editions, or historical collections in other divisions of the library.

The collection of Americana in the Rare Book Division contains a large number of early English and Hispanic-American imprints published no later than 1800. These and early European imprints may be divided into several categories.

The first is composed of early works of discovery, exploration, and travel, a very rich group with its nucleus in the collection made by James Lenox. A fine collection relating to Columbus is discussed in a following section. Through gift and purchase the library has continued to add materials published before 1551 containing references to America as itemized in Henry Harrisse's *Bibliotheca Americana Vetustissima*; it now has most of the works listed, either in original editions or photostatic copies.

Another category of rare books includes early works which mention or describe the Americas, early historical works relating to national colonial periods, and writings not essentially historical which reflect political, social, or religious aspects of the periods of settlement and expansion. Of the many national literatures represented in this early material three are particularly notable: Polish Americana;[1] works in German;[2] and

French acts of royal administration, together with accounts of French travelers in the United States.[3]

The collection of American periodicals is also rich. Those of the eighteenth century and valuable works of later date are kept in the Rare Book Division. American newspapers published before 1800 and certain rare frontier, Confederate, and other newspapers of a later date are housed in the Rare Book Division; other files are kept in the Newspaper Collection.

Maps and atlases, including a good collection covering the periods of American exploration and colonization, are available in the Map Division, where the literature of American cartography is also housed. Rare maps are to be found in the Manuscripts and Archives Division, the Spencer Collection, and the Rare Book Division.

MANUSCRIPTS

In addition to rare printed materials, the library has a rich and extensive collection of manuscripts relating to the Americas, particularly for the period of the American Revolution and for New York State. Collections of the personal papers of prominent United States citizens are also a strong feature of the manuscript resources. The Obadiah Rich collection contains manuscript material and transcripts of archives concerning the administration of Spanish colonies in America. These and other holdings are described in detail in the discussion of the Manuscripts and Archives Division.

GENERAL WORKS IN AMERICAN HISTORY

The subject classes of American history in the American History Division and in the Local History and Genealogy Division (Billings class marks H and I) contain large numbers of printed documents and archives, printed historical collections, general histories and special studies, books of description and travel, and similar materials. It is the policy of the library to secure any edition of a work containing material not in earlier editions in the collections.

Periodicals are an important feature of the holdings. The files of American historical periodicals are for the most part complete; many of the general periodicals in the library's holdings also have some historical content or reflect political and social conditions of the periods in which they were published. This applies to Hispanic-American as well as to North American periodicals; popular magazines in the South American countries may contain articles of historical value. The heading "Periodicals" in the Public Catalog includes national subdivisions which are a helpful guide to unindexed magazines. Many articles relating to American history are analyzed in the catalogs. The publications of historical societies and other learned institutions have been systematically indexed.

---

1. See Avrahm Yarmolinsky, "Bibliographical Studies in Early Polish Americana," *BNYPL* 38 (1934): 223–40; 39 (1935): 167–72 et seq.; 40 (1936): 427–36.
2. See Paul H. Baginsky, "German Works Relating to America, 1493–1800," *BNYPL* 42

(1938): 909–18 et seq. Published separately by the library in 1942 with revisions and corrections.
3. See Lawrence C. Wroth and Gertrude L. Annan, "Acts of French Royal Administration Concerning Canada, Guiana, the West Indies and Louisiana, Prior to 1791," *BNYPL* 33 (1929): 789–800 et seq. In 1937 the library purchased over 15,000 French ordinances, edicts, and decrees including many concerning North America.

Special types of serials which are of interest to students of American history include the publications of such learned societies and academies as the Carnegie Institution and others with historical sections, and of some museums which have interest in the archaeology and folklore of the American Indian. The historical series of college and university publications are held in extensive files.

The approximate number of pamphlets in each of the larger subject groups follows: American Indians, 3,500; Hispanic America (materials on the area in general or description and travel covering a number of countries), 4,200; Mexico, 1,400; Canada, 1,400; general materials relating to the United States, 7,600; United States local history, 5,000. The pamphlets classed under these headings represent only a portion of those available. Titles of specific subject interest are generally classified with the subject: for example, American essays if purely political would be placed in the American History Division, but those dealing with economic questions would be classified in the Economic and Public Affairs Division. The strong collection of public documents, including both original and reprinted materials, is an important asset for research.

The analysis of the library's American history holdings follows the sequence of the Billings classification. This is not the usual method of this *Guide*, as the Billings classification is in many instances superseded by fixed location class marks; class marks H and I, however, are still in active use.

GENERAL MATERIALS: BIBLIOGRAPHY, PERIODICALS, HISTORY (BILLINGS H-HA)

Approximately 4,200 volumes form a large collection of American historical periodicals (for the most part with complete files) and general histories. Bibliographies present in this class mark are usually lists of subject interest. Important compilations containing bibliographical information are generally kept in the Rare Book Division or marked "Ref. Cat." and kept in the working collection of the Preparation Services. All works are listed in the Public Catalog and the appropriate special catalogs, and all are available for use.

This section contains, in addition, numerous accounts of early explorations of the Americas, including a large collection relating to Columbus, consisting of biography, accounts of voyages, both scholarly and popular, reprinted documents and archives. Columbiana in the Rare Book Division includes early editions of the letters announcing his discoveries in the New World. The library has the only known copy of the first printing of the Columbus letter to Luis de Santangel, called the "Spanish Folio" (Barcelona, 1493), along with five of the eight separate Latin editions published in that year and the German translation of 1497. The Amerigo Vespucci holdings are equally good, with copies of ten of the first thirteen Latin editions of *Mundus Novus* (1503), an account of the explorer's third voyage to the lands which bear his name in the form of a letter to Lorenzo de Medici. The division also has examples of the first Latin and German editions of Vespucci's "Four Voyages" in addition to a fine representation of Fracanzano da Montalboddo's *Paesi nouamente retrouati*, a printed collection of American voyages which did much to create and maintain contemporary interest in the discoveries. Early editions of these first voyages to the New World that are lacking in the library are available either in facsimile or as reprints.[4]

AMERICAN INDIANS (BILLINGS HB)

There are over 12,000 volumes in this rich collection covering both continents and all phases of the history, archaeology, and anthropology of the Indian. There are complete files of periodicals and publications of organizations and institutions, as well as government reports relating to the Indian. References to magazine articles on the American Indian are most completely represented in the American History Division catalog. Monographs on the history, social life and customs, and arts of the Indian are included in both the division catalog and the Public Catalog.

Standard works and histories are present in large numbers. There are various editions of such works as George Catlin's *Letters and Notes on the Manners, Customs, and Condition of the North American Indians* (London, 1841), and of such monumental compilations as Lord Kingsborough's *Antiquities of Mexico* (London, 1830–48). Among other works relating to the Mayan, Aztec, and other early Indian cultures is an extensive collection of facsimiles of pre-Columbian codices.

The American Indian collection was increased during the period from 1912 to 1914 by materials from the library of Wilberforce Eames.[5] In 1912–13 the library secured a series of laws of the Cherokee Nation (1821–93) and Cherokee newspapers (1828–53); the recent acquisition of two pamphlets of extreme rarity published in Tahlequah, C. N. (1853; 1858) containing laws of the Cherokee Nation strengthens those holdings. In 1959, Charles Eberstadt presented a collection of seventy-five treaties between the United States and various Indian tribes and nations ranging in date from 1836 to 1870. These are original State Department issues printed in small editions for official purposes. The library has the texts of many Indian treaties in other forms.

The collection of works relating to American Indian linguistics is particularly complete, not only in formal studies of more than 300 languages and dialects but also in texts, including many Bibles and other religious works. Many of the materials found in this group are housed in the Rare Book Division.

Other noteworthy features of the American Indian holdings in the library include books and pictorial materials relating to manners and customs, social life, and dress. Among the pictorial features are several unique items. A remarkable German broadside with four lines of text containing a hand-colored wood engraving of cannibal Indians dressed in feathers is in the Spencer Collection; considered to date from 1505, this is

---

4. See Wilberforce Eames, "Columbus' Letter on the Discovery of America (1493–1497)," *BNYPL* 28 (1924): 595–99; see also in facsimile *The Letter of Columbus on the Discovery of America* (The Lenox Library, 1892). For the library's holdings of Vespucci, see Joseph Sabin, *Bibliotheca Americana* (New York: Bibliographical Society of America, 1935), 26: 436–83.

5. See *Bibliographical Essays; A Tribute to Wilberforce Eames, 1924* (Cambridge: Harvard Univ. Press, 1924), pp. 19–22.

one of the earliest printed representations of American Indians.[6] In the Prints Division is a gouache on vellum made by Jacques Le Moynes de Morgues depicting Florida Indians and French settlers in 1564.[7] The Rare Book Division has an album of drawings by Francis B. Mayer of Sioux Indians done in pencil and watercolors during the mid-nineteenth century. There is also a collection in three portfolio volumes of 167 leaves of pencil drawings of Indians by George Catlin, each leaf signed by Catlin and accompanied by a leaf of descriptive text in his hand. The collection is entitled *Souvenir of the N. American Indians, as they were in the middle of the Nineteenth Century*. The manuscript title page is signed and dated: "Geo. Catlin, London, 1850." Another interesting feature of the holdings in this area are portraits and pictures of historic Indians, including J. P. Lewis's *The North American Aboriginal Port-folio*.

The accounts of Europeans held captive by Indians form a third group of interest. A collection in the Rare Book Division of more than 500 rare copies, reprints, and the like contains first editions of the sixteenth-century accounts of Nuñez Cabeza de Vaca, Juan Ortiz, and Hans Staden. From the seventeenth century come *A True History of the Captivity and Restoration of Mrs. Mary Rowlandson* (London, 1682) and the account of Quentin Stockwell printed in Increase Mather's *An Essay for the Recording of Illustrious Providences* (Boston, 1684). There is a copy of Jonathan Dickenson's *God's Protecting Providence* (Philadelphia, 1699), and, in addition, a translation of that account published by Christopher Saur in Germantown, Pennsylvania (1756). Narratives of captives in the eighteenth century are represented by the extremely rare second edition of John Williams's *The Redeemed Captive Returning to Zion* (Boston, 1720) and by the famous *The Adventures of Col. Daniel Boon*; a photostatic copy of the latter is housed by the Rare Book Division, and a printed example is found in John Filson's *The Discovery, Settlement and Present State of Kentucke* (Wilmington, 1784) in the Arents Collection.[8] The unusual collection relating to Indian place names is also worthy of mention.

The Chalmers papers and the Schuyler Indian papers in the Manuscripts and Archives Division are the most extensive manuscript materials relating to the American Indian. The Chalmers collection of transcripts and original documents relating to the American colonies includes about 50 items dating from 1750 to 1775; it contains extracts from treaties, proceedings at councils with various tribes, intelligence brought in by spies, and letters of Sir William Johnson. Among the papers of General Philip Schuyler, one of the commissioners of Indian affairs in the Northern Department and agent of the state of New York, are speeches made at Indian councils, notes of

proceedings, minutes of the commissioners' meetings, accounts of supplies, letters, resolutions of Congress, and various papers relating to the lands of the Six Nations, including numerous claims filed in 1795 by white settlers on the Cayuga reservation. About 550 items date 1764–97.

The American History Division maintains a number of scrapbooks and a card file index to American Indian design. The Picture (Illustrations) Index in the division includes many references to American Indians.

HISPANIC (LATIN) AMERICA (BILLINGS HC-HT)

The general collections relating to Hispanic America number over 39,300 volumes. Historically Mexican resources are the most comprehensive, although those for contemporary Cuba are the fastest growing.

The library currently receives about 1,300 periodicals and newspapers from the countries of Latin America. Among the major titles relating to general Latin American history are *Cuadernos hispanoamericanos* (1948–), *Mundo hispánico* (1948–), and the *Publicaciónes* of the Pan American Institute of Geography and History (1930–). Periodicals of more specific interest are noted in following paragraphs. Eight newspapers are currently received from Argentina, Panama, Cuba, Guatemala, Mexico, and New York City. Among the most significant titles are *La Prensa* from Buenos Aires (1869– , with gaps), and *El Universal* (1951–) from Mexico City. The New York City *El Diario* (1932–50) and the current *El Diario-La Prensa* (1963–) are held, along with an incomplete file of *Las Novedades* (1893–1918). Many other titles are accessible through a research pool established in Chicago by the Association of Research Libraries. The Newspaper Collection of the library holds a list of papers in the pool and provides advice for obtaining them. There are, in addition, numerous files of newspapers in the Spanish language published in Latin America during the nineteenth century. The most important are Mexican, such as *El Monitor republicano* and others which appeared during the 1840s. Files of current newspapers are on microfilm.[9]

Rare materials from the age of Latin American discovery are outstanding and include such items as André Thevet's *Les Singularitez de la France antarctique, autrement nommée Amérique* (Paris, 1558) and *La Conquista del Peru* (Seville, 1534), the latter title being one of two recorded copies.[10] Manuscript materials derive largely from the Obadiah Rich collection of original documents and transcriptions covering most of the countries of Latin America and the former viceroyalty of Granada.

The library has on microfilm or in the original a substantially complete collection of the official gazettes from the earliest periods of the federal

---

6. See Wilberforce Eames, "Description of a Wood Engraving Illustrating the South American Indians," *BNYPL* 26 (1922): 755–60. Published separately by the library. See also Stevens, *Lenox*, pp. 136–37.

7. The gouache was the gift of James Hazen Hyde; see *BNYPL* 64 (1960): 243–44.

8. The library's holdings of Indian captivities are given in W. G. Vail, *The Voice of the Frontier* (Philadelphia: University of Pennsylvania Press, 1949).

9. For a listing of the library's holdings see Steven M. Charno, comp., *Latin American Newspapers in United States Libraries: A Union List* (Austin: University of Texas Press, 1969).

10. See Joseph H. Sinclair, trans., *The Conquest of Peru* (The New York Public Library, 1929). The book, printed in April of 1534, is the second printed account; the first, supposedly printed at Nuremberg in February, 1534, is also in the library (*Newe Zeytung aus Hispanien und Italien*).

governments of Latin American countries; this collection includes many of the gazettes for the states or provinces of Argentina, Brazil, and Mexico. There is also a strong collection of statute laws in the Economic and Public Affairs Division, with government statistical publications being another area of special interest. These provide excellent resources in demography, foreign trade statistics, and banking statistics. Boundary disputes are particularly well represented in this fine collection of Latin American public documents.

SOUTH AMERICA (BILLINGS HCM-HLY)

Approximately 26,400 volumes include general histories and works of description and travel, together with reprinted documents and archives.

Books of travel in South American countries frequently contain information of permanent interest. Even if popularly written, they may include interesting archaeological and ethnological observations; many such works are by professionally trained members of exploratory or scientific expeditions. A subject of related interest is geography: this group of works, although not large, includes such important series as the *Boletim geográfico* of the Instituto Brasileiro de Geografia e Estatistica. The published accounts of scientific expeditions in the holdings on natural history are also useful, as are works related to mountains and mountaineering.

An important related subject is biography. In addition to individual biographies, the library maintains a good collection of South American biographical dictionaries. Current editions are kept in the reference collections of the Main Reading Room, and earlier editions are housed in the stacks.

The collection is rich in periodicals, including those which reprint documents and archives. Included are the serial publications of ministries and government departments such as the Brazilian Ministério das Relações Exteriores or the Uruguayan Archivo General. Various academies also issue important series, such as the *Boletin* (1912–) of the Academia Nacional de la Historia, Caracas, or its *Documentos para los anales de Venezuela* (1890–1909) and similar series. Institutes are also active with such publications as the *Revistas* of the Instituto Arqueológico, Histórico e Geográfico Pernambucano (1863–) or the Instituo Histórico e Geográfico Brasileiro (1939–). To these may be added the publications of two kinds of institutions not generally associated with the publication of national archives, such as the *Memoria* and the *Revista* of the Biblioteca Nacional of Argentina, and the documents series of the Museo Mitre of Buenos Aires.

The files of conventional historical periodicals are generally complete. Those devoted to contemporary matters date from the time of World War I, and the files are sometimes incomplete. The excellent collection of popular Hispanic-American periodicals contains additional material of interest to students of South American history.

Area Studies

The collections relating to the individual countries of South America are more or less equal in extent of coverage and importance of materials included; therefore only distinguishing features are noted in the following paragraphs. The library

has sought to collect everything available relating to international affairs, and the coverage would seem to indicate boundary disputes as a major cause of negotiation. There are extensive writings, both official and unofficial, on such disputes as those between Venezuela and British Guiana, and Bolivia and Paraguay.

Large sets and collections are notable features of the various national historical sources. The extensive holdings of early Americana formed by James Lenox and continually augmented include many of the greatest rarities in the field represented not only in first editions but also in contemporaneous translations.

Argentina: More than 2,790 titles represent area studies of the Argentine Republic. Of these, some 860 relate to history, and approximately 300 to description and travel. Best covered among the historical periods are the wars of independence (1810–17) and the period from 1817 to 1860. Among source materials are such works as Pedro de Angelis's *Colección de obras y documentos relativos á la historia antigua y moderna de las provincias del Rio de la Plata* (Buenos Aires, 1836–37) and *Documentos para la historia argentina contemporánea*. Also of historical importance are the collected papers of three former presidents: the *Escritos y discursos* of Nicolás Avellaneda, the *Archivo* of Bartolomé Mitre, and the *Obras* of D. F. Sarmiento.

Brazil: Brazilian area studies number over 3,400 titles. Of these, works specifically relating to description and travel number 647. There are more than 850 historical titles. In this collection is found an unusually large number of works concerning boundary disputes. The period of the Dutch Conquest (1624–54) is particularly well represented with contemporaneous books, pamphlets, and broadsides, as well as later materials.

Chile: Over 1,560 entries in the Public Catalog cover Chilean studies. Of these, about 200 titles represent description and travel, and 600 history. Historical coverage is best for the wars of independence and for the war with Peru (1879–82). Early works of travel include Alonzo de Ovalle's *Relacion verdadera de las pazes que capituló con el Araucano rebelado* [Madrid, 1642], with other accounts by Frézier, Van Baerle, and John Byron.

Peru: Area studies number over 1,750 titles. Of these, 266 represent description and travel, and 640 history. The conquest of Peru receives the best coverage, followed by the wars of independence. One of the library's treasures, *La Conquista del Peru* (Seville, 1534), is one of two recorded copies of the second printed account of the conquest. The library has a copy of the first edition of Garcilaso de la Vega's *Primera parte de los commentarios reales, que tratan del origen de los Yncas* (Lisbon, 1609), along with a copy of the 1723 edition and numerous early translations. The collections of viceregal statutes and *cédulas* in the original or facsimile are fairly extensive. A number of documents in the Obadiah Rich collection of the Manuscripts and Archives Division relate to Peru, most of them being transcripts of archival material.

Venezuela: In this section of more than 1,000 area studies there are 124 works devoted to travel and 340 historical titles. The period of the discovery and German occupation of the country to 1556 receives good coverage, as does the period of the wars of independence. The attempted revolution of Don Francisco de Miranda of 1806 is documented through first editions of the eyewitness narratives of James Biggs, John Edsall, John H. Sherman, and Moses Smith.

Panama: The materials relating to the history of the Republic of Panama, the Panama Canal, and the Panama Railroad are important. A comparatively small number of popular histories and travel literature are classed under Panama in the American History Division; also included are such series as the *Boletín* of the Academia Panameña de la Historia and the *Memorias* issued by the Secretario de las Relaciones Exteriores. These items are considerably augmented by the historical treatises and printed documents in the larger collection relating to Colombia and the Central American countries such as the Elihu Root collection of United States documents (Series F). The numerous public documents of countries with economic or diplomatic dealings with Panama provide additional source materials. Political aspects of the Panama Canal and the Panama Railroad are extensively treated.

Public Documents

The official publications of the various South American governments form a generally strong collection, especially for the twentieth century. Some important series, particularly for the nineteenth century, are fragmentary; however, active attempts are made to complete back files. Official government gazettes are usually present, as are parliamentary proceedings and general economic and statistical publications. The following notes indicate the range of materials to be found in the collection.

Argentina: The *Diario de sesiones* of the Cámara de Diputados is held from 1854 to 1950, with some earlier volumes; that of the Cámara de Senadores is fairly complete from 1854 to 1951. The *Leyes nacionales sancionadas* are complete from 1918 with scattered volumes from 1899 to 1909/10, and there are compilations for earlier periods. The *Boletín oficial* is complete from 1902. The *Registro nacional* covers 1873–1908.

Bolivia: Parliamentary proceedings and papers are fairly complete from 1900 to 1943. The *Anuario administrativo* is complete from 1856 to 1948 preceded by the *Colección oficial de leyes* (1825–57). The library currently receives the *Gaceta oficial.*

Brazil: The *Annaes* of the Camara dos Deputados are complete from 1826 to 1922, for 1954, and from 1960 onward. From the Senado the file is complete from 1891 to 1914, with scattered early volumes from 1827, and from 1956 onward. The *Diário oficial* is available in an incomplete file from 1900 to date as is the *Diário do Congreso* which accompanies it. The *Collecção das leis* commences in 1808 and is fairly complete. To this should be added the 26-volume "Collecção authentica de todas as leys, regimentos, alvaras, e mais ordens, que se expediram para o Brazil desde o estabelecimento destas conquistas. Ordenada por Provizam de 28 de Março de 1754," in the Manuscripts and Archives Division. An extremely important printed collection in 4 volumes, "Codigo brasiliense" (Rio de Janeiro, 1808–21), is housed in the Rare Book Division; that division holds additional *alvarás* covering the treatment of Indians, the slave trade, and other subjects.

Chile: The *Boletín* of the Cámara de Senadores and that of the Cámara de Diputados are fairly complete from 1866 to 1945 and from 1866 to 1935 respectively; the earlier *Sesiones de los cuerpos legislativos, 1811 á 1845* are complete from 1811 to 1841. The *Boletín de las leyes* is complete from 1924 to 1951 with a broken file from 1889 to 1902. The *Recopilación de decretos-leyes por Orden numérico arreglada por la Secretaria del Consejo de Estado* is complete from 1821. The *Diario oficial* is available.

Colombia: The *Anales* of the Cámara de Representantes and those of the Senado are complete from 1903 to 1945, superseded by the *Anales* of the Congreso from 1945 onward. The session laws are fairly complete from 1877 and the contemporary *Leyes expedidas por el Congreso Nacional* (under various titles) from 1821 as far as they have been published. The *Diario oficial* is complete from 1861. There is a good collection of public documents for the department of Antioquia.

Ecuador: The files are generally weak. There are scattered volumes of the *Diario de debates* of both houses of the Congreso. The file of the *Anuario de legislación ecuatoriana* is complete from 1896 to 1925. The *Registro oficial* is complete from 1920 including the *Indice general y clave de legislación.*

Panama: The government publications of Panama form an essentially strong collection. Although the file of the *Anales* of the Asamblea Nacional is fragmentary from 1908 to 1943, there is a more current file of the *Diario de los Debates* (1926–43). The *Leyes expedidas* and the *Gaceta oficial* are complete from 1904. *Memorias* of the various ministries, with few exceptions, are complete from their beginnings.

Paraguay: The files are not strong. The *Diario de sesiones* of the Congreso Nacional is complete from 1926, with scattered volumes for earlier years. It is preceded by the *Diario* of the Cámara de Diputados and of the Senate from 1872 to 1920. The *Diario oficial* is complete from 1918 to 1942 with a few issues before and a scattered file after. The *Registro oficial* is complete from 1869 to 1952 with an irregular file after that time.

Peru: The library holds material on the Viceroyalty of Peru both in original documents of the seventeenth century and for all periods in reprint form. Other compilations of earlier laws and decrees supplement the *Leyes y resoluciones* (fairly complete from 1860 to 1905); this collection is followed by the *Anuario de la legislación peruana,* complete from 1905 to 1925. The *Diario de los debates* for the Cámara de los Diputados is fragmentary, but there is a complete file for the Cámara de Senadores from 1872. There is an irregular file of *El Peruano* up to the time it ceased publication in 1961. The Rare Book Division has a file of the early *Gaceta del gobierno* (1821–26).

Uruguay: The *Diario de sesiones* of the Asamblea General is complete from 1830 to 1933; it is presently published in the *Diario oficial,* available in the library from 1959. The *Diario* of the Cámara de Representantes is complete from 1858. The files of the *Colección legislativa* and its continuation, *Registro nacional de leyes, decretos y otros documentos,* are almost complete from the earliest issue of 1825.

Venezuela: The *Gaceta oficial* is complete from 1902 with fragmentary files of other titles in the collection. *Diarios* of both houses of the Congreso are complete from 1932. The *Recopilación de leyes y decretos* lacks some volumes.

THE SOCIAL SCIENCES

CENTRAL AMERICA (BILLINGS HM)

The general historical collection, principally composed of materials published after 1870, numbers some 2,000 volumes. Early rarities are housed in the Rare Book Division. Books of description and travel are an interesting feature, as are the large holdings of printed documentary material. Special subjects include boundary disputes and the Nicaraguan and other trans-Isthmian canal projects. Technical materials on canals are available in the Economic and Public Affairs Division and the Science and Technology Research Center.

The Rare Book Division is actively adding to a collection of materials on the Scottish colonial project called the Darien Scheme. Also of note are its holdings of bound volumes of "decretos, ordenes, actas," and the like of the Asamblea Constituyente of Guatemala during the period 1824 to 1851 in four volumes, with many broadsides and pamphlets bound in. Another volume contains both official and nonofficial broadsides for the period 1826 to 1840.

Public Documents

The collection of government publications of Central American countries is good, although incomplete. Statistics is among the subjects strongly represented. Official gazettes such as *El Guatemalteco* (1841–71, 1897–) and *La Gaceta* of Honduras (1830/31– , incomplete) are held in substantial runs. The library also has material from the Confederación de Centro-América during the period 1823 to 1840. The library has over 32 percent of the titles listed by James B. Childs in *The Memorias of the Republics of Central America and of the Antilles* (1932), and is actively adding to the collection. Briefly, publications of the individual republics are:

British Honduras: The collection is generally strong, though some files are incomplete.

Costa Rica: The files of important series are broken but not fragmentary.

Guatemala: The collection has few complete sets, although there are scattered files of departmental reports from the 1880s to date. Administrative reports for recent years are generally strong.

Honduras: This collection contains strong, though incomplete, sets of administrative reports.

Nicaragua: This collection is one of the strongest of the Central American group, with long runs of important series.

Salvador: These publications constitute a good collection, although the series are generally incomplete.

WEST INDIES, ETC. (BILLINGS HN-HR)

The collection relating to this area (about 6,300 volumes in general history) is strong in printed materials, including standard histories, contemporary documents such as governors' reports and printed archives, and a great number of books of description and travel dating from the earliest accounts.[11] Since all of these islands have at one time been colonial possessions, much of interest is available in historical works relating to the parent countries.

11. See "List of Works in The New York Public Library Relating to the West Indies," *BNYPL* 16 (1912): 7–49 et seq. Published separately by the library.

Excellent materials are available for all of the islands, but the collection relating to Cuba is the most extensive and perhaps the richest. Most of the historical works are recent, although there are such compilations as Eréchun's *Anales de la Isla de Cuba* (1858–61). At present the Cuban collection is the fastest growing of those for countries outside North America, with works in all languages on the Castro regime.

Cuban documents and archives appear in separate volumes and in serial publications such as the *Boletín del Archivo Nacional.* Historical periodicals include such series as the *Cuba Review, Revista bimestre cubana,* and the more recent *Cuba socialista;* with these may be associated the extensive collection of Cuban literary periodicals. Related materials in the collections devoted to United States foreign relations are also important for Cuban history.

Several manuscripts from the Obadiah Rich collection of the Manuscripts and Archives Division relate to Cuba, most notably an account of a French pirate attack on Havana in 1555 and a treasurer's report of 1794. In the Myers collection is Juan de Castro's diary of the siege of Havana in 1762. The Rare Book Division holds a set of eight reports of trials in Spain of officers in command who had surrendered Havana.

The library's Haitian collection is particularly strong in contemporary pamphlets of the revolutionary period of 1791 to 1804. Other items include *Étrennes américaines,* an almanac for 1769 printed at Port-au-Prince, which is interesting as one of the earliest eighteenth-century imprints in Haiti. From the period of King Christophe is the *Almanach royal d'Haiti* (1817–18; 1820). The Schomburg Center contains important materials on Haiti as well as other islands of the West Indies, particularly on aspects of slavery and emancipation. Its collection includes manuscript military records of the revolutionary period in Haiti, a letter of Toussaint L'Ouverture, and other materials. Materials from the library of Kurt Fisher now in the Schomburg Center include both printed works and several thousand historically significant manuscripts and early documents relating to Haiti, such as presidential proclamations and correspondence, government and church records, and property inventories.

The three letters of Diego Columbus in the Manuscripts and Archives Division dated between 1500 and 1512 discuss matters pertaining to Santo Domingo and the West Indies. Proclamations of William Leyborne, governor-in-chief of the islands of Granada, the Grenadines, St. Vincent and Tobago, date from 1771 to 1775. There is also a letter of Admiral Rodney setting forth his observations on the area, dated from Martinique in 1762. Other manuscripts consist of French ships' logs, papers of the eighteenth century, and papers of American merchants engaged in the Caribbean trade during the nineteenth century.

The library maintains a great interest in the West Indies, acquiring rarities in addition to current publications in all its collecting fields. The history of the lucrative sugar trade of the British West Indies, particularly during the eighteenth century, is documented by many anonymous pamphlets.

Public Documents

The important series of governors' reports for this group of former island possessions is supple-

254

mented by official gazettes (generally present in long runs); statistical and economic reports are also held in strength. There are series of "Blue Books" for all British colonies or former colonies. Over 65 percent of the titles listed by J. B. Childs in *The Memorias of the Republics of Central America and of the Antilles* (1932) are held. The administrative reports not held are acquired when possible.[12]

The following are notes on the collections of publications of some of the governments:

Bermuda: The collection is fairly strong; a number of the administrative series are complete. The *Official Gazette* is available from 1925 onward.

Danish West Indies, Netherlands Antilles, etc.: There are few publications from this group. There is a good collection of Curaçao documents, however, including early imprints and a file of the Netherlands Antilles *Publicatieblad* (1948–) and its predecessor the *Publicatieblad van Curaçao* from 1816–1947, both of which are incomplete. *De Curaçaosche courant* is available from 1876 with gaps.

French West Indies: The series of government reports for Guadeloupe are extensive, though incomplete. The collection of Martinique documents is good.

Haiti and Dominican Republic: The departmental reports of Haiti are generally strong. The laws include some rare materials. The official gazette *Moniteur* is available from 1849 with gaps. The Schomburg Center has a strong Haiti collection.

Jamaica: The collection of publications of Jamaica is strong, including not only the *Annual General Report* but also separate administrative and departmental reports. There is an interesting group of early Jamaican documents in the Rare Book Division.

Puerto Rico: A strong and very complete collection contains such items as the *Gaceta* (1836–99, incomplete).

Trinidad and Tobago: The publications are fragmentary but fairly extensive.

MEXICO (BILLINGS HT)

About 4,600 volumes on Mexico in the general collections form strong holdings supplemented by fine collections of rare materials including pamphlets, early Mexican imprints, and works in the native Indian languages.[13] The general materials include an extensive group of almanacs and *Calendarios* beginning as early as 1809. Noteworthy holdings of periodicals include an excellent collection of literary periodicals of supplementary use for the study of history, social life, and other cultural aspects. The collection of pamphlets contains approximately 200 pieces of the period 1811 to 1929 by and about Fernández de Lizardi. Early files of Mexican newspapers held in the Rare Book Division include *El Monitor republicano* and others which appeared during the 1840s.

The Mexican government has printed many important documents, particularly those relating

12. See James W. Henderson, "The Acquisition and Preservation of Foreign Official Gazettes," *Farmington Plan Newsletter* 31 (1970): 1–24.

13. See "List of Works in The New York Public Library Relating to Mexico," *BNYPL* 13 (1909): 622–62 et seq.

to its foreign affairs, of which the *Archivo histórico diplomático mexicano* of the Secretaría de Relaciones Exteriores is typical. Many of the learned institutions of Mexico issue important documentary materials as well.

General histories are numerous from the earliest periods, as are works of description and travel. In period materials are the important collections on the Conquest; an unusual group of Cortes letters includes the first Latin edition of the second letter, *Praeclara Ferdinãdi* (Nuremberg, 1524) with an important woodcut map of Mexico City and the Gulf of Mexico. Other historical periods well documented in the holdings include that of Maximilian and his Republican successors. The collection relating to Maximilian includes a large number of important pamphlets and the *Gazette*.

Much of importance relating to Mexican history appears with material documenting the history of Spain, and it should be noted that works on the early history of Texas, New Mexico, Arizona, and California are also useful.

A considerable body of material held by the Manuscripts and Archives Division relates to Mexico. There are important transcripts and some original items in the Obadiah Rich collection. Several thousand Mexican documents, commercial papers, lawsuits, and the like, cover the period from 1562 to 1840. The *Monumentos Guadalupanos* consist of original documents and transcripts of the seventeenth, eighteenth, and nineteenth centuries concerning the worship of the Virgin at the famous shrine of Guadalupe. Other materials document the inquisition in Mexico from 1622 to 1680, and furnish a calendar of laws and regulations for New Spain during the years 1586 to 1678. The division has a manuscript account of the war between Mexico and Texas with documents and transcripts from Mexican sources of the period 1836 to 1839, including the correspondence of the Commandant of the Army of the North with the Secretary of War. The papers of Commodore David Conner, USN (ca. 1816–56), also relate to the Texas Revolution and the Mexican War. The papers for the period 1912 to 1915 of Enrique Llorente, Mexican consul at El Paso and representative in Washington of the provisional government under Francisco Villa, are housed in the division.

Public Documents

The collection of Mexican government publications is strong, although many sets lack volumes. It is rich in early imprints. The *Diario oficial* (under its various titles) is fairly complete from 1722 onward. The laws are especially well represented, including an early imprint *Ordenãças y copilación de leyes* (1548), the first law book published in America. Administrative and departmental reports are numerous, and the subject of statistics is represented by extensive holdings.

The collection of the publications of Mexican states is not extensive. It consists principally of some early reports of the *Gobernadores* and of files of official gazettes of the late nineteenth and twentieth centuries. The library presently receives gazettes from approximately half of the states and territories of Mexico.

CANADA (BILLINGS HV-HZ)

The collection relating to Canada is strong. The portion of the holdings administered by the

American History Division numbers approximately 8,600 volumes consisting of reports, letters, and accounts of early and late explorers, general histories, and works of description and travel. There is also an excellent collection relating to the Canadian pioneers. General pamphlets number about 1,400, with many others devoted to special subjects.

Periodicals and serial publications are strong. Various types are present, the most important being the *Reports* and other publications of the Public Archives of Canada relating to both the French and the English periods. Provincial archive publications are also important: those of Quebec, Ontario, British Columbia, and Nova Scotia are outstanding. The archives departments have in many instances issued calendars of important series of unpublished material; the library has extensive files of this matter.

A second source of material in periodicals is the publications of organizations, including among others the Literary and Historical Society of Quebec, the Ontario Historical Society, the Champlain Society; to these may be added the Royal Society of Canada and other British-American learned societies and academies. Those of French America are represented by *Nova Francia* (1925–32) and other publications of the Société d'Histoire du Canada, the *Revue d'histoire de l'Amérique française* (1947–), and the like. The University of Toronto and Laval's Institut d'Histoire issue historical series.

The more specialized historical magazines such as *Canadian Historical Review* (1920–) are also useful to researchers. The library has generally complete files of these as well as of such important Canadian literary magazines containing historical papers as the *Canadian Magazine* (1893–1939).

The early works of exploration and travel briefly described in the introductory section to this description of the American history resources are of particular interest for Canadian historical research. To the works of travelers such as Alfonce and Thévenot may be added those of others who were more specifically explorers of Canada: Champlain, Denys, LeClercy, Hennepin, and La Hontan. The Rare Book Division contains first and early editions of their accounts. The library has a considerable portion of the materials listed in Henry Harrisse's *Notes pour servir à l'histoire et à la cartographie de la Nouvelle-France et des pays adjacents, 1545–1700*, and actively endeavors to secure the remainder either in original editions or in reproduction.

Special mention should be made of what are perhaps the most important single primary sources of early Canadian history—the seventeenth-century *Jesuit Relations* and allied documents. The library has one of the few complete runs of the series together with variant issues of a number of those years. Among the most prized items are the 1632 Le Jeune edition (McCoy 1); the Le Mercier edition of 1656 (McCoy 96); and the Lallemant edition of 1660 (McCoy 104). A bibliography of the *Relations* was printed in 1879 as No. II of the *Contributions to a Catalogue of the Lenox Library*, and the library's copies were more fully described by Victor Hugo Paltsits in R. G. Thwaites's edition of 73 volumes (1896–1901).[14] The more useful portions of the *Rela-*

tions have appeared either in reprints or translations which are kept in the American history collections for general use; original editions are retained in the Rare Book Division.

There are interesting materials relating to the Hudson's Bay Company and other groups organized for exploration. In later materials, the printed works on pioneering and homesteading are an important feature. Documentary materials concerning Upper and Lower Canada as well as the Constitution are strong. A subject of associated interest is that of the American Loyalists during the period of the Revolution, many of whom emigrated to Ontario, Nova Scotia, and New Brunswick. Printed books, as well as transcripts of their claims for reimbursement under the laws of Great Britain (these in the Manuscripts and Archives Division), are among the library's resources.

Individual works on local or provincial history and local historical society publications form a strong collection administered by the American History Division. There is a good working collection of Canadian directories with long files for the more important cities.

There are few manuscripts relating to Canada in the library. Perhaps the most important of these are transcripts of the orders issued by General James Wolfe in the Quebec campaigns from April 30 to September 12, 1759, and by Generals Townshend and Murray at Quebec from September 14, 1759 to April 28, 1760. These transcripts contain orders not found in John Knox's *Journal* (London, 1769) and the text of the orders often varies. The transcripts form a part of the Ford collection, and are held in the Manuscripts and Archives Division. Another manuscript account dated Boston, January 3, 1690, describes the expedition of Sir William Phips against Quebec. It is supplemented by letters and documents in the Chalmers collection concerning the expeditions against Canada of 1690, 1710–11, and 1746–47. Diaries, journals, and other documents in the division concern French Canada during the eighteenth and nineteenth centuries.

Public Documents

The library is a depository for the documents of the national government of Canada. Of the longer series, the collection generally contains extensive files both of legislative and departmental reports and papers. The *Canada Gazette* is complete from 1881; the *Journals* of the Legislative Assembly are available from 1841 to 1866 in an incomplete file, followed by the *Debates* of the House of Commons (1870–). Statutes include the *Acts of the Parliament of the Dominion of Canada* (1867–). There are some municipal documents for the cities of Canada: Quebec and Montreal are best represented, with statistical publications predominating.

The following notes on selected provinces of Canada give some idea of the extent of the resources:

Alberta: Both the *Alberta Gazette* (1905–) and the *Journal* of the Legislative Assembly are complete. The *Sessional Papers* are complete from 1925 to 1937. The *Statutes* are complete from 1906. The *Public Accounts* of the Treasury begin with the second year of the series, 1909. The

---

14. See James C. McCoy, *Jesuit Relations of*

Canada 1632–1673 (Paris: A. Rau, 1937), which gives an indication of the library's holdings.

holdings include generally complete files of separately issued departmental reports.

British Columbia: The file of the *British Columbia Gazette*, commencing in 1863, is incomplete for the early years. For the period in which this province was a crown colony (until 1871), the library has the Governor's *Proclamations* (1858–64) and *Ordinances* (1864–71). The provincial *Statutes* are complete from 1872 to date. The library also has the *Journals* of six of the eight Legislative Councils of the crown colony (1864/65–71); the *Journals* (1872–) of the Legislative Assembly are complete.

New Brunswick: The *Royal Gazette* is complete from 1902 to date. The journals of the earlier Legislative Council and the House of Assembly are fragmentary; the *Journals* of the Legislative Assembly which succeeded it in 1893 are complete. The *Acts* are almost complete from 1922. The collections of departmental reports are incomplete but not fragmentary.

Nova Scotia: The library has a file of the *Royal Gazette* commencing with 1903. There are some scattered volumes of the *Journals* of the House of Assembly prior to 1820, and the file after that date is nearly complete. There is also an almost complete file of the *Journals and Appendices* of the Legislative Council which existed from 1837 to 1928. Of the *Debates and Proceedings* of the House of Assembly (1855–1913) the collection contains a partial file; of the similar series of the Legislative Council (1856–1913) the collection contains a file covering 1875 to 1913. The holdings of the *Statutes*, which commence in 1833, are nearly complete.

Ontario (as Upper Canada, 1791–1841; as part of the Province of Canada, 1841–67): The *Ontario Gazette* (1868–) is incomplete for the earlier years; there are a few scattered numbers of the *Upper Canada Gazette* which preceded it.

The *Journals* of the Legislative Assembly are complete from their commencement in 1868; the *Sessional Papers* run from 1869 to 1951, containing during that period most of the routine departmental reports. The collection contains only partial files of the journals of the House of Assembly and of the Legislative Council (1792–1837), which preceded the Legislative Assembly. The *Statutes* of Ontario are complete from 1867.

Quebec (as Lower Canada, 1791–1841; as part of the Province of Canada, 1841–67): The *Gazette officielle* is complete from its commencement in 1869; there is also a broken file of the earlier *Gazette de Québec*. The *Journals* of the House of Assembly (1792–1837) and those of the Legislative Council (1792–1837) are complete. The *Journals* of the Special Council (1837–39) lack volume 2. The *Journals* of the Legislative Council are complete from their commencement in 1867. The *Statutes* of the province are complete from 1867, and before that those of Lower Canada are available in an incomplete file from 1793 to 1831. The *Sessional Papers* of the Legislative Assembly, which are complete from 1869 to 1936, contain most of the routine departmental reports for that period.

Saskatchewan: The *Saskatchewan Gazette* is complete from 1911. The *Journals* of the Legislative Assembly are complete from their beginning in 1906. The *Statutes* of the province start with 1906 and continue to the present day.

Newfoundland: The *Royal Gazette and Newfoundland Advertiser* with its successor, the *Newfoundland Gazette*, cover the period from 1903 to date. The *Journals* of the House of Assembly begin in 1834 and continue until suspension in 1933, although the files are not complete. The *Journals* of the Legislative Council from 1833 to 1934 lack some volumes.

53

UNITED STATES HISTORY

The collection of about 130,000 books and pamphlets on the history of the United States is one of the most important in the library. It may be categorized as follows:

General history	
(Billings I-IO)	55,800 volumes
State and local history	
(Billings IQ-IZ)	73,800

The above figures represent only the portion of the library's total resources relating to the national, state, and local histories of the United States in political, constitutional, military, religious, and social contexts. The total figures do not include materials which are kept in the Rare Book Division, the Manuscripts and Archives Division, and the other special collections; nor do they include the Public Documents collection in the Economic and Public Affairs Division, works on general church history, or resources in the economic history of the United States.

SCRAPBOOKS

Ephemeral materials related to United States history are preserved in scrapbooks, many of which have come to the library's divisions as gifts. Due to the availability of such resources in other forms, it is the policy of most divisions holding scrapbooks to concentrate indexing on other kinds of material.

PICTORIAL MATERIAL

The American History Division maintains 45 catalog trays indexing the pictures of historical interest in books and periodicals held by the library, in addition to an American Indian Design index. In the important Robert Dennis collection of international stereopticon views are many pictures of the United States. A large number of New York City views, the majority dating from the 1920s and 1930s, are held by the Local History and Genealogy Division.

The Phelps Stokes collection of American historical prints in the Prints Division provides documentation from the earliest periods to the end of the nineteenth century. Among the many articles of United States historical interest is a large group of portraits of George Washington. In addition are political cartoons, including those of Thomas Nast, and drawings made during the Civil War by the artists of *Leslie's Weekly*.

Other pictures archives include the Archibald Robertson drawings of United States scenes during the Revolutionary period in the Spencer Collection, and drawings of American Indians by George Catlin and Francis B. Mayer in the Rare Book Division. The Manuscripts and Archives Division's strong holdings of diaries include many sketches and views; its Emmet and Myers collections contain much illustrative material from the period of the American Revolution.

Of great sociological interest are the more than 300,000 items from the Farm Security Administration Photographic Project made during the 1930s, with a particularly extensive file on the conditions of black Americans. These are held in the Picture Collection, a unit of the Branch Libraries.

PUBLIC DOCUMENTS

The library has always been a federal depository library; its collection of United States federal documents is, therefore, extremely rich. It is also a depository for New York, California, and Washington state publications; it holds most of the state publications of New Jersey, and also regularly receives the publications of other states.

The library's holdings of serial sets of congressional documents and departmental series are complete, insofar as this material has been distributed. Federal legislative proceedings, laws, treaty series, etc. are generally complete. The library secures and preserves the printed bills of Congress, commencing with the set of the 52nd Congress (1891–92). Related materials include extensive holdings of the printed public documents from England, France, and other countries during their period of territorial interest in North America.

Materials in the Rare Book Division are extensive, including a collection of original documents of the first fourteen Congresses (1789–1817) and a good representation of Confederate documents.

EARLY IMPRINTS AND VALUABLE WORKS

A description of Americana in the Rare Book Division is found in chapter 52. Voyages and travels, exploration, and colonization are fully represented in combination with extensive collections of newspapers and periodicals, especially from the eighteenth century. The collection of United States almanacs is particularly strong, with those published before 1820 kept in the Rare Book Division.

The American Revolution is documented by a large collection of contemporaneous colonial and British books and pamphlets which bear on political separation. In the Rare Book Division an important group of broadsides issued during this period is also present, including the first printing of the Declaration of Independence, as well as one of the two known copies of its first New York printing. The collection also includes two copies of the epochal "Northwest Ordinance" of 1787, by which the Continental Congress established a form of government for the little-populated territories north of the Ohio River.

Post-Revolutionary historical materials include a number of rare western works. The library has collected extensively in the literature of the period of western expansion. It has many of the titles listed in H. R. Wagner's *The Plains and the Rockies . . . 1800–1865*, and is attempting to complete its holdings with original editions or reprints and photostatic copies.

Confederate imprints are another feature. Three kinds of subject material are notable: documents of the Confederacy and its various states, individual accounts of Southern men · and women, and schoolbooks.

Other works of interest kept in the Rare Book Division include early imprints relating to the American Indian. Early editions of the writings of historic personages include those of John Smith, the Mathers, and Noah Webster. Biographical materials include an outstanding collection of eulogies on Washington.[1] Works on the history of religion in the United States are numerous; the library's holdings of the early titles printed in America and England listed in H. M. Dexter's *Congregationalism of the Last Three Hundred Years as Seen in Its Literature* (1880), which noted Lenox Library copies, are most creditable. Later church history materials comprise collections on the Mormons and the Shakers. There is also a good collection on the Seventh Day Adventists.

Other materials of historical interest include colonial and Confederate paper money housed in the Rare Book Division, as well as miscellaneous coins, tokens, and medals. Of these, the more important groups consist of Washington medals and the copper and brass tokens of the Civil War period. The outstanding collection of United States postage stamps (1850–1926) presented to the library by Benjamin K. Miller is permanently displayed in the Central Building.[2]

GENERAL UNITED STATES HISTORY

The collection of books and pamphlets relating to the national history of the United States is strong. It consists of printed archives and documents, historical serials, writings on general history as well as on special phases and periods, and works of description and travel.

The Billings Classification Schedule serves as a guide to the brief descriptions which follow.

GENERAL WORKS (BILLINGS IA)

Consistent with the policy of securing any edition containing material not included in works already present in the collections, the library frequently has many editions of general histories. Another type of general literature consists of the published papers of presidents and other significant political figures, which constitute an extensive and important group.

United States historical periodicals are an outstanding feature. The collection includes general

1. See Margaret Bingham Stillwell, "Checklist of Eulogies and Funeral Orations on the Death of George Washington," *BNYPL* 20 (1916): 403–50. Published separately by the library, with additions, as *Washington Eulogies; A Checklist*.

2. See "The Miller Collection of United States Postage Stamps," *BNYPL* 40 (1936): 421–26.

historical periodicals, the publications of national and state historical societies, and those of special historical associations, such as the Catholic Historical Society. The files of these serial publications are generally complete; many of them are indexed in the Public Catalog and the appropriate division catalogs, while commercial indexes often suffice for contemporary volumes.

Early serial publications include a good collection of American almanacs. There are also many pamphlets in this subclass; more than 6,000 titles represent collections, essays, and miscellanies alone (Billings class mark IAG).

THE CONSTITUTION AND CONSTITUTIONAL HISTORY (BILLINGS IB)

This collection contains materials on the federal Constitution and many general works relating to state constitutions as well; holdings classed elsewhere in the library make this a strongly represented subject. Source materials in public documents and in other subject classes are administered by the Economic and Public Affairs Division. Of particular interest are the materials kept in the Rare Book Division which include such rare works as original printed resolutions, debates, and the early editions of *The Federalist*.

FOREIGN RELATIONS (BILLINGS IC)

This subject is very fully covered, both in this subclass and in related subject classes. The library attempts to obtain all available material on commissions dealing with boundary disputes, claims for war indemnities, and the like. The collections contain a vast amount of material relating to the former possessions of this country, the outstanding series being the Elihu Root collection of United States documents (1896–1908), consisting of 184 volumes covering Cuba, Puerto Rico, China, the Hawaiian Islands, Panama, etc., and the Elihu Root collection of United States documents relating to the Philippine Islands (1898–1906) in 178 volumes. These make possible a detailed study of United States efforts for world influence and the factors tending to promote overseas expansion.

POLITICAL HISTORY AND POLITICAL PARTIES (BILLINGS ID)

The materials dealing with this subject are divided between the American History Division and the Economic and Public Affairs Division. The value of the collection is greatly enhanced by the collections classed as political and party publications (Billings IO), described below.

VARIOUS RACES IN THE UNITED STATES (BILLINGS IE)

Although the library has systematically collected in this subject over an extensive period, all materials are not located in this class mark. For example, books on the Jew in America are to be found in the Jewish Division. This subclass (Billings IEC) contains important materials in the literature relating to the Negro. Other items are found under headings such as "Ethnology," "Slavery—U.S.," or "Emancipation of Negroes," and in the Schomburg Center. Among European nationalities, the Germans in the United States have received the greatest attention; German-

American resources developed rapidly from about 1900.

PERIOD BEFORE THE REVOLUTION (BILLINGS IF)

The resources in this subclass constitute a good working collection strengthened by works in the Rare Book Division and related subject materials in the Economic and Public Affairs Division. Primary materials include such compilations as the separately published correspondence of colonial administrators (Sir William Johnson, Shirley, Gage, and others) as well as secondary historical studies. In addition to scholarly works are numerous popular works on colonial life and culture.

The Liebmann collection of American historical documents is fully discussed in the section on alcoholic drinks in chapter 63. Its 226 manuscript items (with some book materials) relate to the production and use of whiskey, rum, and brandy in America from 1665 to 1910. The collections of George Chalmers in the Manuscripts and Archives Division contain transcripts and original documents relating to the revolt of the American colonies bound in 25 volumes, and also include a volume of papers relating to the Indians. Among these papers is Major Robert Rogers' journal of 1760–61.[3] Other Rogers material was given by Mrs. Charles S. Fairchild in 1927 and includes a sutler's permit, travel accounts, power of attorney, etc.

The collection of first and early editions of the Mather family works is substantial and contains many rarities. Richard Mather was one of the translators of the famous "Bay Psalm Book" (Cambridge, 1640). The Lenox copy in the Rare Book Division is one of five known complete examples. Of equal rarity is *A Platform of Church Discipline* (Cambridge, 1649), better known as the "Cambridge Platform," which was in part prepared by Richard Mather. The library holds a copy of the second issue of this early declaration of church government and discipline.

Increase Mather is represented by over 34 first editions, among them *A Brief History of the War With the Indians in New England* (London, 1676) and *Cases of Conscience Concerning Evil Spirits* (Boston, 1693), a book that has been credited with helping to bring the witchcraft trials in Massachusetts to an end. Cotton Mather, the most voluminous writer of the three, is represented in the library by over 60 first editions of his more than 400 existing works. Outstanding among them is *The Wonders of the Invisible World* (Boston, 1693), an account of the witchcraft trials; the Rare Book Division holds copies of the first 3 American editions and the first English edition. His *Magnalia Christi Americana* (London, 1702), and *The Christian Philosopher* (London, 1721) are also present. The manuscript of Cotton Mather's sermon delivered in 1723 on the death of his father is held by the Manuscripts and Archives Division.

THE REVOLUTION (BILLINGS IG)

General Materials

The materials on the Revolutionary period form an outstanding collection. The library has

---

3. See Victor Hugo Paltsits, ed., "Journal of Robert Rogers the Ranger on His Expedition for Receiving the Capitulation of Western French Posts," *BNYPL* 37 (1933): 261–76.

sought to acquire all published original narratives, orderly books, and similar sources of information on campaigns, as well as all published correspondence of political leaders or governmental representatives of the different states. The participation of foreigners as aides, either to the Americans or the British, has received special attention.

Noteworthy holdings for the study of Benjamin Franklin include rare printed works and manuscripts in various locations in the library. There is also an interesting group of materials relating to Major André.

The resources for the study of George Washington are important; their particular strength derives from the presence of certain significant pieces, rather than from their extent.[4] Printed editions of Washington's writings include the early and rare *Journal* (1754). An enormous collection of biographical and historical material relates to Washington's life and career. Portraits in oils by Gilbert Stuart and others are on public display together with two marble busts, one the work of Thomas Crawford; in the Prints Division are over 2,000 engraved portraits. Medals and medallic portraits are kept in the Rare Book Division, which also houses the notable collection of approximately 285 Washington eulogies.[5] Among the most interesting of these are 33 eulogies which belonged to Martha Washington. Twenty-four books from Washington's library are also present, many of them given by the late Edward S. Harkness.

Included among some 550 Washington manuscripts is the final holograph version of the Farewell Address. The earliest manuscript is a land survey in the Emmet collection dated November 20, 1750; a notebook kept while Washington was colonel of the Virginia militia dates from 1757. The largest group is a series in the collection of presidential papers in the Manuscripts and Archives Division. Two business letters are in the Arents Tobacco Collection, and 4 letters and a leaf of notes are in the Berg Collection. Manuscript drafts of portions of Washington Irving's *Life of Washington* are in the Arents and Berg Collections and in the Seligman collection of the Manuscripts and Archives Division. Many musical works celebrating events of Washington's career are a part of the Music Division holdings.

Important works on American Loyalists are supplemented by printed records in the Local History and Genealogy Division and Rare Book Division, which, together with transcripts of records in the Manuscripts and Archives Division, combine to form an outstanding collection of historical works, petitions, depositions, hearings, decisions, and calendars of unpublished materials in various repositories. Fifty-nine volumes of transcripts in the Manuscripts and Archives Division, which the library began to secure from the Public Records Office in London at the end of the nineteenth century, duplicate information gathered by the Commission of Enquiry into the Losses and Services of the American Loyalists.

This subclass contains an adequate collection of printed works relating to the Declaration of Independence. Additional materials elsewhere in the library make the literature relating to it a very rich group. Rare broadsides are in the Rare Book Division; manuscripts are in the Manuscripts and Archives Division; portraits of the signers are in the Manuscripts and Archives and the Prints Divisions.

Manuscript Collections

Brief descriptions of the more important materials and collections on the Revolutionary period now in the Manuscripts and Archives Division follow directly. Such archives as the Emmet and Bancroft collections are not restricted to manuscripts of the Revolutionary period, but contain in addition books, pamphlets, and prints related to other periods of United States history.

The Olive Branch Petition: This document was given posthumously to the library by Lucius Wilmerding in 1948. A petition to George III of England signed by the members of the Continental Congress on July 8, 1775, this was a final attempt to avoid the American Revolution.[6]

Declaration of Independence: This is one of five fair copies Thomas Jefferson made of the document. Dr. Thomas A. Emmet had this manuscript bound with at least one autograph of each of the signers of the Declaration.

Constitution of the United States of America: Bill of Rights: This is an engrossed copy on vellum of the twelve proposed amendments to the Constitution submitted to the several states by Congress as a Bill of Rights on September 25, 1789. It is one of seven known copies of the fourteen originally made.

George Washington, Farewell Address: This is the final version in thirty-two heavily corrected pages which President Washington delivered to the Philadelphia printer David Claypoole. It was published on September 19, 1796, in *Claypoole's American Daily Advertiser*.[7]

Bancroft Collection: Original manuscripts in the Bancroft collection include letters to Samuel Adams from the prominent men of the Revolution, along with drafts of his own letters; the papers of the Boston Committee of Correspondence; the Hawley papers; the Ansbach and other papers on the service of German troops in the Revolution, including the correspondence of General Riedesel; and numerous letters of distinguished Americans. Transcripts in this collection are bound in 210 volumes: they include copies of important materials from European archives on the subject of the Revolution, as well as the British state papers on colonial affairs, and a great number of documents from private sources. Also present is historical matter of a later date, including the unpublished diary and correspondence of President Polk, along with the papers of the historian George Bancroft documenting his duties as minister to Great Britain and Germany and as Commissioner of Boundaries. This most important collection of 486 volumes in manuscript, with other book materials, was purchased in 1894 by the Lenox Library.

---

4. See Robert W. Hill and Lewis M. Stark, "Washingtoniana in The New York Public Library," *BNYPL* 61 (1957): 73–80.

5. Stillwell, "Checklist . . ." (footnote 1 above).

6. Cornelius W. Wickersham, "The Olive Branch," *BNYPL* 56 (1952): 539–43. See also *The Olive Branch Petition of the American Congress to George III, 1775* (The New York Public Library, 1954).

7. See Victor Hugo Paltsits, ed., *Washington's Farewell Address* (The New York Public Library, 1935; reprinted by the library and Arno Press, 1971).

Chalmers Collection: These twenty-five volumes of bound transcripts, original documents, and notes relating to the United States were collected by George Chalmers for his history of the revolt of the colonies, the manuscript of which is also present. There is, in addition, a volume of papers relating to the Indians. Most of the volumes were purchased by the library in 1890; several came with the library of George Bancroft.

Emmet Collection: The manuscripts in this collection number about 10,800 pieces, and include one or more autographs of almost every man of distinction in American affairs during the Revolution, as well as a large number of earlier colonial documents and letters of more recent date. There are three complete sets of autographs of the signers of the Declaration of Independence, one of which has been called "the finest set extant."[8] Among the many official documents of great interest is Thomas Jefferson's fair copy of the Declaration of Independence. The finest material in this collection is mounted in bound volumes with printed titles and narrative text, illustrated with portraits, views, caricatures, drawings, and broadsides. Sixty volumes of publications, the majority relating to the American Revolution, are extra-illustrated. The collection was brought together by Dr. Thomas Addis Emmet and presented to the library by John S. Kennedy in 1896.[9]

Ford Collection: This collection of some 60,000 items consists chiefly of autographs of Americans from the Revolutionary period and the nineteenth century. There are many autographs of the signers of the Declaration of Independence, and a number of letters by Washington and Franklin, letters to General Hand, and many other papers relating to the Revolution. The collection was made between 1840 and 1898 by Gordon Lester Ford and his sons Worthington Chauncey Ford and Paul Leicester Ford; it was presented to the library in 1899 by J. Pierpont Morgan.

Gansevoort-Lansing Papers: In 1919, Victor Hugo Paltsits presented this collection to the library under the terms of the will of Catherine Gansevoort Lansing. It consists of books, pamphlets, and other materials, including a collection of about 25,000 manuscripts documenting the careers of General Peter Gansevoort, an officer during the Revolution, of his son, the Hon. Peter Gansevoort, and of the latter's son, Brigadier-General Henry Sanford Gansevoort. There are also numerous papers of the Lansing, Douw, Van Schaick, and Melville families, along with several hundred items from the papers of Abraham Yates. In all, these manuscripts embrace a period of nearly 250 years of American history; a listing of the papers is given in the *Dictionary Catalog of the Manuscript Division*.[10]

William Livingston Papers: The correspondence and other papers of William Livingston from 1775 to 1782 amount to approximately 950 items; a listing is available in the Manuscripts and Archives Division. The collection was deposited by Mrs. Lewis C. Ledyard in 1938 and given to the library in 1962–65.

Myers Collection: Formed by Colonel Theodorus Bailey Myers, this collection numbers about 1,600 pieces and consists chiefly of autograph letters and documents of distinguished Americans of the colonial period, the Revolution, and the nineteenth century. Included are the signers of the Declaration of Independence, the governors of New York, members of the Continental Congress, and generals of the Revolution, along with autographs of distinguished Europeans. The collection was arranged under the supervision of Dr. Thomas Addis Emmet and, like his own collection, contains illustrative matter such as portraits and prints. It was presented in 1900 by Colonel Myers' family.

Schuyler Collection: This collection of the papers of General Philip Schuyler is arranged in several series which reflect the General's varied activities. The Schuyler canal papers consist of about 740 letters to and from General Schuyler on the affairs of the Northern and Western Inland Lock Navigation Company from 1792 to 1803. The Schuyler Revolutionary papers include 2,431 letters to him from military officers, members of Congress, committees of safety, and private individuals between 1761 and 1802, the greater part relating to the conduct of the war in the Northern Department from 1775 to 1777. A calendar of these manuscripts was made in 1851. In addition are transcripts of letters from General Schuyler and his aides de camp, general orders issued by him, copies of letters and instructions from General Washington, and the like. The Schuyler Indian papers consist of about 550 items concerning Indian affairs during the period 1764–97. The Schuyler land papers number about 850 items including letters, deeds, leases, mortgages, and maps relating to New York State between 1720 and 1840. Other letters of General Schuyler are in the Ford collection (12 originals) and the Bancroft collection (162 transcripts).

PERIOD BETWEEN THE REVOLUTION AND THE CIVIL WAR (BILLINGS II)

This subclass includes a number of strong features. One of the most important is the collection of travelers' observations on the country during this period of expansion (class mark IID). The material on the War of 1812 is also noteworthy, especially the collection of naval histories. A first edition of *The Star Spangled Banner* (Baltimore, 1814) in the Music Division is one of the library's treasures.

The collection relating to the rise of the secession movement is very extensive, with much additional material in the Economic and Public Affairs Division classed with materials on slavery. Pamphlet holdings are outstanding; in classmark IIR ("Slavery Controversy") are filed more than 300 titles, and more than 1,500 titles with the general materials on slavery. Other classes contributing to this period include works on religious history, particularly of the Mormons and Shakers. Periodical and newspaper files for this period are extensive.

8. See Joseph E. Fields, "The Complete Sets of Signers of the Declaration of Independence," *Autograph Collectors' Journal* 3 (1951): 16.
9. See *Calendar of the Emmet Collection of Manuscripts, Etc., Relating to American History* (The New York Public Library, 1900; reprinted by the library, with additions, 1959).
10. See *Dictionary Catalog of the Manuscript Division* (Boston: G. K. Hall & Co., 1967), vol. 2, pp. 517–75. For a particular aspect of the papers, see also Alice P. Kenney, " 'Evidences of of Regard': Three Generations of American Love Letters," *BNYPL* 76 (1972): 92–119.

CIVIL WAR (BILLINGS IK)

This very strong collection covers both the Union and the Confederacy. It includes an extensive collection of the accounts of campaigns, from viewpoints as diverse as those of general officers and private soldiers. The rosters of military organizations, whether issued by the organization or by the adjutants general of the various states, are complete as far as obtainable.[11] Veterans' groups such as the GAR and the Military Order of the Loyal Legion of the United States and auxiliaries such as the United Daughters of the Confederacy are represented by their many publications.

The development of photography and modern processes of reproduction created a wealth of pictorial data on the War. The library has a vast amount of this material, especially in elaborately illustrated books. In addition, drawings by the staff artists of *Leslie's Weekly* are held in the Prints Division. An important collection of Confederate imprints is housed in the Rare Book Division. This includes more than 520 items issued by southern presses during the Confederacy's existence. Of these, approximately 360 publications are official and 160 are unofficial, including textbooks, almanacs, newspapers, and periodicals.

Civil War materials in the Manuscripts and Archives Division consist primarily of diaries and the correspondence of soldiers, most of them in New York regiments. There is also material in the papers of such personalities as Horace Greeley, William H. Harris, Henry J. Raymond, Elizabeth L. Van Lew, and in log books such as those of the S.S. *Tillie* and the S.S. *Passaic*. The division also maintains the files of the United States Sanitary Commission, consisting of over 1,000 boxes of material covering the period from 1862 to 1867. Among the largest groups of material are the papers of the Army and Navy Claim Agency, the Army and Navy Pay Claim archives, the Washington Hospital Directory archives, along with condensed historical matter consisting of reports, plans, maps, newspapers, clippings, and the like. The Schomburg Center should be consulted for original materials on slavery and emancipation during the period.

SINCE THE CIVIL WAR (BILLINGS IL)

This class of materials consists of social and political histories and commentaries on the United States since the Civil War. Included are observations of political leaders, volumes on the administrations of various presidents of the period, and volumes on the Spanish-American War, World War I, and World War II. General works and travelers' accounts, particularly those of foreigners who came to observe and record frontier development,[12] are strongly represented. Many personal narratives and memoirs are classed either with the literature of the region with which they are concerned, with the American Indian material, or with biography. Thus much of the material on persons prominent in the state and national life of this period will be found outside

---

11. See Charles E. Dornbusch, *Military Bibliography of the Civil War*, 3 vols. (The New York Public Library, 1961–1972).

12. See Frank Monaghan, *French Travellers in the United States, 1765–1932; A Bibliographical List* (The New York Public Library, 1933).

this subclass of American history. The extensive collection of diaries in the Manuscripts and Archives Division is another valuable source which adds unique records to the holdings of printed diaries.

POLITICAL AND PARTY PUBLICATIONS, CAMPAIGN HANDBOOKS, ETC. (BILLINGS IO)

The ephemeral nature of many of the publications in this subclass makes them noteworthy because of their rarity, in addition to any individual importance they may have. They provide a strong supplement to the works on American politics. Only the purely political ephemeral materials are kept in this subclass; political pamphlets on economic subjects are ordinarily classified by subject under economics. An important feature of this collection is a large group of Fourth of July orations, and political or patriotic speeches on similar occasions. Another feature is the literature connected with each American presidential campaign: manuals for speakers, pamphlets, scrapbooks, and small items incident to political contests. Special materials include 28 scrapbooks related to the career of Samuel J. Tilden, especially during the presidential election of 1876. Some materials relate to elections other than presidential.

STATE HISTORIES (Billings IQ-IX)

National and state histories of the United States contribute to the holdings of the American History Division, while local, town, or county resources form the collection of the Local History and Genealogy Division. These divisional locations are not reflected in the Billings Classification Schedule, where class marks for state and local history resources are integrated into a single series. *United States Local History Catalog* is described on page 266.

Many of the observations in the preceding sections concerning Americana and American historical literature are applicable to this group. Reference should be made to the detailed description of the resources of the Rare Book Division. Literature of the territories and subsequent states published before 1801 supplement the subject materials of the American History Division, along with early newspapers and periodicals.

As the collections relating to individual states are more or less equal in importance, the following notes are applicable to all. Exceptions are made of Virginia and Massachusetts, for which holdings are more extensive. The collections relating to New York State and New York City are described following the section devoted to local histories. Published state histories are held in strength. Noteworthy supportive features include large numbers of printed archives and documents, files of publications of state historical societies and similar bodies, and contemporary pamphlets on state affairs.

The collection of travel literature is extensive. While the library has sought all available works, it has stressed the observations of foreigners. The collection has a great deal relating to the West and the study of national expansion, including early western imprints held in the Rare Book Division. Maps and atlases are housed in the Map Division.

Newspapers, periodicals, and almanacs constitute large collections. Public documents from the various states are noteworthy: the library is a depository for the official state publications of New York, California, and Washington, and has extensive holdings of the publications of other states, particularly New Jersey. The files of legislative proceedings are generally complete in either original issues or photostatic copies. Files of published state departmental reports are generally available. The document catalog in the Economic and Public Affairs Division is preferable to the Public Catalog and other division catalogs for indicating completeness of files.

Many other subject classes contribute to the study of United States state history to some degree; for example, the collection of railroad materials in the Economic and Public Affairs Division includes a great deal of material relating to western lines. The general collections on religion contain much of interest.

VIRGINIA

The holdings for Virginia are exceptional. Rare materials, general and special historical writings, printed and manuscript archives and documents, serials, and other items chronicle the history of the colony and state from the earliest period to the present day.[13]

Rare works in the library include copies of most of the seventeenth- and eighteenth-century books listed in W. Clayton-Torrence's *A Trial Bibliography of Colonial Virginia* (1908–10), which noted Lenox Library copies. The collection continues to grow; for example, the Arents Tobacco Collection has acquired King James I's copy of *The Generall Histories of Virginia . . .* (1624) by John Smith. Later works, such as Confederate imprints, are also held in significant numbers. Local historical materials are extensive, and there is a strong collection of public documents.

A noteworthy collection of manuscripts includes not only original papers but also transcripts of official records in European archives relating to early Virginia history. Of outstanding importance are the following:

Smyth Papers: The manuscript collection of John Smyth (or Smith) of Nibley, one of the original promoters of plantations and settlements in the second Virginia colony, contains 84 letters, documents, and transcripts. The collection was given to the library by Alexander Maitland in 1897.

Comberford Map: A manuscript map of the southern part of Virginia (now the northern part of North Carolina) made by Nicholas Comberford in 1657, one of two existing copies, is located in the Manuscripts and Archives Division. It is particularly significant for the light it sheds on contemporary place-names.

Proposed Constitution for the State of Virginia: This is a third draft made by Thomas Jefferson in June, 1776. The manuscript was presented to the library by Alexander Maitland in 1894. The first and second drafts are in the Library of Congress.

MASSACHUSETTS

The Bancroft collection in the Manuscripts and Archives Division is especially rich in manuscript materials relating to Massachusetts during

the period of the Revolution; in it are Samuel Adams letters and Joseph Hawley letters and documents. Additional materials are noted in "The Pilgrim Tercentenary Exhibition in The New York Public Library."[14] Histories of the Pilgrims, as a part of New England history, are in the American History Division, while local historical materials (for example, the history of Plymouth) are in the Local History and Genealogy Division.

LOCAL HISTORIES (Billings IQ-IZ)

History of the United States at the town or county level is administered by the Local History and Genealogy Division. The library has rich and extensive materials in this field. Included are published town and county histories, printed archives and documents, church rolls, and vital records. The holdings relating to Virginia and Massachusetts are particularly strong, and those of the other New England states are noteworthy. Exceptionally strong resources in New York local history are discussed in a subsequent section. Among the western states the literature pertaining to Mormon Utah and to California is noteworthy. The Arents Tobacco Collection has a large number of manuscripts from Frederick County, Maryland, ranging in date from the mid-eighteenth century to the early nineteenth century.

The files of local history serials are especially strong. This material, along with pertinent articles in general periodicals, is generally indexed in the catalog of the Local History and Genealogy Division.

Related materials include the general historical works of the American History Division, the very extensive group of municipal reports in the Economic and Public Affairs Division, and such subject areas as regimental histories and church history.

The collection of United States city directories through 1869 in the Local History Division numbers 1,300 volumes and is of exceptional strength and completeness. A microfilm of the New York City directories is available for public use. The General Research and Humanities Division administers a representative group of current United States city directories held in the Main Reading Room. A good collection of city directories for the period since 1870 is kept in the Research Libraries Annex Building.

Pictorial views of the United States are held in the Prints Division, where there is a card index to the views filed there as well as in other locations of the library. The Phelps Stokes collection of historical prints and early views of American cities provides documentation from the earliest periods through the nineteenth century. There are also landscape drawings in the Spencer Collection and in the diaries and other materials of the Manuscripts and Archives Division. There is an extensive group of stereopticon views in the American History Division, and a collection of photographs from the Farm Security Administration Photographic Project in the Picture Collection, a unit of the Branch Libraries.

NEW YORK: STATE, CITY, AND OTHER LOCAL HISTORY (BILLINGS IR-IRM)

The administration of this collection of approximately 7,000 books and pamphlets is divided

---

13. See "List of Works in The New York Public Library Relating to Virginia," *BNYPL* 11 (1907): 64–83 et seq. Published separately by the library.

14. See Victor Hugo Paltsits, *BNYPL* 25 (1921): 39–43.

between the American History Division (state history) and the Local History and Genealogy Division (town or county history). These materials, relating to political, constitutional, military, religious, and social history, as well as books of travel, are supplemented by a large number of works in the Rare Book Division, the rich collections of the Manuscripts and Archives Division, the extensive groups of public documents and other materials in the Economic and Public Affairs Division, materials in newspapers and periodicals, and by other subject collections of the library.

NEW YORK STATE: GENERAL

The subject materials classed in Billings class mark I include most of the published general and special histories, a very great number of printed historical documents, generally complete files of historical periodicals, and large numbers of pamphlets and almanacs. Special topics of importance include materials on the civil list and on the constitutional history of the state.[15]

Early historical literature, especially books and pamphlets having early New York imprints, constitutes a rich collection in the Rare Book Division. Other division resources include newspapers, periodicals, broadsides, almanacs, and public documents published before 1801, and such special materials as paper money, tokens, and medals. The fine collection of early American newspapers are, for the most part, from the collection formed by Dr. Thomas Addis Emmet and Charles R. Hildeburn. Among the book rarities are such items as Daniel Denton's *A Brief Description of New York* (1670), the first separate publication in English relating to the province of New York; the library has two copies, one of them in the scarce, perfect state.[16] The *Laws & Acts* of the colony of New York printed by William Bradford in 1694 is the first compilation of laws published in New York.

The Phelps Stokes and Eno collections in the Prints Division provide scenes of towns and topographical resources. Aquatints from the *Hudson River Portfolio* (1823–24) in the Spencer Collection, representing views of the "American Rhine" from Albany to New York, are considered to be the best color work produced in this country at the time of their printing.

Such a profusion of manuscript sources for a study of the history of New York exists in the library that it is impossible to give more than an indication of available materials. Many of the large Americana collections in the Manuscripts and Archives Division, such as the Bancroft, Chalmers, Duyckinck, Emmet, Ford, and Gansevoort-Lansing papers, contain important New York items. The William Smith memoirs and papers covering the period from 1732 to 1783 are important for New York State history as well as for a study of the beginnings and conduct of the Revolution.[17] The Schuyler collection includes

source materials for the study of Indians, canals, and land transactions in New York State from 1720 to 1840. Additional land papers are found in the Delancey Stow memorial collection for the period from 1812 to 1903. The library has the manuscript index to the papers of the Colony and Manor of Rensselaerswyck, which was given by the heirs of General Stephen Van Rensselaer in 1923.[18] State and national politics are reflected in the papers of Samuel Jones Tilden, James Schoolcraft Sherman, Anthony Jerome Griffin, William Bourke Cockran, and others.

The Manuscripts and Archives Division holds the official records of various local and state units, including those of the town of Harlem (1662–1760), the New York Supreme Court (1735–72), the Vice-Admiralty Court of New York (1753–70), the U.S. District Court for the District of New York (1796–98), and the official diary of the federal Prohibition Administrator for New York (1927–30). There are also records of Orange and Rockland Counties. The copy-books of William Gorham Rice, Timothy S. Williams, and Ashley W. Cole, private secretaries respectively to David B. Hill, Roswell P. Flower, and Levi P. Morton, record the correspondence of the governors of New York from 1886 to 1895. The extensive and growing collection of journals and diaries in the Manuscripts and Archives Division adds important resources for the study of New York history.

NEW YORK STATE: LOCAL HISTORY

Local history materials relating to New York are extensive, including most of the published town and county histories, periodicals, society publications, church rolls, vital records, and similar materials of interest to researchers in local history and genealogy. The pamphlet collection is noteworthy: it contains commemorative and other ephemeral materials in addition to historical studies.

Especially strong materials for western New York, particularly the Rochester area, derive from the collection formed by Rear Admiral Franklin Hanford and purchased by the library in 1931.[19] Rockland County is also well represented, largely through the purchase in 1933 of the collection formed by George H. Budke. This archive includes not only published local histories and genealogies but also manuscript transcripts of official records, typewritten indexes to archives and other manuscript material on the county, along with important items relating to the American Indian, dating from the eighteenth century.

Local documents of New York counties and municipalities constitute an extensive collection. These are more complete from the earliest times up to World War II than for the postwar period because of the tremendous increase in publication. First in importance are the journals of the

---

15. See "Works Relating to the State of New York in The New York Public Library," *BNYPL* 4 (1900): 163–78 et seq.

16. See Victor Hugo Paltsits, "Daniel Denton's Description of New York in 1670," *BNYPL* 28 (1924): 599–604.

17. See *BNYPL* 24 (1920): 125–26. See also William H. W. Sabine, *Historical Memoirs*, 2 vols. (New York: Colburn and Tegg, 1956–58).

18. See Victor Hugo Paltsits, "Inventory of the Rensselaerswyck Manuscripts," *BNYPL* 28 (1924): 359–68 et seq. Published separately by the library.

19. See W. J. Burke, "Books from the Library of Rear-Admiral Franklin Hanford, USN," *BNYPL* 35 (1931): 841–46. See also Victor Hugo Paltsits, "Some Manuscript Sources for the History of Central and Western New York in The New York Public Library," *New York History* 19 (1938): 58–63.

county boards of supervisors. Printing of these journals generally commenced near the middle of the nineteenth century, although Monroe and Westchester Counties have printed their earlier proceedings from manuscript; files are maintained for each county.

The library limits its collecting in the field of municipal documents to the more important cities in the State, although there is comprehensive collecting for all communities in the greater New York City metropolitan area. Most major series are in the holdings. The council proceedings are of the greatest importance. Complete files include Albany (1858–); Buffalo (1854–); Newburgh (1884/85–); and Schenectady (1854–). Long files which are not complete include Amsterdam (1898–); Auburn (1889/90–); Binghamton (1897/98–); Elmira (1875/76–); New Rochelle (1902–); Niagara Falls (1896/97–1951); Rochester (1848/49–1951); Rome (1896/97–1949); Syracuse (1890–1951); Troy (1801–40, 1884/85–1949); and Utica (1895–1943). A few commencing in comparatively recent years are complete: Jamestown (1919–); White Plains (1917–); and Yonkers (1907–11, 1935–).

NEW YORK CITY

A rich and varied body of literature in the general collections of the Research Libraries documents the local history of New York City from the earliest explorations and settlement. The collections widen in scope to trace political, social, and financial aspects from the colonial period to the present. In view of the city's impact upon state and national events, the materials considered in this section of the *Guide* are limited insofar as possible to those which have as the dominant feature the history of New York City proper.

As in the case with other important collections, local history is not completely covered by any single library division. Materials of social history conventionally categorized as local history are administered by the Local History and Genealogy Division; such materials relating to New York City constitute one of the richest collections in the division. Scarce and valuable works are kept in the Rare Book Division, manuscripts in the Manuscripts and Archives Division, and municipal publications, excepting those in the Rare Book Division and other special subject classes, in the Economic and Public Affairs Division. These are supplemented by important groups of prints, maps, photographs, and ephemera.

Although many subject classes in the library contribute valuable materials for the study of New York City history, only a few are mentioned here: biography, with large holdings documenting the lives of New York City residents; technology, with specialized material on the city's mechanical development (such as that documenting the subway and elevated railway, represented by holdings of the Parsons collection); and medicine, with a wealth of records of hospitals and similar institutions. Under the category of religion, church records and similar materials of local import are retained in the Local History and Genealogy Division by virtue of their great historical interest; church history, however, remains in the general collections.

Pictorial Material: Abundant pictorial materials of New York City and its inhabitants from the earliest periods are held in the library. Visual studies of New York City in the Local History and Genealogy Division fill 40 cabinet drawers; a card index arranged by the names of buildings is maintained. Another file contains photographs documenting social conditions from 1905 to 1939. A collection of approximately 15,000 negatives made by the Tenement House Department of New York City dates from 1903 through the 1930s. These appear to have been taken during inspection tours and record tenement conditions in close detail. Floor plans, street views of tenements, apartment buildings, and stores in many areas of the city are included. Most of the negatives are 5-by-7-inch glass plates; a calendar is in preparation.

The American History Division has extensive stereopticon views relating to the city. The Picture Collection of the Branch Libraries has a substantially complete collection of prints made from the original negatives of the Federal Art Project, "Changing New York." The Eno collection of New York City views and the Phelps Stokes collection of American historical prints administered by the Prints Division provide a wealth of illustrative material. The Phelps Stokes collection contains the earliest view of New York (the Hartgers view of New Amsterdam), dating from about 1626 to 1628.

Manuscripts: The manuscript collections noted in the preceding section on New York State history contain much material specifically related to New York City. On deposit from the Corporation of the City of New York since 1899, the Dongan Charter (dated April 27, 1686) is the first of a succession of charters which affirmed the right of the Corporation of the City to administer municipal government. The library attempts to secure representative records of organizations such as business enterprises, city societies, and government agencies. Important business papers include the Constable-Pierrepont collection, composed of the records of James Constable, a merchant of the city from 1799 to 1807, and those of Hezekiah Beers Pierrepont, merchant, distiller, and landowner for the period from 1793 to 1838. Banking in the city is covered by the records of Brown Brothers and Company and those of Brown, Shipley and Company, bankers in New York and London during the period between 1825 and 1889.[20] The extensive papers of Moses Taylor, an important New York merchant of the nineteenth century, reflect the business life of the city during that period.[21]

Business records which are added to the collections usually constitute a sample, covering activities and interests already represented. The Macmillan archives, including 119 correspondence copy-books and some 16,000 letters from Macmillan authors during the first half of the twentieth century, augment the library's extensive literary holdings. The papers of New York Typographical Union No. 6 for the period 1870–1917 strengthen the resources relating to printing technology, the printing industry, trade unionism, and economics. There are also the extensive records of the New York World's Fairs of 1939/40 and 1964/65, the latter not yet available to the public.

20. See Victor Hugo Paltsits, "Business Records of Brown Brothers & Co., New York—1825–1880," *BNYPL* 40 (1936): 495–98.

21. See Wilmer R. Leech, "The Moses Taylor Papers," *BNYPL* 35 (1931): 259–61.

54

LOCAL HISTORY AND GENEALOGY DIVISION
AND GENERAL GENEALOGY AND
HERALDRY RESOURCES

The Local History and Genealogy Division administers the collection of materials on genealogy, heraldry, flags, names, and the local history of the United States, Great Britain, and Ireland at the town and county level. Genealogical and heraldic resources consist of more than 39,000 volumes. There are 19,000 volumes of the local history of Great Britain and Ireland and about 27,000 volumes dealing with the local history of the United States. Supplementary materials in non-Roman alphabets are held in the Slavonic, Jewish, and Oriental Divisions. A large number of scrapbooks, clippings, and manuscripts, including much fugitive and privately printed material, are in the division, with a large number of local history pamphlets of an ephemeral nature in the "n.c." classification (material retained but not cataloged). Resources for the study of local history are discussed fully in the sections on American history and the history of Great Britain.

The acquisition policy for genealogy is generally comprehensive for the United States and strongly representative for Great Britain and Ireland. The collecting policy is representative or selective for most other countries, with the exception of collective genealogies, which are acquired comprehensively for all areas. Bibliography, history, periodicals, and regional works on heraldry are also collected comprehensively, as are works on flags. Local history of the United States, Great Britain, and Ireland is collected comprehensively.

Major works of genealogical reference for all nationalities are represented in the collections, but the most extensive holdings relate to the United States, Great Britain, and Ireland. Among the holdings are British parish registers, and an inclusive group of British and American periodicals of genealogical associations, local history societies, and patriotic organizations, together with serials devoted to heraldry, individual American cities, British antiquities, and similar topics. In 1969, 791 serial publications were currently received in the division in the fields of genealogy, heraldry, and local history of the United States, Great Britain, and Ireland; 670 coming from the United States and 121 from other countries. Of the latter number, 28 were German publications and 42 were publications from Great Britain and Ireland. This figure does not include the numerous other periodicals and serials partially pertaining to genealogy and local history received by other divisions of the Research Libraries.

An important body of material supplementing the periodical resources in the Local History and Genealogy Division is found in the state historical periodicals and publications administered by the American History Division. Local histories of Canada, the West Indies, Mexico, and Central and South America are part of the American History Division's collection. Local histories of other countries of the world are administered by the General Research and Humanities Division.

Since genealogy is a field requiring specialized reference background and techniques, questions on this subject are usually referred to the Local History and Genealogy Division regardless of the dispersion of resources.

Published in 1974 were *A Dictionary Catalog of the Local History and Genealogy Division* (G. K. Hall, 18 volumes) and *United States Local History Catalog* (2 volumes).

A perhaps unique collection of anniversary and special issues of local United States newspapers is available on microfilm. These special issues are cataloged under the name of the locality, and are also entered under the title "Collection of newspapers relating to centennial celebrations and histories of U.S. localities."

Scrapbooks and vertical files include views of American towns and cities, newspaper articles on individual families, historical facts about New York City, etc.

The Local History and Genealogy Division contains pictorial material on United States National Parks in its archives of photographs, stereopticon views, and scrapbooks, and also regularly receives ephemeral material which is stored in vertical files. Ephemera from state parks in the United States is also available, although on a more limited basis. As a matter of course commercially published materials augment this ephemera on state and national parks. The famous natural spectacle of Niagara Falls may be cited as an example: book materials extend from a first mention of the falls in Louis Hennepin's *Nouvelle Decouverte* (1697) to an interesting collection of approximately seventy cataloged guide books dated from 1834 to 1924, along with items such as James Knox Liston's *Niagara Falls: A Poem* (1843).

Holdings of local New York area newspapers include complete runs of the *Villager* and the *Village Voice*, but only a selective group of other titles; when particular local newspapers become important as historical sources there is an attempt to complete the run.

Catalog cards for books in the Local History and Genealogy Division appear in both the division catalog and the Public Catalog; however, cards for vertical file materials and certain analytic entries are not represented in the Public Catalog. Entries for material covering such subjects as bridges, hotels, restaurants, etc. are arranged geographically in the division catalog (for example, "New York (City)—Bridges"), while they are arranged in the Public Catalog only by subject with a geographical subdivision ("Bridges—U.S.—N.Y.—New York").

SPECIAL INDEXES AND FILES

CARD FILES

International Biographical Index to Scientists and Aviators

Before 1967 this card index, arranged alphabetically by name, was maintained in the Science and Technology Division (inactive, 58 card drawers; 70,000 references). Entries refer generally to biographical sketches and obituary notices, and similar short pieces on scientists and aviators in periodicals and publications of learned societies shelved in the Research Libraries.

Coat of Arms Index

This alphabetical index arranged by surnames refers to coats of arms in books located, for the most part, in the Local History and Genealogy Division; one tray indexes the public arms of nations, royal families, educational institutions, and other organizations (21 card drawers).

Index to Probate Notices

This file provides information on the dates of death and the probate notices of New Yorkers (Dea-Z only), primarily drawn from newspaper accounts ca. 1916–27 (inactive, 8 card drawers).

New York City Views

Arranged by subject groups (such as hotels, museums, parks, theatres), this index refers for the most part to books in the Local History and Genealogy Division (10 card drawers).

"Let's Exchange" File

This file provides information on genealogies in preparation by users of the Local History and Genealogy Division, and permits users to exchange information with other family historians (500 cards).

VERTICAL FILES

Genealogy Vertical File

This file, arranged by family name, has uncataloged family genealogical data and other ephemera in the form of letters and jottings; most of the material refers to American families (10 file trays).

New York City Views

A file of mounted photographs of views of the five boroughs of New York City since the late nineteenth century, but taken for the most part in the 1920s and 1930s (49 file trays). Many of the photographs were taken by Percy L. Sperr. On the reverse of each photograph is an identification of the view, the date it was taken (when known), the name of the photographer, and sometimes a notation to indicate whether reproduction is permitted. The file is arranged alphabetically by street or place name or numerically by street and avenue; there is a card index arranged alphabetically by name of building and subject.

A separate file contains 443 photographs taken by Lewis Wickes Hine documenting social conditions primarily in New York City from 1905 to 1939. A calendar of the file is held at the desk. The Eugene L. Armbruster collection of 14,000 photographs, purchased in 1934, records buildings and their surroundings in Long Island during the period 1890–1930. An equally exceptional collection of about 300 photographs of Long Island taken by Dr. Daniel Berry Austin depicts Dutch Colonial homesteads and other historic sites from about 1899 to 1913. Flatbush, New Utrecht, and Port Washington are particularly well represented in this photographic record of structures which have almost all disappeared. Included with the collection are photographs of Austin's trip to the far West. Thousands of contemporary postcard views of New York City are arranged by subject.

New York City Vertical File

A mounted clipping file of articles from newspapers and magazines arranged by subject (apartment houses, parks, population, etc.) (18 file boxes).

Public Symbols and Personal Arms File

The file consists of 26 file boxes containing pictorial representations of public symbols of the world, including flags, coats-of-arms, and other emblems that symbolize a geographic location, city, state, or county; the material is arranged in alphabetical order by location. An additional 21 file boxes contain representations of personal arms in folders arranged by surname (47 file boxes).

In addition to special indexes and files, the Local History and Genealogy Division has 61 scrapbooks, of which 3 volumes relate to families, 1 to flags, 1 to royalty, and 56 to views of New York City and other localities in the United States.

GENEALOGY RESOURCES

The 39,000 volumes of genealogy include materials on heraldry, as well as vital records and city directories. Bibliographies, indexes, and general reference works for all nationalities are present, with particularly rich collections of individual and collective English and American genealogical works. European resources are strongest in collective genealogies, although individual genealogies for prominent continental families are included. Genealogical textbooks, guidebooks, manuals, and books of popular instruction are an outstanding feature of the resources. Numerous dictionaries in English and the major Western European languages deal with the origin and meaning of given names and surnames.[1]

The collection is strong in volumes on the peerage and royal lineages; there is an excellent run of the *Almanach de Gotha* from 1777. Other Gotha publications are well represented, as are *Burke's Peerage*, *Burke's Landed Gentry*, and G. E. Cokayne's *Complete Peerage* and similar works relating to European nobility. There is an excellent historical collection of publications, yearbooks, and proceedings of American patriotic societies such as the Sons of the Revolution, Daughters of the American Revolution, and

---

1. See Elsdon C. Smith, "Personal Names; An Annotated Bibliography," *BNYPL* 54 (1950): 315–32 et seq. Published separately by the library, 1952; reprinted by Gale Research Co., 1965.

others. The Local History and Genealogy Division has been a depository since 1961 for materials from the New York State Daughters of the American Revolution concerning cemetery, town, and family records, a collection which in 1969 consisted of more than 450 typescript volumes.

Among significant library publications in the field of genealogy are Harold Lancour, *A Bibliography of Ship Passenger Lists, 1538–1825* (1937); revised and enlarged by Richard J. Wolfe, with a list of passenger arrival records in the National Archives by Frank E. Bridgers (1963; third edition, second, corrected printing, 1966); George F. Black, *The Surnames of Scotland; Their Origin, Meaning, and History* (1946; reprinted 1962 and 1971); and Lester J. Cappon, *American Genealogical Periodicals; a Bibliography with a Chronological Finding-List* (1962; second printing, with geographical finding-list, 1964).

NOTABLE ACCESSIONS

The strength of the collections is based upon important gifts which have come to the Research Libraries over the years in addition to their continuing purchases. In 1896 the purchase of the W. P. Robinson collection of American town and family histories (3,221 volumes and 921 pamphlets) formed one of the cornerstones of the holdings. By 1900 a separate catalog for materials on local history and genealogy was located in the Lenox Library, and the books were shelved in a separate area. The Cleveland Dodge gift of some 400 British genealogies and town and county histories came in 1909. In 1916 the widow of Professor Frank Dempster Sherman gave a large collection of materials relating to the Sherman genealogies.[2] The John Malcolm Bullock gift of a collection relating to Scottish genealogy and local history was added in 1920. In the early 1950s the Research Libraries purchased the Washburn collection consisting of the office files of Mabel R. T. Washburn and the National Historical Society, Inc. The material includes many unpublished genealogies. In 1958 the most extensive genealogy devoted to one family, that of the Palmers in the United States, was deposited by Nellie Morse Palmer, who had assisted her husband Horace Wilbur Palmer in the preparation of this work in 17 bound volumes totaling 8,220 pages.

RARE BOOKS AND MANUSCRIPTS

Among rare early genealogies in the Rare Book Division is the *Memoirs of Capt. Roger Clap* (1731), which contains a short account of the author and his family, qualifying it as the first printed American genealogy. Another early American work is *A Genealogy of the Family of Mr. Samuel Stebbins*, by Luke Stebbins, (1771).

A body of material in the Manuscripts and Archives Division relates to the American Loyalists during the period of the Revolution. Most important of the items are 60 volumes of transcripts of the original manuscripts, books, and papers of the Commission of Enquiry into the Losses and Services of the American Loyalists (1783–90) preserved with the Audit Office Records in the Public Record Office of England. A microfilm copy is available for public use. The

George H. Budke papers in the division contain early records of the history of Rockland and Orange Counties, New York, and the adjoining Bergen County, New Jersey, including much genealogical material.

Typescripts of tombstone inscriptions, indexes of wills, lists of church members, records of marriages, and similar unpublished materials in the Local History and Genealogy Division form a primary source of genealogical information. For example, Gertrude A. Barber's compilations and indexes of New York State records are listed on more than 100 cards in the division catalog. Additional transcripts are the work of Kenneth E. Hasbrouck working in New York State, and Francis F. Spies working in Vermont, New York, Connecticut, and New Jersey, as well as the aforementioned New York State DAR collections.

VITAL RECORDS

Every effort is made to collect the printed or typescript indexes to vital records pertaining to births, marriages, and deaths in the various states of the United States. A printed series worthy of special mention is the index to vital records of New York City, issued by the city, which commenced in 1888. The library receives these indexes with the understanding that the volumes covering births and deaths will be used only for historical and genealogical purposes. The records of marriages, which included only the name of the groom, is no longer published; the last volume was for 1936. Various vital records for the period 1795–1866 are available in the Municipal Archives and Records Center, which was formerly a part of the New York Public Library.

CITY DIRECTORIES

The collection of United States city directories through 1869 numbers approximately 1,300 and is of exceptional strength and completeness. Films of the New York City directories are available for public use. A good collection of city directories for the period after 1870 is kept in the Research Libraries Annex at 521 West 43rd Street. The General Research and Humanities Division administers a representative group of current United States city directories, which are held in the Main Reading Room.

HERALDRY RESOURCES

The collection of approximately 1,400 volumes, together with scrapbooks, correspondence, and other material, form very strong resources in this area. Major works on heraldry are supplemented by materials on the related subjects of flags, national and royal coats-of-arms, city seals, college seals and colors, and the like. The card catalog in the Local History and Genealogy Division shows more than 2,600 entries for heraldry with a great number of index entries for articles in periodicals and journals; Great Britain and Ireland are the best represented with more than 550 entries. The Slavonic Division catalog holds an additional 120 cards representing items in the Cyrillic alphabet.

The collection is strong in older works as well as in current materials. There are a number of the standard works of the sixteenth and seventeenth centuries in early editions in the Rare Book Division, including the works of John Guillim, Nicholas Upton, and others. Published informa-

2. See *BNYPL* 20 (1916): 843.

tion on current and popular phases of the subject is supplemented by a number of files and special collections. Additional pictorial representations of coats of arms are found in the Spencer Collection's rich holdings of festival books, and books on tournaments; the Spencer Collection also holds European manuscript patents of nobility, carta executoria, and the like. The Mortimer and Anna Neinken collection of some 14,000 antique seals housed in the Manuscripts and Archives Division contains wax impressions of coats of arms and crests of the noble and royal houses of Europe, as well as examples of ecclesiastical seals, guild and city seals, and the like.[3]

---

3. See Gerald D. McDonald, "The Mortimer and Anna Neinken Collection of Antique Seals," *BNYPL* 58 (1954): 159–61.

Entries for material on flags total about 660 cards in the Local History and Genealogy Division catalog. The range of coverage is world-wide in the Roman alphabet. Some rarities in the Spencer Collection include a seventeenth-century Japanese "Banners of the Daimyo Families" and two Japanese printed books, one on flags and the other on ships' flags of the world; both date from the mid-nineteenth century. In 1942, Major Chandler Davis gave a most important collection of books, pamphlets, correspondence, and other materials on flags from the library of the late Gherardi Davis. The following year Major Davis added a further group of materials containing in part original colored drawings and photographs of regimental colors of the German and Russian armies; the manuscripts, drawings, and photographs are in the Manuscripts and Archives Division.

55

BIOGRAPHY AND PORTRAITS

BIOGRAPHY

Biography is collected comprehensively by the Research Libraries, with American biography forming one of the largest groups within this subject collection of 83,000 volumes. The preponderance of materials consists of individual biographies, as the following indicates:

Biographical dictionaries and other reference works	7,500 volumes
Collective biography	11,000
Individual biography	64,500

Biographies of subject interest are generally located with the literature pertaining to that subject, biographies of artists, for example, being maintained by the Art and Architecture Division, and those of musicians by the Music Division. Biographical information concerning a figure of the stature of Sarah Bernhardt is thus available in the General Research and Humanities Division, and further specialized materials related to her life and career are administered by the Theatre Collection of the Performing Arts Research Center.

The heavy use of biographical materials by readers and staff has resulted in the transferral of many volumes from the general collections to places of convenient use. This plan of special location applies particularly to biographical dictionaries and collective biographies. Working collections are located at the Information Desk in Room 315, at the Main Reading Room Desk, on the open shelves of the Main Reading Room, and in Preparation Services (the latter intended primarily for staff use, although available to the public). In the case of annuals and other compilations which appear at intervals, a progressive arrangement often locates the most recent volume on the open shelves; the next most recent volume, in one of the working collections; and earlier volumes not needed elsewhere, in the general collections. Locations are indicated on the catalog cards.

Other valuable sources of biographical information include encyclopedias, particularly those published abroad (a reference collection is located in the Main Reading Room), local history and genealogy, and the publications of institutions and organizations. An example of the latter type of material is found in the working collection of alumni registers kept in Preparation Services. The resources of the Manuscripts and Archives Division are notable for biographical materials, particularly for American historical, literary, business, and scientific figures.

Biographical materials in scholarly periodicals are extensively indexed by individual card entries in the Public Catalog. Special attention is given to indexing material related to figures for whom other biographical information is lacking. The catalogs of some of the divisions of the Research Libraries contain references (mainly to periodical articles) which are not included in the Public Catalog. This is particularly true in the case of the catalogs of the Art and Architecture Division, and the Music Division and the Theatre and Dance Collections at the Performing Arts Research Center. Many divisions maintain files of biographical information. For example, much elusive biographical information will be found in the extensive clipping file of the Schomburg Center for Research in Black Culture.

SPECIAL INDEXES AND FILES

Art and Architecture Division

A general clipping file preserves material relating to artists, including biographies, portraits, and the like.

Dance Collection

The clipping file in the collection contains biographical information on dancers supplemented by scrapbooks and clippings given by Ruth St.

Denis, Ted Shawn, Doris Humphrey, Charles Weidman, and others.

Economic and Public Affairs Division

A general clipping file contains biographical material relating to government officials and important financial and commercial figures. The scope and content of the file is determined by current interests, and ephemeral material is discarded when no longer pertinent.

General Research and Humanities Division

A card file arranged by subject and by occupation locates books in the Research Libraries containing current biographical sketches.

Local History and Genealogy Division

A vertical file is arranged by name of family (primarily American, although including other nationalities). All types of uncataloged materials are contained in the files, such as clippings, typescripts, and other ephemera. Supplementing the vertical file are a variety of scrapbooks for prominent American families, such as the Carnegies, Roosevelts, and Whitneys.

Another inactive card file is an index to probate notices giving details clipped primarily from notices in the *New York Times*. The file concentrates upon the 1920s and lacks the letters A-C. There is also a large but inactive international biographical index to scientists and aviators in the Local History and Genealogy Division (discussed in chapter 54).

Music Division

A biographical file consists of entries containing a great miscellany of biographical information about musicians and their work. A portrait index refers to portraits in many sources in the Music Division and in other locations of the Research Libraries. A clipping file in the division holds material arranged by composer's or performer's name, and broadly by subject area.

Prints Division

The division maintains a file of clippings, pamphlets, catalogs, and other material relating to print makers. The names of the persons represented are listed in the catalog of the division.

Theatre Collection

An extensive vertical file consists of clippings on theatrical figures, including motion picture, television, radio, and circus personalities. Two notable scrapbook collections, the Robinson Locke collection of dramatic scrapbooks, and the David Belasco collection of typescripts, photographs, original designs, and scrapbooks, supplement the vertical file.

RESOURCES

Biographical Dictionaries and Collective Biographies

The collections of retrospective biographical works of this nature are substantial, with many of the standard sets such as *Dictionary of National Biography, Dictionary of American Biogra-*

phy, and *Allgemeine deutsche Biographie* available in the reference collection of the Main Reading Room. Contemporary biographical collections of the "who's who" nature are also well represented, with nearly complete holdings of the publications of the United States, Canada, and Western European countries. For other areas, in particular South America, many items are far from current, although they appear to represent the latest compilations available. The General Research and Humanities Division endeavors to maintain current files despite erratic publishing.

Associated with these contemporary biographical publications are the specialized, professional, or trade "who's whos." The Research Libraries collect these publications extensively for the United States, Great Britain, and Canada, attempting to obtain material for other countries when possible. The Science and Technology Research Center acquires the membership directories of the larger scientific and engineering societies. Other biographical information is found in the very extensive holdings of United States county histories in the Local History and Genealogy Division. Biographical dictionaries of the lives of prominent men of the various states are a feature of the American History Division. Biographical data about prominent Europeans is often found in the necrologies of local and national learned society publications. Significant items are indexed in the Public Catalog.

Individual Biographies

The strong resources in this area include several outstanding collections: biography of women has been given special attention; the naval history section includes many biographies of naval officers; Negro biography is found both in the Research Libraries' general holdings and in those of the Schomburg Center; individual as well as collective biographies of New York men and women are well represented in the American History and the Local History and Genealogy Divisions.

First and early editions of the noted biographies in the English language such as Thomas Fuller's *History of the Worthies of England*, Johnson's *Lives of the Poets*, Boswell's *Life of Samuel Johnson*, and Lytton Strachey's *Eminent Victorians* are found in the Rare Book Division and the Berg Collection.

The extensive collection of shorthand periodicals in the Research Libraries has been indexed for biographical materials up to the date of the printed catalog of the collection (1935).[1] There are, in addition, collective biographies for shorthand reporters, stenographers, and court reporters.

A number of scrapbooks containing newspaper and magazine clippings, postcards, and the like, supplement the books in the general collections. Most of the figures represented are North American; the most extensive holdings are those for Abraham Lincoln and Elihu Root.

Jewish Division: Some 2,000 volumes in the resources of the Jewish Division include virtually all biographies written in Hebrew or Yiddish and

---

1. Karl Brown and Daniel C. Haskell, "Shorthand Books in The New York Public Library," *BNYPL* 36 (1932): 243–49 et seq. Published separately, with corrections and additions, by the library, 1935; and reprinted by the library and Arno Press in 1971.

certain biographies relating specifically to the Jews. Certain studies of subject importance are in the relevant divisions; for example, biographies of Jews notable in the arts are located in the Art and Architecture Division, those of scientific figures in the Science and Technology Research Center.

Oriental Division: The Oriental Division collects representatively all new biographical material that is available through purchase, exchange, or gift. The division acquires materials published either in Oriental or Western languages in all areas of Asia and those areas of Africa for which the division customarily collects. The strongest section, books in Arabic and in translation on Arabic subjects, is covered by more than 500 entries in the divisional catalog.

Slavonic Division: The holdings of more than 3,000 biographical volumes are principally in the Cyrillic alphabet and relate to Russian subjects. The division collects books comprehensively, but collects the great number of biographical pamphlets published in Eastern European countries on a representative basis. Russian royal biographies are a feature of the collection, with important items relating to Peter the Great and Catherine II.

Manuscripts

Two extensive collections of manuscripts are of note for biographical studies. The rich holdings of the Manuscripts and Archives Division include materials relating to nearly all fields, primarily from the United States and particularly from the state of New York, and the holdings of the Berg Collection concentrate on the fields of English and American literature. Information on manuscript collections useful for biographical purposes is available in the sections devoted to the Berg Collection in "General Literature," chapter 20, "American Literature," chapter 23, and "English Literature," chapter 24 of this *Guide.*

Manuscripts and Archives Division: The personalities, opinions, and careers of figures as diverse as Washington Irving and William Cullen Bryant, Norman Thomas and H. L. Mencken, are documented by major collections. Diaries and correspondence are held in abundance, along with secondary biographical aids such as business papers.

One of the major series in the Manuscripts and Archives Division is classified as Personal Miscellaneous Papers, in which residents of New York State predominate. The chronological range extends from the eighteenth century; earlier materials, while present, are generally single items rather than archival groups.

Most collections contain biographical materials concerning the lives of associates and contemporaries of the central figure; typical among such collections are the papers of Horace Greeley, Samuel J. Tilden, Noah Webster, John Quinn, and Carl Van Vechten. Other archives such as the Hardwicke collection range from papers relating to Elizabeth I and James I through the personal and official papers of the eighteenth-century British diplomat Sir Luke Schaub. The holdings of the Manuscripts and Archives Division are strengthened by extensive series. Editorial correspondence files of the *Century Magazine* and the Macmillan Company are essential to biographers of nineteenth- and twentieth-century literary figures; the papers of Evert A. and George L. Duyckinck contain letters of Melville, Poe, and other figures of the first half of

the nineteenth century. The Alfred W. Anthony and DeCoursey Fales collections hold much material of biographical importance. The division maintains alphabetical listings of these and similar collections.

PORTRAITS

GENERAL COLLECTIONS

Collections of portraits in book form are classified with materials in the general collections. Volumes of portraits with specific subject interest, for instance those which are principally biographical, are placed in the appropriate subject division. Extra-illustrated books containing portraits are found in the Rare Book Division and in rich holdings in the general collections, where there are, for example, numerous editions of Boswell's *Life of Samuel Johnson* with inserted views and portraits. These portraits may be located through indexes in the Prints Division; individual cards are not filed in the Public Catalog. The *A.L.A. Portrait Index* is found in nearly all divisions having requests for portraits, and has in many cases been annotated with the library's class marks for indexed materials.

ENGRAVED AND PHOTOGRAPHIC PORTRAITS

Holdings of individual portraits in the Research Libraries fall into the two categories of engraved portraits, dating from the fifteenth through the mid-nineteenth centuries, and portraits dating from the invention of photography. Engraved portraits, drawings, and caricatures are found in the Prints Division, with the exception of those for theatre personalities (in the Theatre Collection), dance personalities (in the Dance Collection), and musicians (in the Special Collections Reading Room of the Music Division). The holdings of engraved portraits are generally limited to public personalities, whether celebrated or notorious. There are no general collections of photographic portraits in the Research Libraries, but only scattered specialized collections in the Prints Division and the vertical files of the subject divisions. The vast portrait resources of the Picture Collection of the Branch Libraries are discussed below.

There are important groups of portraits in the special collections and subject divisions of the Research Libraries. Early gifts contributed extensively to the present resources; this is particularly true of the Lenox, Duyckinck, Bancroft, Emmet, and Tilden collections. The Tilden collection is rich in the works of Birch, Lodge, and Caulfield, with an extraordinary group of Gillray's caricatures covering the entire period of the artist's work, from 1777 to 1811. The Beverly Chew collection of literary portraits in the Prints Division contains superb groups of portraits of John Milton and Alexander Pope.[2] The Charles Williston McAlpin collection of George Washington portraits and other materials was a gift in 1942. There is a fine group of Benjamin Franklin portraits in the Prints Division. Bound compilations in the general collections include portraits of Napoleon and the Medici family.

North American Indian portraits form another strong group of materials located in the American

2. See Ruth Shepard Granniss, "The Beverly Chew Collection of Milton Portraits," *BNYPL* 30 (1926): 3–6.

History Division, the Prints Division, and the Rare Book Division. Among the rarer items are a set of John Simon's mezzotints after Verelst's paintings of the four Indian chiefs who visited London in the reign of Queen Anne. In the Rare Book Division are published examples of the Indian portraits of George Catlin, as well as his *Souvenir of N. American Indians* (1850), a three-volume collection of original pencil drawings. The Rare Book Division also has the fine series of portraits in several editions of Thomas L. McKenney's *History of the Indian Tribes of North America* (1836–70) and in Edward S. Curtis's *The North American Indian* (1907–30), illustrated with more than 2,000 photographic plates.

The Carl Van Vechten gift to the Research Libraries included photographic portraits divided by subject area between the Theatre, Dance, and Berg Collections and the Manuscripts and Archives Division. The literary portraits in the Berg Collection contain an unusual group of more than 180 studies of Gertrude Stein. More than 150 additional photographs depict scenes from plays by Gertrude Stein.

Prints Division

The most accessible of the uncataloged portraits in the Research Libraries are contained in more than 200 boxes in the Prints Division; these are arranged alphabetically by sitter. In addition, indexes and reference materials in the Prints Division may be used to locate portraits elsewhere in the general collections.

There are two card indexes for pictorial material including cataloged portraits. The subject index to original single portraits in the Print Room locates individual portrait prints including those bound or incorporated in books. The arrangement is alphabetical by sitter. The subject index to original portrait prints shelved elsewhere in the library locates portraits in selected books which are shelved in locations other than the Prints Division. This index refers to portraits in extra-illustrated books in the Rare Book Division and in books in the Emmet collection of the Manuscripts and Archives Division. Both indexes are supplementary to the *A.L.A. Portrait Index* and other standard print bibliographies such as Hans Wolfgang Singer's *Allgemeiner Bildniskatalog* and the British Museum *Catalogue of Engraved British Portraits*, which are annotated to show divisional holdings.

Science and Technology Research Center

The Science and Technology Research Center has maintained a card index to books and periodical articles about ships, which includes portrait material. This alphabetical file indexes names of ships, uniforms worn on various ships, and portraits of ships' captains; it covers materials in the Science and Technology Research Center and elsewhere in the Research Libraries. The file was kept active until the 1940s, and since that time has been enlarged on a selective and irregular basis.

Dance Collection

Portraits and other iconography are of primary importance in documenting the history of the dance. Representations of dancers, either portraits or action studies, are a strong feature of the Dance Collection. The largest group of portrait material consists of photographs. American dancers are well represented through the gifts of collections on Isadora Duncan, Ted Shawn and Ruth St. Denis, Doris Humphrey, Charles Weidman, Martha Graham, and others. The magnificent group of 500 photographs of Waslaw Nijinsky includes many of the dancers who performed with him. Other gifts document the careers of the ballerinas Alicia Markova and Galina Ulanova. The Cia Fornaroli collection is particularly rich in prints of Fanny Cerito, Marie Taglioni, and other nineteenth-century dancers.

The large vertical file in the collection contains much portrait material in halftone illustrations, supplemented by the many scrapbooks and clipping files which have come to the collection as gifts. The computer-generated book catalog of the collection (see page 151) incorporates a large number of cross-references of assistance in locating portraits.

Music Division

There is an unusually strong collection of portraits in the Special Collections Reading Room of the Music Division. The entire group numbers some 20,000 pieces and includes engravings, lithographs, water colors, tracings, photographs, and halftones; it is international in scope and features portraits of violinists, opera singers, and a number of composers and performers of the seventeenth and eighteenth centuries in contemporary prints. The Muller portrait collection includes a group of portraits of Nicolò Paganini which are of great interest.[3]

Two card files in the Special Collections Reading Room involve portraits. The General Iconography File is an alphabetical index by subject of prints, photographs, and other pictorial material in the Reading Room. The Muller Portrait Index provides reference to the Joseph Muller collection of musicians' portraits, giving subject, birth and death dates, engraver's name, and similar information. A Portrait Index refers to portraits in many sources both in the Music Division and in other parts of the library. The cards are arranged alphabetically by name of the subject of the portrait. This is a source file which does not duplicate the General Iconography File of the Special Collections Reading Room.

Theatre Collection

The majority of theatrical portraits currently acquired are maintained in files arranged alphabetically by the name of actor, theatre, or production, with some cross-referencing; nonbook material pertaining to the stage or motion pictures often contains portraits. All such materials in the Theatre Collection are cataloged by name of the performer, with references to the productions for which there are portraits available. The clipping files of the Theatre Collection also contain many portraits.

A number of the special collections of the Theatre Collection have strong portrait holdings. The Hiram Stead collection includes a vast file of portraits from the British theatre between 1672 and 1932. The Robinson Locke collection of drama scrapbooks documents the American stage

---

3. See Albert Mell, "Paganiniana in the Muller Collection of The New York Public Library," *The Musical Quarterly* 39 (January 1953): 1–25.

from 1870 to 1920 and is arranged by actor rather than production; included are large photographs with autographs of theatrical personalities such as Maude Adams, Lillian Russell, and Geraldine Farrar.

The Universal Pictures gift of its books of movie stills, which began in 1935, covers almost all the films made since the beginning of that studio. An excellent collection of stills from the earliest period of motion pictures documents the productions of German, Russian, and American producers; this was formed by the Picture Collection of the Branch Libraries and subsequently transferred to the Theatre Collection. A Personalities index (for staff use) indicates the source of portraits of movie personalities by cross-references to the movies in which they appeared. The collection is organized generally on the principle of a newspaper morgue; although certain items are indexed for quick finding, the vast majority of material must be sought in the picture folders.

The Carl Van Vechten gift contains several hundred photographs of figures in the American theatre during the second quarter of the twentieth century. A notable special collection consists of photographs and negatives made by Mrs. Florence Vandamm of more than 1,200 stage productions between 1920 and 1962.

Picture Collection of the Branch Libraries

The holdings of this unit of the Branch Libraries in the Central Building include over 300,000 portraits from the sixteenth century to the present. All types of reproduction are found, from woodcuts, engravings, and lithographs to halftones and photographs. The materials have been extracted from books, journals, and periodicals; there are also separate prints and photographs. The collection is arranged in folders alphabetically by name of sitter. If the material has been clipped, the source is indicated by a symbol on the picture mounting. Readers may check out materials from this circulating collection (there is only limited public working space).

THE PURE AND APPLIED SCIENCES

56

SCIENCE AND TECHNOLOGY RESEARCH CENTER AND GENERAL SCIENCE RESOURCES

SCIENCE AND TECHNOLOGY RESEARCH CENTER

The Science and Technology Research Center maintains a collection somewhat in excess of 500,000 volumes in the pure and applied physical sciences and related technologies and industrial arts. Approximately one quarter of the holdings represent pure and applied physical sciences, and about three quarters technology. Even though the number of volumes is not in itself a measure of quality or completeness of coverage, it may be assumed that the 133,700 volumes in the library in the pure sciences alone would include a sizable proportion of the world's important literature in these areas. The technology collection is rich in older, as well as more modern, materials, and thus provides documentation for the history of the subject. The coverage is comprehensive from all countries and in all languages (including Oriental, Slavonic, and Hebrew, although publications in non-Roman alphabet, are at present housed in the Oriental, Slavonic, and Jewish Divisions, respectively).

Periodicals and government publications form the major portion of the Science and Technology Research Center's resources noted in the preceding paragraph. The center has access to files of periodicals such as the *Philosophical Transactions* of the Royal Society of London (1665–), and which include almost all of the relatively few European journals that commenced publication in the early 1700s. Holdings of the journals of general learned societies or national academies (many of which have scientific sections) also form a closely related and strong collection. Of the more than 4,000 periodical titles currently received in the center, 56 percent are in English with others in twenty languages including Afrikaans, Bulgarian, Czech, Danish, Dutch, Finnish, Fleming, French, German, Greek, Italian, Magyar, Norwegian, Polish, Portuguese, Roumanian, Spanish, Swedish, Russian, and Serbo-Croation. This does not take into account the fact that a growing number of scientific journals are polylingual, with many articles appearing in the native language of the contributor. Approximately 190 current scientific and technological periodical titles in the Cyrillic alphabet are in the Slavonic Division. Another 260 titles in Oriental languages are divided roughly as follows: Chinese (50 titles), Japanese (150 titles), Korean (50 titles), Taiwanese (10 titles). The Jewish Division houses similar materials in Hebrew.

The center attempts to obtain almost all the basic indexing and abstracting services in the fields of chemistry, physics, mathematics, geology, meteorology, the nuclear sciences, astronomy, engineering, and technology, along with the basic standard works in these fields. It holds indexing and abstracting services in the natural and medical sciences such as *Biological Abstracts* and *Index Medicus*. Readers thus are able to view a field of science as a whole when working in such disciplines as biochemistry, even if the works cited in the indexes and abstracts are not found in the Research Libraries, but must be sought in other libraries in the metropolitan area.

The center has substantially all directories, biographical dictionaries, and encyclopedias in scientific and industrial fields; it holds government documents in the fields of geology, mining, hydrology, and meteorology.[1] In addition, the center has special directories in such subject areas as ships and aviation, and works on the history of science and technology. Older and rare works in the sciences are usually kept in the Rare Book Division according to the normal practice of the Research Libraries; however, the Parsons collection in the Science and Technology Research Center contains many rare items which must be kept together as a provision of the bequest. There are also miscellaneous groups of materials consisting of pamphlets and brochures on many categories of the center's subject areas. In an uncataloged collection maintained at the Annex at 43rd Street are a number of pamphlets representing manufacturers' catalogs for scientific instruments, optical equipment, clocks and watches, chemical apparatus, laboratory apparatus, and the like, most of which are undated but apparently are of the late nineteenth and early twentieth centuries.

Especially strong are the collections in aeronautics (19,700 volumes); astronomy (21,200 volumes); biography, research, and history (24,000 volumes); chemical engineering (15,100

---

1. Only selected reports of the major technical report producing agencies of the United States federal government—the National Aeronautics and Space Administration (NASA), the Atomic Energy Commission (AEC), Armed Services Technical Information Agency (ASTIA), and the Office of Technical Services Publication Board (OTSPB)—are available.

volumes); chemistry (35,400 volumes); electrical and electronic engineering (32,800 volumes); general technology and manufacture (20,200 volumes); geology (32,200 volumes); mathematics (20,000 volumes); mechanical engineering (33,300 volumes); metals and metallurgy (15,100 volumes); mines and mining (13,400 volumes); and physics (30,200 volumes). Collections in textiles number approximately 2,000 volumes; and in naval science and ships 3,700 volumes. Automobiles and railroads each number over 1,500 volumes.[2]

Certain subject headings in the Science and Technology Research Center catalog group materials in chronological order as well as by author or title.

Among the many compilations produced by members of the staff of the Science and Technology Research Center are William B. Gamble's *History of Aeronautics; A Selected List of References to Material in The New York Public Library* (1938),[3] and Reginald R. Hawkins's *Scientific, Medical, and Technical Books Published in the United States of America 1930–1944* (1946). Currently compiled by the center's staff is *New Technical Books* (1915–), a selective annotated listing of new titles, most in the English language, submitted for monthly exhibit in the center.

Collecting Policy

The collecting policy is generally comprehensive in all disciplines with the exceptions noted below:

The center does not collect publications in the life or medical sciences, dentistry, or pharmacy. This does not apply to the interrelated life and physical sciences such as biochemistry or biophysics, which are collected on the same basis as the physical sciences. The Research Libraries hold only limited collections in the life sciences and, except for a very few standard or rare items, no volumes in the medical sciences other than material on the social and economic aspects of medicine administered by the General Research and Humanities Division. The policy of excluding or reducing holdings in these subject areas was predicated by the availability of adequate special collections in other libraries in New York City.

A strong collection of patents and trade marks, under the jurisdiction of the Science and Technology Research Center until 1962, is presently administered by the library's Annex Section at 43rd Street (see chapter 57 of this *Guide*).

The Science and Technology Research Center seldom collects standards and specifications; dissertations; trade literature as such; laboratory manuals; preprints; abstracting services on cards; engineering college student magazines; daily technical papers; popular scientific or technical periodicals; or house organs as such.

The center also does not collect cover-to-cover periodical translations,[4] although monographic translations are added to the collections if an edition is unobtainable in its original language.

---

2. The figures cited include monographs and bound volumes of periodicals.

3. Reprinted 1971 by the New York Public Library and Arno Press Inc.

4. The Mid-Manhattan Library of the Branch Libraries does collect such periodicals as *Soviet Mathematics.*

Historical Survey

The subject fields covered by the center have always been represented by strong collections. Unique stress was originally placed by the Astor Library on the applied or industrial arts; moreover, libraries were purchased in Europe in all the sciences, and some noteworthy private collections were added. The growth of the collections administered by the Science and Technology Research Center is indicated by the following:

1850	Astor Library	10,000 volumes
1912	New York Public Library	39,000
1921		139,606
1930		201,487
1941		378,000
1966		486,500

In 1934 the William Barclay Parsons collection came as the gift of Mrs. Parsons. The collection consists of 1,191 bound volumes, 27 pamphlets, 53 boxes of maps, and manuscripts which had been brought together by General Parsons. With the exception of the manuscripts, which are housed in the Manuscripts and Archives Division, the collection is maintained in the Science and Technology Research Center. Its major portions consist of "engineering classics" of the seventeenth and eighteenth centuries; materials on railroads and canals of the nineteenth and twentieth centuries; documents on military engineering, mainly of World War I; and manuscripts principally relating to Robert Fulton. There are also 4 incunabula in the collection: Euclid's *Elementa Géometriae* (1482), Valturio's *De l'arte militaire* (1483), Vitruvius' *De Architectura, Libri Decem* (1496), and Polydorus Vergilius' *De Inventoribus Rerum* (1499). Among other items are eighteenth-century sets of playing cards engraved with engineering and geometrical instruments; an extensive group of Bradshaw's maps, timetables, and railway guides of the first half of the nineteenth century; and materials documenting the early history of the railway in the United States and the subway and elevated railway in New York City. The World War I holdings include 21 boxes of English General Staff maps.[5]

The Walter Weichsel transfer collection was donated by Weichsel in 1968. Now consisting of 109 loose-leaf scrapbooks, it is a very fine collection of old bus and street car transfers, ferry and toll tickets, passes, railroad and boat tickets, National Park tickets, and the like, for the United States from 1898 onward. Included are 25 similar books with transportation tickets from 50 of the largest nations of the world. In most instances Weichsel has gathered complete sets of the transfer forms.

Special Indexes and Files

There are few active special indexes and files in the center. So many commercial printed indexes are available in the field that the staff of the center do not generally establish separate ones. Nevertheless a few such indexes remain from the considerable number that once were maintained; although not always kept up to date, these contain information not generally accessible elsewhere.

---

5. See "Catalogue of the William Barclay Parsons Collection," *BNYPL* 45 (1941): 95–108 et seq.

Clock-and-Watchmakers File

An alphabetical index to books about early timepieces and makers; it includes materials shelved in the Science and Technology Research Center and elsewhere in the Research Libraries (2 card drawers, inactive).

Directories File

An alphabetical index arranged by subject and then by country of directories available in the Research Libraries (4 card drawers, inactive). There is a notation of the years available, and often some indication of content or coverage.

Industrial Arts History

An index arranged alphabetically under subjects (such as bleaching, chewing gum, machinery, paper) for references to early industrial developments found in books and articles in the Research Libraries; the indexed material extends to 1940 (11 card drawers, inactive).

Mathematical Tables Index

A card index of mathematical tables which have appeared in books shelved in the center; the index is arranged alphabetically by subject (natural functions, solids, solutions, and the like) (2 card drawers, inactive).

Ships Index

An alphabetical index by name of ship (non-naval), uniforms worn on various ships, pictures of ships, portraits of captains, and the like (27 card drawers, active, limited). It indexes books and periodical articles in the Research Libraries and in the Picture Collection of the Branch Libraries. The cards also contain some descriptive detail. The file has been maintained on a very limited basis since the early 1960s.

SCIENCE RESOURCES

HISTORY OF SCIENCE

The collections are comprehensive for the history of science in general and also for the particular sciences, excepting the life sciences and medicine. The strong holdings of society publications from their beginnings in Europe are a significant feature. There are generally complete runs of such journals as the Royal Society of London *Philosophical Transactions* (1665–   ), the *Journal des Sçavans* (Amsterdam, 1665–1792), the Kungliga Svenska Vetenskapsakademien *Handlingar* (1739–   ), and the Hollandsche Maatschappij der Wetenschappen *Verhandelingen* (1754–93).

First and early editions of the great classics of science are especially well represented in mathematics, astronomy, and physics, with additional engineering rarities in the Parsons collection. Some medical and botanical classics are in the Rare Book Division, and also in the Arents Tobacco Collection.[6]

MICROSCOPY

This is a good working collection of 750 books, pamphlets, and periodicals; periodicals and society publications are a feature. The collection of nineteenth-century works is strong. Works of historical interest include Robert Hooke's *Micrographia* (1665), Theodor Balthasar's *Micrometria* (1710), and Henry Baker's frequently reprinted *The Microscope Made Easy* (1742).

MATHEMATICS

General Materials

This has always been an exceptional collection; it is especially strong in periodicals and society publications. The core of the present collection of 20,000 volumes and manuscripts consisted of the libraries of several celebrated mathematicians which Dr. Cogswell secured for the Astor Library in the 1850s; these include Halley's and Legendre's libraries, purchased by S. Ward and enriched by him. During Cogswell's visit to Europe in 1852/53 he also secured some 3,000 volumes from the libraries of Jacobi and of the two Heiligenstadts. The whole collection he evaluated as "entitled to be ranked with the first mathematical libraries abroad," with full collections of all published works of Euler, Gauss, Newton, Leibniz, the Bernouillis, Laplace, Delambre, Lacroix, Legendre, Jacobi, Adel, and others, all the mathematical journals then obtainable, and a very large number of mathematical dissertations and manuscripts.[7]

The collection of mathematical periodicals is outstanding. A check against "Most Cited Serials: Mathematics" in Brown's *Scientific Serials* reveals that out of the 99 titles listed, the Research Libraries lack only 5, and have full representation of the first 50 titles noted by Brown as usually more valuable than those lower on the list.[8] Most of the runs are complete, although some lack a few scattered volumes. An additional strength of the holdings lies in the substantially complete representation of earlier journals since, as Brown notes, mathematics is a comparatively stable science, and earlier journals are used to a greater extent than early publications in physics, chemistry, and physiology. About 46 percent of the mathematics periodicals are in the English language and 54 percent in other languages, mostly in German and French, with some in Italian, Russian, and Japanese. There are also full holdings of the major abstracting services in mathematics.

Rarities and Manuscripts

The library has a large number of first or early printed editions of the great mathematical authors, with Euclid's *Elementa Géometriae* (1482), John Napier's *Rabdologiae* (1617), Galileo's *Discorsi e Dimostrazioni Matematiche* (1683), and Newton's *Principia* (1687) among the first editions;[9] among early editions are Boethius' *De*

---

6. See Sarah A. Dickson, "Panacea or Precious Bane," *BNYPL* 57 (1953): 367 ff. Published separately by the library.

7. See Lydenberg, *History*, p. 28.

8. Charles Harvey Brown, *Scientific Serials* (Chicago: Association of Research Libraries, 1956), pp. 79–82.

9. One of the copies is the rare "Smith" imprint; another contains seven pages of manuscript notes bound in. See Henry P. Macomber, "A Census of the Owners of Copies of the 1687

Institutione Arithmetica (1492), Luca de Paccioli's *Summa de Arithmetica* (1494), Maurolico's "Works" (1566), Napier's *Mirifici Logarithmorum Canonis Constructio* (1619), Tycho Brahe's *De Disciplinis Mathematicis Oratio* (1621), Vossius' *De Quatuor Artibus Popularibus* (1650), Honorat de Meynier's *Paradoxes* (1652), Fermat's "Works" (1657), Wallis' "Works" (1657), Euler's *Tentamen Novae Theoriae Musicae* (1739), and Bernoulli's "Works" (1774). A number of rare colonial American arithmetics deserve mention: the earliest is William Bradford's *The Secretary's Guide* (1737), and the group includes an early Canadian French title, *Thèses de mathematiques qui seront soutenues au seminaires de Quebec* (1775).

There are a number of mathematical manuscripts in the Manuscripts and Archives Division which are of interest largely for their historical importance. These consist of such items as exercise books, problems in geometry, and algebra note books, the earliest of which dates from the late sixteenth century. The largest group of this material is in the papers of Philip Schuyler (1733–1804). Of greater significance perhaps are two manuscripts of Leonhard Euler: "Euler's Einleitung in die Analysis des Unendlichen" dated 1770; and "Anmerkungen und Erlaeuterungen zu Mechanica sive motus scientia."

ASTRONOMY

Strong holdings of journals and society publications are included in the fine collection of 21,200 volumes and manuscripts in this field. In Brown's "List of Most Frequently Cited Serials," the library lacks 7 out of 50 titles, with only 2 missing from the first half of the list.[10] There are complete runs of the most important serials such as *Astrophysical Journal* (1895–), *Astronomische Nachrichten* (1821–), *Royal Astronomical Society of London: Monthly Notices* (1821–), and others. Collections of observatory reports include mostly those of the nineteenth century and before, since the Science and Technology Research Center has not collected twentieth-century reports from seismological and geodetic observatories in depth. There is a good but not extensive collection of astronomical maps and charts, some of them in the Map Division. Ephemerides and nautical almanacs form a very extensive group of materials ranging from incunabula of Johannes Müller Regiomontanus and Abraham ben Samuel Zacuto through numerous sixteenth-century editions of Petrus Apianus to complete sets of the *Nautical Almanac* (1767–) and the *American Ephemeris and Nautical Almanac* (1855–). There are also many nautical almanacs from France, New Zealand, India, and other countries. Egyptian and Babylonian astronomy receive adequate treatment in the Oriental Division's holdings; many index entries in the division catalog refer to articles in learned society and journal publications. There are a number of interesting items in the division on Oriental astronomy, such as Gustaaf Schlegel's *Uranographie chinoise* (1875) and works by Léopold de Saussure.

Johannes de Sacro Bosco's *Sphaera Mundi* is of special interest to the Research Libraries: the Rare Book Division has approximately 117 editions in Latin or in French, German, Italian, and Spanish translations ranging from a copy dated 1472 through the seventeenth century. A fourteenth-century vellum manuscript of Sacro Bosco's "Opera Astronomica et Mathematica," in the Manuscripts and Archives Division contains illuminated capital letters and many astronomical diagrams.

Other than the Sacro Bosco holdings, mentioned above, the Research Libraries have an unusually good collection of titles published before 1700 and some manuscript rarities. Among the books are *De Cometis* (1474), the second edition of the first printed work on astronomy, Ptolemy's *Cosmographia* (1478), Peurbach's *Theoricae Novae Planetarum* (1482), Abraham ben Samuel Zacuto's *Almanach Perpetuum* (1496),[11] Copernicus's *De Revolutionibus Orbium Coelestium* (1543), Besson's *Le Cosmolabe* (1567), Johann Praetorius' *De Cometis* (1578), Kepler's *Astronomia Nova* (1609), Galileo's *Dialogo* (1632), and Tycho Brahe's *Historia Coelestis* (1666).

Materials on time contain much of interest, including works on calendars (including American Indian and Hebrew, as well as the Gregorian and Roman) and instruments (clock, watches, dials, and the like). Special materials on the calendar include a collection presented by W. F. Allen. The library's collection of materials on sundials is extensive: design and other artistic aspects are covered in the collection of the Art and Architecture Division; the scientific aspects, in the Science and Technology Research Center. In the 1930s the library began to collect calendars primarily as examples of typography rather than chronology; the collection housed at the Annex at 43rd Street is under the administration of the General Research and Humanities Division. Encompassing thousands of items from the late nineteenth century on, it is being added to selectively.

The correspondence of Professor Henry Draper from 1869 to 1882 has been noted in chapter 14 of this *Guide*. Three boxes and eight volumes in the Manuscripts and Archives Division contain the papers of William Frederick Allen, presented by him in 1901, consisting of original letters, manuscripts, circulars, and pamphlets relating to the complete history of the movement which resulted in the adoption of Standard Time by the railroads November 18, 1883.

Illustrated manuscripts in the Spencer Collection include a splendid example of Hyginus' "De Sideribus," on vellum, copied in Italy about 1450 with 38 miniatures of constellations outlined with a blue shading (Spencer MS 28); and several sixteenth- and seventeenth-century Persian astronomical works. Among the holdings of the Manuscripts and Archives Division are 4 letters by James Ferguson on scientific matters with astronomical diagrams dated from 1769 to 1776, and 6 volumes of original manuscripts by Karl Friedrich Gauss including his "Astronomische Rechungen zur Erläuterung der Theoria Motus Corporum Coelestium" (1800?).

ASTROLOGY

A collection of about 600 volumes on the subject is administered by the Science and Tech-

---

First Edition of Newton's 'Principia,' " *PBSA* 47 (1953): 269–300.

10. Brown, *Scientific Serials*, pp. 173–75.

11. See Joshua Bloch, "Zacuto and His Almanach Perpetuum," *BNYPL* 57 (1953): 315–18.

nology Research Center; it includes the Fleming Smith collection. There are long runs of periodicals such as *Raphael's Prophetic Messenger* (1833–) and the *American Astrology Magazine* (1933–), along with rarities of the sixteenth- and seventeenth-century works, as well as more contemporary materials.

PHYSICS

This is a generally strong collection in all branches of the subject. It contains extensive and complete files of scientific journals and publications of learned societies, and there is exceptional strength in systematic works in general physics before 1800. In all there are some 30,300 volumes and manuscripts. The Science and Technology Research Center keeps abreast of new fields as diverse as cryogenics, holography, and astronautics. Moreover, fields such as space biology and radiation medicine are collected by virtue of their connection with atomic energy. Molecular, nuclear, and atomic physics have the greatest numerical strength (7,500 volumes); other strong subjects are optics (4,200 volumes); and, electricity and magnetism, and mechanics of solids, each with 3,900 volumes.

The Research Libraries have almost all of the publications listed by Brown as "Most Cited Serials: Physics,"[12] with complete runs except for some of the early numbers of a few less-cited serials. As is the case with most fields in science, the holdings are as complete for older as they are for modern titles. Approximately 28 percent of the material is from the United States; about 54 percent of it is in English. French, German, and Spanish are the languages next in order of titles represented. Scores of indexes and abstracts are available on the open shelves of the Science and Technology Research Center.

Among older works of interest or importance in the library are many published before 1800, such as first editions of Newton's *Principia* (1687), Huygens's *Opuscula Postuma* (1703), Newton's *Opticks* (1704), and Caus's *Les Raisons des forces movantes* (1615), and others. The Manuscripts and Archives Division has the scientific papers and the correspondence from 1847 to 1878 of the physicist Henry Wurtz.

CHEMISTRY

This is the largest and certainly the most frequently used science collection of the Research Libraries. Totalling 35,400 volumes and manuscripts, the holdings afford an excellent working collection of current material, with rich resources in the history of chemistry. There is exceptional strength in periodicals and files of publications of American and European institutions and academies. The collecting policy is exhaustive for all aspects of the field except undergraduate texts.

A check of Brown's list of "Most Cited Serials" reveals only a few lacking titles, with those mostly in allied fields of chemistry, such as pharmacy, biology, physiology in which the library does not collect extensively.[13] Of the total number of periodicals received, 55 percent are in English, and of the total 26 percent come from the United States; Germany, Great Britain, Russia, Japan, and France are next in number of titles received. The center cooperates in reporting

its holdings to the *Comprehensive List of Periodicals for Chemistry and Chemical Engineering* issued by Chemical Abstracts Service: a set of *Chemical Abstracts* is kept on the open shelves of the center for ready reference. In addition to this major abstracting service, the center has others such as *Analytical Abstracts, Bulletin signalétique, Chemical Market Abstracts, Referativnyi Zhurnal,* and *Science Citation Index.*

In recent years the collection has grown proportionally stronger in biochemistry and biophysics. The present disposition of the larger subject groups in the resources is approximately as follows: general chemistry 7,000 volumes; biochemistry 6,700 volumes; physical chemistry 6,400 volumes; and analytic and inorganic chemistry, each 4,600 volumes.

Among the early or rare works are Biringuccio's *De la Pirotechnia* (1540), Jabir's *De Alchemia* (1541), Boyle's *New Experiments and Observations Touching Cold* (1603), Canepari's *De Atrementis* (1660), Robert Hooke's *Micrographia* (1665), Lavoisier's *Opuscules physiques et chymiques* (1774), Dalton's *New System of Checimal Philosophy* (1808–27), and Davy's *Elements of Chemical Philosophy* (1812). There are some forty titles on alchemy (the library has a good collection on this subject) published before 1700.

Holdings on chemistry in the Manuscripts and Archives Division include the correspondence of Jerome Alexander with other scientists (1908–51); the papers (1866–1921) of Wallace Goold Levison; and many of the notes of Peter Henri Van der Weyde (1813–95).

NATURAL HISTORY

The collection relating to natural history is extensive, though highly uneven. There are approximately 5,900 entries listed in the Public Catalog; it is administered by the General Research and Humanities Division. The collecting policy is comprehensive at present, but this has not always been the case. In the early days of the Astor Library, natural history was considered of greater importance than it is today. As Joseph Cogswell noted in 1854, "The Natural Sciences form one of the richest and best furnished [divisions] in the Library. The whole number of volumes embraced in it is four thousand two hundred and forty-nine."[14] However, by 1910, when Dr. Billings in his annual report enunciated his policy of avoiding duplication of strong collections in other libraries in the city, this subject was dropped to second place; the policy became selective, with an emphasis on the best books for the layman. About 1950 the collecting policy became representative, in an attempt to share comprehensive coverage between this library and other libraries in the city, such as the American Museum of Natural History and Columbia University.

Materials which would have been classified in the Public Catalog under the subject heading of "Natural History" in the past are now most generally assigned under more specific general headings, such as "Biology" and "Physics." The subject heading of "Natural History" is perhaps best considered as an historical classification of considerable importance but no longer definitive as a finding aid.

12. Brown, *Scientific Serials*, pp. 89–92.
13. Brown, *Scientific Serials*, pp. 98–101.

14. See Lydenberg, *History*, p. 27.

Periodicals and society publications form an outstanding feature in this subject field. Included are such titles as the *Annales des sciences naturelles* (1824–33), *Archiv für Naturgeschichte* (1835–1908), with long and generally complete files; but special importance attaches to the publications of natural history societies which flourished in the nineteenth century. Later journals include the Belfast Natural History and Philosophical Society's *Proceedings and Reports* (1873/74–), the Boston Society of Natural History's *Proceedings* (1841–1934), and publications of the Linnaean Societies of Lancaster and New York, the *Verein für vaterlandische Naturkunde* in Wurtemberg's *Jahreshefte* (1845–1932), and many others. Although European serials appear to be held in the largest numbers, most localities of the world are represented by at least the major publications, generally up to the early 1930s. At that time, many titles that stressed the biological sciences were discontinued if they were available in other professional or technical libraries in New York City. Rich collections of academy and learned society publications and museum publications are important allied resources.

There are several other features of importance or interest in the collection. There is an inclusive representation of the classics in this field, from Pliny the Elder through Buffon, Pouchet, Darwin, and others. The library has most of the accounts of nineteenth-century voyages and travels of research parties, including sets of the United States Exploring Expedition.[15] The library's specialization in works on the polar and arctic regions adds additional depth to the natural history of these areas. An important resource for natural history not usually analyzed in the library's catalogs is the extensive collection of local history publications in the Local History and Genealogy Division; for example, the "Victoria County Histories" of England have detailed sections devoted to this subject. Perhaps of secondary importance but still of considerable interest is the rather strong collection of essays in natural history.

The Rare Book Division holds a number of early accounts of America from the seventeenth century and later. The naturalist as litterateur is represented in the Berg Collection where, for example, there are numerous first and early editions of John Burroughs, with many manuscripts including twelve notebooks, from 1854 to 1883, and approximately 200 letters. Among materials in the Manuscripts and Archives Division are the letters from Sir Charles Blagden to Sir Joseph Banks on American natural history and politics.[16] A gift of importance to the division in 1937–39 was the correspondence of the National Association of Audubon Societies in America from 1899 through December 31, 1930.

METEOROLOGY

Meteorology is one of the strong collections of the library; 10,000 volumes and manuscripts are maintained. The major part of the holdings consist of government meteorological reports of both the United States and other countries, with excellent coverage from the earliest issue of the

reports to the present. The coverage extends to the states of the United States from the period when reports were issued by state agencies, until the time when such services were taken over by the U.S. Weather Bureau. Thus, for example, there are sets of the Ohio Weather and Crop Service reports and those of the New York City Meteorological Observatory. Excluding the government reports, approximately 40 periodicals are received at present.

Weather and climate are perhaps the strongest subject areas. Certain subject areas dealing with natural phenomena such as weather observations and earth sciences receive unusually close analysis in the card catalogs, both chronologically and geographically. As has been indicated, most of the entries refer to books. Many early books came from the Daniel Draper Library (Central Park Observatory), a number of them inscribed copies.

Material in the Rare Book Division on the subject, other than a few early texts of the sixteenth and seventeenth centuries, consists of printed meteorological observations of the eighteenth and early nineteenth centuries. Materials in the Manuscripts and Archives Division are found in certain diaries, such as that of Dr. Samuel Adams from 1758 to 1819 which, in addition to other personal data, gives a detailed record of the weather in New England including a description of the "Dark Day," May 19, 1780.

PHYSICAL GEOGRAPHY

Mountains and mountaineering, as well as oceanography, are perhaps the areas best covered in this relatively small collection. The first of these topics is under the administration of the General Research and Humanities Division, but the rest of the subject of physical geography is administered by the Science and Technology Research Center. The center has a comprehensive collection of the nautical charts of the U.S. Naval Oceanographic Office, and a representative group of those issued by other countries.

Periodicals and institutional publications are numerous. In the oceanography collection is a strong representation of the publications of leading oceanographic institutions such as the Institut Océanographique (Monaco) and the Scripps Institution of Oceanography. Holdings of tide tables are most complete for the United States, Great Britain, and Canada; those of other countries often show gaps, although the Science and Technology Research Center endeavors to keep its files complete. Classics in oceanography such as Matthew Fontaine Maury's *The Physical Geography of the Sea* (1855) are also available. There are reports of the various oceanographic expeditions, from Samuel P. Lee's *Reports and Charts of the Cruise of the U.S. Brig Dolphin* (1854) to those of the cruise of the *Meteor* (1925–29) and later expeditions.

The collections on caves and speleology contain periodicals exhibiting a wide geographic range. Currently the library receives 14 titles from ten countries, including 2 each from Great Britain, France, Italy and the United States. Some early accounts of the first half of the nineteenth century deal with Mammoth Cave and other caves of the United States.

MOUNTAINS AND MOUNTAINEERING

A comprehensive collection is administered by the General Research and Humanities Division.

---

15. Daniel C. Haskell, "The United States Exploring Expedition, 1838–1842, and Its Publications, 1844–1874," *BNYPL* 44 (1940): 93–112.
16. See *BNYPL* 7 (1903): 407–46.

Approximately 1,800 entries in the Public Catalog pertain to the subject, including, for the most part, accounts of mountain-climbing expeditions and descriptions of individual mountains and mountain ranges. There are a few guide books and books of instruction. The library can show ample documentation of the various expeditions up Mount Everest, from an early article by George Leigh Mallory on a reconnaissance of the mountain (in *Geographic Journal* for 1922), through a number of works on the successful ascent in 1953. Generally texts in languages other than English are held both in the original and in English translation if available. A feature of the collection is the extensive number and completeness of the periodical holdings with titles such as *Die Alpen* (1925–), *Appalachia* (1876–), *Die Bergsteiger* (1930–), *Revue de Géographie Alpine* (1915–), and other journals of mountain-climbing associations such as the *Sierra Club Bulletin* (1893–), and New Zealand's *Canterbury Mountaineer: Journal of the Canterbury Mountaineering and Tramping Club* (1936/37–). The library currently receives approximately 20 periodical titles on the subject.

GEOLOGY

The 30,100 volumes in geology and mineralogy form an extremely strong collection, particularly in holdings of government documents and the publications of professional societies. The collecting policy is exhaustive. American local geology is strong, and there is a good representation of the local geology of Canada and Western European countries; other nations are covered in as much detail. Geological maps with accompanying text are kept in the Science and Technology Research Center, but maps lacking text are maintained by the Map Division. The collection of geological maps is comprehensive for every part of the world, with files including maps produced in early years as well as the most contemporary materials.

The library has complete files of the major indexing services in this field. There are a number of early nineteenth-century textbooks, but textbooks are no longer collected.

Among the early works in geology and mineralogy are Agricola's *De Re Metallica* (1556), Entzelt's *De Re Metallica* (1551), Nicolas Steno's *De Solido intra Solidum Naturaliter* (1669), Swendenborg's *Opera Philosophica et Mineralia* (1734), de Maillet's *Telliamed* (1750), Buffon's *Histoire naturelle* (1749–67), Leibniz's *Protogaea* (1749), Haüy's *Sur la structure des crystaux* (1784), and Agassiz's *Études sur les glaciers* (1840).

Additional information is found in the excellent collection on mines and mining treated in chapter 57 of this *Guide*. Book material on precious or semiprecious stones may be located through the dictionary catalog of the Art and Architecture Division.

PALEONTOLOGY

To avoid duplication of existing resources in other libraries in New York City, the Research Libraries maintain only a representative collection of 2,400 volumes in paleontology. The collection of basic books does not include the paleontological catalogs produced by the various private organizations and societies, nor does it contain museum catalogs.

57

GENERAL TECHNOLOGY RESOURCES

(Including Patents)

The vast resources in technology account for a very large percentage of the holdings of the Science and Technology Research Center. There is a total of approximately 83,000 monograph volumes and 228,600 serial volumes. Because the center arranges serials in a single alphabetical order by title on its shelves, rather than in classified order, it is difficult to determine the number of serial volumes in a specific subject area such as engineering or electrical engineering; therefore only an approximation is provided in the following descriptions. Generally the collections are strong, with special richness in older materials which contribute to the history of technology. There is, moreover, an attempt to collect the proceedings of international symposia and conferences exhaustively. Civil engineering (particularly sewage-disposal and water supply) and transportation (especially railways and aeronautics) are notable aspects of the resources.

During an early period of the Astor Library,

W. G. Astor put more than $12,500 at the disposal of Dr. Cogswell for the purchase of books for a technology department. Cogswell noted that "it will be a leading object of this library to provide a complete 'Bibliotheque Industrielle,' or collection of books for the special benefit of practical industry."[1]

The collecting policy of the Science and Technology Research Center is in general comprehensive for technological works. The center also holds certain bibliographical tools not readily available elsewhere in the New York City area.

A number of book rarities are in the collections, including some fine aeronautical works. The Parsons collection, described in chapter 56 of this *Guide*, has much of importance on early canals, railroads, and military engineering; the library also received manuscripts from General

1. Lydenberg, *History*, p. 27.

Parsons relating to the steamboat and the submarine. A substantial body of manuscripts in the Manuscripts and Archives Division relates to early canals in the eastern United States and to the Panama Canal. Additional holdings include the papers of American engineers such as Bion J. Arnold, Elmer L. Corthell, Robert Fulton, William B. Parsons, Sidney A. Reeve, Frank J. Sprague, Robert B. Stanton, Joseph Gardner Swift, and William John Wilgus; much of this material dates from the turn of the twentieth century. These holdings will be described under the appropriate subject in this chapter.

TECHNOLOGY RESOURCES

Resources in the history of technology number approximately 10,100 volumes, excluding serials; holdings of nineteenth-century materials are exhaustive. Books of formulas date from the eighteenth and nineteenth centuries to the present. A special heading in the center's card catalog headed "Technology & Civilization" locates works on that subject by date (most of them published after 1945 and in other divisions of the Research Libraries); included are periodicals such as *Humanismus und Technik* (1953–) and the like. The center maintains a comprehensive and current collection of technological dictionaries in all languages, although such material is published irregularly.

Engineering

There is a total of approximately 71,900 volumes (excluding serials) related to engineering. Holdings of periodicals and society publications are substantially complete on an international basis. Of the more than 360 titles currently received in the Science and Technology Research Center, 60 percent are in English; of the remaining titles some 30 each are in German, French, and Spanish. Journals in the Cyrillic alphabet are presently maintained by the Slavonic Division. Abstracting services are virtually complete in Western European languages in the fields of engineering. These are generally kept on the open reference shelves in the center. Abstracting services in Russian are represented by *Referativnyi Zhurnal*. The center does not collect "table of contents" journals or express services. Substantial resources on the various aspects of atomic engineering date from early material such as the published reports concerning the famous Manhattan Engineering District ("Manhattan Project").

House organs, newsletters, and industrial bulletins are not customarily collected by the center. What appears in the card catalog under these headings represents long-established serials which the library has continued to receive, or material of particular relevance.

The Science and Technology Research Center receives virtually all of the publications of the National Bureau of Standards and the American Society for Testing Materials (ASTM). It also selectively acquires the engineering standards and specifications of professional associations, in addition to monographs related to the general subject of standards.

The comprehensive collections are strongest for civil engineering and public improvements, including bibliographies, histories, and general works. The coverage is best for technological reports of the U.S. federal government and those of New York City and State; there are also technological reports issued by foreign governments. Technological reports of state agencies are available, although often with gaps in the holdings; there are also some municipal reports.[2]

In addition to the contemporary materials in the Research Libraries are many early works, including García de Céspede's work on surveying, *Libro de instrumentos nuevos* (1606), A. Rathborne's *The Surveyor* (1616), La Hire's *L'École des arpenteurs* (1689), Love's *Geodaesia* (1744), Bergier's *Histoire des grandes chemins de l'empire romain* (1628), Dacres's *Art of Water Drawing* (1660), Fabretti's *De aquis et aquae ductibus ueteris Romae* (1680), Bélidor's *Architecture hydraulique* (1737–53), Bouillet's *Traité des moyens de rendre les rivières navigables* (1693), Smeaton's *A Narrative of the Building of the Eddystone Lighthouse* (1791), and Fontana's *Utilissimo trattato dell'acque correnti* (1696). Other book rarities are in the Parsons collection.

In 1937, Colonel William John Wilgus gave his collection of books and papers covering forty years of engineering. Under the administration of the Manuscripts and Archives Division, a large portion of the papers relate to Colonel Wilgus's work as deputy director of transportation of the American Expeditionary Force (AEF), consisting of letters, orders, and reports on the organization, personnel, port facilities, schedules, and the like. The New York City material is particularly important; it pertains to the construction of the Grand Central Terminal, the electrification of the New York Central Railroad and the Hudson River Railroad, the construction of the Holland Tunnel, the proposed tunnel under the Narrows, New York Harbor, Municipal Art Commission, High Bridge Aqueduct, City Planning, and the Tri-Borough Route.

Beginning in 1951, Gilbert H. Montague gave letters and documents of Robert Fulton to the library, which in addition to the Fulton manuscripts in the Parsons collection form a group of over 70 pieces. Holdings vary from small personal financial notes, akin to present day bank checks, to a 23-page holograph entitled "Submarine Navigation and Attack." Many of the letters and documents throw light on early steamboating and Fulton's continual litigation to defend his patents and legislative grants. Other items relate to the introduction of the submarine, the explosive mine, and the steam vessel as instruments of war. There are also drawings made by Fulton in 1804 of the submarine vessel, submarine bombs, and mode of attack.[3] First and early editions of Fulton's published work add to the library's archives. There are also copies of his biography by Cadwallader D. Colden (1817).

---

2. The Municipal Reference and Research Center (formerly the Municipal Reference Library of the Branch Libraries and no longer part of the New York Public Library) holds books, serials, and other literature on municipal matters, in addition to municipal publications of all cities in the United States with populations exceeding 100,000.

3. See "The Gilbert H. Montague Collection of Fultoniana," *BNYPL* 56 (1952): 149–50, and "Catalogue of the William Barclay Parsons Collection," *BNYPL* 45 (1941): 656–58. Reproduced in William Barclay Parsons, *Robert Fulton and the Submarine* (New York: Columbia Univ. Press, 1922).

Civil Engineering

Strong holdings of material related to civil engineering include approximately 9,300 volumes (excluding serials). Some of the more significant aspects of the holdings are discussed below.

Bridges: Although the coverage is international, it is most substantial for bridges in the United States, and particularly for New York City and State. The New York City materials include contracts, proposals, plans, and specifications for such bridges in the metropolitan area as the Brooklyn Bridge and the George Washington Bridge. There are also albums of photographs.

Canals: A fine collection of books and periodicals is enriched by materials in the Parsons collection consisting of early works on canals of the eighteenth century, and a number of early nineteenth-century reports of committees and commissions relating to canals in the United States and England. A copy of Robert Fulton's *A Treatise on the Improvement of Canal Navigation* (1796) presented to Napoleon Bonaparte contains annotations in the author's hand and is administered by the Rare Book Division. With it is a letter from Fulton attempting to interest Bonaparte in his ideas on the construction of canals. The Schuyler canal papers in the Manuscripts and Archives Division include 740 items on the affairs of the Northern and Western Inland Lock Navigation Companies, minutes of meetings, reports of surveyors and contractors, and correspondence relating to the construction and operation of canals in New York State from 1792 to 1803. Other manuscripts on canals include the papers of Robert Brooke from 1798 to 1806 relating to the proposed Chesapeake and Delaware Canal.

A second large group of materials concerns the Panama Canal. The resources are somewhat dispersed with scientific and technical materials on the canal in the Science and Technology Research Center, and with items of a more general and political nature in the American History Division. Manuscripts range from a late eighteenth-century "Mémoire sur les avantages et les moyens d'ouvrir un canal dans l'Amérique espagnole" to the John Bigelow papers containing correspondence, speeches, pamphlets, and the like during the period 1886 to 1909, in all 85 pieces relating to the selection of the Panama route and to the construction of the canal.

Harbors: A strong and international collection of materials on harbors is represented by over 2,000 cards in the Science and Technology Research Center catalog. There is an extensive geographical breakdown of the subject with, for example, entries leading to material on the port of Bordeaux from 1882 to the present; for Boston from 1837; for Hamburg from 1905; for Melbourne from 1879; and for New York from 1834. Many of the items are government reports. There is also a number of maps and charts.

Roads: Road association publications and proceedings of road congresses are well represented, as is documentary material from the United States consisting of the annual reports of state highway departments and other publications at both state and federal levels; some municipal material is also included. Foreign government documents are available at the national level. Rarities include early editions of Hubert Gautier's *Traité de la construction des chemins* (1721), Christopher Colles's *A Survey of the Roads of the United States of America* (1789), and John L. McAdam's *Remarks on the Present System of Road Making* (1819).

Sewage and Water Supply: Coverage for this subject is comprehensive for the New York City metropolitan area, and the holdings are outstanding in their historical context. In 1902 the Jersey City Public Library presented to the library an important file of government publications relating to the water supply of New York City during the period 1804–48 and of Brooklyn in the 1850s. This gift, combined with materials already in the Ford collection, made the collection "a large and important one."[4] Significant items in the Manuscripts and Archives Division refer to the Croton Aqueduct in New York, including seven volumes of papers on land acquisitions, disbursements, labor time books, etc., for the period 1835–84. Of particular note are a receipted bill for the construction of the Croton Reservoir where the Central Building of the New York Public Library now stands,[5] and a thirty-foot map of the course of the aqueduct of 1884 from Croton Lake to Central Park.[6]

In 1912 the New York City Board of Water Supply, Gas and Electricity gave a collection of contracts and specifications for the city's Catskill water supply. In addition, the papers of William Williams contain material related to his tenure of office as Commissioner of the New York City Board of Water Supply for the period 1914–17.

Pictorial Material: There is a wealth of pictorial documentation on bridges in the Research Libraries ranging from specifications, drawings, and photographs in the Science and Technology Research Center, to material dealing with the New York City area and other states of the Union found in the American History and Local History and Genealogy Divisions. There is some material of this nature on roads and canals. The Prints Division's holdings include representations of roads, bridges, and canals, such as the Panama Canal lithographs made by Joseph Pennell in 1912 and J. W. Hill's watercolors of the Erie Canal made from 1830 to 1832, along with other materials in the Phelps Stokes collection.

Electrical Engineering

The collections number approximately 11,000 volumes (excluding serials). They cover the latest advances in research, such as the industrial applications of laser beams and cryogenics techniques. Generally the Science and Technology Research Center has the commercially produced monographs on the subject of computers and computer programming.

Publications of societies and institutions in the field of electronics are featured. Earlier files of house organs and newsletters of manufacturers of electrical equipment are substantially complete until the 1940s, when a large number of files were discontinued. This is also the case with the files of equipment catalogs; however, the information contained in these sources now appears in commercially produced manufacturers' directories, condensed catalogs, data annuals, and the like, which are held by the library.

4. See *BNYPL* 6 (1902): 45.
5. See "A Bill for the Croton Reservoir," *BNYPL* 31 (1927): 155–58.
6. See "Manuscript Records of the Croton Aqueduct," *BNYPL* 36 (1932): 93.

Early works, which constitute an important feature, include Priestley's *History and Present State of Electricity* (1769), Watson's *Experiments and Observations* (1746), Winkler's *De Imagine Notuum Coelestium Viribus Electricis Efficta* (1750), several works of Benjamin Franklin, Adams's *An Essay on Electricity* (1785), Boullanger's *Traité de la cause et des phénomènes de l'électricité* (1750), Becarria's *Lettre sur l'électricité* (1754), Aldini's *La galvanisme* (1804), Hauksbee's *Physico-mechanical Experiments* (1709), and works by Volta, Ampère, Davis, Faraday, and others. There are six letters of the electrical genius and inventor, Nikola Tesla, in the Manuscripts and Archives Division, three dated 1901 and three dated 1915.

The field of cybernetics is represented by the abstracting journals *Engineering Index* and *Computer Abstracts* and other current periodical titles. Other materials include proceedings of conferences, bibliographies, technical dictionaries, and the like.

Mechanical Engineering

This strong collection numbers about 11,000 volumes (excluding serials); society publications merit special attention. Among the early works on mechanics in the holdings are Zeising's *Theatri Machinarum* (1607–10), Branca's *Le Machine* (1629), Zonca's *Novo teatro de machine* (1607), Besson's *Theatrum Instrumentorum* (1582), and Guidobaldo del Monte's *Le Mechaniche* (1581). There is a great deal of material on automobiles, railways, and steam navigation, with additional rarities in the Parsons collection.

Railways: More than 100 periodical titles on the general subject of railways are found in the holdings; coming from twenty-three countries, 60 are currently received.[7] This figure includes a number of publications of railway enthusiasts from many countries; the Science and Technology Research Center is actively engaged in augmenting these holdings. Street railways are also extensively treated; in this connection the Walter Weichsel transfer collection should be noted, of which over 90 percent comes from electric railway systems. An extensive collection on subways focuses on the New York City subway system with plans, routes, contracts, blueprints, and photographs of construction. The Manuscripts and Archives Division holds papers relating to Swiss and Russian railways in the papers of Elmer Lawrence Cothell; United States railways are featured in those of Bion J. Arnold, James Lewis Cowles, William D. Lewis, Charles F. B. Haskell, Frank J. Sprague (who also gave the library a collection of works on railways in 1935), William John Wilgus, and others.

Automobiles: Periodicals relating to the automobile are held in exceptional strength. Over 110 titles are currently received in the Periodicals Section, including many titles relating to antique cars which reflect a current reader interest. The book collection is comprehensive enough to include such works as Keith Marvin's *License Plates of the World* (1963). Although the collections contain the commercially produced handbooks and repair manuals for most major makes of automobiles, the shop manuals and service bulletins published by automobile manufacturers have not been substantially acquired since 1940. Of great historical interest is a collection of over 3,500 pieces which includes service and parts manuals, catalogs, price lists, scrapbooks, and the like for automobiles and motor trucks from the earliest period of the industry through the 1940s. Included are such makes as Cole, Ford, Hispano-Suiza, King, Locomobile, Moon, Pierce-Arrow, Pontiac, Rolls Royce, and Talbot.

Steamboats: Certain aspects of the steamboat holdings are notable. The Robert Fulton collection in the Manuscripts and Archives Division contains a great deal relating to the development of the steamboat for commercial and military purposes. Material in the Isaiah and John Townsend papers deals with the operation of steamboat companies, among them the North River Steam Boat Company (1815–27). Engravings in the Prints Division include the only known contemporaneous representation of Fulton's *Clermont*, in a French lithograph from 1810. Also on file are prints depicting the arrivals of the *Sirius* and the *Great Western* in New York City in 1838. Another rare item from the Phelps Stokes collection is an oil painting by Joseph Walter of the *Great Western* off Tompkinsville, Staten Island, in 1838.

MINES AND MINING

The holdings for mines and mining are strong, especially for government reports. There are about 9,500 volumes (excluding serials) in the collections; associated holdings in geology for most areas of the world augment these holdings. The periodical and society publication holdings are excellent, with about 90 current titles from 29 countries; the United States and Germany lead the list with 19 and 11 titles each. Most South American countries with extensive mining industries are represented by at least one title. Government publications are strong from most areas, both retrospectively and currently. The book collections are well-rounded, with standard trade publications, and a good representation of the proceedings of mining congresses, technical dictionaries in many languages, and directories; mining handbooks, however, are collected on a selective basis. Among the early works of interest are Löhneyss's *Bericht vom Bergkwerck* (1617), Pettus's *Fodinae Regales* (1670), Agricola's *De Re Metallica* (1556), Platte's *Discovery of Subterraneall Treasure* (1639), Pryce's *Mineralogia Cornubiensis* (1778), and a number of items on mining in Spain, Latin America (particularly Mexico and Peru), and the United States, dating mostly from the eighteenth century. A number of items in the Manuscripts and Archives Division relate to mining: the diaries of John W. Bell and John Henry Cornelison describe the Gold Rush to California in 1849, and later reports of the Bonanza silver mine near Frisco, Utah are also included. The large collection of papers of Robert Brewster Stanton contain his survey field notes, 1889–1922, and other material.

METALLURGY

Metallurgy is generally represented by strong collections, with excellent holdings of nineteenth- and twentieth-century books, journals, and the publications of societies and museums. This last category includes some 86 titles currently received in the Research Libraries from 26 countries; the

---

7. See Thomas R. Thomson, comp., "Checklist of Publications on American Railroads Before 1841," *BNYPL* 45 (1941): 3–68 et seq.

United States is by far the best represented with 23 titles. Early works from the sixteenth to the eighteenth century are an important feature, including Entzelt's *De Re Metallica* (1551), Barba's *Arte de los metales* (1770), and Sarria's *Ensayo de metalurgia* (1784), among others. Of exceptional rarity is Georg de Hennin's historical and technical account, dated 1735, of the mines and metallurgical plants situated in various parts of Siberia. Bound in two volumes, this manuscript is illustrated with carefully executed wash drawings; it is kept in the Slavonic Division.[8] In the Manuscripts and Archives Division are the papers (1773–97) of Ezra Morrill, an iron worker of Salisbury, Massachusetts; there are also papers of the American Iron Association and Phelps, Dodge and Company relating to the production of iron, copper, and coal in nineteenth-century America.

MANUFACTURES

This general section relating to manufactures is strong, particularly in periodicals. Various allusions are found in the library's earlier reports to the formation of a collection of manufacturers' catalogs; collecting in this field was abandoned in the 1930s, although many catalogs have been retained, and some of the combined catalogs of various industries and commercial directories have been added. The tremendous growth of industry and the diversification of yearly models necessitated this change in collecting policy. The histories of various industries in the Economic and Public Affairs Division can be associated with the literature on manufactures. The Manuscripts and Archives Division should also be consulted for papers and records of companies, such as the account books, ledgers, and repair journals of Brewster and Company, manufacturers of carriages and automobile bodies in New Haven and New York from 1837 to 1924.

TEXTILES AND FIBERS

The collections on textiles and fibers form a reasonably strong group of books, pamphlets, and periodicals covering such diverse aspects of the subject as textile manufacturing, dyeing (with a good historical collection), weaving, printing, spinning, and the like. General periodicals on textiles number over 200 titles, of which 150, from 27 different countries, are current. About 60 percent of the titles are in English. Germany is also well represented, and there are 5 titles from Argentina. The Science and Technology Research Center also receives the *Textile Technology Digest* (1944–) and other related abstracts, digests, and directories. Holdings in more specific aspects of the field, such as cotton and linen, are equally extensive.

In view of the prominence of the garment industry in New York City, the center is actively building upon its core collection in textiles and garment manufacture, furs, leather, and the like, to meet the needs of the industry as they are expressed. A heavily used group of books on men's tailoring extends from the eighteenth century to the present. There is a representative collection of works on pattern-making, cloth and

clothing, needlework and lace, and on the techniques of dressmaking and millinery. *Women's Wear Daily* (1910–) is current in the Science and Technology Research Center; there is a complete back file on microfilm. Related holdings on textile design and costume are found in the Art and Architecture Division. The American History Division has noteworthy items on textiles made by the American Indians. Papers such as those of the Rodman-Harvey family (1777–1850) in the Manuscripts and Archives Division relate to the manufacture and marketing of textiles in the United States. Extensive use is made of the correlative holdings in design and fashion illustration in the Picture Collection of the Branch Libraries.

WOOD, LEATHER, PAPER, RUBBER

This is a strong area, with particularly strong representations of periodicals and the publications of societies and associations. There are outstanding materials on the history of rubber and the preservation of paper. Wood and leather are more than adequately covered.

OTHER MECHANICAL TRADES

A small but significant collection of materials on locks and keys is available to serious researchers. There is good historical coverage, with many older commercial catalogs. Serials include volumes such as *Locksmith Ledger* (1955–).

CHEMICAL TECHNOLOGY

The great strength of the library in periodical literature makes this section outstanding. The holdings number approximately 5,000 volumes (excluding serials). Both the theoretical and practical aspects of chemical engineering are well covered. There is a comprehensive collection of the proceedings of international congresses; the large number of such congresses, however, precludes exhaustive collecting.

Works on explosives and fireworks are available. There is an interesting historical collection on fireworks, although not a great deal is being published at present; Vannoccio Biringuccio's *De la Pirotechnica* (1540) is present in first and early editions, and there are many other works of the seventeenth and eighteenth centuries.

A most important collection on plastics and resins includes abstracts, directories, and substantial holdings of periodicals and society publications. Over 60 periodical titles from nineteen countries relate to the plastics; over one third derive from the United States and England, and 8 from Germany.

PATENTS

One of the largest collections of patents in the United States is held by the New York Public Library. The Patents Collection consists of patent specifications, abstracts of patents, and patent lists, along with related periodicals and books. Similar materials on trademarks and trade names are available. More than one-half of the Patents Collection derives from the United States, England, France, and Germany, although publications from approximately thirty-five other countries are held. That the holdings have always been of importance may be seen from the following:

---

8. See Avrahm Yarmolinsky, "A Russian Manuscript Treatise on Metallurgy," *BNYPL* 40 (1936): 1007–11.

1921	19,520 volumes
1930	27,798
1941	37,000 (estimated figure)
1966	70,000

It has been estimated that the collection increases at the rate of 2,400 volumes per year.

Some notable gifts have been received over the years, among the earliest being the presentation of a complete set of English patents to the Astor Library by the British Commissioners of Patents in 1855. In 1941, Fritz V. Briesen gave nearly 1,000 bound volumes of complete copies of United States patents for the years 1871 to 1912. In 1968 the library received from the U.S. Commissioners of Patents numbers of the *Ishō Kōhō* (Design Gazette) of the Patents Office of Japan from May 26, 1961 to date, to be sent on a continuing basis.

Significant historical patents collections include volumes of *Patentes y Marcas* (1900–47), which list patents granted in Argentina as well as in other South American countries; also included are nineteenth-century patent publications from the Australian states of New South Wales, South Australia, and Victoria, and publications of imperial Russia from the late nineteenth century to 1916.

The library currently receives substantially complete collections of patents, including specifications and drawings, from the following countries:

Belgium Specifications	493,079 to date	(1950–)
Denmark	1	(1894–)
England	1	(1617–)
France	317,502	(1902–)
Germany	1	(1877–)[9]
Sweden	1	(1885–)
United States	115,264	(1871–)

Either abstracts of patents or patents lists are received from the following countries:

Australia: *Official Journal of Patents, Trademarks, and Designs* (1904–)

Canada: *Canadian Patent Office Record* (1873–)

Hungary: *Szabadalmi Közlöny es Védegyértesitö* [formerly *Szabadalm Közlony*] (1896–)

Ireland: *The Official Journal of Industrial and Commercial Property* (1928–)

Israel: *Lishkat Ha-Patentim* (1964–)

Italy: *Bollettino dei Brevetti per Invenzioni, Modelli e Marchi* (1940–, incomplete file)

Japan: *Tokkyo koho* [Patent Gazette] (1950–)

Netherlands: *Octrooi en Merk* (1927–)

New Zealand: *Patent Office Journal* (1912–)

Switzerland: *Schweizerisches Patent-, Muster- und Marken-Blatt* (1962–)

Republic of South Africa: *Patents Journal, including Trade Marks and Designs* (1952–)

U.S.S.R.: *Byulleten Izobretenii I Tovarnykh Znakov* (1959–)

The library maintains complete files of two publications issued by the U.S. Patent Office, *Index of Patents* and *Manual of Classification*.[10] The collection also contains the comprehensive *Index of Classification* issued on microfilm covering the years 1836 through 1968. This index lists all numbers of the patents issued under specific classification categories. Among the periodicals received by the Patents Collection are the West German *Beiträge zum Stand der Technik in der tabakverarbeitenden Industrie* (1961–), the *Airplane Patent Digest* including the English supplement (1930–), and the important *Industrial Property* (1962–), published by the United International Bureau for the Protection of Intellectual Property in Switzerland. In addition to a substantial reference collection are supplementary book materials, which include specialized commercial patent lists and indexes. There is also material on international and United States patent and trademark law.

TRADEMARKS

Generally, trademark publications are available in the library for countries represented by patent publications. The collection includes a unique catalog of trademarks registered in the U.S. Patent Office through part of 1947. Although of considerable historical interest, this file has been superseded by two commercial publications in the collection: *Trademark Renewal Register* (1964 and 1966) and *Trademark Register* (1961–64, 1967–). These publications index by subject the trademarks presently in effect.

Special Indexes and Files

Trademark File. A card file consisting of trademark and trade name entries clipped from the *Official Gazette* of the U.S. Patent Office and arranged by merchandise classification (inactive, 240 card drawers). The file was commenced in 1915 and extends to 1947.

Cheminform Institute File. An alphabetical card file of chemical trade names coded to show the location of information about the product; the manufacturer's or distributor's name; patent information (inactive, 143 card drawers). The file extends to 1962. Two notebooks identifying the code symbols on the cards accompany the file.

Underwood's Digest File. This card file consists of abstracts of patent and trademark law cases clipped from *Underwood's Digest* and arranged by numerical code (inactive, 39 card drawers). The file extends from the early 1900s to approximately 1961. Twenty-eight drawers of the file deal with patent cases, and eleven with trademark cases.

A special index, completed in 1941, to British Amended Patents consisting of some 4,000 cards is also in the Patents Collection.

---

9. Except for numbers 302,901–455,200 (1918–28) and 750,987–1,000,000 (1945–57). Readers will find these numbers in the U.S. Patent Office.

10. It should be noted that although the index goes back to 1790, there are patents only from 1871.

58

MEDICINE AND THE BIOLOGICAL SCIENCES

COLLECTING POLICY

MEDICINE

Approximately 34,000 volumes relating to medicine are held by the library. Works on the therapeutic aspects of medicine or those intended for the professional or specialist have not usually been collected. In view of the strong emphasis upon social history in the library's collections, however, materials that contribute to history and sociology, such as the reports of institutions, are actively collected.

Medicine, like law, requires the special administration of experts, both for the selection of materials and for reference assistance. The New York Academy of Medicine Library at 2 East 103rd Street, noted as the second largest medical library in the United States, is the local library which serves the general public. Readers seeking less specialized information and reference services will find the necessarily smaller medical collections of the Research Libraries of use. There is good coverage of such topics as exercise, the maintenance of health, diets, and the like; it should be stressed that the library makes no distinction between practical plans and fads, and that both aspects are represented in the holdings. Associated with these topics are the publications issued by various departments of public health in the government documents collections of the library, which offers up-to-date information useful to the layman. There are also monographs and periodicals relating to the Red Cross.

Only the most extensive bibliographies of medicine are collected, on a representative basis. Much reliance is placed on inclusive bibliographies such as *Index Medicus*. Certain older works in all medical fields have been retained due to their value as early imprints, or for documentary purposes other than medical, as is the case with fine illustrated medical books.

THE BIOLOGICAL SCIENCES

The library does not specialize in the fields of the biological sciences. The 31,800 volumes held are adequate only for research of a general nature, although there are strong collections in allied subjects such as agriculture and voyages and travels. Subjects closely related to the medical sciences such as anatomy, physiology, and bacteriology are represented by only small holdings of basic reference texts.

The policy for collecting works in the biological sciences is similar to that for medicine. Until 1877 biology, botany, and zoology were collected comprehensively, and therefore the holdings are rich in the early classics of those fields. Since then it has been the library's policy to acquire only standard works of reference, both domestic and foreign, and similar materials which supplement the collections in other subjects.

The Science and Technology Research Center is attempting to build a central core of basic reference works in biology that may be of assistance to the researcher into biochemistry, biophysics, or biological mathematics. In addition, the center wishes to maintain complete files of comprehensive biological abstracts and indexes so that a researcher may compile bibliographies of works to consult even though the material itself may not be in the Research Libraries.

HISTORICAL SURVEY

The deemphasis of the medical and biological sciences in the collections is not a recent event. As early as 1854, Dr. Cogswell declared that medicine would not be considered of major importance to the Astor Library since it "is so well provided for in the hospitals and other libraries of the city." In 1877, Mr. Brevoort affirmed this position; however, in 1883 a part of $15,000 given by J. J. Astor was used for additions in this field.[1] Since then systematic collection has not been attempted.

In 1949 the medical collections in the Research Libraries, then estimated at about 26,000 volumes, were reviewed. Approximately 3,800 books were transferred to the Academy of Medicine Library; only the resources in medical biography, local history, medical bibliographies, histories of medicine, and books on nervous and mental diseases, longevity, food and diet, vegetarianism, chiropody, exercise, and the Red Cross were retained. About 59 periodical titles (approximately four percent of the extensive holdings) were also retained.

As early as 1851, Cogswell reported a good collection of works on "natural history and all its divisions," later stating that "in entomology we are said to have the best and fullest collection in the country to which naturalists have free access." In his report of 1854 he remarked on the costliness of works such as Wallich's *Plantae Asiaticae Rariores*, Roxburgh's *Plants of the Coast of Coromandel*, a complete set of Gould's works on the birds, Chenu's *Illustrations Conchyliologiques*, Audubon's *Birds of America* (of which the library has both quartos and folio sets), Sibthorp's *Flora Graeca*, Lambert's *A Description of Genus Pinus*, and at least 100 volumes of similar interest and rarity.

In 1877 the deemphasis of natural history began when Brevoort stated that it was no longer to be a field for extensive buying, since other libraries in New York City covered the subject. Certain large collections did, nevertheless, continue to strengthen the resources: the Stuart collection, received in 1892, contained among its 14,000 books and pamphlets a notable group relating to natural history, as well as collections of shells and minerals. The Tilden library also contained a fine collection of illustrated folio works relating to natural history, ornithology, botany, and the like.

Historical materials (as distinguished from rare and unusual works) are, on the whole, ample. Both general and special studies represent the development of the subject for the eighteenth century and following. American and Continental periodicals, society publications, and other serials are generally present with full, if not complete,

---

1. See Lydenberg, *History*, p. 27, 64–5, 89.

files (this was the case until 1934, when some of the titles were discontinued in the light of their availability to the public in other city libraries).

Manuscript holdings relating to biology are small. In the Manuscripts and Archives Division, however, many of the notable biologists are represented by autographs, letters, and other material of interest. An important collection consists of the correspondence of the National Association of Audubon Societies from 1899 through 1930, which the library received in 1938.

RESOURCES

MEDICINE

Among the 130 periodical titles in medicine listed as present in the Research Libraries, approximately 20 are in the field of medical history, such as the *Archiwum historii medycyny* (1964–), the *Bulletin of the History of Medicine* (1933–), and *Sudhoffs Archiv* (1908–). There are also substantially complete files of the *American Journal of Nursing* (1900–) and the *Journal of the American Medical Association* (1885–). Journals relating to vivisection number 4 titles including the *Anti-Vivisectionist* (1949–).

The library retains a few general directories of the profession, the most important being the *American Medical Directory*, the *Biographical Directory of the American Psychiatric Association*, *Directory of Medical Specialists*, and *Medical Directory of New York State*. The latest issue of these titles is on the open shelves in the Main Reading Room. Back issues are in the general collections, as are foreign directories such as the British *Medical Register*. The Science and Technology Research Center has selected standard dispensatories and pharmacopoeias for the use of the physical scientist. The library relies upon the major indexes of medical literature such as *Index Medicus* and its predecessors, *Cumulated Index Medicus*, and the catalogs of organizations such as the National Library of Medicine.

The history of medicine is well documented in the holdings, with a good retrospective collection. Annual reports of medical schools (primarily from the nineteenth century) and New York City hospitals are an outstanding feature, since they represent both the social and historical aspects of the subject. Reports from hospitals outside New York City and those in foreign countries are not particularly well represented. Official reports of state boards of health and medical examiners, while not complete, are present in large numbers. In addition, a number of works relating to the history of medicine, while not classified with the subject in the Public Catalog, may be found under headings such as "U.S. History—Civil War —Medical and Sanitary Affairs." There are materials on specific diseases such as tuberculosis; for the most part these are older items of the late nineteenth and early twentieth centuries, and concern the prevention of the disease. The library has collected works on syphilis, particularly those treating its supposed connection with the discovery of America. Thus the Rare Book Division holds a first edition of Girolamo Fracastoro's *Syphilis sive Morbus Gallicus* (Verona, 1530) which gave a name to the disease and also a copy of the rarer and more complete Rome edition of 1531. Other works of interest include those on the early treatment of syphilis such as Ulrich von Hotten's *De Guaiaci Medicina et Morbo Gallico*

(1519). Ruy Díaz de Isla's *Tractado . . . contra el mal serpentina* (1542) is available in a second edition; in this work the physician describes his treatment of a number of Columbus's men in Barcelona after their return from Haiti in 1493.

Beyond the items already noted, medical rarities are few. There is a treatise on popular medicine entitled *Versehung von Lieb, Seele, Ehre und Gut* (Nuremberg, 1489); and in the fine collection of early Mexican imprints in the Rare Book Division are four of the first eight medical books printed in Mexico City before 1600, including the first two, Alonso de la Veracruz's *Phisica* (1557) and Francisco Bravo's *Opera Medicinalia* (1570). The Arents Tobacco Collection has a number of early medical works, most from the seventeenth century; included are herbals, pharmacopoeias, and books of medicine for the layman. They are described more fully in chapter 60 of this *Guide*. Early anatomy books in the Research Libraries are described in the section on drawing and painting resources in chapter 28.

Doctors have often entered the field of letters; a library exhibition of the published works, most from the Berg Collection, of some eighty English and American doctor/authors was held in 1964.[2] Among the papers of physicians and surgeons in the Manuscripts and Archives Division are Benjamin Rush's "Observations on the Cause & Cure of the Tetanus," a paper read March 17, 1786, along with notes of lectures delivered by him in 1809 and 1810 kept by George Clark. Other papers include those of John Wakefield Francis of New York (1809–61) and Gustav Scholer (1887–1929) of New York City; in addition are miscellaneous materials such as 6 volumes of scrapbooks containing prescriptions filled at the store of McIntyre Ewen and Son from 1857 to 1890. In 1919, Simon Gratz of Philadelphia presented the division with a collection of 61 autograph letters of eminent American physicians and surgeons covering the period 1756 to 1880. Among the names represented are Silvester Gardiner, Samuel Latham Mitchell, David Hosack, and Jacob Bigelow.[3] An Arabic manuscript treatise on the human body is dated 1375; it contains one miniature and several circular marginal ornaments. The papers of Eugenie M. Heller and John Houston Finley contain material on the Red Cross during World War I. The Ingersoll-Farrell family correspondence contains the letters during 1917–18 and 1940 of Mrs. Clinton P. Farrell as president of the Vivisection Investigation League, Inc., of New York.

BOTANY

As has been previously noted, holdings in the field of botany are not strong. A check of the section entitled "Most Frequently Cited Serials" in Charles Harvey Brown's *Scientific Serials* (1956) reveals that the library has active or complete files of only nine of the first twenty-five titles, most of them in biochemistry, biophysics, or agriculture rather than in the field of botany proper. Some twelve titles in botany are cur-

2. See John D. Gordan, "Doctors as Men of Letters: English and American Writers of Medical Background," *BNYPL* 68 (1964): 574–601. Published separately by the library.

3. See "Letters of American Physicians and Surgeons," *BNYPL* 23 (1919): 547–54.

rently available in the Periodicals Section; these are from the United States, Canada, Poland, Brazil, England, and Germany, among them items such as the *Botanical Review* (1935–) and the *Boletim* (1944–) of the Museo Nacional in Rio de Janeiro. The General Research and Humanities Division collects only standard reference texts of broad general interest.

Although the general research services of the library are not strong in botanical works, there are a number of rarities in the special and subject collections that should be mentioned. The Prints Division houses a few curious examples of nature printing from actual specimens, including one of the first books to be so illustrated, Christiano Gottlieb Ludwig's *Ectypa Vegetalilium* (1760). The division has copies of both the "lottery" or quarto and the folio editions of Robert John Thornton's *Temple of Flora*. It has also Rudolf Koch and Fritz Kredel's *Das Blumenbuch* (1929). The Rare Book Division's holdings in botany were enriched in 1965 by the gift of Mr. and Mrs. Pál Keleman of some forty books ranging in date from the early sixteenth century to the first quarter of the nineteenth, including the work of many of the most famous European botanists, among them Otto Brunfels, Charles de l'Écluse, John Parkinson, and J. C. Volckamer.[4]

Both the Arents Tobacco Collection and the Arents Collection of Books in Parts contain fine botanical books, and the collections are actively adding to the holdings. In the Arents Tobacco Collection the criterion for selection has been the mention of the tobacco plant, the earliest example being Rembert Dodoens's *Crüyde Boeck* (1554). Fine examples of botanical books originally issued in parts include Redouté's *Descrip-*

tions des Plantes Rares et Cultivées à Malmaison (1812–17), Henry John Elwes's *A Monograph of the Genus Lilium* (1877–80), and John Guille Millais's *Rhododendrons* (1917–24).

Manuscripts are notable in the Spencer Collection's holdings of botanical works. A fifteenth-century "Tacuinum Sanitatis" ("table of health") from northern Italy contains 200 representations of plants and simples in pen-and-ink and color.[5] An eighteenth-century German "Hortus Floridus" is illustrated with hundreds of watercolor drawings of plants and flowers. Among the large number of Japanese manuscripts and scrolls are herbals selected for their aesthetic, artistic, and botanical interest. The earliest of these is a manuscript scroll from 1165, "Koyaku Zukan" (Incense of Medicine). There are others produced during the eighteenth and nineteenth centuries.

ZOOLOGY

Zoology materials are held in less strength than those for botany, although some of the early publications, particularly the materials relating to birds such as sets of Gould and Audubon works and Edward Lear's *Illustrations of the Family of Psittacidae, or Parrots* (1832), are of considerable importance. A check of the section relevant to zoology in Charles Harvey Brown's *Scientific Serials* (1956) reveals that only eight of the first twenty-five periodicals are actively collected by the library, with several of those not devoted to zoology proper but to related fields such as microscopy and biochemistry; periodicals held by the library come from the United States, Israel, Brazil, France, and England.

---

4. See Lewis M. Stark, "Kelemen Gift: Early Books in Botany," *BNYPL* 69 (1965): 73–76.

5. See Karl Kup, "A Medieval Codex of Italy," *Natural History* 72 (1963): 31–41.

59

AGRICULTURE

Agriculture holdings may best be characterized as uneven. The collecting policy is comprehensive for periodical and society publications; for serial government reports of the United States, Canada, and England; and for materials such as bibliographies, histories, and general serial and monograph coverage of the subject.

The library selectively acquires current books, seeking comprehensive coverage only of the sociological and economic aspects of agriculture, and makes no attempt to acquire secondary works or textbooks in the field of agricultural technology. The collections are stronger in works on the economic or statistical aspects of agriculture than on the technical aspects of plant and animal breeding. For current information on these technical aspects of agriculture, the library relies upon those publications of national and state bureaus whose holdings are indexed in the standard agricultural indexes. Some idea of the

growth of the collections in this field may be gained from the following table:

1921	25,751 volumes
1930	39,808
1966	86,600

The library receives most of the important bibliographies and abstracting journals not only for the general subject of agriculture but also for certain specialized fields such as poultry raising, livestock, dairy products, and tropical agriculture. The *Dictionary Catalog of the National Agricultural Library* (1862–1965) and its supplement, *National Agricultural Library Catalog* (1966–), provide comprehensive retrospective and current coverage of the field. Titles such as *Agricultural Index* (1916–), *Bibliography of Agriculture* (1942–), *Der Forschungsdienst* (1936–), and *Sel'skokhozyaistvennaya Literatura SSSR* (1926–) augment the resources.

RESOURCES

PERIODICALS AND SOCIETY PUBLICATIONS

Periodicals in agriculture may be divided into two types, those primarily of research interest and those having a more popular appeal. In all, the Research Libraries have about 900 periodical titles under the heading "Agriculture—Periodical and Society Publications" in the Public Catalog; of this number some 140 titles are currently received from more than thirty-five countries. The United States is represented by approximately 30 current periodical titles, the USSR by approximately 54. There is a good number from Latin America, including Argentina, Brazil, Chile, Costa Rica, Panama, Paraguay, Peru, and Puerto Rico; Oriental titles come primarily from India and Japan.

Periodical holdings range in date from the eighteenth century to the present. From the eighteenth century are titles such as the *Museum Rusticum et Commerciale* (1763–66) and the *Corps d'observations* (1757–58) of the Société d'Agriculture de Commerce, et des Arts de Bretagne. There are good holdings of the farm journals which commenced or flourished during the nineteenth century in America; of these the library has substantial files, including *American Agriculturist* (1842– , incomplete file), *Country Gentleman* (1853–1954), and *Farm Journal* (1877–). There is also a complete file of Robert B. Thomas's *(Old) Farmer's Almanack* (1793–), with some issues bearing their original owners' notations. A card file of American almanacs before 1821 is kept in the Rare Book Division, along with almanac rarities.

Scholarly periodicals include long files of publications of the Deutsche Landwirtschafts-Gesellschaft, the Académie d'Agriculture de France, the International Institute of Agriculture, the Royal Agricultural Society of England, and many others. Provincial agricultural societies, both domestic and foreign, are also represented by substantial files. Holdings of periodicals and society publications in such specialized agricultural topics as poultry, dairies and dairying, and cattle were once collected on a more comprehensive basis than at present; indeed the poultry holdings were considered outstanding until the early 1940s.

Government publications, the majority of which are serial, include a noteworthy collection of the agricultural reports of the United States and Canada (for which the library is a depository), along with the less comprehensively held reports of other national governments. The library substantially receives all the serial and monographic publications of the agricultural experiment stations and state agricultural departments or boards in this country; only the annual reports of foreign provincial or state agricultural agencies, including those of Canada, are generally received. At present, the Economic and Public Affairs Division is attempting to strengthen its collections of the international statistical publications from all levels of government.

BOOKS

The collection of books on agricultural subjects is adequate, though perhaps not as strong as the serial publications. There is a good representation of works which have appeared since 1800, among them many nineteenth-century addresses delivered before American agricultural societies by Samuel Griswold Goodrich, Noah Webster, and others. Early books include an incunabulum, *Opera Agricolationum* (1496), and first and early editions of the works of Samuel Hartlib, Gervase Markham, Jacques Vanière, and Charles Estienne (whose *L'Agriculture et maison rustique* [1570] is held by both the Arents Tobacco Collection and the Rare Book Division). Agricultural Americana in the Rare Book Division includes Jared Eliot's *Essays upon Field-Husbandry in New England* (1760), *American Husbandry* (1775) by "An American," and Samuel Deane's *The New-England Farmer* (1790).

OTHER MATERIALS

Several specialized collections are of more than passing interest. There are, for example, materials on North and South American Indian agriculture; many of the catalog entries for this subject represent periodical articles. Over 2,000 cards in the Public Catalog refer to the horse. Of particular interest are stud books, among them the *American Stud Book* (1873–), the *American Morgan Horse Register* (1894–), and the *Arab Horse Stud Book* (1919–). Exemplifying the library's often astonishing range of subject matter are catalog headings such as "Horse Stealing and Horse Thieves," which contains the constitution and by-laws of the eighteenth-century Montgomery County (Pennsylvania) Society for the Recovery of Stolen Horses and Bringing Thieves to Justice, and material on Josephine Amelia Perkins, the celebrated horse thief.

Several hundred uncataloged agricultural machinery catalogs date from the late nineteenth and early twentieth centuries. John Wynn Baker's *A Short Description and List, with the Prices of the Instruments of Husbandry, Made in the Factory at Laughlinstown Near Celbridge, in the Country of Kildare* (1767) is a typical cataloged item.

Manuscript holdings on agriculture consist of entries in American account books of the eighteenth and early nineteenth centuries, and in commonplace books, memoranda, and the like. Additional material appears in the papers of Albert Shaw, Bolton Hall, and Horace Greeley.

The Prints Division has a variety of prints and engravings on agricultural subjects throughout its collections. For example, there are farming views in the Phelps Stokes collection of American historical prints, in the scrapbooks of wood engravings by Alexander Anderson, in the holdings of bank note vignettes, and in engravings after artists like William Sidney Mount. In the collection of illustrated books in the Spencer Collection is the seventeenth-century *Yu Chih K'êng Chih T'u* ("Cultivating Rice and Manufacturing Silk"); consisting of forty-six engravings with colors added later by hand, it was made for an emperor of China.

ARENTS TOBACCO COLLECTION

The Arents Tobacco Collection, the product of over forty years of collecting by George Arents, was first presented to the library in 1943–44; upon Arents's death in 1960, the collection was endowed to continue its function. The largest and most comprehensive library in the world on the history, literature, and lore of tobacco, the Arents Tobacco Collection is housed in rooms on the third floor of the library's Central Building along with the Arents Collection of Books in Parts, given in 1957. Among the furnishings of the rooms are association items from Arents' collection, including a wooden figure of an Indian chief, an eighteenth-century figure of a Scotsman holding a cigar box, and an early vending machine that opens when coins are inserted.[1]

In 1944 the Arents Tobacco Collection contained more than 4,000 pieces in twenty languages. By 1956 it had grown to include more than 7,000 items in twenty-six languages, including Bulgarian, Japanese, Latin, and Lithuanian. The Tobacco Collection presently includes more than 12,000 books and manuscripts. In addition are approximately 125,000 cigarette cards, along with other materials related to tobacco, such as sheet music, drawings, and prints. The collection is remarkable for the superb condition of its holdings. Arents attempted to obtain the finest or most interesting copy available of a book or pamphlet sought; this policy has been followed by the curator.

Although the collection is devoted to tobacco and includes almost every important work dealing with the subject, it also contains many historical and literary works in which tobacco receives only incidental mention. Among the fields represented in the collection are American and English literature (with special emphasis on Restoration drama) and medicine. Materials as diverse as rare herbals, government proclamations and edicts from Europe and the Americas, and early records of travel in the New World complement the holdings of other parts of the Research Libraries.

In addition to its comprehensive holdings on the history of tobacco, the Arents Tobacco Collection has a representative collection on the technical aspects of the subject; covered are such topics as "Smoking and Health," "Chemical Composition of Tobacco," "Tobacco Manufacture," and "Tobacco Marketing."

ARENTS TOBACCO PUBLICATIONS

The library has published the Arents Tobacco Collection series of books on the history or lore of tobacco, primarily facsimiles of significant, and often amusing, manuscripts in the collection, beginning with *A Few Words about Pipes, Smoking, & Tobacco* (1947).

The contents of the collection are described in a catalog compiled by Jerome E. Brooks entitled *Tobacco: Its History Illustrated by the Books,*

Manuscripts and Engravings in the Library of George Arents, Jr.[2] A continuing supplement to that catalog has been issued; in all, ten parts of the supplement, entitled *Tobacco: A Catalogue of the Books, Manuscripts and Engravings Acquired Since 1942,* have appeared since 1958.[3] Items in both the catalog and its supplement are arranged chronologically, commencing with the earliest work held in the collection, Waldseemüller's *Cosmographiae introductio* (1507). This supplemented catalog has been the public source of information about the collection; cards for the Arents Tobacco Collection do not appear in the Public Catalog. In the future, entries for new acquisitions will appear in the *Dictionary Catalog of The Research Libraries.*

RESOURCES

The following general descriptions are intended to serve as a sampling of the materials found in the Arents Tobacco Collection.

BOOKS AND RARE PERIODICALS

Isolated issues of periodicals are retained when they contain articles relating to tobacco. The collection also holds rare serials such as *Pipe Lover's Magazine, Bulletin de l'Association française contre l'Abus du Tabac,* and *Cope's Smoke Room Booklets and Other Publications.*

Almost every American and English author of note is represented by first editions from the first work in the English language devoted entirely to tobacco, Anthony Chute's *Tabaco* (1595), through Aldous Huxley's *Time Must Have a Stop* (1944), and later publications. The list includes such rarities as Thomas Nash's *Pierce Penilesse* (1592), Robert Burton's *Anatomy of Melancholy* (1621), Laurence Stern's *A Sentimental Journey* (1768), Nathaniel Hawthorne's "The Celestial Railway" (1846), Herman Melville's *Mardi* (1849), and Robert Louis Stevenson's *Treasure Island* (1883). The range of works which refer to tobacco is large enough to include both *A Counterblaste to Tobacco* (1604) issued anonymously by James I, and a popular celebration of tobacco in Clement Clarke Moore's "A Visit from St. Nicholas," published in *The New-York Book of Poetry* (1837).

The Arents Tobacco Collection contains a wealth of British plays. Although the works of Shakespeare, curiously enough, make no reference to tobacco, the other great Elizabethan and Jacobean playwrights are well represented. There are the two "humour" plays of Ben Jonson, *Every Man out of His Humour* (1600) and *Every Man in His Humour* (1616). There is a first folio edition of the plays of Beaumont and Fletcher,

1. See Jerome E. Brooks, "The Library Relating to Tobacco Collected by George Arents," *BNYPL* 48 (1944): 3–15.

2. 4 vols. (New York: The Rosenbach Company, 1937–43); a separate index volume appeared in 1952.

3. Published by The New York Public Library, 1958–69. Parts I–VII were compiled by Sarah A. Dickson, and Parts VIII–X by Perry Hugh O'Neil.

as well as editions of some of their other plays. Other well-known sixteenth- and seventeenth-century dramatists whose works are in the collection are John Marston, Thomas Middleton, John Webster, and Edward Sharpham. Dramatists of the Restoration such as Congreve, Wycherley, and Farquhar are represented. Among European works of literature is a first separate edition of Molière's *Le Festin de Pierre* (1683).

Americana from the age of European discovery is particularly well represented by such items as Peter Martyr's *De orbo novo decades* (1516), the works of Thevet, Benzoni, and Acosta, and a fine set of De Bry, along with Dutch, Spanish, French, and English editions of Esquemeling's work on American buccaneers, *De Americaensche Zeerovers* (1678).

The collection of early herbals is good; the holdings are described in the section on botany in chapter 58 of this *Guide*. Medical books are a specialty; of particular interest are those advocating tobacco as a cure for all diseases and distresses, such as Nicolás Monardes's *Segunda parte del libro de las cosas que se traen de nuestras Indias Occidentales* (1571) and Gilles Everaerts's *De herba panacea* (1587).[4] There are rich holdings of medical books from the seventeenth century, including Edmund Gardiner's *The Triall of Tobacco* (1610), Stephen Bradwell's *A Watchman for the Pest* (1625), and Lorenz Strauss' *Palaestra medica* (1686), along with popular medical books such as James Primrose's *De vulgi erroribus in medicina* (1639) and *The Kitchin-Physician*, by "T. K." (1680).

Early dictionaries and grammars which mention tobacco are also present as, for example, John Florio's *A Worlde of Words* (1598), Jean Nicot's *Thresor de la langue francoyse* (1606), Ludovico Bertonio's *Vocubulario dela lengua Aymara* (1612), and a first edition of Samuel Johnson's *Dictionary of the English Language* (1755).

Government publications are not currently collected by the Arents Tobacco Collection; such publications on tobacco may be found in the Economic and Public Affairs Division, which receives publications of the United States Government and those of the Canadian National Government. There are, however, a good many government documents of an historical nature in the Arents Tobacco Collection, such as those relating to the tobacco monopoly in France and for similar government monopolies in other countries of Europe and the Americas.

MANUSCRIPTS

There are many important manuscripts in the Arents Tobacco Collection. Of note are literary manuscripts such as "The Poor Labouring Bee" (ca. 1599) by Robert Devereux, Earl of Essex, a manuscript of "Court Eclogs" (1716) by Lady Mary Wortley Montagu in the hand of Alexander Pope, Charles Lamb's "Farewell to Tobacco" (ca. 1805), Oscar Wilde's *The Importance of Being Earnest*,[5] and "Father Abraham," a first draft of part of William Faulkner's *The Hamlet* (1940). Other manuscripts include documents of Queen Elizabeth I, Sir Walter Raleigh, Catherine de Medici, and Louis XIV, among others.

A large group of manuscripts bears on the United States. Included are a letter, a receipt, and a document signed by George Washington; letters of Thomas Jefferson and Charles Carroll of Carrollton; and other manuscripts of figures famous in American history. In addition are Revolutionary tobacco payments and Confederate documents for rations. Of prime importance in this American group are the manuscripts of Robert Morris, including official copies of contracts, accounts, court evidence statements, and other items relating to suits involving Morris and various other parties as a result of his tobacco trade activities. There are 54 autograph letters of Morris, among them a tobacco contract negotiated by him between the United States and the Fermes Générales of France.

Further documents include commercial papers related to the tobacco trade in Virginia, Maryland, New York, and Georgia in the eighteenth century, and two receipt books of the New York City tobacconist James Bryer dated 1795 and 1807. A large group of manuscript documents comes from Frederick County, Maryland; ranging in date from the mid-eighteenth century, this group consists of bills of indictment, slave bills, tavern licenses, bills of sale, and the like.

Japanese manuscripts date from the early eighteenth century onward. A delicately illustrated rice paper manuscript (ca. 1773) called "Haensô No Ben" (A Farewell to Tobacco) contains poems on a universally expressed and often unrealized wish to abandon the "precious bane."

SHEET MUSIC

Popular tunes range from "The Tobacco Box" of 1795 to modern titles such as "The Maple Leaf Rag," "My Little Murad," "Pack Up Your Troubles in Your Old Kit Bag," "Cigarette," and "The Sweetheart of Sigma Chi." Of exceptional interest is a rich recent acquisition of sheet music produced in Victorian England. Other musical rarities are noted in chapter 31 of this *Guide*, "Music Division and General Music Resources."

PRINTS AND DRAWINGS

Pictorial representations of tobacco, tobacco pipes, and tobacco smoking include original drawings, watercolors, engravings, mezzotints, and aquatints. There are prints by Hogarth, Gillray, and Cruikshank, and by North American lithographers such as Currier and Ives. Drawings of Rowlandson, Lewis Baumer, Kate Greenaway, and Rackham are present. Twenty-seven sheets of pencil drawings by George Catlin depict pipes and stems found among the various Indian tribes of North America.

The cultivation and use of tobacco in the Western Hemisphere are documented by watercolor illustrations. Early examples of such drawings are the 31 superb illustrations in a Cuban manuscript of 1764, Nicolas José Rapun's "Instruccion general de el cultivo de tavacos." Perhaps the most notable contemporary drawings are 12 watercolors on Aztec and Mayan subjects executed in 1939 by Ariel Baynes, after the originals as reproduced in Lord Kingsborough's *Antiquities of Mexico* (1831–48).

---

4. See Sarah Augusta Dickson, *Panacea or Precious Bane: Tobacco in Sixteenth Century Literature* (The New York Public Library, 1954).

5. A facsimile of this has been published; see *The Importance of Being Earnest . . . as Originally Written by Oscar Wilde* (The New York Public Library, 1956).

TOBACCO EPHEMERA

A collection of posters, labels, trade cards, and stickers documents the history of tobacco. An exceptionally fine collection of cigarette cards numbers more than 125,000 pieces; included are more than 3,000 complete sets. Cards in this collection originated in England, France, Germany, Holland, Japan, Siam, Spain, the United States, and other nations.

61

GARDENING, HORTICULTURE, AND FORESTRY

Histories, bibliographies, and dictionaries for the subjects of gardening, horticulture, and forestry are collected comprehensively by the library. Other forms of printed material are collected on a selective or representative basis. By virtue of being a depository for United States Federal Government publications, the library holds substantially complete files of the bulletins and reports of agricultural stations, national parks, and similar organizations. There are good holdings of materials published by other national governments, although state and municipal records are present in large numbers only from the United States and Canada.

The Research Libraries do not generally collect works on the technical aspects of gardening, horticulture, and forestry because of the other large collections in New York City which provide such holdings to the public. Information relating to the library's resources in this area may be found in the sections of this *Guide* on "The Biological Sciences" and "Agriculture," in chapters 58 and 59.

Periodicals are featured in the holdings. Journals of the nineteenth and twentieth centuries on gardening are usually represented by substantial, if incomplete, files. In gardening, for example, some 200 titles are listed in the Public Catalog, not all of them currently published and received. Horticulture is also represented by a substantial number. Included under these headings are titles such as *Florists' Exchange* (1888–1961), *Horticulture* (1904–   ), *The Garden* (1872–1927), and *Gardener's Chronicle of America* (1905–51). The contents of periodicals in these subjects are not generally indexed in the library's catalogs. The publications of horticulture societies and gardening clubs likewise make an important contribution, although files are by no means complete. Included are national, state, and local organizations.

Periodicals related to forestry include titles such as *Schweizerische Anstalt für das forstliche Versuchswesen. Mitteilungen* (1891–1959) and *Revue des eaux et forêts* (1862–1948), along with trade journals, typical among which is *The Lumberman's Review* (1892–1930). The increasingly important topic of conservation is represented by *Conservation in the Americas* (1946–   ), *Michigan Conservation* (1931–   , incomplete), among others, and by foreign titles such as *Ochrona przyrody* (1950) and *Razvedka nedr* (1947–   ).

GARDENING

Entries in the Public Catalog under the subject of gardening are arranged chronologically. For example, under the heading "Gardening, to 1800" are works arranged by date of publication. The General Research and Humanities Division has had the primary collecting responsibility for this area, including the topic of landscape gardening (formerly the responsibility of the Art and Architecture Division); this topic is of first importance, including as it does most of the works on individual and historic gardens, along with similar specialized materials. Books of a general nature, most of them of interest to the amateur gardener, are maintained in the reference collection of the Main Reading Room. General works are available in the collections, dating from the sixteenth century and including such items as Nicolas de Bonnefons's *Le iardinier françois* (1651) and works by Sir William Chambers and others. The Prints Division has a wealth of prints of gardens and flowers, although these are not arranged by subject but by the name of the artist or print maker.

HORTICULTURE

Special subjects, such as fruits and flower growing, are well covered by monographs, journals, and the publications of specialized organizations. A collection of some interest includes uncataloged seed catalogs. The library presently receives the catalogs of only four companies; but there are, in addition, the catalogs of a number of other companies ranging in date from 1860 to the 1950s, at which time most appear to have been discontinued. All of these catalogs are administered by the Annex Section of the Research Libraries: detailed information about them is available in the "Scrapbook File" of the General Research and Humanities Division.

Materials related to the subject of horticulture may be found in other sections of this *Guide*. Among those is "Agriculture," described in chapter 59; of particular note is the discussion of various monograph series issued by departments of agriculture and experimental stations, works on plant culture, and the like. In addition, "Botany," treated in chapter 58, contains references to materials of historical importance to the topic of horticulture, including botanical information available in illustrated folio works.

FORESTRY

This subject is more than adequately covered; the preceding observations on types of materials present are applicable here. Periodicals have been discussed above; the publications of forestry organizations and the reports of national and state bureaus of forestry are substantial, particularly for the United States. Approximately 550 entries under the heading "Natural Resources—Conservation" refer to government publications, including conservation laws of the states of the United States. There are also reports of national and international congresses on conservation and publications of the associations and organizations concerned with the subject.

The Local History and Genealogy Division has not only pictorial material on United States national parks in its archives of photographs, stereopticon views, and scrapbooks, but also regularly receives ephemeral material which is stored in vertical files. Ephemera from state parks in the United States is also available, although on a more limited basis. As a matter of course commercially published materials augment this ephemera on state and national parks.

62

FISH AND FISHERIES

This collection, which includes studies in ichthyology, technical material on fish culture, and works on fishing as an industry, has some strong points. At present only bibliographies, serial government reports, books dealing with whales and whaling, and materials on the economic development of the fish resources of the world are collected comprehensively; but earlier periodicals and society publications on the general subject are useful for a study of the history of world fish and fishing. Two checklists of publications on fishes and fisheries, published by the library in 1899 and 1909, are of historical interest.[1]

Approximately 100 periodical titles appear in the Public Catalog under the heading "Fisheries —Periodical and Society Publications," of which some 30 are currently published and received. Among these are the *Dansk Fiskeritidende* (1904–), *World Fishing* (1952–), and the *AFZ: allgemeine Fischwirtschaftszeitung* (1957–). Abstracts of articles in serial publications may be found in reference works such as *Commercial Fisheries Abstracts* (1952–) and *World Fisheries Abstracts* (1950–). As a depository institution, the library holds substantially complete runs of publications related to fishing sponsored by the governments of the United States and Canada, as well as the United Nations. The publications of the Food and Agriculture Organization of the United Nations are equally well represented, as are those of fishery bureaus in the United States and other nations. The Economic and Public Affairs Division maintains complete runs of the statistical publications of such agencies.

The collection of books and pamphlets from the nineteenth and twentieth centuries is more than adequate. As already noted, historical materials constitute a feature of considerable interest; among these are rare and significant titles such as Ippolito Salviani's *Aquatilium animalium Historiae* (1554), Francis Willughby's *De historia piscium* (1686), and Peter Artedi's *Ichthyologia* (1738).

Certain specialized categories within the broad subject of fish and fisheries deserve more detailed attention. In 1937, Miss Caroline C. and Miss Louise DeForest Haynes gave a collection of over 100 rare works on the salmon, in memory of their brother William DeForest Haynes. The resources on whales and whaling include a number of accounts of whaling voyages, mostly of the nineteenth century, including one in verse, Charles Murphey's *A Journal of a Whaling Voyage on Board Ship Dauphin* (1877). Manuscripts in the Manuscripts and Archives Division include the logbooks of the whalers *Adeline* (1834–37), *Petrel* (1866–68; 1871–72), and *Greyhound* (1887–92).

Various other portions of this *Guide* discuss material related to fish and fisheries. Perhaps the most important is the collection on fishing as a sport (see chapter 41, "Sports and Games"), which contains a notable representation of Isaac Walton. Other resources are present in the rich collection of publications of scientific expeditions (see chapter 56, "Natural History"), and the extensive series of academy and learned society publications (see chapter 6, "Learned Societies and Museum Publications").

1. See "Checklist of Works on Fish and Fisheries in The New York Public Library," *BNYPL* 3 (1899): 296–312 ff; and "List of Works in The New York Public Library Relating to Fishing and Fish Culture," *BNYPL* 13 (1909): 259–307.

63

FOOD, COOKERY, AND DOMESTIC ECONOMY

The subject of food and cookery is collected comprehensively; some 27,000 volumes, along with manuscripts and other materials, make up an outstanding collection. The subject is administered by the General Research and Humanities Division, and there are significant related collections in other divisions of the library. The Science and Technology Research Center holds materials related to the technologies of food and cookery, and the Economic and Public Affairs Division collects reports on the financial structure and history of various food corporations, distilleries, and the like.

The subject of food and cookery is varied, and there is a multiplicity of subject headings in the Public Catalog relevant to it. There are approximately 6,500 entries under the subject heading "Food," and in addition a great number of related subjects such as sugar, coffee, and tea receive separate entries. Related fields such as gastronomy, the history of food, nutrition, and wine culture hold much of interest. The General Research and Humanities Division maintains an inactive Food History File; entries in two card drawers refer to information published prior to 1935. (It should be noted that the library does not collect materials related to the medical aspects of food and cookery.)

Periodical holdings are substantial. The library receives major abstracting reviews such as *Journal of the Science of Food and Agriculture* (1950–) and *Nutrition Abstracts and Reviews* (1931–), as well as the numerous United Nations publications related to food. Periodicals received originate not only in Europe and the United States, but also in Asia; examples of these are the *Journal of Nutrition and Dietics* (1964–) from India and the *Philippine Journal of Nutrition* (1962–).

COOKBOOKS

The library's outstanding collection of approximately 8,000 cookbooks includes cookbooks issued by individuals and private organizations which are not generally commercially available, and national and regional cookbooks from all countries. These range from "Cookery, African" to "Cookery—Yugoslavian," and include such specialties as "Cookery—Cake," "Cookery (Camp)," and "Cookery at Sea." America is best represented with about 1,600 titles divided roughly as follows: 80 titles published before 1860; more than 500 titles published between 1901 and 1925; and more than 800 since 1926. In addition are more than 200 books on American regional cookery of all periods. The library's copy of Mary Randolph's *The Virginia Housewife* (1824) appears to be the only recorded copy of that edition. The collection of cookbooks in the Jewish Division, while not large, is significant. Cookery is analyzed by subject; there is also a chronological arrangement under subject.

In 1941 the library received, under the terms of the will of the late Mrs. Helen Hay Whitney, a collection of 17 manuscripts and more than 200 printed books, the majority of them English,

ranging in date from the fifteenth to the twentieth century. The majority of the printed volumes are of the seventeenth and eighteenth centuries. The earliest book is Girolamo Ruscelli's *The Secretes of the Reverende Maister Alexis of Piemount* (1558); other notable books in the Whitney collection are *The Good Hous-wives Treasurie* (1588) and Hannah Glasse's *The Art of Cookery, Made Plain and Easy* (1747).

There is a fifteenth-century manuscript compilation of recipes, copied on vellum with the names of dishes rubricated. Among later manuscripts are the recipe collections associated with Joane Yate, Lady Anne Morton, Hester Denbigh, and Mary Ellen Meredith.[1]

Associated with the books and manuscripts in the Whitney collection are cookbooks in the Arents Tobacco Collection, notably *The Ladies Cabinet Opened* (1639). In the Manuscripts and Archives Division are recipes of the Pennypacker family of the late nineteenth century, along with various eighteenth- and nineteenth-century recipes from Mexico.

MENUS

The library's collection of menus, maintained at the Annex Section, includes printed and manuscript menus dating from 1849. The nucleus of the collection came from the 19,500 menus presented to the library in 1909 by Miss Frank E. Buttolph; the collection has been augmented by subsequent gifts. It is arranged by date.

The present collection has a notable representation of menus from fraternities and fraternal organizations; wine and food societies; commercial, professional, and political groups; educational and religious institutions; hotels, steamships, and restaurants.

Of special interest is a bound file of bills of fare of the Fifth Avenue Hotel from August 1859 to August 1882. Present also is a collection of old Waldorf-Astoria menus. Some menus for this and other hotels in New York City are mounted in scrapbooks with other related materials, and maintained by the Local History and Genealogy Division.

Some menus, because of the fame of the people attending, the occasion, or the fine printing, have been retained by the Rare Book Division. Some of these are for banquets in New York City for the Prince of Wales, later King Edward VII, for Queen Elizabeth II, and for a luncheon honoring Colonel John Glenn, Jr., and his fellow astronauts.

ALCOHOLIC DRINKS

The ethical aspects of the subject of alcoholic drinks are covered under "Temperance," in chapter 18 of this *Guide*. Of some 57 periodicals re-

---

1. See Lewis M. Stark, "The Whitney Cookery Collection," *BNYPL* 50 (1946): 103–26; published separately by the library in 1946; 2nd edition, 1959.

lated to the subject of alcoholic drinks, 18 from 5 nations are currently received by the library. The subject of wines is best represented, with more than 1,500 entries in the Public Catalog for topics such as winemaking, trade statistics, wines of various nations, and the like. Some rarities are present, such as Alfonso Ferri's *De ligni sancti multiplici medicina, & vini exhibitione* (1538). Periodical titles on wine and winemaking number more than 30, with 19 currently published and received from nine countries. There is additional information on individual wines.

Works on the eighteenth-century Whiskey Insurrection in Pennsylvania in the Rare Book Division include Hugh Henry Brackenridge's *Incidents of the Insurrection* (1795), along with James Elliot's account and printed documents and speeches of Albert Gallatin and Edmund Randolph.

The Liebmann collection of American historical documents presented to the library by Alfred J. Liebmann in 1954 contains 226 manuscript items and a dozen printed pieces relative to the production and use of whiskey, rum, and brandy in the United States during the period 1665–1910. Included are orders for liquors, tavern licenses, U.S. Army commissary requisitions, and letters and documents signed by presidents, military commanders and others. The majority of items reflect American history prior to 1865. A small but significant group of manuscripts documents the Whiskey Insurrection.[2]

NARCOTICS

Aside from government publications and general reference works on drugs and drug addiction, the library does not collect extensively in this field. There is an attempt to maintain a representative collection on the social aspects of drug taking and related subjects. Medical texts on narcotics are not generally collected.

Of the narcotics, opium receives the largest number of entries in the Public Catalog; included are social and historical aspects of that topic such as the Opium War (1840–42). Related subject headings in the Public Catalog include "Hallucinations and Illusions," "Lysergic Acid Diethylamide," "Hallucinogens," and the like. The American History Division has material on the ceremonial use of peyote by the American Indians.

---

2. See Robert W. Hill, "The Liebmann Collection of American Historical Documents," *BNYPL* 58 (1954): 386–91.

DOMESTIC ECONOMY

Many of the subjects related to domestic economy have been described in other sections of this *Guide*. As an example, spinning and weaving have been considered as technological aspects of manufacture in chapter 57, and costume design has been considered as part of the general subject of art resources in chapter 28.

The collection relating to domestic economy, administered by the General Research and Humanities Division, is, on the whole, adequate. It consists of some 5,600 volumes. The history and bibliography of the subject are collected comprehensively.

There is a particularly interesting, although by no means complete, representation of nineteenth-century journals, including titles as diverse as *Economist and General Adviser* (1824–25) and *Sanktpeterburgskoye yezhenedel'noye sochineniya, kasayushcheyesya do razmnozheniya domostroitel'stva* ("St. Petersburg Weekly Publication *Re* the Increase of Housebuilding"; May-October 1778). Some 7 periodical titles are currently received.

Books published before 1850 number just over 100, beginning with the early sixteenth-century translation by Raffaele Maffie of Xenephon's *Oeconomicus*. Books printed since 1851 include a first edition of Isabella Mary Beeton's *The Book of Household Management* (1861). There are, in addition, numerous later editions of this household classic known popularly as "Mrs. Beeton's Cookery Book." There is a good collection of the works of the American Mary Virginia Terhune, among them works on household management such as *Common Sense in the Household* (1871).

There is an unusual collection of international fashion periodicals of the nineteenth and twentieth centuries. The subjects of homemaking and beauty culture include historical materials. Hairdressing as a subject includes a good collection of journals, among them *The American Hairdresser* (1904–) and other titles, most of these French or American. The Economic and Public Affairs Division has the constitution and membership books of the Journeymen Barbers', Hairdressers' and Cosmetologists' International Union of America (1892–). Dressmaking and millinery are represented by works in the general collections. The subject of perfumery, essences, and essential oils forms another strong collection. Materials include the bibliographical check-list, the *Fritzsche Library Bulletin* (1957–), and 13 other journal titles published primarily since 1945, but with long runs of *American Perfumer and Essential Oil Review* (1907–55) and *Perfumery and Essential Oil Record* (1916–54).

64

MILITARY AND NAVAL SCIENCE

MILITARY SCIENCE

The collection of 43,700 volumes and numerous manuscripts on military art and science is strong. There is an excellent representation of regimental histories and personal narratives. A

wide-ranging accumulation of official publications and a number of unofficial publications provides an adequate representation of current materials from most countries for the general reader. For research, however, the principal value of the collection is historical.

The General Research and Humanities Division collects comprehensively in this field. The Economic and Public Affairs Division assumes secondary collecting responsibility in the fields of jurisprudence, military law, court martial, military administration and registers, and United States federal and state government reports. The estimated growth of the collections is indicated by the following:

1921	12,600 volumes
1930	17,900
1966	43,700

Perhaps the most significant gift in this field was the transfer by the Military Service Institution of its library of more than 8,000 pieces in 1912, with a later deposit in 1913 of 500 books and pamphlets including government documents, Civil War records, and many papers formerly owned by General John M. Schofield. The Parsons collection in the Science and Technology Research Center contains a number of items of military interest, particularly in connection with engineering.

Periodical holdings are comprehensive. The library has almost complete holdings on microfilm of *Stars and Stripes* and complete holdings of *Yank* in all editions;[1] a complete file of the World War I edition of *Stars and Stripes* is in the Rare Book Division. Among publications concerning subjects as diverse as arms and armor, military collectors, and military engineering are *Allgemeine Schweizerische Militaerzeitschrift* (1865–), *Army and Navy Journal* (1863–), and *Journal of the Royal Artillery* (1858–); representative of earlier items is the *Military and Naval Magazine of the United States* (1833–36). There are numerous handbooks and manuals, with good American and British collections. Military laws, regulations, and decisions of courts martial are well represented, as are routine reports and other publications of war ministries, state militia departments, and similar administrative divisions. Associated with these materials are the rich collection of session laws in the Economic and Public Affairs Division, administrative reports from most countries of the world, and publications of international organizations such as the League of Nations and the United Nations.

Technical subjects of consequence include strong collections relating to defense, military tactics, firearms, artillery, and ballistics, with special features such as the World War I engineering materials in the Wilgus collection in the Manuscripts and Archives Division. The Science and Technology Research Center does not cover military science as such, but contains much material on aspects of the subject such as chemical warfare, nuclear warfare, and the military uses of science.

Materials in the historical classifications for all nations include special divisions for important wars in which are located not only historical works but also those dealing with particular phases of military art and science applicable to the war in question. Materials on military hospitals are composed principally of historical works,

the field of medicine not being a collecting area for the library. The collections on war and peace consist of materials of varying importance on philosophical and ethical problems, and are noted in detail in chapter 18 of this *Guide*.

ARMY LISTS AND REGIMENTAL HISTORIES

Published American army lists in the collection date from 1809 to the present, including the rare 1863 issue, suppressed because of serious errors in the text. English army lists are available from 1754, and there are substantial files from Austria, France, Prussia, Saxony, Switzerland, and other countries.

Regimental histories (both official and unofficial), personal accounts, and related materials concerned with military units form a significant and growing collection. Those for the United States number well over 2,000, with strong holdings for the Civil War and World Wars I and II. Unit histories for the United States Air Force are also held in strength.[2]

There are fine collections of monographs and periodicals relating to regiments from Canada, Australia, and New Zealand.[3] A 1954 estimate indicated that more than 800 British regimental histories were held by the library. Some 150 regimental histories in the Slavonic Division are, for the most part, nineteenth-century Russian publications, many of them purchased from the library of the Grand Duke Vladimir Alexandrovich in 1931.

RARE BOOKS, MANUSCRIPTS, MAPS, AND OTHER MATERIALS

Military classics, such as the writings of Valturio and Vegetius, are present in editions dating back to the fifteenth century. A notable vellum copy of Valturio's *De Re Militari* (1472) in the Spencer Collection is considered to be the second illustrated book printed in Italy; also in the Spencer Collection are Dürer's treatise on fortifications, *Etliche underrich, zu befestigung der*

---

2. See the following compilations by Charles E. Dornbusch, published in three volumes as *Military Bibliography of the Civil War* by The New York Public Library:

Vol. I: *Regimental Publications and Personal Narratives of the Civil War; A Checklist: Northern States* (1962; reprinted by the library and Arno Press Inc., 1971).

Vol. II: *Regimental Publications and Personal Narratives: Southern, Border, and Western States and Territories; and Union and Confederate Biographies* (1967).

Vol. III: *General References; Armed Forces; and Campaigns and Battles* (1972).

See also the compiler's *Unit Histories of the United States Air Force, including Privately Printed Personal Narratives* (Hampton Bays, N.Y.: Hampton Books, 1958), and *Histories: Personal Narratives: United States Army* (Cornwallville, N.Y.: Hope Farm Press, 1967).

3. See the following compilations by Charles E. Dornbusch published by the Hope Farm Press, Cornwallville, N.Y.: *The Canadian Army 1855– 1955; Regimental Histories and a Guide to the Regiments* (1959); *The Canadian Army, 1855– 1965; Lineages, Regimental Histories* (1966); *Australian Military Bibliography* (1963); and *The New Zealand Army: A Bibliography* (1961).

---

1. See Charles E. Dornbusch, "*Stars and Stripes*: Check List of the Several Editions," *BNYPL* 52 (1948): 331–40; 53 (1949): 335–38, and "Yank, the Army Weekly," *BNYPL* 54 (1950): 272–79. Published separately by the library.

Stett, Schloss und Flecken (1527), Jean Perrissin's *Der erste Tail* (1570), and Leonhardt Fronsperger's *Kriegsbuch* (1578).

Jacopo Mariano Taccola's "Da machinis" (ca. 1449) is one of the vellum manuscripts in the Spencer Collection. The Manuscripts and Archives Division's holdings are of considerable interest. Many diaries, orderly books, plans of maneuvers, correspondence, journals, contracts, regimental returns, muster and pay rolls, and the like relate to the American Revolution; included is material on Colonial, British, and German troops. Other items cover later periods of United States history; of interest are letter books, orderly books, and conscription records of the Confederate States during the Civil War. Papers of army officers include those of Robert Rogers, William Alexander (Lord Stirling), Henry Dearborn, Horatio Gates, Mordecai Gist, John Lamb, Daniel Morgan, and Baron Von Riedesel.

Within the extensive papers of Philip Schuyler and the Gansevoort family of Albany there are separate series of military correspondence and papers. Those of General Schuyler and General Peter Gansevoort relate to the command of important forces during the Revolution. Gansevoort's materials continue to show militia duties and campaigns until the War of 1812, while those of a grandson, Henry Sanford Gansevoort (1834–71), reflect his artillery and cavalry commands during the Civil War. In addition are the Civil War papers of Ezra Ayers Carman, Francis Vinton Greene, Robert E. Lee, and John Wolcott Phelps. Further eighteenth- and nineteenth-century manuscripts are in the Bancroft, Emmet, Ford, and Myers collections. Later periods covered include a group of World War I letters from military personnel.[4]

Drawings in the Spencer Collection and the Prints Division include representations of batteries and redoubts of the American Revolution by Archibald Robertson, and 138 original drawings made by the staff artists of *Leslie's Weekly* during the Civil War. Two fortification collections purchased in 1946 include 100 original watercolor plans (1690–1710) for forts and 140 manuscript plans (1710–65) of European battlefields and fortifications. Military materials in the Prints Division may be located through the name of the artist or printmaker; military portraits are found in sources as diverse as Goya's *Los desastres de la guerra* (1863) and Otto Dix's *Der Krieg* (1914).

The Butterfield collection in the Map Division is made up of maps used by General Daniel Butterfield during the Civil War. The group of seventy-one maps includes hand-drawn specimens and a number seized from the Confederate armies. In addition, the division has maps covering the American Revolutionary War in New York State, the Civil War, and both World Wars. There are English general staff maps for World War I in the Parsons collection of the Science and Technology Research Center.

The Rare Book Division holds thirty-nine decorations of honor which have been in the collections since 1912: the division is not adding to this collection. Among the decorations are the French Legion of Honor, the Russian Order of St. Vladimir, the Prussian Iron Cross, and 2 Napoleonic medals.

NAVAL SCIENCE

The collection of 29,200 volumes and numerous manuscripts relating to naval art and history is stronger in certain areas than that relating to military science. Naval history has been given particular consideration; as a result of the James Owen Proudfit Fund, many important and valuable works have been secured. Most areas in naval art and history are collected comprehensively, with the exception of government reports and publications and works on naval artillery and ordnance, torpedos, submarine vessels, and submarine warfare, where the coverage is representative. Naval log books and journals for vessels of the American, English, and French navies from the late seventeenth century to the modern period are in the Manuscripts and Archives Division, as are more than seventy letters, documents, and drawings of Robert Fulton relating to the submarine, the explosive mine, and the steam vessel as instruments of war.

The growth of the collections is indicated by the following table of estimated strength:

1921	8,400 volumes
1930	12,000
1966	29,200

Periodical holdings are outstanding. There are excellent representations from many maritime nations, generally with complete files of important titles. These include not only journals, but the publications of societies and institutions, navy registers, and other materials. Among titles currently received are the United States Naval Institute *Proceedings* (1874–), *Revista general de marina* (1877–), and *Naval Research Logistics Quarterly* (1954–), as well as other more specialized periodicals. Official publications (reports, navigation directions, navy lists, and the like) are held in strength for many nations. Particularly noteworthy are the American and British navy lists; eighty volumes of the latter once belonged to the Duke of Clarence, later King William IV of England, whose annotations are present in some cases.[5]

A significant part of the holdings consists of personal accounts of the sea and sea voyages, shipwrecks, lifesaving and similar subjects. Included in the extensive collection of materials on pirates and piracy are two classics in the field: Exquemelin's *De Americaensche Zee-roovers* (1678), along with its 1684 English translation, *Bucaniers of America*, and Captain Charles Johnson's *General History of the . . . Pyrates* (1724).

There are approximately 110 books on navigation published before 1800, including noted rarities such as Pedro de Medina's *Arte de navegar* (1545), with sixteenth-century translations of the work into Italian, French, Dutch, and other languages; and Martín Cortés's *Breve compendio de la sphera y de la arte de navegar* (1551) with 6 editions of the Richard Eden translation of the work into English dating from 1561 to 1615. These and similar works of the period gain added importance from their relation to the holdings for the Age of Discovery in the Americas, an

---

4. See Deoch Fulton, ed., "War Letters of Augustus Trowbridge," *BNYPL* 43 (1939): 591–617 et seq. Published separately by the library.

5. See Edmund Pearson, "A King's Books," *BNYPL* 24 (1920): 3–6.

outstanding strength of the Research Libraries. The Rare Book Division has a first edition of Nathaniel Bowditch's *The New American Practical Navigator* (1802); most later editions of this work, which has been continually republished, are in the general collections. Approximately 1,400 entries in the Public Catalog are found under the heading of navigation, with many references referring to more specialized aspects of the subject. The collection of navigational tables dates from 1559.

Shipbuilding and marine engineering, fields administered by the Science and Technology Research Center, are well covered both in current and historical works and in periodicals. The Ships Index File, now inactive, locates printed information on individual ships and on some ships' captains. A 33-volume scrapbook series of clippings contains pictures of ships of all ages, harbors and ports, and related topics.

Naval history, a strong subject for all countries, includes additional material on individual naval battles or engagements. Particular interest attaches to the battle of Lepanto: in 1958 the library purchased the Sir William Stirling-Maxwell collection of 59 contemporaneous pamphlets and books celebrating this victory by the Italian and Spanish fleets over the Turks. The Rare Book Division seeks actively to augment the holdings, which now number about 70 pieces. A group of items on naval prizes includes material from England, France, and the Netherlands from the seventeenth and later centuries, including laws, ordinances, diplomatic correspondence, and the like, and material for the United States and Prussia dating from the eighteenth century. Naval biography is outstanding for all countries.

Many other areas of the library's collections enrich the resources in naval art and history. Classes of importance are history, geography, costume, and law (with strength in international law, although the library does not collect treatises on the subject). The public documents holdings of the Economic and Public Affairs Division provide a wealth of source material.

MANUSCRIPTS

Ships' logs, journals, official reports, proceedings of courts of enquiry, correspondence, and other items in the Manuscripts and Archives Division form a considerable body of source material. The larger part of this archive deals with American vessels and personnel, but there are many items relating to the English navy, and some to the French and Dutch navies. The Proudfit Fund has been used to purchase official naval manuscripts such as log books and flag or signal books.

The earliest American item is a letter book of the Navy Board of the Eastern Department of Boston for the period from October 24, 1778 to October 29, 1779, containing copies of some 249 letters. The journal of James Inderwick, surgeon on the brig *Argus*, chronicles events during the War of 1812.[6] The library also has the log book

of the *Argus* during part of the year 1813 and another journal kept by William Clarke, surgeon's mate on the vessel during 1812 and 1813. Other logs dating from 1815 to 1919 include those of the USS *Independence, Boxer, Lynx, Prometheus, Macedonian,*[7] *Guerriere, Boston, Potomac, Lexington, Congress, Kansas,* and the prize schooner *Patuxent*.

For the Civil War period are the day books of all articles ordered and supplied at the U.S. Navy Yard in Washington from July 18, 1861, to November 30, 1868, the papers of Gideon Welles for the period 1825 to 1885, and similar materials. The letters of Percival Drayton, most of these written on shipboard during the period 1861–65, deal with the naval operations of the war.[8] Among the papers of naval officers are those of Louis M. Goldsborough (1821–73), John Adolph Dahlgren (1829–67), David Conner (1842–47), and Thomas Turner (1868–70). The papers of Homer C. Blake (1840–69) and George C. Foulk (1884–87) contain not only material of United States naval interest but dispatches, letters, and reports of naval actions concerning Korea in the latter part of the nineteenth century. The manuscripts of William C. Church relate to his work during 1863–64 as founder, editor, and proprietor of *The United States Army and Navy Journal*. Narratives of voyages include that of Paul F. Taylor, on the USS *Quincy*, which carried President Franklin D. Roosevelt to the Crimean Conference in 1945.

Early English naval documents in the Manuscripts and Archives Division include the log book (1691–93) of the *Royal Sovereign* under Vice Admiral Ralph Delavall, operating against the French. There are also the logs of HMS *Temeraire* (1762–63), *Glory* (1794), *Isis* (1805), and others spanning a period from 1805 to 1900. Supplementing these materials are treatises, statistics, and receipts of payment from the seventeenth century; and receipts of payment, journals, diaries, rosters, and orderly books from the eighteenth century. The division has the memoirs of Gordon Gallie Macdonald, a lieutenant in the British Navy, for the period 1745 to 1831; the records of cases in the New York Vice Admiralty Courts for the period 1753 to 1770; and letter books of Sir Herbert Sawyer (1810–15), Francis Stanfell (1812–31), and James Creighton (1813–19), among others.

French naval manuscripts include a journal kept aboard *Le Jazon* (1745–46) and log books of armed vessels engaged in the transportation of troops to the French colonies in the West Indies and French Guiana during the period 1761 to 1776. A bound manuscript volume in French describes French naval participation in the American Revolution and other matters.

Two manuscript volumes in Dutch refer to signal flags of the Netherlands navy during the eighteenth century; they are illustrated with colored drawings.

---

6. See Victor Hugo Paltsits, ed., "Cruise of the U.S. Brig *Argus* in 1813. Journal of Surgeon James Inderwick," *BNYPL* 21 (1917): 383–405.

7. See Henry F. Graff, ed., "Bluejackets with Perry in Japan," *BNYPL* 54 (1950): 367–83 et seq. Published separately by the library.

8. Printed with an introductory note by the donor, Gertrude L. Hoyt, *BNYPL* 10 (1906): 587–625 et seq.

APPENDIXES

PUBLISHED CATALOGS OF THE
RESEARCH LIBRARIES' COLLECTIONS

An impressive number of the catalogs for the various collections found in the New York Public Library's Research Libraries have been produced in book form either by the library or in cooperation with other publishers. The divisions, collections, or subject areas represented are: American History Division; Arents Collection of Books Relating to Tobacco; Arents Collection of Books in Parts; Berg Collection of English and American Literature; Government Publications; Jewish Division; Manuscripts and Archives Division; Map Division; Music Division; Oriental Division; Rare Book Division; Schomburg Center for Research in Black Culture; Slavonic Division; Spencer Collection of Illustrated Books and Manuscripts and Fine Bindings; Theatre: Drama Collection, and Books on the Theatre; World War I Collection; and, more recently represented, the Dance Collection and the Local History and Genealogy Division. Only the following major subject areas are left uncovered: art and architecture, economic and public affairs, science and technology, prints, nonbook-form material in the Theatre Collection, phonorecords, and other audiovisual materials. All but the last four of these categories will, however, be included in the projected "Dictionary Catalog . . . 1911–1971."

GENERAL CATALOGS

DICTIONARY CATALOG OF THE RESEARCH LIBRARIES, 1911–1971 (projected)

This will be a photographic reproduction of the approximately 11,000,000 entries under author, title, and subject in the main Public Catalog of the Research Libraries, which was established in 1911 with the opening of the Central Building at Fifth Avenue and 42nd Street and located in Room 315. Incorporated into the catalog at that time were entries representing the holdings of two predecessor libraries, the Astor Library (founded in 1848) and the Lenox Library (established in 1870). Excluded from this catalog are entries for books in non-Roman alphabets (Cyrillic, Oriental, Hebrew); entries for some special collections (such as the Arents Collections and the Berg Collection); and some nonbook-form materials (such as manuscripts, maps, phonorecords, prints, and the like). When issued, this will be the only dictionary catalog (authors, titles, subjects) of a major research collection ever published. It will contain, moreover, many references to periodical articles.

DICTIONARY CATALOG OF THE RESEARCH LIBRARIES, 1971–

This catalog (New York: The New York Public Library) is a cumulative list of authors, titles, and subjects representing books and book-like materials (including microforms and music scores) added to the collections since January 1, 1971. The first official issue of the catalog (January 1972) includes a selection of materials added to the collections during 1971. Some materials cataloged in 1971 were added to the Public Catalog only; other materials cataloged in 1971 appear in both the Public Catalog and the *Dictionary Catalog*; still others appear in the *Dictionary Catalog* only. Therefore, readers should consult the Public Catalog for titles published before 1972 that are not found in the *Dictionary Catalog*. The first issue of the *Dictionary Catalog* was followed by various cumulations and supplements which were superseded by a basic set cumulating all previous issues: there are bimonthly supplements to the basic set, and each segment of the basic set is cumulated on a rotation basis. The underlying principle of the cumulation cycle is to prevent the necessity of searching for an item in more than two sources—a cumulated basic volume and the more recent cumulative supplement.

New acquisitions in certain areas excluded from the Public Catalog are being or will be covered by the *Dictionary Catalog*. New materials from the Schomburg Center for Research in Black Culture (newly designated a part of the Research Libraries) have been covered since October 1972, and Cyrillic materials (with the entries in Romanized forms) have been covered since January 1973. From mid-1973 new book acquisitions of the Arents, Berg, and Spencer Collections have been cataloged in the *Dictionary Catalog*, and from January 1974 data for nonbook materials (e.g., sheet maps, motion pictures, and phonorecords) have been included on a selective basis, coverage to be systematically expanded. Since 1974, Hebrew works have been cataloged according to the ANSI Z39 Committee's computer-compatible transcription. See the introduction to the latest volume of the catalog for information on new cataloging policies. Oriental works will be covered in the future, along with manuscripts and prints at a later point.

DIVISION, COLLECTION, AND SUBJECT CATALOGS

Except where noted, the following catalogs published in book form were produced by G. K.

Hall & Company of Boston; these are arranged alphabetically by the name of the division, collection, or subject area:

The Arents Collection of Books in Parts and Associated Literature: A Complete Checklist, by Sarah Augusta Dickson (The New York Public Library, 1957); A Supplement . . . 1957–1963, by Perry O'Neil (The New York Public Library, 1964).

Tobacco, Its History; Illustrated by the Books, Manuscripts, and Engravings in the Library of George Arents, Jr. (New York: The Rosenbach Company, 1937–43; 1952 [index]), 5 vols.

Tobacco; A Catalogue of the Books, Manuscripts and Engravings Acquired Since 1942 in the Arents Tobacco Collection at The New York Public Library (The New York Public Library, 1958); Parts I–VII (1507–1672) by Sarah A. Dickson and VIII–X (1673–1724) by Perry Hugh O'Neil have been published to date.

Dictionary Catalog of the History of the Americas Collection (1961), 28 vols.; Supplement (1964), 9 vols.

Dictionary Catalog of the Henry W. and Albert A. Berg Collection of English and American Literature (1969), 5 vols.; Supplement (1975), 1 vol.

Dictionary Catalog of the Dance Collection of the Research Libraries (The New York Public Library and G. K. Hall & Co., 1974), 10 vols.

Catalog of Government Publications in the Research Libraries (1972), 40 vols.

Catalog of Hebrew and Yiddish Titles of the Jewish Collection (1960), 3 vols.

Dictionary Catalog of the Jewish Collection (1960), 14 vols.; Supplement (1975), 8 vols.

Dictionary Catalog of the Local History and Genealogy Division (1974), 18 vols.

Dictionary Catalog of the Manuscript Division (1967), 2 vols.

Dictionary Catalog of the Map Division (1971), 10 vols.

Dictionary Catalog of the Music Collection (1964), 33 vols.; Supplement I (1966), 1 volume superseded by a final Supplement (1973), cumulating material cataloged in the 1966 supplement with new materials acquired through 1971.

Dictionary Catalog of the Oriental Collection (1960), 16 vols.

Dictionary Catalog of the Rare Book Division (1971), 21 vols.; Supplement (1973), 1 vol.

Dictionary Catalog of the Schomburg Collection of Negro Literature and History (1962), 9 vols.; First Supplement (1967), 2 vols., Second Supplement (1972), 4 vols.

Dictionary Catalog of the Slavonic Collection, 2d ed. (1974), 44 vols.

Dictionary Catalog and Shelf List of the Spencer Collection of Illustrated Books and Manuscripts and Fine Bindings (1970), 2 vols.

Catalog of the Theatre and Drama Collections (1967), 21 vols.: Part I. Drama Collection: Listing by Cultural Origin, 6 vols.; Drama Collection: Author Listing, 6 vols.; Part II. Theatre Collection: Books on the Theatre, 9 vols.; Supplement (1973), 3 vols.

United States Local History Catalog (1974), 2 vols.

Subject Catalog of the World War I Collection (1961), 4 vols.

LOCATION CHART

This listing provides locations (as of April 1975) for units of the New York Public Library whose collections are discussed in this Guide; it will be revised in any subsequent reprintings. Since the location of several of these units may be changed in the future, users of the library's collections should check current directories.

Building	Room or Floor
Central Building: Fifth Avenue and 42nd Street	
The Research Libraries	
Humanities and Social Sciences Research Center	
American History Division	315A
Art and Architecture Division	313
Economic and Public Affairs Division	228
General Research and Humanities Division	315
Information Desk	315
Main Reading Room	315M
Periodicals Section	108
Public Catalog	315
Jewish Division	84
Local History and Genealogy Division	315G
Map Division	117
Oriental Division	219
Slavonic Division	217
Stack Maintenance and Delivery Division	
Works in the Stacks are requested in 315 (See also Annex)	
Microform Reading Room	315M
Science and Technology Research Center	121
Special Collections	
Arents Collections (Arents Collection of Books in Parts; Arents Tobacco Collection)	324
Berg Collection of English and American Literature	320
Manuscripts and Archives Division	319
Prints Division	308
Rare Book Division	303
Spencer Collection of Illustrated Books and Manuscripts and Fine Bindings	324
Preparation Services ("Reference Catalog" class mark)	
Reference works available to the public may be requested in Room 315	

Central Serial Record (*consult
librarian in any public division*)
The Branch Libraries
Literature and Language Department,
Mid-Manhattan Library   78 and 80
(See also Mid-Manhattan Library,
8 East 40th Street)
Picture Collection   73
Annex, The Research Libraries: 521 West
43rd Street
Stack Maintenance and
Delivery Division
Newspaper Collection
Patents Collection
(See also Central Building)
*Works shelved in the Annex are listed
in the Public Catalog in Room 315,
which should be consulted before any
visit to the Annex.*
Library & Museum of the Performing Arts,
The New York Public Library
at Lincoln Center:
111 Amsterdam Avenue
The Research Libraries
Performing Arts Research Center   3rd Floor
Dance Collection
Music Division
Americana Collection

Special Collections
Toscanini Memorial Archives
Rodgers and Hammerstein Archives
of Recorded Sound
Theatre Collection
The Branch Libraries
General Library of the
Performing Arts   1st and 2nd
Floors
Shelby Cullom Davis Museum of
the Performing Arts
Children's Library   2nd Floor
Schomburg Center for Research in
Black Culture, The Research
Libraries: 103 West 135th Street
Donnell Library Center, The Branch
Libraries: 20 West 53rd Street
Central Children's Room   2nd Floor
Mid-Manhattan Library, The Branch
Libraries: 8 East 40th Street
General Reference Service   4th Floor
History and Social Science
Department   5th Floor
Science Department   4th Floor
(See also Literature and Language
Department, Mid-Manhattan
Library, Rooms 78 and 80,
Central Building)

305

INDEX TO SUBJECTS
AND COLLECTIONS

This is an index to primary descriptions of resources; it is alphabetized word by word. Passing references and items cited as examples are not indexed, nor are titles or authors unless the library has particularly large and significant collections relating to them or a work of exceptional rarity or research value. The Public Catalog and the dictionary catalogs (see the first Appendix) must be used for titles and authors or for further subject research.

Numbers refer to pages. For an overview of the arrangement of the chapters devoted to divisions of the library or to subject areas, the table of contents should be consulted first. For extensive research, particularly for materials acquired before 1940, the index to Karl Brown's *Guide to the Reference Collections of The New York Public Library* (1941) should be consulted.

The index entries are primarily to specific subjects in which the library has significant holdings, to divisions and administrative Collections, to collections and gifts housed within an administrative unit (indexed by last name of donor and/or by subject), and, selectively, to forms of materials

(photographs, cigarette cards, etc.). In this index the subheading "guides" under a subject refers to catalogs, indexes, files, and other research tools for the library's own holdings; the page references under the main entry are to descriptions of the resources themselves. "Serials" used as a subheading refers to newspapers, periodicals, society publications, etc. The subheading "govt. publications," refers to public documents, gazettes, etc. "Papers" refers to correspondence, records, original documents, and other manuscript or archival material.

Italic page references under a division or major subject refer to the main section of the book describing that division or subject and its resources; significant references to other parts of the book are in roman. For the most part, however, the more specific subject and location are indexed. For example, manuscripts from the Philippines, which are housed in the Manuscripts and Archives Division, some of them in its Rich collection, are described in the Oriental resources chapter; they are indexed only under "Rich collection" and "Philippines: manuscripts."